THE TIMES

ATLAS OF THE WORLD

WORLD

COMPACT EDITION

Times Books, 77-85 Fulham Palace Road,
London W6 8JB

The Times is a registered trademark of
Times Newspapers Ltd

First published 1994
Second Edition 2000
Third Edition 2004

Fourth Edition 2007

Printed in Singapore

British Library Cataloguing in Publication Data.
A catalogue record for this book is
available from the British Library.

ISBN 978-0-00-723374-8

Imp 001

All mapping in this atlas is generated from Collins Bartholomew digital databases.
Collins Bartholomew, the UK's leading independent geographical information supplier,
can provide a digital, custom, and premium mapping service to a variety of markets.
For further information:
Tel: +44 (0) 141 306 3752
e-mail: collinsbartholomew@harpercollins.co.uk

or visit our website at: www.collinsbartholomew.com

www.harpercollins.co.uk
visit the book lover's website

THE TIMES

ATLAS
OF THE
WORLD

COMPACT EDITION

TIMES BOOKS
London

4 CONTENTS

All independent countries and populated dependent and disputed territories are included in this list of the states and territories of the world; the list is arranged in alphabetical order by the conventional name form. For independent states, the full name is given below the conventional name, if this is different; for territories, the status is given. The capital city name is the same form as shown on the reference maps.

The statistics used for the area and population are the latest available and include estimates. The information on languages and religions is based on the latest information on 'de facto' speakers of the language or 'de facto' adherents to the religion. The information available on languages and religions varies greatly from country to country. Some countries include questions in censuses, others do not, in which case best estimates are used. The order of the languages and religions reflect their relative importance within the country; generally, languages or religions are included when more than one per cent of the population are estimated to be speakers or adherents.

Membership of selected international organizations is shown for each independent country. Territories are not shown as having separate memberships of these organizations.

ABBREVIATIONS

Currencies

| CFA | Communauté Financière Africaine |
| CFP | Comptoirs Français du Pacifique |

Organizations

APEC	Asia-Pacific Economic Cooperation
ASEAN	Association of Southeast Asian Nations
CARICOM	Caribbean Community
CIS	Commonwealth of Independent States
Comm.	The Commonwealth
EU	European Union
OECD	Organization of Economic Cooperation and Development
OPEC	Organization of Petroleum Exporting Countries
SADC	Southern African Development Community
UN	United Nations

AFGHANISTAN
Islamic State of Afghanistan

Area Sq Km	652 225	Religions	Sunni Muslim, Shi'a Muslim
Area Sq Miles	251 825		
Population	29 863 000	Currency	Afghani
Capital	Kābul	Organizations	UN
Languages	Dari, Pashtu, Uzbek, Turkmen	Map page	76–77

ALBANIA
Republic of Albania

Area Sq Km	28 748	Religions	Sunni Muslim, Albanian Orthodox, Roman Catholic
Area Sq Miles	11 100		
Population	3 130 000		
Capital	Tirana (Tiranë)	Currency	Lek
Languages	Albanian, Greek	Organizations	UN
		Map page	109

ALGERIA
People's Democratic Republic of Algeria

Area Sq Km	2 381 741	Religions	Sunni Muslim
Area Sq Miles	919 595	Currency	Algerian dinar
Population	32 854 000	Organizations	OPEC, UN
Capital	Algiers (Alger)	Map page	114–115
Languages	Arabic, French, Berber		

American Samoa
United States Unincorporated Territory

Area Sq Km	197	Religions	Protestant, Roman Catholic
Area Sq Miles	76		
Population	65 000	Currency	United States dollar
Capital	Fagatogo	Map page	49
Languages	Samoan, English		

ANDORRA
Principality of Andorra

Area Sq Km	465	Religions	Roman Catholic
Area Sq Miles	180	Currency	Euro
Population	67 000	Organizations	UN
Capital	Andorra la Vella	Map page	104
Languages	Spanish, Catalan, French		

ANGOLA
Republic of Angola

Area Sq Km	1 246 700	Religions	Roman Catholic, Protestant, traditional beliefs
Area Sq Miles	481 354		
Population	15 941 000		
Capital	Luanda	Currency	Kwanza
Languages	Portuguese, Bantu, local languages	Organizations	SADC, UN
		Map page	120

Anguilla
United Kingdom Overseas Territory

Area Sq Km	155	Religions	Protestant, Roman
Area Sq Miles	60		Catholic
Population	12 000	Currency	East Caribbean dollar
Capital	The Valley	Map page	147
Languages	English		

ANTIGUA AND BARBUDA

Area Sq Km	442	Religions	Protestant, Roman
Area Sq Miles	171		Catholic
Population	81 000	Currency	East Caribbean dollar
Capital	St John's	Organizations	CARICOM,
Languages	English, creole		Comm., UN
		Map page	147

ARGENTINA
Argentine Republic

Area Sq Km	2 766 889	Religions	Roman Catholic,
Area Sq Miles	1 068 302		Protestant
Population	38 747 000	Currency	Argentinian peso
Capital	Buenos Aires	Organizations	UN
Languages	Spanish, Italian,	Map page	152–153
	Amerindian		
	languages		

ARMENIA
Republic of Armenia

Area Sq Km	29 800	Religions	Armenian Orthodox
Area Sq Miles	11 506	Currency	Dram
Population	3 016 000	Organizations	CIS, UN
Capital	Yerevan (Erevan)	Map page	81
Languages	Armenian, Azeri		

Aruba
Self-governing Netherlands Territory

Area Sq Km	193	Religions	Roman Catholic,
Area Sq Miles	75		Protestant
Population	99 000	Currency	Aruban florin
Capital	Oranjestad	Map page	147
Languages	Papiamento, Dutch,		
	English		

Ascension
Dependency of St Helena

Area Sq Km	88	Religions	Protestant, Roman
Area Sq Miles	34		Catholic
Population	1 122	Currency	Pound sterling
Capital	Georgetown	Map page	113
Languages	English		

AUSTRALIA
Commonwealth of Australia

Area Sq Km	7 692 024	Religions	Protestant, Roman
Area Sq Miles	2 969 907		Catholic, Orthodox
Population	20 155 000	Currency	Australian dollar
Capital	Canberra	Organizations	APEC, Comm.,
Languages	English, Italian,		OECD, UN
	Greek	Map page	50–51

Australian Capital Territory (Federal Territory)

Area Sq Km	2 358	Population	321 680
Area Sq Miles	910	Capital	Canberra

Jervis Bay Territory (Territory)

Area Sq Km	73	Population	611
Area Sq Miles	28		

New South Wales (State)

Area Sq Km	800 642	Population	6 609 304
Area Sq Miles	309 130	Capital	Sydney

Northern Territory (Territory)

Area Sq Km	1 349 129	Population	200 019
Area Sq Miles	520 902	Capital	Darwin

Queensland (State)

Area Sq Km	1 730 648	Population	3 635 121
Area Sq Miles	668 207	Capital	Brisbane

South Australia (State)

Area Sq Km	983 482	Population	1 514 854
Area Sq Miles	379 725	Capital	Adelaide

Tasmania (State)

Area Sq Km	68 401	Population	472 931
Area Sq Miles	26 410	Capital	Hobart

Victoria (State)

Area Sq Km	227 416	Population	4 822 663
Area Sq Miles	87 806	Capital	Melbourne

Western Australia (State)

Area Sq Km	2 529 875	Population	1 906 114
Area Sq Miles	976 790	Capital	Perth

AUSTRIA
Republic of Austria

Area Sq Km	83 855	Religions	Roman Catholic,
Area Sq Miles	32 377		Protestant
Population	8 189 000	Currency	Euro
Capital	Vienna (Wien)	Organizations	EU, OECD, UN
Languages	German, Croatian,	Map page	102–103
	Turkish		

AZERBAIJAN
Republic of Azerbaijan

Area Sq Km	86 600	Religions	Shi'a Muslim, Sunni
Area Sq Miles	33 436		Muslim, Russian and
Population	8 411 000		Armenian Orthodox
Capital	Baku (Bakı)	Currency	Azerbaijani manat
Languages	Azeri, Armenian,	Organizations	CIS, UN
	Russian, Lezgian	Map page	81

Azores (Arquipélago dos Açores)
Autonomous Region of Portugal

Area Sq Km	2 300	Religions	Roman Catholic,
Area Sq Miles	888		Protestant
Population	241 762	Currency	Euro
Capital	Ponta Delgada	Map page	112
Languages	Portuguese		

 BELIZE

Area Sq Km	22 965	Religions	Roman Catholic,
Area Sq Miles	8 867		Protestant
Population	270 000	Currency	Belize dollar
Capital	Belmopan	Organizations	CARICOM, Comm.,
Languages	English, Spanish,		UN
	Mayan, creole	Map page	147

 THE BAHAMAS
Commonwealth of The Bahamas

Area Sq Km	13 939	Religions	Protestant, Roman
Area Sq Miles	5 382		Catholic
Population	323 000	Currency	Bahamian dollar
Capital	Nassau	Organizations	CARICOM, Comm.,
Languages	English, creole		UN
		Map page	146–147

 BENIN
Republic of Benin

Area Sq Km	112 620	Religions	Traditional beliefs,
Area Sq Miles	43 483		Roman Catholic,
Population	8 439 000		Sunni Muslim
Capital	Porto-Novo	Currency	CFA franc
Languages	French, Fon,	Organization	UN
	Yoruba, Adja,	Map page	114
	local languages		

 BAHRAIN
Kingdom of Bahrain

Area Sq Km	691	Religions	Shi'a Muslim, Sunni
Area Sq Miles	267		Muslim, Christian
Population	727 000	Currency	Bahraini dinar
Capital	Manama	Organizations	UN
	(Al Manāmah)	Map page	79
Languages	Arabic, English		

 Bermuda
United Kingdom Overseas Territory

Area Sq Km	54	Religions	Protestant, Roman
Area Sq Miles	21		Catholic
Population	64 000	Currency	Bermuda dollar
Capital	Hamilton	Map page	125
Languages	English		

 BANGLADESH
People's Republic of Bangladesh

Area Sq Km	143 998	Religions	Sunni Muslim, Hindu
Area Sq Miles	55 598	Currency	Taka
Population	141 822 000	Organizations	Comm., UN
Capital	Dhaka (Dacca)	Map page	75
Languages	Bengali, English		

 BHUTAN
Kingdom of Bhutan

Area Sq Km	46 620	Religions	Buddhist, Hindu
Area Sq Miles	18 000	Currency	Ngultrum,
Population	2 163 000		Indian rupee
Capital	Thimphu	Organizations	UN
Languages	Dzongkha,	Map page	75
	Nepali, Assamese		

 BARBADOS

Area Sq Km	430	Religions	Protestant, Roman
Area Sq Miles	166		Catholic
Population	270 000	Currency	Barbados dollar
Capital	Bridgetown	Organizations	CARICOM,
Languages	English, creole		Comm., UN
		Map page	147

 BOLIVIA
Republic of Bolivia

Area Sq Km	1 098 581	Religions	Roman Catholic,
Area Sq Miles	424 164		Protestant, Baha'i
Population	9 182 000	Currency	Boliviano
Capital	La Paz/Sucre	Organizations	UN
Languages	Spanish, Quechua,	Map page	152
	Aymara		

 BELARUS
Republic of Belarus

Area Sq Km	207 600	Religions	Belorussian Orthodox,
Area Sq Miles	80 155		Roman Catholic
Population	9 755 000	Currency	Belarus rouble
Capital	Minsk	Organizations	CIS, UN
Languages	Belorussian, Russian	Map page	88–89

Bonaire
part of Netherlands Antilles

Area Sq Km	288	Religions	Roman Catholic,
Area Sq Miles	111		Protestant
Population	10 114	Currency	Netherlands Antilles
Capital	Kralendijk		guilder
Languages	Dutch, Papiamento	Map page	147

BELGIUM
Kingdom of Belgium

Area Sq Km	30 520	Religions	Roman Catholic,
Area Sq Miles	11 784		Protestant
Population	10 419 000	Currency	Euro
Capital	Brussels (Bruxelles)	Organizations	EU, OECD, UN
Languages	Dutch (Flemish),	Map page	100
	French (Walloon),		
	German		

Bonin Islands (Ogasawara-shotō)
part of Japan

Area Sq Km	104	Religions	Shintoist, Buddhist,
Area Sq Miles	40		Christian
Population	2 300	Currency	Yen
Capital	Omura	Map page	69
Languages	Japanese		

BOSNIA-HERZEGOVINA
Republic of Bosnia and Herzegovina

Area Sq Km	51 130	Religions	Sunni Muslim, Serbian
Area Sq Miles	19 741		Orthodox, Roman
Population	3 907 000		Catholic, Protestant
Capital	Sarajevo	Currency	Marka
Languages	Bosnian, Serbian,	Organizations	UN
	Croatian	Map page	109

 ## BOTSWANA
Republic of Botswana

Area Sq Km	581 370	Religions	Traditional beliefs,
Area Sq Miles	224 468		Protestant, Roman
Population	1 765 000		Catholic
Capital	Gaborone	Currency	Pula
Languages	English, Setswana,	Organizations	Comm., SADC, UN
	Shona, local	Map page	120
	languages		

 ## BRAZIL
Federative Republic of Brazil

Area Sq Km	8 514 879	Religions	Roman Catholic,
Area Sq Miles	3 287 613		Protestant
Population	186 405 000	Currency	Real
Capital	Brasília	Organizations	UN
Languages	Portuguese	Map page	150–151

 ## BRUNEI
State of Brunei Darussalam

Area Sq Km	5 765	Religions	Sunni Muslim, Buddhist,
Area Sq Miles	2 226		Christian
Population	374 000	Currency	Brunei dollar
Capital	Bandar Seri Begawan	Organizations	APEC, ASEAN,
Languages	Malay, English,		Comm., UN
	Chinese	Map page	61

 ## BULGARIA
Republic of Bulgaria

Area Sq Km	110 994	Religions	Bulgarian Orthodox,
Area Sq Miles	42 855		Sunni Muslim
Population	7 726 000	Currency	Lev
Capital	Sofia (Sofiya)	Organizations	UN
Languages	Bulgarian, Turkish,	Map page	110
	Romany,		
	Macedonian		

 ## BURKINA
Democratic Republic of Burkina Faso

Area Sq Km	274 200	Religions	Sunni Muslim,
Area Sq Miles	105 869		traditional beliefs,
Population	13 228 000		Roman Catholic
Capital	Ouagadougou	Currency	CFA franc
Languages	French, Moore	Organizations	UN
	(Mossi), Fulani, local	Map page	114
	languages		

 ## BURUNDI
Republic of Burundi

Area Sq Km	27 835	Religions	Roman Catholic,
Area Sq Miles	10 747		traditional beliefs,
Population	7 548 000		Protestant
Capital	Bujumbura	Currency	Burundian franc
Languages	Kirundi (Hutu,	Organizations	UN
	Tutsi), French	Map page	119

 ## CAMBODIA
Kingdom of Cambodia

Area Sq Km	181 035	Religions	Buddhist, Roman
Area Sq Miles	69 884		Catholic, Sunni
Population	14 071 000		Muslim
Capital	Phnum Pénh	Currency	Riel
	(Phnom Penh)	Organizations	ASEAN, UN
Languages	Khmer, Vietnamese	Map page	63

 ## CAMEROON
Republic of Cameroon

Area Sq Km	475 442	Religions	Roman Catholic,
Area Sq Miles	183 569		traditional beliefs,
Population	16 322 000		Sunni Muslim,
Capital	Yaoundé		Protestant
Languages	French, English,	Currency	CFA franc
	Fang, Bamileke,	Organizations	Comm., UN
	local languages	Map page	118

 ## CANADA

Area Sq Km	9 984 670	Religions	Roman Catholic,
Area Sq Miles	3 855 103		Protestant, Eastern
Population	32 268 000		Orthodox, Jewish
Capital	Ottawa	Currency	Canadian dollar
Languages	English, French,	Organizations	APEC, Comm.,
	local languages		OECD, UN
		Map page	126–127

Alberta (Province)

Area Sq Km	661 848	Population	3 113 600
Area Sq Miles	255 541	Capital	Edmonton

British Columbia (Province)

Area Sq Km	944 735	Population	4 141 300
Area Sq Miles	364 764	Capital	Victoria

Manitoba (Province)

Area Sq Km	647 797	Population	1 150 800
Area Sq Miles	250 116	Capital	Winnipeg

New Brunswick (Province)

Area Sq Km	72 908	Population	756 700
Area Sq Miles	28 150	Capital	Fredericton

Newfoundland and Labrador (Province)

Area Sq Km	405 212	Population	531 600
Area Sq Miles	156 453	Capital	St John's

Northwest Territories (Territory)

Area Sq Km	1 346 106	Population	41 400
Area Sq Miles	519 734	Capital	Yellowknife

 CANADA

Nova Scotia (Province)

Area Sq Km 55 284	Population 944 800
Area Sq Miles 21 345	Capital Halifax

Nunavut (Territory)

Area Sq Km 2 093 190	Population 28 700
Area Sq Miles 808 185	Capital Iqaluit (Frobisher Bay)

Ontario (Province)

Area Sq Km 1 076 395	Population 12 068 300
Area Sq Miles 415 598	Capital Toronto

Prince Edward Island (Province)

Area Sq Km 5 660	Population 139 900
Area Sq Miles 2 185	Capital Charlottetown

Québec (Province)

Area Sq Km 1 542 056	Population 7 455 200
Area Sq Miles 595 391	Capital Québec

Saskatchewan (Province)

Area Sq Km 651 036	Population 1 011 800
Area Sq Miles 251 366	Capital Regina

Yukon Territory (Territory)

Area Sq Km 482 443	Population 29 900
Area Sq Miles 186 272	Capital Whitehorse

Canary Islands (Islas Canarias)
Autonomous Community of Spain

Area Sq Km 7 447	Languages Spanish
Area Sq Miles 2 875	Religions Roman Catholic
Population 1 944 700	Currency Euro
Capital Santa Cruz de Tenerife/Las Palmas	Map page 114

CAPE VERDE
Republic of Cape Verde

Area Sq Km 4 033	Religions Roman Catholic, Protestant
Area Sq Miles 1 557	
Population 507 000	Currency Cape Verde escudo
Capital Praia	Organizations UN
Languages Portuguese, creole	Map page 46

Cayman Islands
United Kingdom Overseas Territory

Area Sq Km 259	Religions Protestant, Roman Catholic
Area Sq Miles 100	
Population 45 000	Currency Cayman Islands dollar
Capital George Town	Map page 146
Languages English	

CENTRAL AFRICAN REPUBLIC

Area Sq Km 622 436	Religions Protestant, Roman Catholic, traditional beliefs, Sunni Muslim
Area Sq Miles 240 324	
Population 4 038 000	
Capital Bangui	Currency CFA franc
Languages French, Sango, Banda, Baya, local languages	Organizations UN
	Map page 118

Ceuta
Autonomous Community of Spain

Area Sq Km 19	Religions Roman Catholic, Muslim
Area Sq Miles 7	
Population 74 931	Currency Euro
Capital Ceuta	Map page 106
Languages Spanish, Arabic	

CHAD
Republic of Chad

Area Sq Km 1 284 000	Religions Sunni Muslim, Roman Catholic, Protestant, traditional beliefs
Area Sq Miles 495 755	
Population 9 749 000	
Capital Ndjamena	Currency CFA franc
Languages Arabic, French,Sara, local languages	Organizations UN
	Map page 115

Chatham Islands
part of New Zealand

Area Sq Km 963	Religions Protestant
Area Sq Miles 372	Currency New Zealand dollar
Population 717	Map page 49
Capital Waitangi	
Languages English	

CHILE
Republic of Chile

Area Sq Km 756 945	Religions Roman Catholic, Protestant
Area Sq Miles 292 258	
Population 16 295 000	Currency Chilean peso
Capital Santiago	Organizations APEC, UN
Languages Spanish, Amerindian languages	Map page 152–153

CHINA
People's Republic of China

Area Sq Km 9 584 492	Religions Confucian, Taoist, Buddhist, Christian, Sunni Muslim
Area Sq Miles 3 700 593	
Population 1 323 345 000	
Capital Beijing (Peking)	Currency Yuan, Hong Kong dollar, Macao pataca
Languages Mandarin, Wu, Cantonese, Hsiang, regional languages	Organizations APEC, UN
	Map page 68–69

Anhui (Province)

Area Sq Km 139 000	Population 59 860 000
Area Sq Miles 53 668	Capital Hefei

Bejing (Municipality)

Area Sq Km 16 800	Population 13 820 000
Area Sq Miles 6 487	Capital Beijing (Peking)

Chongqing (Municipality)

Area Sq Km 23 000	Population 30 900 000
Area Sq Miles 8 880	Capital Chongqing

Fujian (Province)

Area Sq Km 121 400	Population 34 710 000
Area Sq Miles 46 873	Capital Fuzhou

Gansu (Province)

Area Sq Km 453 700	Population 25 620 000
Area Sq Miles 175 175	Capital Lanzhou

Guangdong (Province)

Area Sq Km 178 000	Population 86 420 000
Area Sq Miles 68 726	Capital Guangzhou (Canton)

Guangxi Zhuangzu Zizhiqu (Autonomous Region)

Area Sq Km 236 000	Population 44 890 000
Area Sq Miles 91 120	Capital Nanning

Guizhou (Province)

Area Sq Km 176 000	Population 35 250 000
Area Sq Miles 67 954	Capital Guiyang

Hainan (Province)

Area Sq Km 34 000	Population 7 870 000
Area Sq Miles 13 127	Capital Haikou

Hebei (Province)

Area Sq Km 187 700	Population 67 440 000
Area Sq Miles 72 471	Capital Shijiazhuang

Heilongjiang (Province)

Area Sq Km 454 600	Population 36 890 000
Area Sq Miles 175 522	Capital Harbin

Henan (Province)

Area Sq Km 167 000	Population 92 560 000
Area Sq Miles 64 479	Capital Zhengzhou

Hong Kong (Special Administrative Region)

Area Sq Km 1 075	Population 6 780 000
Area Sq Miles 415	Capital Hong Kong

Hubei (Province)

Area Sq Km 185 900	Population 60 280 000
Area Sq Miles 71 776	Capital Wuhan

Hunan (Province)

Area Sq Km 210 000	Population 64 400 000
Area Sq Miles 81 081	Capital Changsha

Jiangsu (Province)

Area Sq Km 102 600	Population 74 380 000
Area Sq Miles 39 614	Capital Nanjing

Jiangxi (Province)

Area Sq Km 166 900	Population 41 400 000
Area Sq Miles 64 440	Capital Nanchang

Jilin (Province)

Area Sq Km 187 000	Population 27 280 000
Area Sq Miles 72 201	Capital Changchun

Liaoning (Province)

Area Sq Km 147 400	Population 42 380 000
Area Sq Miles 56 911	Capital Shenyang

Macao (Special Administrative Region)

Area Sq Km 17	Population 440 000
Area Sq Mile 7	Capital Macao

Nei Mongol Zizhiqu (Inner Mongolia) (Autonomous Region)

Area Sq Km 1 183 000	Population 23 760 000
Area Sq Miles 456 759	Capital Hohhot

Ningxia Huizu Zizhiqu (Autonomous Region)

Area Sq Km 66 400	Population 5 620 000
Area Sq Miles 25 637	Capital Yinchuan

Qinghai (Province)

Area Sq Km 721 000	Population 5 180 000
Area Sq Miles 278 380	Capital Xining

Shaanxi (Province)

Area Sq Km 205 600	Population 36 050 000
Area Sq Miles 79 383	Capital Xi'an

Shandong (Province)

Area Sq Km 153 300	Population 90 790 000
Area Sq Miles 59 189	Capital Jinan

Shanghai (Municipality)

Area Sq Km 6 300	Population 16 740 000
Area Sq Miles 2 432	Capital Shanghai

Shanxi (Province)

Area Sq Km 156 300	Population 32 970 000
Area Sq Miles 60 348	Capital Taiyuan

Sichuan (Province)

Area Sq Km 560 000	Population 83 290 000
Area Sq Miles 219 692	Capital Chengdu

Tianjin (Municipality)

Area Sq Km 11 300	Population 10 010 000
Area Sq Miles 4 363	Capital Tianjin

Xinjiang Uygur Zizhiqu (Sinkiang) (Autonomous Region)

Area Sq Km 1 600 000	Population 19 250 000
Area Sq Miles 617 763	Capital Ürümqi

Xizang Zizhiqu (Tibet) (Autonomous Region)

Area Sq Km 1 228 400	Population 2 620 000
Area Sq Miles 474 288	Capital Lhasa

Yunnan (Province)

Area Sq Km 394 000	Population 42 880 000
Area Sq Miles 152 124	Capital Kunming

Zhejiang (Province)

Area Sq Km 101 800	Population 46 770 000
Area Sq Miles 39 305	Capital Hangzhou

Christmas Island
Australian External Territory

Area Sq Km	135	Religions	Buddhist, Sunni
Area Sq Miles	52		Muslim, Protestant,
Population	1 508		Roman Catholic
Capital	The Settlement	Currency	Australian dollar
Languages	English	Map page	58

Cocos Islands (Keeling Islands)
Australian External Territory

Area Sq Km	14	Religions	Sunni Muslim,
Area Sq Miles	5		Christian
Population	621	Currency	Australian dollar
Capital	West Island	Map page	58
Languages	English		

COLOMBIA
Republic of Colombia

Area Sq Km	1 141 748	Religions	Roman Catholic,
Area Sq Miles	440 831		Protestant
Population	45 600 000	Currency	Colombian peso
Capital	Bogotá	Organizations	APEC, UN
Languages	Spanish, Amerindian	Map page	150
	languages		

COMOROS
Union of the Comoros

Area Sq Km	1 862	Religions	Sunni Muslim, Roman
Area Sq Miles	719		Catholic
Population	798 000	Currency	Comoros franc
Capital	Moroni	Organizations	UN
Languages	Comorian, French,	Map page	121
	Arabic		

CONGO
Republic of the Congo

Area Sq Km	342 000	Religions	Roman Catholic,
Area Sq Miles	132 047		Protestant, traditional
Population	3 999 000		beliefs, Sunni Muslim
Capital	Brazzaville	Currency	CFA franc
Languages	French, Kongo,	Organizations	UN
	Monokutuba, local	Map page	118
	languages		

CONGO, DEMOCRATIC REPUBLIC OF THE

Area Sq Km	2 345 410	Religions	Christian, Sunni
Area Sq Miles	905 568		Muslim
Population	57 549 000	Currency	Congolese franc
Capital	Kinshasa	Organizations	SADC, UN
Languages	French, Lingala,	Map page	118–119
	Swahili, Kongo,		
	local languages		

Cook Islands
Self-governing New Zealand overseas territory

Area Sq Km	293	Religions	Protestant, Roman
Area Sq Miles	113		Catholic
Population	18 000	Currency	New Zealand dollar
Capital	Avarua	Map page	49
Languages	English, Maori		

COSTA RICA
Republic of Costa Rica

Area Sq Km	51 100	Religions	Roman Catholic,
Area Sq Miles	19 730		Protestant
Population	4 327 000	Currency	Costa Rican colón
Capital	San José	Organizations	UN
Languages	Spanish	Map page	146

CÔTE D'IVOIRE
Republic of Côte d'Ivoire

Area Sq Km	322 463	Religions	Sunni Muslim, Roman
Area Sq Miles	124 504		Catholic, traditonal
Population	18 154 000		beliefs, Protestant
Capital	Yamoussoukro	Currency	CFA franc
Languages	French, creole, Akan,	Organizations	UN
	local languages	Map page	114

CROATIA
Republic of Croatia

Area Sq Km	56 538	Religions	Roman Catholic,
Area Sq Miles	21 829		Serbian Orthodox,
Population	4 551 000		Sunni Muslim
Capital	Zagreb	Currency	Kuna
Languages	Croatian, Serbian	Organizations	UN
		Map page	109

CUBA
Republic of Cuba

Area Sq Km	110 860	Religions	Roman Catholic,
Area Sq Miles	42 803		Protestant
Population	11 269 000	Currency	Cuban peso
Capital	Havana (La Habana)	Organizations	UN
Languages	Spanish	Map page	146

Curaçao
part of Netherlands Antilles

Area Sq Km	444	Religions	Roman Catholic,
Area Sq Miles	171		Protestant
Population	126 816	Currency	Netherlands Antilles
Capital	Willemstad		guilder
Languages	Dutch, Papiamento	Map page	147

CYPRUS
Republic of Cyprus

Area Sq Km	9 251	Religions	Greek Orthodox, Sunni
Area Sq Miles	3 572		Muslim
Population	835 000	Currency	Cyprus pound
Capital	Nicosia (Lefkosia)	Organizations	Comm., UN
Languages	Greek, Turkish,	Map page	80
	English		

CZECH REPUBLIC

Area Sq Km	78 864	Religions	Roman Catholic,
Area Sq Miles	30 450		Protestant
Population	10 220 000	Currency	Czech koruna
Capital	Prague (Praha)	Organizations	UN
Languages	Czech, Moravian,	Map page	102–103
	Slovakian		

DENMARK
Kingdom of Denmark

Area Sq Km	43 075	Religions	Protestant
Area Sq Miles	16 631	Currency	Danish krone
Population	5 431 000	Organizations	EU, OECD, UN
Capital	Copenhagen	Map page	93
	(København)		
Languages	Danish		

DJIBOUTI
Republic of Djibouti

Area Sq Km	23 200	Religions	Sunni Muslim,
Area Sq Miles	8 958		Christian
Population	793 000	Currency	Djibouti franc
Capital	Djibouti	Organizations	UN
Languages	Somali, Afar, French,	Map page	117
	Arabic		

DOMINICA
Commonwealth of Dominica

Area Sq Km	750	Religions	Roman Catholic,
Area Sq Miles	290		Protestant
Population	79 000	Currency	East Caribbean dollar
Capital	Roseau	Organizations	CARICOM, Comm.,
Languages	English, creole		UN
		Map page	147

DOMINICAN REPUBLIC

Area Sq Km	48 442	Religions	Roman Catholic,
Area Sq Miles	18 704		Protestant
Population	8 895 000	Currency	Dominican peso
Capital	Santo Domingo	Organizations	UN
Languages	Spanish, creole	Map page	147

Easter Island (Isla de Pascua)
part of Chile

Area Sq Km	171	Religions	Roman Catholic
Area Sq Miles	66	Currency	Chilean peso
Population	3 791	Map page	157
Capital	Hanga Roa		
Languages	Spanish		

EAST TIMOR
Democratic Republic of Timor-Leste

Area Sq Km	14 874	Religions	Roman Catholic
Area Sq Miles	5 743	Currency	United States dollar
Population	947 000	Organisations	UN
Capital	Dili	Map page	59
Languages	Portuguese, Tetun,		
	English		

ECUADOR
Republic of Ecuador

Area Sq Km	272 045	Religions	Roman Catholic
Area Sq Miles	105 037	Currency	United States dollar
Population	13 228 000	Organizations	APEC, UN
Capital	Quito	Map page	150
Languages	Spanish, Quechua,		
	Amerindian		
	languages		

EGYPT
Arab Republic of Egypt

Area Sq Km	1 000 250	Religions	Sunni Muslim, Coptic
Area Sq Miles	386 199		Christian
Population	74 033 000	Currency	Egyptian pound
Capital	Cairo (Al Qāhira)	Organizations	UN
Languages	Arabic	Map page	116

EL SALVADOR
Republic of El Salvador

Area Sq Km	21 041	Religions	Roman Catholic,
Area Sq Miles	8 124		Protestant
Population	6 881 000	Currency	El Salvador colón,
Capital	San Salvador		United States dollar
Languages	Spanish	Organizations	UN
		Map page	146

EQUATORIAL GUINEA
Republic of Equatorial Guinea

Area Sq Km	28 051	Religions	Roman Catholic,
Area Sq Miles	10 831		traditional beliefs
Population	504 000	Currency	CFA franc
Capital	Malabo	Organizations	UN
Languages	Spanish, French,	Map page	118
	Fang		

ERITREA
State of Eritrea

Area Sq Km	117 400	Religions	Sunni Muslim, Coptic
Area Sq Miles	45 328		Christian
Population	4 401 000	Currency	Nakfa
Capital	Asmara	Organizations	UN
Languages	Tigrinya, Tigre	Map page	116

ESTONIA
Republic of Estonia

Area Sq Km	45 200	Religions	Protestant, Estonian
Area Sq Miles	17 452		and Russian Orthodox
Population	1 330 000	Currency	Kroon
Capital	Tallinn	Organizations	UN
Languages	Estonian, Russian	Map page	88

ETHIOPIA
Federal Democratic Republic of Ethiopia

Area Sq Km	1 133 880	Religions	Ethiopian Orthodox,
Area Sq Miles	437 794		Sunni Muslim,
Population	77 431 000		traditional beliefs
Capital	Addis Ababa	Currency	Birr
	(Ādīs Ābeba)	Organizations	UN
Languages	Oromo, Amharic,	Map page	117
	Tigrinya, local		
	languages		

Falkland Islands
United Kingdom Overseas Territory

Area Sq Km	12 170	Religions	Protestant, Roman
Area Sq Miles	4 699		Catholic
Population	3 000	Currency	Falkland Islands
Capital	Stanley		pound
Languages	English	Map page	153

GABON
Gabonese Republic

Area Sq Km	267 667	Religions	Roman Catholic,
Area Sq Miles	103 347		Protestant, traditonal
Population	1 384 000		beliefs
Capital	Libreville	Currency	CFA franc
Languages	French, Fang, local	Organizations	UN
	languages	Map page	118

Faroe Islands
Self-governing Danish Territory

Area Sq Km	1 399	Religions	Protestant
Area Sq Miles	540	Currency	Danish krone
Population	47 000	Map page	94
Capital	Tórshavn		
	(Thorshavn)		
Languages	Faroese, Danish		

Galapagos Islands (Islas Galápagos)
part of Ecuador

Area Sq Km	8 010	Religions	Roman Catholic
Area Sq Miles	3 093	Currency	United States dollar
Population	18 640	Map page	125
Capital	Puerto Baquerizo		
	Moreno		
Languages	Spanish		

FIJI
Republic of the Fiji Islands

Area Sq Km	18 330	Religions	Christian, Hindu, Sunni
Area Sq Miles	7 077		Muslim
Population	848 000	Currency	Fiji dollar
Capital	Suva	Organizations	UN, Comm.
Languages	English, Fijian,	Map page	49
	Hindi		

THE GAMBIA
Republic of The Gambia

Area Sq Km	11 295	Religions	Sunni Muslim,
Area Sq Miles	4 361		Protestant
Population	1 517 000	Currency	Dalasi
Capital	Banjul	Organizations	Comm., UN
Languages	English, Malinke,	Map page	114
	Fulani, Wolof		

FINLAND
Republic of Finland

Area Sq Km	338 145	Religions	Protestant, Greek
Area Sq Miles	130 559		Orthodox
Population	5 249 000	Currency	Euro
Capital	Helsinki (Helsingfors)	Organizations	EU, OECD, UN
Languages	Finnish, Swedish	Map page	92–93

Gaza
semi-autonomous region

Area Sq Km	363	Religions	Sunni Muslim, Shi'a
Area Sq Miles	140		Muslim
Population	1 406 423	Currency	Israeli shekel
Capital	Gaza	Map page	80
Languages	Arabic		

FRANCE
French Republic

Area Sq Km	543 965	Religions	Roman Catholic,
Area Sq Miles	210 026		Protestant, Sunni
Population	60 496 000		Muslim
Capital	Paris	Currency	Euro
Languages	French, Arabic	Organizations	EU, OECD, UN
		Map page	104–105

GEORGIA
Republic of Georgia

Area Sq Km	69 700	Religions	Georgian Orthodox,
Area Sq Miles	26 911		Russian Orthodox,
Population	4 474 000		Sunni Muslim
Capital	T'bilisi	Currency	Lari
Languages	Georgian, Russian,	Organizations	CIS, UN
	Armenian, Azeri,	Map page	81
	Ossetian, Abkhaz		

French Guiana
French Overseas Department

Area Sq Km	90 000	Religions	Roman Catholic
Area Sq Miles	34 749	Currency	Euro
Population	187 000	Map page	151
Capital	Cayenne		
Languages	French, creole		

GERMANY
Federal Republic of Germany

Area Sq Km	357 022	Religions	Protestant, Roman
Area Sq Miles	137 849		Catholic
Population	82 689 000	Currency	Euro
Capital	Berlin	Organizations	EU, OECD, UN
Languages	German, Turkish	Map page	102

French Polynesia
French Overseas Country

Area Sq Km	3 265	Religions	Protestant, Roman
Area Sq Miles	1 261		Catholic
Population	257 000	Currency	CFP franc
Capital	Papeete	Map page	49
Languages	French, Tahitian,		
	Polynesian		
	languages		

GHANA
Republic of Ghana

Area Sq Km	238 537	Religions	Christian, Sunni
Area Sq Miles	92 100		Muslim, traditional
Population	22 113 000		beliefs
Capital	Accra	Currency	Cedi
Languages	English, Hausa,	Organizations	Comm., UN
	Akan, local	Map page	114
	languages		

Gibraltar
United Kingdom Overseas Territory

Area Sq Km	7	Religions	Roman Catholic,
Area Sq Miles	3		Protestant, Sunni
Population	28 000		Muslim
Capital	Gibraltar	Currency	Gibraltar pound
Languages	English, Spanish	Map page	106

GREECE
Hellenic Republic

Area Sq Km	131 957	Religions	Greek Orthodox, Sunni
Area Sq Miles	50 949		Muslim
Population	11 120 000	Currency	Euro
Capital	Athens (Athina)	Organizations	EU, OECD, UN
Languages	Greek	Map page	111

Greenland
Self-governing Danish Territory

Area Sq Km	2 175 600	Religions	Protestant
Area Sq Miles	840 004	Currency	Danish krone
Population	57 000	Map page	127
Capital	Nuuk (Godthåb)		
Languages	Greenlandic, Danish		

GRENADA

Area Sq Km	378	Religions	Roman Catholic,
Area Sq Miles	146		Protestant
Population	103 000	Currency	East Caribbean dollar
Capital	St George's	Organizations	CARICOM, Comm.,
Languages	English, creole		UN
		Map page	147

Guadeloupe
French Overseas Department

Area Sq Km	1 780	Religions	Roman Catholic
Area Sq Miles	687	Currency	Euro
Population	448 000	Map page	147
Capital	Basse-Terre		
Languages	French, creole		

Guam
United States Unincorporated Territory

Area Sq Km	541	Religions	Roman Catholic
Area Sq Miles	209	Currency	United States dollar
Population	170 000	Map page	59
Capital	Hagåtña		
Languages	Chamorro, English,		
	Tagalog		

GUATEMALA
Republic of Guatemala

Area Sq Km	108 890	Religion	Roman Catholic,
Area Sq Miles	42 043		Protestant
Population	12 599 000	Currency	Quetzal, United States
Capital	Guatemala City		dollar
Languages	Spanish, Mayan	Organizations	UN
	languages	Map page	146

Guernsey
United Kingdom Crown Dependency

Area Sq Km	78	Religions	Protestant, Roman
Area Sq Miles	30		Catholic
Population	62 692	Currency	Pound sterling
Capital	St Peter Port	Map page	95
Languages	English, French		

GUINEA
Republic of Guinea

Area Sq Km	245 857	Religions	Sunni Muslim,
Area Sq Miles	94 926		traditional beliefs,
Population	9 402 000		Christian
Capital	Conakry	Currency	Guinea franc
Languages	French, Fulani,	Organizations	UN
	Malinke, local	Map page	114
	languages		

GUINEA-BISSAU
Republic of Guinea-Bissau

Area Sq Km	36 125	Religions	Traditional beliefs,
Area Sq Miles	13 948		Sunni Muslim,
Population	1 586 000		Christian
Capital	Bissau	Currency	CFA franc
Languages	Portuguese, crioulo,	Organizations	UN
	local languages	Map page	114

GUYANA
Co-operative Republic of Guyana

Area Sq Km	214 969	Religions	Protestant, Hindu,
Area Sq Miles	83 000		Roman Catholic,
Population	751 000		Sunni Muslim
Capital	Georgetown	Currency	Guyana dollar
Languages	English, creole,	Organizations	CARICOM, Comm.,
	Amerindian		UN
	languages	Map page	150

HAITI
Republic of Haiti

Area Sq Km	27 750	Religions	Roman Catholic,
Area Sq Miles	10 714		Protestant, Voodoo
Population	8 528 000	Currency	Gourde
Capital	Port-au-Prince	Organizations	CARICOM, UN
Languages	French, creole	Map page	147

HONDURAS
Republic of Honduras

Area Sq Km	112 088	Religions	Roman Catholic,
Area Sq Miles	43 277		Protestant
Population	7 205 000	Currency	Lempira
Capital	Tegucigalpa	Organizations	UN
Languages	Spanish, Amerindian	Map page	147
	languages		

HUNGARY
Republic of Hungary

Area Sq Km	93 030	Religions	Roman Catholic,
Area Sq Miles	35 919		Protestant
Population	10 098 000	Currency	Forint
Capital	Budapest	Organizations	OECD, UN
Languages	Hungarian	Map page	103

ICELAND
Republic of Iceland

Area Sq Km	102 820	Religions	Protestant
Area Sq Miles	39 699	Currency	Icelandic króna
Population	295 000	Organizations	OECD, UN
Capital	Reykjavik	Map page	92
Languages	Icelandic		

 ## INDIA
Republic of India

Area Sq Km	3 064 898	Religions	Hindu, Sunni Muslim,
Area Sq Miles	1 183 364		Shi'a Muslim, Sikh,
Population	1 103 371 000		Christian
Capital	New Delhi	Currency	Indian rupee
Languages	Hindi, English, many	Organizations	Comm., UN
	regional languages	Map page	72–73

INDONESIA
Republic of Indonesia

Area Sq Km	1 919 445	Religions	Sunni Muslim,
Area Sq Miles	741 102		Protestant, Roman
Population	222 781 000		Catholic, Hindu,
Capital	Jakarta		Buddhist
Languages	Indonesian, local	Currency	Rupiah
	languages	Organizations	APEC, ASEAN,
			OPEC, UN
		Map page	58–59

 ## IRAN
Islamic Republic of Iran

Area Sq Km	1 648 000	Religions	Shi'a Muslim, Sunni
Area Sq Miles	636 296		Muslim
Population	69 515 000	Currency	Iranian rial
Capital	Tehrān	Organizations	OPEC, UN
Languages	Farsi, Azeri, Kurdish,	Map page	81
	regional languages		

IRAQ
Republic of Iraq

Area Sq Km	438 317	Religions	Shi'a Muslim, Sunni
Area Sq Miles	169 235		Muslim, Christian
Population	28 807 000	Currency	Iraqi dinar
Capital	Baghdād	Organizations	OPEC, UN
Languages	Arabic, Kurdish,	Map page	81
	Turkmen		

IRELAND

Area Sq Km	70 282	Religions	Roman Catholic,
Area Sq Miles	27 136		Protestant,
Population	4 148 000	Currency	Euro
Capital	Dublin	Organizations	EU, OECD, UN
	(Baile Átha Cliath)	Map page	97
Languages	English, Irish		

 ## Isle of Man
United Kingdom Crown Dependency

Area Sq Km	572	Religions	Protestant, Roman
Area Sq Miles	221		Catholic
Population	77 000	Currency	Pound sterling
Capital	Douglas	Map page	98
Languages	English		

 ## ISRAEL
State of Israel

Area Sq Km	20 770	Religions	Jewish, Sunni Muslim,
Area Sq Miles	8 019		Christian, Druze
Population	6 725 000	Currency	Shekel
Capital	Jerusalem*	Organizations	UN
	(Yerushalayim)	Map page	80
	(El Quds)		
Languages	Hebrew, Arabic		

*De facto capital. Disputed.

 ## ITALY
Italian Republic

Area Sq Km	301 245	Religions	Roman Catholic
Area Sq Miles	116 311	Currency	Euro
Population	58 093 000	Organizations	EU, OECD, UN
Capital	Rome (Roma)	Map page	108–109
Languages	Italian		

 ## JAMAICA

Area Sq Km	10 991	Religions	Protestant, Roman
Area Sq Miles	4 244		Catholic
Population	2 651 000	Currency	Jamaican dollar
Capital	Kingston	Organizations	CARICOM, Comm.,
Languages	English, creole		UN
		Map page	146

Jammu and Kashmir
Disputed territory (India/Pakistan)

Area Sq Km	222 236	Map page	74–75
Area Sq Miles	85 806		
Population	13 000 000		
Capital	Srinagar		

 ## JAPAN

Area Sq Km	377 727	Religions	Shintoist, Buddhist,
Area Sq Miles	145 841		Christian
Population	128 085 000	Currency	Yen
Capital	Tōkyō	Organizations	APEC, OECD, UN
Languages	Japanese	Map page	66–67

Jersey
United Kingdom Crown Dependency

Area Sq Km	116	Religions	Protestant, Roman
Area Sq Miles	45		Catholic
Population	87 500	Currency	Pound sterling
Capital	St Helier	Map page	95
Languages	English, French		

JORDAN
Hashemite Kingdom of Jordan

Area Sq Km	89 206	Religions	Sunni Muslim,
Area Sq Miles	34 443		Christian
Population	5 703 000	Currency	Jordanian dinar
Capital	'Ammān	Organizations	UN
Languages	Arabic	Map page	80

Juan Fernández Islands
part of Chile

Area Sq Km	179	Religions	Roman Catholic,
Area Sq Miles	69		Protestant
Population	633	Currency	Chilean peso
Capital	San Juan Bautista	Map page	157
Languages	Spanish, Amerindian languages		

LATVIA
Republic of Latvia

Area Sq Km	63 700	Religions	Protestant, Roman
Area Sq Miles	24 595		Catholic, Russian
Population	2 307 000		Orthodox
Capital	Riga	Currency	Lats
Languages	Latvian, Russian	Organizations	UN
		Map page	88

KAZAKHSTAN
Republic of Kazakhstan

Area Sq Km	2 717 300	Religions	Sunni Muslim, Russian
Area Sq Miles	1 049 155		Orthodox, Protestant
Population	14 825 000	Currency	Tenge
Capital	Astana (Akmola)	Organizations	CIS, UN
Languages	Kazakh, Russian, Ukrainian, German, Uzbek, Tatar	Map page	76–77

LEBANON
Republic of Lebanon

Area Sq Km	10 452	Religions	Shi'a Muslim, Sunni
Area Sq Miles	4 036		Muslim, Christian
Population	3 577 000	Currency	Lebanese pound
Capital	Beirut (Beyrouth)	Organizations	UN
Languages	Arabic, Armenian, French	Map page	80

KENYA
Republic of Kenya

Area Sq Km	582 646	Religions	Christian, traditional
Area Sq Miles	224 961		beliefs
Population	34 256 000	Currency	Kenyan shilling
Capital	Nairobi	Organizations	Comm., UN
Languages	Swahili, English, local languages	Map page	119

LESOTHO
Kingdom of Lesotho

Area Sq Km	30 355	Religions	Christian, traditional
Area Sq Miles	11 720		beliefs
Population	1 795 000	Currency	Loti, South African
Capital	Maseru		rand
Languages	Sesotho, English, Zulu	Organizations	Comm., SADC, UN
		Map page	123

KIRIBATI
Republic of Kiribati

Area Sq Km	717	Religions	Roman Catholic,
Area Sq Miles	277		Protestant
Population	99 000	Currency	Australian dollar
Capital	Bairiki	Organizations	Comm., UN
Languages	Gilbertese, English	Map page	49

LIBERIA
Republic of Liberia

Area Sq Km	111 369	Religions	Traditional beliefs,
Area Sq Miles	43 000		Christian, Sunni
Population	3 283 000		Muslim
Capital	Monrovia	Currency	Liberian dollar
Languages	English, creole, local languages	Organizations	UN
		Map page	114

KUWAIT
State of Kuwait

Area Sq Km	17 818	Religions	Sunni Muslim, Shi'a
Area Sq Miles	6 880		Muslim, Christian,
Population	2 687 000		Hindu
Capital	Kuwait (Al Kuwayt)	Currency	Kuwaiti dinar
Languages	Arabic	Organizations	OPEC, UN
		Map page	78

LIBYA
Socialist People's Libyan Arab Jamahiriya

Area Sq Km	1 759 540	Religions	Sunni Muslim
Area Sq Miles	679 362	Currency	Libyan dinar
Population	5 853 000	Organizations	OPEC, UN
Capital	Tripoli (Ṭarābulus)	Map page	115
Languages	Arabic, Berber		

KYRGYZSTAN
Kyrgyz Republic

Area Sq Km	198 500	Religions	Sunni Muslim, Russian
Area Sq Miles	76 641		Orthodox
Population	5 264 000	Currency	Kyrgyz som
Capital	Bishkek (Frunze)	Organizations	CIS, UN
Languages	Kyrgyz, Russian, Uzbek	Map page	77

LIECHTENSTEIN
Principality of Liechtenstein

Area Sq Km	160	Religions	Roman Catholic,
Area Sq Miles	62		Protestant
Population	35 000	Currency	Swiss franc
Capital	Vaduz	Organizations	UN
Languages	German	Map page	105

LAOS
Lao People's Democratic Republic

Area Sq Km	236 800	Religions	Buddhist, traditional
Area Sq Miles	91 429		beliefs
Population	5 924 000	Currency	Kip
Capital	Vientiane (Viangchan)	Organizations	ASEAN, UN
Languages	Lao, local languages	Map page	62–63

LITHUANIA
Republic of Lithuania

Area Sq Km	65 200	Religions	Roman Catholic,
Area Sq Miles	25 174		Protestant, Russian
Population	3 431 000		Orthodox
Capital	Vilnius	Currency	Litas
Languages	Lithuanian, Russian, Polish	Organizations	UN
		Map page	88

Lord Howe Island
part of Australia

Area Sq Km	17	Religions	Protestant,
Area Sq Miles	6		Roman Catholic
Population	397	Currency	Australian dollar
Languages	English	Map page	51

LUXEMBOURG
Grand Duchy of Luxembourg

Area Sq Km	2 586	Religions	Roman Catholic
Area Sq Miles	998	Currency	Euro
Population	465 000	Organizations	EU, OECD, UN
Capital	Luxembourg	Map page	100
Languages	Letzeburgish,		
	German, French		

MACEDONIA (F.Y.R.O.M.)
Republic of Macedonia

Area Sq Km	25 713	Religions	Macedonian Orthodox,
Area Sq Miles	9 928		Sunni Muslim
Population	2 034 000	Currency	Macedonian denar
Capital	Skopje	Organizations	UN
Languages	Macedonian,	Map page	111
	Albanian, Turkish		

MADAGASCAR
Republic of Madagascar

Area Sq Km	587 041	Religions	Traditional beliefs,
Area Sq Miles	226 658		Christian, Sunni
Population	18 606 000		Muslim
Capital	Antananarivo	Currency	Malagasy ariary,
Languages	Malagasy, French		Malagasy franc
		Organizations	UN
		Map page	121

Madeira
Autonomous Region of Portugal

Area Sq Km	779	Religions	Roman Catholic,
Area Sq Miles	301		Protestant
Population	245 012	Currency	Euro
Capital	Funchal	Map page	114
Languages	Portuguese		

MALAWI
Republic of Malawi

Area Sq Km	118 484	Religions	Christian, traditional
Area Sq Miles	45 747		beliefs, Sunni Muslim
Population	12 884 000	Currency	Malawian kwacha
Capital	Lilongwe	Organizations	Comm.,SADC, UN
Languages	Chichewa, English,	Map page	121
	local languages		

MALAYSIA
Federation of Malaysia

Area Sq Km	332 965	Religions	Sunni Muslim,
Area Sq Miles	128 559		Buddhist,
Population	25 347 000		Hindu, Christian,
Capital	Kuala Lumpur/		traditional beliefs
	Putrajaya	Currency	Ringgit
Languages	Malay, English,	Organizations	APEC, ASEAN,
	Chinese, Tamil,		Comm., UN
	local languages	Map page	60–61

MALDIVES
Republic of the Maldives

Area Sq Km	298	Religions	Sunni Muslim
Area Sq Miles	115	Currency	Rufiyaa
Population	329 000	Organizations	Comm., UN
Capital	Male	Map page	56
Languages	Divehi (Maldivian)		

MALI
Republic of Mali

Area Sq Km	1 240 140	Religions	Sunni Muslim,
Area Sq Miles	478 821		traditional beliefs,
Population	13 518 000		Christian
Capital	Bamako	Currency	CFA franc
Languages	French, Bambara,	Organizations	UN
	local languages	Map page	114

MALTA
Republic of Malta

Area Sq Km	316	Religions	Roman Catholic
Area Sq Miles	122	Currency	Maltese lira
Population	402 000	Organizations	Comm., UN
Capital	Valletta	Map page	84
Languages	Maltese, English		

MARSHALL ISLANDS
Republic of the Marshall Islands

Area Sq Km	181	Religions	Protestant, Roman
Area Sq Miles	70		Catholic
Population	62 000	Currency	United States dollar
Capital	Delap-Uliga-Djarrit	Organizations	UN
Languages	English, Marshallese	Map page	48

Martinique
French Overseas Department

Area Sq Km	1 079	Religions	Roman Catholic,
Area Sq Miles	417		traditional beliefs
Population	396 000	Currency	Euro
Capital	Fort-de-France	Map page	147
Languages	French, creole		

MAURITANIA
Islamic Arab and African Republic of Mauritania

Area Sq Km	1 030 700	Religions	Sunni Muslim
Area Sq Miles	397 955	Currency	Ouguiya
Population	3 069 000	Organizations	UN
Capital	Nouakchott	Map page	114
Languages	Arabic, French, local		
	languages		

MAURITIUS
Republic of Mauritius

Area Sq Km	2 040	Religions	Hindu, Roman
Area Sq Miles	788		Catholic, Sunni
Population	1 245 000		Muslim
Capital	Port Louis	Currency	Mauritius rupee
Languages	English, creole,	Organizations	Comm., SADC, UN
	Hindi, Bhojpuri,	Map page	113
	French		

Mayotte
French Departmental Collectivity

Area Sq Km	373	Religions	Sunni Muslim,
Area Sq Miles	144		Christian
Population	186 026	Currency	Euro
Capital	Dzaoudzi	Map page	121
Languages	French, Mahorian		

Melilla
Autonomous Community of Spain

Area Sq Km	13	Religions	Roman Catholic,
Area Sq Miles	5		Muslim
Population	68 463	Currency	Euro
Capital	Melilla	Map page	114
Languages	Spanish, Arabic		

MEXICO
United Mexican States

Area Sq Km	1 972 545	Religions	Roman Catholic,
Area Sq Miles	761 604		Protestant
Population	107 029 000	Currency	Mexican peso
Capital	Mexico City	Organizations	APEC, OECD, UN
Languages	Spanish, Amerindian	Map page	144–145
	languages		

MICRONESIA, FEDERATED STATES OF

Area Sq Km	701	Religions	Roman Catholic,
Area Sq Miles	271		Protestant
Population	110 000	Currency	United States dollar
Capital	Palikir	Organizations	UN
Languages	English, Chuukese,	Map page	48
	Pohnpeian, local		
	languages		

MOLDOVA
Republic of Moldova

Area Sq Km	33 700	Religions	Romanian Orthodox,
Area Sq Miles	13 012		Russian Orthodox
Population	4 206 000	Currency	Moldovan leu
Capital	Chişinău (Kishinev)	Organizations	CIS, UN
Languages	Romanian,	Map page	90
	Ukrainian, Gagauz,		
	Russian		

MONACO
Principality of Monaco

Area Sq Km	2	Religions	Roman Catholic
Area Sq Miles	1	Currency	Euro
Population	35 000	Organizations	UN
Capital	Monaco-Ville	Map page	105
Languages	French,Monégasque,		
	Italian		

MONGOLIA

Area Sq Km	1 565 000	Religions	Buddhist, Sunni Muslim
Area Sq Miles	604 250	Currency	Tugrik (tögrög)
Population	2 646 000	Organizations	UN
Capital	Ulan Bator	Map page	68–69
	(Ulaanbaatar)		
Languages	Khalka (Mongolian),		
	Kazakh, local		
	languages		

MONTENEGRO
Republic of Montenegro

Area Sq Km	13 812	Religions	Montenegrin
Area Sq Miles	5 333		Orthodox,
Population	620 145		Sunni Muslim
Capital	Podgorica	Currency	Euro
Languages	Serbian	Organizations	UN
	(Montenegrin),	Map page	109
	Albanian		

Montserrat
United Kingdom Overseas Territory

Area Sq Km	100	Religions	Protestant, Roman
Area Sq Miles	39		Catholic
Population	4 000	Currency	East Caribbean dollar
Capital	Brades*	Organizations	CARICOM
Languages	English	Map page	147

*Temporary capital

MOROCCO
Kingdom of Morocco

Area Sq Km	446 550	Religions	Sunni Muslim
Area Sq Miles	172 414	Currency	Moroccan dirham
Population	31 478 000	Organizations	UN
Capital	Rabat	Map page	114
Languages	Arabic, Berber,		
	French		

MOZAMBIQUE
Republic of Mozambique

Area Sq Km	799 380	Religions	Traditional beliefs,
Area Sq Miles	308 642		Roman Catholic,
Population	19 792 000		Sunni Muslim
Capital	Maputo	Currency	Metical
Languages	Portuguese, Makua,	Organizations	Comm., SADC, UN
	Tsonga, local	Map page	121
	languages		

MYANMAR (BURMA)
Union of Myanmar

Area Sq Km	676 577	Religions	Buddhist, Christian,
Area Sq Miles	261 228		Sunni Muslim
Population	50 519 000	Currency	Kyat
Capital	Naypyidaw/Rangoon	Organizations	ASEAN, UN
	(Yangôn)	Map page	62–63
Languages	Burmese, Shan,		
	Karen, local languages		

NAMIBIA
Republic of Namibia

Area Sq Km	824 292	Religions	Protestant, Roman
Area Sq Miles	318 261		Catholic
Population	2 031 000	Currency	Namibian dollar
Capital	Windhoek	Organizations	Comm., SADC, UN
Languages	English, Afrikaans,	Map page	121
	German, Ovambo,		
	local languages		

NAURU
Republic of Nauru

Area Sq Km	21	Religions	Protestant, Roman
Area Sq Miles	8		Catholic
Population	14 000	Currency	Australian dollar
Capital	Yaren	Organizations	Comm., UN
Languages	Nauruan, English	Map page	48

 NEPAL

Area Sq Km	147 181	Religions	Hindu, Buddhist,
Area Sq Miles	56 827		Sunni Muslim
Population	27 133 000	Currency	Nepalese rupee
Capital	Kathmandu	Organizations	UN
Languages	Nepali, Maithili,	Map page	75
	Bhojpuri, English,		
	local languages		

 NETHERLANDS
Kingdom of the Netherlands

Area Sq Km	41 526	Religions	Roman Catholic,
Area Sq Miles	16 033		Protestant, Sunni
Population	16 299 000		Muslim
Capital	Amsterdam/	Currency	Euro
	The Hague	Organizations	EU, OECD, UN
	('s-Gravenhage)	Map page	100
	(Den Haag)		
Languages	Dutch, Frisian		

 Netherlands Antilles
Self-governing Netherlands Territory

Area Sq Km	800	Religions	Roman Catholic,
Area Sq Miles	309		Protestant
Population	183 000	Currency	Netherlands Antilles
Capital	Willemstad		guilder
Languages	Dutch, Papiamento,	Map page	147
	English		

New Caledonia
French Overseas Country

Area Sq Km	19 058	Religions	Roman Catholic,
Area Sq Miles	7 358		Protestant, Sunni
Population	237 000		Muslim
Capital	Nouméa	Currency	CFP franc
Languages	French, local	Map page	48
	languages		

NEW ZEALAND

Area Sq Km	270 534	Religions	Protestant, Roman
Area Sq Miles	104 454		Catholic
Population	4 028 000	Currency	New Zealand dollar
Capital	Wellington	Organizations	APEC, Comm.,
Languages	English, Maori		OECD, UN
		Map page	54

 NICARAGUA
Republic of Nicaragua

Area Sq Km	130 000	Religions	Roman Catholic,
Area Sq Miles	50 193		Protestant
Population	5 487 000	Currency	Córdoba
Capital	Managua	Organizations	UN
Languages	Spanish, Amerindian	Map page	146
	languages		

 NIGER
Republic of Niger

Area Sq Km	1 267 000	Religions	Sunni Muslim,
Area Sq Miles	489 191		traditional beliefs
Population	13 957 000	Currency	CFA franc
Capital	Niamey	Organizations	UN
Languages	French, Hausa,	Map page	115
	Fulani, local		
	languages		

 NIGERIA
Federal Republic of Nigeria

Area Sq Km	923 768	Religions	Sunni Muslim,
Area Sq Miles	356 669		Christian, traditional
Population	131 530 000		beliefs
Capital	Abuja	Currency	Naira
Languages	English, Hausa,	Organizations	Comm., OPEC, UN
	Yoruba, Ibo, Fulani,	Map page	115
	local languages		

 Niue
Self-governing New Zealand Overseas Territory

Area Sq Km	258	Religions	Christian
Area Sq Miles	100	Currency	New Zealand dollar
Population	1 000	Map page	48
Capital	Alofi		
Languages	English, Niuean		

Norfolk Island
Australian External Territory

Area Sq Km	35	Religions	Protestant, Roman
Area Sq Miles	14		Catholic
Population	2 601	Currency	Australian dollar
Capital	Kingston	Map page	48
Languages	English		

 Northern Mariana Islands
United States Commonwealth

Area Sq Km	477	Religions	Roman Catholic
Area Sq Miles	184	Currency	United States dollar
Population	81 000	Map page	59
Capital	Capitol Hill		
Languages	English, Chamorro,		
	local languages		

 NORTH KOREA
People's Democratic Republic of Korea

Area Sq Km	120 538	Religions	Traditional beliefs,
Area Sq Miles	46 540		Chondoist, Buddhist
Population	22 488 000	Currency	North Korean won
Capital	P'yŏngyang	Organizations	UN
Languages	Korean	Map page	65

NORWAY
Kingdom of Norway

Area Sq Km	323 878	Religions	Protestant, Roman
Area Sq Miles	125 050		Catholic
Population	4 620 000	Currency	Norwegian krone
Capital	Oslo	Organizations	OECD, UN
Languages	Norwegian	Map page	92–93

OMAN
Sultanate of Oman

Area Sq Km	309 500	Religions	Ibadhi Muslim, Sunni
Area Sq Miles	119 499		Muslim
Population	2 567 000	Currency	Omani riyal
Capital	Muscat (Masqat)	Organizations	UN
Languages	Arabic, Baluchi,	Map page	79
	Indian languages		

PAKISTAN
Islamic Republic of Pakistan

Area Sq Km	803 940	Religions	Sunni Muslim, Shi'a
Area Sq Miles	310 403		Muslim, Christian,
Population	157 935 000		Hindu
Capital	Islamabad	Currency	Pakistani rupee
Languages	Urdu, Punjabi,	Organizations	Comm., UN
	Sindhi, Pushtu,	Map page	74
	English		

PALAU
Republic of Palau

Area Sq Km	497	Religions	Roman Catholic,
Area Sq Miles	192		Protestant, traditional
Population	20 000		beliefs
Capital	Melekeok	Currency	United States dollar
Languages	Palauan, English	Organizations	UN
		Map page	59

PANAMA
Republic of Panama

Area Sq Km	77 082	Religions	Roman Catholic,
Area Sq Miles	29 762		Protestant, Sunni
Population	3 232 000		Muslim
Capital	Panama City	Currency	Balboa
Languages	Spanish, English,	Organizations	UN
	Amerindian	Map page	146
	languages		

PAPUA NEW GUINEA
Independent State of Papua New Guinea

Area Sq Km	462 840	Religions	Protestant, Roman
Area Sq Miles	178 704		Catholic, traditional
Population	5 887 000		beliefs
Capital	Port Moresby	Currency	Kina
Languages	English, Tok Pisin	Organizations	Comm., UN
	(creole), local	Map page	59
	languages		

PARAGUAY
Republic of Paraguay

Area Sq Km	406 752	Religions	Roman Catholic,
Area Sq Miles	157 048		Protestant
Population	6 158 000	Currency	Guaraní
Capital	Asunción	Organizations	UN
Languages	Spanish, Guaraní	Map page	152

PERU
Republic of Peru

Area Sq Km	1 285 216	Religions	Roman Catholic,
Area Sq Miles	496 225		Protestant
Population	27 968 000	Currency	Sol
Capital	Lima	Organizations	APEC, UN
Languages	Spanish, Quechua,	Map page	150
	Aymara		

PHILIPPINES
Republic of the Philippines

Area Sq Km	300 000	Religions	Roman Catholic,
Area Sq Miles	115 831		Protestant, Sunni
Population	83 054 000		Muslim, Aglipayan
Capital	Manila	Currency	Philippine peso
Languages	English, Filipino,	Organizations	APEC, ASEAN, UN
	Tagalog, Cebuano,	Map page	64
	local languages		

Pitcairn Islands
United Kingdom Overseas Territory

Area Sq Km	45	Religions	Protestant
Area Sq Miles	17	Currency	New Zealand dollar
Population	47	Map page	49
Capital	Adamstown		
Languages	English		

POLAND
Polish Republic

Area Sq Km	312 683	Religions	Roman Catholic,
Area Sq Miles	120 728		Polish Orthodox
Population	38 530 000	Currency	Zloty
Capital	Warsaw (Warszawa)	Organizations	OECD, UN
Languages	Polish, German	Map page	103

PORTUGAL
Portuguese Republic

Area Sq Km	88 940	Religions	Roman Catholic,
Area Sq Miles	34 340		Protestant
Population	10 495 000	Currency	Euro
Capital	Lisbon (Lisboa)	Organizations	EU, OECD, UN
Languages	Portuguese	Map page	106

Puerto Rico
United States Commonwealth

Area Sq Km	9 104	Religions	Roman Catholic,
Area Sq Miles	3 515		Protestant
Population	3 955 000	Currency	United States dollar
Capital	San Juan	Map page	147
Languages	Spanish, English		

QATAR
State of Qatar

Area Sq Km	11 437	Religions	Sunni Muslim
Area Sq Miles	4 416	Currency	Qatari riyal
Population	813 000	Organizations	OPEC, UN
Capital	Doha (Ad Dawḥah)	Map page	79
Languages	Arabic		

Réunion
French Overseas Department

Area Sq Km	2 551	Religions	Roman Catholic
Area Sq Miles	985	Currency	Euro
Population	785 000	Map page	113
Capital	St-Denis		
Languages	French, creole		

 Rodrigues Island
part of Mauritius

Area Sq Km	104	Religions	Christian
Area Sq Miles	40	Currency	Rupee
Population	36 306	Map page	159
Capital	Port Mathurin		
Languages	English, creole		

 ROMANIA

Area Sq Km	237 500	Religions	Romanian Orthodox,
Area Sq Miles	91 699		Protestant, Roman
Population	21 711 000		Catholic
Capital	Bucharest (București)	Currency	Romanian leu
Languages	Romanian,	Organizations	UN
	Hungarian	Map page	110

 RUSSIAN FEDERATION

Area Sq Km	17 075 400	Religions	Russian Orthodox,
Area Sq Miles	6 592 849		Sunni Muslim,
Population	143 202 000		Protestant
Capital	Moscow (Moskva)	Currency	Russian rouble
Languages	Russian, Tatar,	Organizations	APEC, CIS, UN
	Ukrainian, local	Map page	82–83
	languages		

 RWANDA
Republic of Rwanda

Area Sq Km	26 338	Religions	Roman Catholic,
Area Sq Miles	10 169		traditional beliefs,
Population	9 038 000		Protestant
Capital	Kigali	Currency	Rwandan franc
Languages	Kinyarwanda,	Organizations	UN
	French, English	Map page	119

 Saba
part of Netherlands Antilles

Area Sq Km	13	Religions	Roman Catholic,
Area Sq Miles	5		Protestant
Population	1 387	Currency	Netherlands Antilles
Capital	Bottom		guilder
Languages	Dutch, English	Map page	147

 St Barthélémy
Dependency of Guadeloupe

Area Sq Km	21	Religions	Roman Catholic
Area Sq Miles	8	Currency	Euro
Population	6 852	Map page	147
Capital	Gustavia		
Languages	French, creole		

 St Helena
United Kingdom Overseas Territory

Area Sq Km	121	Religions	Protestant, Roman
Area Sq Miles	47		Catholic,
Population	5 000	Currency	St Helena pound
Capital	Jamestown	Map page	113
Languages	English		

 ST KITTS AND NEVIS
Federation of St Kitts and Nevis

Area Sq Km	261	Religions	Protestant, Roman
Area Sq Miles	101		Catholic
Population	43 000	Currency	East Caribbean dollar
Capital	Basseterre	Organizations	CARICOM, Comm.,
Languages	English, creole		UN
		Map page	147

 ST LUCIA

Area Sq Km	616	Religions	Roman Catholic,
Area Sq Miles	238		Protestant
Population	161 000	Currency	East Caribbean dollar
Capital	Castries	Organizations	CARICOM, Comm.,
Languages	English, creole		UN
		Map page	147

 St Martin
Dependency of Guadeloupe

Area Sq Km	54	Religions	Roman Catholic
Area Sq Miles	21	Currency	Euro
Population	29 078	Map page	147
Capital	Marigot		
Languages	French, creole		

 St Pierre and Miquelon
French Territorial Collectivity

Area Sq Km	242	Religions	Roman Catholic
Area Sq Miles	93	Currency	Euro
Population	6 000	Map page	131
Capital	St-Pierre		
Languages	French		

ST VINCENT AND THE GRENADINES

Area Sq Km	389	Religions	Protestant, Roman
Area Sq Miles	150		Catholic
Population	119 000	Currency	East Caribbean dollar
Capital	Kingstown	Organizations	CARICOM, Comm.,
Languages	English, creole		UN
		Map page	147

SAMOA
Independent State of Samoa

Area Sq Km	2 831	Religions	Protestant, Roman
Area Sq Miles	1 093		Catholic
Population	185 000	Currency	Tala
Capital	Apia	Organizations	Comm., UN
Languages	Samoan, English	Map page	49

SAN MARINO
Republic of San Marino

Area Sq Km	61	Religions	Roman Catholic
Area Sq Miles	24	Currency	Euro
Population	28 000	Organizations	UN
Capital	San Marino	Map page	108
Languages	Italian		

SÃO TOMÉ AND PRÍNCIPE
Democratic Republic of São Tomé and Príncipe

Area Sq Km	964	Religions	Roman Catholic,
Area Sq Miles	372		Protestant
Population	157 000	Currency	Dobra
Capital	São Tomé	Organizations	UN
Languages	Portuguese, creole	Map page	113

SAUDI ARABIA
Kingdom of Saudi Arabia

Area Sq Km	2 200 000	Religions	Sunni Muslim, Shi'a
Area Sq Miles	849 425		Muslim
Population	24 573 000	Currency	Saudi Arabian riyal
Capital	Riyadh (Ar Riyāḍ)	Organizations	OPEC, UN
Languages	Arabic	Map page	78–79

SENEGAL
Republic of Senegal

Area Sq Km	196 720	Religions	Sunni Muslim, Roman
Area Sq Miles	75 954		Catholic, traditional
Population	11 658 000		beliefs
Capital	Dakar	Currency	CFA franc
Languages	French, Wolof, Fulani,	Organizations	UN
	local languages	Map page	114

SERBIA
Republic of Serbia

Area Sq Km	88 361	Religions	Serbian Orthodox,
Area Sq Miles	34 116		Sunni Muslim
Population	9 379 437	Currency	Serbian dinar, Euro
Capital	Belgrade (Beograd)	Organizations	UN
Languages	Serbian, Albanian,	Map page	109
	Hungarian		

SEYCHELLES
Republic of the Seychelles

Area Sq Km	455	Religions	Roman Catholic,
Area Sq Miles	176		Protestant
Population	81 000	Currency	Seychelles rupee
Capital	Victoria	Organizations	Comm., SADC, UN
Languages	English, French,	Map page	113
	creole		

SIERRA LEONE
Republic of Sierra Leone

Area Sq Km	71 740	Religions	Sunni Muslim,
Area Sq Miles	27 699		traditional beliefs
Population	5 525 000	Currency	Leone
Capital	Freetown	Organizations	Comm., UN
Languages	English, creole,	Map page	114
	Mende, Temne,		
	local languages		

SINGAPORE
Republic of Singapore

Area Sq Km	639	Religions	Buddhist, Taoist, Sunni
Area Sq Miles	247		Muslim, Christian,
Population	4 326 000		Hindu
Capital	Singapore	Currency	Singapore dollar
Languages	Chinese, English,	Organizations	APEC, ASEAN,
	Malay, Tamil		Comm., UN
		Map page	60

Sint Eustatius
part of Netherlands Antilles

Area Sq Km	21	Religions	Protestant, Roman
Area Sq Miles	8		Catholic
Population	2 829	Currency	Netherlands Antilles
Capital	Oranjestad		guilder
Languages	Dutch, English	Map page	147

Sint Maarten
part of Netherlands Antilles

Area Sq Km	34	Religions	Protestant, Roman
Area Sq Miles	13		Catholic
Population	31 882	Currency	Netherlands Antilles
Capital	Philipsburg		guilder
Languages	Dutch, English	Map page	147

SLOVAKIA
Slovak Republic

Area Sq Km	49 035	Religions	Roman Catholic,
Area Sq Miles	18 933		Protestant, Orthodox
Population	5 401 000	Currency	Slovakian koruna
Capital	Bratislava	Organizations	UN
Languages	Slovakian,	Map page	103
	Hungarian, Czech		

SLOVENIA
Republic of Slovenia

Area Sq Km	20 251	Religions	Roman Catholic,
Area Sq Miles	7 819		Protestant
Population	1 967 000	Currency	Tólar
Capital	Ljubljana	Organizations	UN
Languages	Slovenian, Croatian,	Map page	108–109
	Serbian		

SOLOMON ISLANDS

Area Sq Km	28 370	Religions	Protestant, Roman
Area Sq Miles	10 954		Catholic
Population	478 000	Currency	Solomon Islands dollar
Capital	Honiara	Organizations	Comm., UN
Languages	English, creole, local	Map page	48
	languages		

SOMALIA
Somali Democratic Republic

Area Sq Km	637 657	Religions	Sunni Muslim
Area Sq Miles	246 201	Currency	Somali shilling
Population	8 228 000	Organizations	UN
Capital	Mogadishu	Map page	117
	(Muqdisho)		
Languages	Somali, Arabic		

SOUTH AFRICA, REPUBLIC OF

Area Sq Km	1 219 080	Religions	Protestant, Roman
Area Sq Miles	470 689		Catholic, Sunni
Population	47 432 000		Muslim, Hindu
Capital	Pretoria (Tshwane)/	Currency	Rand
	Cape Town	Organizations	Comm., SADC, UN
Languages	Afrikaans, English,	Map page	122–123
	nine official local		
	languages		

SOUTH KOREA
Republic of Korea

Area Sq Km	99 274	Religions	Buddhist, Protestant,
Area Sq Miles	38 330		Roman Catholic
Population	47 817 000	Currency	South Korean won
Capital	Seoul (Sŏul)	Organizations	APEC, UN
Languages	Korean	Map page	65

SPAIN
Kingdom of Spain

Area Sq Km	504 782	Religions	Roman Catholic
Area Sq Miles	194 897	Currency	Euro
Population	43 064 000	Organizations	EU, OECD, UN
Capital	Madrid	Map page	106–107
Languages	Castilian, Catalan,		
	Galician, Basque		

SRI LANKA
Democratic Socialist Republic of Sri Lanka

Area Sq Km	65 610	Religions	Buddhist, Hindu,
Area Sq Miles	25 332		Sunni Muslim, Roman
Population	20 743 000		Catholic
Capital	Sri Jayewardenepura	Currency	Sri Lankan rupee
	Kotte	Organizations	Comm., UN
Languages	Sinhalese, Tamil,	Map page	73
	English		

SUDAN
Republic of the Sudan

Area Sq Km	2 505 813	Religions	Sunni Muslim,
Area Sq Miles	967 500		traditional beliefs,
Population	36 233 000		Christian
Capital	Khartoum	Currency	Sudanese dinar
Languages	Arabic, Dinka,	Organizations	UN
	Nubian, Beja, Nuer,	Map page	116–117
	local languages		

SURINAME
Republic of Suriname

Area Sq Km	163 820	Religions	Hindu, Roman
Area Sq Miles	63 251		Catholic, Protestant,
Population	449 000		Sunni Muslim
Capital	Paramaribo	Currency	Suriname guilder
Languages	Dutch,	Organizations	CARICOM, UN
	Surinamese,	Map page	151
	English, Hindi		

Svalbard
part of Norway

Area Sq Km	61 229	Religions	Protestant
Area Sq Miles	23 641	Currency	Norwegian krone
Population	2 515	Map page	82
Capital	Longyearbyen		
Languages	Norwegian		

SWAZILAND
Kingdom of Swaziland

Area Sq Km	17 364	Currency	Emalangeni,
Area Sq Miles	6 704		South African rand
Population	1 032 000	Organizations	Comm., SADC, UN
Capital	Mbabane	Map page	123
Languages	Swazi, English		
Religions	Christian,		
	traditional beliefs		

SWEDEN
Kingdom of Sweden

Area Sq Km	449 964	Religions	Protestant,
Area Sq Miles	173 732		Roman Catholic
Population	9 041 000	Currency	Swedish krona
Capital	Stockholm	Organizations	EU, OECD, UN
Languages	Swedish	Map page	92–93

SWITZERLAND
Swiss Confederation

Area Sq Km	41 293	Religions	Roman Catholic,
Area Sq Miles	15 943		Protestant,
Population	7 252 000	Currency	Swiss franc
Capital	Bern (Berne)	Organizations	OECD, UN
Languages	German, French,	Map page	105
	Italian, Romansch		

SYRIA
Syrian Arab Republic

Area Sq Km	185 180	Religions	Sunni Muslim, Shi'a
Area Sq Miles	71 498		Muslim, Christian
Population	19 043 000	Currency	Syrian pound
Capital	Damascus (Dimashq)	Organizations	UN
Languages	Arabic, Kurdish,	Map page	80
	Armenian		

TAIWAN
Republic of China

Area Sq Km	36 179	Religions	Buddhist, Taoist,
Area Sq Miles	13 969		Confucian, Christian
Population	22 858 000	Currency	Taiwan dollar
Capital	T'aipei	Organizations	APEC
Languages	Mandarin, Min,	Map page	71
	Hakka, local		
	languages		

TAJIKISTAN
Republic of Tajikistan

Area Sq Km	143 100	Religions	Sunni Muslim
Area Sq Miles	55 251	Currency	Somoni
Population	6 507 000	Organizations	CIS, UN
Capital	Dushanbe	Map page	77
Languages	Tajik, Uzbek, Russian		

TANZANIA
United Republic of Tanzania

Area Sq Km	945 087	Religions	Shi'a Muslim, Sunni
Area Sq Miles	364 900		Muslim, traditional
Population	38 329 000		beliefs, Christian
Capital	Dodoma	Currency	Tanzanian shilling
Languages	Swahili, English,	Organizations	Comm., SADC, UN
	Nyamwezi, local	Map page	119
	languages		

THAILAND
Kingdom of Thailand

Area Sq Km	513 115	Religions	Buddhist, Sunni
Area Sq Miles	198 115		Muslim
Population	64 233 000	Currency	Baht
Capital	Bangkok	Organizations	APEC, ASEAN, UN
	(Krung Thep)	Map page	62–63
Languages	Thai, Lao, Chinese,		
	Malay, Mon-Khmer		
	languages		

TOGO
Republic of Togo

Area Sq Km	56 785	Religions	Traditional beliefs,
Area Sq Miles	21 925		Christian, Sunni
Population	6 145 000		Muslim
Capital	Lomé	Currency	CFA franc
Languages	French, Ewe, Kabre,	Organizations	UN
	local languages	Map page	114

Tokelau
New Zealand Overseas Territory

Area Sq Km	10	Religions	Christian
Area Sq Miles	4	Currency	New Zealand dollar
Population	1 000	Map page	49
Capital	none		
Languages	English, Tokelauan		

TONGA
Kingdom of Tonga

Area Sq Km	748	Religions	Protestant, Roman
Area Sq Miles	289		Catholic
Population	102 000	Currency	Pa'anga
Capital	Nuku'alofa	Organizations	Comm., UN
Languages	Tongan, English	Map page	49

TRINIDAD AND TOBAGO
Republic of Trinidad and Tobago

Area Sq Km	5 130	Religions	Roman Catholic,
Area Sq Miles	1 981		Hindu, Protestant,
Population	1 305 000		Sunni Muslim
Capital	Port of Spain	Currency	Trinidad and Tobago
Languages	English, creole,		dollar
	Hindi	Organizations	CARICOM, Comm.,
			UN
		Map page	147

Tristan da Cunha
Dependency of St Helena

Area Sq Km	98	Religions	Protestant, Roman
Area Sq Miles	38		Catholic
Population	284	Currency	Pound sterling
Capital	Settlement of	Map page	113
	Edinburgh		
Languages	English		

TUNISIA
Tunisian Republic

Area Sq Km	164 150	Religions	Sunni Muslim
Area Sq Miles	63 379	Currency	Tunisian dinar
Population	10 102 000	Organizations	UN
Capital	Tunis	Map page	115
Languages	Arabic, French		

TURKEY
Republic of Turkey

Area Sq Km	779 452	Religions	Sunni Muslim, Shi'a
Area Sq Miles	300 948		Muslim
Population	73 193 000	Currency	Turkish lira
Capital	Ankara	Organizations	OECD, UN
Languages	Turkish, Kurdish	Map page	80

TURKMENISTAN
Republic of Turkmenistan

Area Sq Km	488 100	Religions	Sunni Muslim, Russian
Area Sq Miles	188 456		Orthodox
Population	4 833 000	Currency	Turkmen manat
Capital	Aşgabat (Ashkhabad)	Organizations	CIS, UN
Languages	Turkmen, Uzbek,	Map page	76
	Russian		

Turks and Caicos Islands
United Kingdom Overseas Territory

Area Sq Km	430	Religions	Protestant
Area Sq Miles	166	Currency	United States dollar
Population	26 000	Map page	147
Capital	Grand Turk		
Languages	English		

TUVALU

Area Sq Km	25	Religions	Protestant
Area Sq Miles	10	Currency	Australian dollar
Population	10 000	Organizations	Comm.
Capital	Vaiaku	Map page	49
Languages	Tuvaluan, English		

UGANDA
Republic of Uganda

Area Sq Km	241 038	Religions	Roman Catholic,
Area Sq Miles	93 065		Protestant, Sunni
Population	28 816 000		Muslim, traditional
Capital	Kampala		beliefs
Languages	English, Swahili,	Currency	Ugandan shilling
	Luganda, local	Organizations	Comm., UN
	languages	Map page	119

UKRAINE

Area Sq Km	603 700	Religions	Ukrainian Orthodox,
Area Sq Miles	233 090		Ukrainian Catholic,
Population	46 481 000		Roman Catholic
Capital	Kiev (Kyiv)	Currency	Hryvnia
Languages	Ukrainian, Russian	Organizations	CIS, UN
		Map page	90–91

UNITED ARAB EMIRATES
Federation of Emirates

Area Sq Km	77 700	Religions	Sunni Muslim, Shi'a
Area Sq Miles	30 000		Muslim
Population	4 496 000	Currency	United Arab Emirates
Capital	Abu Dhabi		dirham
	(Abū Ẓabī)	Organizations	OPEC, UN
Languages	Arabic, English	Map page	79

Abu Dhabi (Abū Ẓabī) (Emirate)

Area Sq Km	67 340	Population	1 248 000
Area Sq Miles	26 000	Capital	Abu Dhabi (Abū Ẓabī)

Ajman (Emirate)

Area Sq Km	259	Population	189 000
Area Sq Miles	100	Capital	Ajman

Dubai (Emirate)

Area Sq Km	3 885	Population	971 000
Area Sq Miles	1 500	Capital	Dubai

Fujairah (Emirate)

Area Sq Km	1 165	Population	103 000
Area Sq Miles	450	Capital	Fujairah

Ras al Khaimah (Emirate)

Area Sq Km	1 684	Population	179 000
Area Sq Miles	650	Capital	Ras al Khaimah

Sharjah (Emirate)

Area Sq Km	2 590	Population	551 000
Area Sq Miles	1 000	Capital	Sharjah

Umm al Qaiwain (Emirate)

Area Sq Km	777	Population	49 000
Area Sq Miles	300	Capital	Umm al Qaiwain

UNITED KINGDOM
of Great Britain and Northern Ireland

Area Sq Km	243 609	Religions	Protestant, Roman
Area Sq Miles	94 058		Catholic, Muslim
Population	59 668 000	Currency	Pound sterling
Capital	London	Organizations	Comm., EU, OECD,
Languages	English, Welsh,		UN
	Gaelic	Map page	94–95

England (Constituent country)

Area Sq Km	130 433	Population	49 138 831
Area Sq Miles	50 360	Capital	London

Northern Ireland (Province)

Area Sq Km	13 576	Population	1 685 267
Area Sq Miles	5 242	Capital	Belfast

Scotland (Constituent country)

Area Sq Km	78 822	Population	5 062 011
Area Sq Miles	30 433	Capital	Edinburgh

Wales (Principality)

Area Sq Km	20 778	Population	2 903 085
Area Sq Miles	8 022	Capital	Cardiff

UNITED STATES OF AMERICA
Federal Republic

Area Sq Km	9 826 635	Religions	Protestant, Roman
Area Sq Miles	3 794 085		Catholic, Sunni
Population	298 213 000		Muslim, Jewish
Capital	Washington D.C.	Currency	United States dollar
Languages	English, Spanish	Organizations	APEC, OECD, UN
		Map page	132–133

Alabama (State)

Area Sq Km	135 765	Population	4 486 508
Area Sq Miles	52 419	Capital	Montgomery

Alaska (State)

Area Sq Km	1 717 854	Population	643 786
Area Sq Miles	663 267	Capital	Juneau

Arizona (State)

Area Sq Km	295 253	Population	5 456 453
Area Sq Miles	113 998	Capital	Phoenix

Arkansas (State)

Area Sq Km	137 733	Population	2 710 079
Area Sq Miles	53 179	Capital	Little Rock

California (State)

Area Sq Km	423 971	Population	35 116 033
Area Sq Miles	163 696	Capital	Sacramento

Colorado (State)

Area Sq Km 269 602	Population 4 506 542	
Area Sq Miles 104 094	Capital Denver	

Connecticut (State)

Area Sq Km 14 356	Population 3 460 503
Area Sq Miles 5 543	Capital Hartford

Delaware (State)

Area Sq Km 6 446	Population 807 385
Area Sq Miles 2 489	Capital Dover

District of Columbia (District)

Area Sq Km 176	Population 570 898
Area Sq Miles 68	Capital Washington

Florida (State)

Area Sq Km 170 305	Population 16 713 149
Area Sq Miles 65 755	Capital Tallahassee

Georgia (State)

Area Sq Km 153 910	Population 5 126 000
Area Sq Miles 59 425	Capital Atlanta

Hawaii (State)

Area Sq Km 28 311	Population 1 244 898
Area Sq Miles 10 931	Capital Honolulu

Idaho (State)

Area Sq Km 216 445	Population 1 341 131
Area Sq Miles 83 570	Capital Boise

Illinois (State)

Area Sq Km 149 997	Population 12 600 620
Area Sq Miles 57 914	Capital Springfield

Indiana (State)

Area Sq Km 94 322	Population 6 159 068
Area Sq Miles 36 418	Capital Indianapolis

Iowa (State)

Area Sq Km 145 744	Population 2 936 760
Area Sq Miles 56 272	Capital Des Moines

Kansas (State)

Area Sq Km 213 096	Population 2 715 884
Area Sq Miles 82 277	Capital Topeka

Kentucky (State)

Area Sq Km 104 659	Population 4 092 891
Area Sq Miles 40 409	Capital Frankfort

Louisiana (State)

Area Sq Km 134 265	Population 4 482 646
Area Sq Miles 51 840	Capital Baton Rouge

Maine (State)

Area Sq Km 91 647	Population 1 294 464
Area Sq Miles 35 385	Capital Augusta

Maryland (State)

Area Sq Km 32 134	Population 5 458 137
Area Sq Miles 12 407	Capital Annapolis

Massachusetts (State)

Area Sq Km 27 337	Population 6 427 801
Area Sq Miles 10 555	Capital Boston

Michigan (State)

Area Sq Km 250 493	Population 10 050 446
Area Sq Miles 96 716	Capital Lansing

Minnesota (State)

Area Sq Km 225 171	Population 5 019 720
Area Sq Miles 86 939	Capital St Paul

Mississippi (State)

Area Sq Km 125 433	Population 2 871 782
Area Sq Miles 48 430	Capital Jackson

Missouri (State)

Area Sq Km 180 533	Population 5 672 579
Area Sq Miles 69 704	Capital Jefferson City

Montana (State)

Area Sq Km 380 837	Population 909 453
Area Sq Miles 147 042	Capital Helena

Nebraska (State)

Area Sq Km 200 346	Population 1 729 180
Area Sq Miles 77 354	Capital Lincoln

Nevada (State)

Area Sq Km 286 352	Population 2 173 491
Area Sq Miles 110 561	Capital Carson City

New Hampshire (State)

Area Sq Km 24 216	Population 1 275 056
Area Sq Miles 9 350	Capital Concord

New Jersey (State)

Area Sq Km 22 587	Population 8 590 300
Area Sq Miles 8 721	Capital Trenton

UNITED STATES OF AMERICA
Federal Republic

New Mexico (State)

Area Sq Km	314 914	Population	1 855 059
Area Sq Miles	121 589	Capital	Santa Fe

New York (State)

Area Sq Km	141 299	Population	19 157 532
Area Sq Miles	54 556	Capital	Albany

North Carolina (State)

Area Sq Km	139 391	Population	8 320 146
Area Sq Miles	53 819	Capital	Raleigh

North Dakota (State)

Area Sq Km	183 112	Population	634 110
Area Sq Miles	70 700	Capital	Bismarck

Ohio (State)

Area Sq Km	116 096	Population	11 421 267
Area Sq Miles	44 825	Capital	Columbus

Oklahoma (State)

Area Sq Km	181 035	Population	3 493 714
Area Sq Miles	69 898	Capital	Oklahoma City

Oregon (State)

Area Sq Km	254 806	Population	3 521 515
Area Sq Miles	98 381	Capital	Salem

Pennsylvania (State)

Area Sq Km	119 282	Population	12 335 091
Area Sq Miles	46 055	Capital	Harrisburg

Rhode Island (State)

Area Sq Km	4 002	Population	1 069 725
Area Sq Miles	1 545	Capital	Providence

South Carolina (State)

Area Sq Km	82 931	Population	4 107 183
Area Sq Miles	32 020	Capital	Columbia

South Dakota (State)

Area Sq Km	199 730	Population	761 063
Area Sq Miles	77 116	Capital	Pierre

Tennessee (State)

Area Sq Km	109 150	Population	5 797 289
Area Sq Miles	42 143	Capital	Nashville

Texas (State)

Area Sq Km	695 622	Population	21 779 893
Area Sq Miles	268 581	Capital	Austin

Utah (State)

Area Sq Km	219 887	Population	2 316 256
Area Sq Miles	84 899	Capital	Salt Lake City

Vermont (State)

Area Sq Km	24 900	Population	616 592
Area Sq Miles	9 614	Capital	Montpelier

Virginia (State)

Area Sq Km	110 784	Population	7 293 542
Area Sq Miles	42 774	Capital	Richmond

Washington (State)

Area Sq Km	184 666	Population	6 068 996
Area Sq Miles	71 300	Capital	Olympia

West Virginia (State)

Area Sq Km	62 755	Population	1 801 873
Area Sq Miles	24 230	Capital	Charleston

Wisconsin (State)

Area Sq Km	169 639	Population	5 441 196
Area Sq Miles	65 498	Capital	Madison

Wyoming (State)

Area Sq Km	253 337	Population	498 703
Area Sq Miles	97 814	Capital	Cheyenne

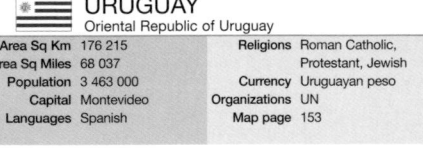

URUGUAY
Oriental Republic of Uruguay

Area Sq Km	176 215	Religions	Roman Catholic,
Area Sq Miles	68 037		Protestant, Jewish
Population	3 463 000	Currency	Uruguayan peso
Capital	Montevideo	Organizations	UN
Languages	Spanish	Map page	153

UZBEKISTAN
Republic of Uzbekistan

Area Sq Km	447 400	Religions	Sunni Muslim, Russian
Area Sq Miles	172 742		Orthodox
Population	26 593 000	Currency	Uzbek som
Capital	Toshkent	Organizations	CIS, UN
Languages	Uzbek, Russian,	Map page	76–77
	Tajik, Kazakh		

VANUATU
Republic of Vanuatu

Area Sq Km	12 190	Religions	Protestant, Roman
Area Sq Miles	4 707		Catholic, traditional
Population	211 000		beliefs
Capital	Port Vila	Currency	Vatu
Languages	English, Bislama	Organizations	Comm., UN
	(creole), French	Map page	48

VATICAN CITY
Vatican City State or Holy See

Area Sq Km	0.5	Religions	Roman Catholic
Area Sq Miles	0.2	Currency	Euro
Population	552	Map page	108
Capital	Vatican City		
Languages	Italian		

VENEZUELA
Republic of Venezuela

Area Sq Km	912 050	Religions	Roman Catholic,
Area Sq Miles	352 144		Protestant
Population	26 749 000	Currency	Bolívar
Capital	Caracas	Organizations	OPEC, UN
Languages	Spanish, Amerindian	Map page	150
	languages		

VIETNAM
Socialist Republic of Vietnam

Area Sq Km	329 565	Religions	Buddhist, Taoist,
Area Sq Miles	127 246		Roman Catholic,
Population	84 238 000		Cao Dai, Hoa Hao
Capital	Ha Nôi (Hanoi)	Currency	Dong
Languages	Vietnamese, Thai,	Organizations	APEC, ASEAN, UN
	Khmer, Chinese,	Map page	62–63
	local languages		

Virgin Islands (U.K.)
United Kingdom Overseas Territory

Area Sq Km	153	Religions	Protestant, Roman
Area Sq Miles	59		Catholic
Population	22 000	Currency	United States dollar
Capital	Road Town	Map page	147
Languages	English		

Virgin Islands (U.S.)
United States Unincorporated Territory

Area Sq Km	352	Religions	Protestant,
Area Sq Miles	136		Roman Catholic
Population	112 000	Currency	United States dollar
Capital	Charlotte Amalie	Map page	147
Languages	English, Spanish		

Wallis and Futuna Islands
French Overseas Territory

Area Sq Km	274	Religions	Roman Catholic
Area Sq Miles	106	Currency	CFP franc
Population	15 000	Map page	49
Capital	Matâ'utu		
Languages	French, Wallisian,		
	Futunian		

West Bank
Disputed Territory

Area Sq Km	5 860	Religions	Sunni Muslim, Jewish,
Area Sq Miles	2 263		Shi'a Muslim, Christian
Population	2 421 491	Currency	Jordanian dinar,
Capital	none		Isreali shekel
Languages	Arabic, Hebrew	Map page	80

Western Sahara
Disputed territory (Morocco)

Area Sq Km	266 000	Religions	Sunni Muslim
Area Sq Miles	102 703	Currency	Moroccan dirham
Population	341 000	Map page	114
Capital	Laâyoune		
Languages	Arabic		

YEMEN
Republic of Yemen

Area Sq Km	527 968	Religions	Sunni Muslim, Shi'a
Area Sq Miles	203 850		Muslim
Population	20 975 000	Currency	Yemeni riyal
Capital	Şan'a'	Organizations	UN
Languages	Arabic	Map page	78–79

ZAMBIA
Republic of Zambia

Area Sq Km	752 614	Religions	Christian, traditional
Area Sq Miles	290 586		beliefs
Population	11 668 000	Currency	Zambian kwacha
Capital	Lusaka	Organizations	Comm., SADC, UN
Languages	English, Bemba,	Map page	120–121
	Nyanja, Tonga, local		
	languages		

ZIMBABWE
Republic of Zimbabwe

Area Sq Km	390 759	Religions	Christian, traditional
Area Sq Miles	150 873		beliefs
Population	13 010 000	Currency	Zimbabwean dollar
Capital	Harare	Organizations	SADC, UN
Languages	English, Shona,	Map page	121
	Ndebele		

ANTARCTICA

Total Land Area
12 093 000 sq km
4 669 292 sq miles
(excluding ice shelves)

HIGHEST MOUNTAIN
Vinson Massif
4 897 m /16 066 ft

OCEANIA

Total land area
8 844 516 sq km
3 414 887 sq miles
(includes New Guinea and
Pacific Island nations)

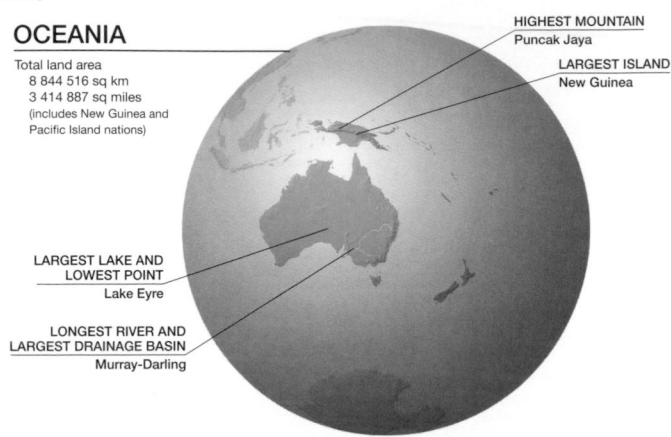

HIGHEST MOUNTAIN
Puncak Jaya

LARGEST ISLAND
New Guinea

LARGEST LAKE AND
LOWEST POINT
Lake Eyre

LONGEST RIVER AND
LARGEST DRAINAGE BASIN
Murray-Darling

HIGHEST MOUNTAINS	HEIGHT metres	feet	LARGEST ISLANDS	AREA sq km	sq miles	LARGEST LAKES	AREA sq km	sq miles	LONGEST RIVERS	LENGTH km	miles
Puncak Jaya	5 030	16 502	New Guinea	808 510	312 167	Lake Eyre	0–8 900	0–3 436	Murray-Darling	3 750	2 330
Puncak Trikora	4 730	15 518	South Island	151 215	58 384	Lake Torrens	0–5 780	0–2 232	Darling	2 739	1 702
Puncak Mandala	4 700	15 420	North Island	115 777	44 702				Murray	2 589	1 608
Puncak Yamin	4 595	15 075	Tasmania	67 800	26 178				Murrumbidgee	1 690	1 050
Mt Wilhelm	4 509	14 793							Lachlan	1 480	919

ASIA

Total Land Area
45 036 492 sq km
17 388 686 sq miles

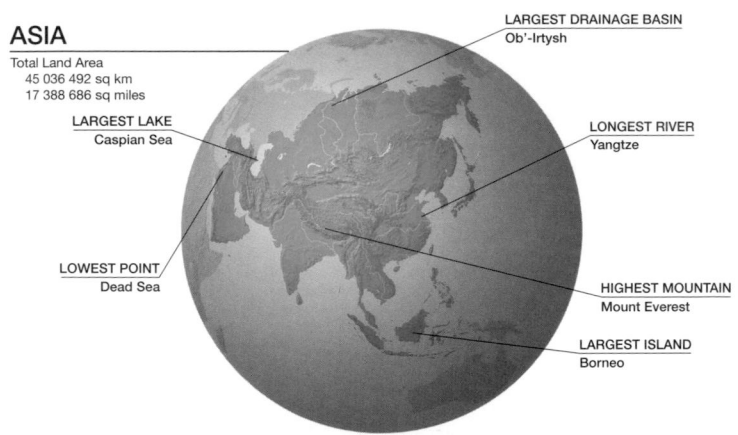

LARGEST DRAINAGE BASIN
Ob'-Irtysh

LARGEST LAKE
Caspian Sea

LONGEST RIVER
Yangtze

LOWEST POINT
Dead Sea

HIGHEST MOUNTAIN
Mount Everest

LARGEST ISLAND
Borneo

HIGHEST MOUNTAINS	HEIGHT metres	feet	LARGEST ISLANDS	AREA sq km	sq miles	LARGEST LAKES	AREA sq km	sq miles	LONGEST RIVERS	LENGTH km	miles
Mt Everest	8 848	29 028	Borneo	745 561	287 863	Caspian Sea	371 000	143 244	Yangtze	6 380	3 964
K2	8 611	28 251	Sumatra	473 606	182 860	Lake Baikal	30 500	11 776	Ob'-Irtysh	5 568	3 460
Kangchenjunga	8 586	28 169	Honshū	227 414	87 805	Lake Balkhash	17 400	6 718	Yenisey-Angara-Selenga	5 550	3 448
Lhotse	8 516	27 939	Celebes	189 216	73 057	Aral Sea	17 158	6 625	Yellow	5 464	3 395
Makalu	8 463	27 765	Java	132 188	51 038	Ysyk-Köl	6 200	2 393	Irtysh	4 440	2 759

EUROPE

Total Land Area
9 908 599 sq km
3 825 731 sq miles

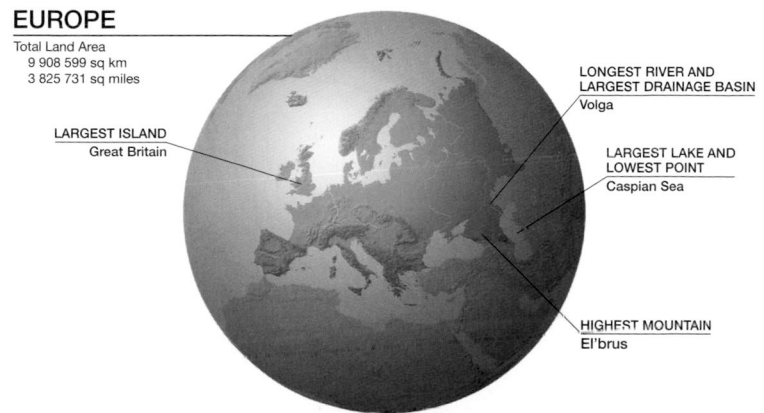

LONGEST RIVER AND
LARGEST DRAINAGE BASIN
Volga

LARGEST ISLAND
Great Britain

LARGEST LAKE AND
LOWEST POINT
Caspian Sea

HIGHEST MOUNTAIN
El'brus

HIGHEST MOUNTAINS	HEIGHT metres	feet	LARGEST ISLANDS	AREA sq km	sq miles	LARGEST LAKES	AREA sq km	sq miles	LONGEST RIVERS	LENGTH km	miles
El'brus	5 642	5 642	Great Britain	218 476	84 354	Caspian Sea	371 000	143 244	Volga	3 688	2 291
Gora Dykh-Tau	5 204	17 073	Iceland	102 820	39 699	Lake Ladoga	18 390	7 100	Danube	2 850	1 770
Shkhara	5 201	17 063	Novaya Zemlya	90 650	35 000	Lake Onega	9 600	3 706	Dnieper	2 285	1 419
Kazbek	5 047	16 558	Ireland	83 045	32 064	Vänern	5 585	2 156	Kama	2 028	1 260
Mont Blanc	4 808	15 774	Spitsbergen	37 814	14 600	Rybinskoye Vdkhr.	5 180	2 000	Don	1 931	1 199

AFRICA

Total Land Area
30 343 578 sq km
11 715 721 sq miles

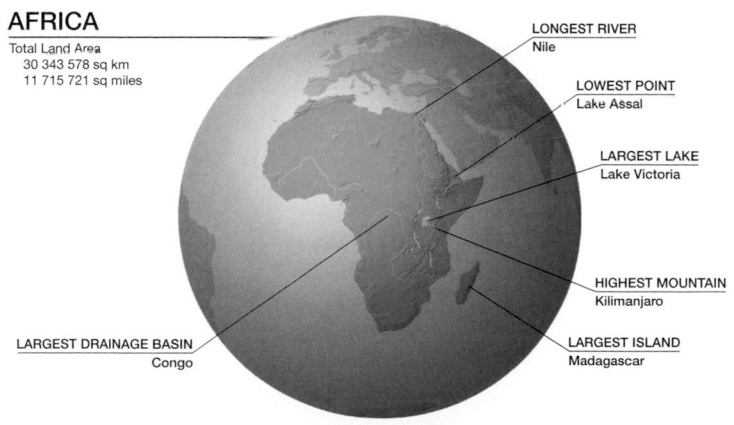

LONGEST RIVER
Nile

LOWEST POINT
Lake Assal

LARGEST LAKE
Lake Victoria

HIGHEST MOUNTAIN
Kilimanjaro

LARGEST DRAINAGE BASIN
Congo

LARGEST ISLAND
Madagascar

HIGHEST MOUNTAINS	HEIGHT metres	feet	LARGEST ISLANDS	AREA sq km	sq miles	LARGEST LAKES	AREA sq km	sq miles	LONGEST RIVERS	LENGTH km	miles
Kilimanjaro	5 892	19 331	Madagascar	587 040	226 657	Lake Victoria	68 800	26 564	Nile	6 695	4 160
Mt Kenya	5 199	17 057				Lake Tanganyika	32 900	12 702	Congo	4 667	2 900
Margherita Peak	5 110	16 765				Lake Nyasa	30 044	11 600	Niger	4 184	2 599
Meru	4 565	14 977				Lake Volta	8 485	3 276	Zambezi	2 736	1 700
Ras Dejen	4 533	14 872				Lake Turkana	6 475	2 500	Webi Shabeelle	2 490	1 547

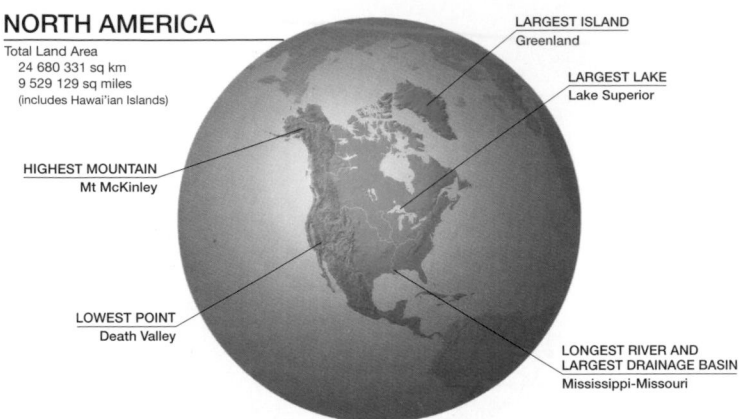

NORTH AMERICA

Total Land Area
24 680 331 sq km
9 529 129 sq miles
(includes Hawai'ian Islands)

LARGEST ISLAND
Greenland

LARGEST LAKE
Lake Superior

HIGHEST MOUNTAIN
Mt McKinley

LOWEST POINT
Death Valley

LONGEST RIVER AND
LARGEST DRAINAGE BASIN
Mississippi-Missouri

HIGHEST MOUNTAINS	HEIGHT metres	feet	LARGEST ISLANDS	AREA sq km	sq miles	LARGEST LAKES	AREA sq km	sq miles	LONGEST RIVERS	LENGTH km	miles
Mt McKinley	6 194	20 321	Greenland	2 175 600	840 004	Lake Superior	82 100	31 699	Mississippi-Missouri	5 969	3 709
Mt Logan	5 959	19 550	Baffin Island	507 451	195 928	Lake Huron	59 600	23 012	Mackenzie-Peace-Finlay	4 241	2 635
Pico de Orizaba	5 747	18 855	Victoria Island	217 291	83 897	Lake Michigan	57 800	22 317	Missouri	4 086	2 539
Mt St Elias	5 489	18 008	Ellesmere Island	196 236	75 767	Great Bear Lake	31 328	12 095	Mississippi	3 765	2 339
Volcán Popocatépetl	5 452	17 887	Cuba	110 860	42 803	Great Slave Lake	28 568	11 030	Yukon	3 185	1 979

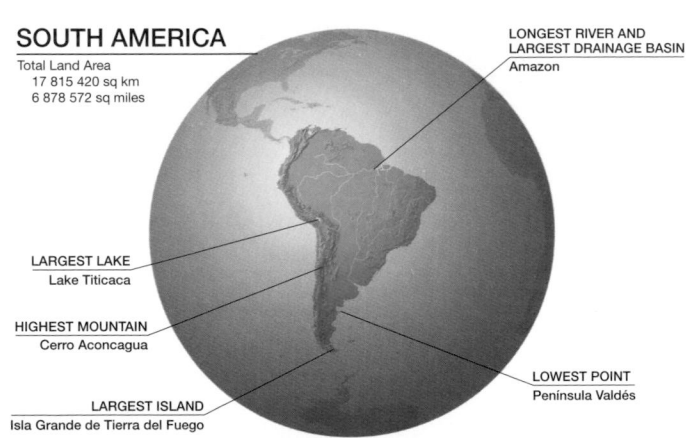

SOUTH AMERICA

Total Land Area
17 815 420 sq km
6 878 572 sq miles

LONGEST RIVER AND
LARGEST DRAINAGE BASIN
Amazon

LARGEST LAKE
Lake Titicaca

HIGHEST MOUNTAIN
Cerro Aconcagua

LARGEST ISLAND
Isla Grande de Tierra del Fuego

LOWEST POINT
Península Valdés

HIGHEST MOUNTAINS	HEIGHT metres	feet	LARGEST ISLANDS	AREA sq km	sq miles	LARGEST LAKES	AREA sq km	sq miles	LONGEST RIVERS	LENGTH km	miles
Cerro Aconcagua	6 959	22 831	Isla Grande de Tierra del Fuego	47 000	18 147	Lake Titicaca	8 340	3 220	Amazon	6 516	4 049
Nevado Ojos del Salado	6 908	22 664	Isla de Chiloé	8 394	3 240				Río de la Plata-Paraná	4 500	2 796
Cerro Bonete	6 872	22 546	East Falkland	6 760	2 610				Purus	3 218	1 999
Cerro Pissis	6 858	22 500	West Falkland	5 413	2 090				Madeira	3 200	1 988
Cerro Tupungato	6 800	22 211							Sao Francisco	2 900	1 802

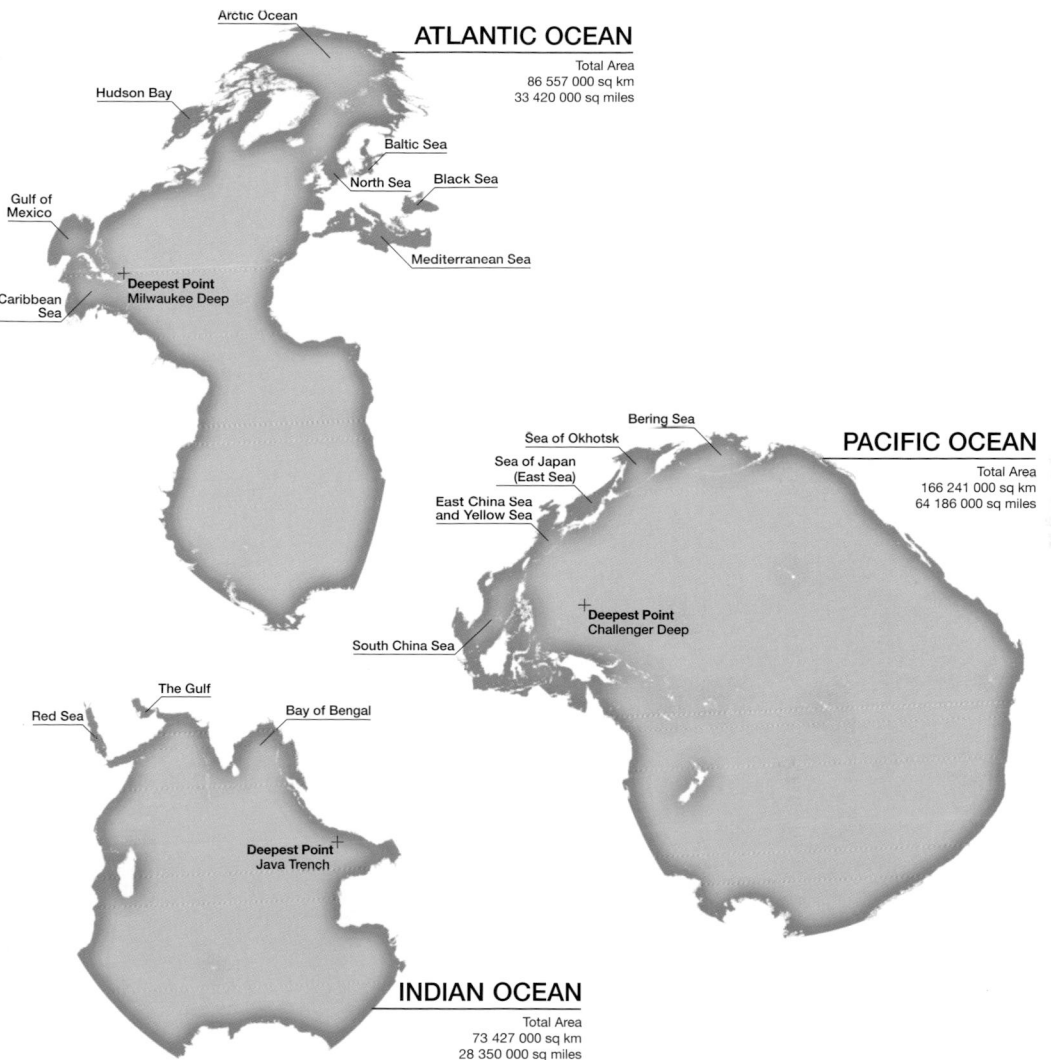

ATLANTIC OCEAN
Total Area
86 557 000 sq km
33 420 000 sq miles

Arctic Ocean
Hudson Bay
Baltic Sea
North Sea   Black Sea
Gulf of Mexico
Mediterranean Sea
Deepest Point
Milwaukee Deep
Caribbean Sea

PACIFIC OCEAN
Total Area
166 241 000 sq km
64 186 000 sq miles

Bering Sea
Sea of Okhotsk
Sea of Japan (East Sea)
East China Sea and Yellow Sea
Deepest Point
Challenger Deep
South China Sea

The Gulf
Red Sea
Bay of Bengal
Deepest Point
Java Trench

INDIAN OCEAN
Total Area
73 427 000 sq km
28 350 000 sq miles

ATLANTIC OCEAN	AREA sq km	sq miles	DEEPEST POINT metres	feet
Extent	86 557 000	33 420 000	8 605	28 231
Arctic Ocean	9 485 000	3 662 000	5 450	17 880
Caribbean Sea	2 512 000	970 000	7 680	25 196
Mediterranean Sea	2 510 000	969 000	5 121	16 800
Gulf of Mexico	1 544 000	596 000	3 504	11 495
Hudson Bay	1 233 000	476 000	259	849
North Sea	575 000	222 000	661	2 168
Black Sea	508 000	196 000	2 245	7 365
Baltic Sea	382 000	147 000	460	1 509

INDIAN OCEAN	AREA sq km	sq miles	DEEPEST POINT metres	feet
Extent	73 427 000	28 350 000	7 125	23 376
Bay of Bengal	2 172 000	839 000	4 500	14 763
Red Sea	453 000	175 000	3 040	9 973
The Gulf	238 000	92 000	73	239

PACIFIC OCEAN	AREA sq km	sq miles	DEEPEST POINT metres	feet
Extent	166 241 000	64 186 000	10 920	35 826
South China Sea	2 590 000	1 000 000	5 514	18 090
Bering Sea	2 261 000	873 000	4 150	13 615
Sea of Okhotsk	1 392 000	537 000	3 363	11 033
Sea of Japan (East Sea)	1 013 000	391 000	3 743	12 280
East China Sea and Yellow Sea	1 202 000	464 000	2 717	8 913

MAJOR CLIMATIC REGIONS AND SUB-TYPES

Winkel Tripel Projection
1:145 000 000

Köppen classification system

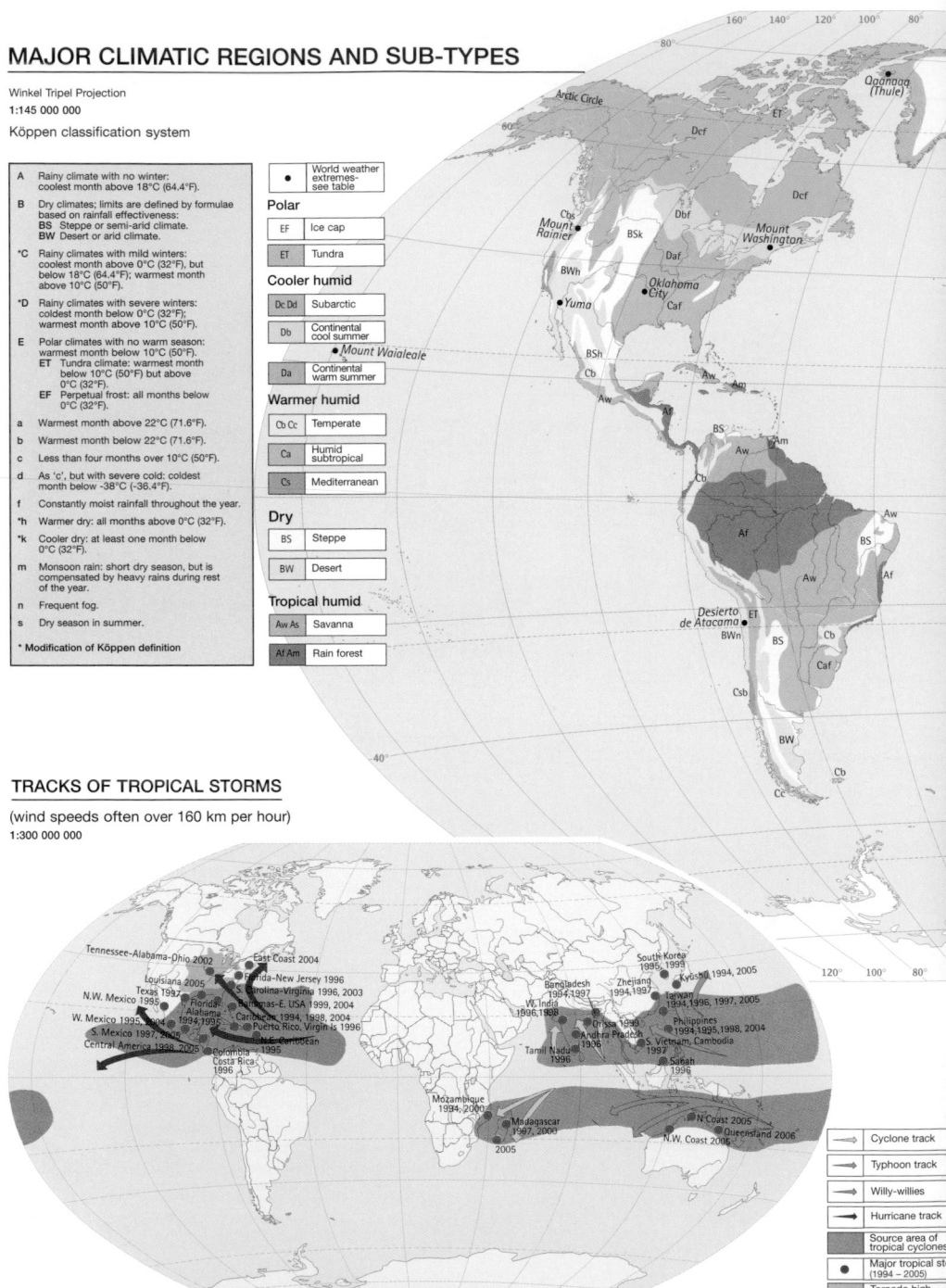

	●	World weather extremes- see table

Polar

EF	Ice cap
ET	Tundra

Cooler humid

Dc Dd	Subarctic
Db	Continental cool summer
Da	Continental warm summer

Warmer humid

Cb Cc	Temperate
Ca	Humid subtropical
Cs	Mediterranean

Dry

BS	Steppe
BW	Desert

Tropical humid

Aw As	Savanna
Af Am	Rain forest

A Rainy climate with no winter: coolest month above 18°C (64.4°F).

B Dry climates; limits are defined by formulae based on rainfall effectiveness:
BS Steppe or semi-arid climate.
BW Desert or arid climate.

*C Rainy climates with mild winters: coolest month above 0°C (32°F), but below 18°C (64.4°F); warmest month above 10°C (50°F).

*D Rainy climates with severe winters: coldest month below 0°C (32°F); warmest month above 10°C (50°F).

E Polar climates with no warm season: warmest month below 10°C (50°F).
ET Tundra climate: warmest month below 10°C (50°F) but above 0°C (32°F).
EF Perpetual frost: all months below 0°C (32°F).

a Warmest month above 22°C (71.6°F).

b Warmest month below 22°C (71.6°F).

c Less than four months over 10°C (50°F).

d As 'c', but with severe cold: coldest month below -38°C (-36.4°F).

f Constantly moist rainfall throughout the year.

*h Warmer dry: all months above 0°C (32°F).

*k Cooler dry: at least one month below 0°C (32°F).

m Monsoon rain: short dry season, but is compensated by heavy rains during rest of the year.

n Frequent fog.

s Dry season in summer.

* Modification of Köppen definition

TRACKS OF TROPICAL STORMS

(wind speeds often over 160 km per hour)
1:300 000 000

⟶	Cyclone track
⟶	Typhoon track
⟶	Willy-willies
⟶	Hurricane track
	Source area of tropical cyclones
●	Major tropical stor (1994 – 2005)
	Tornado high risk areas

WORLD WEATHER EXTREMES

Highest shade temperature	57.8°C/136°F **Al 'Aziziyah**, Libya (13th September 1922)	Highest surface wind speed		
Hottest place – Annual mean	34.4°C/93.9°F **Dalol**, Ethiopia		High altitude	372 km per hour/231 miles per hour **Mount Washington**, New Hampshire, USA (12th April 1934)
Driest place – Annual mean	0.1 mm/0.004 inches **Atacama Desert**, Chile		Low altitude	333 km per hour/207 miles per hour **Qaanaaq (Thule)**, Greenland (8th March 1972)
Most sunshine – Annual mean	90% **Yuma**, Arizona, USA (over 4 000 hours)		Tornado	512 km per hour/318 miles per hour **Oklahoma City**, Oklahoma, USA (3rd May 1999)
Least sunshine	Nil for 182 days each year, **South Pole**	Greatest snowfall		31 102 mm/1 224.5 inches **Mount Rainier**, Washington, USA (19th February 1971–18th February 1972)
Lowest screen temperature	-89.2°C/-128.6°F **Vostok Station**, Antarctica (21st July 1983)	Heaviest hailstones		1 kg/2.21 lb **Gopalganj**, Bangladesh (14th April 1986)
Coldest place – Annual mean	-56.6°C/-69.9°F **Plateau Station**, Antarctica	Thunder-days Average		251 days per year **Tororo**, Uganda
Wettest place – Annual mean	11 873 mm/467.4 inches **Meghalaya**, India	Highest barometric pressure		1 083.8 mb **Agata**, Siberia, Rus. Fed. (31st December 1968)
Most rainy days	Up to 350 per year **Mount Waialeale**, Hawaii, USA	Lowest barometric pressure		870 mb 483 km/300 miles west of **Guam**, Pacific Ocean (12th October 1979)
Windiest place	322 km per hour/200 miles per hour in gales, **Commonwealth Bay**, Antarctica			

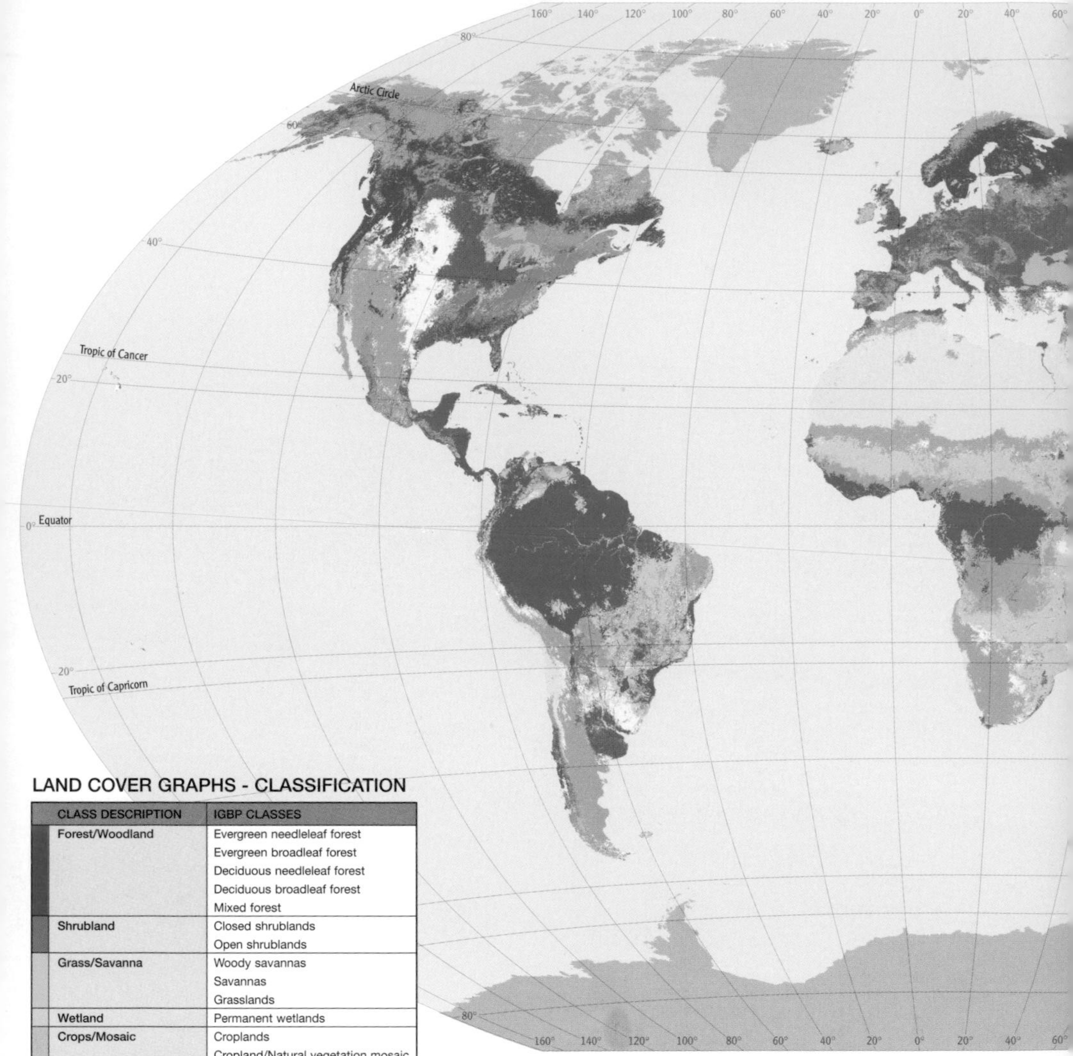

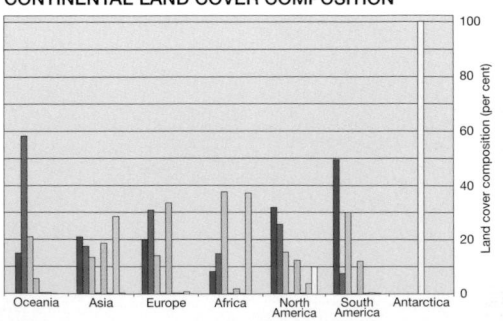

LAND COVER GRAPHS - CLASSIFICATION

CLASS DESCRIPTION	IGBP CLASSES
Forest/Woodland	Evergreen needleleaf forest
	Evergreen broadleaf forest
	Deciduous needleleaf forest
	Deciduous broadleaf forest
	Mixed forest
Shrubland	Closed shrublands
	Open shrublands
Grass/Savanna	Woody savannas
	Savannas
	Grasslands
Wetland	Permanent wetlands
Crops/Mosaic	Croplands
	Cropland/Natural vegetation mosaic
Urban	Urban and built-up
Snow/Ice	Snow and Ice
Barren	Barren or sparsely vegetated

GLOBAL LAND COVER COMPOSITION

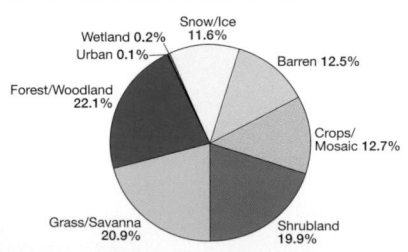

Wetland 0.2%
Urban 0.1%
Snow/Ice 11.6%
Barren 12.5%
Forest/Woodland 22.1%
Crops/Mosaic 12.7%
Grass/Savanna 20.9%
Shrubland 19.9%

CONTINENTAL LAND COVER COMPOSITION

Land cover composition (per cent)

Oceania   Asia   Europe   Africa   North America   South America   Antarctica

WORLD LAND COVER

Winkel Tripel Projection
1:145 000 000

	Water bodies
	Evergreen needleleaf forest
	Evergreen broadleaf forest
	Deciduous needleleaf forest
	Deciduous broadleaf forest
	Mixed forest
	Closed shrublands
	Open shrublands
	Woody savannas
	Savannas
	Grasslands
	Permanent wetlands
	Croplands
	Urban and build-up
	Cropland/Natural vegetation mosaic
	Snow and Ice
	Barren or sparsely vegetated

ENVIRONMENTAL IMPACTS

Winkel Tripel Projection
1:300 000 000

**ercentage change
forest area, 1990–2005**

	-2.0 – -8.0
	-0.4 – -1.9
	no significant change
	+0.4 – +1.9
	+2.0 – +8.0
	no data

hreat of desertification

	very high risk
	high risk

oral reefs at risk

●	high risk
●	medium/low risk

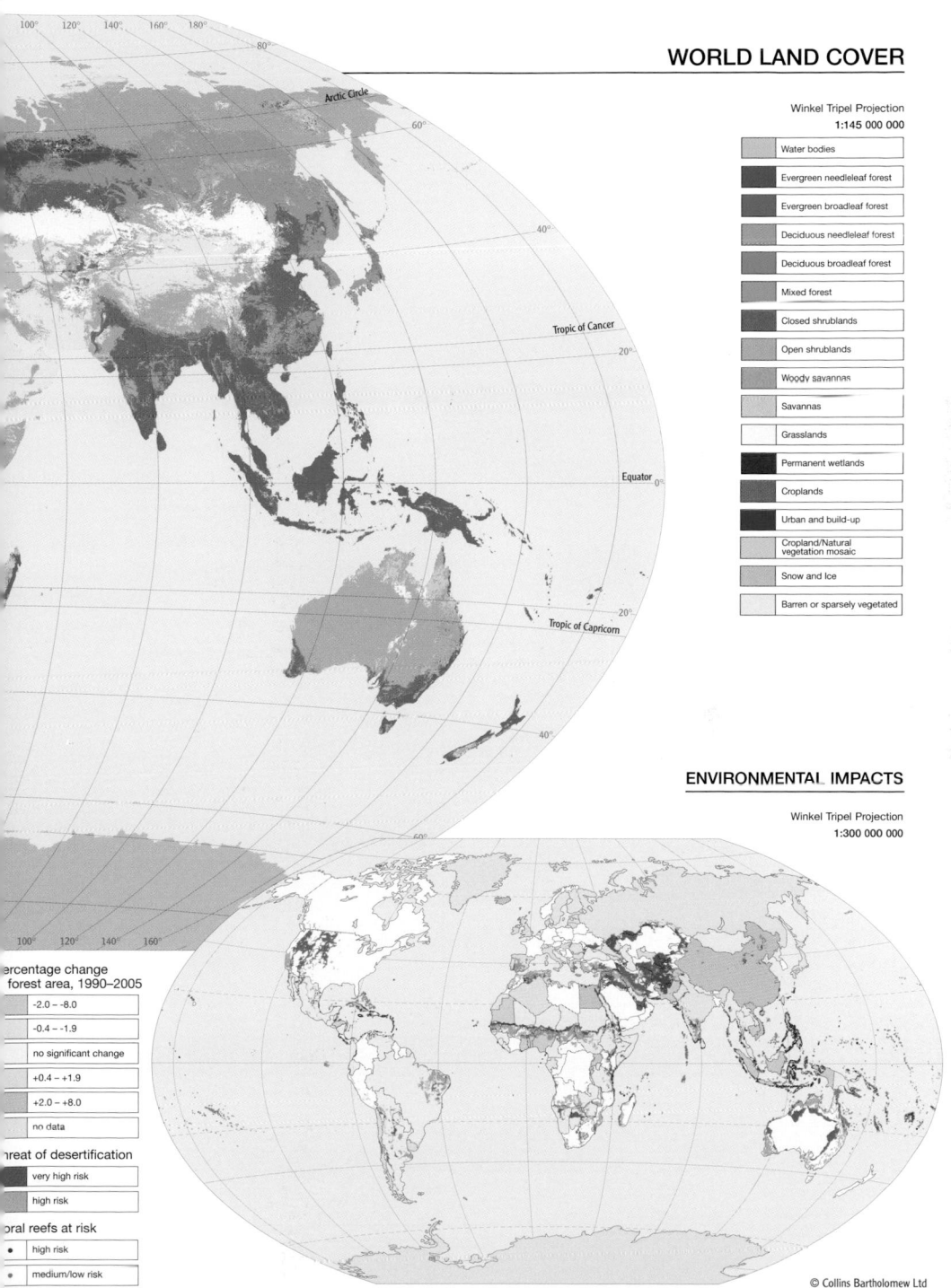

© Collins Bartholomew Ltd

WORLD POPULATION DISTRIBUTION AND THE WORLD'S MAJOR CITIES

Winkel Tripel Projection

1:145 000 000

Population Density

per sq mile

1 250	250	62.5	2.5	0

Inhabitants

500	100	25	1	0

Uninhabited

per sq km

Gridded Population of the World (GPW), Version 3. Palisades, NY: CIESN, Columbia University. Available at http://sedac.ciesn.columbia.edu/plue/gpw

Major Urban Agglomerations

- 5 million–10 million
- 10 million–20 million
- over 20 million

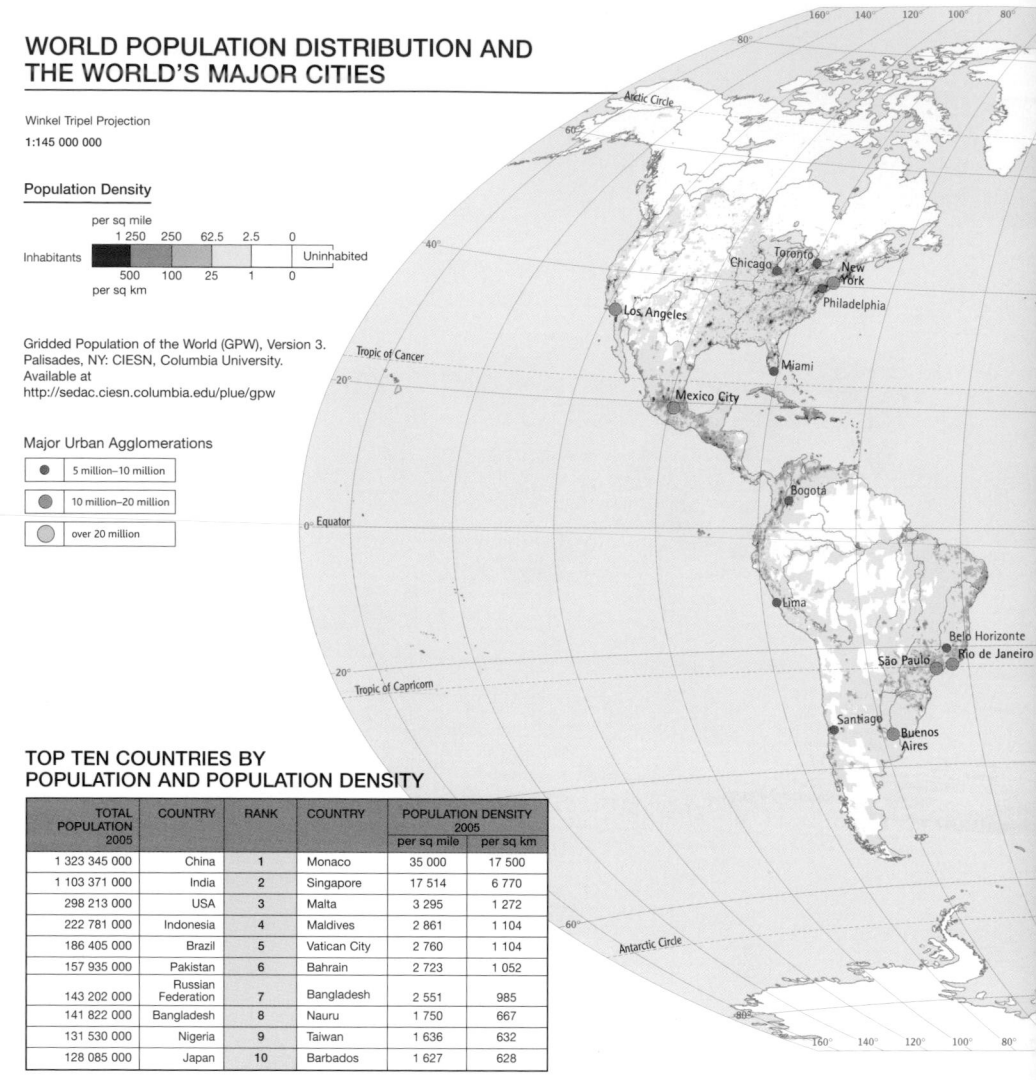

TOP TEN COUNTRIES BY POPULATION AND POPULATION DENSITY

TOTAL POPULATION 2005	COUNTRY	RANK	COUNTRY	POPULATION DENSITY 2005	
				per sq mile	per sq km
1 323 345 000	China	1	Monaco	35 000	17 500
1 103 371 000	India	2	Singapore	17 514	6 770
298 213 000	USA	3	Malta	3 295	1 272
222 781 000	Indonesia	4	Maldives	2 861	1 104
186 405 000	Brazil	5	Vatican City	2 760	1 104
157 935 000	Pakistan	6	Bahrain	2 723	1 052
143 202 000	Russian Federation	7	Bangladesh	2 551	985
141 822 000	Bangladesh	8	Nauru	1 750	667
131 530 000	Nigeria	9	Taiwan	1 636	632
128 085 000	Japan	10	Barbados	1 627	628

KEY POPULATION STATISTICS FOR MAJOR REGIONS

	POPULATION 2005 (millions)	GROWTH (per cent)	INFANT MORTALITY RATE	TOTAL FERTILITY RATE	LIFE EXPECTANCY (years)	% AGED 60 OR OVER	
						2005	2050
World	6 453	1.21	57	2.65	65.4	10	22
More developed regions	1 209	0.30	8	1.56	75.6	20	32
Less developed regions	5 243	1.43	62	2.90	63.4	8	20
Africa	887	2.18	94	4.97	49.1	5	10
Asia	3 917	1.21	54	2.47	67.3	9	24
Europe	725	0	9	1.40	73.7	21	35
Latin America and the Caribbean	558	1.42	26	2.55	71.5	9	24
North America	332	0.97	7	1.99	77.6	17	27
Oceania	32	1.32	29	2.32	74	14	25

Except for population (2005) and % aged 60 and over figures, the data are annual averages projected for the period 2000–2005.

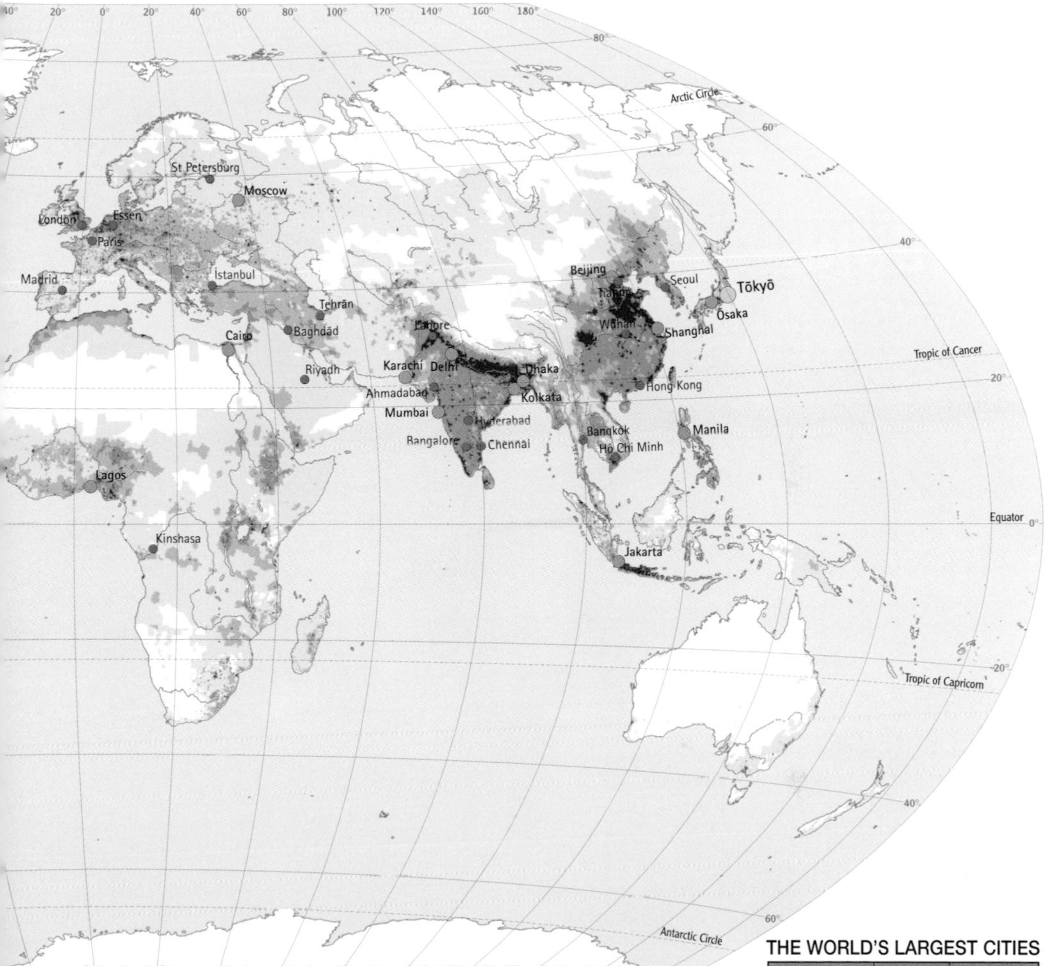

WORLD POPULATION GROWTH BY CONTINENT 1750–2050

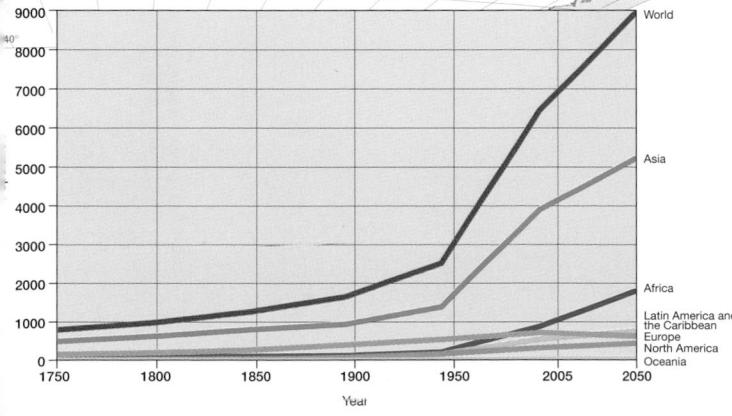

THE WORLD'S LARGEST CITIES

CITY	COUNTRY	POPULATION
Tōkyō	Japan	35 327 000
Mexico City	Mexico	19 013 000
New York	USA	18 498 000
Mumbai	India	18 336 000
São Paulo	Brazil	18 333 000
Delhi	India	15 334 000
Kolkata	India	14 299 000
Buenos Aires	Argentina	13 349 000
Jakarta	Indonesia	13 194 000
Shanghai	China	12 665 000
Dhaka	Bangladesh	12 560 000
Los Angeles	USA	12 146 000
Karachi	Pakistan	11 819 000
Rio de Janeiro	Brazil	11 469 000
Ōsaka	Japan	11 286 000
Cairo	Egypt	11 146 000
Lagos	Nigeria	11 135 000
Beijing	China	10 849 000
Manila	Philippines	10 677 000
Moscow	Rus. Fed.	10 672 000

© Collins Bartholomew Ltd

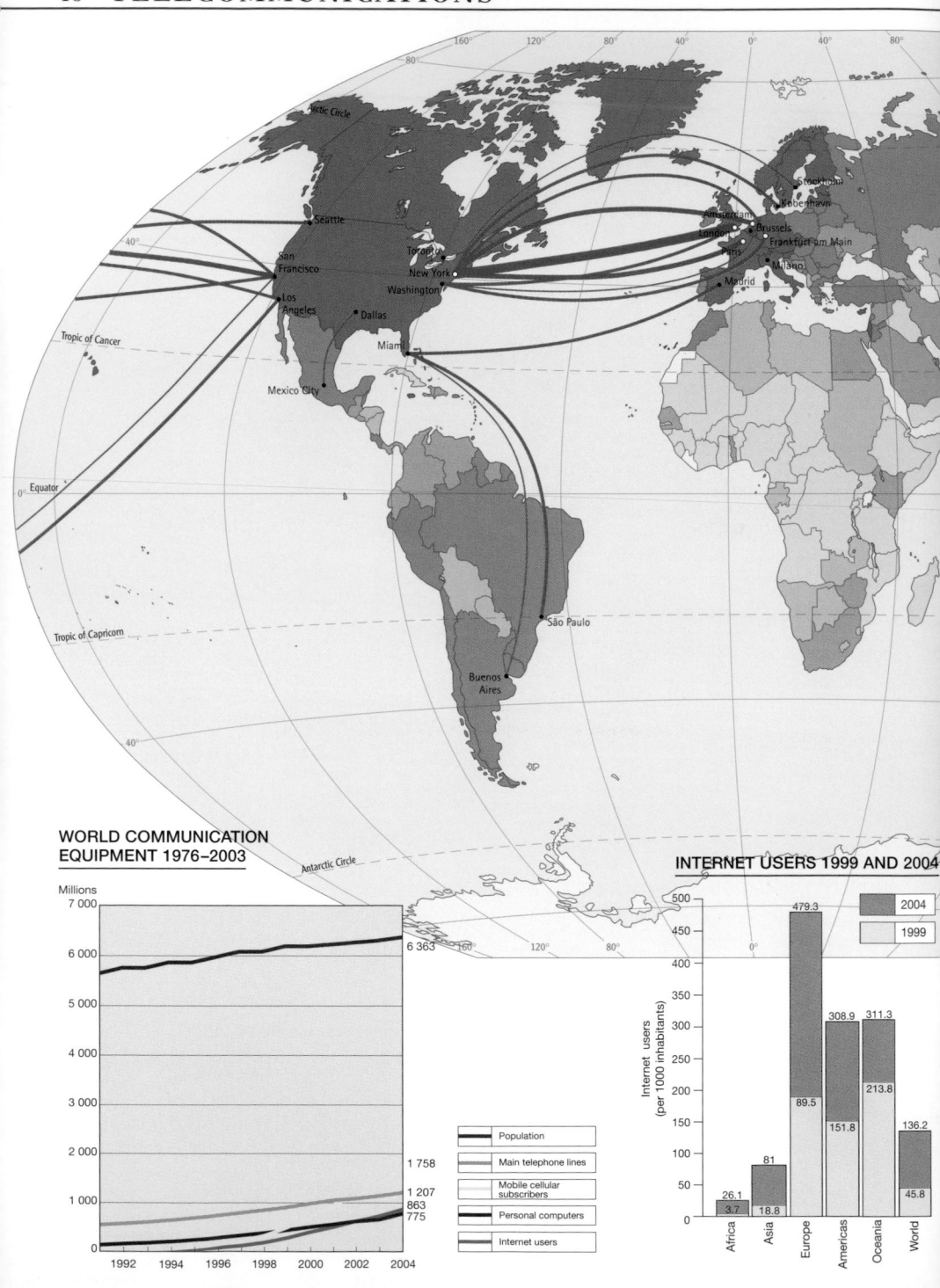

WORLD COMMUNICATION EQUIPMENT 1976–2003

Millions

7 000

6 363

6 000

5 000

4 000

3 000

2 000

1 758

1 207

1 000

863
775

1992 1994 1996 1998 2000 2002 2004

— Population
— Main telephone lines
— Mobile cellular subscribers
— Personal computers
— Internet users

INTERNET USERS 1999 AND 2004

■ 2004
□ 1999

Internet users (per 1000 inhabitants)

500

479.3

450

400

350

308.9 311.3

300

250

213.8

200

151.8

150

136.2

100

89.5

81

50

26.1 45.8

3.7 18.8

0

Africa Asia Europe Americas Oceania World

INTERNET USERS AND INTERNET ROUTES

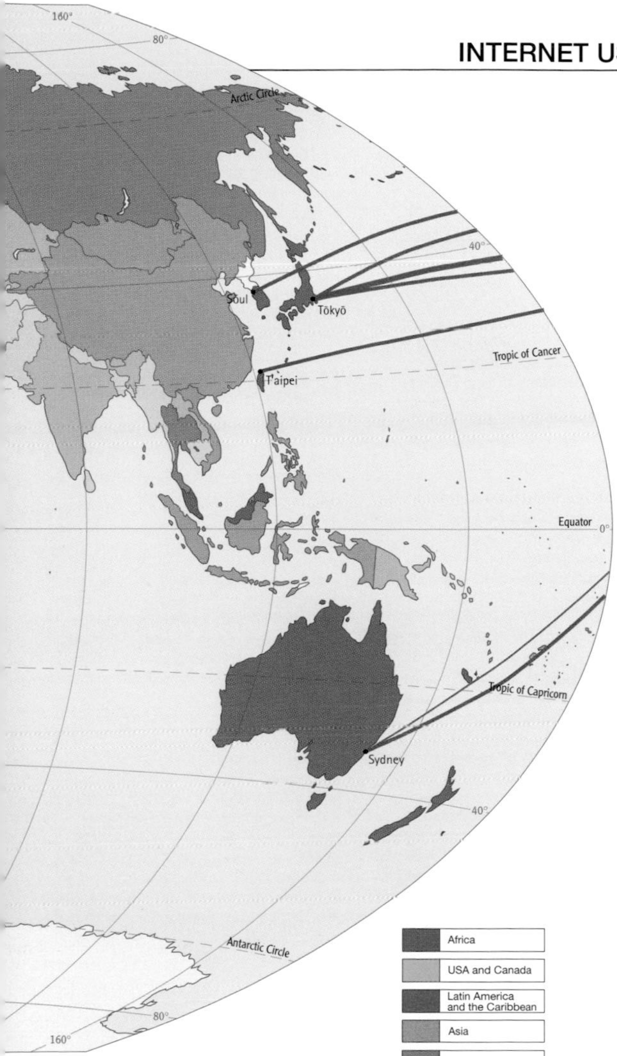

Winkel Tripel Projection
1:149 000 000

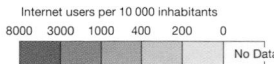

Internet Usage

Internet users per 10 000 inhabitants

8000	3000	1000	400	200	0

No Data

Major interregional internet routes

Gigabytes per second

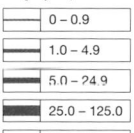

	0 – 0.9
	1.0 – 4.9
	5.0 – 24.9
	25.0 – 125.0
○	Hub Cities

TOP BROADBAND ECONOMIES 2004

Countries with the highest broadband penetration rate - subscribers per 100 inhabitants

TOP ECONOMIES	RATE
South Korea	24.8
Hong Kong, China	22.0
Netherlands	19.8
Denmark	19.1
Iceland	18.8
Canada	17.0
Taiwan	16.5
Switzerland	16.4
Belgium	15.6
Finland	15.3
Japan	15.3
Norway	14.9
Israel	14.0
Sweden	13.7
Liechtenstein	13.7
USA	12.9
United Kingdom	11.9
Singapore	11.9
France	11.2
Austria	10.0

Legend:
- Africa
- USA and Canada
- Latin America and the Caribbean
- Asia
- Europe
- Oceania

INTERNET USERS

% world share

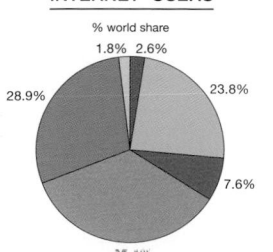

1.8% 2.6%
28.9%
23.8%
7.6%
35.4%

TELEPHONE MAIN LINES

% world share

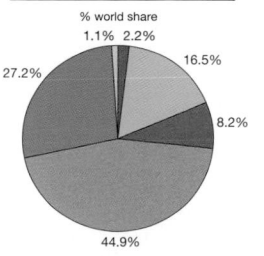

1.1% 2.2%
16.5%
27.2%
8.2%
44.9%

CELLULAR SUBSCRIBERS

% world share

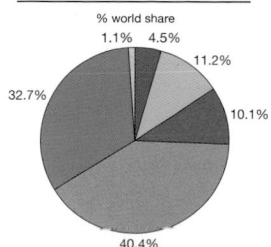

1.1% 4.5%
11.2%
32.7%
10.1%
40.4%

© Collins Bartholomew Ltd

MAP POLICIES AND ABBREVIATIONS

Place Names

The spelling of place names on maps has always been a matter of great complexity, because of the variety of the world's languages and the systems used to write them down. There is no standard way of spelling names or of converting them from one alphabet, or symbol set, to another. Instead, conventional ways of spelling have evolved in each of the world's major languages, and the results often differ significantly from the name as it is spelled in the original language. Familiar examples of English conventional names include Munich (München), Florence (Firenze) and Moscow (from the transliterated form, Moskva).

In this atlas, local name forms are used where these are in the Roman alphabet, though for major cities and main physical features, conventional English names are given first. The local forms are those which are officially recognized by the government of the country concerned, usually as represented by its official mapping agency. This is a basic principle laid down by the United Kingdom government's Permanent Committee on Geographical Names (PCGN) and the equivalent United States Board on Geographic Names (BGN). Prominent English-language and historic names are not neglected, however. These, and significant superseded names and alternate spellings, are included in brackets on the maps where space permits, and are cross-referenced in the index.

Country names are shown in conventional English form and include any recent changes promulgated by national governments and adopted by the United Nations. The names of continents, oceans, seas and under-water features in international waters also appear in English throughout the atlas, as do those

of other international features where such an English form exists and is in common use. International features are defined as features crossing one or more international boundary.

Boundaries

The status of nations, their names and their boundaries, are shown in this atlas as they are at the time of going to press, as far as can be ascertained. Where an international boundary symbol appears in the sea or ocean it does not necessarily infer a legal maritime boundary, but shows which offshore islands belong to which country. The extent of island nations is shown by a short boundary symbol at the extreme limits of the area of sea or ocean within which all land is part of that nation.

Where international boundaries are the subject of dispute it may be that no portrayal of them will meet with the approval of any of the countries involved, but it is not seen as the function of this atlas to try to adjudicate between the rights and wrongs of political issues. Although reference mapping at atlas scales is not the ideal medium for indicating the claims of many separatist and irredentist movements, every reasonable attempt is made to show where an active territorial dispute exists, and where there is an important difference between 'de facto' (existing in fact, on the ground) and 'de jure' (according to law) boundaries. This is done by the use of a different symbol where international boundaries are disputed, or where the alignment is unconfirmed, to that used for settled international boundaries. Ceasefire lines are also shown by a separate symbol. For clarity, disputed boundaries and areas are annotated where this is considered necessary. The atlas aims to take a strictly neutral viewpoint of all such cases, based on advice from expert consultants.

Map Projections

Map projections have been selected specifically for the area and scale of each map, or suite of maps. As the only way to show the Earth with absolute accuracy is on a globe, all map projections are compromises. Some projections seek to maintain correct area relationships (equal area projections), true distances and bearings from a point (equidistant projections) or correct angles and shapes (conformal projections); others attempt to achieve a balance between these properties. The choice of projections used in this atlas has been made on an individual continental and regional basis. Projections used, and their individual parameters, have been defined to minimize distortion and to reduce scale errors as much as possible. The projection used is indicated at the bottom left of each map page.

Scale

In order to directly compare like with like throughout the world it would be necessary to maintain a single scale throughout the atlas. However, the desirability of mapping the more densely populated areas of the world at larger scales, and other geographical considerations, such as the need to fit a homogeneous physical region within a uniform rectangular page format, mean that a range of scales have been used. Scales for continental maps range between 1:25 000 000 and 1:55 000 000, depending on the size of the continental land mass being covered. Scales for regional maps are typically in the range 1:15 000 000 to 1:25 000 000. Mapping for most countries is at scales between 1:6 000 000 and 1:12 000 000, although for the more densely populated areas of Europe the scale increases to 1:3 000 000.

ABBREVIATIONS

Arch.	Archipelago			L	Lake			Ra.	Range		mountain range
B.	Bay				Loch	(Scotland)	lake	S.	South, Southern		
	Bahia, Baia	Portuguese	bay		Lough	(Ireland)	lake		Salar, Salina,		
	Bahia	Spanish	bay		Lac	French	lake		Salinas	Spanish	salt pan, salt pans
	Baie	French	bay		Lago	Portuguese, Spanish	lake	Sa	Serra	Portuguese	mountain range
C.	Cape			M.	Mys	Russian	cape, point		Sierra	Spanish	mountain range
	Cabo	Portuguese,		Mt	Mount			Sd	Sound		
		Spanish	cape, headland		Mont	French	hill, mountain	S.E.	Southeast,		
	Cap	French	cape, headland	Mt.	Mountain				Southeastern		
Co	Cerro	Spanish	hill, peak, summit	Mte	Monte	Portuguese, Spanish	hill, mountain	St	Saint		
E.	East, Eastern			Mts	Mountains				Sankt	German	
Est.	Estrecho	Spanish	strait		Monts	French	hills, mountains		Sint	Dutch	saint
G.	Gebel	Arabic	hill, mountain	N.	North, Northern			Sta	Santa	Italian, Portuguese,	
Gt	Great			O.	Ostrov	Russian	island			Spanish	saint
I.	Island, Isle			Pk	Puncak	Indonesian, Malay	hill, mountain	Ste	Sainte	French	saint
	Ilha	Portuguese	island	Pt	Point			Str.	Strait		
	Islas	Spanish	island	Pta	Punta	Italian, Spanish	cape, point	Tk	Teluk	Indonesian, Malay	bay, gulf
Is	Islands, Isles			R.	River			Tg	Tanjong, Tanjung	Indonesian, Malay	cape, point
	Islas	Spanish	islands		Rio	Portuguese	river	Vdkhr.	Vodokhranilishche	Russian	reservoir
Kep.	Kepulauan	Indonesian	islands		Rio	Spanish	river	W.	West, Western		
Khr.	Khrebet	Russian	mountain range		Rivière	French	river		Wadi, Wâdi, Wādi	Arabic	watercourse

MAP SYMBOLS

Transport

═══ Motorway

──── Main road

── ── Track

──── Main railway

┴┴┴┴ Canal

✈ Main airport

Boundaries

▬▬▬ International boundary

·▬ ◄ Disputed international boundary or alignment unconfirmed

Undefined international boundary in the sea.
All land within this boundary is part of state or territory named.

▬▬▬ Administrative boundary
Shown for selected countries only.

●●●● Ceasefire line or other boundary described on the map

Land and Water Features

Lake

Impermanent lake

Salt lake or lagoon

Impermanent salt lake

Dry salt lake or salt pan

── River

---- Impermanent river

Ice cap / Glacier

_|123 Pass
Height in metres

∴ Site of special interest

⌣ Oasis

∿∿∿ Wall

Relief

Contour intervals used in layer-colouring, for land height and sea depth

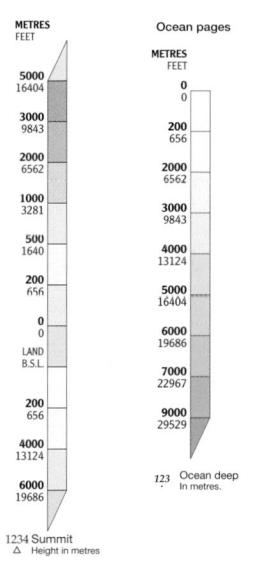

METRES / FEET

5000 16404
3000 9843
2000 6562
1000 3281
500 1640
200 656
0 0
LAND B.S.L.
200 656
4000 13124
6000 19686

Ocean pages

METRES / FEET

0 0
200 656
2000 6562
3000 9843
4000 13124
5000 16404
6000 19686
7000 22967
9000 29529

123 Ocean deep
In metres.

1234 Summit
△ Height in metres

Styles of Lettering

Cities and towns are explained separately

Country	**FRANCE**
Overseas Territory/Dependency	**Guadeloupe**
Disputed Territory	AKSAI CHIN
Administrative name
Shown for selected countries only.	**SCOTLAND**
Area name	PATAGONIA

Physical features

Island	*Gran Canaria*
Lake	*Lake Erie*
Mountain	*Mt Blanc*
River	*Thames*
Region	*LAPPLAND*

Cities and Towns

| Population | National Capital | Administrative Capital
Shown for selected countries only | Other City or Town |
|---|---|---|---|
| over 10 million | **DHAKA** ▣ | **Karachi** ⊙ | **New York** ⊙ |
| 5 million to 10 million | **MADRID** ▣ | **Toronto** ⊙ | **Philadelphia** ⊙ |
| 1 million to 5 million | **KĀBUL** ▢ | **Sydney** ○ | **Koahsiung** ○ |
| 500 000 to 1 million | **BANGUI** ▢ | **Winnipeg** ○ | **Jeddah** ○ |
| 100 000 to 500 000 | WELLINGTON ▢ | Edinburgh ○ | Apucarana ○ |
| 50 000 to 100 000 | PORT OF SPAIN ▢ | Bismarck ○ | Invercargill ○ |
| under 50 000 | MALABO ▫ | Charlottetown ○ | Ceres ○ |

CONTINENTAL MAPS

Boundaries

── International boundary   ------ Disputed international boundary   ········ Ceasefire line

Cities and Towns

National Capital   **Beijing** ▢   Other City or Town   **New York** ○

METRES
FEET

METRES / FEET	
6000	19686
4000	13124
2000	6562
1000	3281
500	1640
200	656
0	0
LAND B.S.L.	
200	656
3000	9843
5000	16404
7000	22967

Winkel Tripel Projection

EARTH'S DIMENSIONS

Mass	5.974 X 10²¹ tonnes
Total area	509 450 000 sq km / 196 672 000 sq miles
Land area	149 450 000 sq km / 57 688 000 sq miles
Water area	360 984 000 sq km / 138 984 000 sq miles
Volume	1 083 207 X 10⁶ cu km / 259 875 X 10⁶ cu miles

HIGHEST MOUNTAINS

	LOCATION	HEIGHT	
		metres	feet
Mt Everest	China/Nepal	8 848	29 028
K2	China/Jammu and Kashmir	8 611	28 251
Kangchenjunga	India/Nepal	8 586	28 169
Lhotse	China/Nepal	8 516	27 939
Makalu	China/Nepal	8 463	27 765

LARGEST ISLANDS

	LOCATION	AREA	
		sq km	sq miles
Greenland	North America	2 175 600	840 004
New Guinea	Oceania	808 510	312 167
Borneo	Asia	745 561	287 863
Madagascar	Africa	587 040	266 657
Baffin Island	North America	507 451	195 928

Equatorial diameter	12 756 km / 7 926 miles
Polar diameter	12 714 km / 7 900 miles
Equatorial circumference	40 075 km / 24 903 miles
Meridional circumference	40 008 km / 24 861 miles

1: 126 000 000

LARGEST LAKES

	LOCATION	AREA	
		sq km	sq miles
Caspian Sea	Asia/Europe	371 000	143 244
Lake Superior	North America	82 100	31 698
Lake Victoria	Africa	68 800	26 563
Lake Huron	North America	59 600	23 011
Lake Michigan	North America	57 800	22 316

LONGEST RIVERS

	LOCATION	LENGTH	
		km	miles
Nile	Africa	6 695	4 160
Amazon	South America	6 516	4 049
Yangtze	Asia	6 380	3 965
Mississippi-Missouri	North America	5 969	3 709
Ob'-Irtysh	Asia	5 568	3 460

TIME COMPARISONS

Time varies around the world due to the earth's rotation causing different parts of the world to be in light or darkness at any one time. To account for this, the world is divided into twenty-four Standard Time Zones based on 15° intervals of longitude. The table below gives examples of times observed at different parts of the world when it is 12 noon in the zone at the Greenwich Meridian (0° longitude). Daylight Saving Time, normally one hour ahead of local Standard Time, observed by certain countries for parts of the year, is not considered.

Winkel Tripel Projection

01:00	02:00	03:00	04:00	05:00	06:00	07:00	08:00	09:00	10:00	11:00	12:00
GMT -11	GMT -10	GMT -9	GMT -8	GMT -7	GMT -6	GMT -5	GMT -4	GMT -3	GMT -2	GMT -1	GMT 12
Am. Samoa Samoa	Cook Is Hawai'ian Is Tahiti	Anchorage	Vancouver San Francisco Los Angeles Pitcairn Is	Edmonton Denver	Chicago Houston Monterrey Mexico City Easter Island	Ottawa Washington Havana Bogotá Lima	Puerto Rico Caracas La Paz Asunción	Nuuk Brasília Rio de Janeiro Buenos Aires	South Georgia S. Sandwich Is	Azores Cape Verde	Reykjavík London Rabat Nouakch Accra

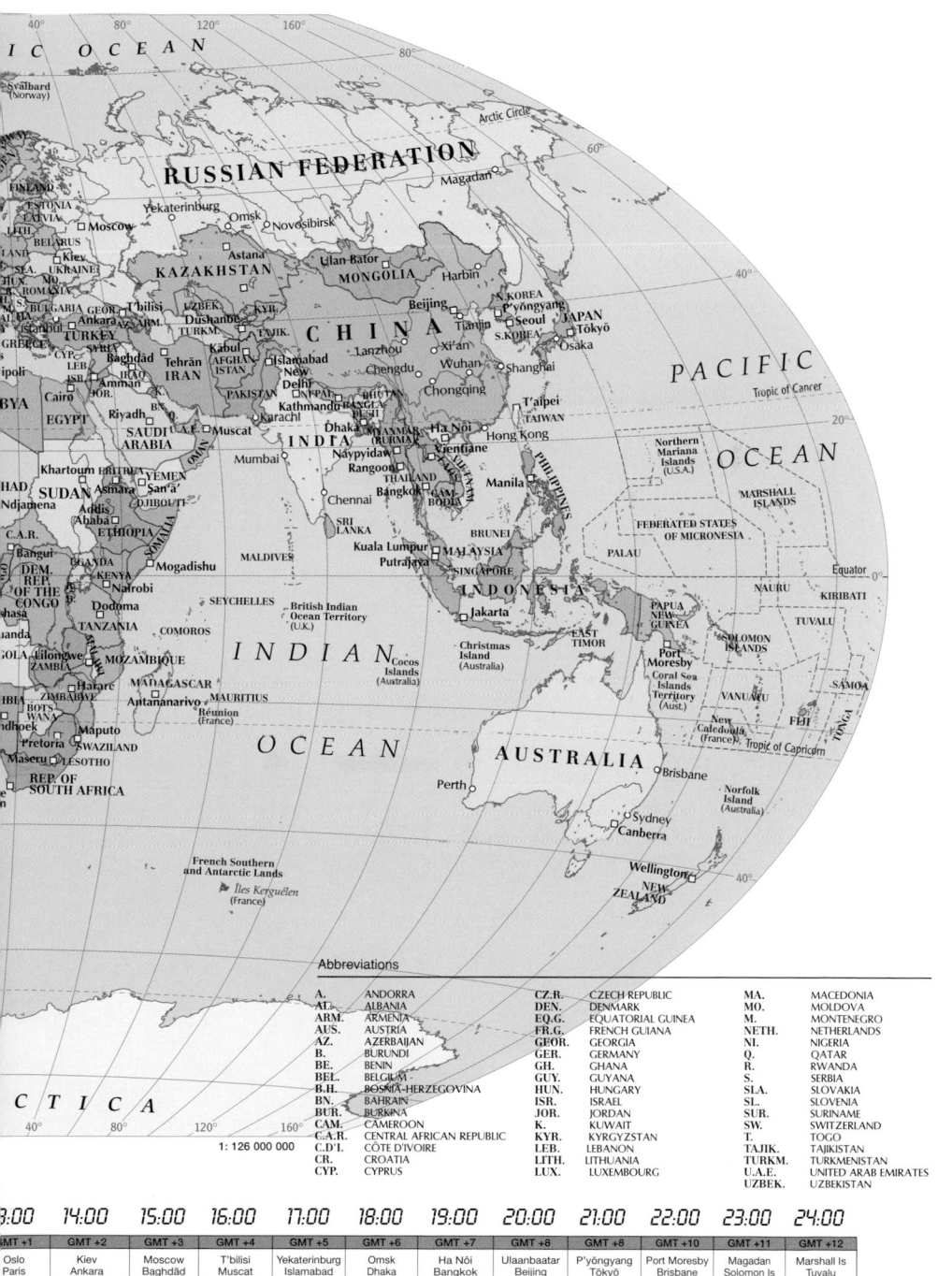

Abbreviations

A.	ANDORRA	CZ.R.	CZECH REPUBLIC	MA.	MACEDONIA
AL.	ALBANIA	DEN.	DENMARK	MO.	MOLDOVA
ARM.	ARMENIA	EQ.G.	EQUATORIAL GUINEA	M.	MONTENEGRO
AUS.	AUSTRIA	FR.G.	FRENCH GUIANA	NETH.	NETHERLANDS
AZ.	AZERBAIJAN	GEOR.	GEORGIA	NI.	NIGERIA
B.	BURUNDI	GER.	GERMANY	Q.	QATAR
BE.	BENIN	GH.	GHANA	R.	RWANDA
BEL.	BELGIUM	GUY.	GUYANA	S.	SERBIA
B.H.	BOSNIA-HERZEGOVINA	HUN.	HUNGARY	SLA.	SLOVAKIA
BN.	BAHRAIN	ISR.	ISRAEL	SL.	SLOVENIA
BUR.	BURKINA	JOR.	JORDAN	SUR.	SURINAME
CAM.	CAMEROON	K.	KUWAIT	SW.	SWITZERLAND
C.A.R.	CENTRAL AFRICAN REPUBLIC	KYR.	KYRGYZSTAN	T.	TOGO
C.D'I.	CÔTE D'IVOIRE	LEB.	LEBANON	TAJIK.	TAJIKISTAN
CR.	CROATIA	LITH.	LITHUANIA	TURKM.	TURKMENISTAN
CYP.	CYPRUS	LUX.	LUXEMBOURG	U.A.E.	UNITED ARAB EMIRATES
				UZBEK.	UZBEKISTAN

1: 126 000 000

13:00	14:00	15:00	16:00	17:00	18:00	19:00	20:00	21:00	22:00	23:00	24:00
GMT +1	GMT +2	GMT +3	GMT +4	GMT +5	GMT +6	GMT +7	GMT +8	GMT +8	GMT +10	GMT +11	GMT +12
Oslo	Kiev	Moscow	T'bilisi	Yekaterinburg	Omsk	Ha Nôi	Ulaanbaatar	P'yŏngyang	Port Moresby	Magadan	Marshall Is
Paris	Ankara	Baghdād	Muscat	Islamabad	Dhaka	Bangkok	Beijing	Tōkyō	Brisbane	Solomon Is	Tuvalu
Algiers	Cairo	Riyadh	Seychelles	Karachi		Jakarta	Manila	Palau	Canberra	New Caledonia	Fiji
Abuja	Harare	Addis Ababa	Mauritius				Singapore				Wellington
Kinshasa	Cape Town	Dodoma					Perth				

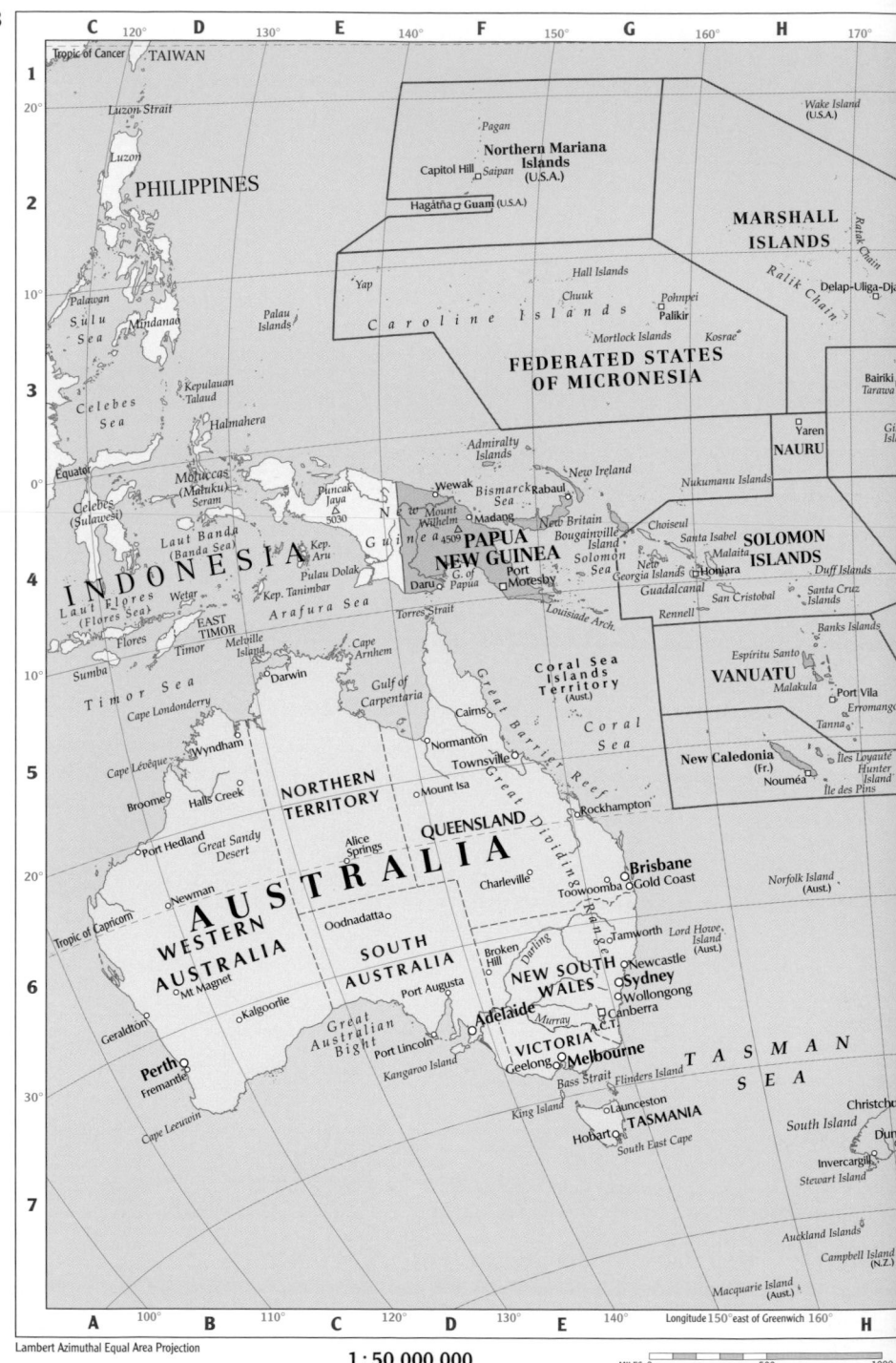

Lambert Azimuthal Equal Area Projection

1 : 50 000 000

MILES 0   500   1000

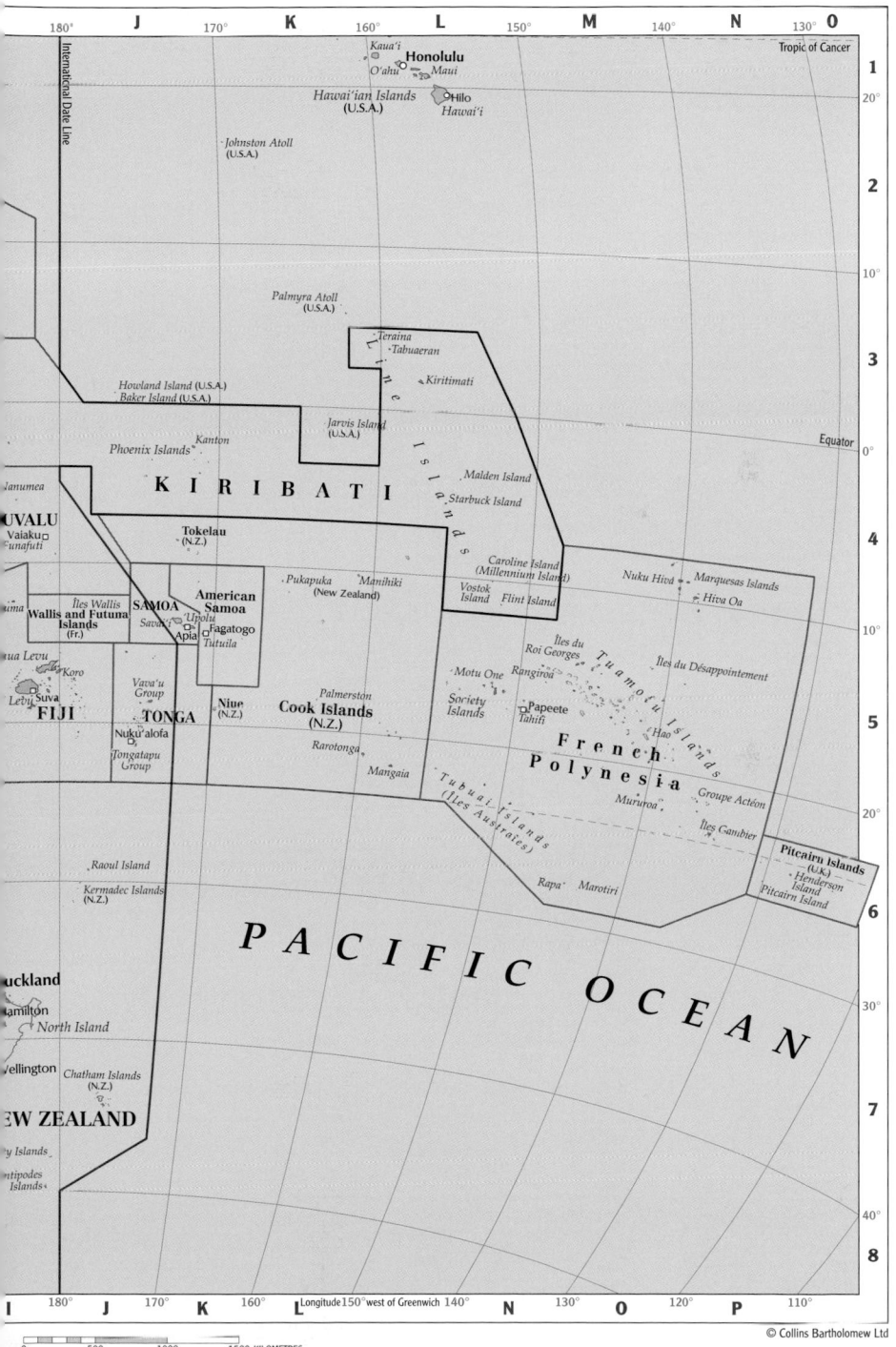

International Date Line

Kaua'i
O'ahu **Honolulu**
Maui
Hawai'ian Islands
(U.S.A.)
Hilo
Hawai'i

·Johnston Atoll
(U.S.A.)

Palmyra Atoll
(U.S.A.)

Teraina
·Tabuaeran

Kiritimati

Howland Island (U.S.A.)·
Baker Island (U.S.A.)·

Jarvis Island
(U.S.A.)

Phoenix Islands
·Kanton

·lanumea

K I R I B A T I

Malden Island

Starbuck Island

Caroline Island
(Millennium Island)

Nuku Hiva · *Marquesas Islands*

· *Hiva Oa*

UVALU
Vaiaku□
unafuti

Tokelau
(N.Z.)

·Pukapuka   ·Manihiki
(New Zealand)

Vostok
Island Flint Island

Îles du
Roi Georges
·
Rangiroa   Îles du Désappointement

·ima

Wallis and Futuna
Îles Wallis   **SAMOA**
Islands   Savai'i □ Upolu
(Fr.)   □ Apia
Fagatogo

American
Samoa
· Fagatogo
Tutuila

Motu One·
· Society
· Islands   Tahifi **Papeete**

FIJI   Vava'u
Group   **Niue**   Palmerston   Society
(N.Z.)   **Cook Islands**   Islands
TONGA   *(N.Z.)*

French
Polynesia

·ua Levu

Koro

·Lévu Suva

Nuku'alofa·
·Tongatapu
Group

Rarotonga·

Mangaia

·Hao

Groupe Actéon

Tubuai Islands
(Îles Australes)

Mururoa· ·

Îles Gambier

Raoul Island·

·Kermadec Islands
(N.Z.)

Rapa· Marotiri

Pitcairn Islands
(U.K.)
·Henderson
Island
·Pitcairn Island

P A C I F I C   O C E A N

·uckland

·amilton
North Island ·

·Vellington Chatham Islands
(N.Z.)

EW ZEALAND

·y Islands

·ntipodes
Islands·

0   500   1000   1500 KILOMETRES

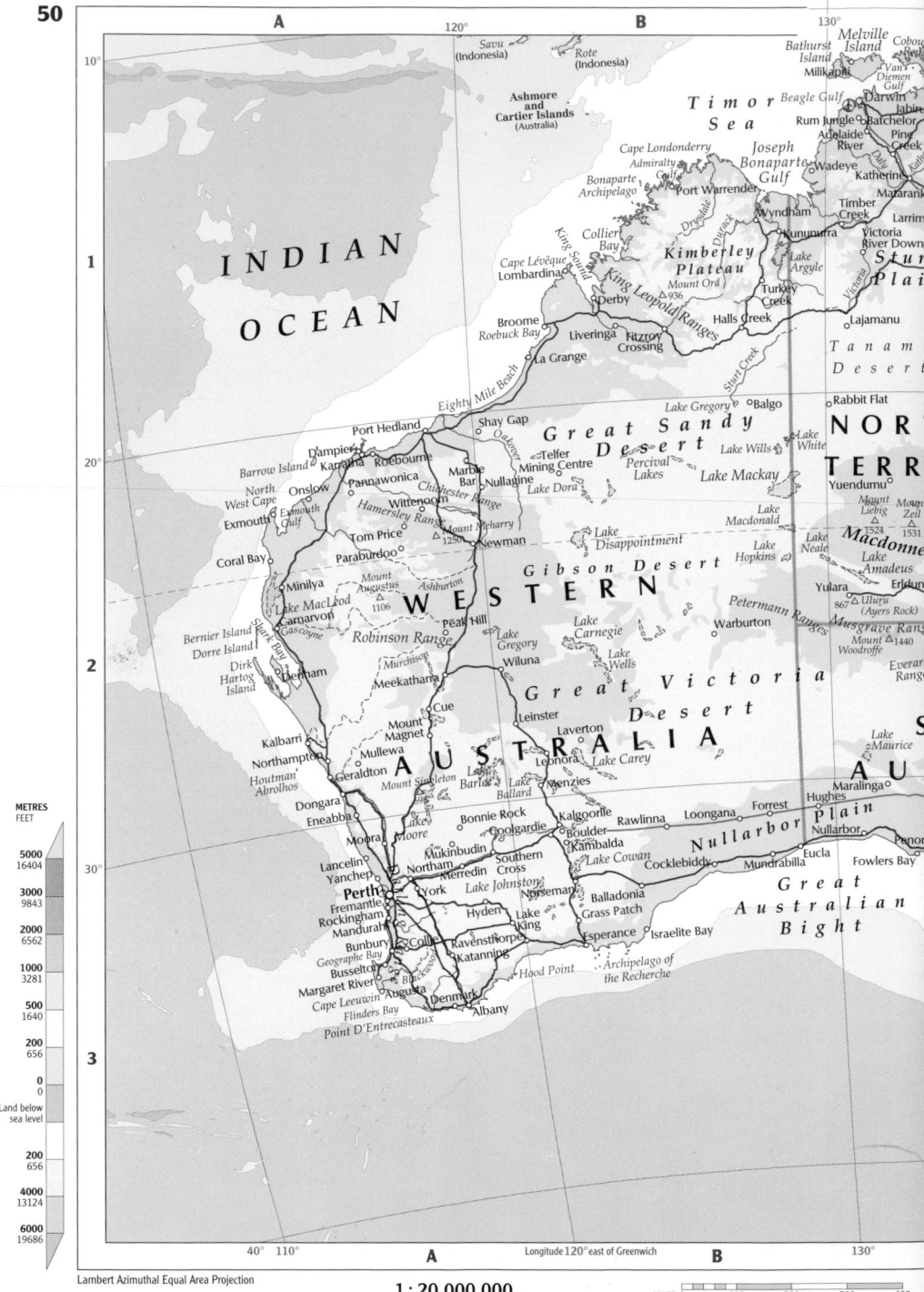

A 120° B 130°

INDIAN OCEAN

Savu (Indonesia)
Rote (Indonesia)

Timor Sea

Ashmore and Cartier Islands (Australia)

Bathurst Island *Melville Island* *Cobou*
Van Diemen Gulf
Beagle Gulf Darwin *Jabin*
Milikapiti
Rum Jungle Batchelor
Adelaide River Pine Creek
Wadeye Katherine
Mararani
Cape Londonderry
Admiralty Gulf
Joseph Bonaparte Gulf
Port Warrender
Timber Creek Larrim
Bonaparte Archipelago
Wyndham
Kununurra *Victoria River Down*
Collier Bay
Kimberley Plateau
Mount Ord △936
Lake Argyle
Stur Plai
Lombardina
Cape Lévêque
Derby
Turkey Creek
Halls Creek
Lajamanu
Broome
Roebuck Bay
Liveringa Fitzroy Crossing
Tanam Desert
Eighty Mile Beach
La Grange
Lake Gregory Balgo
Rabbit Flat
Port Hedland
Shay Gap
Great Sandy Desert
Lake Wills Lake White
NOR
Dampier
Telfer Mining Centre
Percival Lakes
Lake Mackay
Yuendumu
TERR
Barrow Island Karratha Roebourne
Marble Bar Nullagine
Lake Dora
Pannawonica
Wittenoom *Chichester Range*
North West Cape
Onslow
Hamersley Range
Mount △Meharry 1250
Newman
Lake Disappointment
Mount Liebig *Mount Zeil*
1524 1531
Macdonne
Exmouth *Exmouth Gulf*
Tom Price
Paraburdoo
Lake Macdonald
Lake Neale
Lake Amadeus
Coral Bay
Minilya
Mount Augustus 1106
Ashburton
Gibson Desert
Lake Hopkins
Yulara Erldun
△Uluru (Ayers Rock)
867△
Lake MacLeod
Carnarvon
WESTERN
Petermann Ranges
Warburton
Musgrave Rang
Mount △1440
Woodroffe
Everar
Range
Gascoyne
Robinson Range
Peak Hill
Lake Gregory
Lake Carnegie
Bernier Island
Dorre Island
Murchison
Wiluna
Lake Wells
Great Victoria
Dirk Hartog Island
Denham
Meekatharra
Desert
A U
Cue
AUSTRALIA
Leinster
Laverton
Mount Magnet
Lake Maurice
Kalbarri
Mullewa
Leonora Lake Carey
Northampton
Geraldton
Mount Singleton
Lake Barlee
Menzies
S
Houtman Abrolhos
Dongara
Lake Ballard
Maralinga
Eneabba
Bonnie Rock
Kalgoorlie
Rawlinna Loongana Forrest
Hughes
A U
Moora
Mukinbudin
Coolgardie
Boulder
Nullarbor
Lancelin
Yanchep
Northam Southern Cross
Kambalda
Lake Cowan
Cocklebiddy
Mundrabilla
Eucla
Nullarbor Plain
Fowlers Bay
Great
Australian
Bight
Perth
Merredin
Fremantle
Rockingham
York
Lake Johnston
Norseman
Mandurah
Hyden
Balladonia
Bunbury
Geographe Bay
Collie
Lake King
Grass Patch
Esperance Israelite Bay
Busselton
Ravensthorpe
Katanning
Margaret River
Blackwood
Denmark
Archipelago of the Recherche
Cape Leeuwin Augusta
Hood Point
Flinders Bay
Albany
Point D'Entrecasteaux

METRES
FEET

5000	16404
3000	9843
2000	6562
1000	3281
500	1640
200	656
0	0

Land below sea level

200	656
4000	13124
6000	19686

Lambert Azimuthal Equal Area Projection

40° 110° A Longitude 120° east of Greenwich B 130°

1 : 20 000 000

MILES 0 100 200 300 400

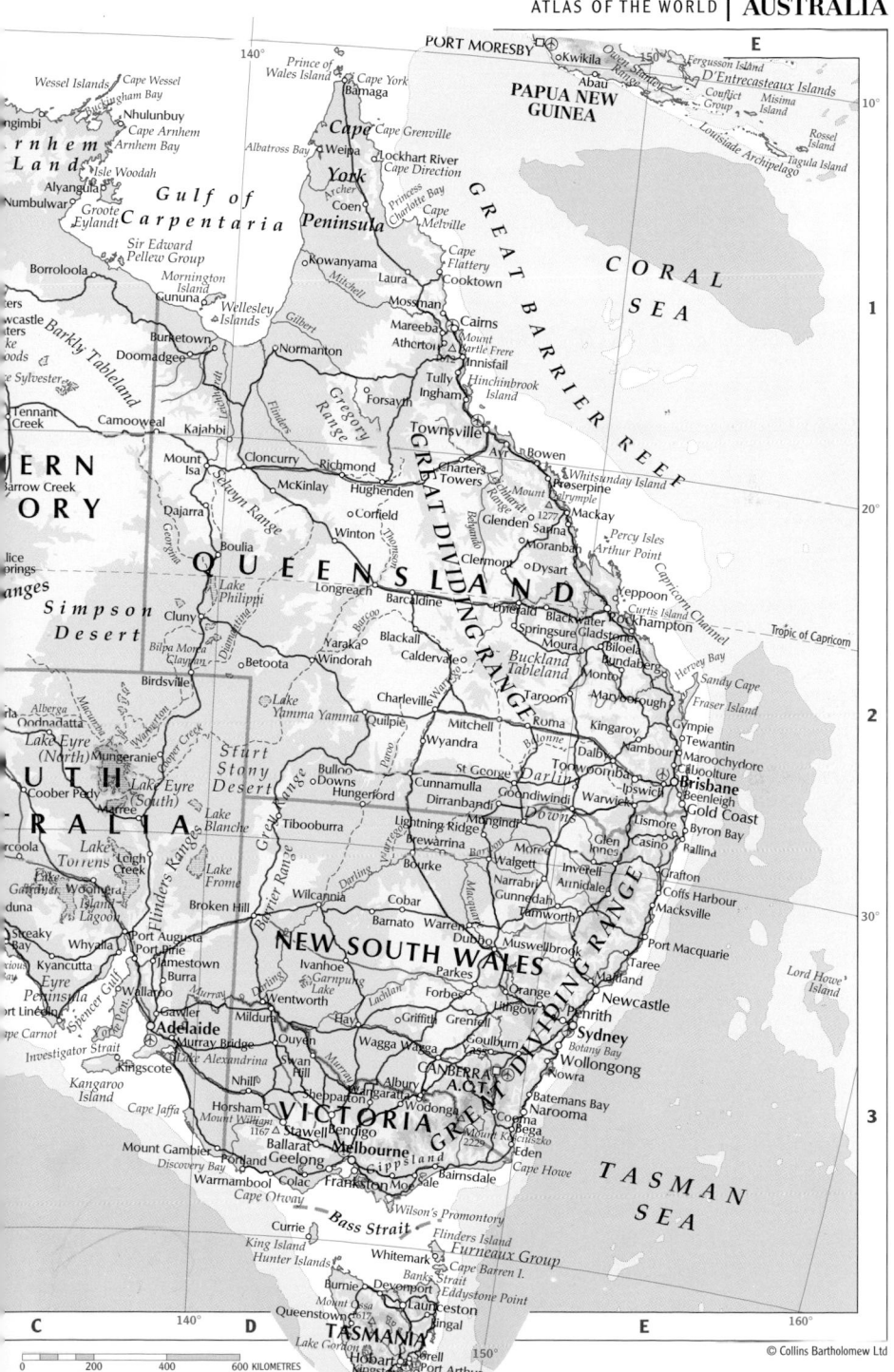

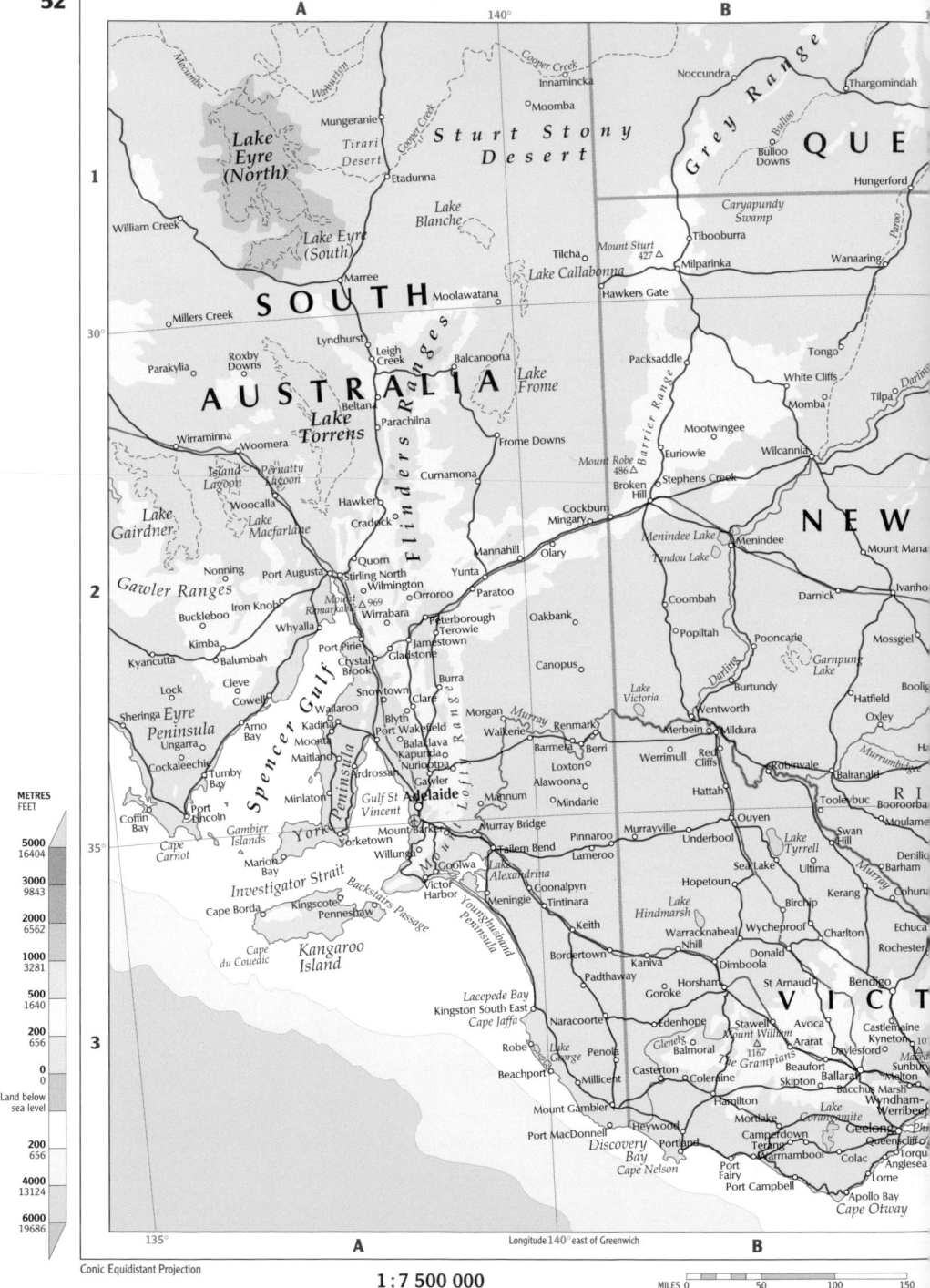

A　　　140°　　　B

METRES
FEET

5000	16404
3000	9843
2000	6562
1000	3281
500	1640
200	656
0	0
Land below sea level	
200	656
4000	13124
6000	19686

Macumba
Warburton
Mungeranie
Tirari Desert
Cooper Creek
Innamincka
Moomba
Sturt Stony Desert
Noccundra
Thargomindah
Grey Range
Billoo
Bulloo Downs
QUE
Lake Eyre (North)
Etadunna
Lake Blanche
Caryapundy Swamp
Hungerford
William Creek
Lake Eyre (South)
Tilcha
Mount Sturt 427 △
Tibooburra
Milparinka
Wanaaring
Lake Callabonna
Marree
Moolawatana
Hawkers Gate
Millers Creek
S O U T H
Lyndhurst
Leigh Creek
Balcanoona
Lake Frome
Packsaddle
Tongo
Parakylia
Roxby Downs
White Cliffs
Momba
Tilpa
Darling
A U S T R A L I A
Beltana
Parachilna
Flinders Ranges
Frome Downs
Mootwingee
Wilcannia
Wirraminna
Woomera
Lake Torrens
Curnamona
Mount Robe 486 △
Euriowie
N E W
Island Lagoon
Pernatty Lagoon
Hawker
Cradock
Barrier Range
Broken Hill
Stephens Creek
Lake Gairdner
Lake Macfarlane
Woocalla
Quorn
Mannahill
Olary
Cockburn
Mingary
Menindee Lake
Meninee
Mount Mana
Nonning
Port Augusta
Stirling North
Wilmington
Yunta
Yandou Lake
Danick
Ivanhoe
Gawler Ranges
Iron Knob
Mount Remarkable △ 969
Wirrabara
Orroroo
Paratoo
Oakbank
Coombah
Buckleboo
Peterborough
Terowie
Popiltah
Pooncarie
Mossgiel
Kimba
Whyalla
Jamestown
Canopus
Burtundy
Garnpung Lake
Kyancutta
Port Pirie
Crystal Brook
Gladstone
Lake Victoria
Darling
Hatfield
Boolig
Lock
Balumbah
Snowtown
Clare
Burra
Morgan
Renmark
Wentworth
Oxley
Cleve
Cowell
Eyre Peninsula
Wallaroo
Blyth
Waikerie
Merbein
Mildura
Murrumbidge
Ha
Sheringa
Arno Bay
Kadina
Port Wakefield
Balaklava
Berri
Werrimull
Red Cliffs
Robinvale
Balranald
R I
Ungarra
Moonta
Kapunda
Nuriootpa
Loxton
Hattah
Tooleybuc
Booroorba
Cockaleechie
Tumby Bay
Maitland
Ardrossan
Gawler
Alawoona
Mindarie
Ouyen
Moulamei
Port Lincoln
Minlaton
Gulf St Vincent
Adelaide
Mannum
Murray Bridge
Murrayville
Underbool
Lake Tyrrell
Swan Hill
Coffin Bay
Gambier Islands
Yorketown
Mount Barker
Pinnaroo
Sea Lake
Ultima
Denilio
Barham
Cape Carnot
Marion Bay
Willunga
Goolwa
Tailem Bend
Lameroo
Hopetoun
Kerang
Cohuna
Investigator Strait
Kingscote
Penneshaw
Backstairs Passage
Victor Harbor
Meningie
Coonalpyn
Tintinara
Lake Hindmarsh
Birchip
Echuca
Cape Borda
Youngbusband Peninsula
Keith
Warracknabeal
Wycheproof
Charlton
Rochester
Cape du Couedic
Kangaroo Island
Bordertown
Kaniva
Nhill
Donald
St Arnaud
Bendigo
Padthaway
Goroke
Horsham
Dimboola
V I C T
Lacepede Bay
Kingston South East
Cape Jaffa
Naracoorte
Edenhope
Stawell
Avoca
Castlemaine
Kyneton
Robe
Lake George
Penola
Glenelg
Mount William 1167
The Grampians
Ararat
Daylesford
Beachport
Millicent
Casterton
Coleraine
Beaufort
Ballarat
Bacchus Marsh
Sunbury
Melton
Mount Gambier
Hamilton
Skipton
Werribee
Wyndham
Port MacDonnell
Heywood
Mortlake
Lake Corangamite
Geelong
Queencliff
Torqu
Discovery Bay
Cape Nelson
Portland
Port Fairy
Port Campbell
Camperdown
Terang
Warrnambool
Colac
Lorne
Anglesea
Apollo Bay
Cape Otway

Longitude 140° east of Greenwich

1 : 7 500 000

MILES 0　　50　　100　　150

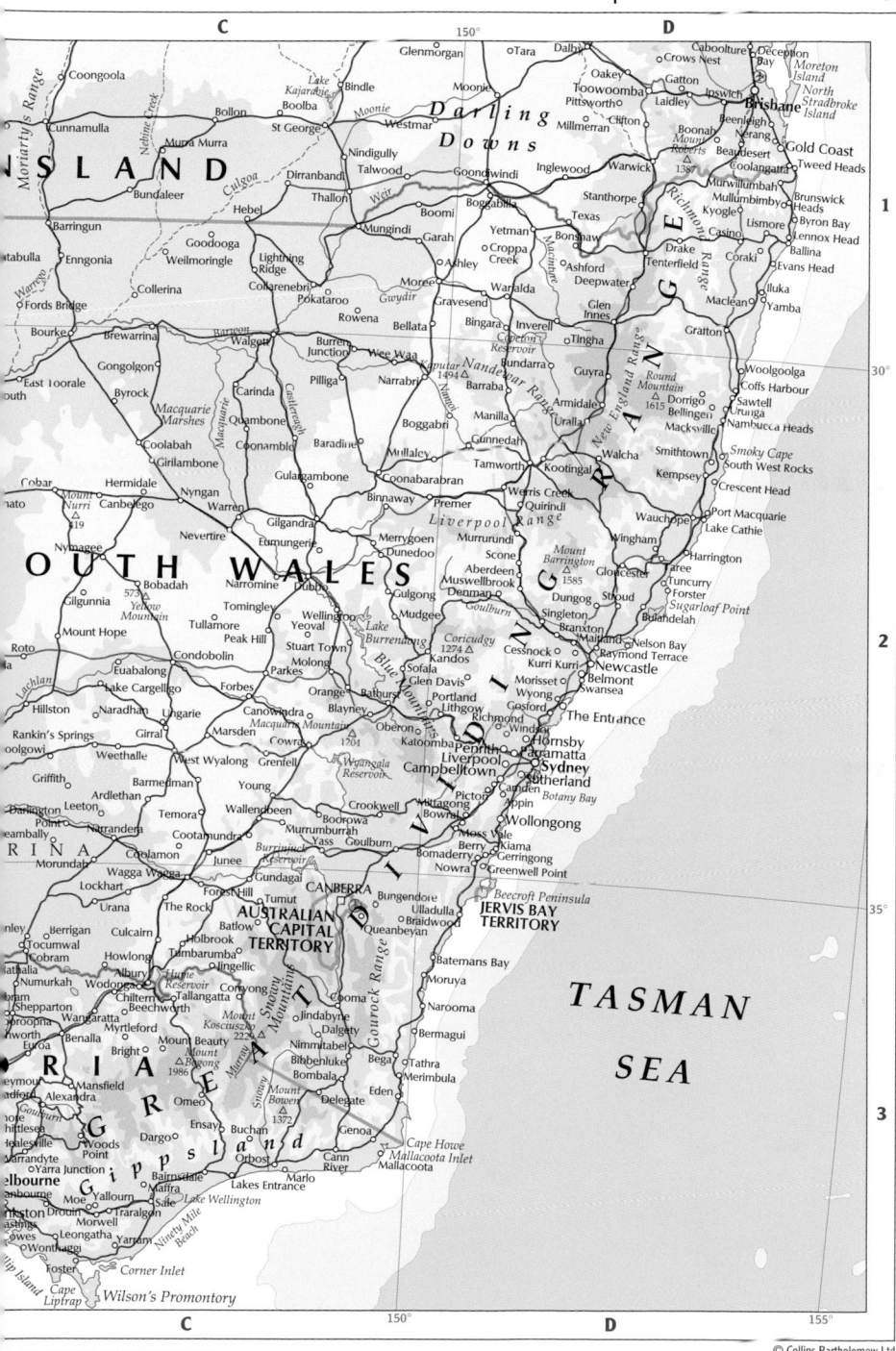

ISLAND

SOUTH WALES

VICTORIA

Great Dividing Range

New England Range

Darling Downs

Liverpool Range

Nandewar Range

Blue Mountains

Macquarie Marshes

Coricudgy

Snowy Mountains

Gourock Range

TASMAN

SEA

Brisbane
Gold Coast
Tweed Heads
Coolangatta
Byron Bay
Lennox Head
Ballina
Evans Head
Iluka
Yamba
Maclean
Grafton
Woolgoolga
Coffs Harbour
Sawtell
Urunga
Nambucca Heads
Smoky Cape
South West Rocks
Crescent Head
Port Macquarie
Lake Cathie
Kempsey
Taree
Harrington
Tuncurry
Forster
Sugarloaf Point
Bulahdelah
Nelson Bay
Newcastle
Belmont
Swansea
Wyong
The Entrance
Gosford
Hornsby
SYDNEY
Parramatta
Penth
Liverpool
Campbelltown
Sutherland
Botany Bay
Wollongong
Kiama
Gerringong
Nowra
Greenwell Point

Coongoola
Cunnamulla
Murra Murra
Bollon
St George
Nindigully
Talwood
Goondiwindi
Inglewood
Warwick
Stanthorpe
Texas
Yetman
Croppa Creek
Ashford
Deepwater
Drake
Tenterfield
Coraki
Casino
Kyogle
Mullumbimby
Murwillumbah
Brunswick Heads
Lismore
Richmond Range

CANBERRA
AUSTRALIAN CAPITAL TERRITORY
JERVIS BAY TERRITORY

Beecroft Peninsula

Ulladulla
Batemans Bay
Moruya
Narooma
Bermagui
Bega
Tathra
Merimbula
Eden
Cape Howe
Mallacoota Inlet
Mallacoota

Wilson's Promontory
Corner Inlet
Foster
Cape Liptrap

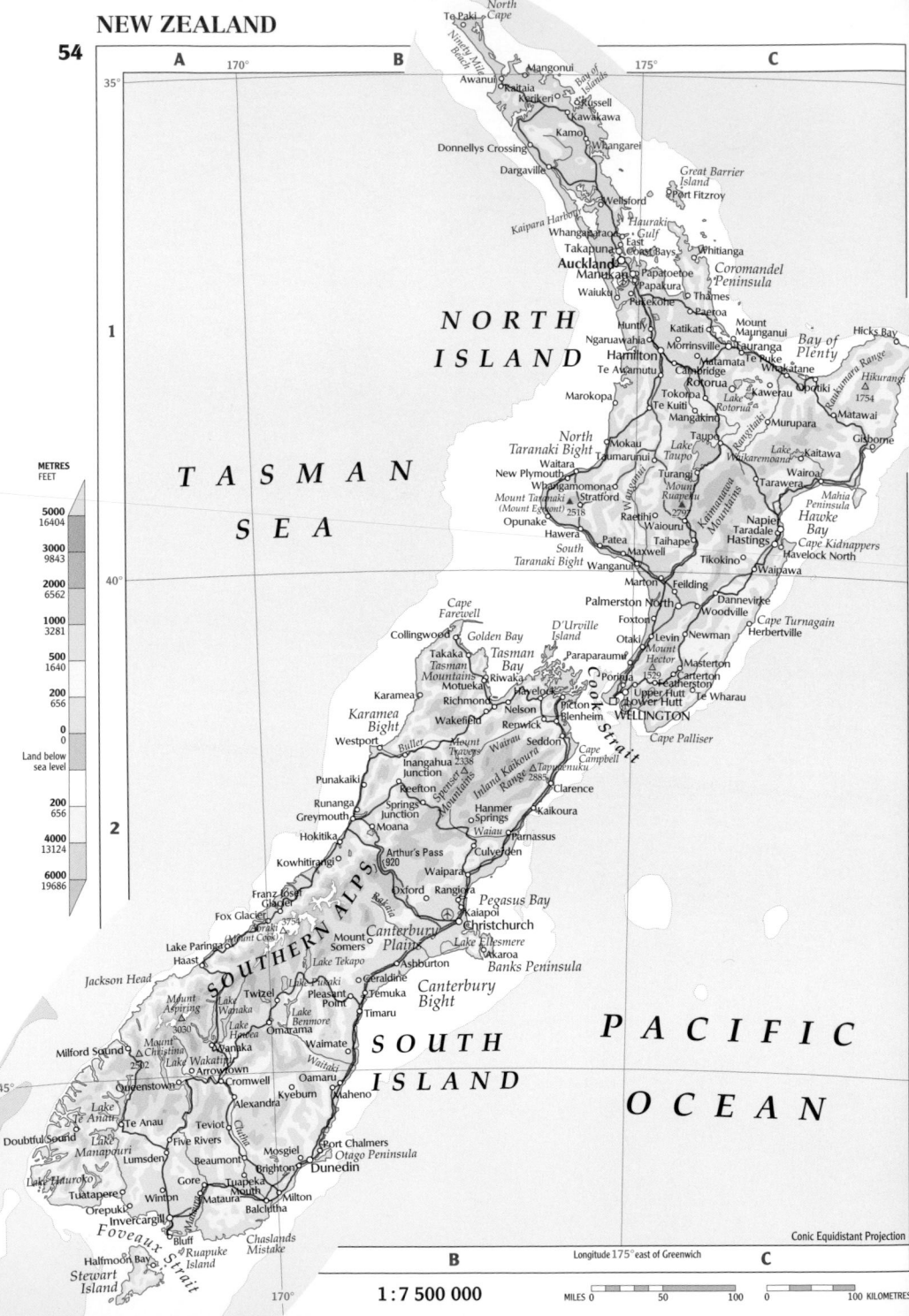

NEW ZEALAND

A   170°   B   175°   C

35°

Te Paki
North
Cape
Ninety Mile Beach
Mangonui
Awanui
Kaitaia
Kerikeri
Russell
Bay of Islands
Kawakawa
Kamo
Donnellys Crossing
Whangarei
Dargaville
Great Barrier
Island
Wellsford
Port Fitzroy
Kaipara Harbour
Whangaparaoa
Hauraki
Gulf
East
Coast Bays
Takapuna
Whitianga
Coromandel
Peninsula
Auckland
Papatoetoe
Manukau
Papakura
Waiuku
Thames
Pukekohe
Paeroa
Huntly
Mount Maunganui
Ngaruawahia
Morrinsville
Tauranga
Hicks Bay
Katikati
Hamilton
Te Awamutu
Cambridge
Matamata
Te Puke
Whakatane
Rotorua
Kawerau
Opotiki
Raukumara Range
Marokopa
Tokoroa
Lake
Rotorua
Murupara
Hikurangi
1754
Te Kuiti
Waiouru
Kaitaia
Matawai
Mangakino
Taupo
Lake
Waikaremoana
Gisborne

NORTH ISLAND

Mokau
North
Taranaki Bight
Taumarunui
Lake
Taupo
New Plymouth
Waitara
Turangi
Mount
Ruapehu
2797
Tarawera
Mahia
Peninsula
Whangamomona
Stratford
Mount Taranaki
(Mount Egmont)
2518
Raetihi
1529
Mount
Napier
Hawke
Bay
Opunake
Taradale
Cape Kidnappers
Hawera
Patea
Taihape
Hastings
South
Taranaki Bight
Maxwell
Tikokino
Havelock North
Wanganui
Waipawa

40°

Marton
Feilding
Dannevirke
Palmerston North
Woodville
Cape Turnagain
Foxton
Herbertville
Cape
Farewell
Otaki
Levin
Newman
Collingwood
Golden Bay
D'Urville
Island
Paraparaumu
Mount
Hector
Masterton
Takaka
Tasman
Bay
Porirua
Carterton
Tasman
Mountains
Riwaka
Upper Hutt
Featherston
Karamea
Motueka
Havelock
Lower Hutt
Te Wharau
Richmond
Nelson
Picton
WELLINGTON
Karamea
Bight
Wakefield
Renwick
Blenheim
Westport
Seddon
Cape
Campbell
Cape Palliser

2

Buller
Mount
Travers
Wairau
Punakaiki
Inangahua 2338
Junction
Spenser
Mountains
Tapuaenuku
2885
Reefton
Inland Kaikoura
Range
Clarence
Runanga
Springs
Junction
Hanmer
Springs
Kaikoura
Greymouth
Moana
Waiau
Parnassus
Hokitika
Arthur's Pass
(920)
Culverden
Kowhitirangi
Oxford
Waipara
Rangiora
Pegasus Bay
Franz Josef
Glacier
Kaiapoi
SOUTHERN ALPS
Christchurch
Fox Glacier
Aoraki 3754
(Mount Cook)
Canterbury
Plains
Lake Ellesmere
Akaroa
Lake Paringa
Mount
Somers
Banks Peninsula
Haast
Lake Tekapo
Ashburton
Jackson Head
Lake Pukaki
Geraldine
Canterbury
Bight
Mount
Aspiring
3030
Twizel
Pleasant
Point
Temuka
Lake
Wanaka
Timaru

SOUTH ISLAND

Milford Sound
Mount
Christina
2502
Lake
Hawea
Omarama
Waimate
Wanaka
Waitaki
Lake Wakatipu
Arrowtown
Oamaru
Queenstown
Cromwell
Kyeburn
Maheno
Lake
Anau
Alexandra

45°

Te Anau
Teviot
Clutha
Lake
Manapouri
Five Rivers
Doubtful Sound
Lumsden
Beaumont
Port Chalmers
Lake Hauroko
Gore
Mosgiel
Otago Peninsula
Tuatapere
Tuapeka
Mouth
Brighton
Dunedin
Orepuki
Mataura
Milton
Winton
Balclutha
Invercargill
Foveaux Strait
Bluff
Chaslands
Mistake
Halfmoon Bay
Ruapuke Island
Stewart
Island

TASMAN

SEA

PACIFIC

OCEAN

B   Longitude 175° east of Greenwich   C

170°

1 : 7 500 000

MILES 0   50   100   0   100 KILOMETRES

METRES FEET	
5000	16404
3000	9843
2000	6562
1000	3281
500	1640
200	656
0	0
Land below sea level	
200	656
4000	13124
6000	19686

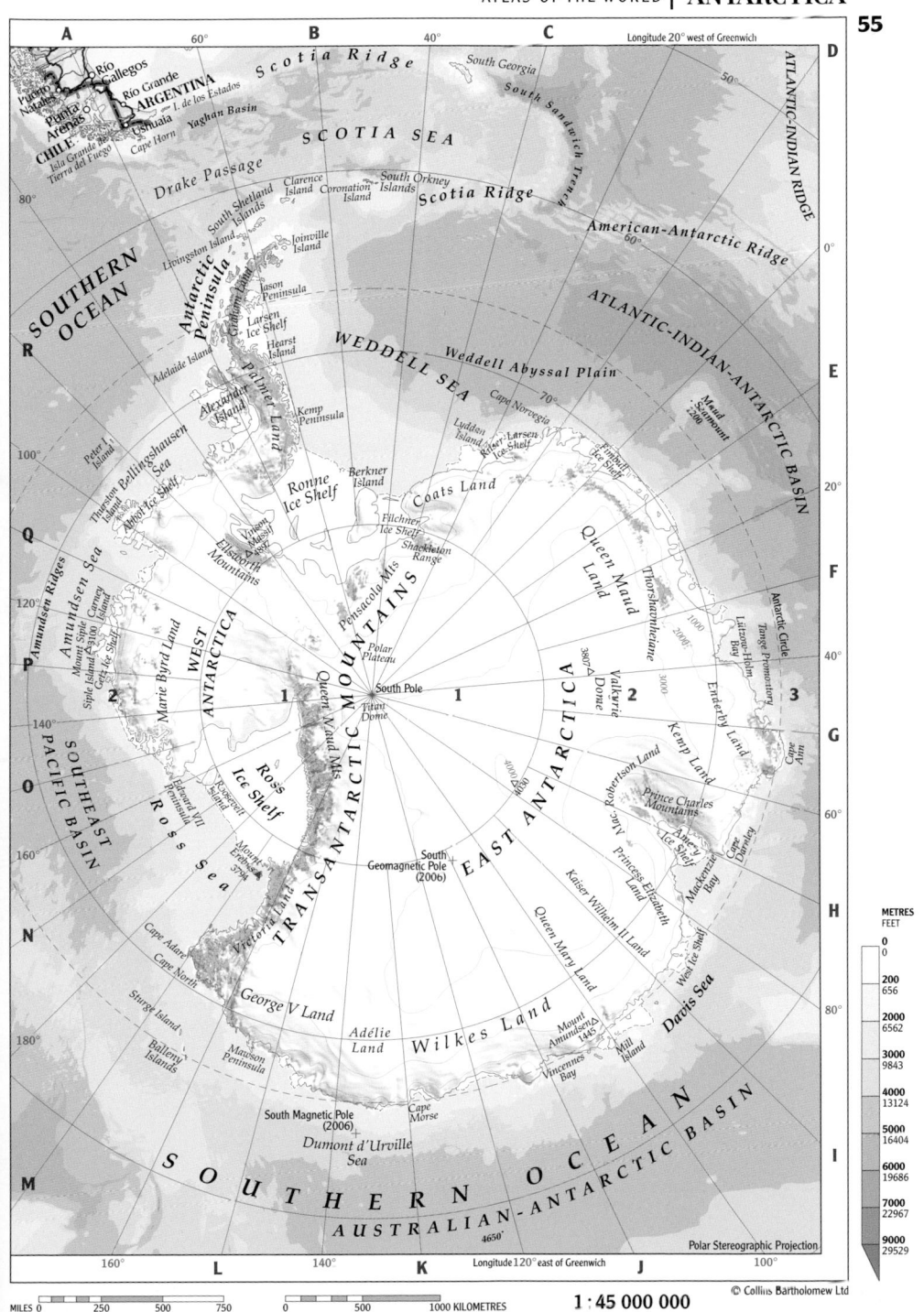

SOUTHERN OCEAN

ARGENTINA

CHILE

Scotia Ridge

South Georgia

South Sandwich Trench

SCOTIA SEA

ATLANTIC-INDIAN RIDGE

Drake Passage

Clarence Island
Coronation Island
South Orkney Islands
Scotia Ridge

American-Antarctic Ridge

ATLANTIC-INDIAN-ANTARCTIC BASIN

South Shetland Islands
Livingston Island
Joinville Island
Jason Peninsula

SOUTHERN OCEAN

Antarctic Peninsula
Larsen Ice Shelf
Hearst Island

WEDDELL SEA
Weddell Abyssal Plain

Adelaide Island
Kemp Peninsula
Cape Norvegia
Maud Seamount 2206

Palmer Land

Alexander Island

Peter I Island

Thurston Island
Bellingshausen Sea
Abbot Ice Shelf

Ronne Ice Shelf

Berkner Island

Coats Land

Lyddan Island
Larsen Ice Shelf
Riiser-Larsen Ice Shelf

Queen Maud Land

Thorshavnheiane

Antarctic Circle

Amundsen Sea

Vinson Massif 4897
Ellsworth Mountains

Filchner Ice Shelf
Shackleton Range
Pensacola Mts

Prince Olav Coast
Lützow-Holm Bay

Lunga Promontory

Amundsen Ridges

Mount Sidley
Spirit Island
Carney Island
Getz Ice Shelf
Siple Island

WEST ANTARCTICA

Marie Byrd Land

Polar Plateau

South Pole

Titan Dome

Queen Maud Mts

Valkyrie Dome
3807

TRANSANTARCTIC MOUNTAINS

Enderby Land

Kemp Land

Cape Ann

SOUTHEAST PACIFIC BASIN

Ross Ice Shelf

Edward VII Peninsula
Roosevelt Island

Ross Sea

EAST ANTARCTICA

Alec. Robertson Land
Prince Charles Mountains
Amery Ice Shelf
Mackenzie Bay
Cape Darnley

Mount Erebus 3794

South Geomagnetic Pole (2006)

Kaiser Wilhelm II Land
Princess Elizabeth Land

West Ice Shelf
Davis Sea

Cape Adare
Cape North

Victoria Land

George V Land

Queen Mary Land
Wilkes Land

Mount Amundsen 1445
Mill Island

Sturge Island

Balleny Islands

Adélie Land

Mawson Peninsula

Vincennes Bay

South Magnetic Pole (2006)

Cape Morse

Dumont d'Urville Sea

SOUTHERN OCEAN

AUSTRALIAN-ANTARCTIC BASIN
4650

METRES	
FEET	
0	0
200	656
2000	6562
3000	9843
4000	13124
5000	16404
6000	19686
7000	22967
9000	29529

MILES 0   250   500   750

0   500   1000 KILOMETRES

1 : 45 000 000

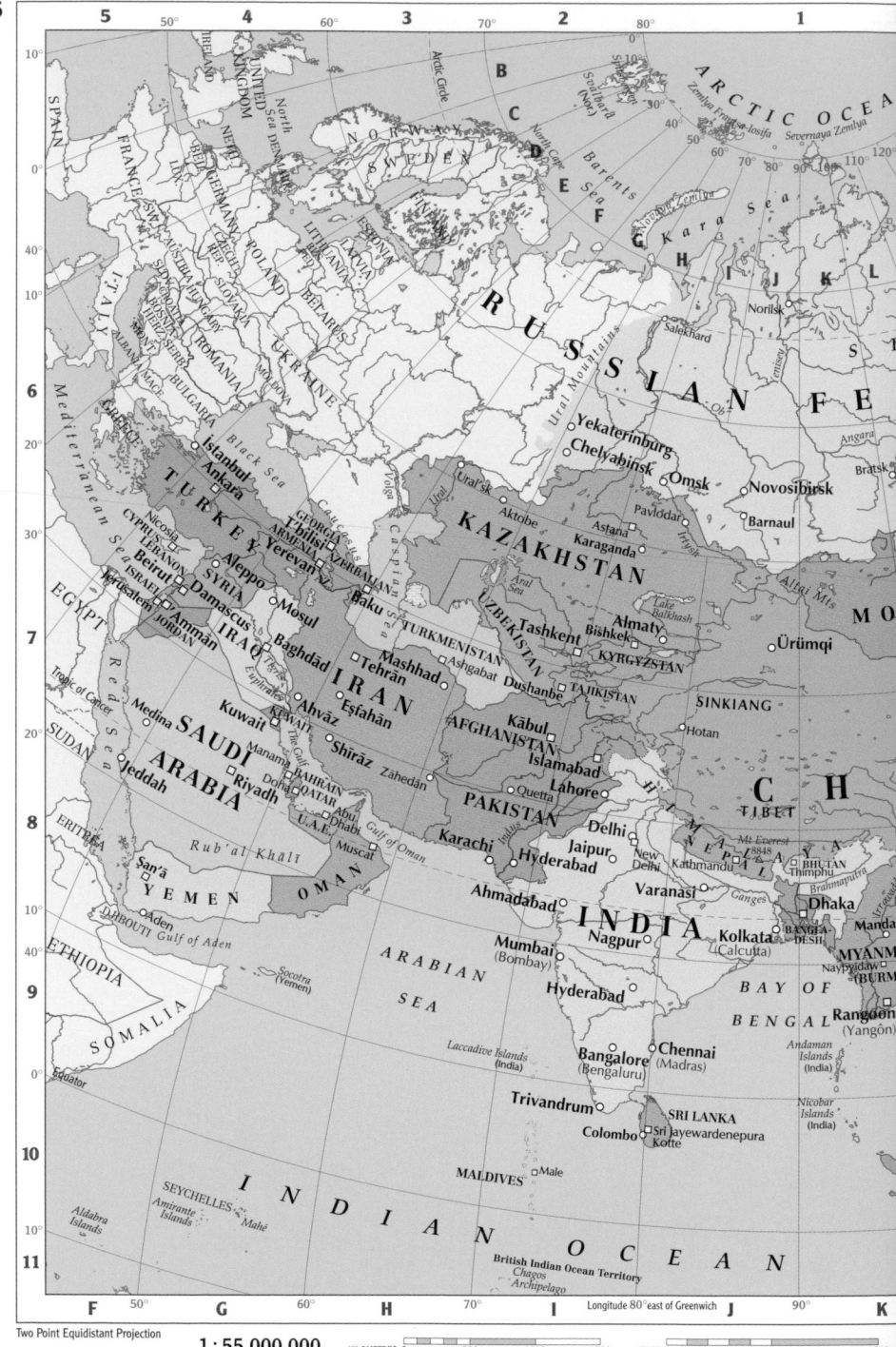

5 50° **4** 60° **3** 70° **2** 80° **1**

10°

A R C T I C   O C E A

B

C

D

E

F

G

H   I   J   K

Norilsk

Salekhard

R U S S I A N   F E

Yekaterinburg

Chelyabinsk

Omsk

Novosibirsk

Bratsk

Ural'sk

Aktobe

Astana

Pavlodar

Barnaul

Karaganda

KAZAKHSTAN

SPAIN

FRANCE

ITALY

Mediterranean Sea

GREECE

Black Sea

Istanbul

Ankara

TURKEY

Tbilisi

Yerevan

ARMENIA

AZERBAIJAN

Aleppo

Mosul

Baku

Almaty

Bishkek

Tashkent

Lake
Balkhash

Ürümqi

KYRGYZSTAN

M O

Aral
Sea

Caspian Sea

TURKMENISTAN

UZBEKISTAN

Hotan

SINKIANG

Nicosia

CYPRUS

LEBANON

Beirut

Damascus

SYRIA

Jerusalem

ISRAEL

Amman

JORDAN

IRAQ

Baghdad

Mashhad

Ashgabat

Dushanbe

TAJIKISTAN

C H

EGYPT

Tropic of Cancer

Medina

Kuwait

KUWAIT

Ahvāz

Tehrān

Eşfahān

IRAN

Kābul

AFGHANISTAN

Islamabad

TIBET

SUDAN

Red Sea

SAUDI
ARABIA

Jeddah

Manama

BAHRAIN

The Gulf

QATAR

Doha

Abu
Dhabi

U.A.E.

Shīrāz

Zāhedān

Quetta

Lāhore

Mt Everest
8848

New
Delhi

Kathmandu

Delhi

Jaipur

NEPAL

BHUTAN

Thimphu

Brahmaputra

Riyadh

PAKISTAN

Karachi

Muscat

Gulf of Oman

Indus

Hyderabad

Ahmadabad

Varanasi

Ganges

Dhaka

BANGLA-
DESH

Manda

ERITREA

San'a

YEMEN

OMAN

Rub' al Khālī

ARABIAN
SEA

INDIA

Nagpur

Kolkata
(Calcutta)

MYANM
(BURM

Naypyidaw

Aden

DJIBOUTI

Gulf of Aden

Socotra
(Yemen)

Mumbai
(Bombay)

Hyderabad

BAY OF

BENGAL

Rangoon
(Yangôn)

ETHIOPIA

SOMALIA

Equator

Laccadive Islands
(India)

Bangalore
(Bengaluru)

Chennai
(Madras)

Andaman
Islands
(India)

Trivandrum

SRI LANKA

Sri Jayewardenepura
Kotte

Colombo

Nicobar
Islands
(India)

MALDIVES

Male

I N D I A N   O C E A N

SEYCHELLES

Aldabra
Islands

Amirante
Islands

Mahé

British Indian Ocean Territory
Chagos
Archipelago

Longitude 80° east of Greenwich

F 50° G 60° H 70° I J 90° K

Two Point Equidistant Projection

1 : 55 000 000

KILOMETRES 0   500   1000   1500   MILES 0   500   1000

2　　　　　　　4　　50°　5　40°　6　30°

180°
170°
60°

Arctic Circle

R U S S I A N

East Siberian Sea

New Siberian Islands

Wrangel Island

U.S.A.

B E R I N G　S E A

Aleutian Islands (U.S.A.)

Lena

Yakutsk

Sea of Okhotsk

Magadan

Kamchatka Peninsula

Petropavlovsk-Kamchatskiy

Midway Islands (U.S.A.)

170°

7

180°

Tropic of Cancer

Kure Atoll

Sakhalin

Kuril Islands

Lake Baikal

tsk

Khabarovsk

Sapporo

Hokkaidō

20°
170°

Qiqihar

Harbin

Vladivostok

Heilong Jiang

Sea of Japan (East Sea)

Honshū

P A C I F I C

Ulan Bator

Changchun

NORTH KOREA

Tokyo

J A P A N

O C E A N

Wake Atoll (U.S.A.)

8

OLIA

INNER MONGOLIA

Shenyang

P'yŏngyang

Seoul

Osaka

Baotou

Beijing

Dalian

SOUTH KOREA

Fukuoka

Kyūshū

160°

Tianjin

Yellow Sea

Lanzhou

Taiyuan

Xi'an

Huang He

Shanghai

East China Sea

Bonin Islands (Japan)

10°

Volcano Islands (Japan)

Ngewae Island

hengdu

Wuhan

Nanjing

ngqing

Changsha

T'aipei

TAIWAN

Northern Mariana Islands (U.S.A.)

9

Kunming

Fuzhou

Guangzhou

Guam (U.S.A.)

Nanning

Hong Kong

Ha Nôi

Hainan

Luzon

Caroline Islands

Equator

0°

South China Sea

Manila

Quezon City

PHILIPPINES

Melekeok

AILAND

Bangkok

Palawan

Mindanao

PALAU

10

CAMBODIA

Phnom Penh

Hô Chi Minh City

Sulu Sea

Davao

Admiralty Island

New Britain

Gulf of Thailand

Celebes Sea

Halmahera

Jayapura

PAPUA NEW GUINEA

Bandar Seri Begawan

BRUNEI

Manado

Puncak Jaya 5030

G u i n e a

10°

M A L A Y S I A

Borneo

Moluccas (Maluku)

Seram

dan

Kuala Lumpur

Kuching

Kepulauan Aru

Putrajaya

SINGAPORE

Balikpapan

Celebes (Sulawesi)

Pulau Dolak

Palembang

Banjarmasin

Makassar

Kepulauan Tanimbar

Laut Banda

Cape Arnhem

AUSTRALIA

11

matra

I N D O N E S I A

Laut Java

Jakarta

Dili

EAST TIMOR

Arafura Sea

Bandung

Java

Surabaya

Sumbawa

Timor

Laut Sawu

Sumba

0

140°

P

150°

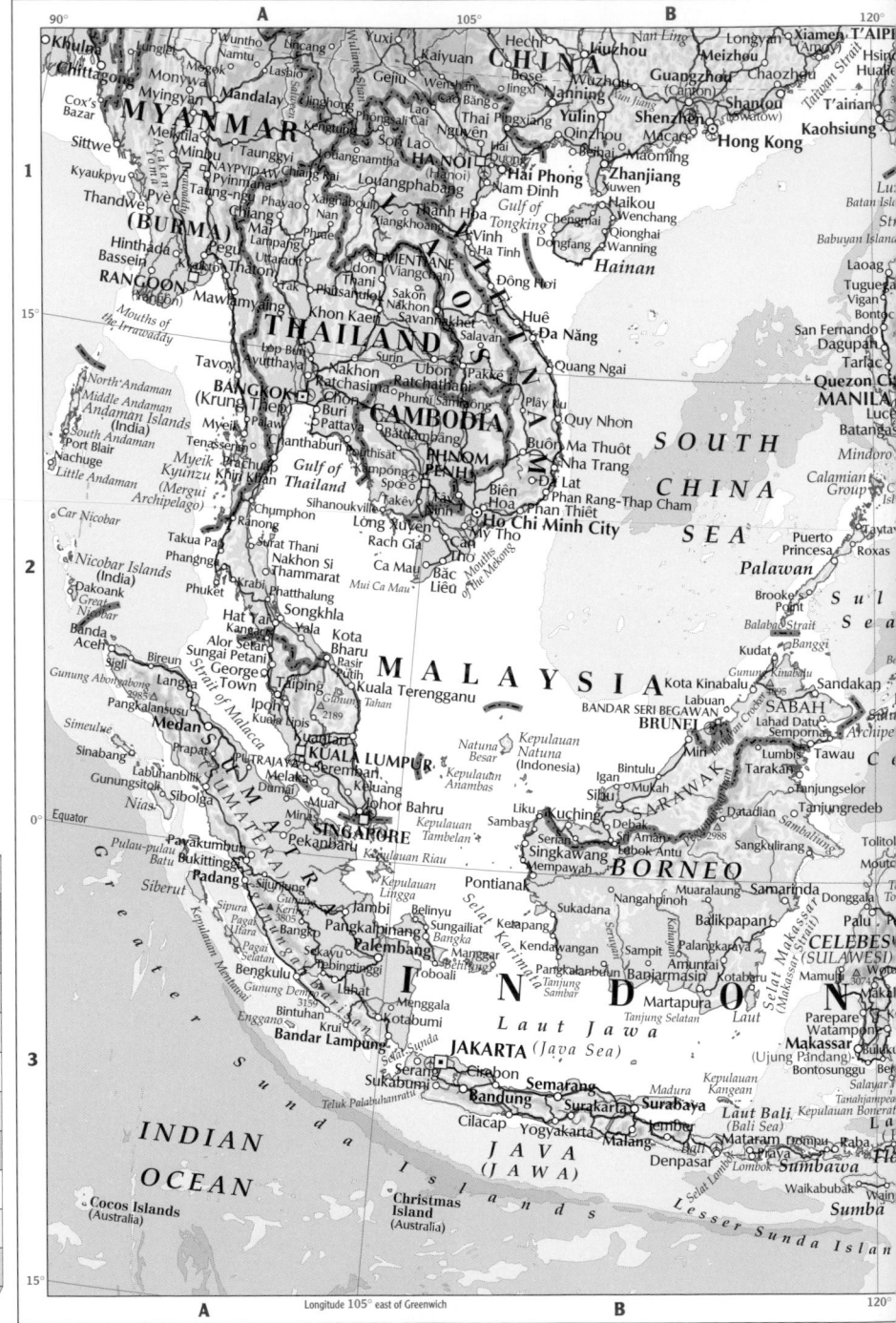

A map of Southeast Asia showing parts of China, Myanmar (Burma), Thailand, Laos, Vietnam, Cambodia, Malaysia, Indonesia, Borneo, and the surrounding seas.

90° **105°** **B** **120°**

CHINA

Khulna · Chittagong · Cox's Bazar · Sittwe · Kyaukpyu · Thandwe

MYANMAR (BURMA)

Mandalay · Monywa · Myingyan · Mektila · Minbu · Pye · Taunggyi · Pyinmana · NAYPYIDAW · Chiang Mai

Hinthada · Bassein · **RANGOON (Yangon)** · Pegu · Thaton · Mawlamyine

THAILAND · **BANGKOK (Krung Thep)** · Ayutthaya · Nakhon Ratchasima · Chon Buri · Pattaya

CAMBODIA · Battambang · **PHNOM PENH**

HA NOI (Hanoi) · Hai Phong · Nam Dinh · Thanh Hoa · Vinh · Ha Tinh · Dong Hoi · Huê · Da Nang · Quang Ngai

Gulf of Tongking · Haikou · Wenchang · Qionghai · Dongfang · **Hainan**

Zhanjiang · Xuwen · Chengmai

LAOS · **VIENTIANE (Viangchan)** · Louangphabang · Xaignabouri · Savannakhet · Salavan · Pakxe

VIETNAM · Play Ku · Quy Nhon · Buôn Ma Thuôt · Nha Trang · Da Lat · Phan Rang-Thap Cham · Phan Thiêt · **Ho Chi Minh City** · Biên Hoa · My Tho

Guangzhou (Canton) · Chaozhou · Shantou · Shenzhen · Macau · **Hong Kong** · Maoming

Hechi · Liuzhou · Longyan · **Xiamen (Amoy)** · **T'AIPEI** · Kaiyuan · Nanning · Qinzhou · Beihai · Yulin · Behai

Kaohsiung · **T'ainan**

Laoag · Tuguegarao · Vigan · Bontoc · San Fernando · Dagupan · Tarlac · **Quezon City** · **MANILA** · Batangas · Lucena

SOUTH CHINA SEA

North Andaman · Middle Andaman · **Andaman Islands (India)** · South Andaman · Port Blair · Nachague · Little Andaman · Car Nicobar

Nicobar Islands (India) · Great Nicobar · Banda Aceh · Sigli · Bireun · Langsa · Medan · Pangkalanbun · Sibolga · Sinabang · Nias

MALAYSIA · **KUALA LUMPUR** · Ipoh · Taiping · George Town · Alor Setar · Kota Bharu · Kuala Terengganu · Kuantan · Melaka · Johor Bahru · **SINGAPORE**

BANDAR SERI BEGAWAN · **BRUNEI** · **SABAH** · Kota Kinabalu · Labuan · Lahad Datu · Sandakan · Tawau

SARAWAK · Kuching · Sibu · Bintulu · Miri

BORNEO · Pontianak · Singkawang · Samarinda · Balikpapan · Banjarmasin · Palangkaraya · Sampit

SUMATRA · Padang · Jambi · Palembang · Pangkalpinang · Bengkulu · Bandar Lampung

INDONESIA · **JAKARTA** · Bandung · Semarang · Surakarta · Surabaya · Yogyakarta · Malang · Denpasar

JAVA (JAWA) · **Laut Jawa (Java Sea)** · **Laut Bali (Bali Sea)**

CELEBES (SULAWESI) · **Makassar (Ujung Pandang)** · Parepare · Watampone

Mindoro · **Calamian Group** · Puerto Princesa · Roxas · **Palawan**

INDIAN OCEAN

Cocos Islands (Australia) · Christmas Island (Australia)

Lesser Sunda Islands · Waikabubak · **Sumbawa** · Mataram · Bima · **Sumba**

Strait of Malacca · Gulf of Thailand · Mouths of the Irrawaddy · Mouths of the Mekong · Greater Sunda Islands

METRES / FEET
5000 / 16404
3000 / 9843
2000 / 6562
1000 / 3281
500 / 1640
200 / 656
0 / 0
Land below sea level
200 / 656
4000 / 13124
6000 / 19686

1 · 2 · 3 (row indices along left margin)
15° · 0° Equator · 15° (latitude lines)

Albers Equal Area Conic Projection

Longitude 105° east of Greenwich

1 : 25 000 000

MILES 0 · 250 · 500

135° | 150° | E

Tropic of Cancer

*Ryukyu Islands
(Nansei-shotō)
(Japan)*

IWAN

1

*Philippine
Sea*

P A C I F I C

**Northern
Mariana
Islands
(U.S.A.)**

Pagan

O C E A N

15°

CAPITOL HILL *Saipan
Tinian*

Rota

PHILIPPINES

HAGÅTÑA ✛

**Guam
(U.S.A.)**

Catanduanes
Legaspi
Sorsogon
Irosin Catarman
Masbate *Samar* Catbalogan
Roxas Tacloban
Bacolod *Cebu*
tlos Bohol Surigao
Bohol Sea Buttuan
quieta Illigan Cagayan de Oro
dian Cotabato *Mindanao*
amboanga **Davao**
ela Mati
*Moro
Gulf* General Santos

Mariana Trench

**FEDERATED STATES
OF MICRONESIA**

Ulithi *Fais*
Yap ✛
Colonia
Ngulu *Sorol* *Faraulep*
Eauripik *Caroline
Islands*

2

PALAU ✛
MELEKEOK *Babeldaob*

*East Caroline
Basin*

Equator 0°

*Kepulauan
Talaud*
Sangir
Morotai
*Kepulauan
Sangi*
anjung Manado Karakelong
inahasa Tondano Daruba
Luwuk Gorontalo Tobelo
Ternate **Halmahera**
Sao-Siu
Waigeo
St Matthias
Group Mussau Island

*Pelleluhu
Islands*
Hermit Islands
Admiralty
Islands
Isabel Channel
New Hanover
Umbukul Kavieng
Manus Island Lorengau New
Bismarck Archipelago Ireland
Rabaul

S   I   A

AUSTRALIA

Timor Sea

C 135° | D

0   250   500   750 KILOMETRES

© Collins Bartholomew Ltd

METRES / FEET

5000 / 16404
3000 / 9843
2000 / 6562
1000 / 3281
500 / 1640
200 / 656
0 / 0
Land below sea level
200 / 656
4000 / 13124
6000 / 19686

Albers Equal Area Conic Projection

1 : 12 000 000

MILES 0   100   200   300

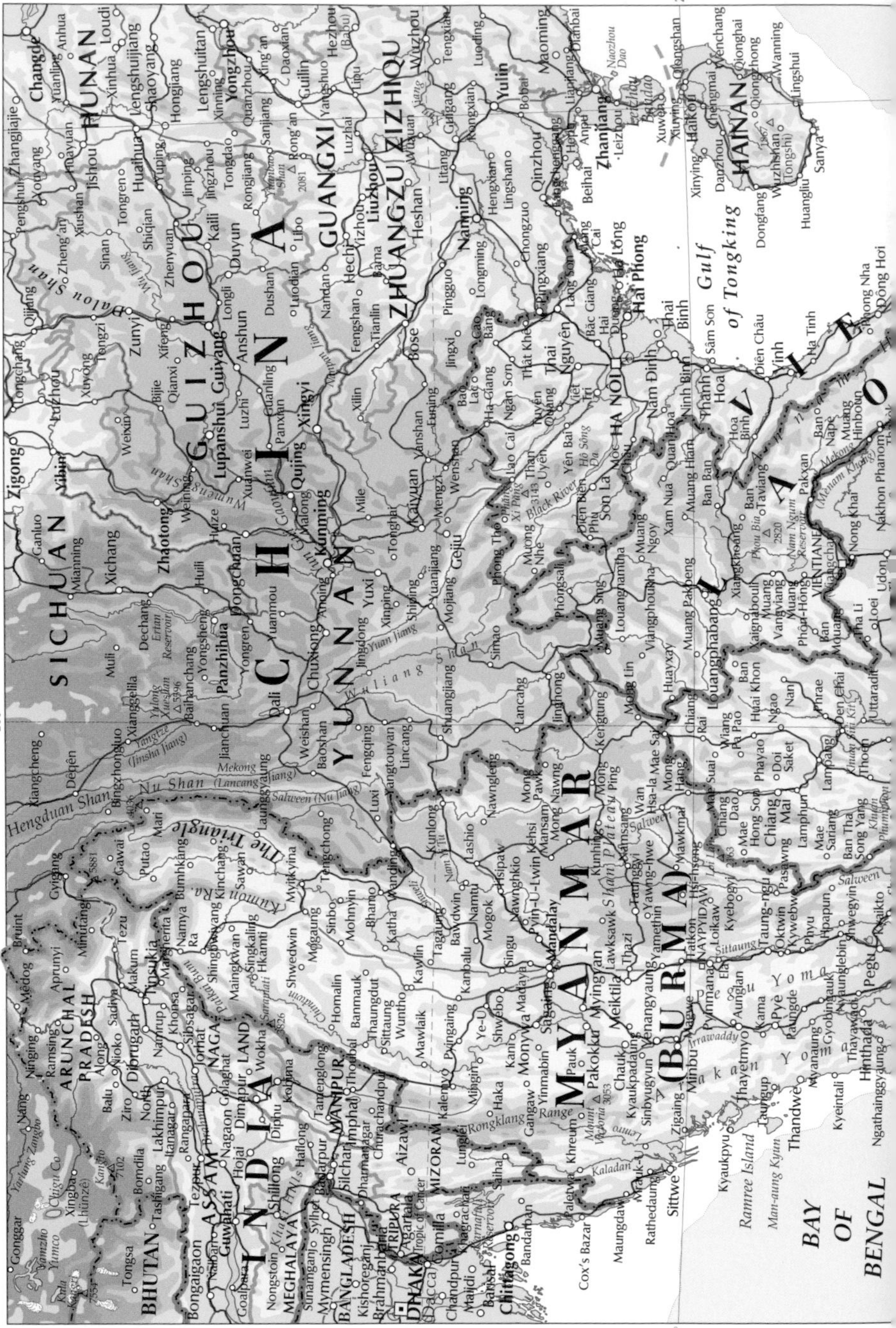

METRES
FEET

5000
16404

3000
9843

2000
6562

1000
3281

500
1640

200
656

0
0

Land below
sea level

200
656

4000
13124

6000
19686

Albers Equal Area Conic Projection

1 : 12 000 000

MILES 0   100   200   300

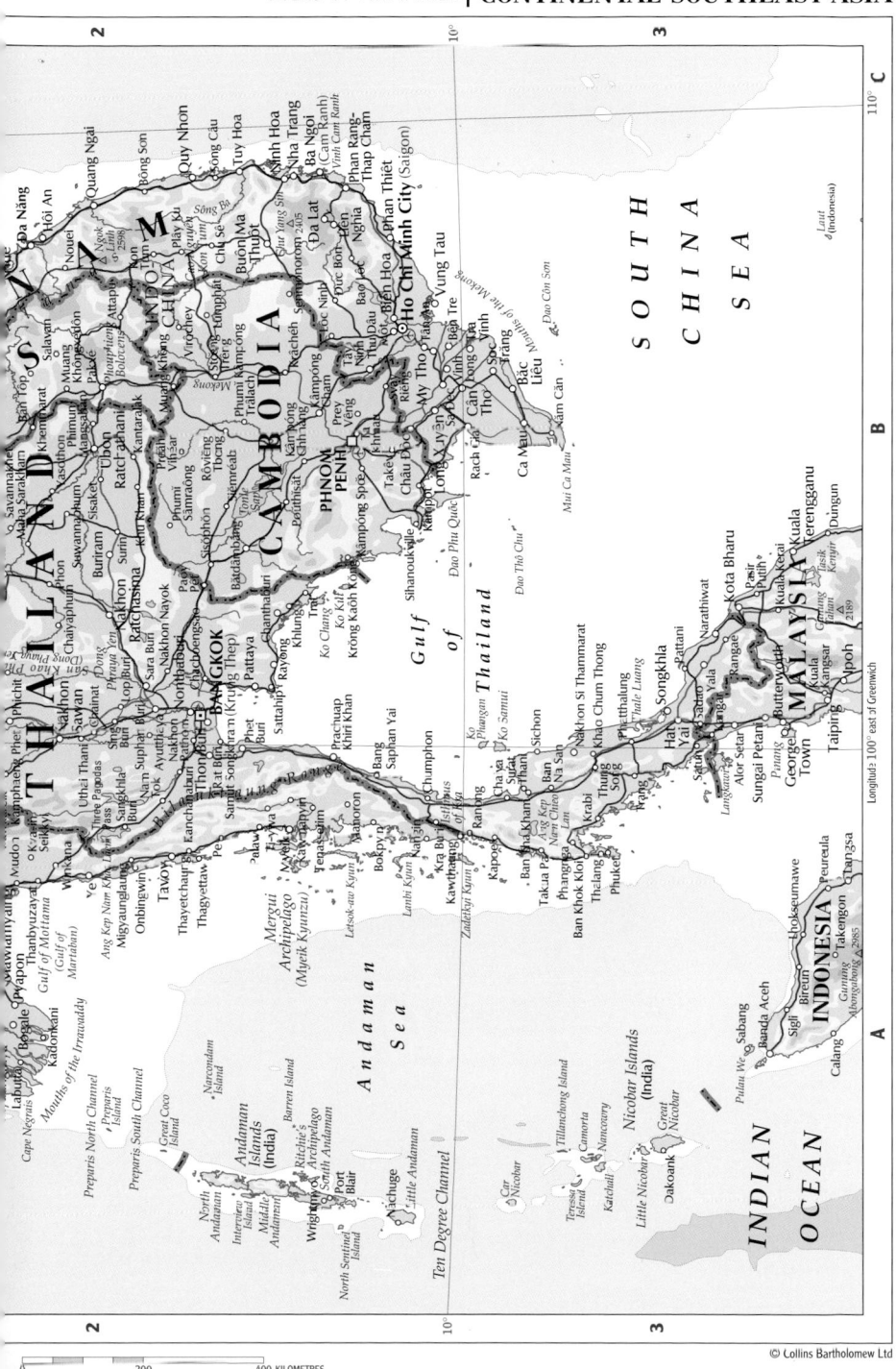

0   200   400 KILOMETRES

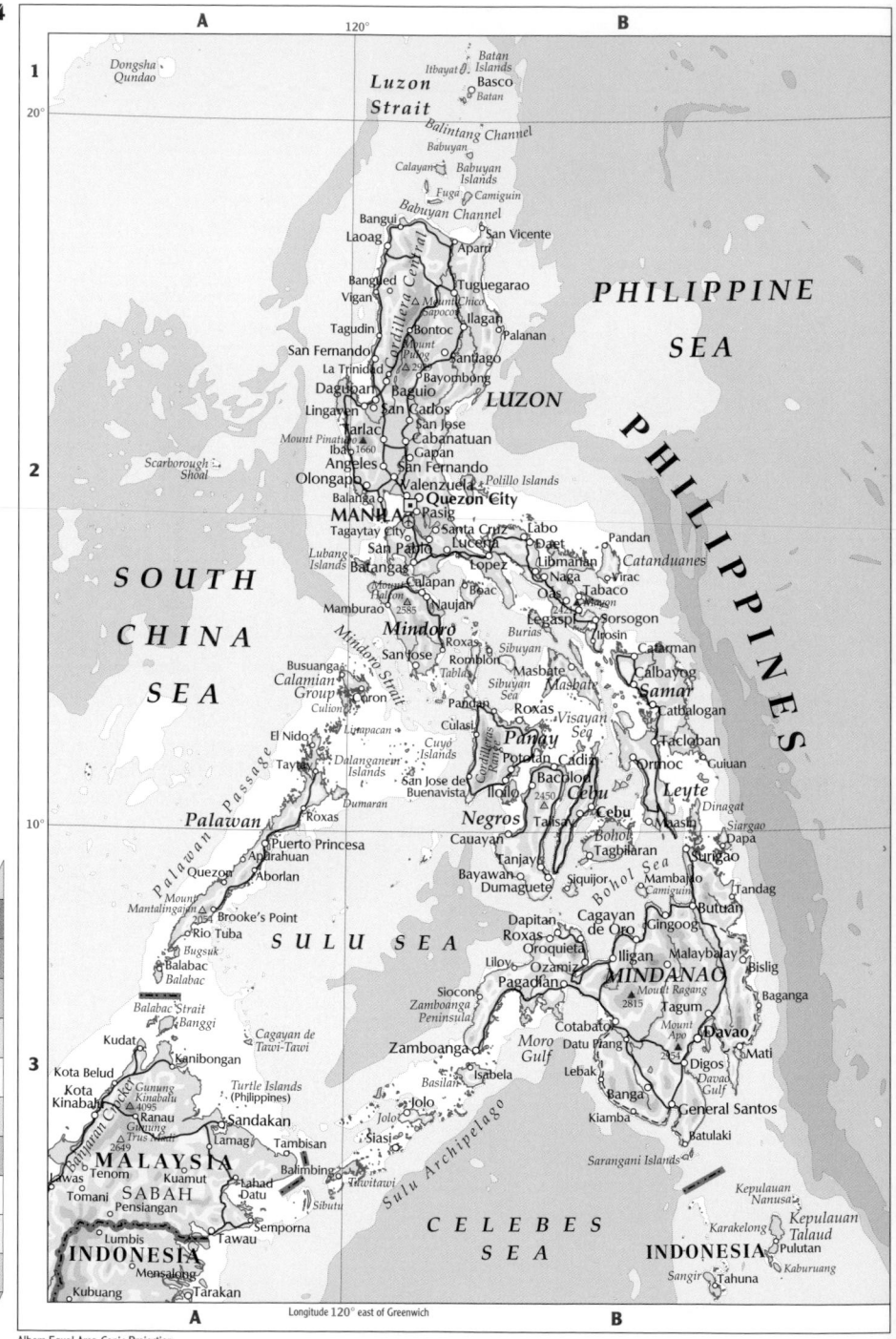

PHILIPPINES

A 120° **B**

1

20°

Dongsha
Qundao

Luzon
Strait

*Batan
Islands*
Itbayat Basco
Batan

Balintang Channel

Babuyan

Calayan Babuyan
Islands
Fuga Camiguin

Babuyan Channel

Bangui
Laoag Aparri
San Vicente

Bangued Tuguegarao
Vigan
Ilagan
Tagudin Bontoc Palanan
Mount
San Fernando Pulog Santiago
La Trinidad 2929 Bayombong
Dagupan Baguio **LUZON**
Lingayen San Carlos
Tarlac San Jose
Mount Pinatubo Cabanatuan
Iba 1660 Gapan
Angeles San Fernando
Olongapo Valenzuela Polillo Islands
Balanga Quezon City
MANILA Pasig
Tagaytay City Santa Cruz Labo
Lubang Batangas San Pablo Lucena Daet Pandan
Islands Lopez Libmanan *Catanduanes*
Calapan Naga Virac
Mamburao Boac Oas Tabaco
Mount Naujan Burias Legaspi Sorsogon
Halcon 2585 *Mindoro* Roxas Irosin
San Jose Sibuyan Masbate Catarman
Busuanga Romblon *Sea* Calbayog
Calamian Coron Tablas *Masbate* *Samar*
Group Culion Pandan Roxas Catbalogan
Culasi *Visayan* Tacloban
El Nido Cuyo *Seg* Ormoc Guiuan
Tayta *Islands* Pototan Cadiz *Leyte*
Dalanganem Bacolod Dinagat
Islands San Jose de Iloilo 2450 Cebu Maasin
Dumaran Buenavista Cebu Siargao
Roxas *Negros* Talisay Dapa
Puerto Princesa *Bohol* Tagbilaran Surigao
Aborlan Cauayan *Sea* Tandag
Quezon Tanjay Siquijor Mambajo
Aborlan Bayawan Dumaguete Camiguin Butuan
Dapitan Gingoog
SULU SEA Roxas Cagayan Iligan
Oroquieta de Oro Malaybalay Bislig
Liloy Ozamiz *MINDANAO* Baganga
Siocon Pagadian Mount Ragang
Zamboanga 2815 Tagum
Peninsula Cotabato Mount
Zamboanga *Moro* Datu Piang Apo Davao
Gulf Lebak 2954 Digos Mati
Isabela Banga
Basilan General Santos
Jolo *Jolo* Kiamba Batulaki
Siasi *Sulu Archipelago* Sarangani Islands

**PHILIPPINE
SEA**

**SOUTH
CHINA
SEA**

*Scarborough
Shoal*

*Mount
Mantalingajan*
Brooke's Point
Rio Tuba
Bugsuk
Balabac
Balabac

Palawan Passage

Palawan

Linapacan

Mindoro Strait

Roxas

Kudat
Kota Belud
Kota
Kinabalu
Gunung
Kinabalu
4095
Ranau
Gunung
Trus Madi
2649
MALAYSIA
SABAH
Tenom
Tomani
Pensiangan
INDONESIA
Lumbis
Mensalong
Kubuang Tarakan

Kanibongan
Sandakan
Tamag Tambisan
Balimbing
Tuwitawi
*Cagayan de
Tawi-Tawi*
*Turtle Islands
(Philippines)*
Sibutu

Lahad
Datu
Semporna
Tawau

*CELEBES
SEA*

INDONESIA
Karakelong
Pulutan
Sangir Tahuna

*Kepulauan
Nanusa*
*Kepulauan
Talaud*
Kaburuang

Balabac Strait
Banggi

Baturan Creek

3

10°

**P
H
I
L
I
P
P
I
N
E
S**

METRES	
FEET	
5000	16404
3000	9843
2000	6562
1000	3281
500	1640
200	656
0	0
Land below	
sea level	
200	656
4000	13124
6000	19686

Albers Equal Area Conic Projection

Longitude 120° east of Greenwich

1:12 000 000

KILOMETRES 0 200 400
MILES 0 100 200 300

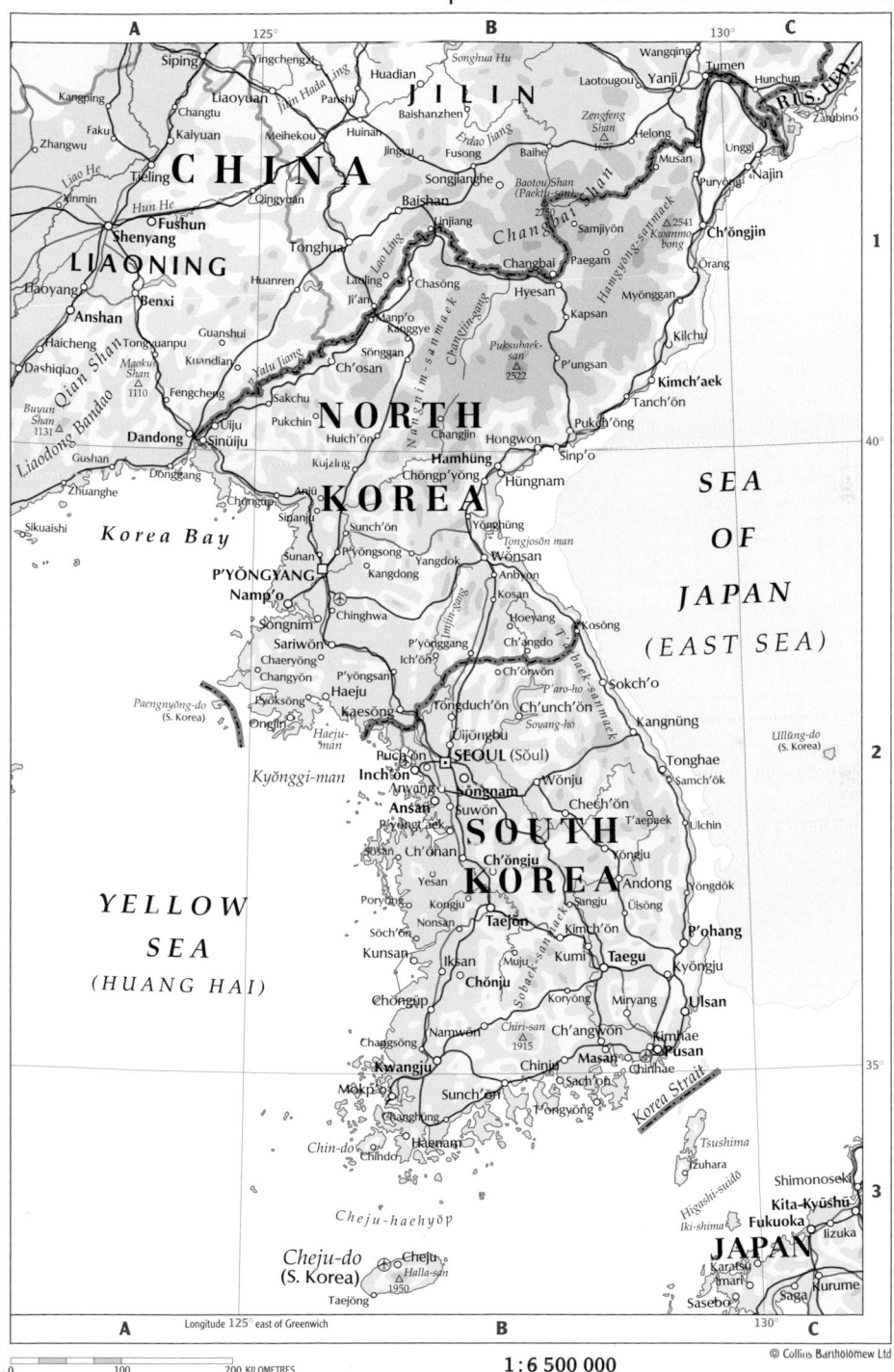

Longitude 125° east of Greenwich

1 : 6 500 000

© Collins Bartholomew Ltd

| 0 | 100 | 200 KILOMETRES |
| 0 | 50 | 100 | 150 MILES |

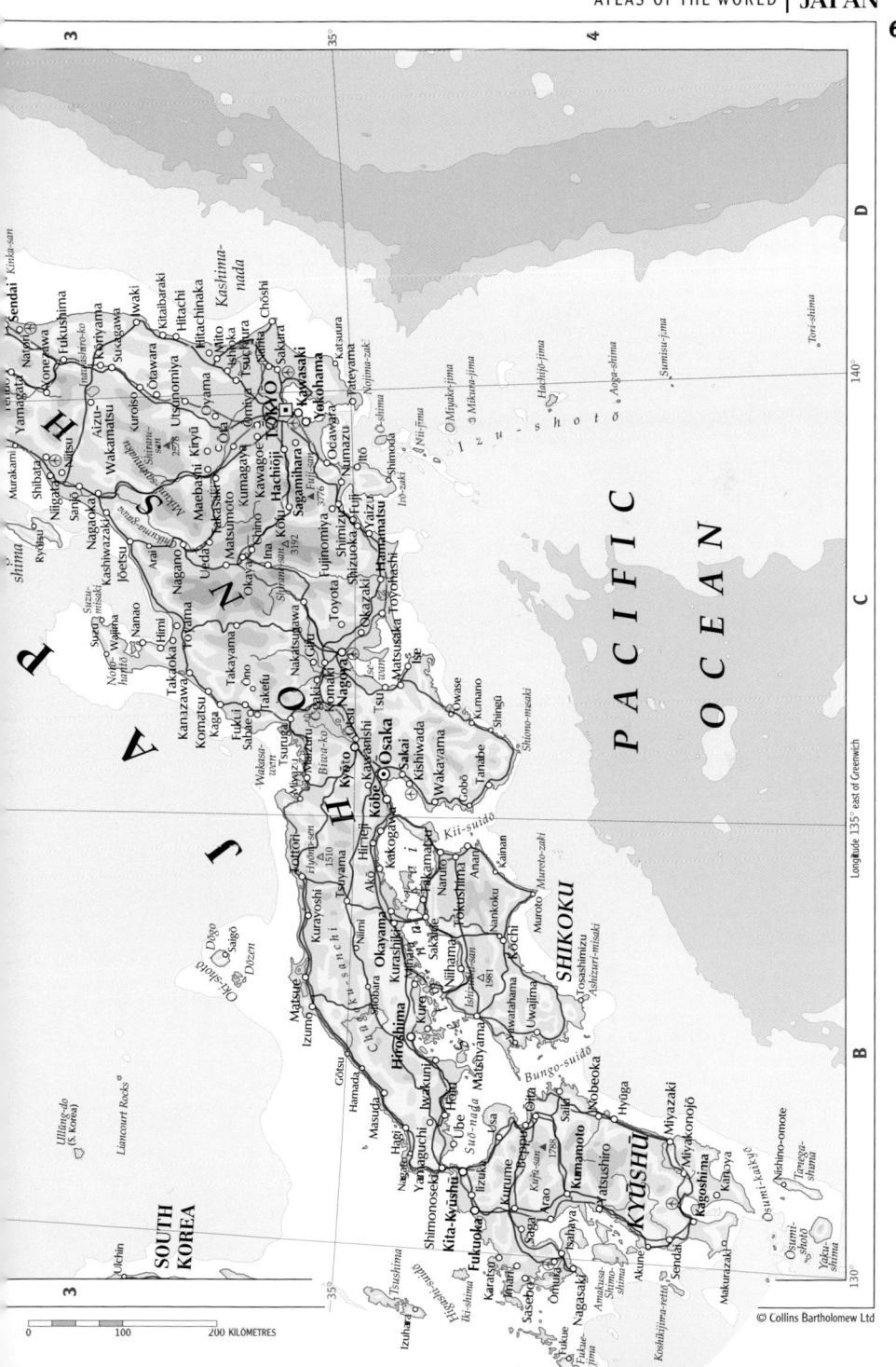

Longitude 135° east of Greenwich

SOUTH KOREA

PACIFIC OCEAN

HONSHU

SHIKOKU

KYUSHU

0   100   200 KILOMETRES

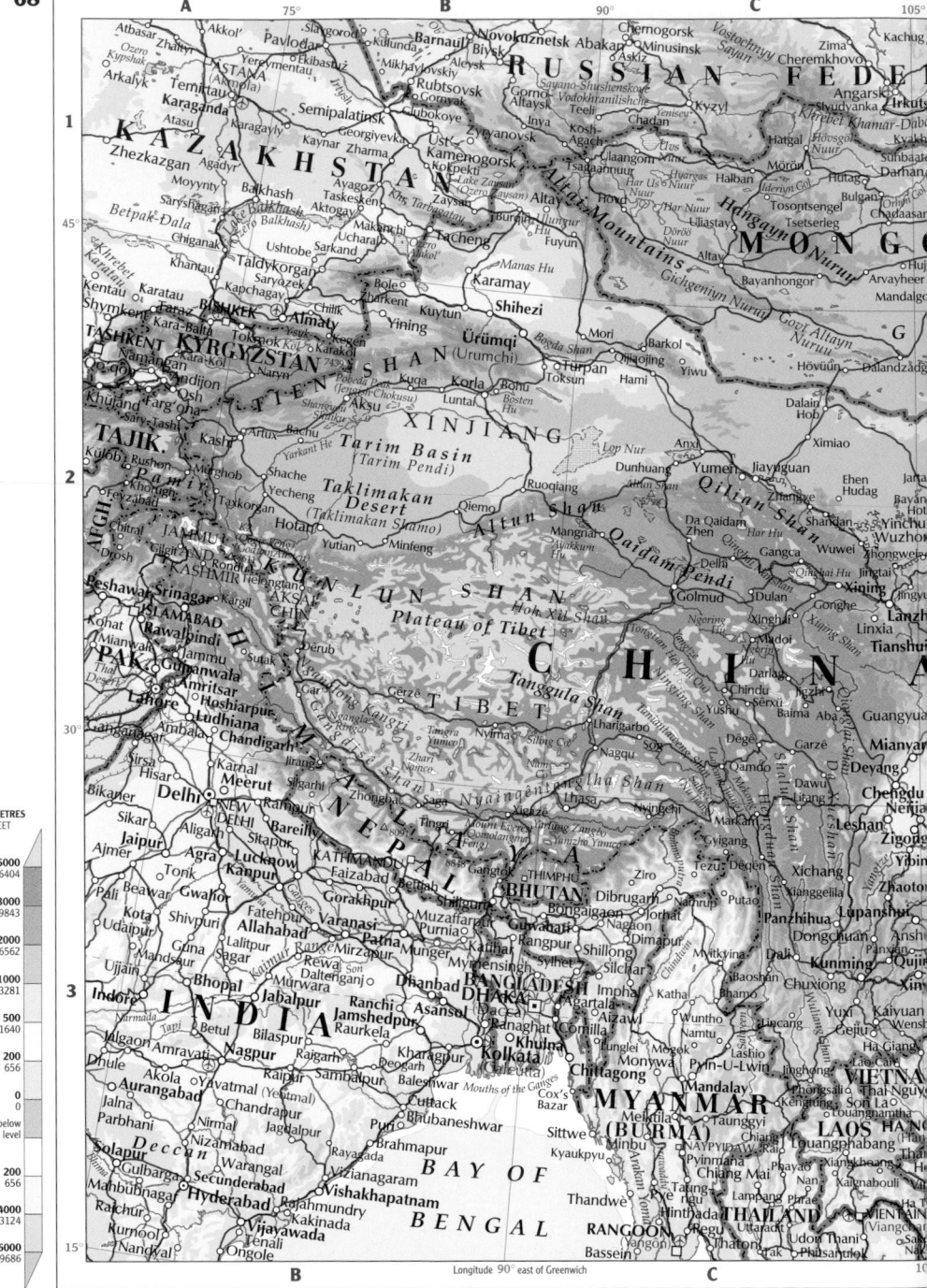

RUSSIAN FEDE

Atbasar Akkol Slavgorod Kulunda Barnaul Biysk Novokuznetsk Abakan Chernogorsk Minusinsk Vostochnyy Sayan Zima Kachug
Ozero Zhaltyr Yereymentau Kibashtak Mikhaylovskiy Askiz Sayano-Shushenskoye Vodokhranilishche Cheremkhovo Angarsk Irkuts
Arkalyk ASTANA (Akmola) Pavlodar Rubtsovsk Gorno-Altaysk Teeli Yenisey Chadan Khrebet Khamar-Daba Kyakhta

KAZAKHSTAN

MONGO

KYRGYZSTAN

TASHKENT

XINJIANG

Tarim Basin
(Tarim Pendi)

Taklimakan Desert
(Taklimakan Shamo)

KUNLUN SHAN

Plateau of Tibet

CHINA

TIBET

HIMALAYA

NEPAL

BHUTAN

BANGLADESH

INDIA

MYANMAR (BURMA)

THAILAND

VIETNA

LAOS

BAY OF BENGAL

METRES / FEET

5000 / 16404
3000 / 9843
2000 / 6562
1000 / 3281
500 / 1640
200 / 656
0 / 0
Land below sea level
200 / 656
4000 / 13124
6000 / 19686

Albers Equal Area Conic Projection

1 : 25 000 000

MILES 0   250   500

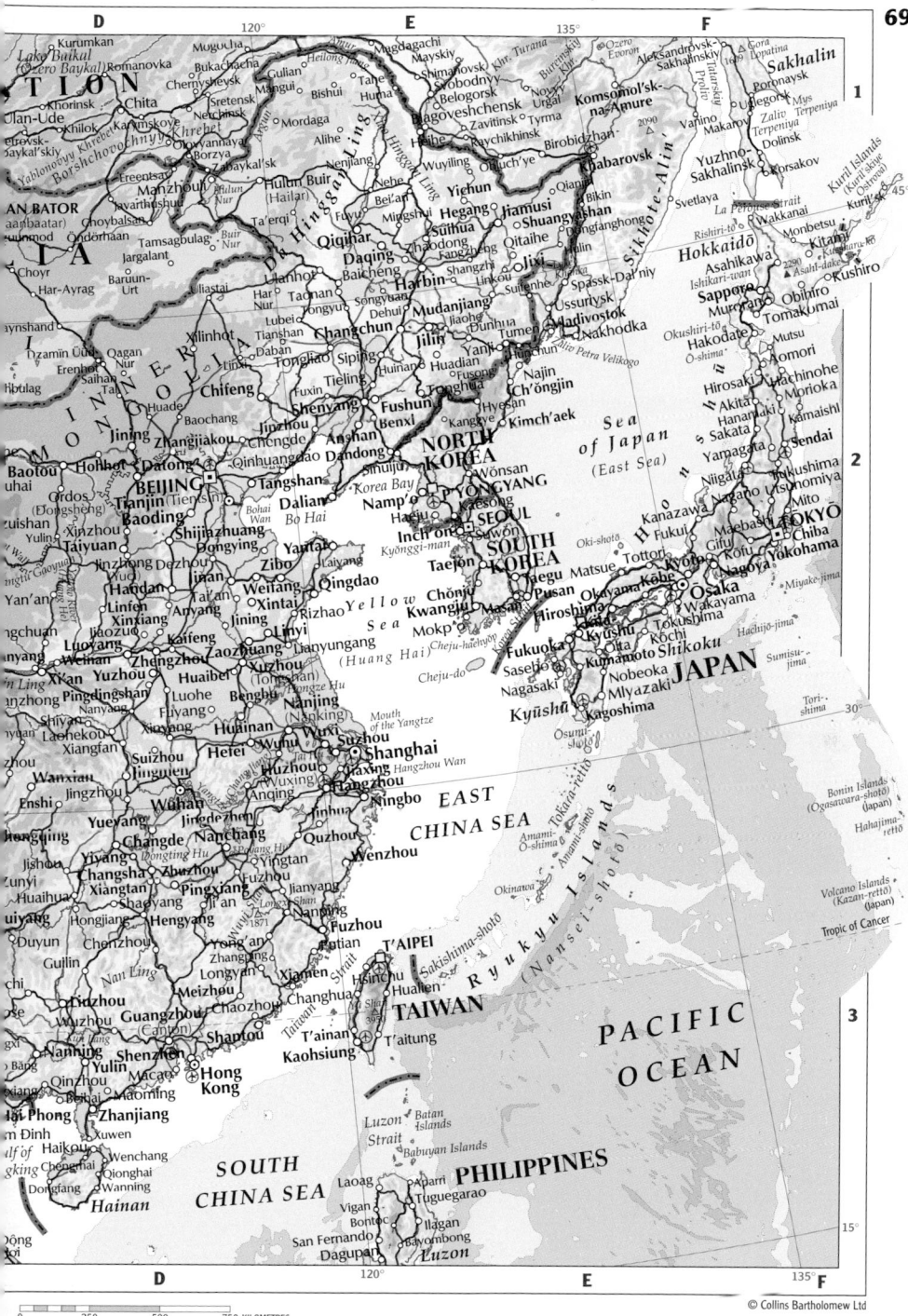

0   250   500   750 KILOMETRES

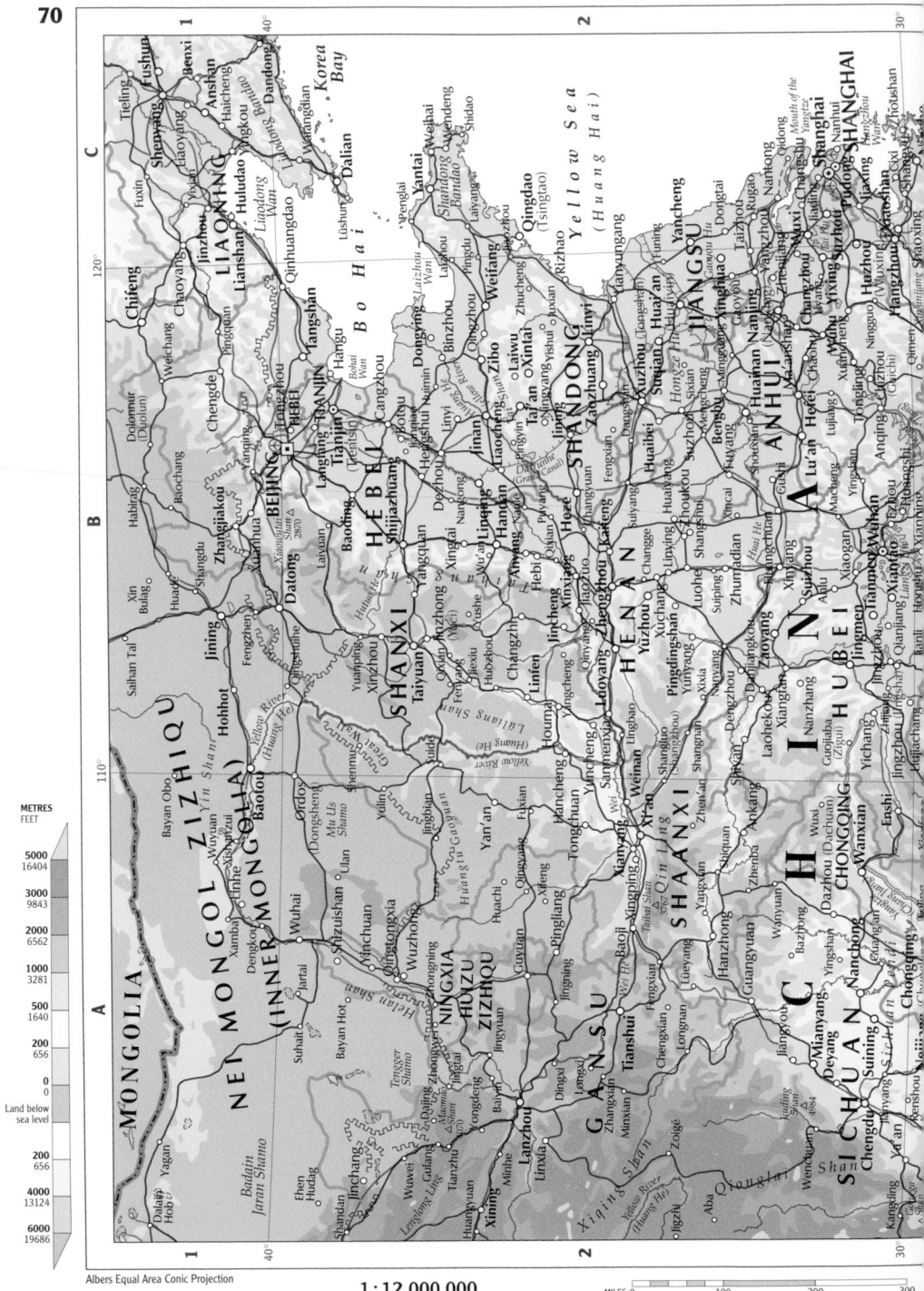

METRES
FEET

5000
16404

3000
9843

2000
6562

1000
3281

500
1640

200
656

0
0

Land below
sea level

200
656

4000
13124

6000
19686

Albers Equal Area Conic Projection

1 : 12 000 000

MILES 0   100   200   300

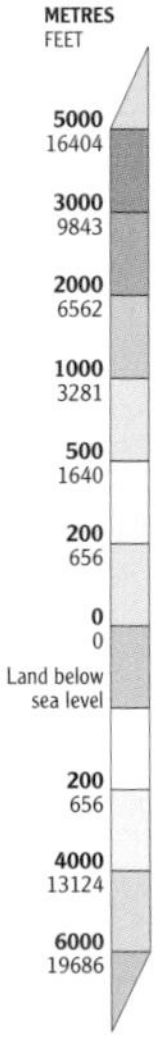

METRES
FEET

5000	16404
3000	9843
2000	6562
1000	3281
500	1640
200	656
0	0

Land below
sea level

200	656
4000	13124
6000	19686

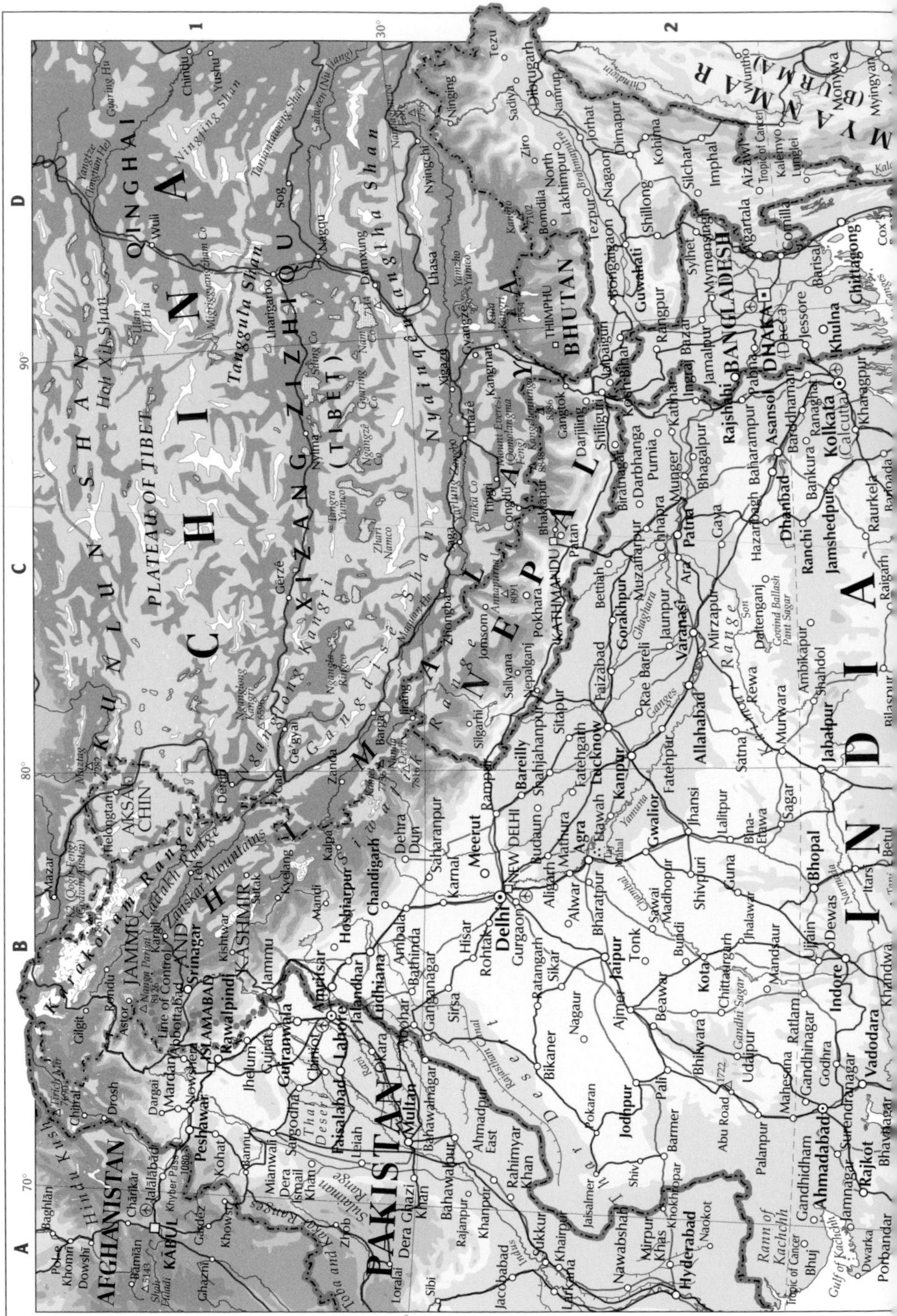

Albers Equal Area Conic Projection

1 : 15 000 000

MILES 0   100   200   300

QINGHAI

C H I N A

XIZANG ZIZHIQU (TIBET)

PLATEAU OF TIBET

K U N L U N   S H A N

H I M A L A Y A

N E P A L

BHUTAN

BANGLADESH

MYANMAR (BURMA)

I N D I A

AFGHANISTAN

PAKISTAN

JAMMU AND KASHMIR

KABUL

ISLAMABAD

THIMPHU

KATHMANDU

NEW DELHI

Delhi

DHAKA (Dacca)

KOLKATA (Calcutta)

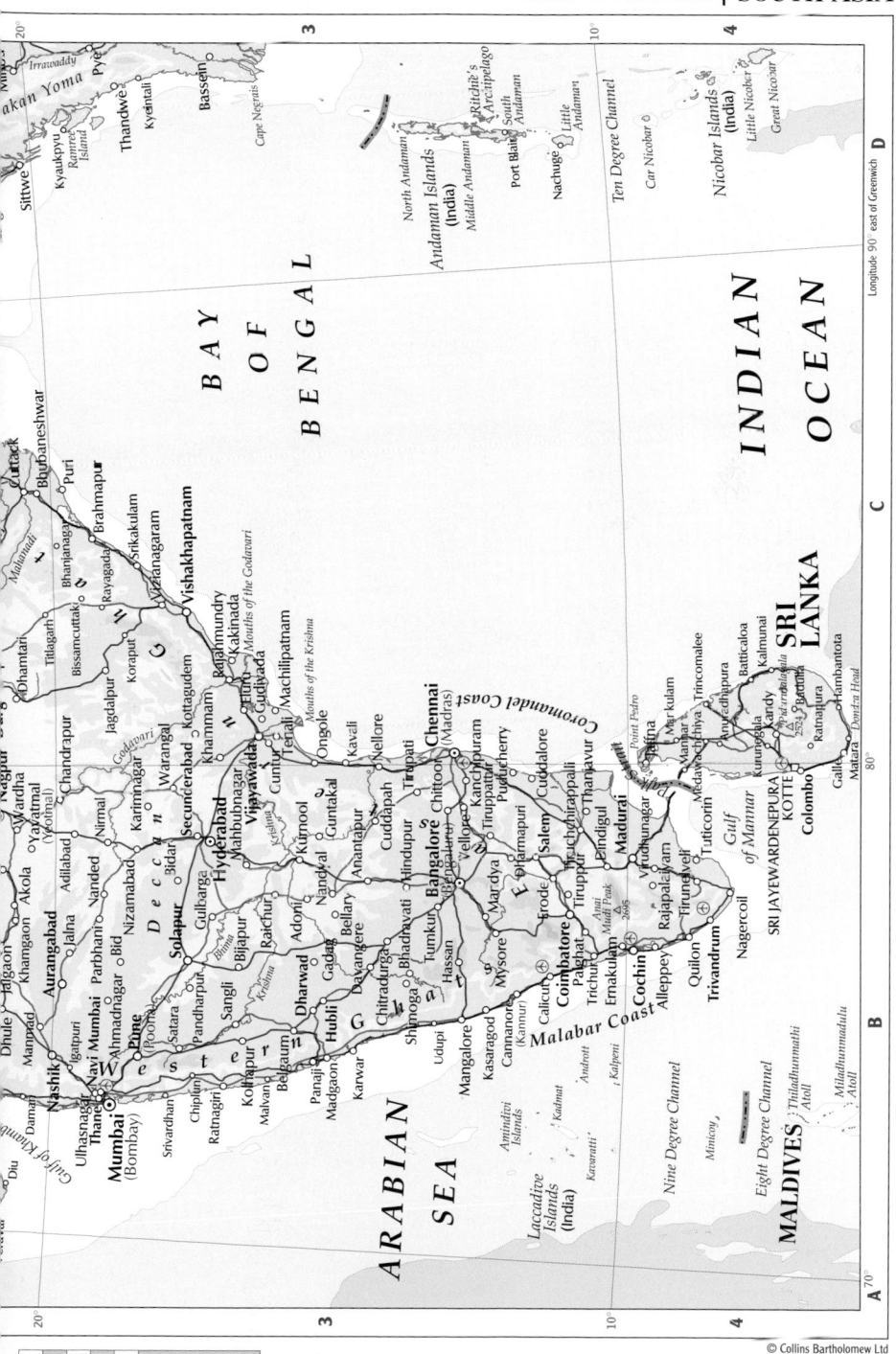

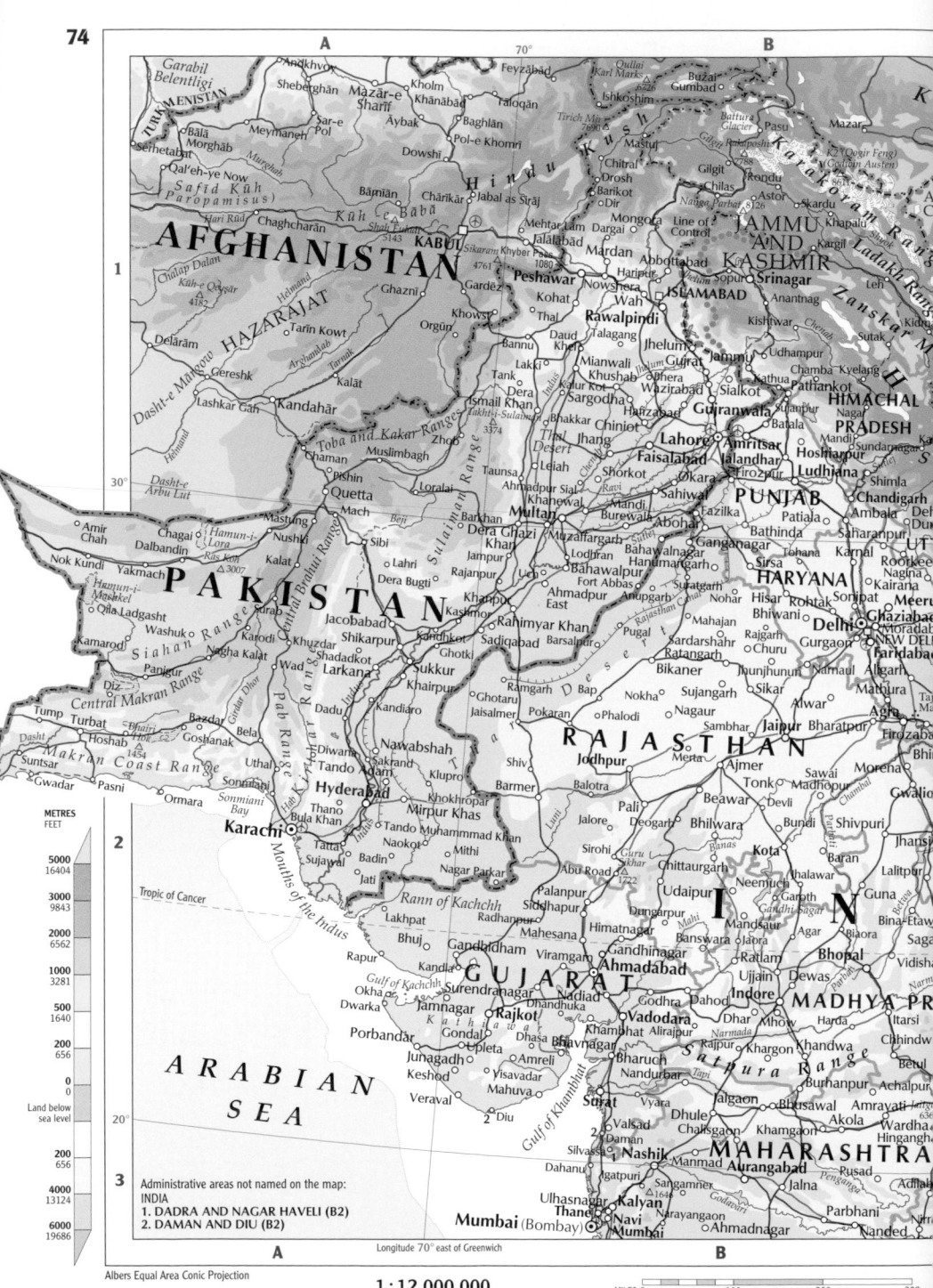

1 : 12 000 000

Albers Equal Area Conic Projection

Longitude 70° east of Greenwich

Administrative areas not named on the map:
INDIA
1. DADRA AND NAGAR HAVELI (B2)
2. DAMAN AND DIU (B2)

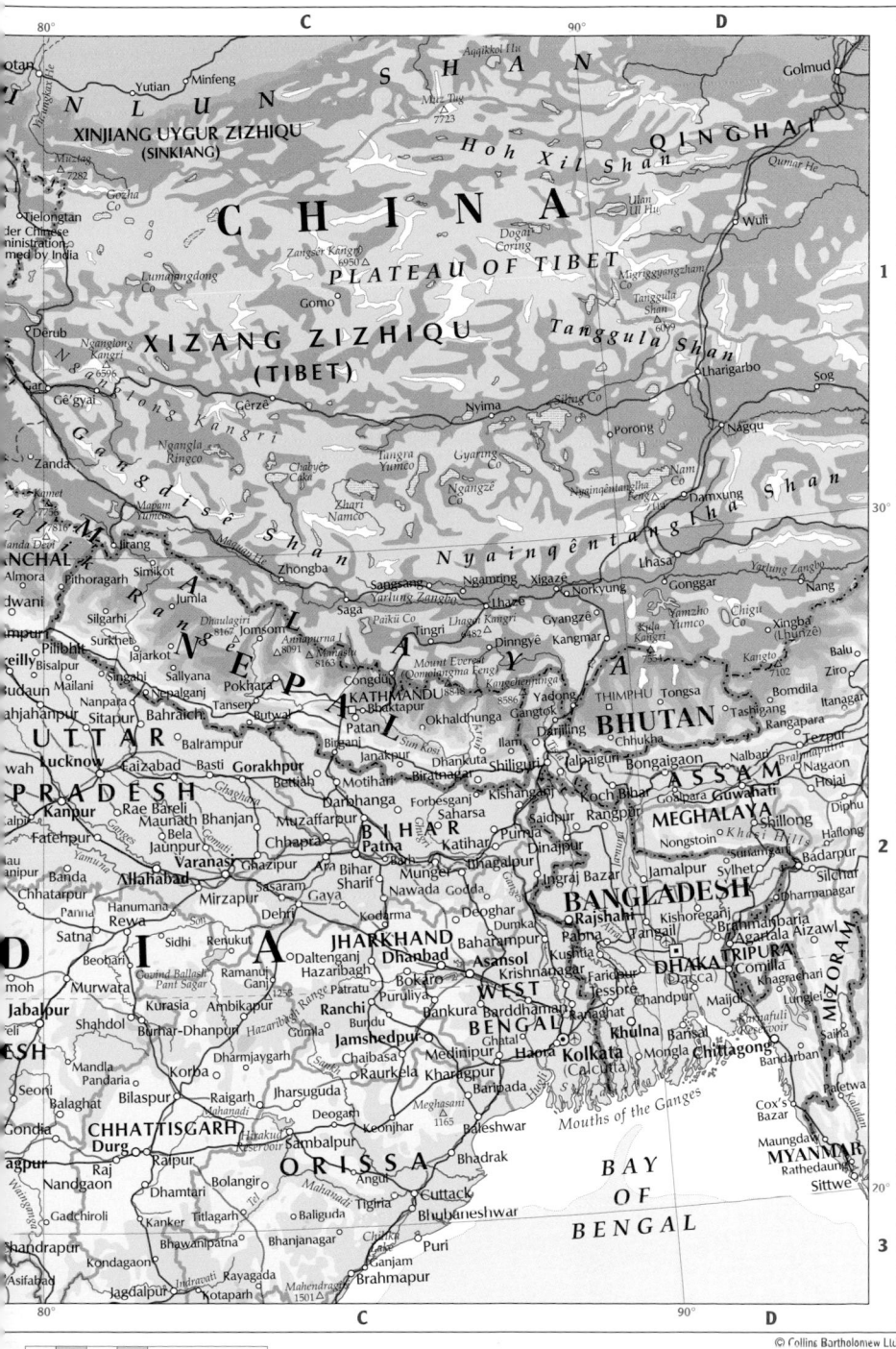

© Collins Bartholomew Ltd

0   200   400 KILOMETRES

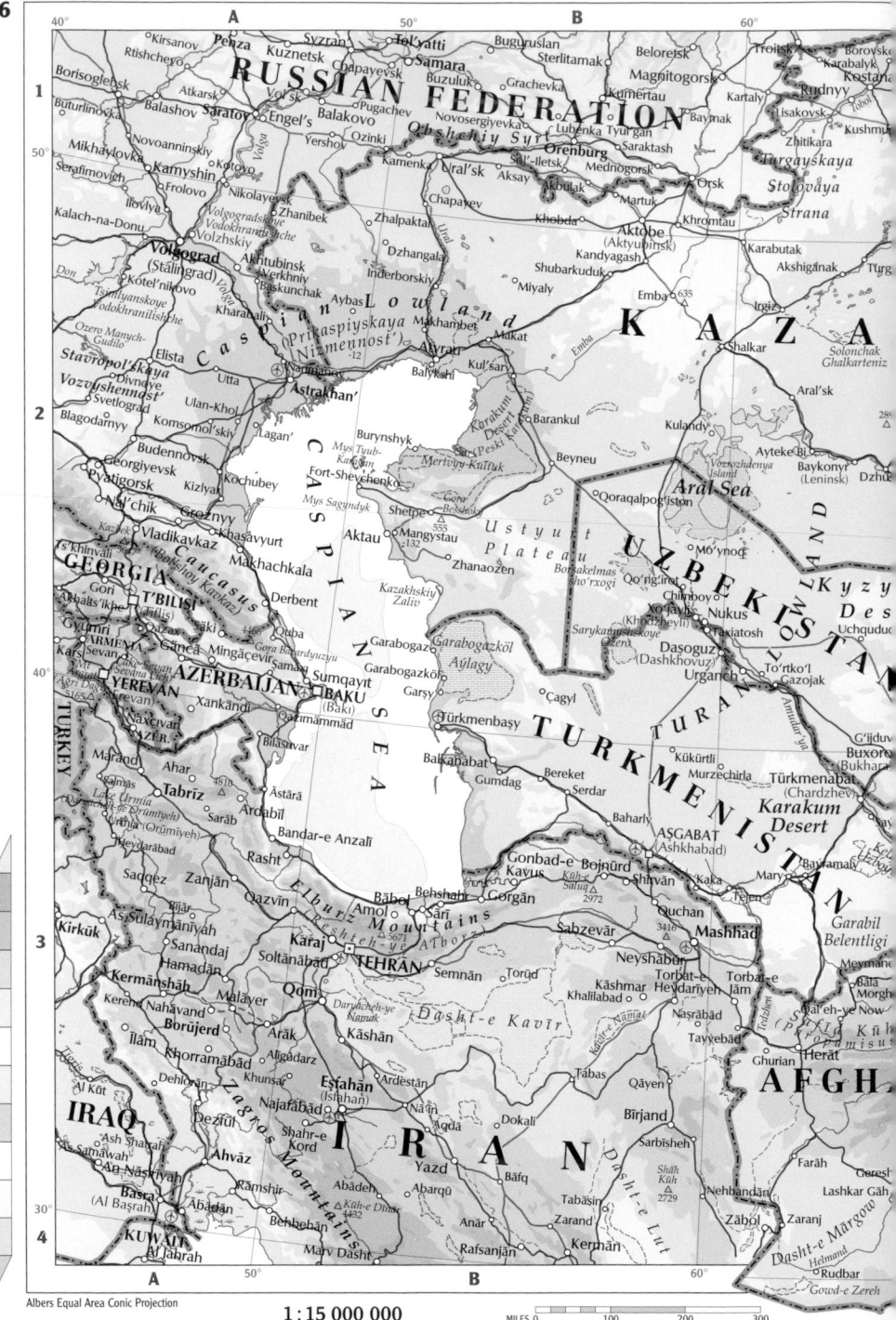

METRES
FEET

5000 16404

3000 9843

2000 6562

1000 3281

500 1640

200 656

0 0

Land below
sea level

200 656

4000 13124

6000 19686

Albers Equal Area Conic Projection

1 : 15 000 000

MILES 0   100   200   300

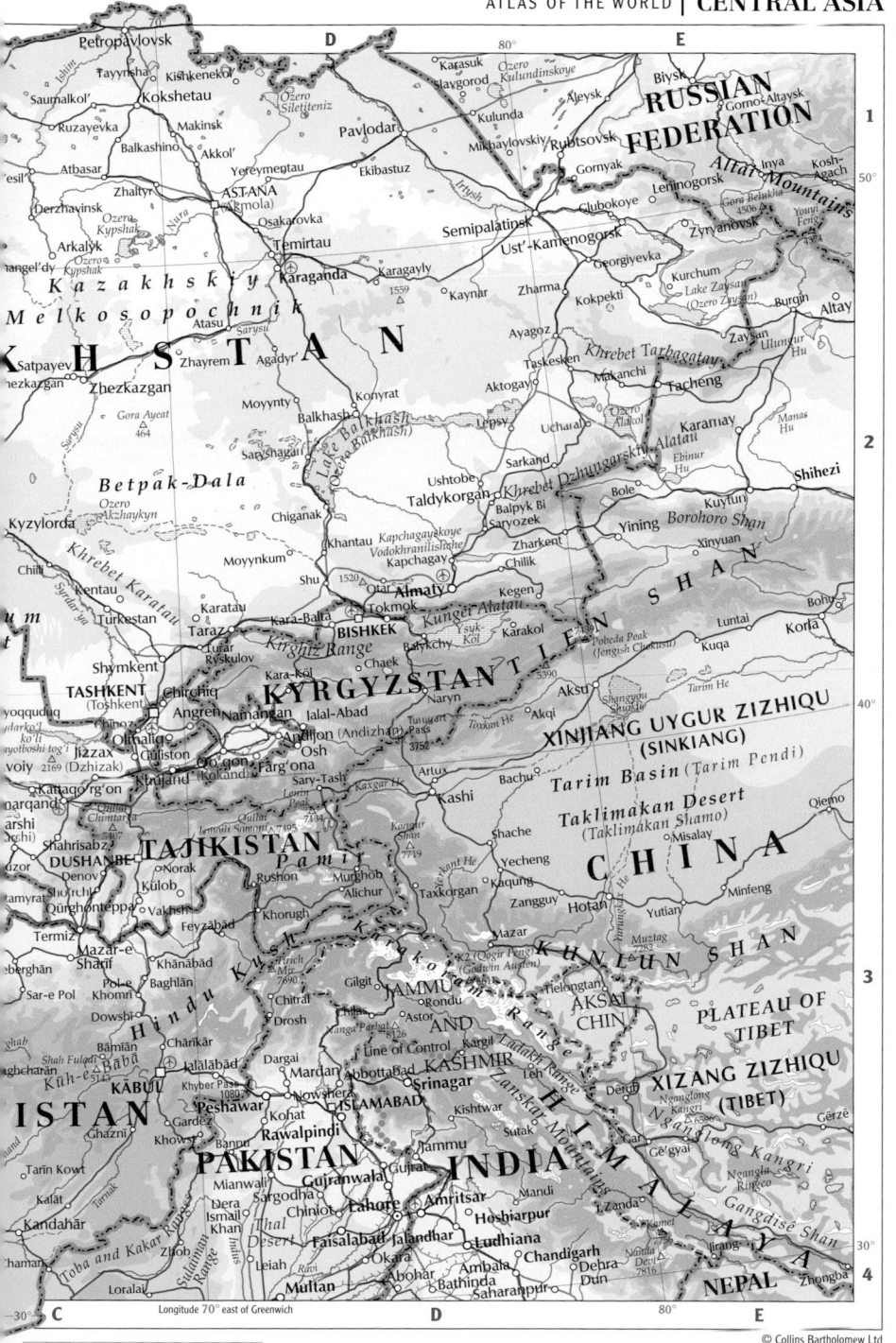

Petropavlovsk
Tayynsha
Saumalkol'
Kishkenekol'
Kokshetau
Karasuk
Karagord
Slavgorod
Kulundinskoye
Biysk
Gorno-Altaysk
RUSSIAN
FEDERATION
Ruzayevka
Makinsk
Pavlodar
Aleysk
Kulunda
Mikhaylovskiy
Rubtsovsk
Gornyak
Leninogorsk
Altai Mountains
Inya
Kosh-Agach
Atbasar
Zhaltyr
Akkol'
Yereymentau
Ekibastuz
Irtysh
Glubokoye
Zyryanovsk
Gora Belukha
4506 m
Youyi
Feng
Derzhavinsk
ASTANA
(Aqmola)
Osakarovka
Semipalatinsk
Ust'-Kamenogorsk
Georgiyevka
Kurchum
Lake Zaysan
(Ozero Zaysan)
Burqin
Altay
Arkalyk
Ozero
Kypshak
Temirtau
Karagandy
Kaynar
Zharma
Kokpekti
Zaysan
Ulungur
Hu
Satpayev
Zhaltyr
Atasu
Sarysu
Ayagoz
Taskesken
Khrebet Tarbagatay
Manqati
Tacheng
Manas
Hu
Zhezkazgan
Konyrat
Aktogay
Ozero
Alakol'
Ebinur
Hu
Shihezi
Betpak-Dala
Balkhash
Lepsy
Ucharal
Khrebet Dzhungarskiy Alatau
Karamay
Kyzylorda
Ozero
Akzhaykyn
Saryshagan
Sarkand
Bole
Borohoro Shan
Xinyuan
Moyynkum
Chiganak
Ushtobe
Balpyk Bi
Yining
Shu
Taldykorgan
Saryozek
Kuytun
Luntai
Korla
Khantau
Kapchagayskoye
Vodokhranilishche
Zharkent
T I E N
Rentau
Turkestan
Karatau
Kapchagay
Chilik
S H A N
Kara-Balta
Almaty
Kegen
Pobeda Peak
(Jengish Chokusu)
Kuqa
Shymkent
Taraz
Ryskulov
Tokmok
Kunge Alatau
Ysyk-Köl
Karakol
Aksu
Tarim He
TASHKENT
Chirchiq
BISHKEK
Chaek
Balykchy
XINJIANG UYGUR ZIZHIQU
(SINKIANG)
Olmaliq
Angren
Namangan
Jalal-Abad
Naryn
Akqi
Bachu
Tarim Basin (Tarim Pendi)
Jizzax
Andijon (Andizhan)
Osh
Kashi
Shache
Taklimakan Desert
(Taklimakan Shamo)
Qiemo
TAJIKISTAN
Pamir
CHINA
Yecheng
Misalay
DUSHANBE
Norak
Rushon
Murghob
Taxkorgan
Zangguu
Hotan
Yutian
Minfeng
KUNLUN SHAN
K2 (Qogir Feng)
(Godwin Austen)
Mazar
Muztag
PLATEAU OF
TIBET
Hindu Kush
Karakoram Range
JAMMU
AKSAI
CHIN
XIZANG ZIZHIQU
(TIBET)
KASHMIR
Srinagar
Leh
Gerze
ISLAMABAD
Jammu
H I M A L A Y A
NEPAL

© Collins Bartholomew Ltd

0   250   500 KILOMETRES

A | B

Port Said GAZA Dead Sea
Suez Canal Al 'Arish Beersheba Al Karak At Tafilah
As Sa'dah Turayf
As Suways Al Ismā'īlīyah ISRAEL JORDAN Al 'Isāwīyah 40°
Suez Petra Ma'ān An Najaf Al Ḥayy
(As Suways) Eilat Al 'Aqabah Sakākah 'Ar'ar Ash Shaṭrah
Za'farānah Sinai Nuwaybi' Al Mudawwarah Dawmat As Samāwah Amārah
Jabal Katrin Al Muzayyinah Haql Ḥālat 'Ammār al Jandal IRAQ Sūq ash
Mount Catherine Jabal Al Bi'r Rafḥā' An Nāṣirīyah Shuyūkh
Ra's Ghārib 2637 al Lawz Raf Ash An Nafūd KU
Jabal Ghārib At Ṭūr 2579 Tabūk 979 Shu'bah Basra
1751 Jamsah Jubbah Ḥafar al Bāṭin Al Başrah
Sharm ash Jabal al Dubbagh Qal'at al Mu'azzam Mawqaq Ḥā'il Raudhatain
Shaykh 2350 Taymā' Al Jahrāt Ash Şubayḥī
Al Ghurdaqah Al Muwaylih Ad Dār Jabal Ghazzālah Ṭābah Al Kahfah Al Quwārah Jabal al Kū'
(Hurghada) Dūba al Ḥamrā' az Zalma 325 Qarya
Būr Safājah Qal'at al 1288 Samīrah Az Zilfī al Ulyá Ash
Al Qusayr Azlam Al 'Ula As Sulaymī Ḥulayfah Buraydah Al Arṭāwīyah Shumlūl
Marsā 'Alam Al Wajh Khaybar Nuqrah Nafy Al Majma'ah Rum
Ḥanak Hujr Uqlat Ar Rass Asharat
Hulayfah Umm as Şuqūr 'Unayzah Ariah
Lajj Jabal Radwā Buwāṭah Al Ḥanākīyah SAUDI
Jabal Ḥamāṭah Yanbu' al Bahr 1814 Sūq As Ad Dir'īyah Al Jubaylah
1977 Suwayq Medina Shubaykīyah Ad RIYADH
Tropic of Cancer Baranis (Al Madīnah) Jabal Shi'r Dawādimī (Ar Riyāḍ)
Rayyis Badr Hunayn Al Qā'īyah 'Afīf Al Quwayfiyah As Salamīyah
Bi'r Shalatayn Maḥd adh Ad Dilam
Mastūrah Dhahab Halabān Ar Ruwaydah Ḥillah
Umm Ad Dafīnah ARABIA
Wadi Rābigh Birak Zalim Khashm Māwan
al 'Allāqi Jabal Umm Ḥāḍhah 1025 Layla
HALAIB Mukhar Jabal ARABIA
TRIANGLE Tuwwal Kursh Al Bādi'
UNDER SUDANESE Khulays Jabal
ADMINISTRATION Madrakah Hasan
Jebel Asoteriba Halaib As Sūq
2215 Marsa Al Ḥawīyah PENINSUL
Delwein Jeddah As Ar Rawdah
Salāla (Jiddah) Mecca Aṭ Ṭā'if 'Amā'ir
Dungunab Muhammad (Makkah) Turabah As Sulayyil
Qol Mastābah 'Aqīq Jabal Kumdah
Nubian Desert Al Līth Al Mindak Qal'at Banī Ma'ārid
20° Jebel Al Junaynah Bishah Tathlīth 'Urūq al Awārik
Oda Al 'Alyayri RUB
2259 Dawqah Khamāsīn (EM
SUDAN Port Sudan Qam Baljurshī
Ḥadil An Nimāṣ Ḥamdah
Wadi 'Amur Al Qunfidhah Dirs
Karnob Sanha Abhā Khamis Mushayt
Musmar Sinkat Suakin Al Birk Ash Shuqayq Ad Darb Zahrān Najrān Ash
Erheib Tokar 2780 Harajā Sharawrah
Haiya Karora Ramlat Dahm
Derudeb Algena Jīzān Abū 'Arīsh Husn Āl
Hagar Nish Nakfa Midi Al Hazm al Jawf
Aşmeret Hills Plateau Mount Shara Jaza'ir Şabyā' Şa'dah
2603 Farasān Khamir Raydah
ERITREA Afabet Hajjah Amrān Ma'rib
Aroma Akordat Keren Dahlak Aş Şaḥīl 3760 YEME
Kassala Teseney Massawa Archipelago Az Zaydīyah Al Maḥwīt ŞAN'Ā'
New Halfa Barentu ASMARA Dekemhare Kamarān Bājil Ma'bar Bayḥan al Qişāb
Khashm el Girba Mendefera Adi Mersa Fatma Hodeidah Manākhah Dhamār Rada'
Showak Om Keyih (Al Ḥudaydah) Bayt al Faqīh Ibb Qaṭabah Al Bayḍā' Ḥabb
Gedaref Hajer Inda Silase Adigrat Ed Az Zuqur Zabīd Yarīm Al Bayḍā' Jabal Thamar
Aksum Denakil Hays Ta'izz 2512 Musayna' Zinjibār
Gallabat Adi Ark'ay ETHIOPIA Mocha Qaḥtabah Lawdar
Ras Dejen 4533 Mek'ele Al Mukhā' Dhubāb Lahij Aden
2131 Assab Al Turbah ('Adan)
Longitude 40° east of Greenwich Bab al Ash Shaykh 'Uthman
Mandab

METRES FEET
5000 16404
3000 9843
2000 6562
1000 3281
500 1640
200 656
0 0
Land below sea level
200 656
4000 13124
6000 19686

Albers Equal Area Conic Projection

1 : 12 000 000

© Collins Bartholomew Ltd

MILES 0   100   200   300   0   200   400 KILOMETRES

A   30°   B

Târgu Mureş   Miercurea-   Bacău   **CHIŞINĂU**   Tiraspol   Berezivka   Mykolayiv   Tokmak   **Mariupol'**   Taganrog   Rost
Sebeş   Şighişoara   Ciuc   Vaslui   Tighina   Nova   Kakhovka   Berdyans'k   na-Do
Deva   Sibiu   Sfântu   **MOLDOVA**   Comrat   Artsyz   Kherson   Melitopol'   Staromins'kaya
Lugoj   Caransebeş   Gheorghe   Focşani   Bilhorod-   **Odesa**   Armyans'k   **UKRAINE**   Novooleksiyivka   Primors'k   Atkarsk
Reşiţa   Făgăraş   Tecuci   Dnistrov's'kyy   Karkinits'ka Zatoka   Perekops'k   Dzhankoy   Pavlovsk
Drobeta-   **ROMANIA**   Galaţi   Brăila   Izmayil   Chornomors'ke   *Crimea*   Nyzhn'ohirs'kyy   Timashevsk
Turnu Severin   Piteşti   Buzău   Bucureşti   Dunărea   Yevpatoriya   Krasno
Craiova   Ploieşti   **BUCHAREST**   Simferopol'   Feodosiya   Krymsk
Slatina   Rosiori   Călăraşi   Constanţa   Sevastopol'   Sudak   Novorossiysk
Calafat   Caracal   Ruse   Dobrich   Mangalia   Khadyzhensk
SERBIA   Montana   Pleven   Razgrad   Kavarna   Tuapse
Vratsa   Lovech   Shumen   Varna   **B L A C K   S E A**
SOFIA   **BULGARIA**   Sliven   Burgas
Pernik   Kazanlŭk   Stara Zagora
Kyustendil   Plovdiv   Dimitrovgrad
Blagoevgrad   Haskovo   Kŭrdzhali   Kirklareli   Cide   İnebolu   İnce Burun
Smolyan   Babaeski   Zonguldak   Bartın   Sinop
Sandanski   **Edirne**   Saray   Ereğli   **Karabük**   Boyabat   Bafra   **Samsun**
Serres   Drama   Komotini   Çorlu   **İstanbul**   Kadıköy   Düzce   Gerede   Vezirköprü   Merzifon   Terme   Ordu   Trabz
Kavala   Xanthi   Tekirdağ   Silivri   Körfez   Bolu   Tosya   Amasya   Giresun
Thessaloniki   *Thasos*   Gallipoli   Sea of Marmara   **Bursa**   Mudurnu   Çankırı   Osmancık   Niksar   Şebinkarahisar
Polygyros   Gökçeada   Çanakkale   Gemlik   Bilecik   Beypazarı   Kalecik   **Çorum**   Sungurlu   Sivas   Zara   Erzi
Volos   *Limnos*   Ezine   Can   İnegöl   **ANKARA**   Kırıkkale   Yozgat   Yıldızeli   Divriği
GREECE   *Lesbos*   Edremit   Susurluk   Tavşanlı   Eskişehir   Akdağmadeni   Kangal   Erz
Evvoia   Mytilini   Ayvalık   Balıkesir   Kütahya   Sivrihisar   Polatlı   Kırşehir   Boğazlıyan
Chalkida   *Chios*   Bergama   Soma   Simav   Emirdağ   **T U R K E Y**   Kaman   Yahyalı
ATHENS   Bornova   Demirci   Banaz   Afyon   Yunak   Kayseri   *Erciyes*   Pınarbaşı   **Elazığ**
Piraeus   Aigina   Chios   Manisa   Salihli   Uşak   Sandıklı   Akşehir   Nevşehir   Elbistan
Ermoupoli   *Andros*   **İzmir**   Alaşehir   Civril   Dinar   Lake Tuz   Aksaray   *Hasan Dağı*   Niğde   **Malatya**
Tinos   *Samos*   Küçükmenderes   Isparta   Burdur   *(Tuz Gölü)*   Bor   Karapınar   Adıyaman   Siver
Paros   Kuşadası   **Aydın**   Denizli   Eğirdir Gölü   **Konya**   Kahramanmaraş
Naxos   Milos   *Dodecanese*   Yatağan   Bucak   Beyşehir   Ereğli   **Gaziantep**   Şanlı
Santorini   *(Thira)*   Muğla   *(Dodekanisos)*   Beyşehir Gölü   Korkuteli   Karaman   **Adana**   Birecik   Akça
Kritiko Pelagos   Marmaris   Dalaman   Serik   Manavgat   Ermenek   Tarsus   Osmaniye   Kilis
Chania   Irakleio   Agios   Fethiye   Elmalı   **Antalya**   *Taurus Mountains*   Erdemli   Mersin   **İskenderun (Alexandretta)**
Rethymno   Nikolaos   Kaş   Alanya   *(Toros Dağları)*   *(İçel)*   **Aleppo**
CRETE   *(KRITI)*   Ierapetra   *Karpathos*   *Meğisti*   *Antalya*   Anamur   Silifke   Antakya   İdlib   **Ar Raqqah**
(Scarpanto)   *Körfezi*   Cape Apostolos   Andreas   Kyrenia   *(Antioch)*   Ma'arrat an   Nu'mān
NICOSIA   Aigialousa   **Latakia**   **Hamāh**
(Lefkosia)   *(Keryneia)*   Famagusta   Tartūs   Bāniyās   **S Y R I**
Cape Arnauti   Polis   Evrychou   **Homs**
Paphos   Limassol   Larnaca   Tripoli   Tadmur
CYPRUS   *(Lemesos)*   *(Trâblous)*   Al Qaryatayn
LEBANON   An Nabk
BEIRUT   Sab' Ābār
M E D I T E R R A N E A N   S E A   *(Beyrouth)*   **DAMASCUS**   *(Dimashq)*
Sidon   Az Zabadānī
Tyre   Sea of Galilee   *(Yam Kinneret)*   As Suwaydā'
Al Qunaytirah   *Syrian Dese*
Haifa   *(Bādiyat ash Sh*
Nazareth   *(Hefa)*   Irbid   Al Mafraq
(Nazerat)   Jenin   **ISRAEL**   Az Zarqā'
Al Bardi   **Alexandria**   Tel Aviv-Yafo   **WEST**   **AMMAN**   Turayf
Umm   Marsā   *(Al Iskandariya)*   Kafr ash   Rehovot   **JERUSALEM**   **BANK**   At Tafilah
Sa'ad   Matrūh   Al 'Āmiriya   Shaykh   Baltīm   Dumyāt   **GAZA**   Beersheba   *Dead Sea*
LIBYA   *Libyan Plateau*   Al Hammām   Damanhūr   Mansūrah   Port Said   Al 'Arīsh   Al Karak
(Ad Diffah)   Shubrā al Khaymah   Banhā   Tanta   Būr Sa'īd   Al Ismā'īliyah   **JORDAN**
Qattara   **Giza**   Az Zaqāzīq   Suez   Petra   Ma'ān   Wādī al Sirhān
Qārah   *Depression*   *(Al Jīzah)*   *(As Suways)*   Al Īsāwīyah
Wāhāt Sīwah   **CAIRO**   Pyramids of Giza   Al
(Siwa Oasis)   *(Al Qāhirah)*   Memphis   *Sinai*   Dawmat al Jan
Siwah   Al Fayyūm   Za'farānah   Ellat   Mudawwarah   **SAUDI**
E G Y P T   Banī Suwayf   Nuwaybi' al   Hālat 'Ammār
Al Bawītī   *(Beni Suef)*   Muzayyinah   Haql   *Mount Katrīna*   Al Bi'r
Maghāghah   *Mount Catherine*   Aqabah   Al
Banī Mazār   *2637*

A   Longitude 30° east of Greenwich   B

METRES / FEET

METRES	FEET
5000	16404
3000	9843
2000	6562
1000	3281
500	1640
200	656
0	0

Land below sea level

200	656
4000	13124
6000	19686

MILES 0   100   200   300

ocherkassk
ernograd
Sal'sk

Ozero
Manych-Gudilo Elista   Utta
horetsk Ipatovo   Divnoye
Kropotkin Stavropol'skaya   Komsomol'skiy Ulan-
Labinsk Stavropol'   Budennovsk   Khol   Lagan'
Psebay Nevinnomyssk   Kochubey
kop Cherkessk Georgiyevsk
Karachayevsk Pyatigorsk   Kizlyar
Kislovodsk Prokhladnyy
Sokhumi Nal'chik Groznyy   Khasavyurt
Tqvarch'eli Vladikavkaz   Makhachkala
Zugdidi Buynaksk
K'ut'aisi   Izberbash
P'ot'i Samtredia Gori T'elavi   Derbent
Bat'umi Akhalts'ikhe Zaqatala
GEORGIA T'BILISI
Rust'avi
Şäki
Ganca Mingäçevir   Sumqayıt
Yusufeli Sevan   Göyçay Şamaxı
Oltu Kars   **AZERBAIJAN**   BAKU
ARMENIA YEREVAN
Horasan Ağdam
Erzurum   Ağrı   Qazımämmäd
AZER.   Salyan
Hınıs Doğubeyazıt Sisian Biläsuvar
Malazgirt Mäku Naxçıvan Çäläabad
Ahlat   Länkäran
Tatvan Khoy Marand Ähar Ästära
Bitlis Van   Sarāb Ardabīl
arbakır Van Salmas Tabrīz
Siirt Urmia
Batman Başkale Mīāneh
Mardin Hakkāri Orūmīyeh Fowman Rasht
Al Qāmishlī Zākho Oshnovīyeh Heydarābād Tonkābon
Dahūk Mīāndowāb Zanjān Qazvīn
Mahābād Saqqez
Mosul Arbīl Bījār Abhar   Karaj TEHRĀN
As Sulaymānīyah   Sanandaj Solṭānābād
Kirkūk Halabja Qorveh Hamadān
Tuz Khurmātū Kangāvar Malāyer
Bayjī Rāvānsar Araak Qom
Sāmarrā' Kerend Nahāvand
Al Muqdādīyah Eslāmābād-e Borūjerd Dow Rūd
Hit Gharb Ilām Golpāyegān
Ba'qūbah Khorramābād Aligūdarz Najafābād
BAGHDĀD Dehlorān Dārān
Al Kāzimīyah
Karbalā' Hillah Al Kūt Dezfūl Shahr-e Kord
IRAQ Shūshtar
An Najaf Al Ḥayy Al ʿAmārah Masjed Soleymān
Ad Dīwānīyah Shahreżā
As Samāwah Sūq ash Shuyūkh Ahvāz Ramhormoz
An Nāṣirīyah Ramshahr
Ash Shabakah Khorramshahr Omīdīyeh Yāsūj
RABIA Basra Behbehān
(Al Baṣrah) Bandar-e Kāzerūn
Rafḥā' Abādān Emām Khomeynī Shīrāz
Hawalli Genāveh Borāzjān
KUWAIT Al Fāw Būshehr Farrāshband
Al Jahrā' KUWAIT Ahram
(Al Kuwayt) Dowlatābād
Aş Şubayḥīyah Al Aḥmadī
Ash Shu'bah Mīnāʼ Saʿūd

RUSSIAN
FEDERATION

Astrakhan

Volga

Balykshi

Sor Donyztau

KAZAKHSTAN

Barankul
Beyneu

UZBEKISTAN

Borsakelmas sho'rxoği

Ustyurt Plateau
Ustyurt Karabaur

TURKMENISTAN

Türkmenbaşy Jebel Balkanabat
Bereket
Hazar Gumdag Serdar
Magtymguly
Gorgān Gonbad-e Kavus
Gomīshān
Nowshahr Bābol Behshahr Māmey
Amol Sārī Emāmrūd
Damghan Torūd
Semnān Torūd

IRAN

Dasht-e Kavīr

Nāʼīn Dokali
Ardestān Meybod
Yazd Bāfq Anār
Abādeh Abarqū
Safāshahr Shahr-e Bābak
Arsenjān Abādeh Tashk
Neyrīz Beshneh
Fasā Dārāb Rostāq
Jahrom Jūyom Häjjīābād

C   50°   **D**   1

40°

2

30°

C   50°   **D**   3

0   200   400 KILOMETRES

© Collins Bartholomew Ltd

A 40° 30° B 20° C 10° D 0° E 10° F 20°

Arctic Circle

Greenland
(Denmark)

Bjørnøya
(Nor.)

Denmark Strait

Jan Mayen
(Nor.)

60°

ICELAND
Reykjavík

NORWEGIAN
SEA

Trondheim

From

N
O
R
W
A
Y

S
W
E
D
E
N

Gulf of Bot

3

ATLANTIC
OCEAN

Faroe
Islands
(Den.)
Tórshavn

Bergen

Oslo

Stockh

Shetland
Islands

Gotland

Stockh

50°

Orkney
Islands

NORTH
SEA

Gothenburg

Gotland

Baltic Sea

RUS. 1

SCOTLAND

Glasgow

Edinburgh

DENMARK

Copenhagen

Malmö

N.
Ireland

IRELAND

Dublin

UNITED
KINGDOM

Hamburg

POLAN

Manchester

WALES

Cardiff

ENGLAND

Birmingham

London

NETHERLANDS
Amsterdam
The Hague

Hannover

Berlin

Poznan

Warsaw

Łódź

Kato

4

LIE. LIECHTENSTEIN
MACE. MACEDONIA
MONT. MONTENEGRO

Channel Is.
(U.K.)

English Channel

Brussels

BELGIUM

Essen

Rhine

GERMANY

Frankfurt

Prague

CZECH
REPUBLIC

Seine

Luxembourg LUXEMBOURG

Paris

Munich

Vienna

SLOVAK

Bratislava

Buda

Bay of
Biscay

Loire

FRANCE

Bern

LIE.

SWITZERLAND

Mont Blanc

AUSTRIA

SLOVENIA

Ljubljana

HUNGARY

Zagreb

CROATIA

Belgra

Cape Finisterre

Bordeaux

Lyon

Rhône

Milan

Turin

SAN
MARINO

BOSNIA-
HERZ.

Sarajevo

SER

40°

Oporto

Bilbao

Pyrenees

Andorra
la Vella ANDORRA

Marseille

MONACO

Corsica

VATICAN
CITY

I
T
A
L
Y

Adriatic Sea

MONT.

Podgorica

Skop

Lisbon

PORTUGAL

Madrid

SPAIN

Barcelona

Rome

Tirana

ALBANIA

Cabo de
São Vicente

Valencia

Balearic Islands

Sardinia

Naples

5

Seville

Gibraltar
(U.K.)

MEDITERRANEAN
SEA

Palermo

Sicily

Ionian
Sea

MOROCCO

ALGERIA

TUNISIA

MALTA
Valletta

10°

D

Greenwich 0° meridian

E

10°

F

20°

Chamberlin Trimetric Projection

1 : 25 000 000

MILES 0   250   500

0   250   500   750 KILOMETRES

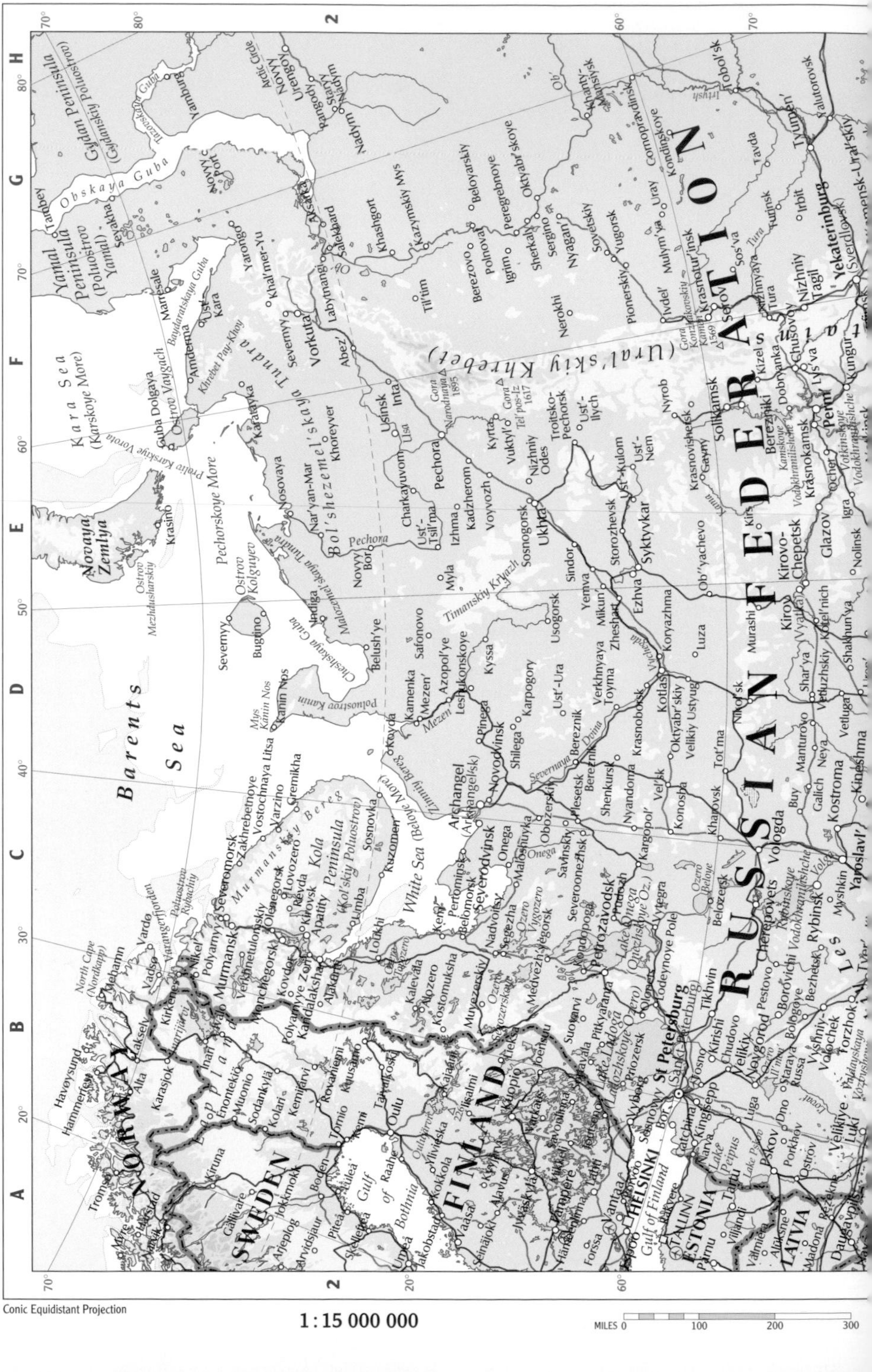

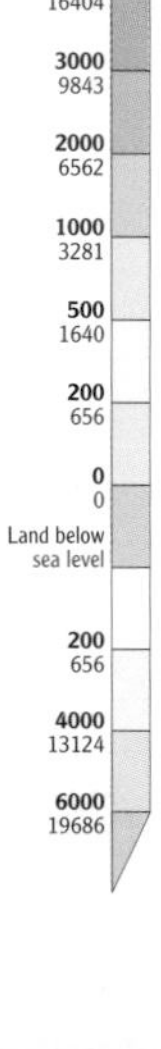

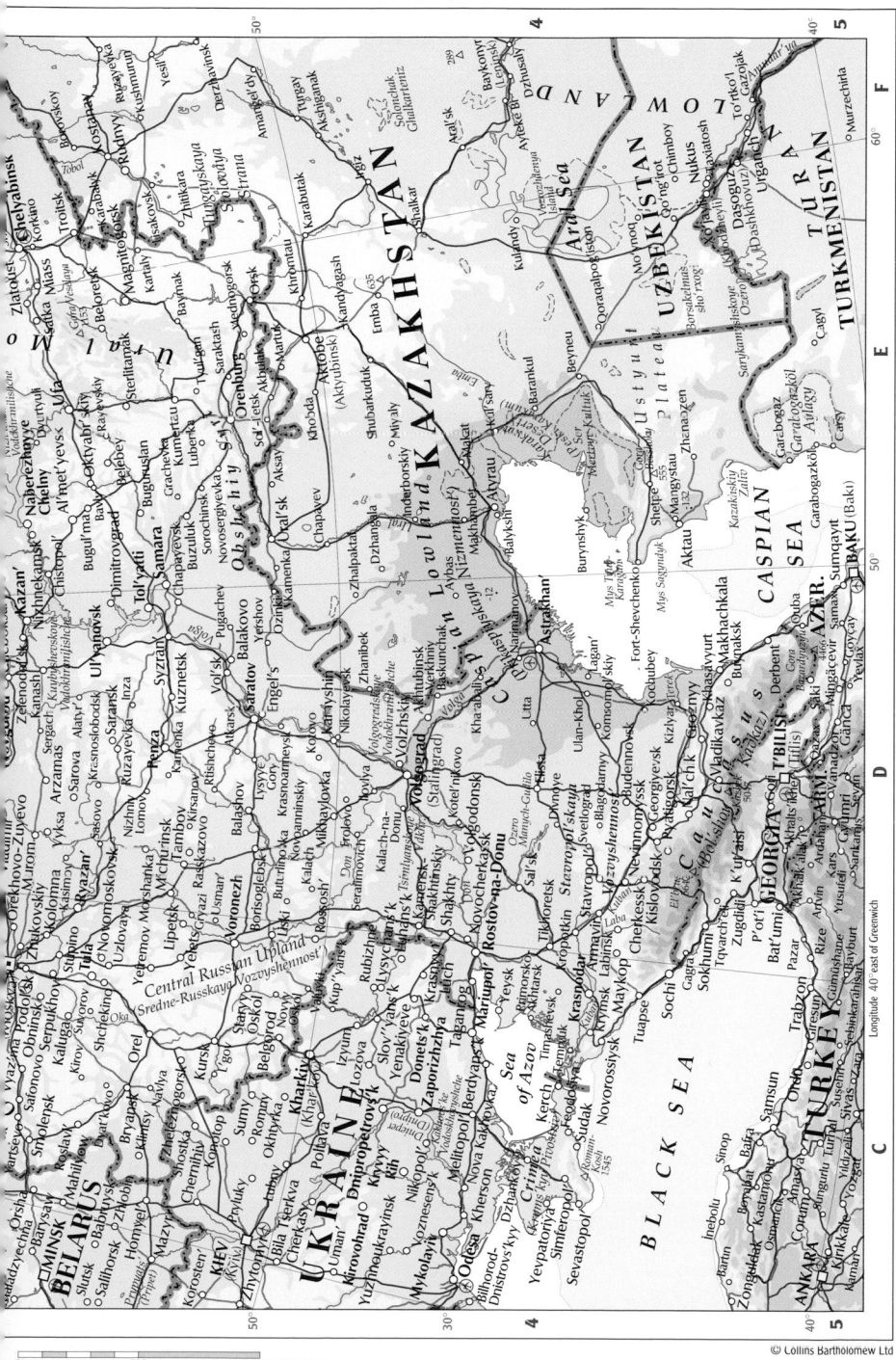

© Collins Bartholomew Ltd

0   250   500 KILOMETRES

FINLAND

SWEDEN

Uppsala
Norrtalje
Mariehamn

Åland
Islands

Kökar

Korpo

Mäntsälä
Järvenpää
Tuusula Porvoo
Kirkkonummi Espoo
HELSINKI
(Helsingfors)

Kouvola
Anjalankoski
Hamina
Loviisa

Kotka

Vyborg

Vyborgskiy Zaliv

Ostrov
Moshchnyy

Zelenogorsk

STOCKHOLM

Tumba
Västerhaninge

Nynäshamn

Hanko

Ekenäs

Gulf of Finland

Sosnovyy Bor
Lomonosov
Petrodvore

Gotska
Sandön

BALTIC SEA

Kalana
Hiiumaa
Emmaste

TALLINN
Paldiski
Keila
Aruküla
Kehra
Tapa

Maardu
Loksa
Vaida
Rapla
Jäide

Rakvere
Kiviõli
Kohtla-
Järve

Narva
Bay
Sillamäe

Kärdla
Vormsi
Haapsalu
Hullo
Kalna

Mustjala
Orissaare

Rakke
Emumägi
166

Raja

Narva
Narvskove
Vodokhranilishche

Os'mino

Kingisepp

Ust'-
Luga

Voloso

Siver

Mshinsk

Gdov

Luga

Visby
Slite

Gotland
(Sweden)

Fårö

Klintehamn

Virtsu
Saaremaa
Säre
Muhu
Kihnu

Vändra
Põltsamaa

ESTONIA

Pärnu

Viljandi

Tartu

Jõgeva

Lake
Peipus

Plyussa

Yamm

ESTONIA

Võrtsjärv

Ülenurme

Lake
Pskov

Strugi-
Krasnyy

Irbe Strait

Ruhnu

Mäzirbe
Kolkasrags

Roja

Ovišrags

Ventspils
Dundaga

Talsi

Gulf
of
Riga

Limbaži

Salacgriva

Valmiera

Mõisaküla
Elva
Põlva

Valka
Valga

Smiltene

Võru

Cēsis

Rauna

Alūksne

Gulbene

Pechory

PSKOV

Porkhov

Slavkovich

Dedovic

Chikhachev

Pāvilosta
Akmenrags

Kuldīga

Aizpute

Tukums

Jūrmala
Olaine

RIGA

Sigulda

Elkas kalns
265

Madona

Balvi

Bytalovo

Pushkinskiye
Gory

Bezhanits

Novorzhe

Liepāja

Skrunda
Saldus

Dobele

Jelgava

Iecava

Ogre

Barkava

Kārsava

Krasnogorodskoye

Opochka

Nīca

Mažeikiai

Skuodas

Akmenė

Bauska

Aizkraukle

Jēkabpils

Līvāni

Viļāni

Preiļi

Mežvidi

Ludza

Rēzekne

Malta

Dagda

Sebezh

Viški

Postoshka

LATVIA

Kretinga

Plungė

Telšiai

Šiauliai

Kuršēnai

Pasvalys

Pakruojis

Biržai

Rokiškis

Zarasai

Kupiškis

Krāslava

Rasony

Yezyarys

Klaipėda

Gargždai
Medvegalio
kalnis
235

Radviliškis

Kelmė

Panevėžys

DAUGAVPILS

Druya

Verkhnyadzvinsk

Navapolatsk

Harad

Courland
Lagoon

Kintai

Silalė

LITHUANIA

Visaginas

Utena

Braslaw

Myory

Polatsk

Obal'

Nida

Šilutė

Rasainiai

Ignalina

Dūkštas

Sharkawshchyna

Ushachy

Shumilina

Pagégiai

Zelenogradsk

Svetlogorsk
Mys Taran

Svetly

Sovetsk

Neman

Tauragė

Jurbarkas

Kėdainiai

Ukmergė

Molėtai

Švenčionys

Pastavy

Varapayeva

Hlybokaye

Byeshankovi

Gulf of
Gdańsk

Baltiysk

Mamonovo

Primorsk

RUS. FED.

Kaliningrad

Chernyakhovsk

Gvardeysk

Gusev

Ozersk

Goldap

Šakiai

Kybartai

Vilkaviškis

Marijampolė

Kazlu
Rūda

Šaki

Norelkiškės

Grigiškės

KAUNAS

Nemunas

Neris

Pabradė

Astravyets

Varapayeva

Narach

Myadzyel

Dokshytsy

Lyepyel'

Byahoml'

Chashniki

Kokhan

Talachyn

Syar

Frombork

Braniewo

Bartoszyce

Korsze

Węgorzewo

Suwałki

Sejny

Druskininkai

Varėna

Merkinė

Eišiškės

Trakai

Salčininkai

VILNIUS

Ašmyany

Smarhon'

Vilyeyka

Maladzyechna

Valozhyn

Zaslawye

Smalyavichy

Plyeshchanitsy

Barysaw

Zhodzina

Byelynichy

Byerazino

Elbląg

Malbork

Pasłęk

Dobre
Miasto

Olsztyn

Gižycko

Olecko

Ełk

Augustów

Hrodna

Lida

Iwye

Dzyatlavichy

Zdzyarzhynsk

Karelichy

MINSK

Chervyen'

Smilavichy

Kwidzyn

Środa

Iława

Góra
Chełmońska
312

Pojezierze Mazurskie

Jezioro
Śniardwy

Grajewo

Mońki

Szczuczyn

Shchuchyn

Yarozawka

Navahrudak

Stowbtsy

Nyasvizh

Kapyl'

Staryya
Darohi

Asipovichy

Babruysk

Brodnica

Działdowo

Nidzica

Mława

Ostrołęka

Narew

Łomża

Nizina
Mazowiecka

Zambrów

Wysokie
Mazowieckie

Białystok

Svislach

Vawkavysk

Zel'va

Slonim

Masty

Nyoman

Baranavichy

Lyakhavichy

Klyetsk

Slutsk

Staryya

Kapyl'

Klichav

Rahach

Zhlob

Byerazina

Clechanów

POLAND

Płock

Legionowo

Pruszków

Zgierz

Łódź

Skierniewice

WARSAW
(Warszawa)

Minsk
Mazowiecki

Wyszków

Siedlce

Węgrów

Łuków

Biała
Podlaska

Brest

Kobryn

Ivanava

Pinsk

Drahichyn

Kamyanyets

Pruzhany

Zhabinka

Malaryta

Kamin'-
Kashyrs'kyy

Ratne

Lyubeshiv

Pietrykawa

Dzyatlavichy

Luninyets

Byaroza

Tsyelyakhany

Hantsavichy

Salihorsk

Lyuban'

Mal'kavichy

Aktsyabrski

Hlusk

Starobin

Svyetlahorsk

Kapatkyevichy

Vasilyevichy

Kalinkavichy

Mazyr

Khoy

Yel'sk

Nizina
Mazowiecka

Vistula
(Wisła)

Kutno

Radom

Piotrków
Trybunalski

Tomaszów
Mazowiecki

Pionki

Puławy

Lublin

Mazowiecka

Pińczów

Kielce

Łysica
611

Ostrowiec
Świętokrzyski

Starachowice

Skarżysko-
Kamienna

Koriskie

Kraśnystaw

Chełm

Liuboml'

Kovel'

Turiys'k

Volodymyrets'

Kuznetsov's'k

Manevychi
220

Sarny

Rokytne

Olevs'k

Stolin

Dubrovytsya

Lyel'chytsy

Vysokaye

UKRA

Nardvich

Ovruch

Polis

Luhyny

Narodychi

Prypyats' (Pripet) Marshes

Prypyats' (Pripyats')

Dnyaprow-ski

Yasel'da

BELARUS

METRES
FEET

5000
16404

3000
9843

2000
6562

1000
3281

500
1640

0
0

Land below
sea level

200
656

4000
13124

6000
19686

Conic Equidistant Projection

1 : 6 000 000

Longitude 25° east of Greenwich

MILES 0   50   100   150

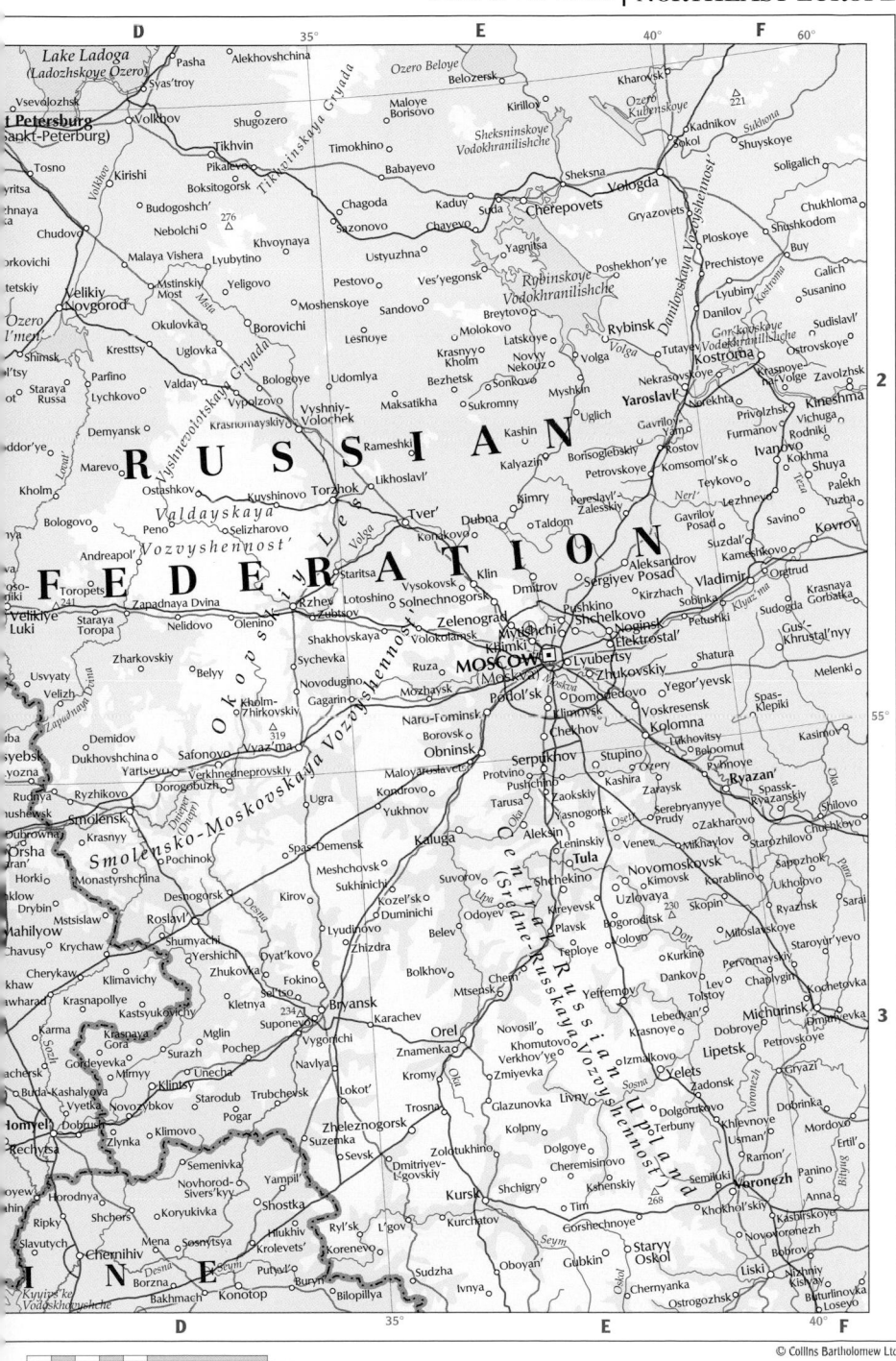

0   100   200 KILOMETRES

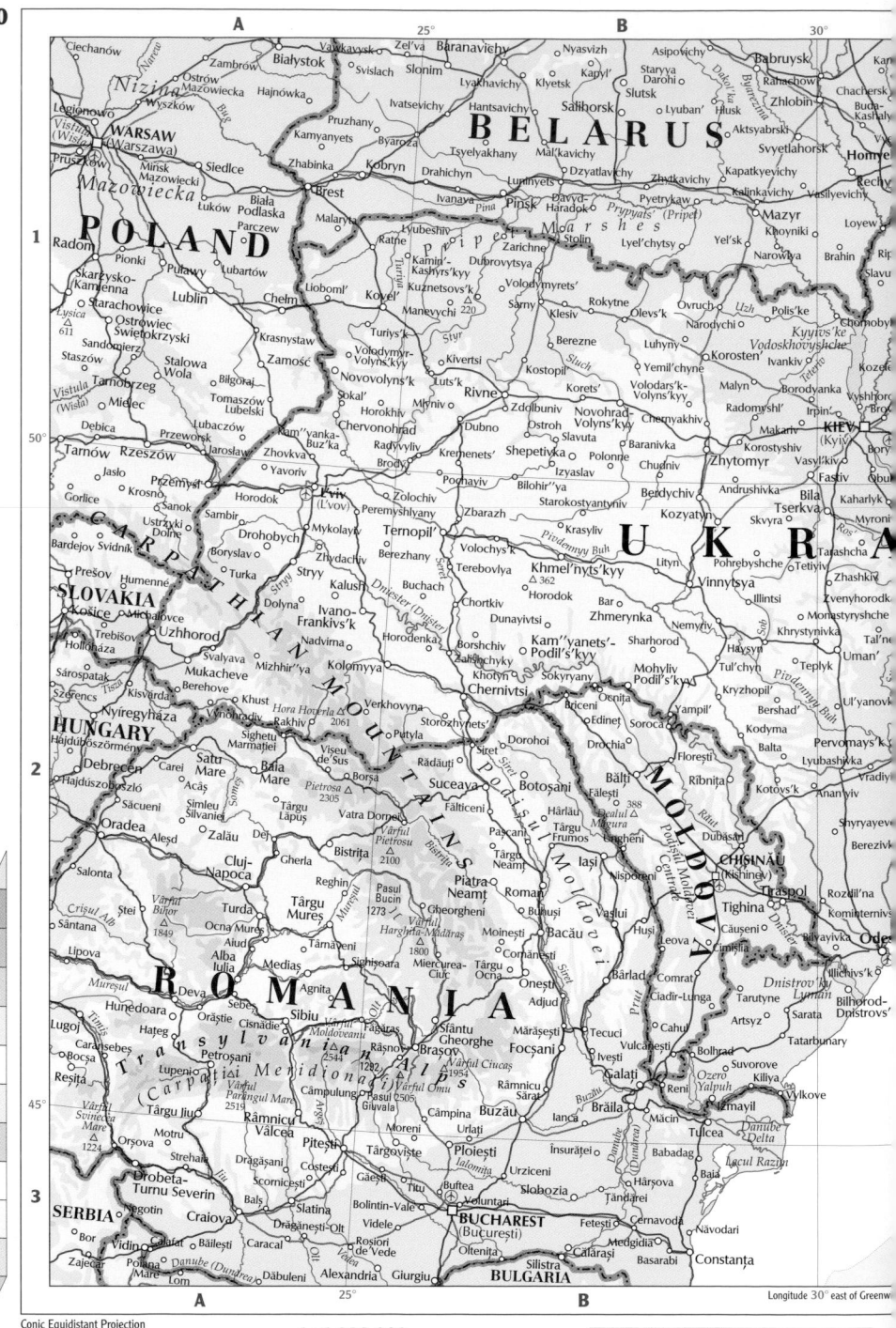

A 25° B 30°

Ciechanów · Vawkavysk · Zel'va · Baranavichy · Nyasvizh · Asipovichy · Babruysk · Kan

Zambrów · Białystok · Slonim · Klyetsk · Kapyl' · Starryya · Rahachow · Zhlobin · Chachersk

Ostrów Mazowiecka · Hajnówka · Svislach · Lyakhavichy · Slutsk · Darohi · Zhlobin · Buda-

Legionowo · Wyszków · Pruzhany · Kamyanyets · Byaroza · Tsyelyakhany · Salihorsk · Lyuban' · Hlusk · Svyetlahorsk · Homye

WARSAW (Warszawa) · Siedlce · Zhabinka · Kobryn · Drahichyn · Luninyets · Dzyatlavichy · Pyetrykaw · Kalinkavichy · Vasilyevichy

Pruszków · Mińsk Mazowiecki · Brest · Ivanava · Pina · Pinsk · Davyd-Haradok · Zarichne · Lyel'chytsy · Yel'sk · Narowlya · Mazyr · Loyew

POLAND · Radom · Łuków · Biała Podlaska · Malaryta · Lyubeshiv · Ratne · Stolin · **Pripet Marshes** · Khoyniki · Brahin · Slavu

Pionki · Puławy · Lubartów · Kamin'-Kashyrs'kyy · Zarichne · Dubrovytsya · Rokytne · Ovruch · Narodychi · Chornoby

Skarżysko-Kamienna · Lublin · Chełm · Lioboml' · Kovel' · Kuznetsovs'k · Volodymyrets' · Olevs'k · Polis'ke · Vodoskhovyshche

Starachowice · Ostrowiec Świętokrzyski · Krasnystaw · Turiys'k · Maneyvychi · Sarny · Klesiv · Luhyny · Korosten' · Ivankiv · Kyyiv'ske · Kozel

Sandomierz · Zamość · Volodymyr-Volyns'kyy · Kivertsi · Berezne · Yemil'chyne · Malyn · Borodyanka · Radomyshl' · Irpin'

Staszów · Stalowa Wola · Bilgoraj · Novovolyns'k · Luts'k · Rivne · Zdolbuniv · Novohrad-Volyns'kyy · Volodars'k-Volyns'kyy · Korets' · Makariv · **KIEV** (Kyyiv) · Vyshhoro

Tarnobrzeg · Tomaszów Lubelski · Sokal' · Mlyniv · Dubno · Ostroh · Slavuta · Polonne · Zhytomyr · Brusyliv · Fastiv · Obu

Mielec · Przeworsk · Horokhiv · Radyvyliv · Kremenets' · Shepetivka · Chudniv · Berdychiv · Vasyl'kiv · Bory

Debica · Tarnów · Rzeszów · Jarosław · Zhovkva · Brody · Izyaslav · Polonne · Andrushivka · Bila Tserkva · Kaharlyk · Myroni

CARPATHIAN MOUNTAINS · Jasło · Krosno · Sambir · Yavoriv · **Lviv** (L'vov) · Zolochiv · Pochayiv · Bilohir''ya · Starokostyantyniv · Kozyatyn · Skvyra · Tarashcha · Ros

Gorlice · Przemyśl · Horodok · Peremyshlyany · Zbarazh · Krasyliv · Litynn · Pohrebyshche · Tetiyiv · Zvenyhorodk · Zhashkiv

Bardejov · Svidník · Ustrzyki Dolne · Drohobych · Mykolayiv · **Ternopil'** · Berezhany · Volochys'k · **Khmel'nyts'kyy** · Vinnytsya · Illintsi · Tal'n · Khrystynivka

Prešov · Humenné · Boryslav · Turka · Stryy · Kalush · Zhydachiv · Terebovlya · Buchach · Horodok · Bar · Zhmerynka · Nemyriv · Uman'

SLOVAKIA · Košice · Michalovce · Uzhhorod · Svalyava · Ivano-Frankivs'k · Nadvirna · Horodenka · Dunayivtsi · Sharhorod · Haysyn · Teplyk

Trebišov · Mukacheve · Mizhhir"ya · Kolomyya · Borshchiv · Kam''yanets'-Podil's'kyy · Mohyliv-Podil's'kyy · Kryzhopil' · Bershad' · Kodyma · Ul'yanov

Sárospatak · Szerencs · Kisvárda · Berehove · Khust · Rakhiv · Verkhovyna · Khotyn · Sokyryany · Yampil' · Pervomays'k

Nyíregyháza · Vynohradiv · Hora Hoverla 2061 · **Chernivtsi** · Oenita · Edinet · Soroca · Balta · Lyubashivka · Vradiy

HUNGARY · Hajdúböszörmény · Sighetu Marmaţiei · Viseu de Sus · Putyla · Storozhynets' · Briceni · Drochia · Floreşti · Kotovs'k · Ananyiv · Shyryayeve

Debrecen · Carei · Satu Mare · Baia Mare · Borşa · Rădăuţi · Siret · Dorohoi · **MOLDOVA** · Ribniţa · Berezivka

Hajdúszoboszló · Acăs · Simleu Silvaniei · Târgu Lăpuş · Vatra Dornei · Suceava · Botoşani · Bălţi · Faleşti · Dubăsari

Săcueni · Zalău · Dej · Bistriţa · Fălticeni · Hârlău · Ungheni · Străşeni · **CHIŞINĂU** (Kishinev) · Tiraspol · Rozdil'na · Kominternivs'k

Oradea · Alesd · Gherla · Reghin · Piatra Neamţ · Paşcani · Târgu Frumos · Iaşi · Nisporeni · Tighina · Illichivs'k · Ode

ROMANIA · Salonta · Cluj-Napoca · Turda · Bistriţa · Roman · Bacău · Vaslui · Huşi · Leova · Căuşeni · Bilyayivka

Sântana · Ştei · Ocna Mureş · Târgu Mureş · Gheorgheni · Buhuşi · Comrat · Ciadir-Lunga · Tarutyne · Sarata

Lipova · Aiud · Târnăveni · Miercurea-Ciuc · Moineşti · Oneşti · Bârlad · Comrat · Tatarbunary

Deva · Alba Iulia · Mediaş · Sighişoara · Sfântu Gheorghe · Adjud · Tecuci · Cahul · Reni · Izmayil · Vylkove

Hunedoara · Orăştie · Sibiu · Agnita · Braşov · Mărăşeşti · Focşani · Galaţi · Brăila · Măcin · Tulcea · **Danube Delta**

Lugoj · Caransebeş · Haţeg · Cisnădie · Făgăraş · Râşnov · Ivesti · Vulcaneşti · Bolhrad · Suvorove · Ozero Yalpuh · Kiliya

Bocşa · Petroşani · Câmpulung · Râmnicu Sărat · Ianca · **Transylvanian Alps** · Tândărei · Hârşova · Băile Herculane

Reşiţa · Târgu Jiu · Râmnicu Vâlcea · Piteşti · Târgovişte · Buzău · Câmpina · Ploieşti · Urlaţi · Babadag · Lacul Razim

Drobeta-Turnu Severin · Orşova · Motru · Strehaia · Drăgăşani · Costeşti · Găeşti · Ploieşti · Urziceni · Slobozia · Ţăndărei · Năvodari

SERBIA · Bor · Vidin · Calafat · Băileşti · Craiova · Balş · Slatina · Bolintin-Vale · **BUCHAREST** (Bucureşti) · Voluntari · Fetesti · Cernavoda · Medgidia · Constanţa

Zaječar · Poiana Mare · Danube (Dunărea) · Dăbuleni · Alexandria · Roşiori de Vede · Videle · Giurgiu · Olteniţa · Călăraşi · Basarabi

BULGARIA · Silistra

A 25° B Longitude 30° east of Greenw

BELARUS

UKRAINE

METRES FEET

5000	16404
3000	9843
2000	6562
1000	3281
500	1640
200	656
0	0

Land below sea level

200	656
4000	13124
6000	19686

Conic Equidistant Projection

1 : 6 000 000

MILES 0 · 50 · 100 · 150

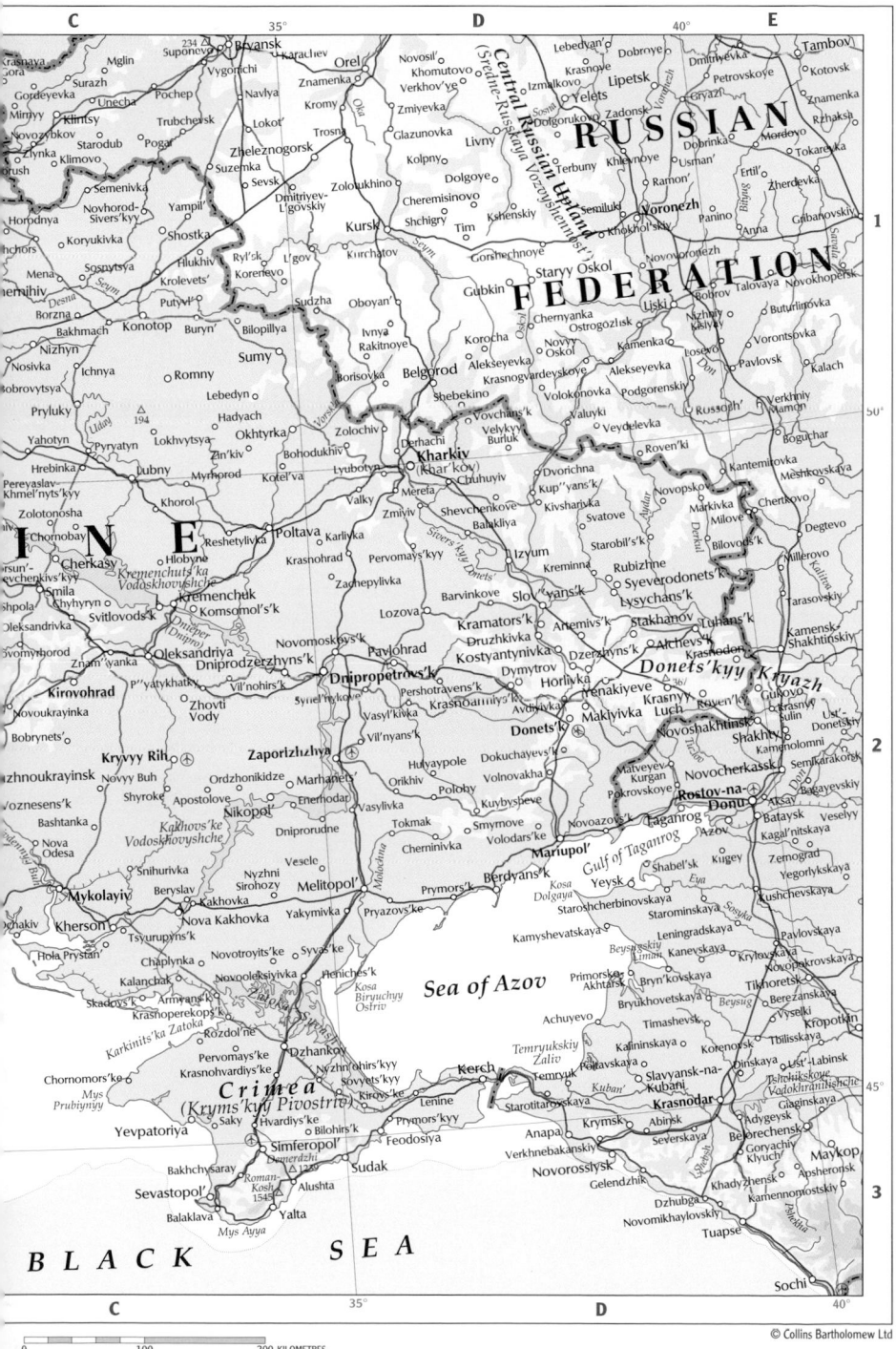

© Collins Bartholomew Ltd

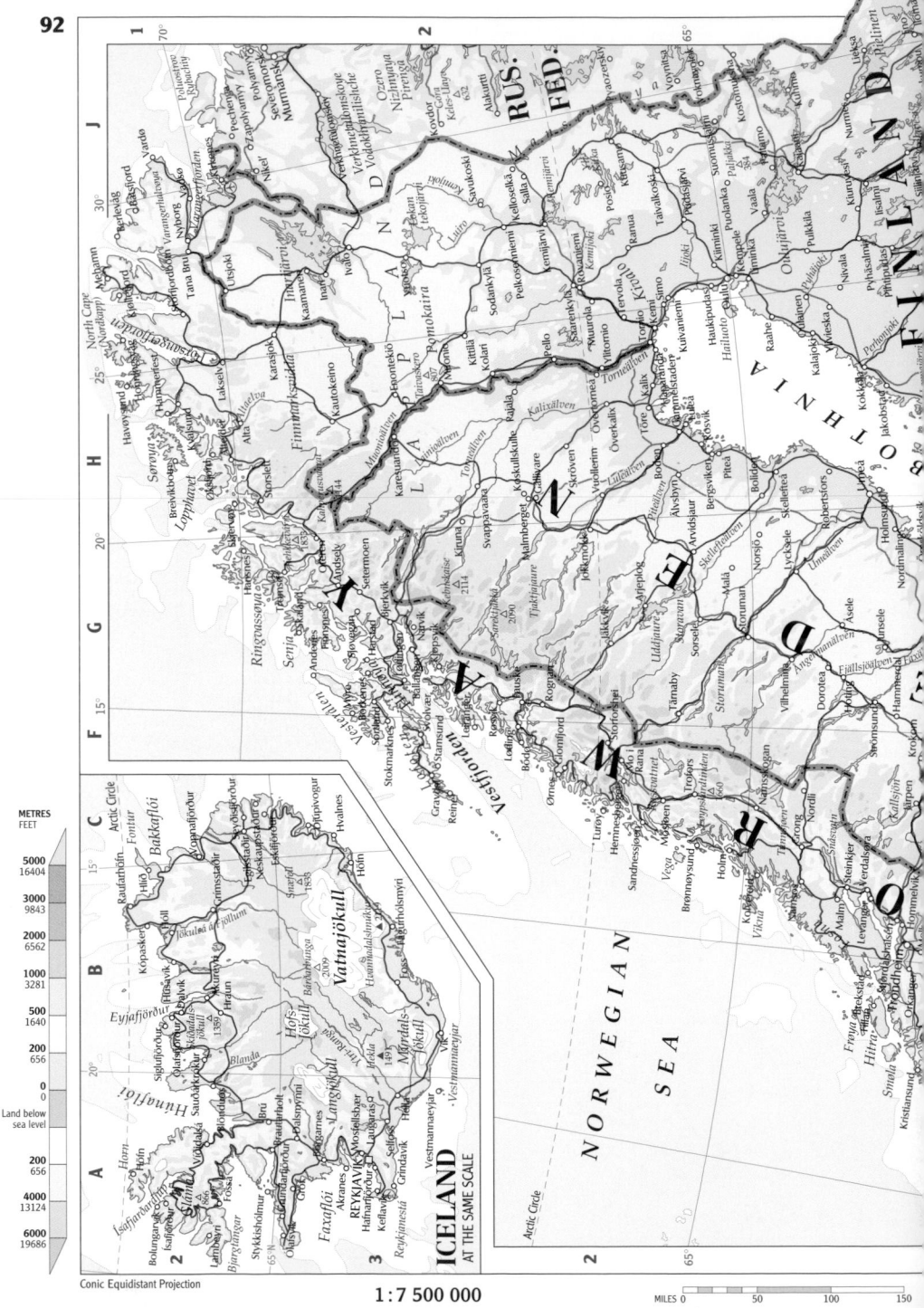

ICELAND
AT THE SAME SCALE

Conic Equidistant Projection

1:7 500 000

METRES
FEET

5000
16404

3000
9843

2000
6562

1000
3281

500
1640

200
656

0

Land below
sea level

200
656

4000
13124

6000
19686

MILES 0   50   100   150

NORWEGIAN SEA

RUS. FED.

FINLAND

BOTHNIA

SWEDEN

NORWAY

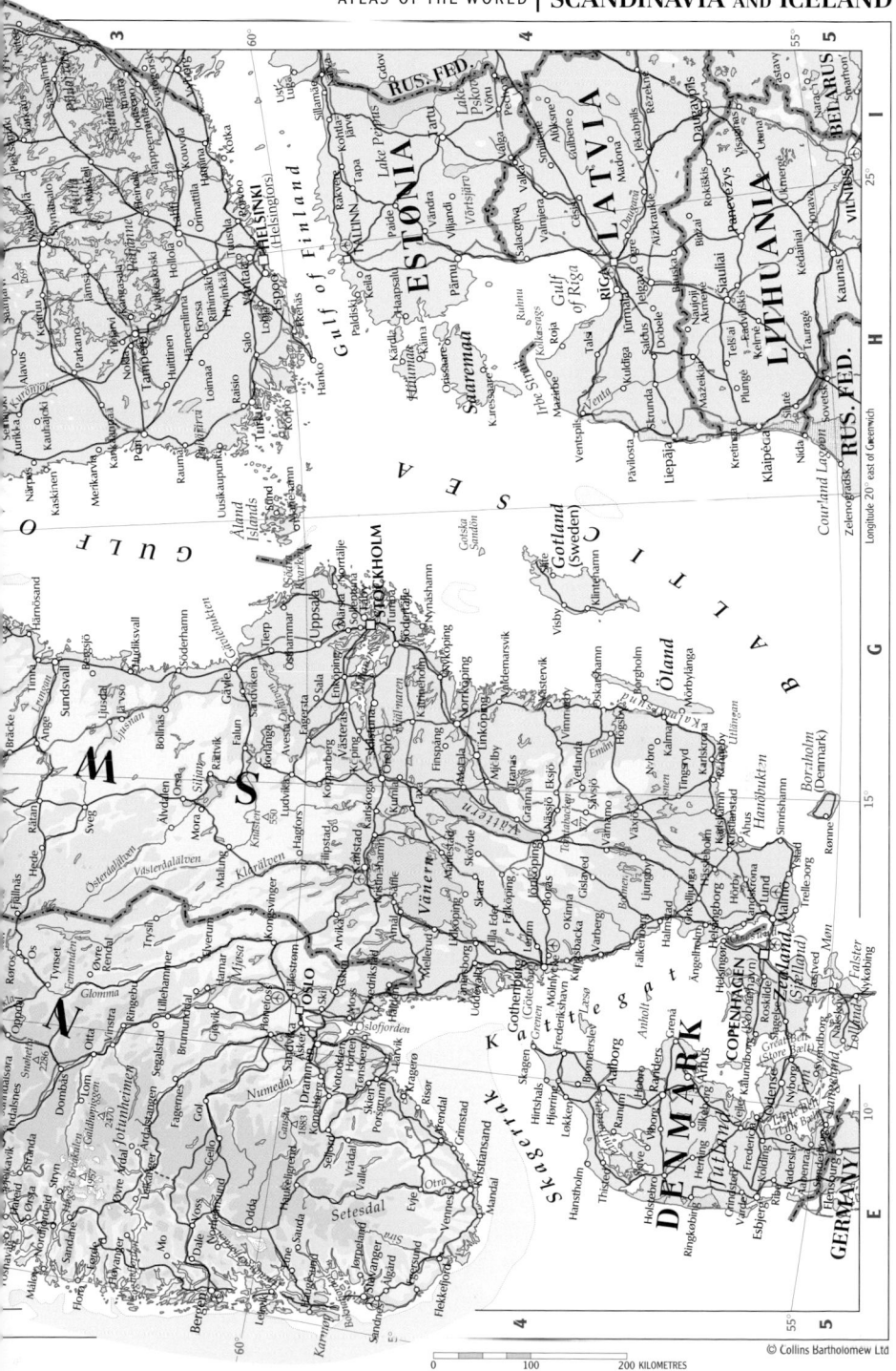

© Collins Bartholomew Ltd

0   100   200 KILOMETRES

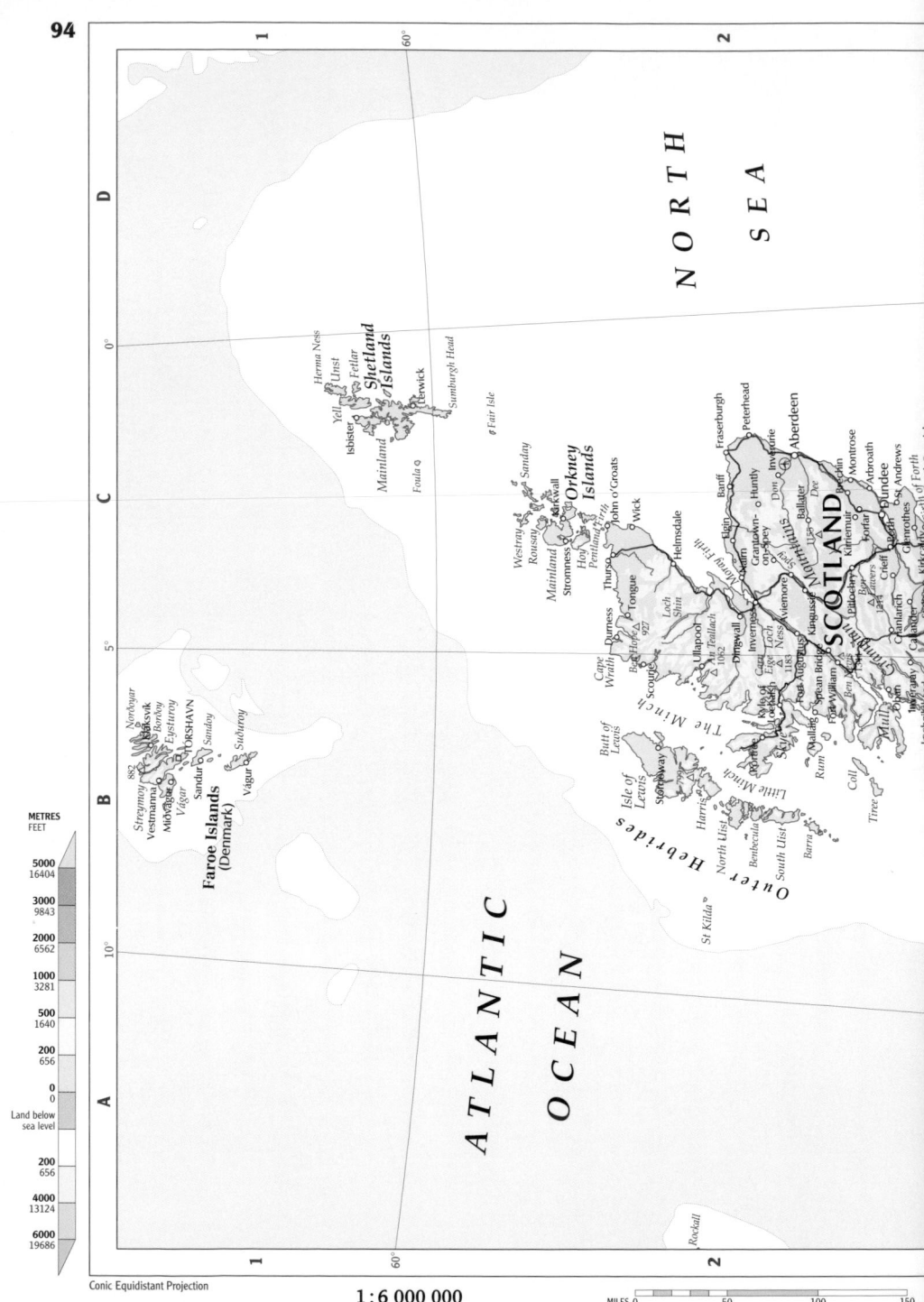

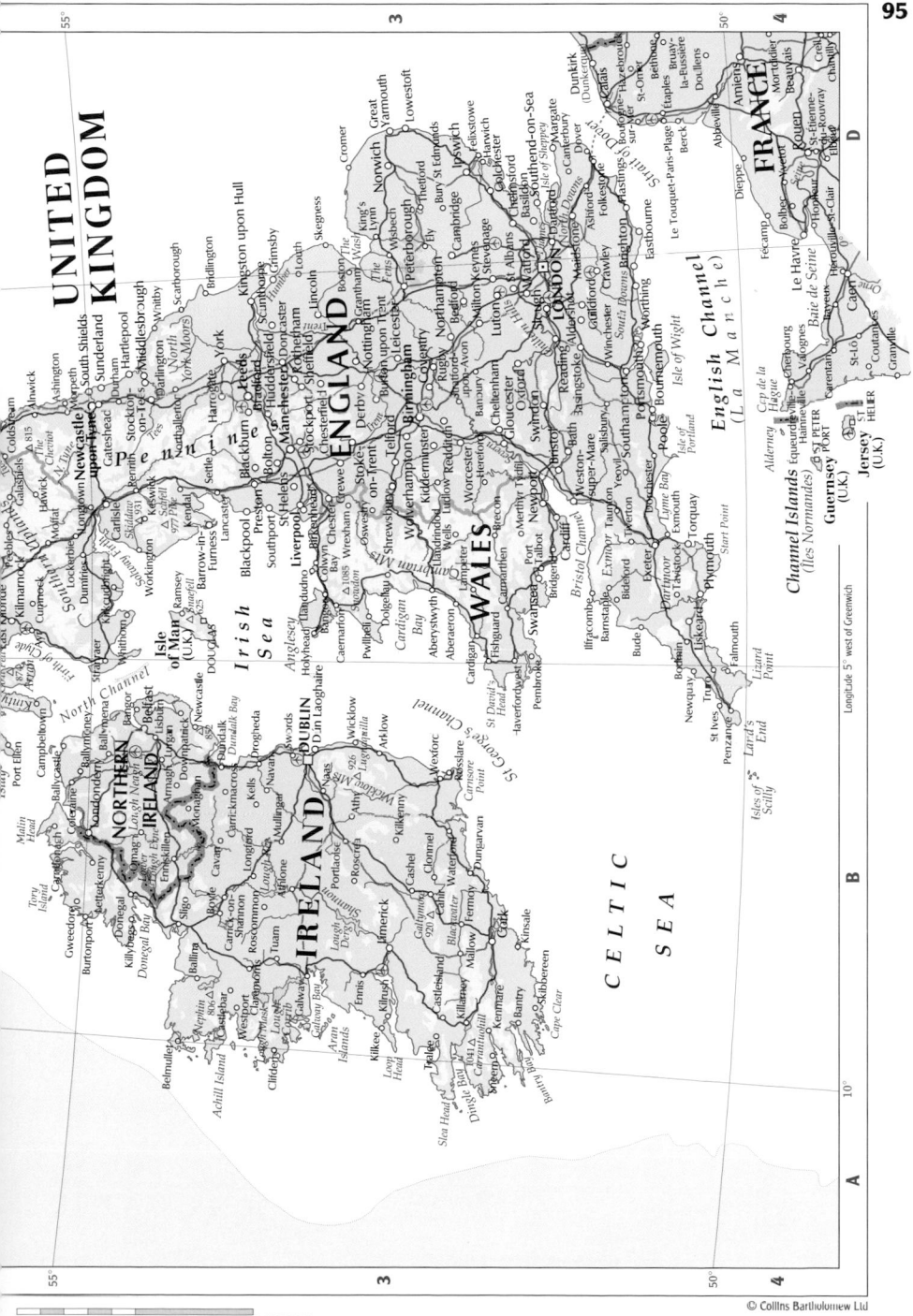

© Collins Bartholomew Ltd

0   100   200 KILOMETRES

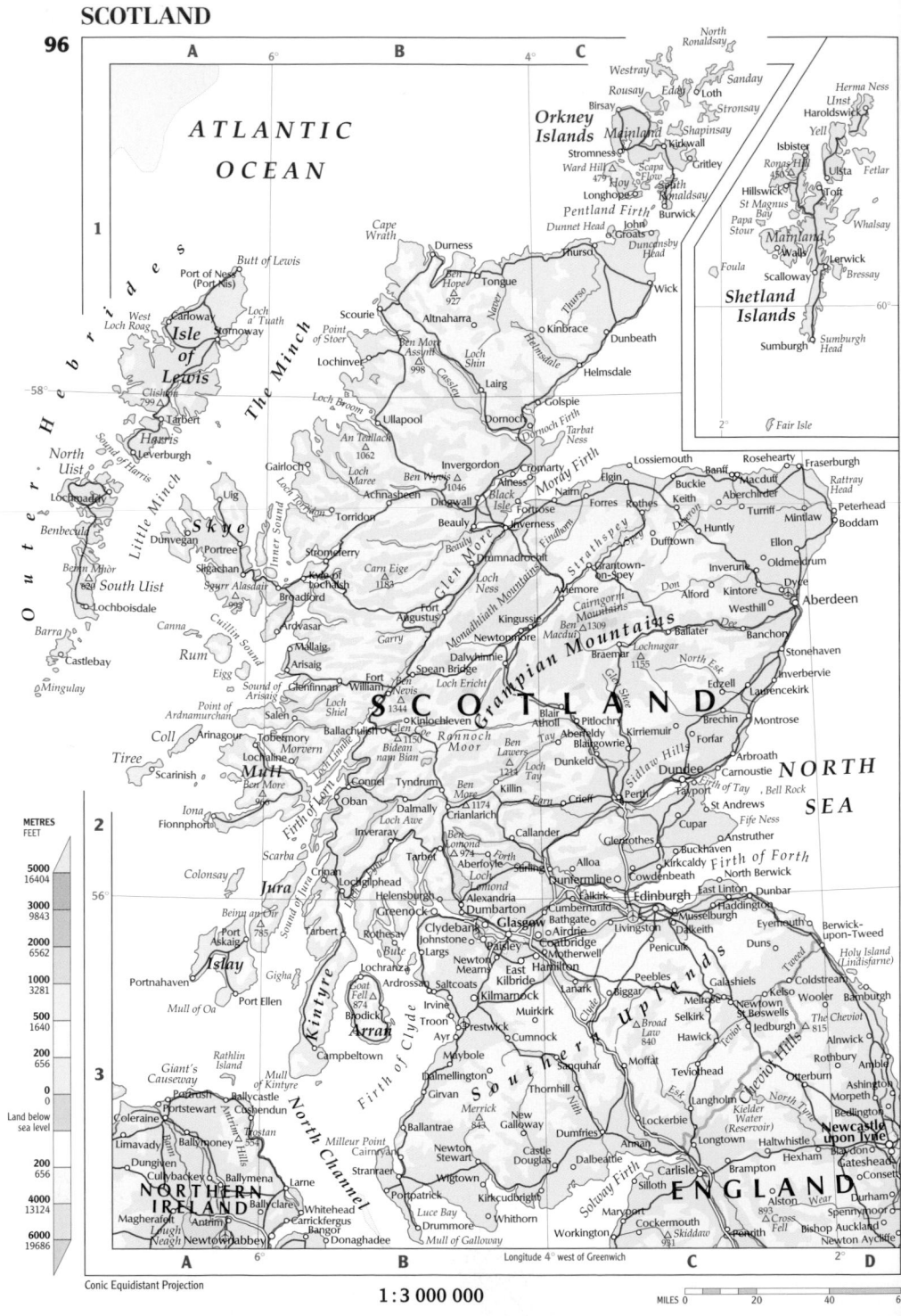

ATLANTIC
OCEAN

NORTH
SEA

ENGLAND

NORTHERN
IRELAND

Orkney
Islands

Shetland
Islands

Isle
of
Lewis

O u t e r   H e b r i d e s

Skye

S C O T L A N D

Grampian Mountains

Southern Uplands

Cheviot Hills

METRES
FEET

5000
16404

3000
9843

2000
6562

1000
3281

500
1640

200
656

0

Land below
sea level

200
656

4000
13124

6000
19686

Conic Equidistant Projection

Longitude 4° west of Greenwich

1 : 3 000 000

MILES 0   20   40   60

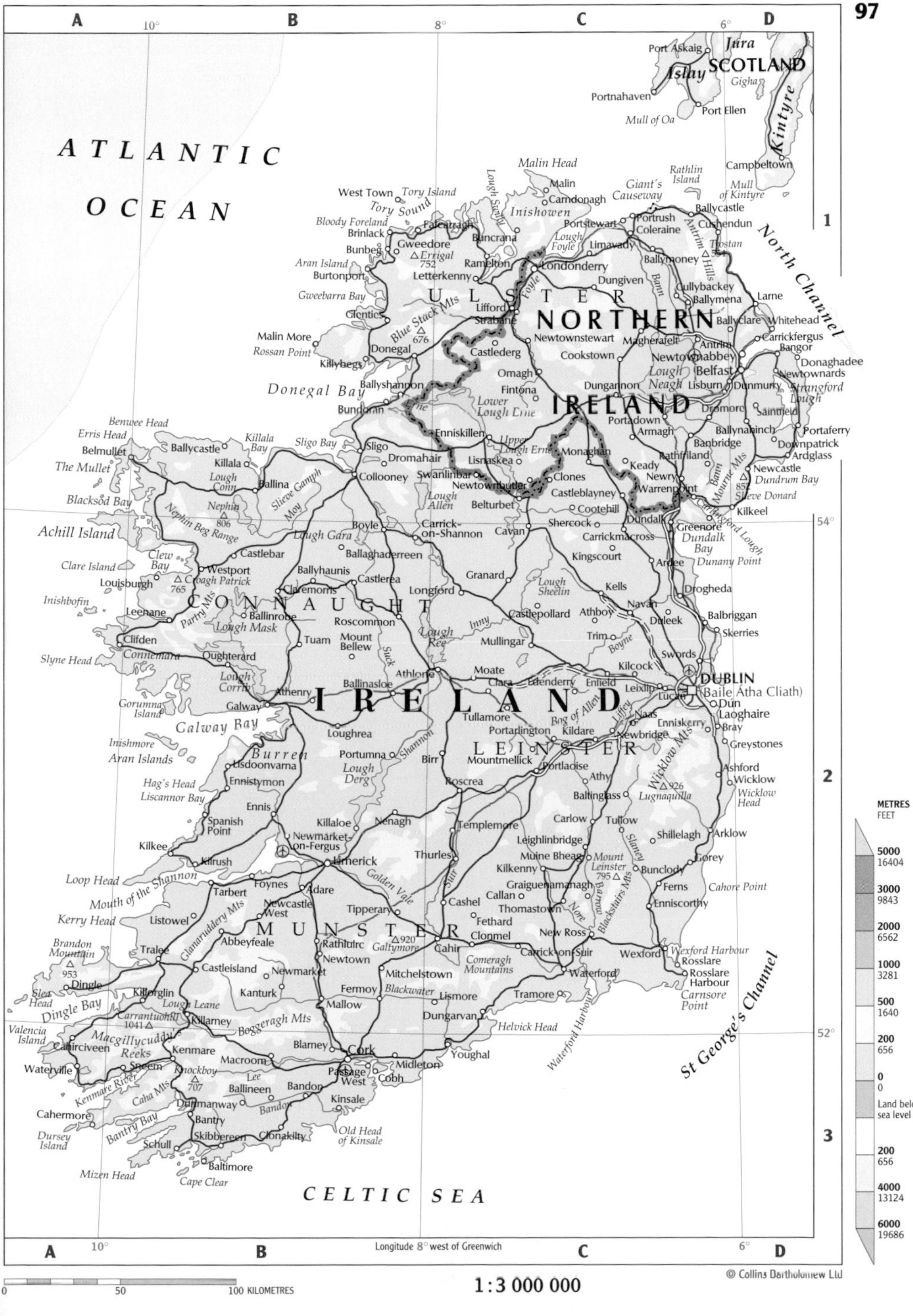

A 10° B 8° C 6° D

SCOTLAND

Port Askaig Jura
Islay Gigha
Portnahaven Port Ellen
Mull of Oa Campbeltown

Mull of Kintyre

A T L A N T I C

O C E A N

Malin Head
West Town Tory Island Malin
Tory Sound Carndonagh Giant's Rathlin Mull
Bloody Foreland Inishowen Causeway Island of Kintyre
Brinlack Falcarragh Portstewart Ballycastle
Gweedore Buncrana Portrush Cushendun
Bunbeg △Errigal Coleraine Portrush
Aran Island 752 Ramelton Limavady Tristan
Burtonport Letterkenny Londonderry Ballymoney
Gweebarra Bay Dungiven Cullybackey
U L S T E R Lifford Ballymena Larne
Glenties Ballyclare Whitehead
Malin More Strabane **N O R T H E R N** Carrickfergus
Rossan Point Donegal Newtownstewart Magherafelt Antrim Bangor
Killybegs Castlederg Cookstown Newtownabbey Donaghadee
Donegal Bay Ballyshannon Omagh **I R E L A N D** Belfast Newtownards
Bundoran Fintona Dungannon Lisburn Dunmurry Strangford
Benwee Head Portadown Dromore Saintfield
Erris Head Lower Lough Erne Ballynahinch Portaferry
Belmullet Ballycastle Killala Sligo Bay Enniskillen Armagh Banbridge Downpatrick
The Mullet Killala Bay Sligo Upper Lough Erne Rathfriland Ardglass
Lough Dromahair Monaghan Keady Newcastle
Blacksod Bay Conn Ballina Colloney Swanlinbar Clones Newry Dundrum Bay
Nephin Slieve Gamph Newtownbutler Castleblayney Warrenpoint Slieve Donard
Achill Island 806 May Lough Belturbet Cootehill Kilkeel
Nephin Beg Range Allen Shercock Dundalk
Clare Island Boyle Carrick- Cavan Greenore
Clew Castlebar Lough Gara on-Shannon Carrickmacross Dunany Point
Inishbofin Bay Ballyhaderreen Kingscourt Ardee Dunany Point
Louisburgh △Croagh Patrick Ballyhaunis Castlerea Granard Kells Drogheda
765 Claremorris Longford Lough Navan
Leenane **C O N N A U G H T** Roscommon Sheelin Balbriggan
Clifden Ballinrobe Tuam Mount Lough Castlepollard Athboy Duleek Skerries
Connemara Lough Mask Bellew Ree Trim Boyne
Slyne Head Oughterard Athlone Mullingar Swords
Gorumna Lough Ballinasloe Moate Kilcock **DUBLIN**
Island Corrib Galway Athenry Edenderry Enfield Leixlip (Baile Átha Cliath)
Galway Bay **I R E L A N D** Tullamore Bog of Allen Lucan Dún
Inishmore Loughrea Portarlington Kildare Naas Laoghaire
Aran Islands **B u r r e n** Portumna Birr **L E I N S T E R** Newbridge Enniskerry Bray
Lisdoonvarna Lough Mountmellick Portlaoise Greystones
Hag's Head Ennistymon Derg Roscrea Athy Wicklow Mts Ashford
Liscannor Bay Ennis Baltinglass 926△ Wicklow
Spanish Killaloe Nenagh Templemore Carlow Lugnaquilla Wicklow Head
Point Newmarket- Tullow
Kilkee on-Fergus Thurles Shillelagh Arklow
Kilrush Limerick Kilkenny Muine Bheag Bunclody Gorey
Loop Head Foynes Adare Golden Graiguenamanagh Ferns Cahore Point
Mouth of the Shannon Tarbert Newcastle Vale Callan Mount 795△ Enniscorthy
Kerry Head West Tipperary Cashel Thomastown Leinster
Listowel Abbeyfeale Clonmel New Ross Wexford Harbour
Brandon Rathluirc Galtymore Cahir Carrick-on-Suir Wexford Rosslare
Mountain Tralee **M U N S T E R** 920△ Comeragh Waterford Rosslare
953△ Newtown Mitchelstown Mountains Harbour
Dingle Castleisland Newmarket Fermoy Blackwater Lismore Tramore Carnsore
Slea Killorglin Kanturk Mallow Dungarvan Point
Head Dingle Bay Lough Leane Boggeragh Mts Helvick Head
Valencia Carrantuohill Killarney Blarney Youghal
Island 1041△ Macroom Cork Waterford Harbour
Waterville Macgillycuddy's Lee Midleton
Reeks Kenmare Knockboy Ballineen Passage Cobh
Cahermore Sheen 707△ Bandon West
Knockboy Dunmanway Kinsale
Caha Mts Bantry Bandon
Dursey Bantry Bay Skibbereen Clonakilty Old Head
Island Schull of Kinsale
Mizen Head Baltimore
Cape Clear

C E L T I C S E A

North Channel

St George's Channel

METRES	FEET
5000	16404
3000	9843
2000	6562
1000	3281
500	1640
200	656
0	0
Land below sea level	
200	656
4000	13124
6000	19686

© Collins Bartholomew Ltd

0 50 100 KILOMETRES

1:3 000 000

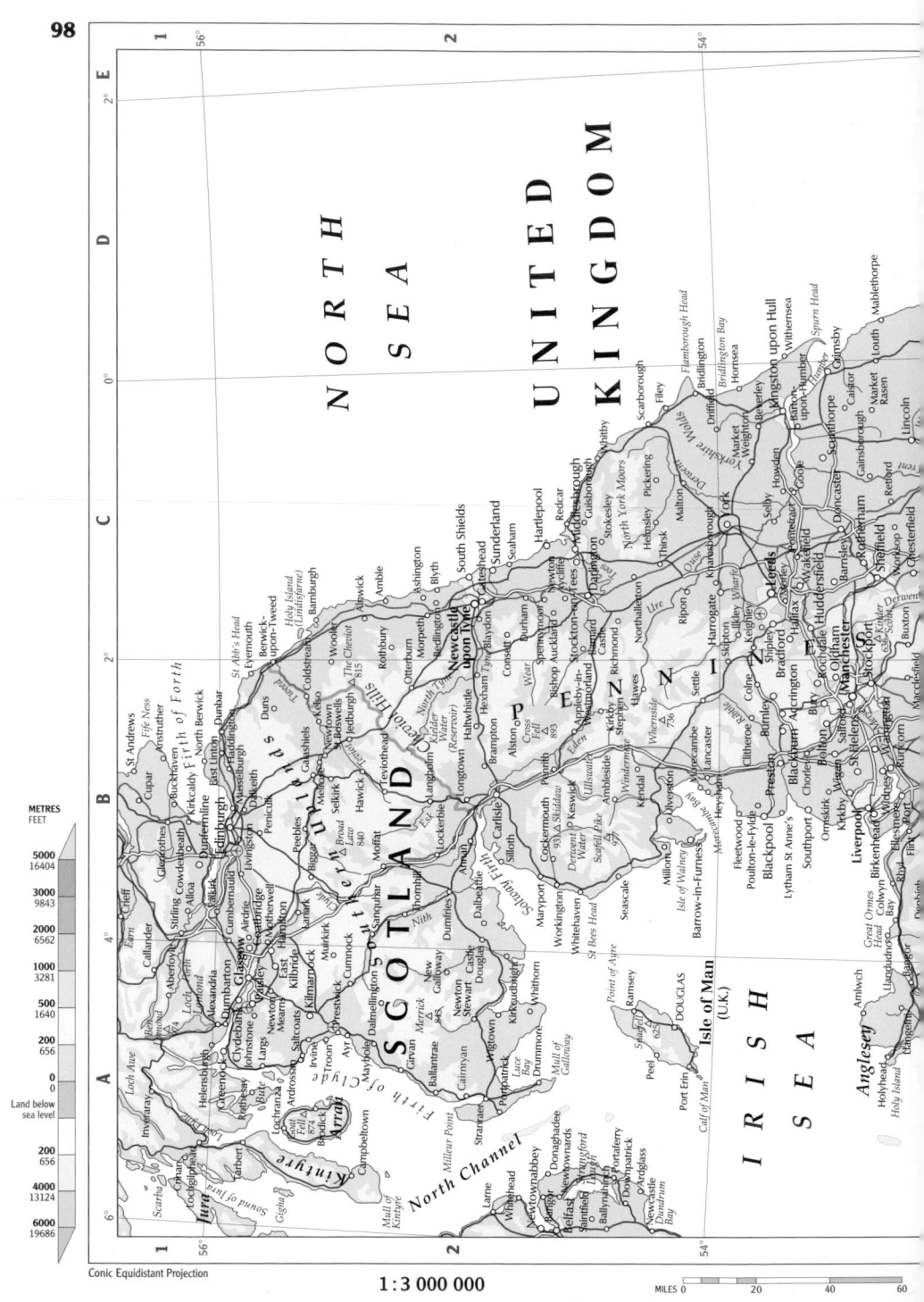

NORTH SEA

UNITED KINGDOM

SCOTLAND

S o u t h e r n   U p l a n d s

P E N N I N E S

IRISH SEA

North Channel

Isle of Man (U.K.)

Anglesey

Conic Equidistant Projection

1:3 000 000

MILES 0   20   40   60

METRES
FEET

5000 16404
3000 9843
2000 6562
1000 3281
500   1640
200   656
0   0
Land below
sea level
200   656
4000 13124
6000 19686

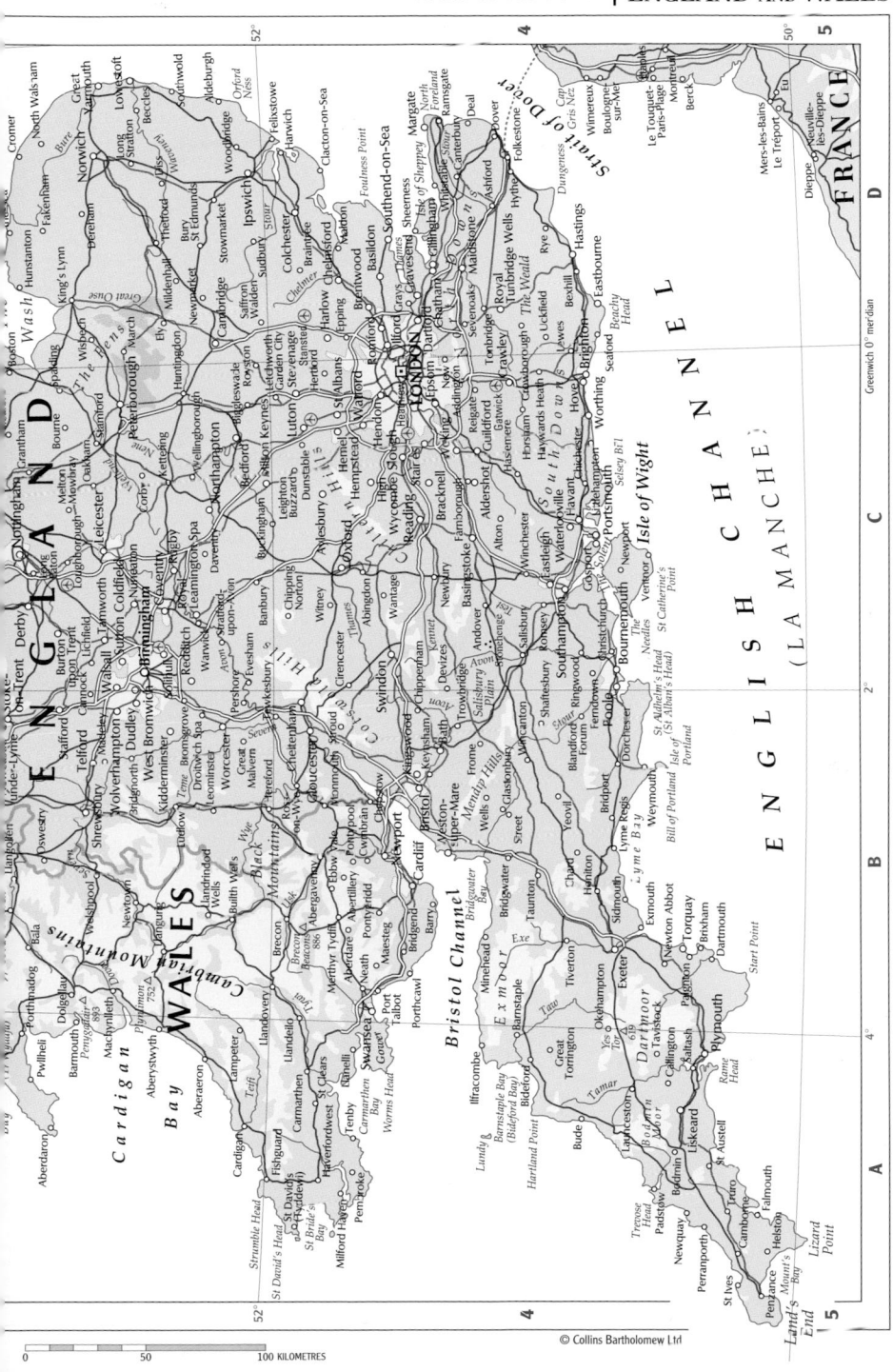

© Collins Bartholomew Ltd

0   50   100 KILOMETRES

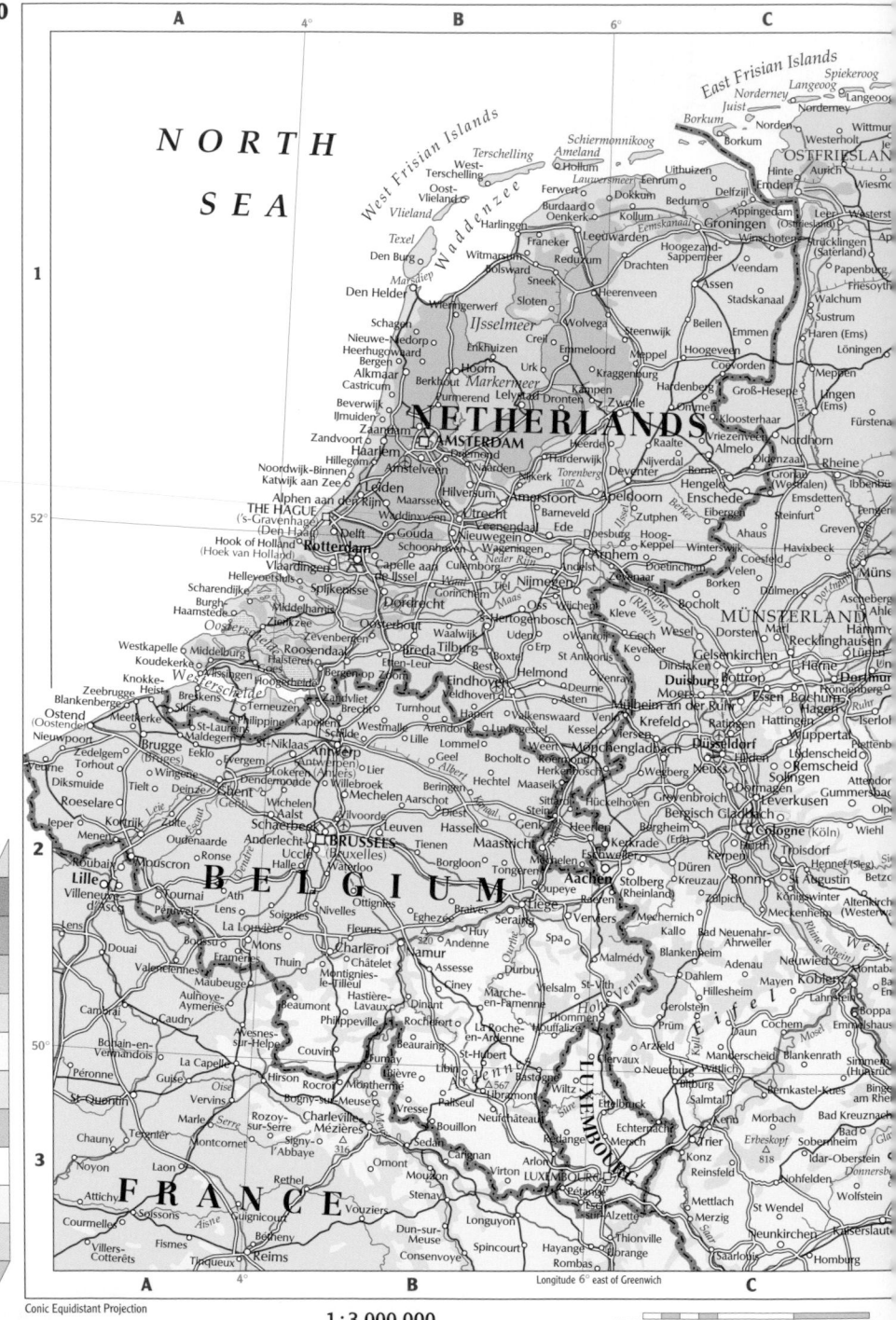

A   4°   B   6°   C

NORTH

SEA

West Frisian Islands

East Frisian Islands

NETHERLANDS

BELGIUM

FRANCE

LUXEMBOURG

MÜNSTERLAND

52°

50°

1

2

3

METRES
FEET

5000	16404
3000	9843
2000	6562
1000	3281
500	1640
200	656
0	0

Land below
sea level

200	656
4000	13124
6000	19686

A   4°   B   Longitude 6° east of Greenwich   C

Conic Equidistant Projection

1 : 3 000 000

MILES 0   20   40   60

0   50   100 KILOMETRES

MILES 0   50   100   150

Conic Equidistant Projection

1:6 000 000

Longitude 10° east of Greenwich

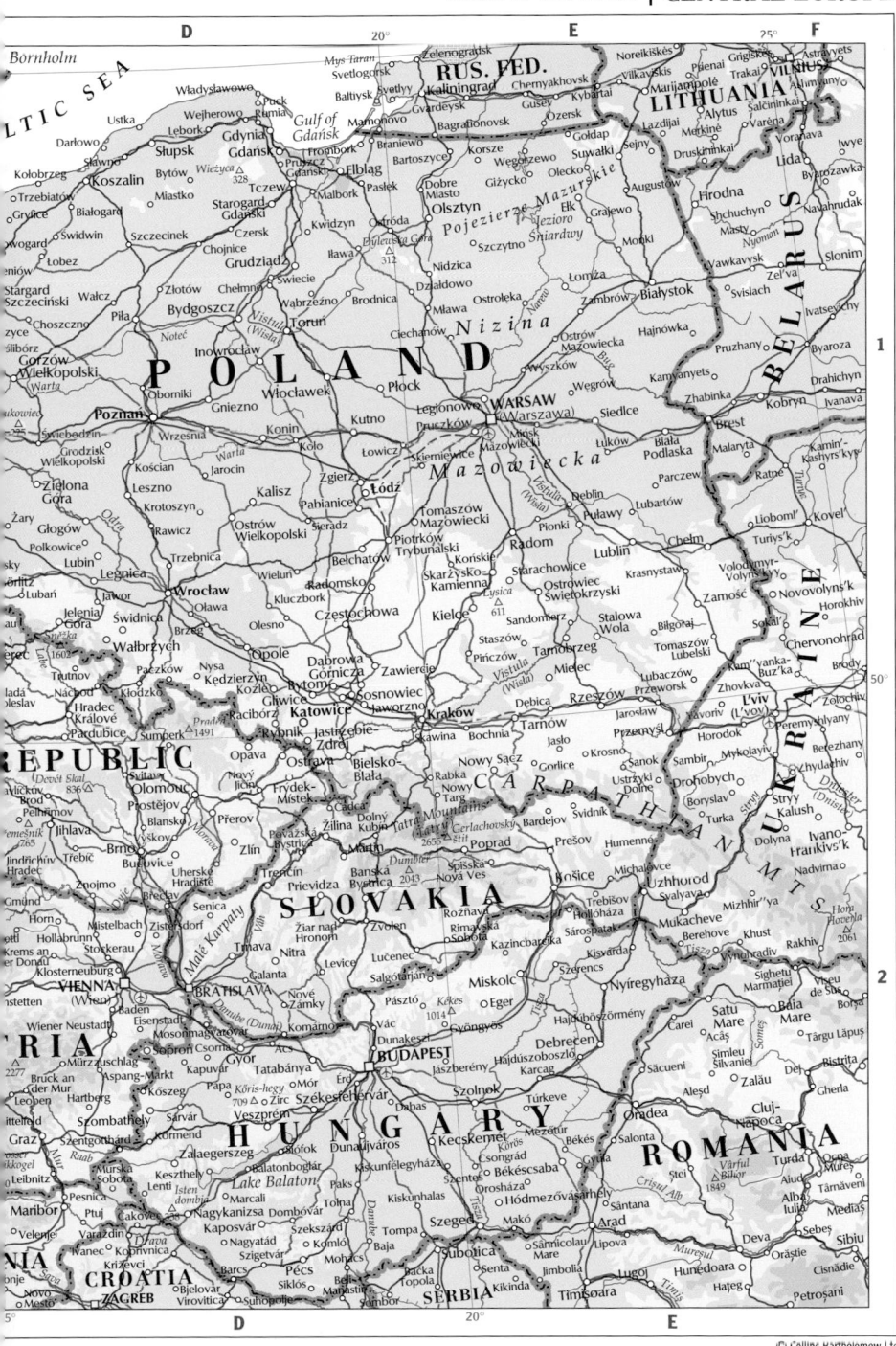

© Collins Bartholomew Ltd

0   100   200 KILOMETRES

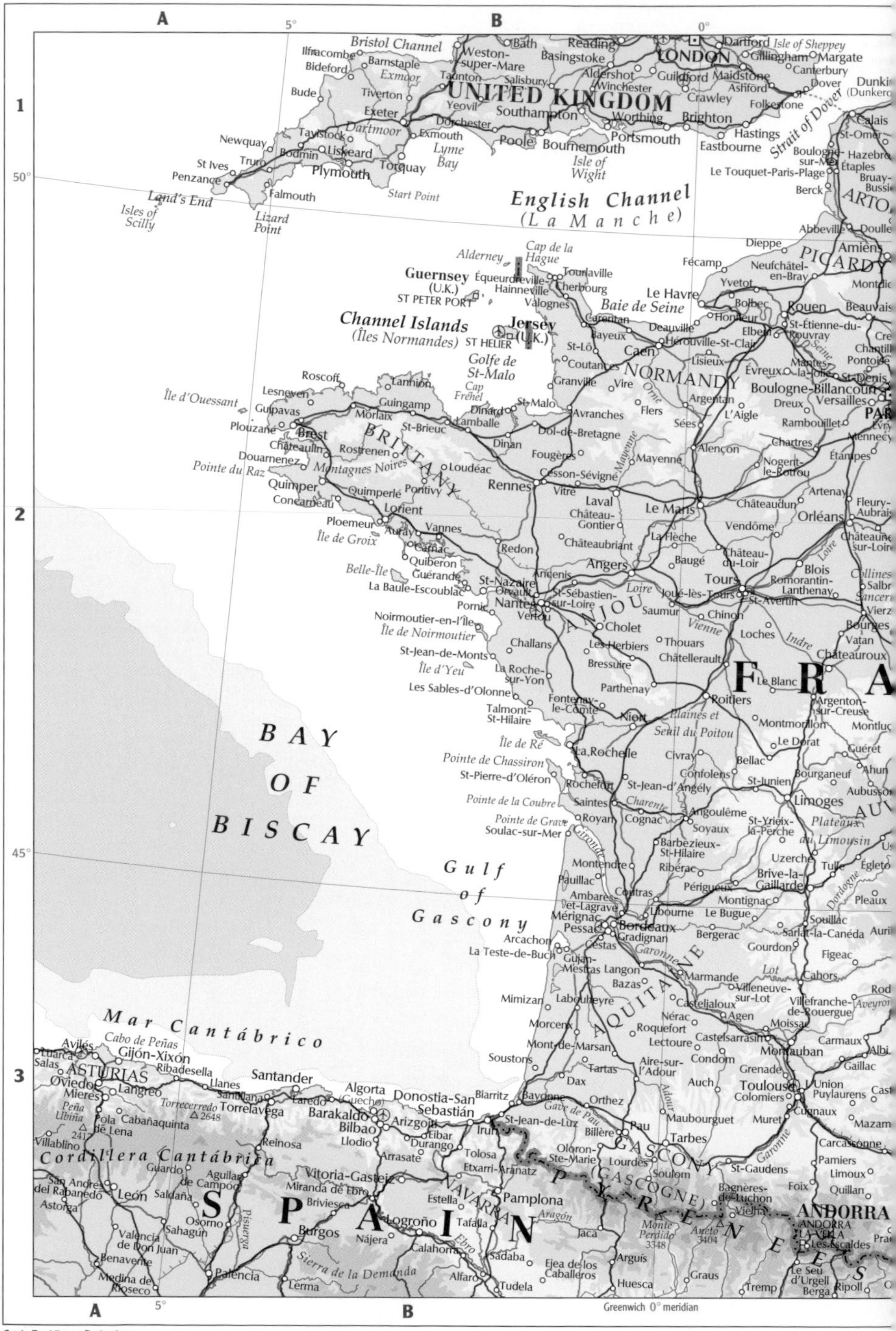

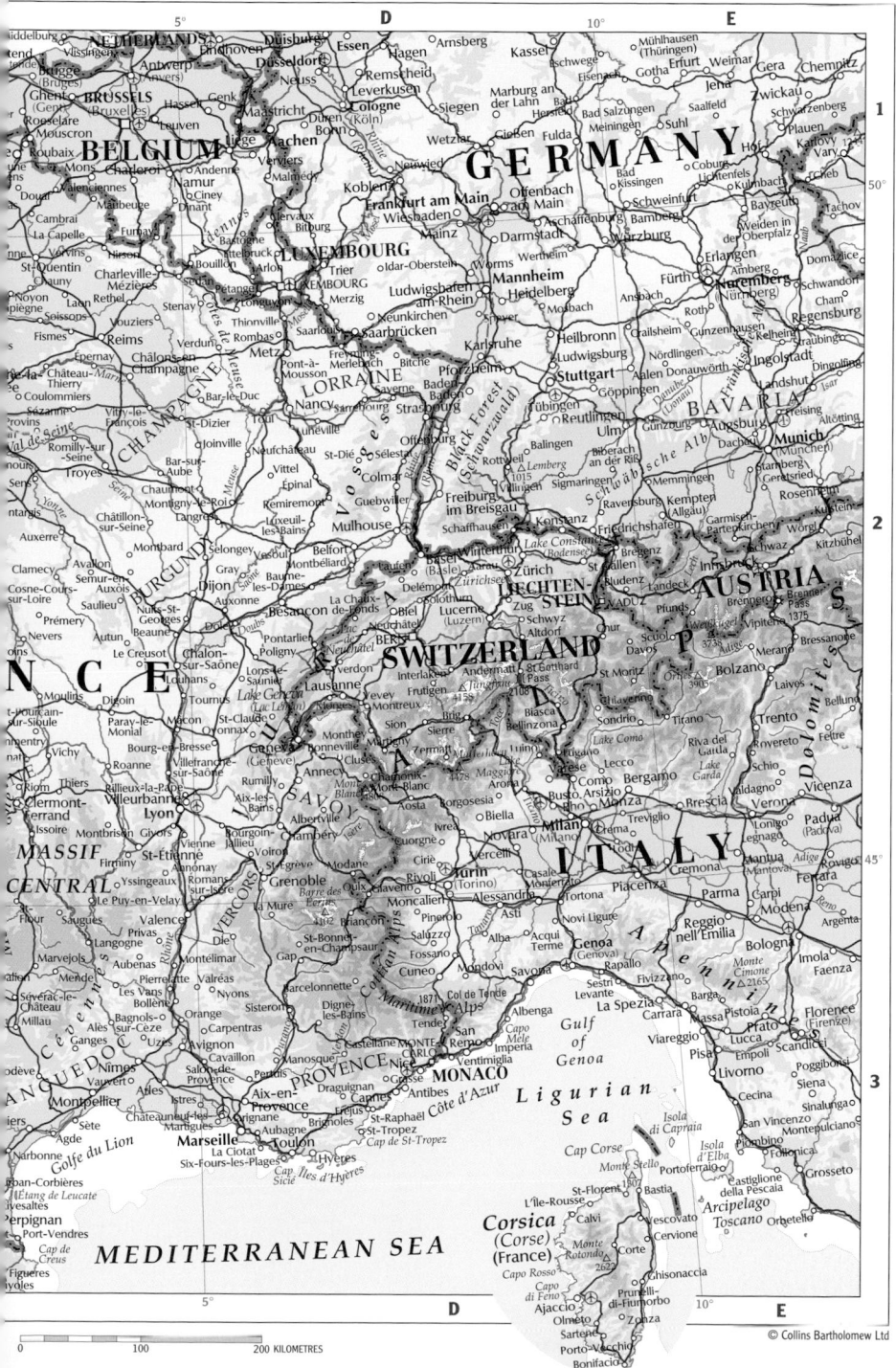

© Collins Bartholomew Ltd

0   100   200 KILOMETRES

A 10° B 5°

ATLANTIC OCEAN

Cabo Ortegal
Punta de Estaca de Bares
Ortigueira
Cervo
Mar Cantábrico
Ferrol
Viveiro
Luarca
Avilés
Cabo de Peñas
Gijón-Xixón
Santander
Algort-
(Guech)
A Coruña
A Gándara de Altea
Ribadeo
Cangas del Narcea
Salas
Pola de Siero
Ribadesella
Llanes
Santillana
Laredo
Betanzos
Villablino
Oviedo
Mieres
Torrecerredo
2648
Torrelavega
Barakaldo
Bilbao
Cape Finisterre (Cabo Fisterra)
Santiago de Compostela
Ordes
Melide
Lugo
Becerreá
ASTURIAS
△ 2412
Peña Ubiña
Cabañaquinta
Reinosa
Llodio
Vitoria-Gasteiz
Muros
Vilagarcía de Arousa
Santa Uxía de Ribeira
Lalín
Chantada
Sarria
GALICIA
Cordillera Cantábrica
San Andrés del Rabanedo
León
Aguilar de Campoo
Miranda de Ebro
Briviesca
Loga-
Pontevedra
Monforte de Lemos
Ponferrada
Astorga
Guardo
Saldaña
Ebro
Burgos
Nájera-
Marín
Cangas
Redondela
Vigo
Miño
Caniza
Xinzo de Limia
Barco
Verín
△ El Teleno 2188
Sierra de la Cabrera
Truchas
Benavente
Valencia de Don Juan
Palencia
Sahagún
Osorno
Lerma
Sierra de la Dem-
Tui
Tondevela
Braganca
Zamora
Medina de Rioseco
CASTILLA Y LEÓN
Valladolid
Duero
Aranda de Duero
Ayllón
Alma
Medin
Sigüenz
Viana do Castelo
Braga
Chaves
Macedo de Cavaleiros
Mirandela
Torre de Moncorvo
Pesmoselle
Toro
Tordesillas
Cuéllar
Cerezo de Abajo
Povoa de Varzim
Guimarães
Vila Real
Douro
Medina del Campo
Olmedo
Maia
Matosinhos
Oporto
Porto
Pedroso
Lamego
Ledesma
Salamanca
Tormes
Arévalo
Segovia
Peñafiel △ 2430
Guadalajara
Emb
Bur-
Vila Nova de Gaia
São João da Madeira
Ovar
Viseu
Meda
Lumbrales
Ciudad Rodrigo
Ávila
Sierra de Guadarrama
Alcalá de Henares
Aveiro
Ílhavo
Águeda
Mangualde
Vilar Formoso
Guarda
Peñaranda de Bracamonte
Mostoles
Fuenlabrada
Parla
MADRID
Getafe
Mealhada
Coimbra
Mondego
Torre 1993
Covilhã
Nuñomoral
Béjar
Sierra de Gredos
Figueira da Foz
Lousã
Serra da Estrela
Sabugal
Plasencia
Coria
Valle de Tiétar
Torrijos
Aranjuez
Ocaña
Tajo
Tarar-
Marinha Grande
Pombal
Castelo Branco
Navalmoral de la Mata
Talavera de la Reina
Tagus (Tajo)
Toledo
Batalha
Torres Novas
Tomar
Alcántara
Montes de Toledo
CASTILLA-LA MANCH
Leiria
Entroncamento
Abrantes
Cáceres
Trujillo
Herrera del Duque
Madridejos
Alcazar
San Juan
Peniche
Santarém
Ponte de Sôr
Portalegre
Campo Maior
EXTREMADURA
Miajadas
Navalvillar de Pela
Ciudad Real
Socuéllamos
Villarroble
Torres Vedras
Coruche
Estremoz
Elvas
Mérida
Don Benito
Villanueva de la Serena
Almadén
Daimiel
Manzanares
Vila Franca de Xira
Amadora
LISBON
Cacém
(Lisboa)
Montijo
Badajoz
Cabeza del Buey
Hinojosa del Duque
Jabalón
Valdepeñas
Cascais
Almada
Redondo
Olivenza
Zafra
Almendralejo
Los Pedroches
Pozoblanco
Puertollano
Villanueva de los Infantes
Cabo Espichel
Setúbal
Alcácer do Sal
Évora
Barragem de Alqueva
Fregenal de la Sierra
Peñarroya-Pueblonuevo
Linares
Baía de Setúbal
Torrão
Amareleja
Azuaga
Sierra Morena
Córdoba
Andújar
Baeza
Úbeda
Sines
Cabo de Sines
Grândola
Beja
Moura
Rosal de la Frontera
Constantina
Palma del Río
Guadalquivir
Jaén
Baza
Aljustrel
Castro Verde
Serpa
Cortegana
Martos
Alcaudete
Priego de Córdoba
Sierra de E
Odemira
Mértola
Valverde del Camino
Écija
Lucena
Cabra
Alcalá la Real
Baza
Aljezur
Almodôvar
Guadiana
Seville (Sevilla)
Carmona
Marchena
Osuna
Loja
Granada
Guadix
Mulhacén △ 3482
Alm-
Cabo de São Vicente
Sagres
ALGARVE
Portimão
Loulé
Huelva
Almonte
Coria del Río
Utrera
Puente-Genil
Antequera
Vélez-Málaga
Motril
Albufeira
Tavira
Ayamonte
Lagos
Faro
Santa Maria
Playa de Castilla
Las Marismas
Lebrija
Morón de la Frontera
ANDALUCÍA
Ronda
Málaga
Almuñécar
Adra
Sanlúcar de Barrameda
El Puerto de Santa María
Arcos de la Frontera
Torremolinos
Costa del Sol
Golf Alm
Costa de la Luz
Cádiz
San Fernando
Jerez de la Frontera
Chiclana de la Frontera
Marbella
Estepona
Golfo de Cádiz
Vejer de la Frontera
Barbate de Franco
La Línea de la Concepción
Algeciras
Gibraltar (U.K.)
Cabo Trafalgar
Strait of Gibraltar
Pta Almina
Tangier (Tanger)
Ceuta (Spain)
Cabo Negro
Cap des Trois Fourches
Asilah
Tétouan
MOROCCO

PORTUGAL
SPAIN

A 10° B 5°

Conic Equidistant Projection

1 : 6 000 000

MILES 0   50   100   150

METRES / FEET

METRES	FEET
5000	16404
3000	9843
2000	6562
1000	3281
500	1640
200	656
0	0
Land below sea level	
200	656
4000	13124
6000	19686

METRES / FEET

5000 / 16404
3000 / 9843
2000 / 6562
1000 / 3281
500 / 1640
200 / 656
0 / 0
Land below sea level
200 / 656
4000 / 13124
6000 / 19686

Conic Equidistant Projection

1 : 6 000 000

Longitude 10° east of Greenwich

MILES 0   50   100   150

A L P S

F R A N C E

Corsica (Corse) (France)

Sardinia (Sardegna) (Italy)

I T A L Y

A p e n n i n e s

SAN MARINO

MONACO

VATICAN CITY

ROME (Roma)

Naples (Napoli)

Genoa (Genova)

Milano

Turin (Torino)

Venice (Venezia)

SLOVENIA

LJUBLJANA

Trieste

Sicily (Sicilia)

Palermo

ALGERIA

TUNISIA

L i g u r i a n Sea

Gulf of Genoa

T Y R R H E N I A N SEA

M E D I T E R R A N E A N   S E A

Sicilian Channel

Côte d'Azur

A D R I A T I C

Gulf of Venice

Bolzano, Brennero, Vipiteno, Bressanone, Merano, Adige, Dolomites, Cortina d'Ampezzo, Tolmezzo, Gemona del Friuli, Cividale del Friuli, Udine, Gorizia, Monfalcone, Tolmin, Logatec, Koper, Rijeka, Pazin, Poreč, Rovinj, Pula, Istria, Cres, Lošinj

Trento, Belluno, Feltre, Vittorio Veneto, Pordenone, Conegliano, Treviso, Vicenza, Padua (Padova), Rovigo, Chioggia, Porto Tolle, Comacchio, Ravenna, Rimini, Pesaro, Fano, Senigallia, Ancona

Sondrio, Tirano, Chiavenna, Bellinzona, Lugano, Lake Como, Lecco, Bergamo, Brescia, Verona, Legnago, Mantua (Mantova), Ferrara, Modena, Bologna, Imola, Faenza, Forlì, Cesena, Cesenatico

Aosta, Mont Blanc 4807, Chamonix, Martigny, Verbania, Lake Maggiore, Varese, Como, Monza, Milano, Lodi, Crema, Cremona, Piacenza, Parma, Reggio nell'Emilia

Annecy, Albertville, Chambéry, Grenoble, Voiron, Modane, Susa, Rivoli, Turin (Torino), Moncalieri, Asti, Alessandria, Tortona, Novi Ligure, Acqui Terme

Briançon, Gap, St-Bonnet-en-Champsaur, Embrun, Barcelonnette, Cuneo, Mondovì, Alba, Fossano, Saluzzo, Pinerolo

Digne-les-Bains, Castellane, Draguignan, Grasse, Cannes, Nice, MONTE-CARLO, Ventimiglia, San Remo, Imperia, Albenga, Savona, Genoa (Genova)

Toulon, Hyères, Îles d'Hyères, Cap Sicié, St-Tropez, Cap de St-Tropez, Fréjus, St-Raphael, Antibes, Cap Corse

La Spezia, Massa, Carrara, Monte Cimone 2165, Pistoia, Prato, Florence (Firenze), Lucca, Pisa, Viareggio, Livorno, Empoli, Arno, Siena, Arezzo, Perugia, Assisi, Foligno

Isola di Capraia, Isola d'Elba, Portoferraio, Piombino, Follonica, Grosseto, Orbetello, Arcipelago Toscano, Isola di Montecristo

Corsica (Corse), Bastia, L'Île-Rousse, St-Florent, Calvi, Monte Cinto 2706, Vescovato, Corte, Cervione, Capo Rosso, Ajaccio, Olmeto, Sartène, Bonifacio, Porto-Vecchio, Propriano

Strait of Bonifacio, Isola Asinara, Punta Caprara, Santa Teresa Gallura, La Maddalena, Arzachena, Olbia, Porto Torres, Sassari, Alghero, Capo Caccia, Ploaghe, Oschiri, Budoni, Orosei, Golfo di Orosei, Nuoro, Macomer, Bonorva, Siniscola

Oristano, Abbasanta, Punta La Marmora 1834, Laconi, Tortolì, Mandas, Capo di Monte Santu, Capo Comino, Capo della Frasca, Guspini, Monte Linas 1236, San Gavino Monreale, Serramanna, Villaputzu, Iglesias, Assemini, Cagliari, Quartu Sant'Elena, Portoscuso, Isola di San Pietro, Isola di Sant'Antioco, Sant'Antioco, Pula, Golfo di Cagliari, Capo Carbonara, Capo Spartivento

Viterbo, Civitavecchia, Tarquinia, Lago di Bolsena, Orvieto, Todi, Terni, Narni, Rieti, L'Aquila, Monte Corno 2912, Teramo, Ascoli Piceno, Fermo, Macerata, Civitanova Marche

Guidonia Montecelio, Tivoli, Avezzano, Monte Amaro 2793, Sulmona, Chieti, Pescara, Frosinone, Sora, Cassino, Latina, Aprilia, Anzio, Pomezia, Velletri, Sabaudia, Gaeta, Golfo di Gaeta, Isole Ponziane, Naples (Napoli), Pozzuoli, Sorrento, Isola d'Ischia, Isola di Capri

Isola di Ustica, Isole Lipari, Isola Filicudi, Isola Salina, Capo San Vito, Monte Sparagio, Trapani, Partinico, Palermo, Cefalù, Termini Imerese, Leonforte, Marsala, Alcamo, Rocca Busambra 1613, Mazara del Vallo, Partanna, Castelvetrano, Castellammare, Sciacca, Canicattì, Caltanissetta, Agrigento, Caltagirone, Licata, Niscemi, Gela, Golfo di Gela

Isola Marettimo, Capo Granitola, La Galite, Collo, Cap de Fer, Chetaïbi, Skikda, Annaba, Cap de Garde, El Tarf, El Kala, Tabarka, Cap Bon, Golfe de Tunis, Bizerte, Rass Jebel, Menzel Bourguiba, Mateur, Nefza, Jedeida, Azzaba, El Hadjar

0   100   200 KILOMETRES

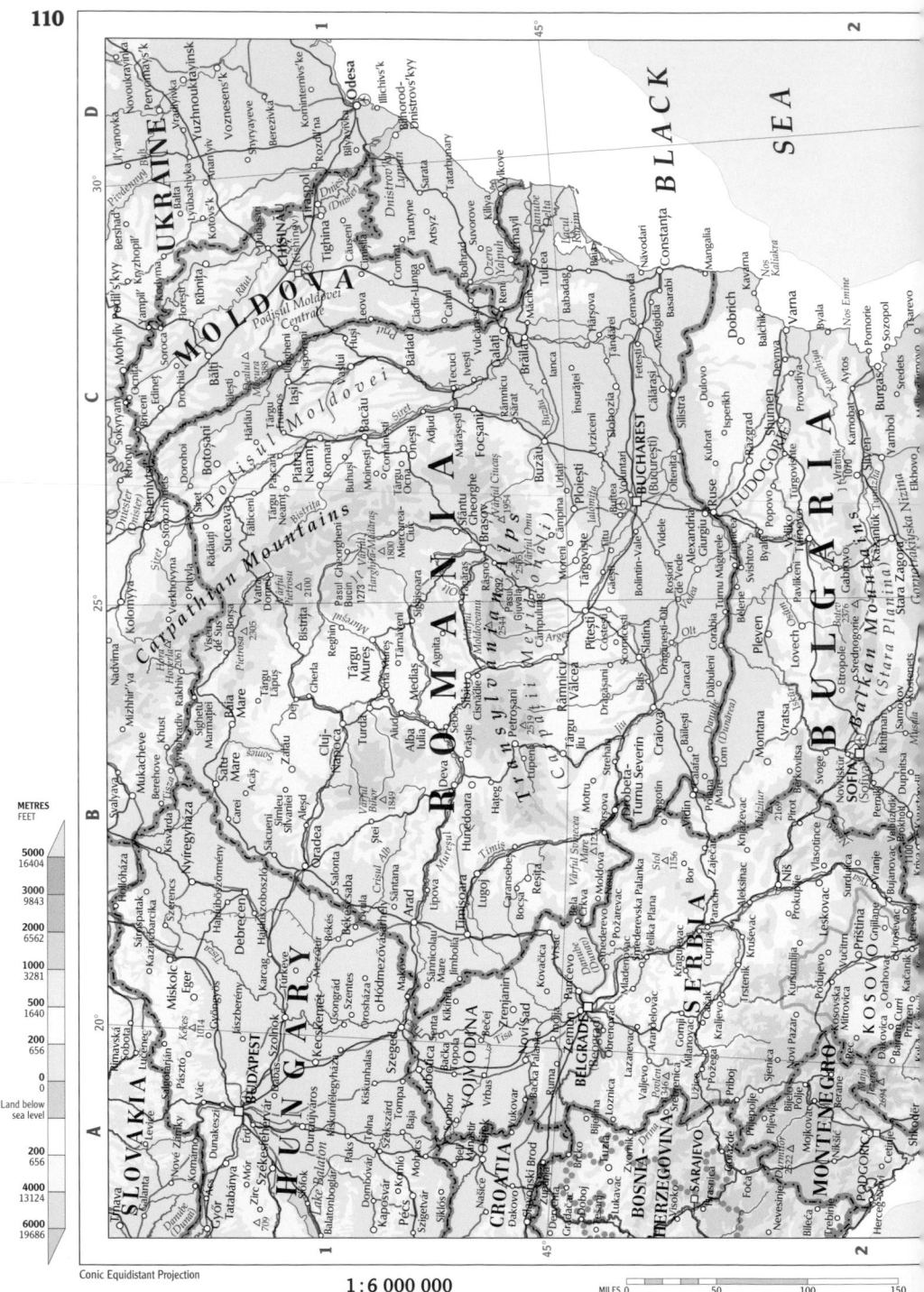

METRES
FEET

5000 | 16404
3000 | 9843
2000 | 6562
1000 | 3281
500 | 1640
200 | 656
0 | 0
Land below
sea level
200 | 656
4000 | 13124
6000 | 19686

Conic Equidistant Projection

1 : 6 000 000

MILES 0   50   100   150

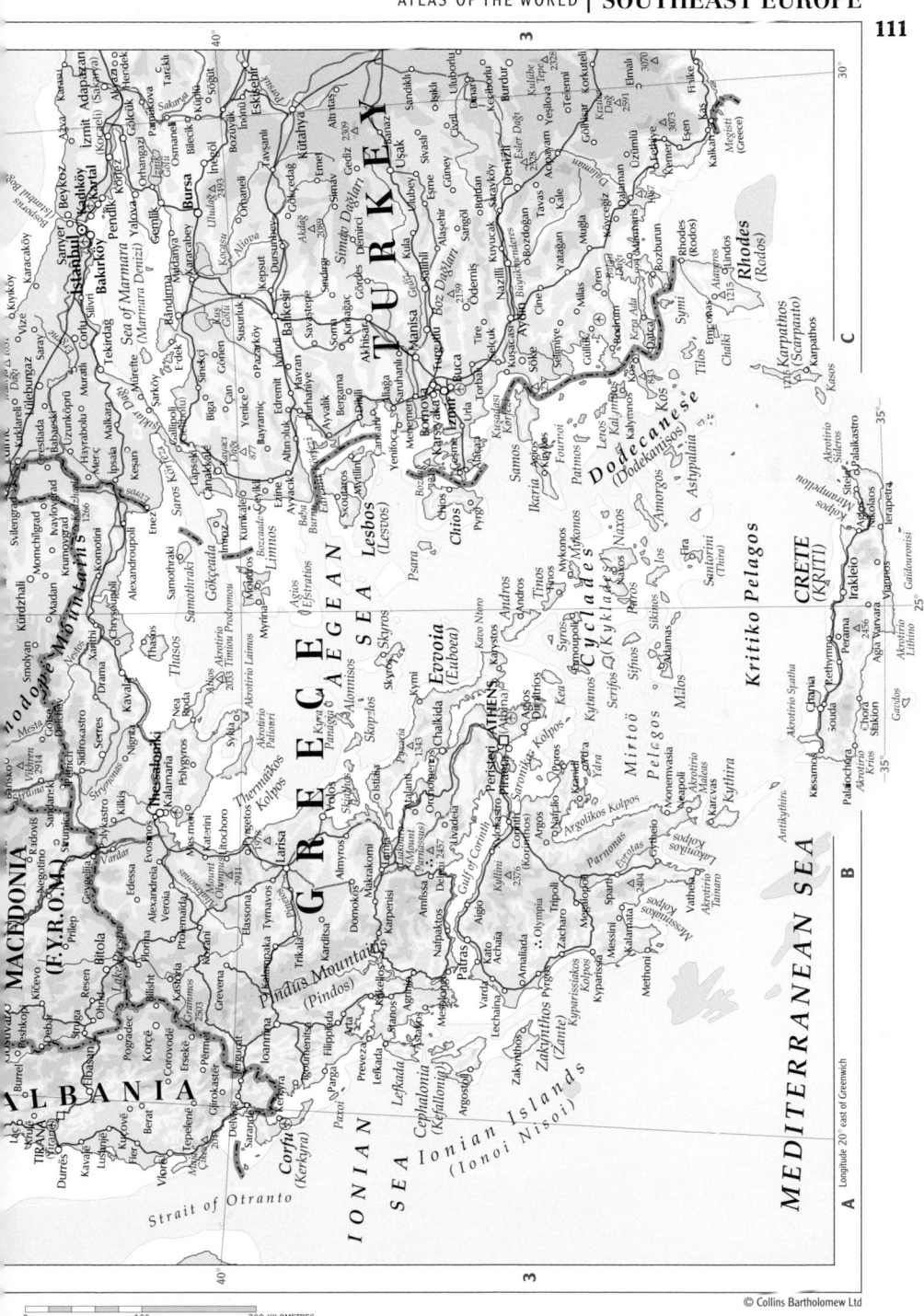

0   100   200 KILOMETRES

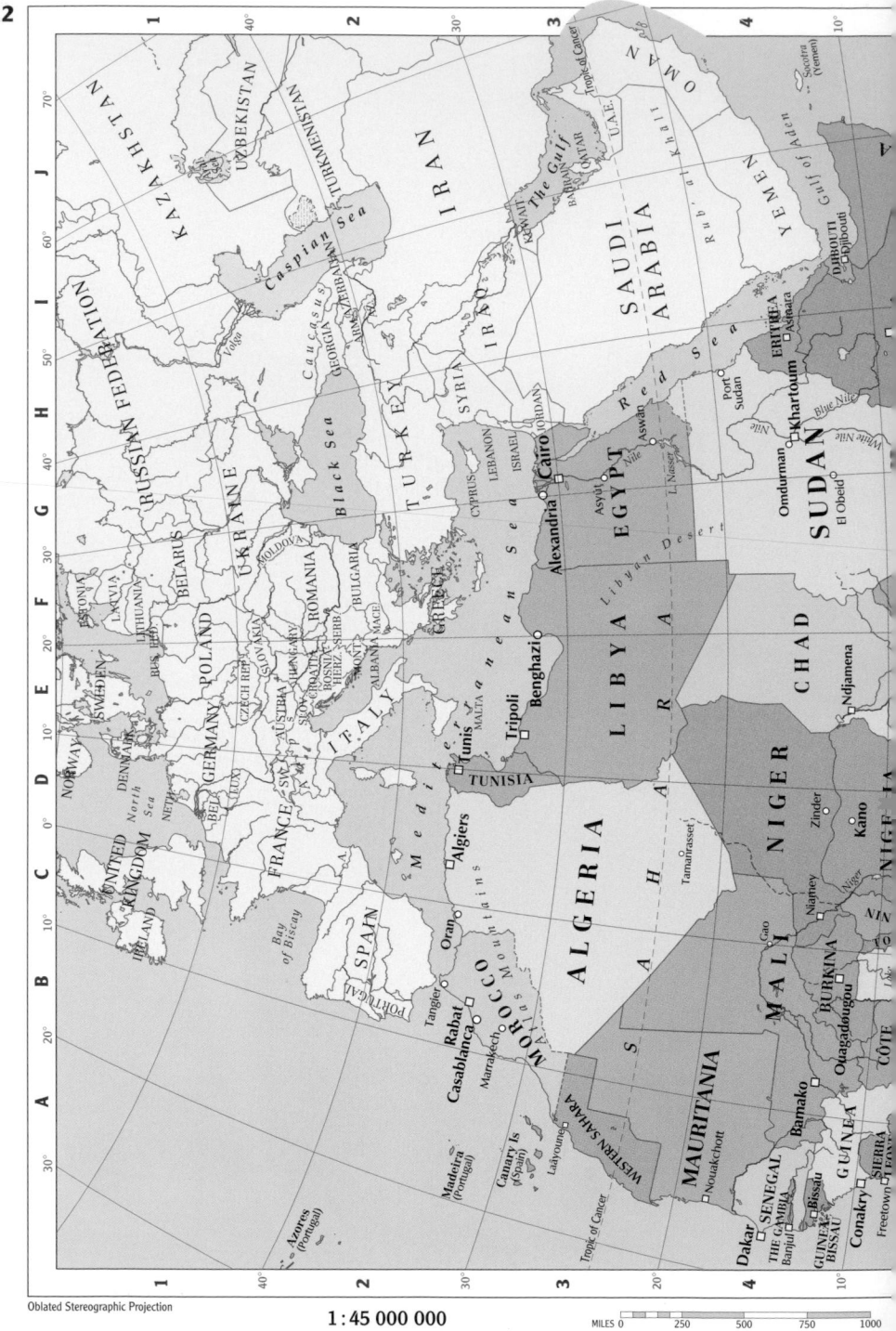

Oblated Stereographic Projection

1 : 45 000 000

MILES 0   250   500   750   1000

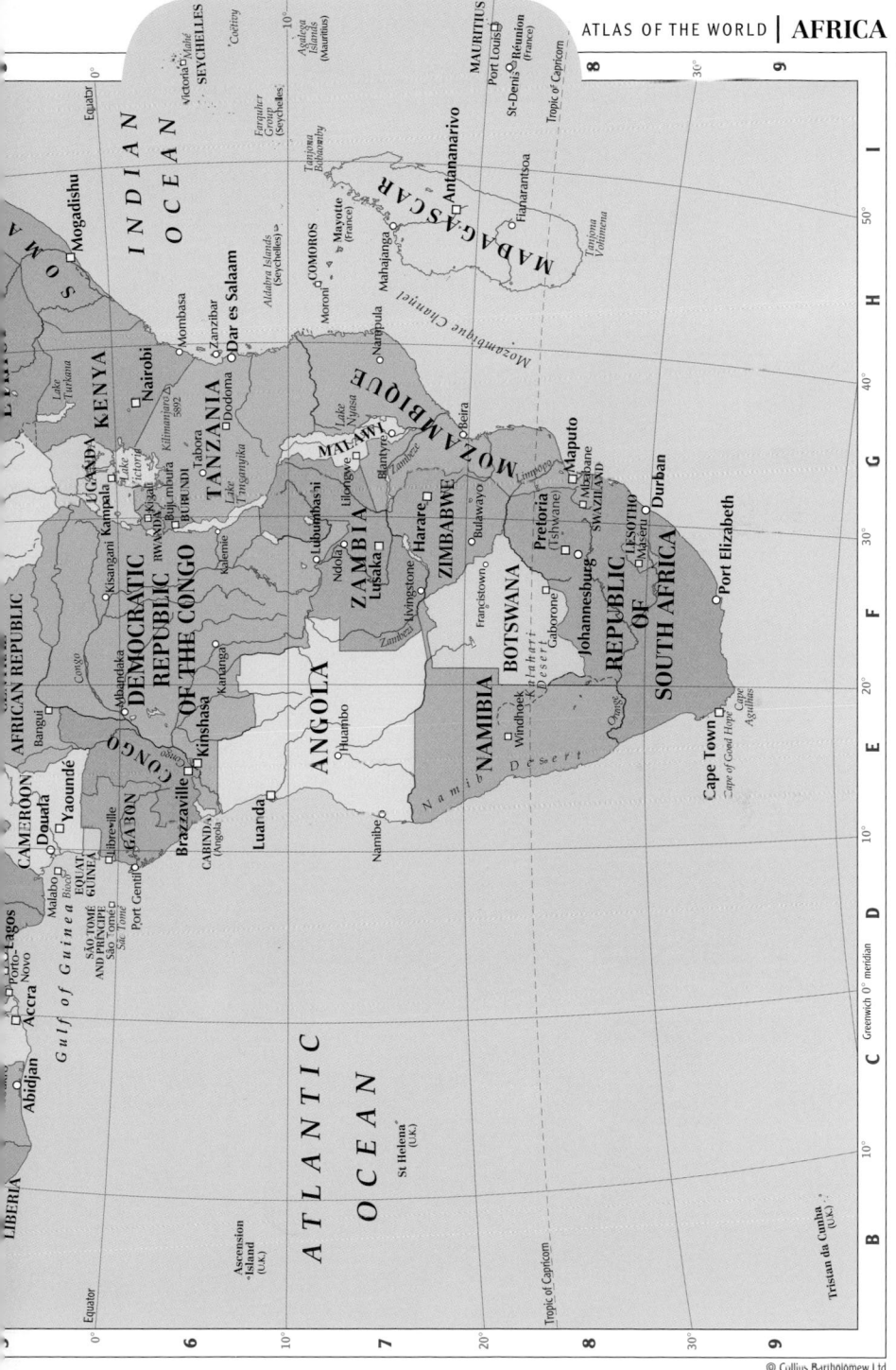

0   500   1000   1500 KILOMETRES

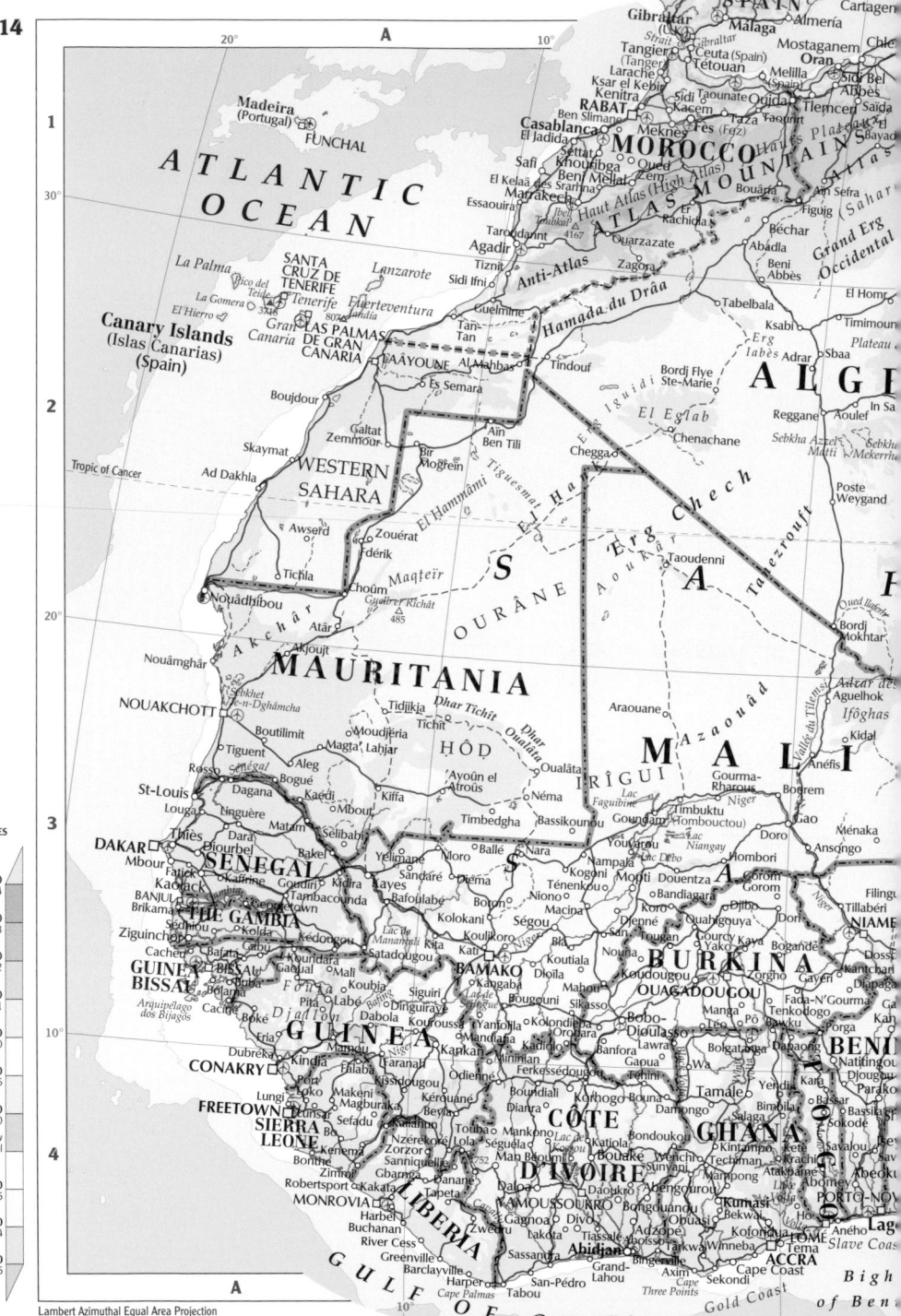

A

| 20° | A | 10° |

SPAIN Cartagen

Gibraltar Málaga Almería
Tangier Ceuta (Spain) Mostaganem Oran Chle
Larache Tétouan Melilla Sidi Bel
Ksar el Kebir Taounate Oujda Tlemcen Saïda
RABAT Sidi Taourirt Taourirt
Kenitra Slimane Fès (Fez) Figuig
Casablanca Meknès El Bayad
El Jadida Settat Oued Zem
Safi Khouribga Beni Mellal **MOROCCO** Béni
Essaouira Marrakech Haut Atlas (High Atlas) Abbès
ATLANTIC Taroudannt 4167 Ouarzazate Ar-Rachidia Béchar
Agadir Anti-Atlas Zagora Grand Erg
OCEAN Tiznit Hamada du Drâa Tabelbala Occidental
Madeira Sidi Ifni Guelmine El Homr
(Portugal) FUNCHAL Tan-Tan Timimoun
ALGI
Lanzarote Es Semara Tindouf Bordj Flye
SANTA Fuerteventura Ste-Marie Reggane Aoulet In Sa
CRUZ DE Guelta Zemmour Chenachane Sebkha Azzel Sebkh
La Palma TENERIFE Ain Ben Tili Mati Mekerrh
Pico del Tenerife Bir Chegga Poste
Teide LAS PALMAS Mogrein Erg Chech Weygand
Canary Islands Gran DE GRAN Tiguesmat
(Islas Canarias) Canaria CANARIA WESTERN Erg Iguidi El Eglab
(Spain) Boujdour SAHARA Taoudenni
Tropic of Cancer El Hammâmi Bordj
Awserd Zouérat Mokhtar
Ad Dakhla Tichla Fdérik Aguelhok
Nouâdhibou Choûm Taezrouft Ifôghas
Atâr Guelb er Richât Araouane Azaouâd Kidal
Nouâmghâr Akjoujt 485 OURÂNE **MALI** Nénfis
NOUAKCHOTT **MAURITANIA**
Boutilimit Tidjikja Dhar Tichît Dhar Araouane Gourma-
Moudjéria Tichit Oualâta Rharous Bourem
Tiguent Magta Lahjar HÔD IRÎGUI Timbuktu Gao
St-Louis Aleg Ayoûn el Néma (Tombouctou) Ménaka
Rosso Bogué Atroûs Timbedgha Gourma Ansongo
Dagana Kaédi Kiffa Bassikounou Gao
DAKAR Matam Nioro Nara Mopti Hombori Filingu
Mbour Linguère Sélibabi Yélimané Balé Kogoni Douentza **NIAME**
Fatick Dara Bakel Sandaré Diéma Bandiagara Djibo
Kaolack Goudiri Niono Koro Ouahigouya Dori
SENEGAL Tambacounda Ségou Macina Djenné **BURKINA** Gaya **NIAME**
BANJUL Kédougou Kolokani Nouna Gourcy Yako Bogandé Dossi
Brikama Kolda Kita Koutiala Sikasso **OUAGADOUGOU** Fada-N'Gourma Diapa
THE GAMBIA Mali Dioila Bobo- Zorgho **BENI**
Ziguinchor Koubia Siguiri Dinguiraye Kolondiéba Dioulasso Manga Po Tenkodogo Natitingou
GUINEA Labé Kouroussa Orodara Banfora Lawra Wa Diougou
BISSAU Pita Dabola Mamou Kankan Odienné Ferkessédougou Tehini Bolgatanga Parako
GUINEA Dubréka Kindia Kissidougou Beyla Boundiali Korhogo Bouna Tamale Yendi
CONAKRY Nzérékoré Lola Séguéla Katiola **GHANA**
Lungi Makeni Macenta Man Bouaké Wenchi Techiman **PORTO-NO**
FREETOWN Magburaka Danané **CÔTE** Bondoukou Kumasi **LOMÉ**
SIERRA Kenema Sanniquellie **D'IVOIRE** Abengourou Obuasi **ACCRA**
LEONE Zimmi Tapeta Gagnoa **YAMOUSSOUKRO** Grand- Cape Coast
MONROVIA Harbel Zwedru Bongouanou Lahou Sekondi Big
Buchanan Takota Abidjan of Ben
River Cess **LIBERIA** Sassandra
Greenville San-Pédro Cape
Barclayville Grand- Three Points Gold Coast
Harper Cape Palmas Tabou Lahou

A
10°

GULF OF GUINEA

METRES
FEET

5000
16404

3000
9843

2000
6562

1000
3281

500
1640

200
656

0
0

Land below
sea level

200
656

4000
13124

6000
19686

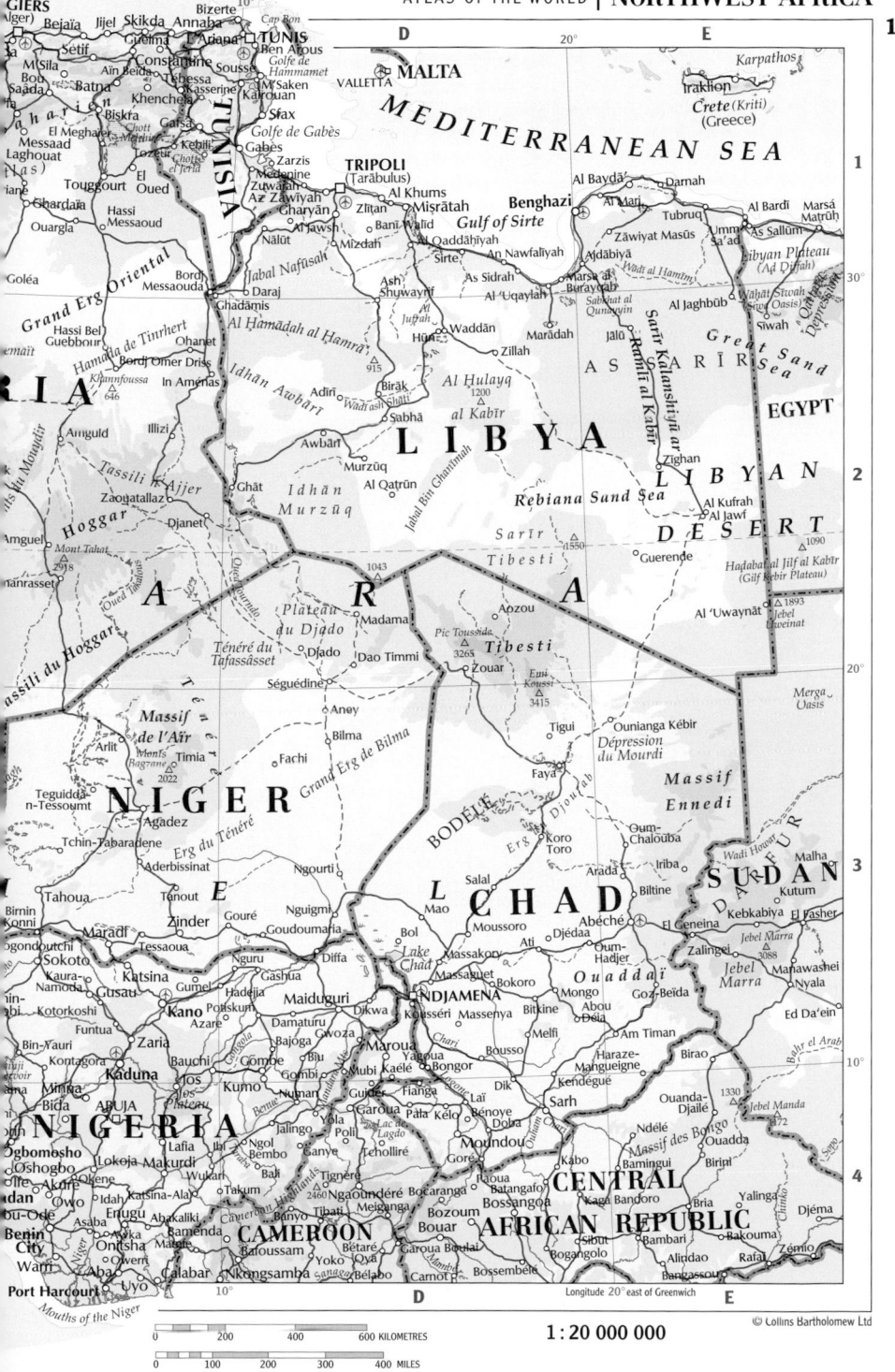

MEDITERRANEAN SEA

LIBYA

LIBYAN DESERT

EGYPT

S A H A R A

NIGER

CHAD

SUDAN

NIGERIA

CAMEROON

CENTRAL AFRICAN REPUBLIC

TRIPOLI
(Tarābulus)

Benghazi

VALLETTA

MALTA

TUNIS

Crete (Kriti)
(Greece)

Karpathos

Iraklion

NDJAMENA

ABUJA

Longitude 20° east of Greenwich

© Collins Bartholomew Ltd

0   200   400   600 KILOMETRES

0   100   200   300   400 MILES

1 : 20 000 000

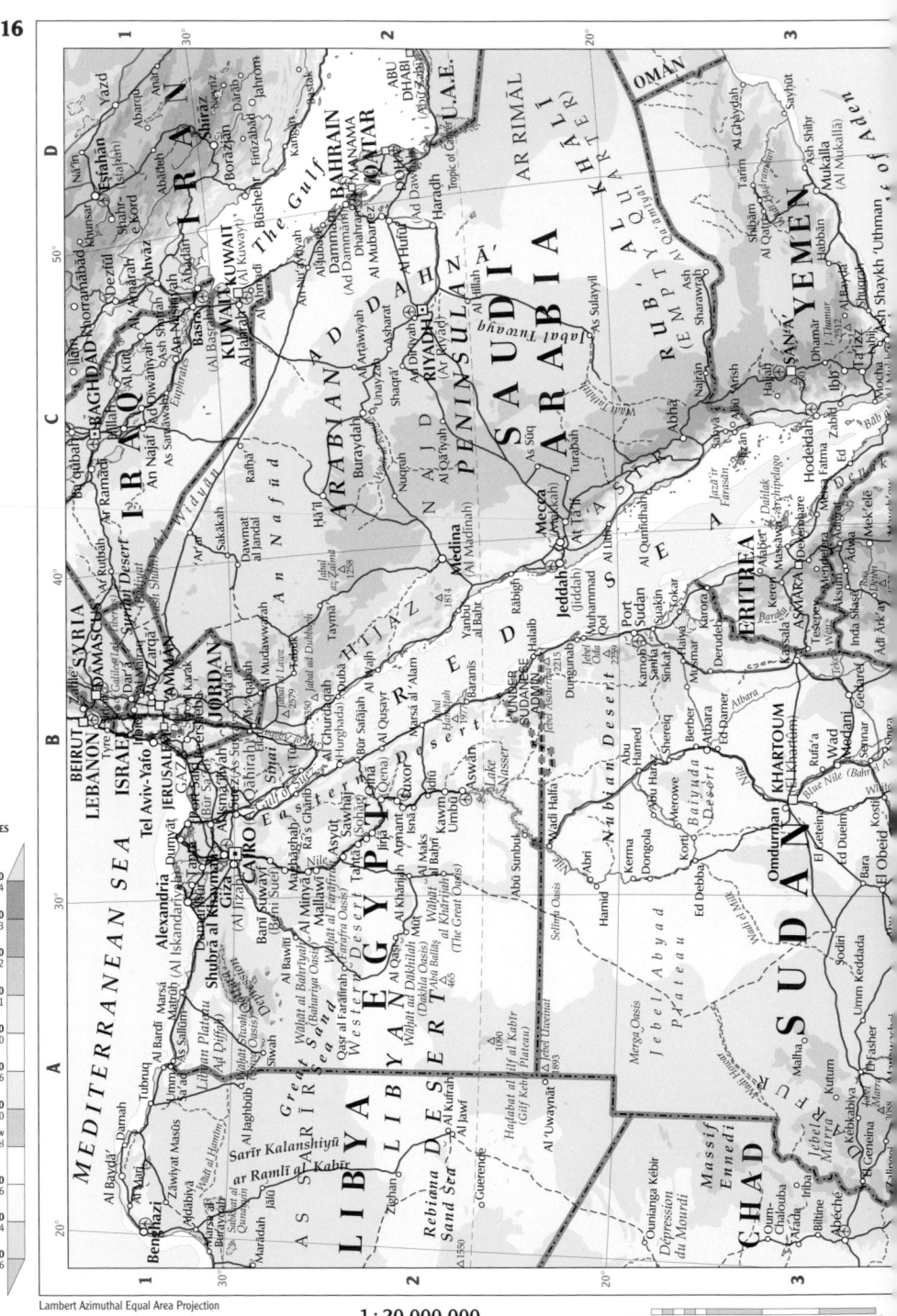

METRES
FEET

5000 16404
3000 9843
2000 6562
1000 3281
500 1640
200 656
0 0
Land below
sea level
200 656
4000 13124
6000 19686

Lambert Azimuthal Equal Area Projection

1 : 20 000 000

MILES 0   100   200   300   400

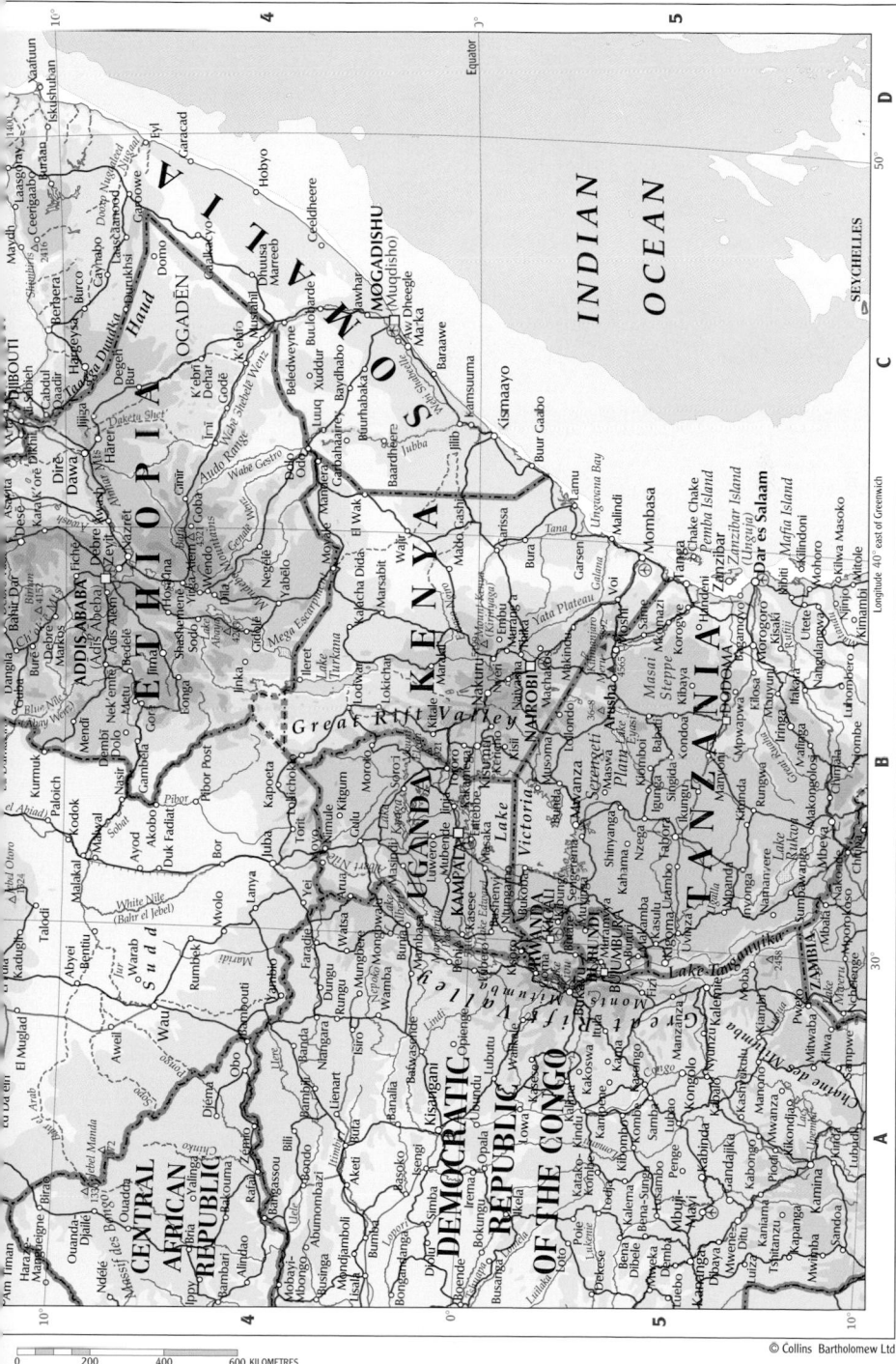

INDIAN

OCEAN

SEYCHELLES

ETHIOPIA

SOMALIA

OGADEN

Haud

DJIBOUTI

ADDIS ABABA

KENYA

NAIROBI

Great Rift Valley

UGANDA

KAMPALA

Lake Victoria

TANZANIA

Dar es Salaam

Zanzibar Island
(Unguja)

Pemba Island

Mombasa

RWANDA

KIGALI

BURUNDI

BUJUMBURA

Lake Tanganyika

DEMOCRATIC

REPUBLIC

OF THE CONGO

CENTRAL

AFRICAN

REPUBLIC

ZAMBIA

White Nile
(Bahr el Jebel)

Blue Nile
(Abay Wenz)

Sudd

Equator

MOGADISHU
(Muqdisho)

Longitude 40° east of Greenwich

© Collins Bartholomew Ltd

0   200   400   600 KILOMETRES

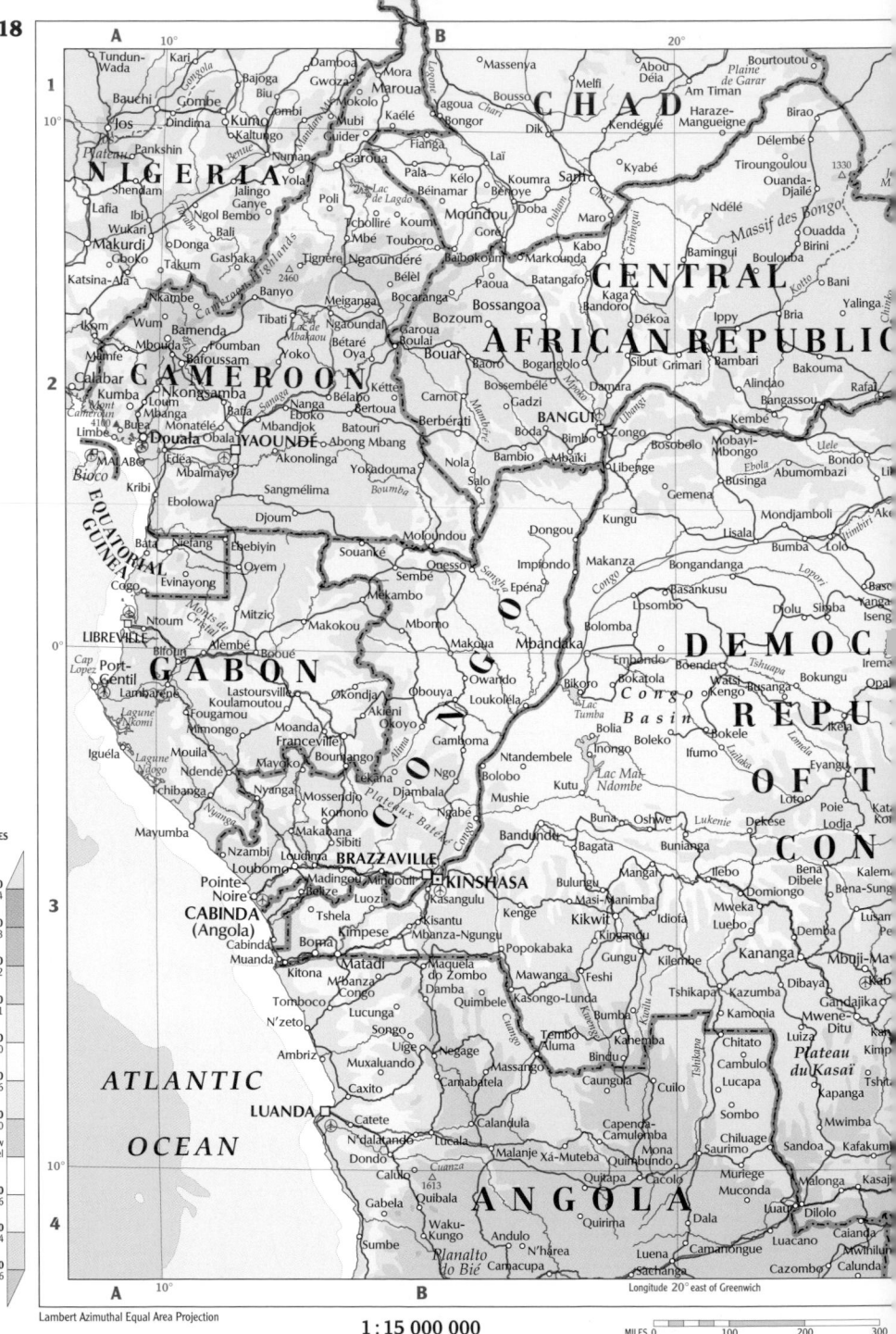

A 10°   **B**   20°

1

NIGERIA

CAMEROON

CHAD

CENTRAL

AFRICAN REPUBLIC

2

BANGUI

EQUATORIAL
GUINEA

LIBREVILLE

GABON

DEMOC

REPU

C O N G O

OF T

CON

BRAZZAVILLE

KINSHASA

3

CABINDA
(Angola)

ATLANTIC

OCEAN

LUANDA

ANGOLA

4

A 10°   **B**   Longitude 20° east of Greenwich

METRES
FEET

5000	16404
3000	9843
2000	6562
1000	3281
500	1640
200	656
0	0

Land below
sea level

200	656
4000	13124
6000	19686

Lambert Azimuthal Equal Area Projection

1 : 15 000 000

MILES 0   100   200   300

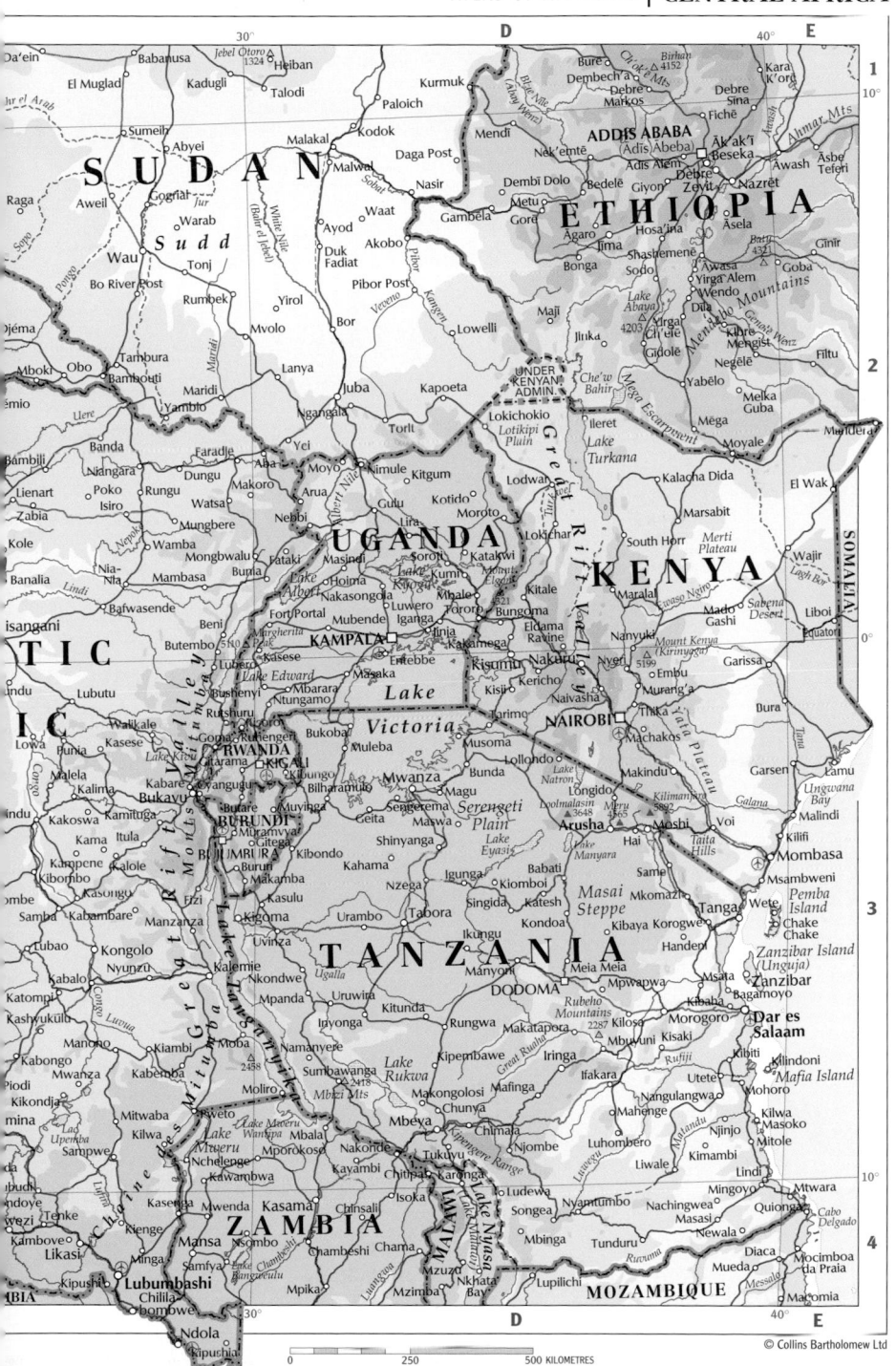

0   250   500 KILOMETRES

© Collins Bartholomew Ltd

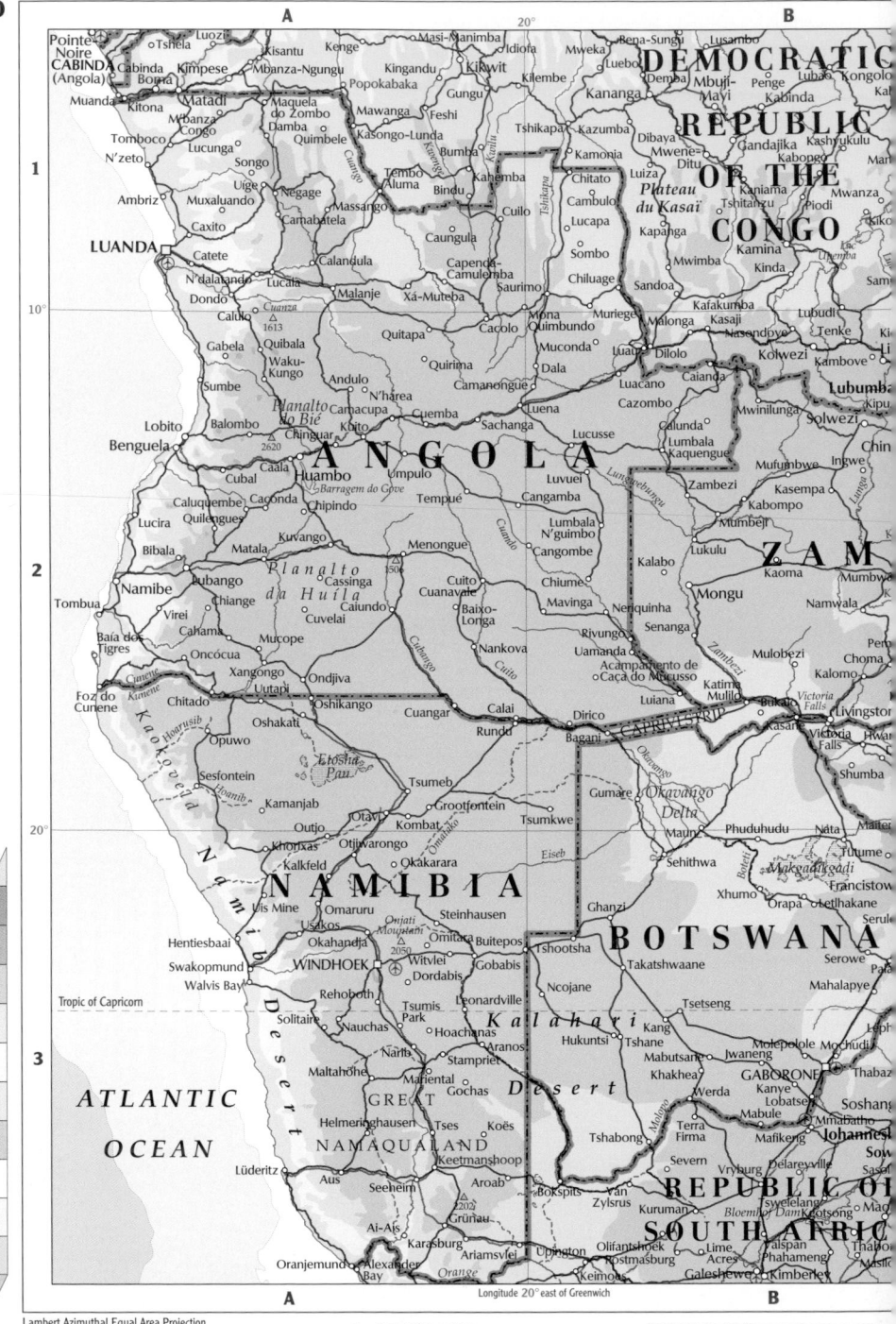

A — 20° — B

DEMOCRATIC
REPUBLIC
OF THE
CONGO

Pointe-
Noire
CABINDA
(Angola) Cabinda
Boma
Muanda
Kitona
Tombouco
N'zeto
Ambriz
Muxaluando
Caxito
LUANDA Catete
N'dalatando Lucala
Dondo
Calulo
Gabela Quibala
Waku-
Kungo
Sumbe Andulo
N'harea
Camacupa
Lobito Balombo
Benguela Chinguar
Cubal Huambo
Caala
Caluquembe Caconda
Quilengues Chipindo
Lucira
Bibala Matala
Namibe Lubango
Chiange
Cahama
Mucope
Oncócua
Tombua Virei
Baía dos
Tigres
Foz do
Cunene
Chitado

Tshela Luozi
Kisantu Kenge
Masi-Manimba
Idiofa
Mweka Tuebo
Bena-Sungu Lusambo
Cabinda Kimpese Mbanza-Ngungu Kingandu Kikwit Kilembe Demba Mbuji-Mayi Penge Lubao Kongolo
Popokabaka Gungu Kananga Kabinda
Maquela do Zombo Mawanga Feshi Tshikapa Kazumba Dibaya Mwene-Ditu Gandajika Kashyukulu
Damba Quimbele Kasongo-Lunda Bumba Kamonia Kabongo
Lucunga Songo Tembo- Aluma Bindu Kahemba Chitato Kaniama Tshitangu Piodi Kiko
Uige Negage Massango Cuilo Cambulo Plateau du Kasaï Kapanga Kamina Kinda
Muxaluando Camabatela Caungula Capenda- Camulemba Saurimo Chiluage Sombo Mwimba Kafakumba
Calandula Xá-Muteba Cacolo Mona Quimbundo Sandoa Lubudi
Malanje Quitapa Quirima Muconda Luau Dilolo Kolwezi Tenke
Dala Luacano Caianda Kolwezi Kambove **Lubumba**
Camanongue Luena Cazombo Mwinilunga Solwezi Kipu
Cuemba Sachanga Lucusse Calunda Lumbala Kaquengue Mufumbwe Ingwe **Chin**
Umpulo Luvuei Zambezi Kabompo Kasempa
Tempué Cangamba Lumbala N'guimbo Mumbeji **ZAM**
Kuvango Menongue Cangombe Kalabo Lukulu Kaoma Mumbwe
Cuito Chiume Mongu Namwala
Cassinga Cuanavale Mavinga Neriquinha Senanga Mulobezi Choma
Caiundo Baixo-Longa Rivungo Uamanda Kalomo
Cuvelai Nankova Acampamento de Caça do Mucusso Katima Mulilo Victoria Falls Livingstone
Xangongo Ondjiva Luiana Bukalo Victoria Falls Hwange
Uutapi Oshikango Cuangar Calai Dirico Bagani Shumba

Land below
sea level

ATLANTIC

OCEAN

Lüderitz

Oranjemund Alexander Bay

Chitado
Opuwo
Sesfontein
Kamanjab
Outjo
Khorixas Otjiwarongo
Kalkfeld
Otjosondu Mine Omaruru
Hentiesbaai Okahandja
Swakopmund **WINDHOEK**
Walvis Bay Rehoboth
Solitaire Nauchas
Naris
Maltahöhe Mariental
Helmeringhausen Gochas
Tses
Aus Keetmanshoop
Seeheim Aroab
Ai-Ais Grünau
Karasburg Ariamsvlei

Oshakati Rundu
Etosha Pan
Tsumeb
Grootfontein Tsumkwe
Otavi Gumare Okavango Delta
Kombat Maun Phuduhudu Nata Maitengue
Steinhausen Sehithwa Makgadikgadi Tutume
Omaruru Ghanzi Xhumo Orapa Letlhakane Francistown
Witvlei Buitepos Tshootsha **BOTSWANA** Serowe
Gobabis Takatshwaane Mahalapye
Dordabis Ncojane Tsetseng
Leonardville Kang Molepolole Mochudi
Tsumis Park Hoachanas Hukuntsi Tshane Mabutsane Jwaneng **GABORONE**
Stampriet Khakhea Werda Kanye Lobatse
Koës Mabule
Tshabong Terra Firma Mmabatho Mafikeng **Johannes**
Bokspits Van Zylsrus Kuruman Vryburg Delareyville **SOW**
Upington Olifantshoek Lime Acres **REPUBLIC OF**
Keimoes Postmasburg Galeshewe Kimberley **SOUTH AFRIC**

ANGOLA

NAMIBIA

Kalahari

Desert

Great

NAMAQUALAND

Longitude 20° east of Greenwich

METRES
FEET

5000
16404

3000
9843

2000
6562

1000
3281

500
1640

200
656

0
0

Land below
sea level

200
656

4000
13124

6000
19686

Tropic of Capricorn

Lambert Azimuthal Equal Area Projection

1 : 15 000 000

MILES 0   100   200   300

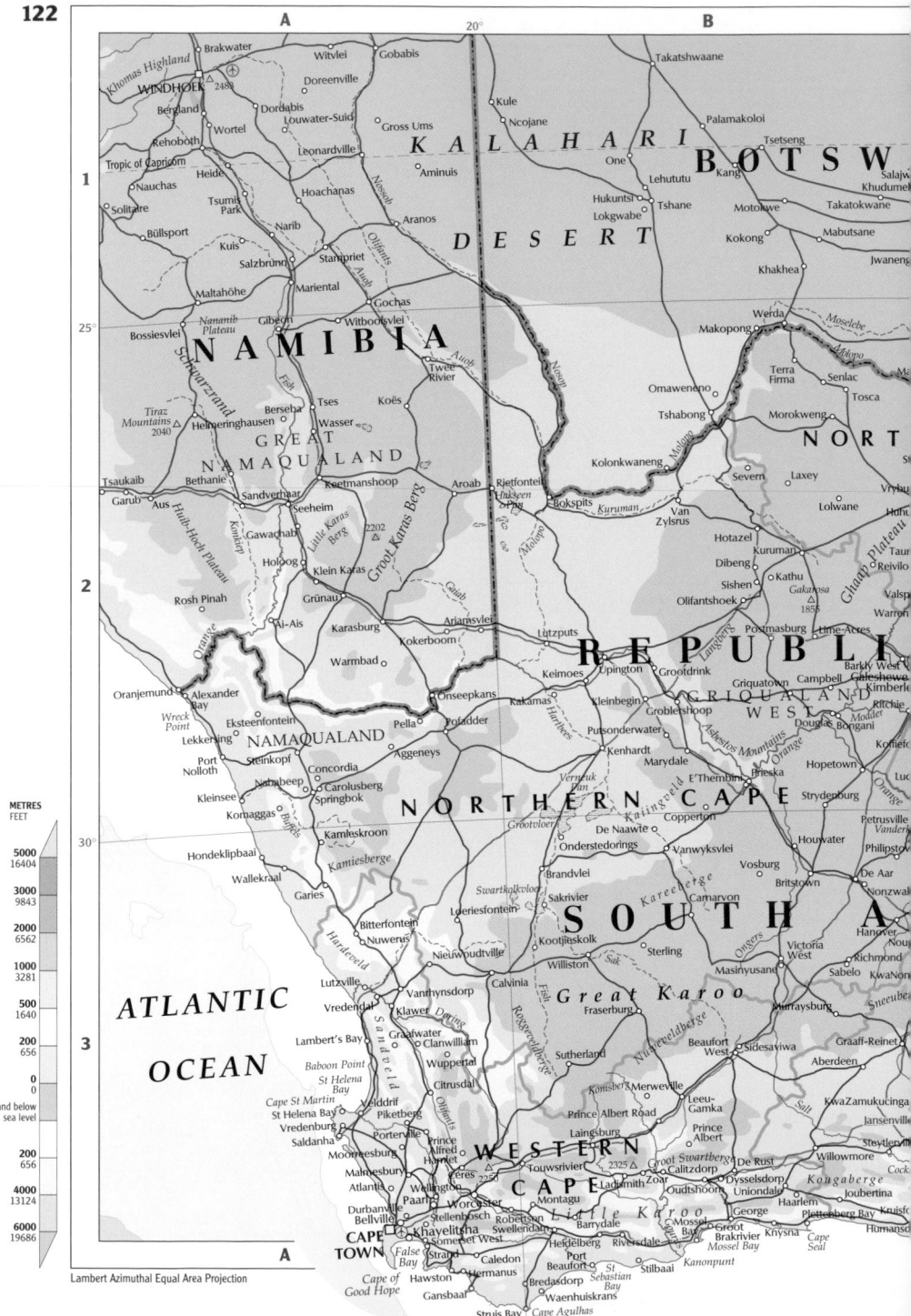

A   20°   **B**

Brakwater
Witvlei
Gobabis
Takatshwaane
Khomas Highland
WINDHOEK △2489
Bergland
Doreenville
Kule
Palamakoloi
Dordabis
Louwater-Suid
Ncojane
Tsetseng
Rehoboth
Wortel
Gross Ums
One
Lehututu
Kang
Khudumel
Tropic of Capricorn
Heide
Leonardville
Aminuis
Hukuntsi
Tshane
Motokwe
Takatokwane
Nauchas
Tsumis Park
Hoachanas
Lokgwabe
Solitaire
Narib
Aranos
Kokong
Mabutsane
Büllsport
Kuis
Salzbrunn
Stampriet
Khakhea
Jwaneng
Maltahöhe
Mariental
Gochas

K A L A H A R I
B O T S W
D E S E R T
N O R T

Namanib Plateau
Gibeon
Witbooisvlei
Werda
Bossiesvlei
Makopong
Moselebe
Schwarzrand
Twee Rivier
Omaweneno
Terra Firma
Senlac
Tosca
Berseba
Tses
Koës
Tshabong
Morokweng
Heinrichshausen
Wasser
Tiras Mountains 2040
G R E A T
N A M A Q U A L A N D
Kolonkwaneng
Severn
Laxey
Vryb
Tsaukaib
Bethanie
Sandverhaar
Aroab
Rietfontein
Bokspits
Kuruman
Lolwane
Hun
Garub
Aus
Seeheim
Van Zylsrus
Hotazel
Gawachab
Little Karas Berg
2202
Dibeng
Kuruman
Reivilo
Valsp
Hoboog
Klein Karas
Groot Karas Berg
Sishen
Olifantshoek
Kathu
Warren
Rosh Pinah
Grünau
Ariamsvlei
Lutzputs
Postmasburg
Lime Acres
Karasburg
Kokerboom
Keimoes
Upington
Grootdrink
Griquatown
Campbell
Barkly West
Kimberl
Warmbad
R E P U B L I
Oranjemund
Alexander Bay
Onseepkans
Kakamas
Kleinbegin
Groblershoop
G R I Q U A L A N D
Douglas
Koffiefo
Wreck Point
Eksteenfontein
Pella
Pofadder
Hartbees
Putsonderwater
W E S T
Ritchie
Bongani
Lekkersing
Aggeneys
Kenhardt
Brisk
Hopetown
Luc
Port Nolloth
Steinkopf
Concordia
Marydale
E'Thembini
Strydenburg
Kleinsee
Nababeep
Carolusberg
Springbok
Verneuk Pan
Copperton
Petrusville
Komaggas
Kamieskroon
N O R T H E R N C A P E
Grootvloer
De Naawte
Onderstedorings
Vanwyksvlei
Vosburg
Houwater
Philipsto
Hondeklipbaai
Kamiesberge
Brandvlei
Sakrivier
Kareeberge
Camarvon
Britstown
De Aar
Wallekraal
Garies
S O U T H A
Bitterfontein
Swartkolkvloer
Loeriesfontein
Kootjieskolk
Sterling
Williston
Victoria West
Richmond
Nuwerus
Nieuwoudtville
Hanover
Masinyusane
Sabelo
KwaNo
Lutzville
Vanrhynsdorp
Calvinia
G r e a t K a r o o
Fraserburg
Murraysburg
Sneeube
Vredendal
Klawer
Graafwater
Roggeveldberge
Sutherland
Beaufort West
Sidesaviwa
Graaff-Reinet
Lambert's Bay
Clanwilliam
Wuppertal
Komsberg
Merweville
Aberdeen
Baboon Point
Citrusdal
Prince Albert Road
Leeu-Gamka
KwaZamukucinga
A T L A N T I C
Cape St Martin
St Helena Bay
Piketberg
Laingsburg
Prince Albert
Jansenville
O C E A N
Velddrif
Vredenburg
Touwsrivier
2325
W E S T E R N
Calitzdorp
De Rust
Oudtshoorn
Willowmore
Saldanha
Moorreesburg
Ceres
2250
Ladismith
Zoar
Dysselsdorp
Uniondale
Kougaberge
Malmesbury
Wellington
Montagu
C A P E
Little Karoo
George
Plettenberg Bay
Durbanville
Paarl
Worcester
Barrydale
Mossel Bay
Knysna
Bellville
Stellenbosch
Swellendam
Riversdale
Groot Brakrivier
CAPE TOWN
Khayelitsha
Heidelberg
Stilbaai
Mossel Bay
Somerset West
Strand
Caledon
Bredasdorp
Struis Bay
Cape of Good Hope
Hawston
Gansbaai
Waenhuiskrans
Cape Agulhas

ATLANTIC
OCEAN

Lambert Azimuthal Equal Area Projection

METRES / FEET
5000 / 16404
3000 / 9843
2000 / 6562
1000 / 3281
500 / 1640
200 / 656
0 / 0
Land below sea level
200 / 656
4000 / 13124
6000 / 19686

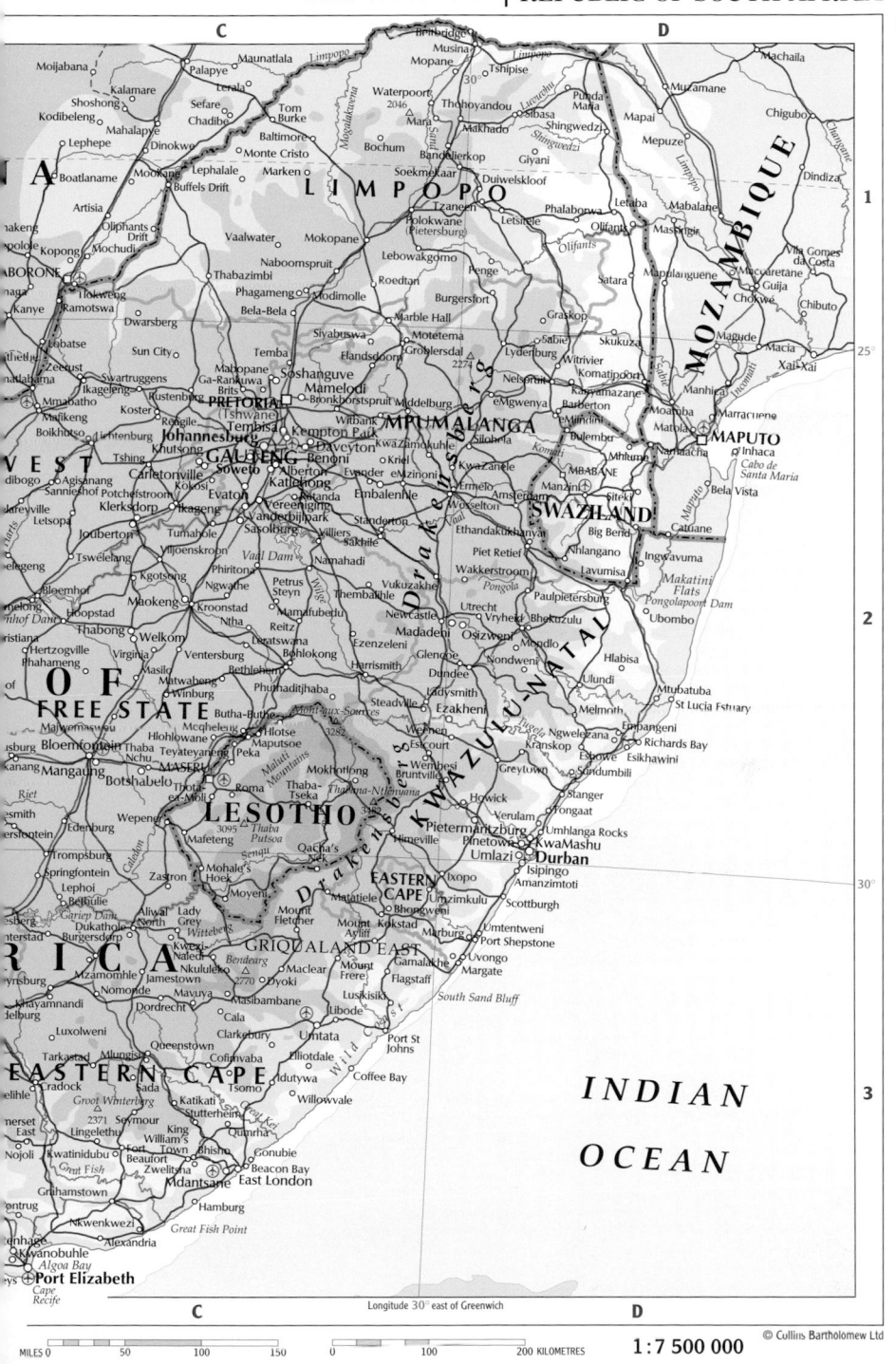

INDIAN

OCEAN

MILES 0   50   100   150   0   100   200 KILOMETRES   1 : 7 500 000

© Collins Bartholomew Ltd

Bi-Polar Oblique Projection

1 : 40 000 000

MILES 0   200   400   600   800

© Collins Bartholomew Ltd

Lambert Azimuthal Equal Area Projection

1 : 25 000 000

MILES 0   250   500

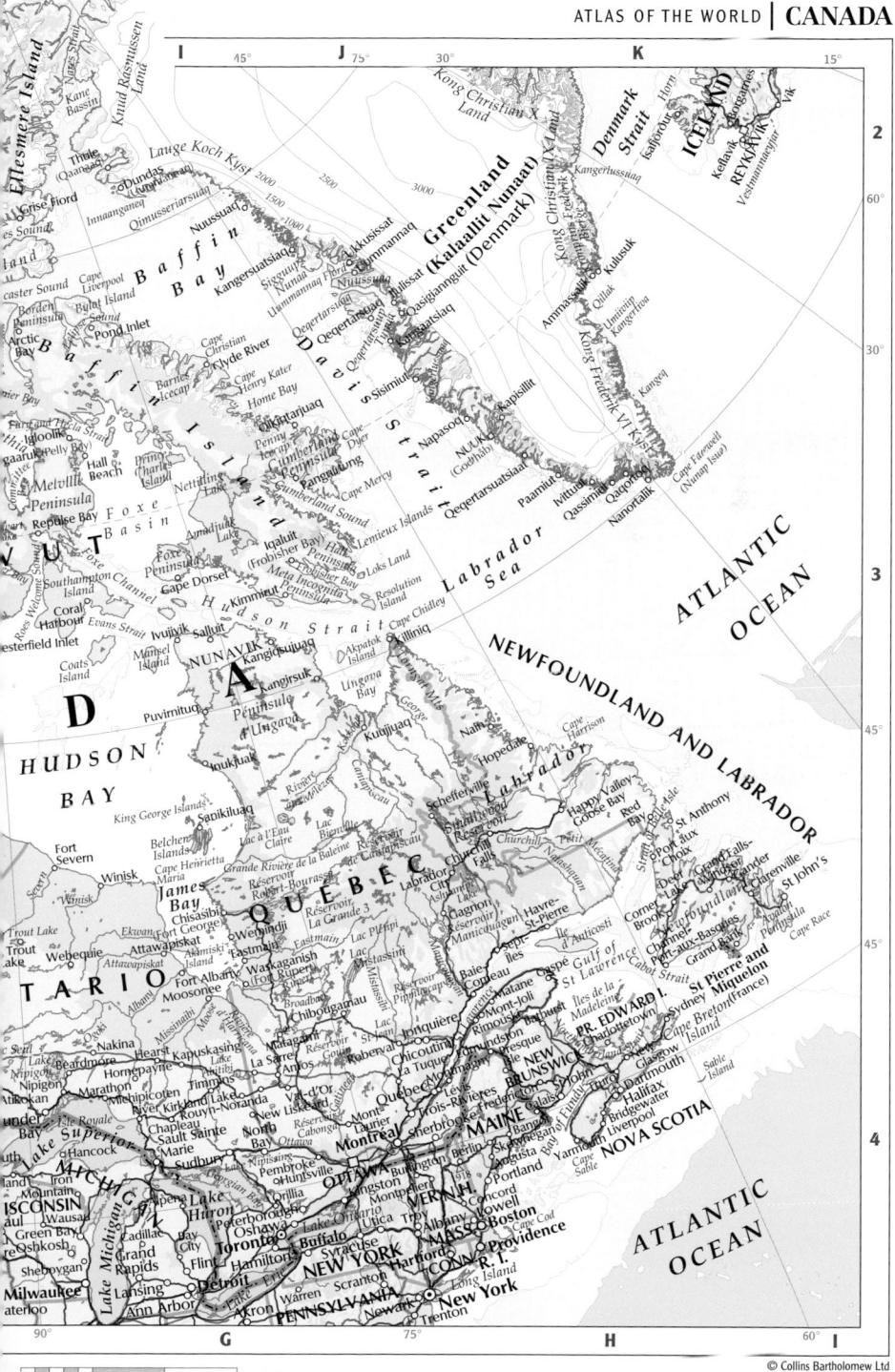

0   750   500   750 KILOMETRES

METRES
FEET

5000
16404

3000
9843

2000
6562

1000
3281

500
1640

200
656

0
0

Land below
sea level

200
656

4000
13124

6000
19686

Lambert Azimuthal Equal Area Projection

1 : 12 000 000

MILES 0   100   200   300

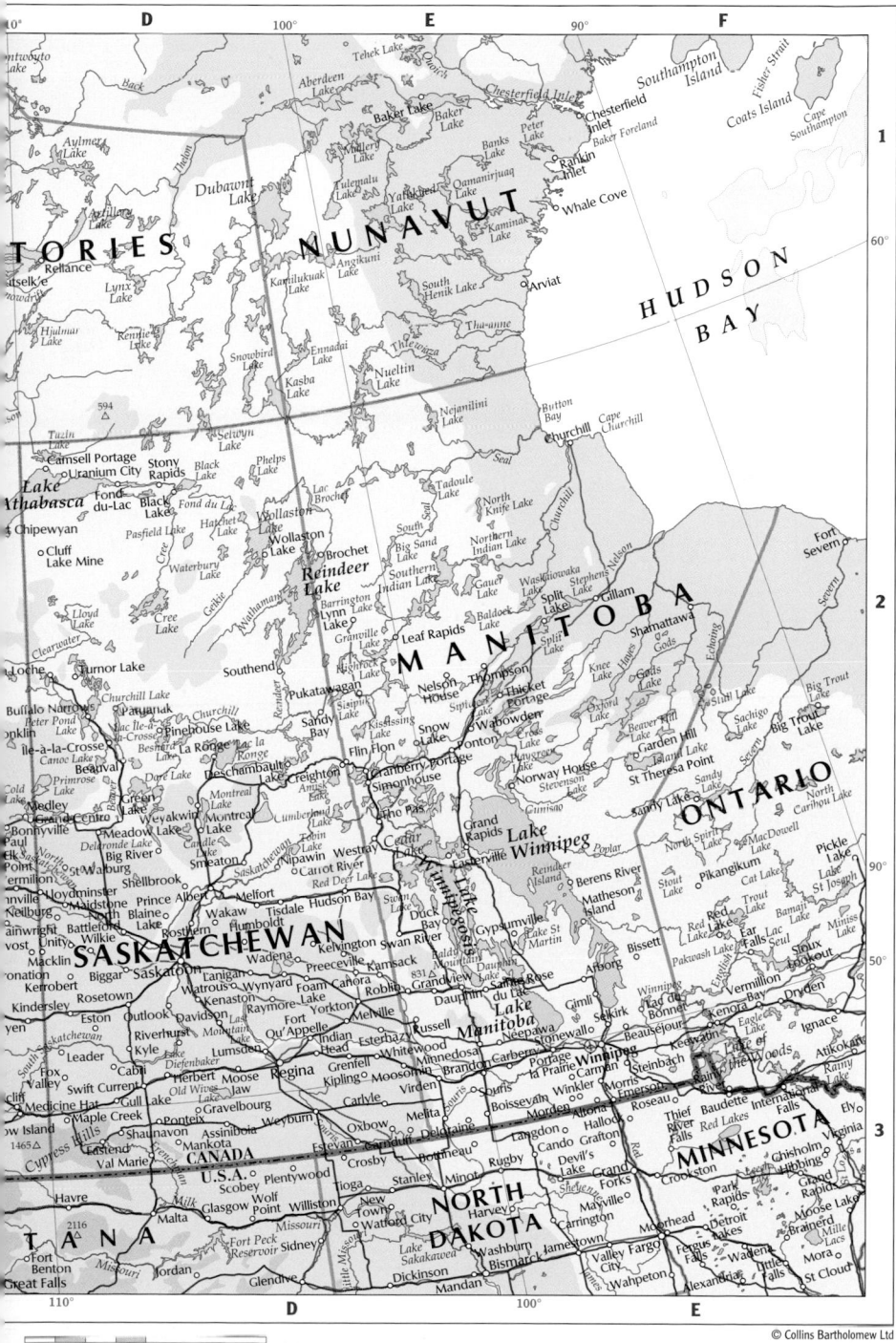

0   200   400 KILOMETRES

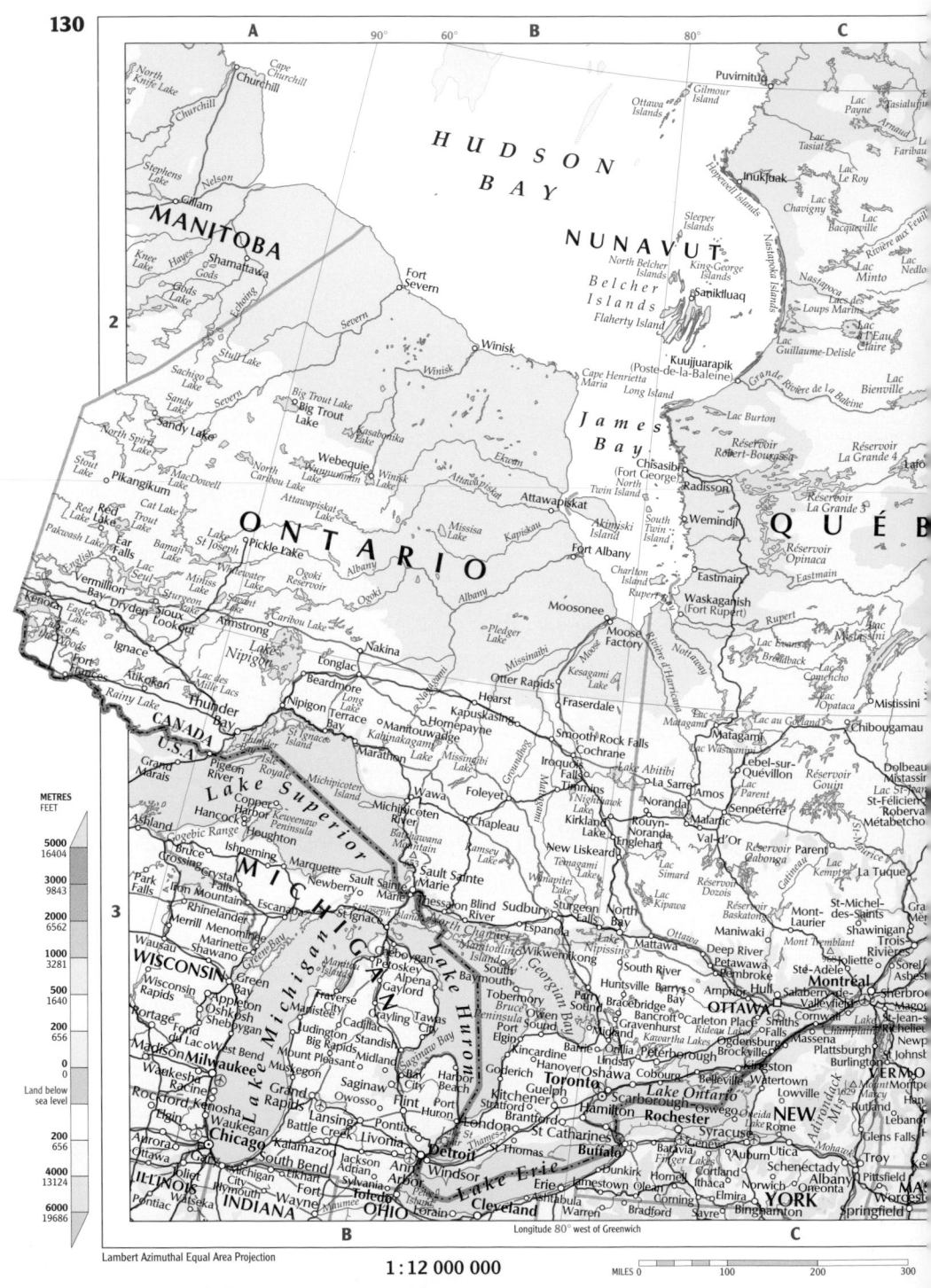

A   90°   60°   B   80°   C

Cape Knife Lake
North Knife Lake
Churchill
Cape Churchill

HUDSON

Puvirnituq
Gilmour Island
Ottawa Islands

BAY

MANITOBA

Gillam
Stephens Lake
Nelson
Churchill

Inukjuak
Lac Payne
Tasiulufuq
Lac Tasiat
Lac Faribu

Knee Lake
Hayes
Shamattawa
Gods
Echoing

NUNAVUT

Lac Le Roy
Lac Chavigny
Lac Minto

Gods Lake
Stull Lake
Fort Severn

Hopewell Islands
Sleeper Islands

Lac Bacqueville
Rivière aux Feuil

Sachigo Lake
Severn

North Belcher Islands
King-George Islands

Lac les Loups Marins

Sandy Lake
Severn
Winisk

Belcher Islands
Sanikiluaq

Lac l'Eau Claire

North Spirit Lake
Big Trout Lake
Big Trout Lake
Kasabonika Lake

Flaherty Island

Lac Guillaume-Delisle

Red Lake
Red Trout Lake
Cat Lake
Webequie
Winisk Lake

Cape Henrietta Maria
Long Island

Kuujjuarapik
(Poste-de-la-Baleine)

Lac Bienville

Pakwash Lake
Bamaji
Lac St Joseph
Pickle Lake
Attawapiskat Lake
Ekwan

James Bay
(Fort George)

Grande Rivière de la Baleine

Ear Falls
Vermillion
Lac Seul

Missa Lake
Ogoki Reservoir
Albany
Attawapiskat

Chisasibi
North Twin Island

Réservoir Robert-Bourassa

ONTARIO

Radisson
Wemindji

Réservoir La Grande 4

Kenora
Lake of the Woods
Dryden
Sioux Lookout
Armstrong
Nakina

Akimiski Island
South Twin Island

Réservoir La Grande 3

QUÉB

Fort Frances
Rainy Lake
Ignace
Atikokan
Nipigon
Longlac

Charlton Island
Rupert

Eastmain
Eastmain

Réservoir Opinaca

Lafor

Thunder Bay
Beardmore
Hearst
Otter Rapids

Moosonee
Moose Factory

Waskaganish
(Fort Rupert)

Lac Evans
Broadback

Lac Mesisni

CANADA
U.S.A.

Nipigon
Terrace Bay
Manitouwadge
Homepayne
Kapuskasing
Fraserdale

Rupert
Nottaway

Lac Comencho
Lac Opataca

Mistissini

Grand Marais
Pigeon River
Marathon
Missinaibi Lake

Smooth Rock Falls
Cochrane

Matagami
Lac au Goéland

Chibougamau

Ashland
Gogebic Range

Lake Superior
Michipicoten Island
Wawa
Foleyet
Timmins
Iroquois Falls
La Sarre

Lebel-sur-Quévillon
Réservoir Gouin

Dolbeau
Mistassini

Copper Harbor
Keweenaw Peninsula
Houghton

Michipicoten
Chapleau
Kirkland Lake
Rouyn-Noranda
Amos
Senneterre

Val Parent

St-Félicien
Roberva
Métabetcho

Hancock
Ishpeming
Marquette

Batchawana Mountain
Ramsey Lake

New Liskeard
Noranda
Malartic
Val-d'Or

Réservoir Cabonga

La Tuque

Park Falls
Iron Mountain
Newberry
Sault Sainte Marie

Temagami
North Bay

Réservoir Dozois

Mont-Laurier
St-Michel-des-Saints

Crystal Falls
Rhinelander
Escanaba
St Ignace
Blind River
Sudbury
Sturgeon Falls

Lac Kipawa
Maniwaki

Gra

Merrill
Menominee
Espanola
Mattawa

Deep River
Petawawa

Shawinigan
Trois-Rivières

WISCONSIN

Marinette
Shawano

Manitoulin Island
Wikwemikong

Nipissing

South River
Pembroke

Ste-Adèle
Joliette

MICHIGAN

Green Bay
Cheboygan
Petoskey
Tobermory

Bruce Peninsula
Owen Sound

Huntsville
Bracebridge
Barrys Bay
Bancroft
Carleton Place
Smiths Falls

Arnprior
Hull

Salaberry-de-Valleyfield

Montréal
Sherbro
Mago

Wisconsin Rapids
Appleton
Oshkosh
Alpena
Gaylord

Georgian Bay
Midland
Gravenhurst

OTTAWA
Rideau Lakes
Cornwall

Richelieu

Portage
Fond du Lac
Sheboygan
Traverse City
Cadillac
Port Elgin

Kawartha Lakes
Peterborough

Brockville
Massena

Plattsburgh
Burlington

VERMO

Madison
Milwaukee
West Bend
Mount Pleasant
Midland
Kincardine
Barrie
Orillia
Lindsay

Kingston
Belleville
Cobourg

Watertown
Lowville

Waukesha
Racine
Grand Rapids
Saginaw
Bay City
Harbor Beach
Goderich

Toronto
Oshawa

Lake Ontario

Oswego
Rome

NEW

Rutland
Lebanon

Rockford
Kenosha
Lansing
Flint
Port Huron
Guelph
Kitchener
Stratford
Hamilton
St Catharines

Scarborough
Rochester
Syracuse
Auburn
Utica

Schenectady
Albany
Troy

Glens Falls

Elgin

Chicago
Battle Creek
Livonia
Pontiac
London
Brantford

Buffalo
Dunkirk
Finger Lakes
Cortland
Ithaca

Oneonta

Pittsfield

MA
Worcest

Aurora
Waukegan
Kalamazoo
Jackson
Ann Arbor
St Thomas
Thames

Detroit
Windsor

Lake Erie

Erie
Jamestown
Olean
Elmira
Binghamton

Norwich

Springfield

ILLINOIS

Joliet
Ottawa
South Bend
Elkhart
Michigan City
Plymouth
Sylvania
Adrian
Toledo
Lorain
Ashtabula
Warren

Cleveland

Bradford
Sayre

YORK

Pontiac
Waseka

INDIANA

Wayne
Maumee

OHIO

Lambert Azimuthal Equal Area Projection

1 : 12 000 000

Longitude 80° west of Greenwich

MILES 0   100   200   300

METRES
FEET

5000
16404

3000
9843

2000
6562

1000
3281

500
1640

200
656

0
0
Land below
sea level

200
656

4000
13124

6000
19686

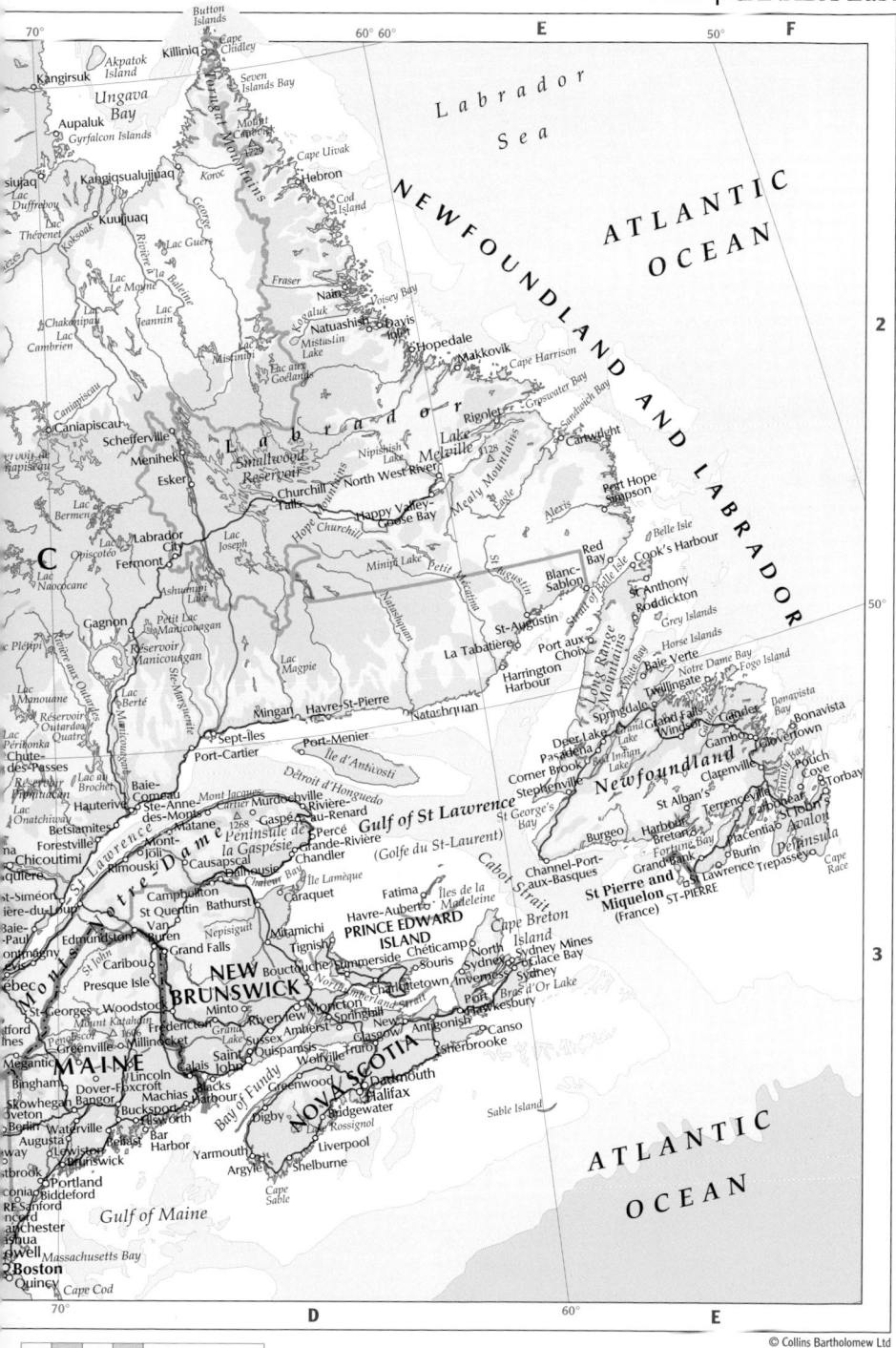

0   200   400 KILOMETRES

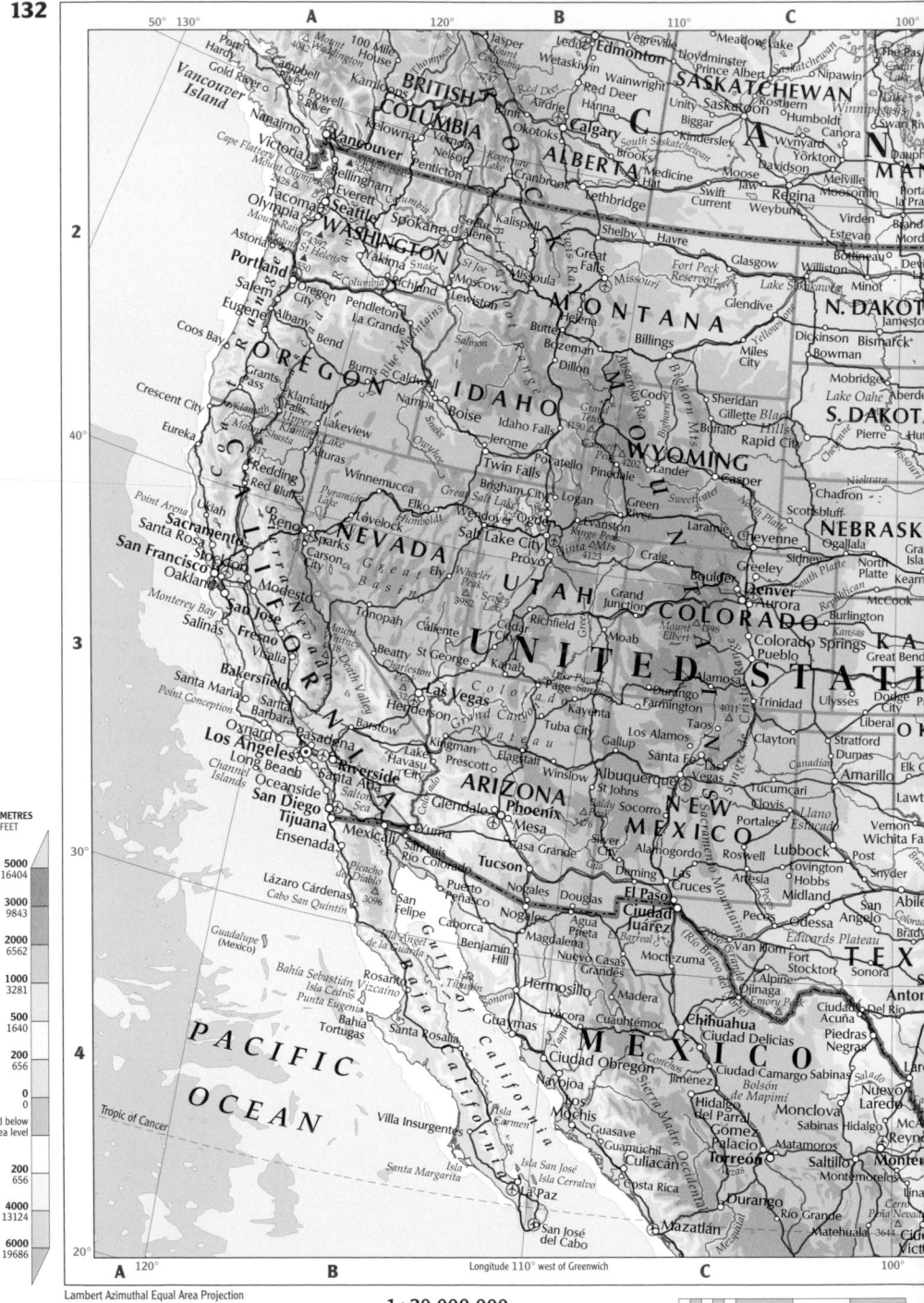

METRES
FEET

5000	16404
3000	9843
2000	6562
1000	3281
500	1640
200	656
0	0
Land below sea level	
200	656
4000	13124
6000	19686

Lambert Azimuthal Equal Area Projection

1 : 20 000 000

Longitude 110° west of Greenwich

MILES 0   100   200   300   400

0 200 400 600 KILOMETRES

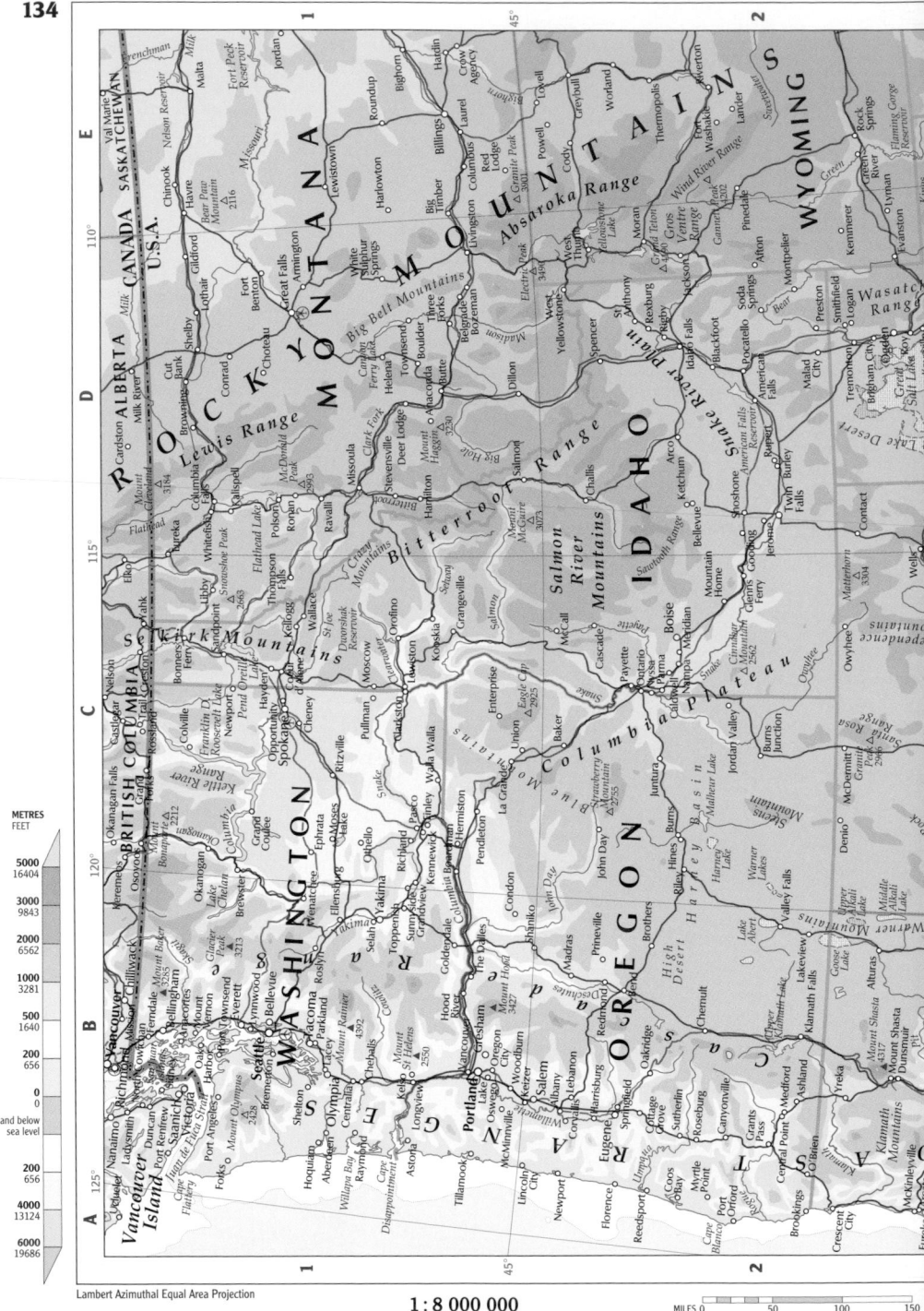

METRES
FEET

5000
16404

3000
9843

2000
6562

1000
3281

500
1640

200
656

0
0

Land below
sea level

200
656

4000
13124

6000
19686

Lambert Azimuthal Equal Area Projection

1 : 8 000 000

MILES 0   50   100   150

45°

45°

CANADA
U.S.A.

ALBERTA   SASKATCHEWAN

BRITISH COLUMBIA

R O C K Y   M O N T A N A

M O U N T A I N S

WYOMING

IDAHO

W A S H I N G T O N

O R E G O N

Vancouver
Island

Seattle

Portland

Salem

Eugene

Spokane

Great Falls

Helena

Butte

Missoula

Billings

Bozeman

Boise

Yellowstone
Lake

Salmon
River
Mountains

Bitterroot   Range

Columbia   Plateau

Blue   Mountains

High
Desert

Snake   River   Plain

Absaroka   Range

Wind   River   Range

Lewis   Range

Big   Belt   Mountains

Wasatch
Range

Great
Salt Lake

Lake   Desert

125°   120°   115°   110°

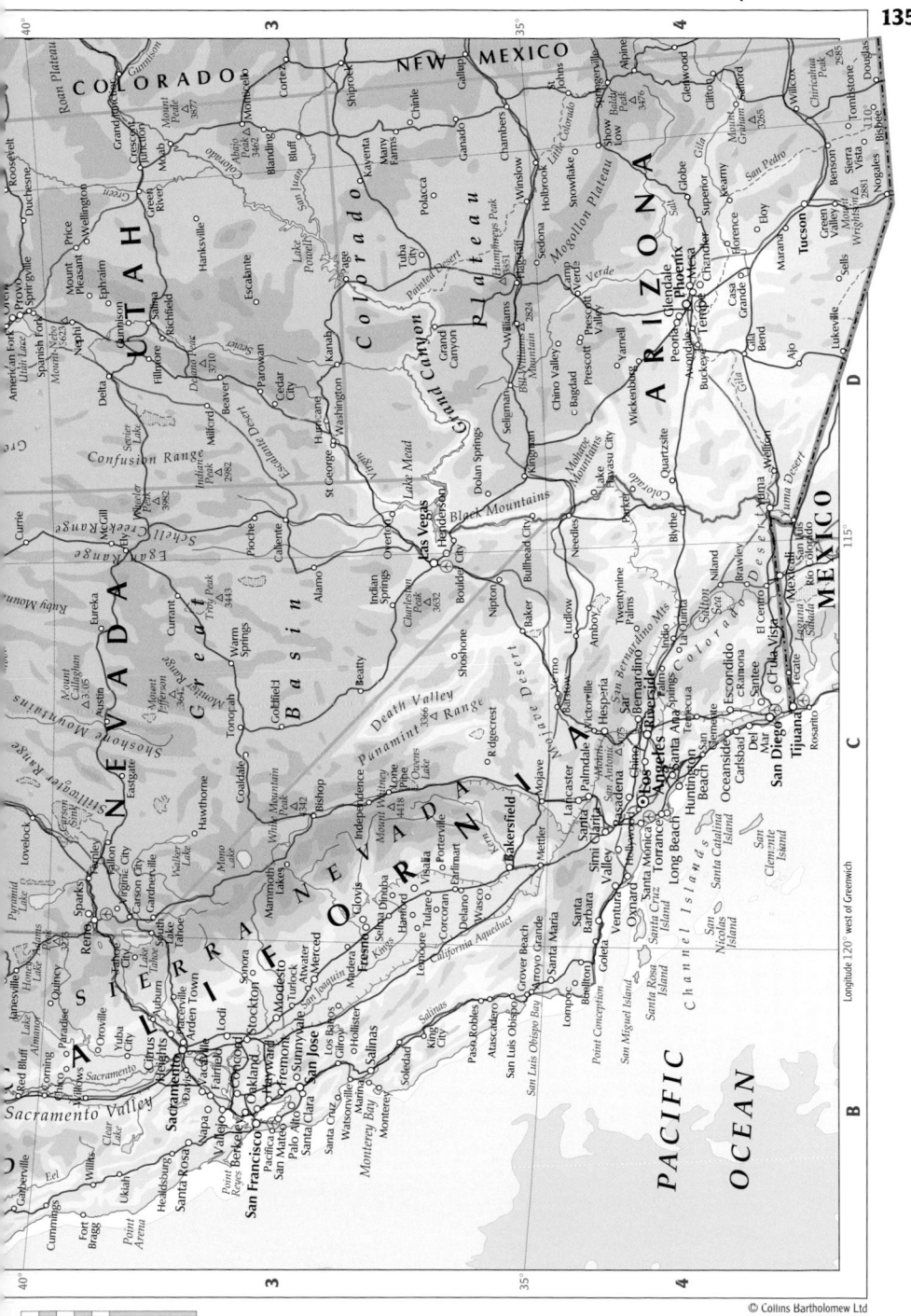

0   100   200 KILOMETRES

Longitude 120° west of Greenwich

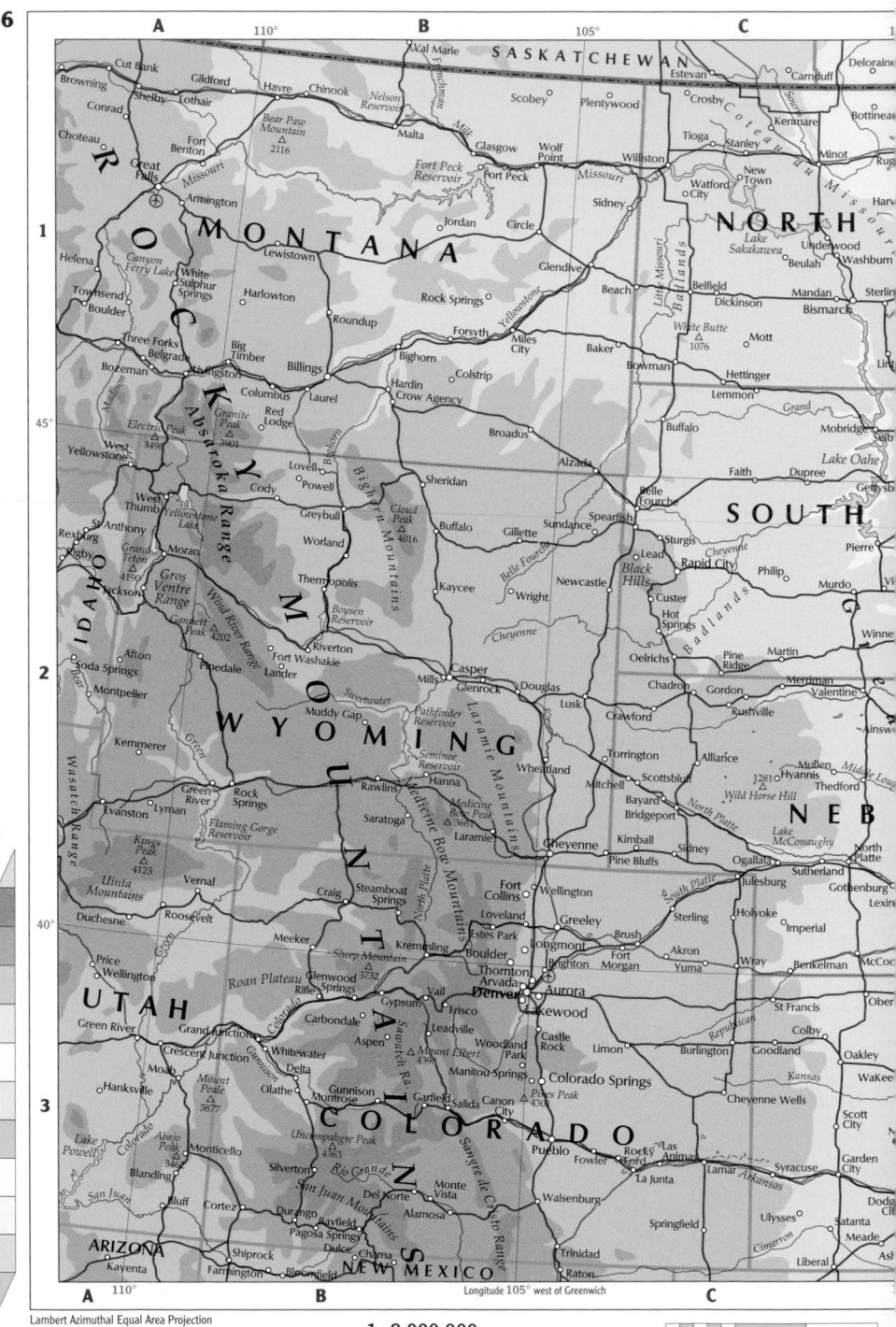

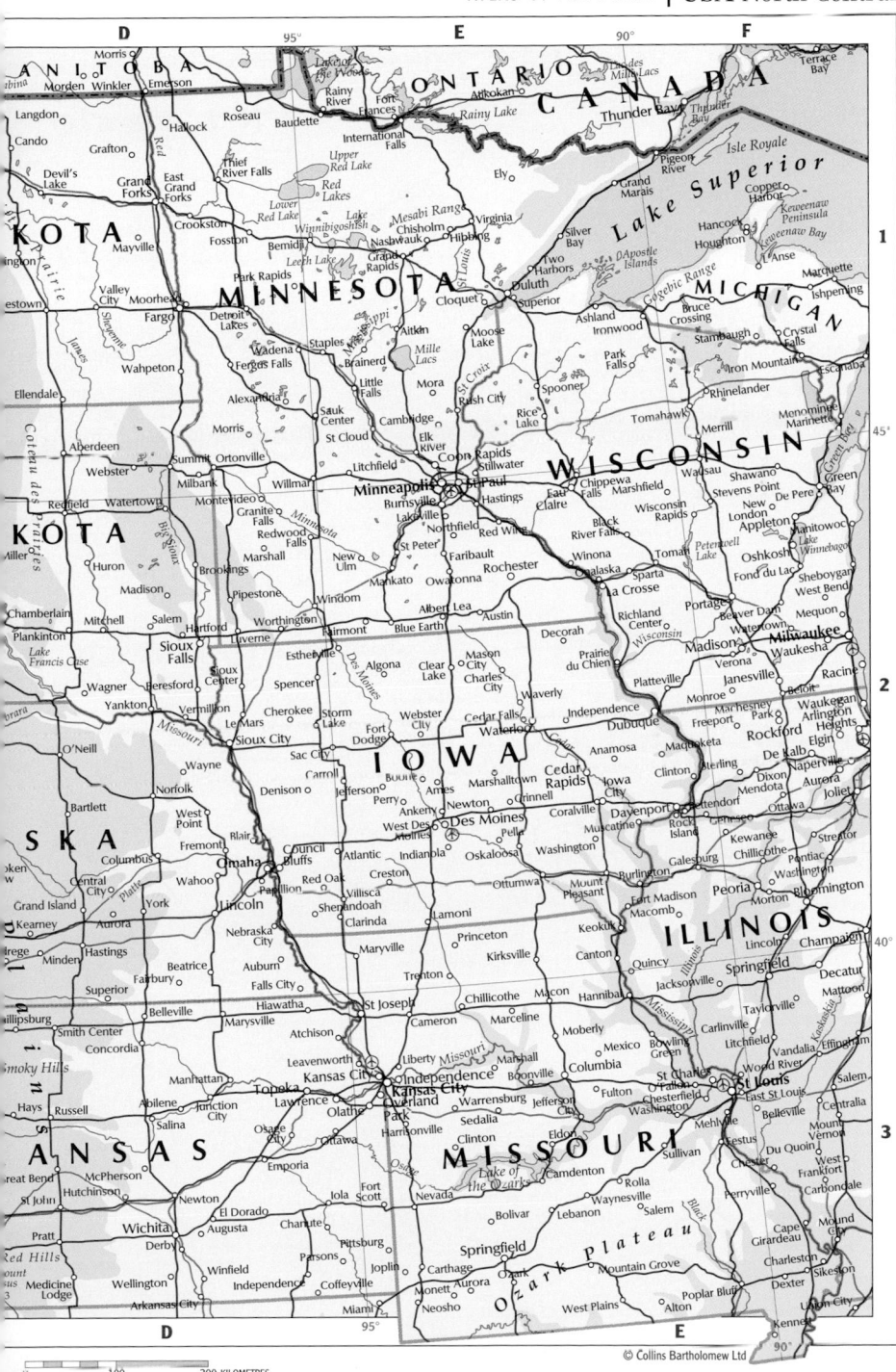

© Collins Bartholomew Ltd

0   100   200 KILOMETRES

A · 90°　　　　　　　　　　85°　　　　　　　　C

MINNESOTA

ONTARIO

Lake Superior

M I C H I G A N

MINNESOTA

WISCONSIN

IOWA

Lake Michigan

Lake Huron

Georgian Bay

Milwaukee

Chicago

ILLINOIS

INDIANA

OHIO

Indianapolis

Columbus

Cincinnati

St Louis

MISSOURI

KENTUCKY

WEST VIRGINIA

TENNESSEE

Longitude 85° west of Greenwich

A · 90°　　　　　　　B　　　　　　　　　　C

Lambert Azimuthal Equal Area Projection

1 : 8 000 000

METRES
FEET

5000　16404
3000　9843
2000　6562
1000　3281
500　1640
200　656
0　0
Land below
sea level
200　656
4000　13124
6000　19686

MILES 0　　50　　100　　150

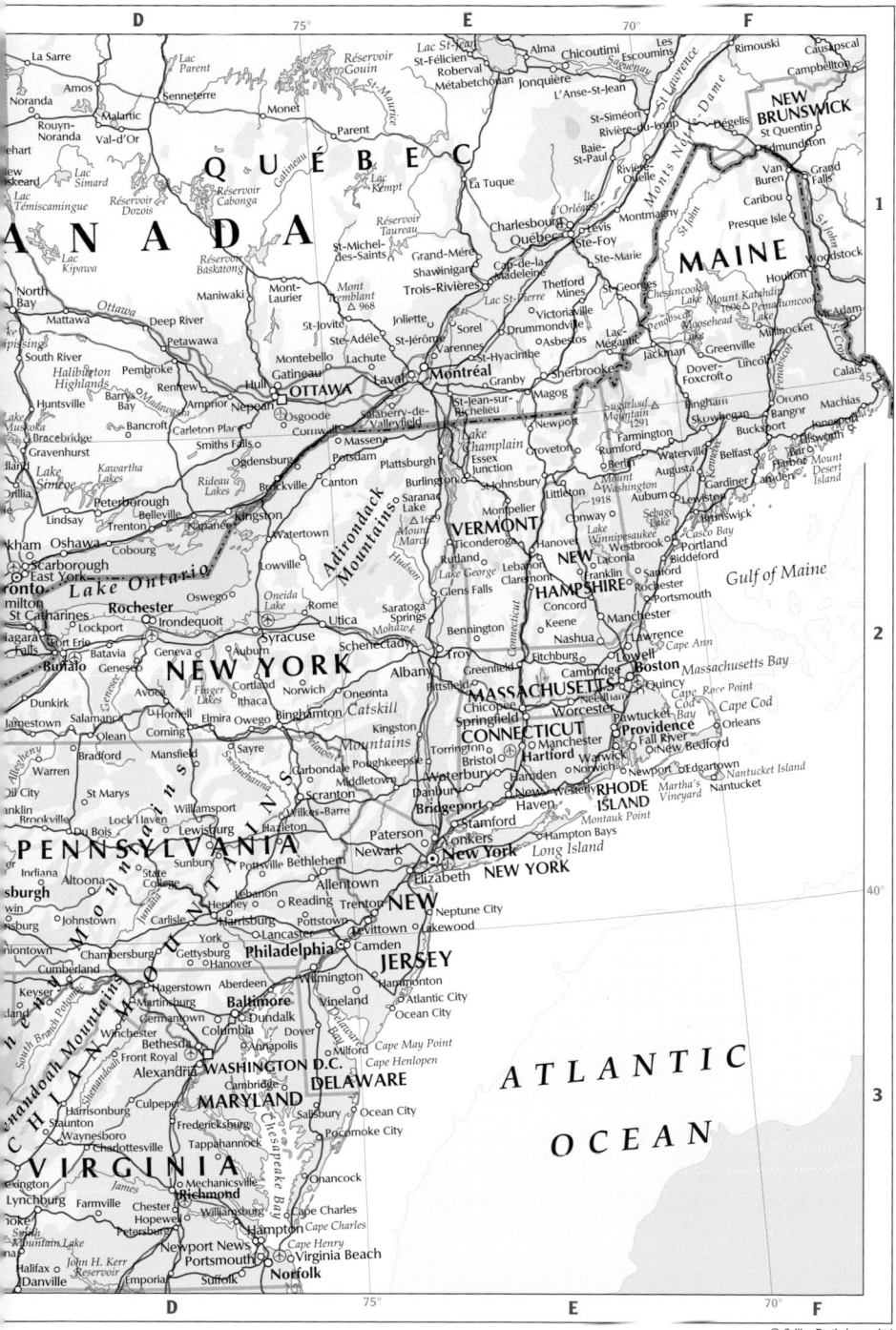

© Collins Bartholomew Ltd

0   100   200 KILOMETRES

A 95° B 90° C

MISSOURI

Vinita
West Plains
Charleston
Hopkinsville
Glasgow
KENTU
Owasso
Bentonville
Poplar Bluff
Sikeston
Russellville
Tulsa
Pryor
Siloam Springs
Rogers
Mountain Home
Alton
Dexter
Mayfield
Murray
Oak Grove
Springfield
Gallatin
Sapulpa
Broken Arrow
Springdale
Harrison
Pocahontas
Kennett
Union City
Paris
Kentucky Lake
Nashville
Franklin
Leban
Muskogee
Tahlequah
Fayetteville
Hoxie
Paragould
Dyersburg
McKenzie
Dickson
Okmulgee
Boston Mountains
White
Marshall
Jonesboro
Blytheville
Humboldt
Jackson
Columbia
McMinnvil
Henryetta

1

Chuotah
Clarksville
Heber Springs
Batesville
Newport
Trumann
Brownsville
Linden
Shelbyville
Manches
Sallisaw
Van Buren
Fort Smith
Magazine
Russellville
Searcy
Conway
Wynne
Forrest City
Memphis
Bartlett
Millington
Savannah
Lewisburg
Tennessee
Lawrenceburg
Fayettev
TENNESS

35°
Eufaula Lake
Poteau
762
Mansfield △ 839
Morrilton
Jacksonville
Marianna
Southaven
Corinth
Florence
Athens
Huntsville
McAlester
Mena
Little Rock
Helena
Holly Springs
Booneville
Russellville
Wheeler Lake
Decatur
Pa
OKLAHOMA
Hot Springs
Lake Ouachita
Stuttgart
Oxford
Batesville
Tupelo
Hamilton
Cullman
Gadsden
Atoka
Ouachita Mountains
Malvern
Clarksdale
Amory
Center Point
Annis
Hugo
Idabel
De Queen
Arkadelphia
Fordyce
Pine Bluff
Dumas
Cleveland
Grenada
Columbus
Birmingham
Vestavia Hills
Cheaha Mountain
Sylacu

ARKANSAS

Red
Paris
Ashdown
Hope
Monticello
Indianola
Greenwood
Winona
Starkville
Bessemer
Alabaster
New Boston
Camden
Warren
MISSISSIPPI
Leland
Louisville
Tuscaloosa
Commerce
Texarkana
El Dorado
Greenville
Greenwood
Macon
Sulphur Springs
Mount Pleasant
Magnolia
Hamburg
Crossett
Yazoo City
Canton
Eutaw
Clanton
Aub
TEXAS
Sabine
Longview
Shreveport
Homer
Minden
Bastrop
Ruston
Lake Providence
Vicksburg
Ridgeland
Meridian
Demopolis
Prattville
Tuske
Tyler
Athens
Kilgore
Henderson
Gilsboro
Driskill Mountain △ 163
Monroe
Tallulah
Jackson
Brandon
Forest
York
Selma
Montgomery
ALABAM
Jacksonville
Marshall
Carthage
Bossier City
Jonesboro
Winnsboro
Mansfield
Crystal Springs
Natchitoches
Olla
Brookhaven
Thomasville
Greenville
Troy
Palestine
Nacogdoches
Toledo Bend Reservoir
Many
LOUISIANA
Natchez
Laurel
Hattiesburg
Jackson
Monroeville
Oz
Crockett
Sam Rayburn Reservoir
Alexandria
Pineville
McComb
Petal
Evergreen
Enterp
Huntsville
Jasper
Leesville
Marksville
Lecompte
Lumberton
Century
Crestview
De Funia Springs
Livingston
Corrigan
De Ridder
Ville Platte
Kentwood
Bogalusa
Picayune
Atmore
The Woodlands
Sulphur
Oakdale
Opelousas
New Roads
Hammond
Gulfport
Biloxi
Pascagoula
Pensacola
Fort Walton Bea
Conroe
Jennings
Lafayette
Port Allen
Baton Rouge
Mississippi Sound
Mobile Bay
Santa Rosa Island
Panama
Houston
Beaumont
Orange
Lake Charles
Crowley
Plaquemine
New Iberia
Thibodaux
Metairie
New Orleans
Gretna
Mobile Point

30°
Humble
Nederland
Vidor
Groves
Abbeville
Morgan City
Raceland
Cut Off
Port Sulphur
Breton Sound
Chandeleur Islands
Pasadena
Baytown
Port Arthur
White Lake
Houma
Sugar Land
Galveston Bay
Marsh Island
Grand Isle
Mississippi Delta
Texas City
Galveston
Atchafalaya Bay
Terrebonne Bay
Lake Jackson
Galveston Island
Freeport

METRES
FEET

5000	16404
3000	9843
2000	6562
1000	3281
500	1640
200	656
0	0

Land below sea level

200	656
4000	13124
6000	19686

3

GULF OF MEXICO

25°

4

95°
B
Longitude 90° west of Greenwich
C

Lambert Azimuthal Equal Area Projection

1 : 8 000 000

MILES 0   50   100   150

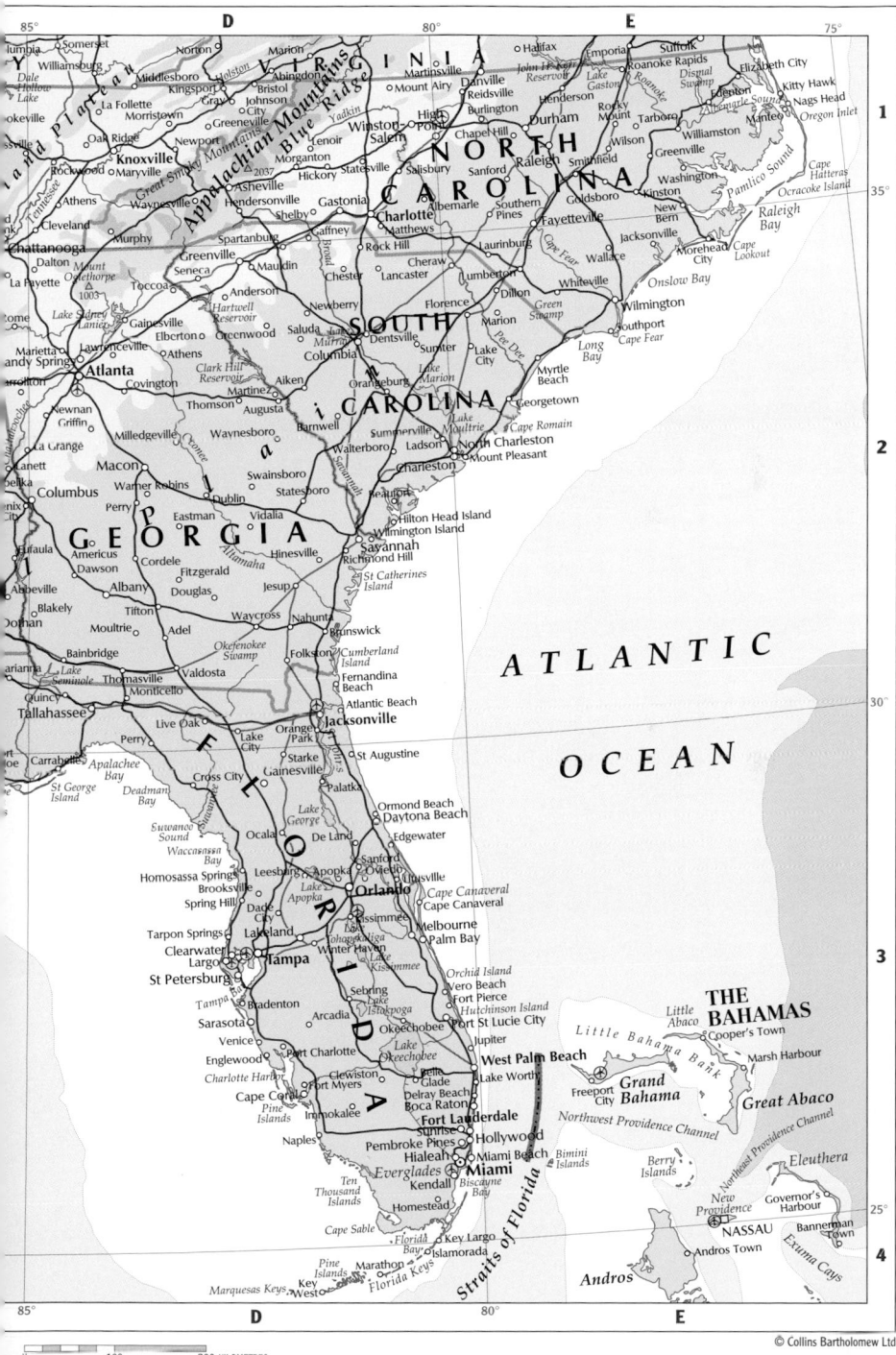

0   100   200 KILOMETRES

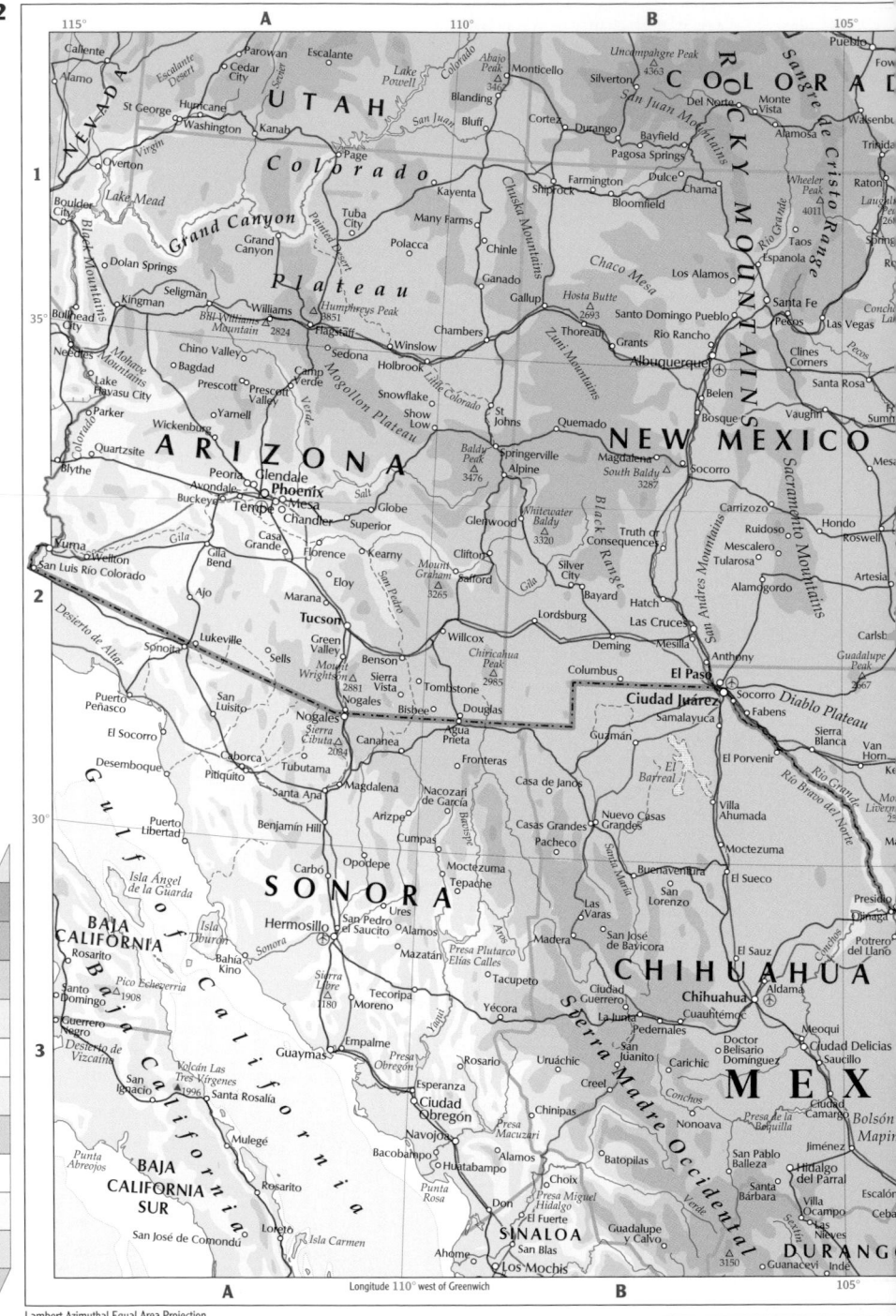

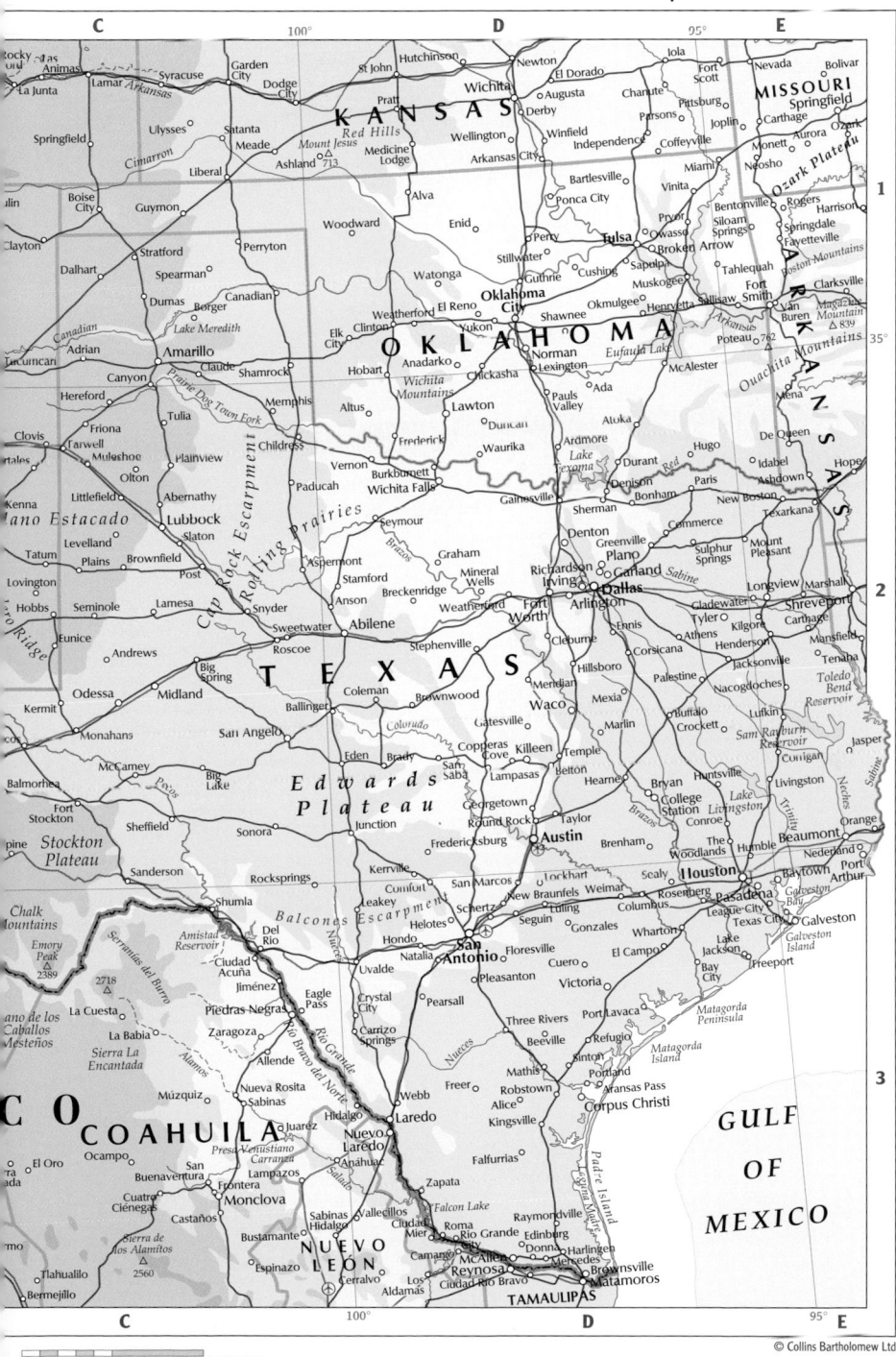

© Collins Bartholomew Ltd

0   100   200 KILOMETRES

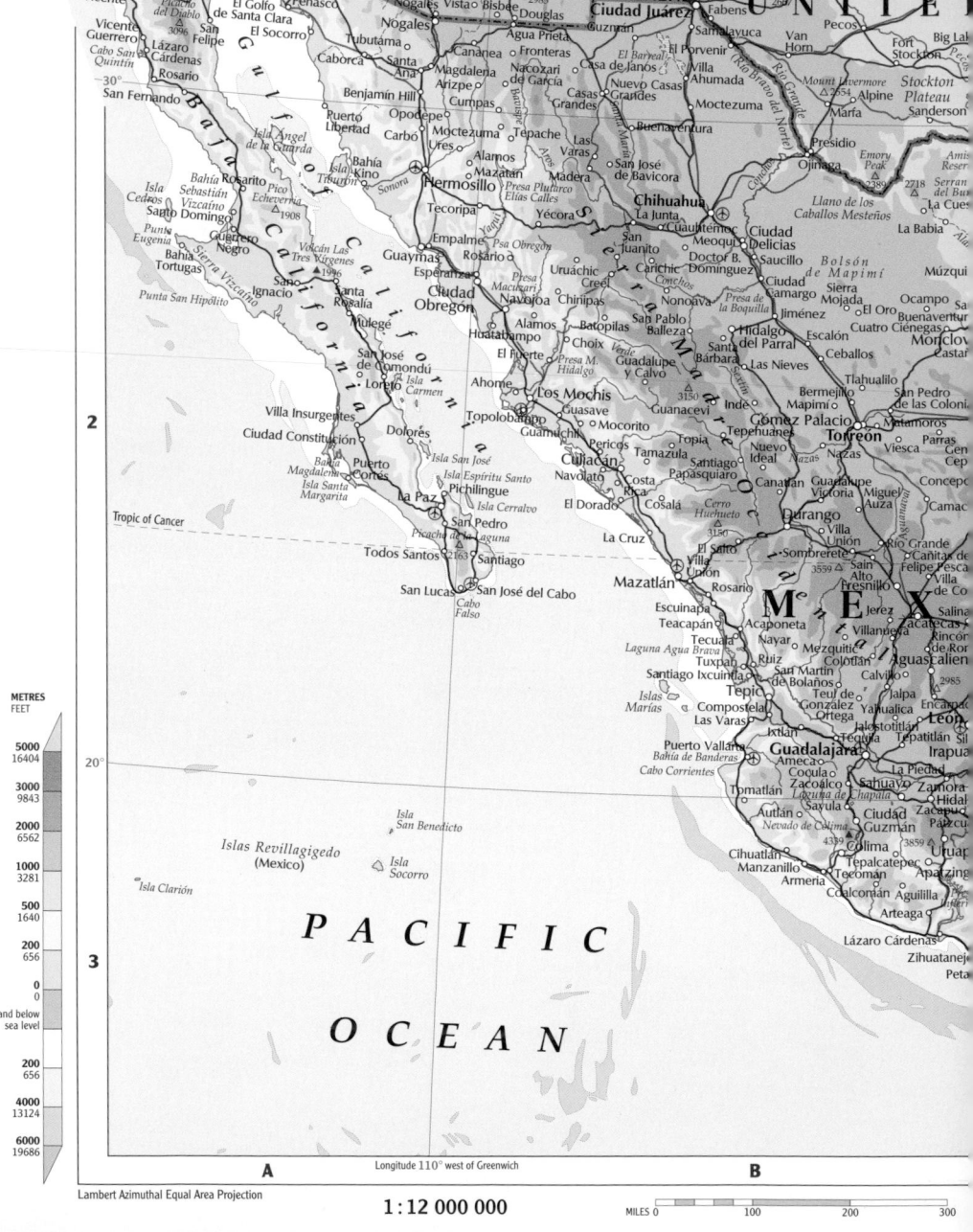

0   200   400 KILOMETRES

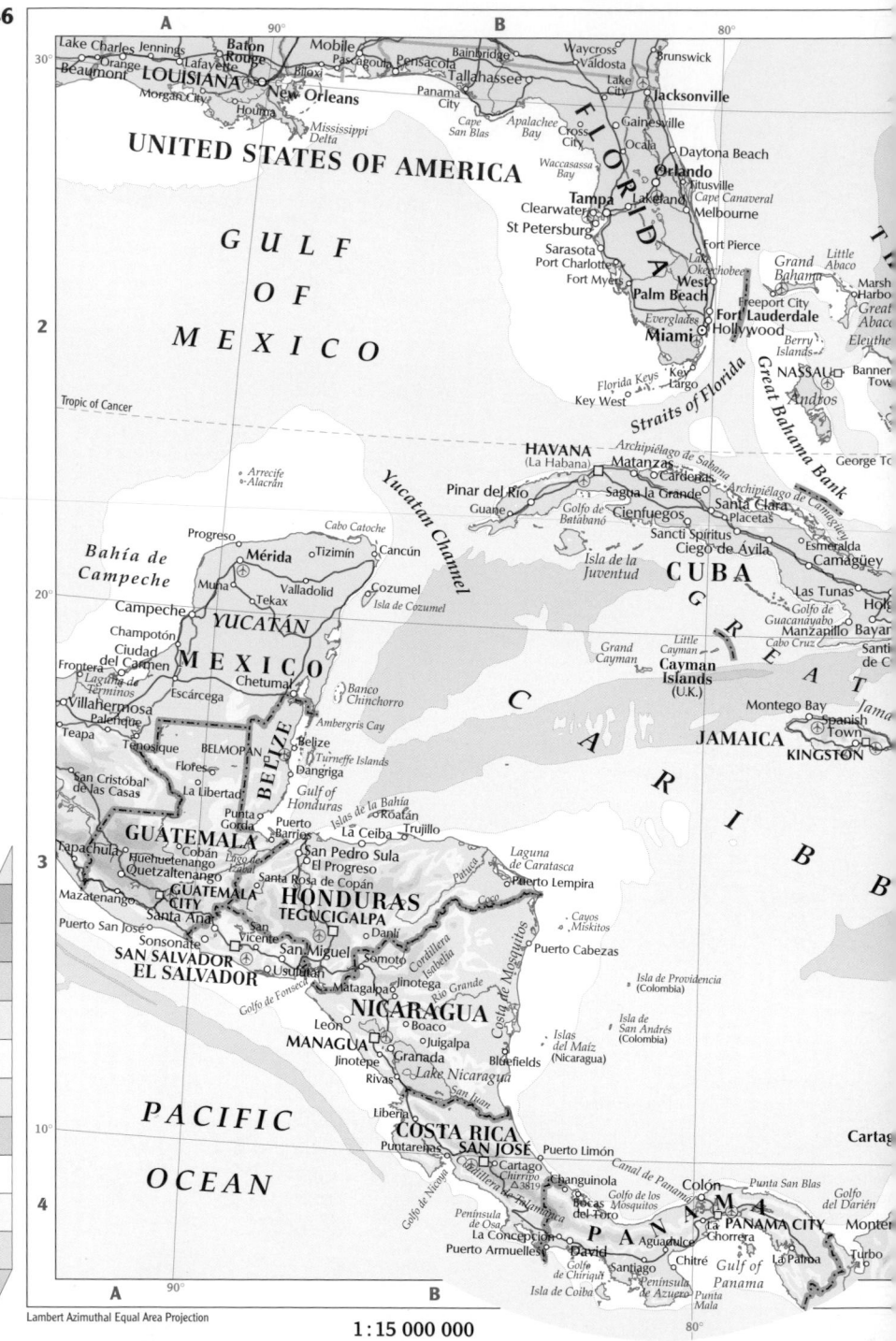

A 90° B 80°

UNITED STATES OF AMERICA

Lake Charles Jennings
Orange Lafayette Baton Mobile Bainbridge Waycross Brunswick
Beaumont **LOUISIANA** Rouge Pascagoula Pensacola Valdosta
Morgan City Houma New Orleans Biloxi Panama Lake Jacksonville
City City
Mississippi Cape Apalachee Cross Gainesville
Delta San Blas Bay City
Ocala Daytona Beach
Waccasassa
Bay Orlando
Titusville
Clearwater Tampa Lakeland Cape Canaveral
St Petersburg Melbourne
Sarasota Fort Pierce
Port Charlotte Lake
Okeechobee West Grand Little
Fort Myers Palm Beach Bahama Abaco
Freeport City Marsh
Everglades Fort Lauderdale Harbor
Hollywood Great
Miami Berry Abaco
Islands Eleuthe

GULF

OF

MEXICO

Florida Keys Key NASSAU Banner
Largo Tow
Key West Andros

Tropic of Cancer Straits of Florida Great Bahama Bank

HAVANA George To
(La Habana) Matanzas
Pinar del Río Cárdenas
Archipiélago de Sabana
Guane Sagua la Grande Santa Clara Esmeralda
Golfo de Cienfuegos Placetas Camagüey
Batabanó Sancti Spíritus
Isla de la Ciego de Ávila **CUBA**
Juventud Las Tunas
Grand Little Golfo de Holl
Cayman Cayman Guacanayabo
Cabo Cruz Manzanillo Bayar Santi
Cayman de C
Islands
(U.K.) Montego Bay Spanish Jama
JAMAICA Town
KINGSTON

Progreso Cabo Catoche
Mérida Tizimín Cancún
Muna Valladolid Cozumel
Bahía de Tekax Isla de Cozumel
Campeche
Campeche **YUCATÁN**
Champotón
Ciudad **MEXICO** Banco
del Carmen Chetumal Chinchorro
Frontera Escárcega
Laguna de
Términos Ambergris Cay
Villahermosa Belize Turneffe Islands
Palenque **BELMOPAN** Dangriga
Teapa Tenosique **BELIZE**
Flores Gulf of
San Cristóbal La Libertad Honduras Islas de la Bahía
de las Casas Punta Puerto Roatán
Gorda Barrios La Ceiba Trujillo
Tapachula **GUATEMALA** San Pedro Sula Laguna
Cobán El Progreso de Caratasca
Huehuetenango Santa Rosa de Copán Puerto Lempira
Quetzaltenango Patuca
Mazatenango **GUATEMALA** **HONDURAS**
CITY **TEGUCIGALPA**
Puerto San José Santa Ana San Danlí Cayos
Sonsonate Vicente Somoto Miskitos Puerto Cabezas
SAN SALVADOR San Miguel Cordillera
EL SALVADOR Usulután Isabelia Isla de Providencia
Jinotega (Colombia)
Golfo de Fonseca Matagalpa Río Grande
León **NICARAGUA** Isla de
Boaco San Andrés
MANAGUA Juigalpa Islas (Colombia)
Jinotepe Granada Bluefields del Maíz
Rivas (Nicaragua)
Liberia Lake Nicaragua San Juan
COSTA RICA
Puntarenas **SAN JOSÉ** Puerto Limón
Cartago Canal de Panamá
Chirripó Changuinola Colón Punta San Blas
3810 Golfo de los Golfo
Bocas Mosquitos **PANAMA CITY** del Darién
La Concepción del Toro Chorrera
Puerto Armuelles David Aguadulce La Palma Turbo
Santiago Chitré Gulf of
Golfo Peninsula Panama
de Chiriquí de Azuero Punta
Isla de Coiba Mala

Arrecife
Alacrán
Yucatan Channel

PACIFIC

OCEAN

Peninsula
de Osa
Golfo de Nicoya

CARIBBEAN

Cartag

Monter

Archipiélago de Camagüey

METRES
FEET

5000 16404
3000 9843
2000 6562
1000 3281
500 1640
200 656
0 0
Land below
sea level
200 656
4000 13124
6000 19686

A 90° B 80°

Lambert Azimuthal Equal Area Projection

1 : 15 000 000

30°

2

20°

3

10°

4

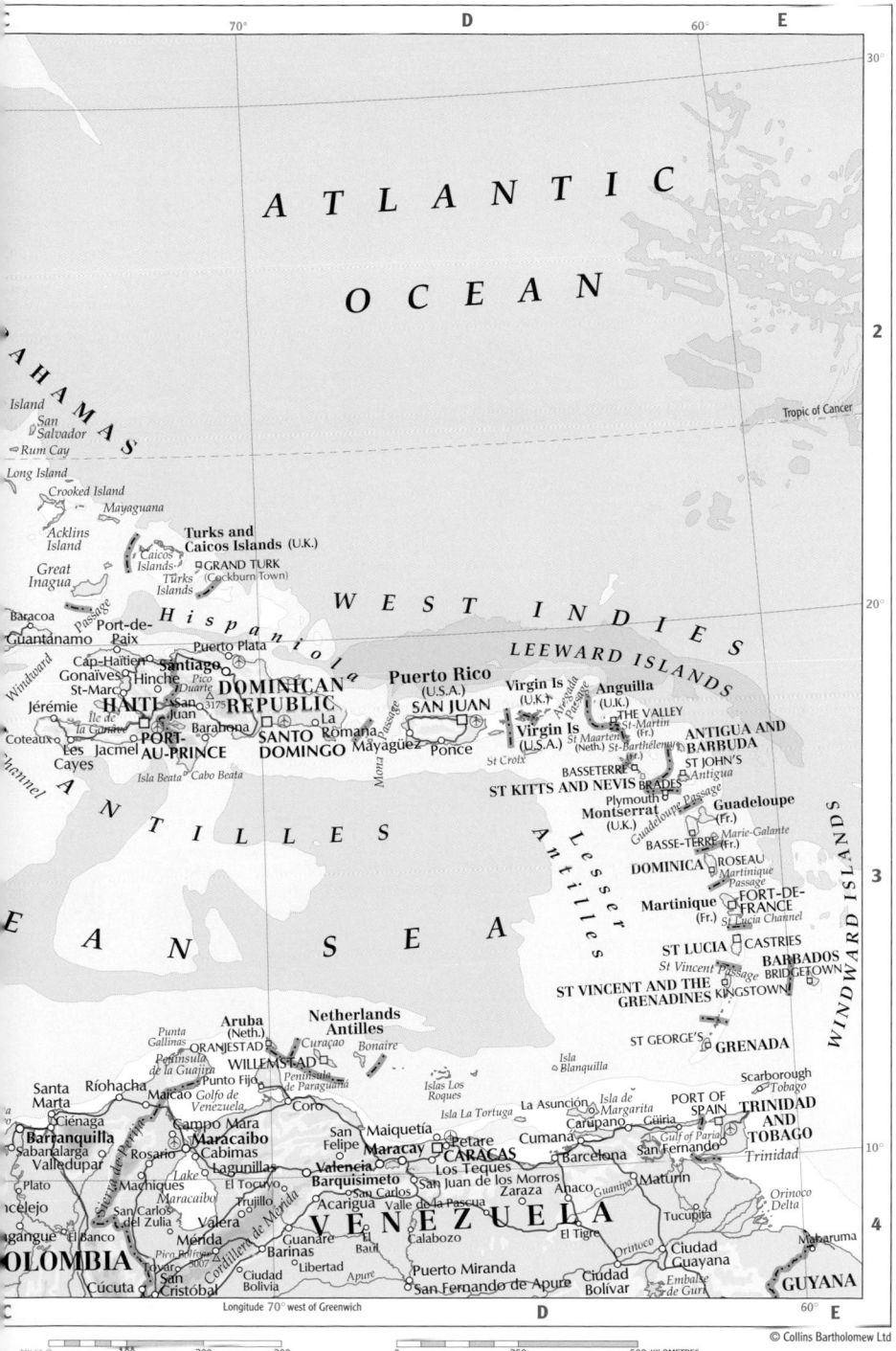

A T L A N T I C

O C E A N

Tropic of Cancer

B A H A M A S

Island
San Salvador
Rum Cay

Long Island

Crooked Island
Mayaguana

Acklins Island

Great Inagua

Baracoa
Guantánamo
Port-de-Paix
Windward Passage

Caicos Islands

Turks and Caicos Islands (U.K.)
GRAND TURK (Cockburn Town)
Turks Islands

W E S T   I N D I E S

Hispaniola

Cap-Haïtien
Gonaïves
St-Marc
Jérémie
Île de la Gonâve

HAITI

Santiago
Hinche
Pico Duarte 3175
San Juan

DOMINICAN REPUBLIC

Puerto Plata

Puerto Rico (U.S.A.)
SAN JUAN

LEEWARD ISLANDS

Virgin Is (U.K.)
Virgin Is (U.S.A.)

Anguilla (U.K.)

THE VALLEY
St-Martin
St Maarten (Neth.)
St-Barthélemy (Fr.)

ANTIGUA AND BARBUDA

ST JOHN'S
Antigua

Coteaux
Les Cayes
Jacmel

PORT-AU-PRINCE

Barahona
San Juan

SANTO DOMINGO

La Romana
Mayagüez
Ponce

St Croix

Mona Passage

Anegada Passage

BASSETERRE
ST KITTS AND NEVIS
BRADES
Plymouth
Montserrat (U.K.)
Guadeloupe Passage

Guadeloupe (Fr.)
BASSE-TERRE (Fr.)
Marie-Galante

Isla Beata
Cabo Beata

G R E A T E R   *A N T I L L E S*

C A R I B B E A N   *S E A*

Channel

DOMINICA
ROSEAU
Martinique Passage

Martinique (Fr.)
FORT-DE-FRANCE
St Lucia Channel

Lesser Antilles

ST LUCIA CASTRIES
St Vincent Passage

ST VINCENT AND THE GRENADINES
KINGSTOWN

BARBADOS
BRIDGETOWN

W I N D W A R D   I S L A N D S

ST GEORGE'S **GRENADA**

Aruba (Neth.)
ORANJESTAD

Netherlands Antilles
Curaçao
WILLEMSTAD
Bonaire

Punta Gallinas
Península de la Guajira
Ríohacha
Maicao
Punto Fijo

Golfo de Venezuela
Campo Mara
Coro
Península de Paraguaná

Isla La Tortuga

Islas Los Roques

Isla Blanquilla

Scarborough
Tobago

TRINIDAD AND TOBAGO
PORT OF SPAIN
Trinidad

Gulf of Paria

La Asunción
Isla de Margarita

GRENADA

Santa Marta
Ciénaga
Barranquilla
Sabanalarga
Valledupar
Plato
celejo
El Banco
angangue

Rosario

Maracaibo
Cabimas
Lagunillas
Lake Maracaibo

San Felipe
Maiquetía
Petare
Maracay
Valencia
CARACAS
Los Teques
San Juan de los Morros
Cumaná
Carúpano
Güiria
San Fernando
Barcelona
Anaco
Maturín
Tucupita

Orinoco Delta

Maturín

Maruma

Machiques
San Carlos del Zulia
Valera
El Tocuyo
Barquisimeto
Trujillo
Mérida
Pico Bolívar 5007
San Carlos
Guanare
Libertad
Apure
San Cristóbal
Ciudad Bolivia

Acarigua
Valle de la Pascua
Zaraza
Guanipa
El Tigre

Cordillera de Mérida

VENEZUELA
Barinas
Calabozo
El Baúl
Puerto Miranda
San Fernando de Apure
Ciudad Bolívar

Ciudad Guayana

Embalse de Guri

Orinoco

GUYANA

OLOMBIA
Cúcuta

MILES 0   100   200   300

0   250   500 KILOMETRES

© Collins Bartholomew Ltd

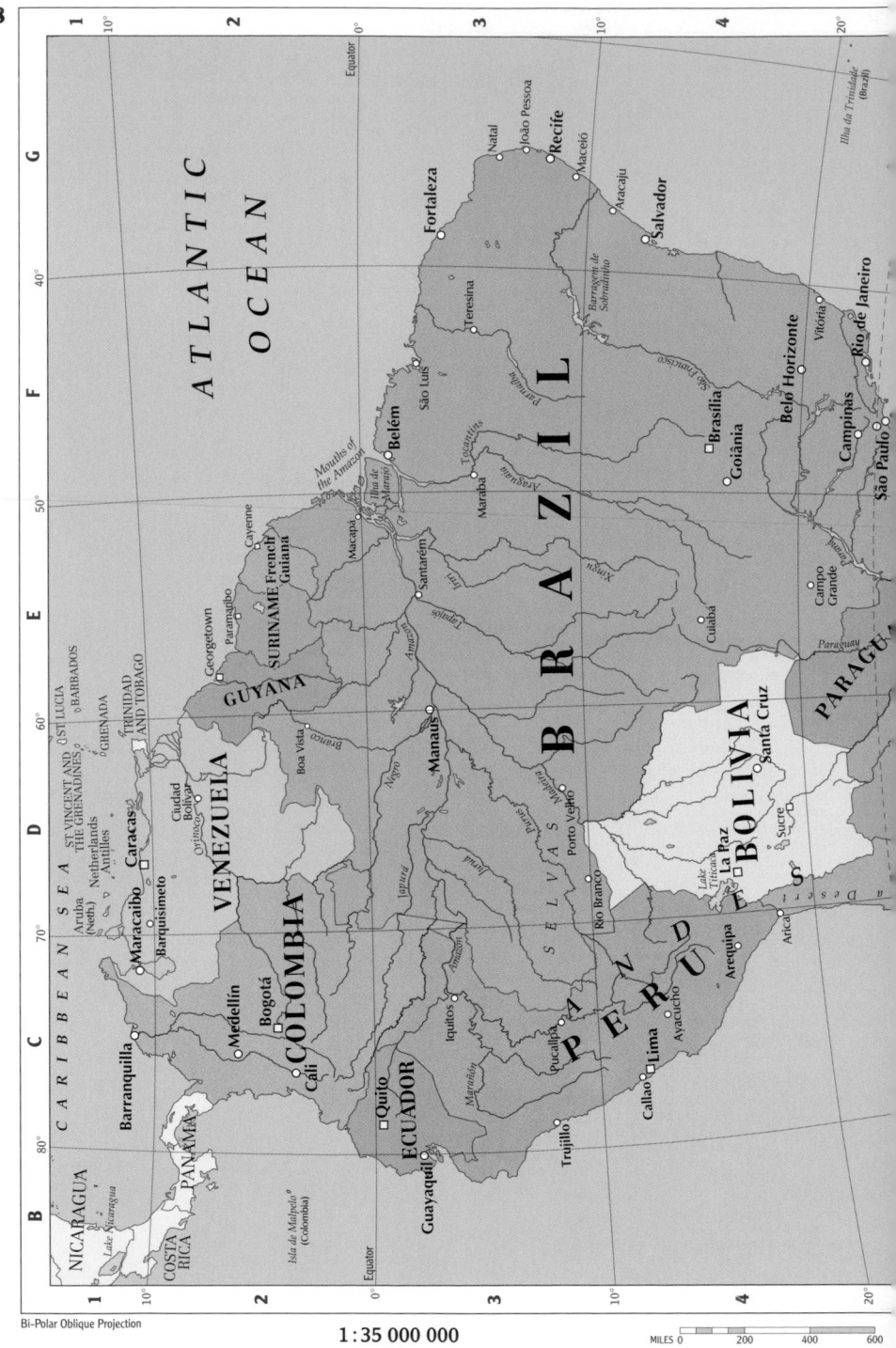

1 10° **2** 0° **3** 10° **4** 20°

1:35 000 000

MILES 0   200   400   600

1 10° **2** 0° **3** 10° **4** 20°

G
F
E
D
C
B

ATLANTIC

OCEAN

CARIBBEAN SEA

NICARAGUA

COSTA
RICA

PANAMA

Isla de Malpelo
(Colombia)

VENEZUELA

COLOMBIA

ECUADOR

PERU

BOLIVIA

BRAZIL

GUYANA

SURINAME

French
Guiana

PARAGUA

Barranquilla

Maracaibo

Barquisimeto

Caracas

Ciudad
Bolívar

Medellín

Bogotá

Cali

Quito

Guayaquil

Trujillo

Callao

Lima

Ayacucho

Pucallpa

Iquitos

Rio Branco

Porto Velho

Arequipa

Arica

La Paz

Sucre

Santa Cruz

Georgetown

Paramaribo

Cayenne

Boa Vista

Manaus

Santarém

Macapá

Belém

São Luís

Teresina

Fortaleza

Natal

João Pessoa

Recife

Maceió

Aracaju

Salvador

Brasília

Goiânia

Cuiabá

Campo
Grande

Belo Horizonte

Vitória

Rio de Janeiro

Campinas

São Paulo

Marabá

Lake
Titicaca

Mouths of
the Amazon

Ilha de
Marajó

SELVAS

ANDES

Atacama Desert

ATLANTIC OCEAN

Equator

Aruba
(Neth.)

Netherlands
Antilles

ST LUCIA

ST VINCENT AND
THE GRENADINES

GRENADA

BARBADOS

TRINIDAD
AND TOBAGO

Lake Nicaragua

Orinoco

Branco

Negro

Amazon

Japurá

Iça

Putumayo

Marañón

Ucayali

Madeira

Purús

Juruá

Tapajós

Xingu

Tocantins

Araguaia

Paraguay

São Francisco

Parnaíba

Ilha da Trinidade
(Brazil)

Barragem de
Sobradinho

80° 70° 60° 50° 40°

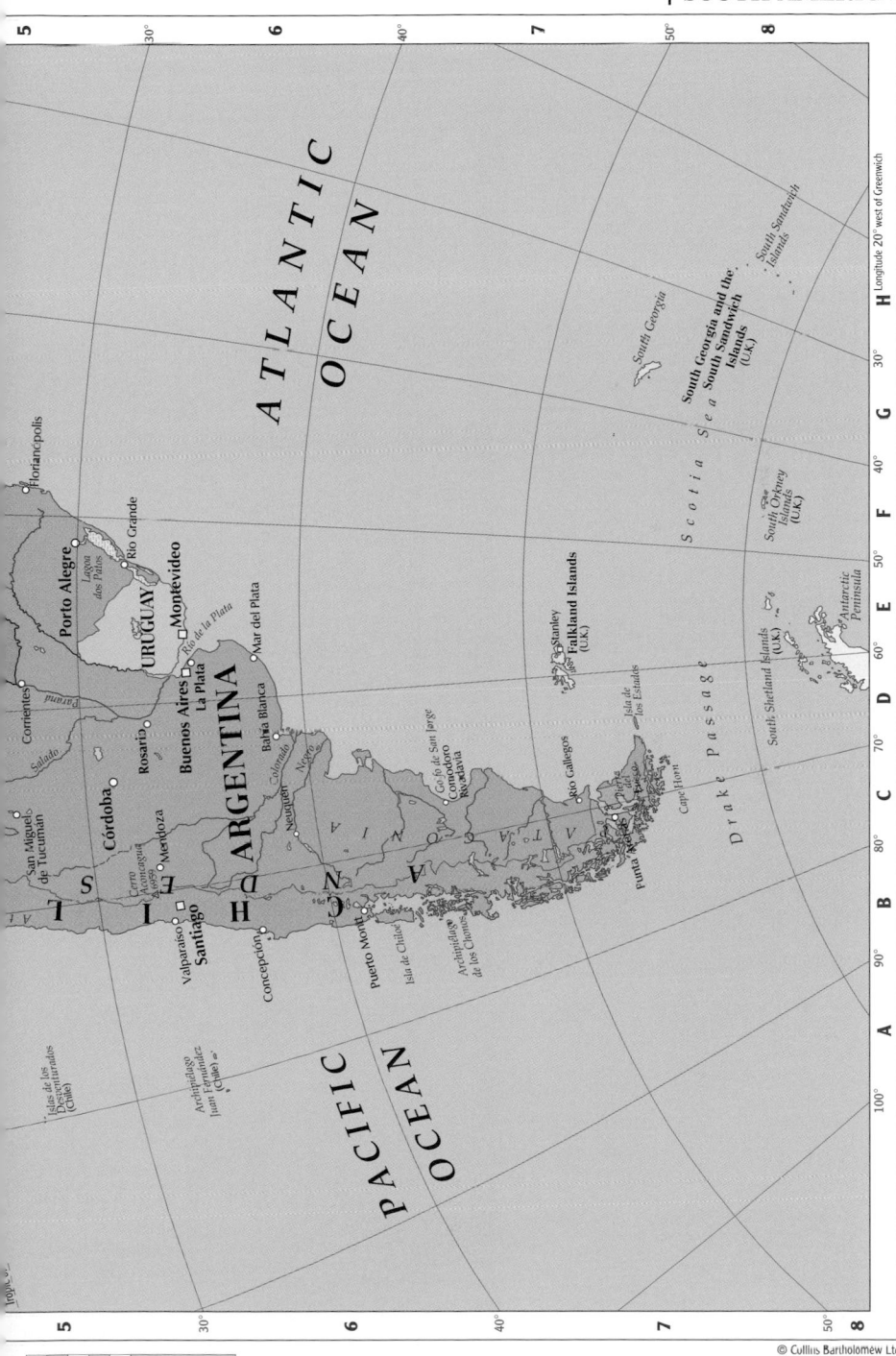

ATLANTIC

OCEAN

PACIFIC

OCEAN

ARGENTINA

URUGUAY

Florianópolis

Porto Alegre

Laguna dos Patos

Rio Grande

Montevideo

Río de la Plata

Buenos Aires

La Plata

Mar del Plata

Corrientes

Rosario

Paraná

Bahía Blanca

Salado

Córdoba

San Miguel de Tucumán

Cerro Aconcagua

Mendoza

Neuquén

Colorado

Negro

Valparaíso

Santiago

Concepción

Puerto Montt

Isla de Chiloé

Archipiélago de los Chonos

Go. de San Jorge

Comodoro Rivadavia

Río Gallegos

Isla de los Estados

Cabo de Hornos

Punta Arenas

Stanley

Falkland Islands
(U.K.)

Drake Passage

South Shetland Islands
(U.K.)

Antarctic Peninsula

Scotia Sea

South Orkney Islands
(U.K.)

South Georgia

South Georgia and the
South Sandwich
Islands
(U.K.)

South Sandwich
Islands

Islas de los Desventurados
(Chile)

Archipiélago Juan Fernández (Chile)

Longitude 20° west of Greenwich

ANDES

CORDILLERA DE LOS ANDES

5   30°

6   40°

7   50°

8

100°   A

90°   B

80°   C

70°   D

60°   E

50°   F

40°   G

30°   H

0   500   1000 KILOMETRES

A 80° B 70° C 60°

CARIBBEAN SEA

Netherlands
Punta   Aruba Antilles   GRENADA
Gallinas   (Neth.)   Curaçao   ST GEORGE'S
Punta   WILLEMSTAD
Santa   Ríohacha   Golfo de   Fijo   TRINIDAD
Marta   Venezuela   Coro   Isla de   Tobago   AND TOBA
Barranquilla   Campo Mara   Margarita   Scarboro
Sabanalarga   Maracaibo   San   La Asunción   Carúpano   PORT OF SPA
Cartagena   Valledupar   Cabimas   Felipe   CARACAS   Maiquetía   Cumaná   Güiria   Trinidad
Machiques   Barquisimeto   Los Teques   Barcelona   San Fernando
Colón   Gulf of   Sincelejo   Magangué   Lake   Valencia   Maracay   Anaco   Maturín
PANAMA CITY   del Darién   Maracaibo   Valera   Acarigua   Guanare   Zaraza   El Tigre   Tucupita   Orinoco
PANAMA   El Banco   Valle de   Delta   Mabaru
Aguadulce   Montería   Tovar   Pico Bolívar   Barinas   Calabozo   la Pascua   Ciudad   Baramanni
Chitre   La Palma   Turbo   Mérida   5007   Libertad   Ciudad Bolívar   Guayana   El Callao   Ar
Punta   Gulf of   Cúcuta   San   San Fernando   La Paragua   Tumereng   Gui
Mala   Panama   Pamplona   Cristóbal   de Apure   Angel Falls   Mount   Annai
Bucaramanga   Arauca   Puerto Páez   El Gran   Roraima
Quibdó   Socorro   Sierra Nevada   Puerto Nuevo   Puerto   Sabana   2810   Normandia
Medellín   del Cocuy   Ayacucho   Guiana   Highla   Mahi
Manizales   Tunja   5493   Meta   Puerto Nuevo   Lethem
Pereira   Zipaquirá   Yopal   Bisinaca   Pakaraima Mountains   Boa Vista   Serra Grande   3150
Armenia   BOGOTÁ   Puerto   Cerro   Caracarai   Nova
Buenaventura   Ibagué   Villavicencio   Inírida   Marahuaca   2579   Paraíso
Cali   Cerro El Nevado   2579   Represa
Palmira   Neiva   San José   Arrecifal   de Balbi
Popayán   6750   del Guaviare   Mesa   Pico da
Tumaco   Florencia   de   Uaupés   Nebina   Manaus
Pasto   Yambi   3014   Tapurucuara   Itacoa
Esmeraldas   Mocoa   Mitú   Barcelos
Ibarra   Caquetá   Lérida   Uaupés
Equator   Ipiales   La Pedrera   Maraã   Manacapuru   Autaze
QUITO   Lago Agrio   Naso   La Pedrera   Santo Antônio   Codajás   Beruri   Borba
Chone   Volcán Cotopaxi   Cabo   El Encanto   Pamar   Santa   do Içá   Coari
Manta   5896   Pantoja   Clara   Tonantins   Fonte   Manicoré
Ambato   Río   Boa   Tapauá
Portoviejo   Chimborazo   Riobamba   Tigre   Leticia   Novo
Paján   6310   Alausí   Iquitos   Tabatinga   Santo Antônio   Aripuanã
Guayaquil   Cuenca   Azogues   Nauta   Benjamim   do Içá
Machala   Gualaceo   Constant   Carauari   Tapauá
Isla Puná   Barranca   Lábrea   Barra
Golfo de   Tumbes   Lagunas   Requena   São Manu
Guayaquil   Loja   Yurimaguas   Eirunepé   Humaitá
Talara   Moyobamba   Pauini   Serra dos   Parec
Sullana   Cordillera   Rioja   Tarapoto   Envira   Porto Velho   Aripuanã
Piura   Contamana   Ipixuna   Boca   Ariquemes   Pimenta   Juína
Catacaos   Jaén   Cruzeiro   do Acre   Bueno
Sechura   Olmos   do Sul   Tarauacá   Feijó   Sena Madureira   Jaru   Vilhena
METRES   Chiclayo   Pucallpa   Rio Branco
FEET   Cajamarca   Puerto   Porto Acre   Madeira   Guayaramerín
5000   Pacasmayo   Otuzco   Portillo   Xapuri   Abunã   Costa   Pontes-e-Lacerda
16404   Trujillo   Huánuco   Alerta   Cobija   Riberalta   Marques   Mato
3000   Chimbote   Huaraz   Cerro   Atalaya   Puerto   Santa Ana   Grosso
9843   Huarmey   de Pasco   Maldonado   Exaltación   de Yacuma   Puerto   Porte
2000   Barranca   La Merced   Machu Picchu   Trinidad   Loreto   Alegre   Esperidia
6562   Huacho   Huancayo   Cusco   Sandia   Ascensión   Puerto Frey
1000   Huaral   Huancavelica   (Cuzco)   Sicuani   Santa Ana   San Pedro
3281   Callao   San Vicente de Cañete   Ayacucho   Abancay   Sicuani   de Yacuma   Santa Cruz
LIMA   Chincha Alta   Antabamba   Yanaoca   Ayaviri   San   Pampa   El Cerro
500   Pisco   Ica   Coracora   Ayaviri   Borja   Lake   Grande   Bañados
1640   Nazca   Nido   Abancay   Juliaca   Titicaca   BOLIVIA   del Izozog   Tucava
200   Marcona   Coropuna   6425   LA PAZ   Montero   San Ignacio
656   Chala   Chuquibamba   Arequipa   Oruro   Warnes
Land below   Camana   Moquegua   Cochabamba   Pampa
sea level   Mollendo   Colquín   Grande
200   Ilo   Tacna   Nevado   Huanuni
656   PACIFIC   Sajama   Corque   Cabezas
4000   OCEAN   Arica   6542
13124
6000   Longitude 70° west of Greenwich
19686

A 80° B 70° C 60°

COLOMBIA   VENEZUELA   ECUADOR   PERU   BOLIVIA

Orinoco   Negro   Amazon   Amazonas

PACIFIC OCEAN

1:20 000 000

MILES 0   100   200   300   400

D   50°   E   40°   F

1

10°

ATLANTIC

OCEAN

Equator   0°

GEORGETOWN
aradise
New Amsterdam
den   Totness   **PARAMARIBO**
ieuw   Albina   St-Laurent-du-Maroni
kerie   Brokopondo   Sinnamary
Professor van   Kourou   **CAYENNE**
Blommestein Meer   Guisanbourg
SURINAME   **French**   Oiapoque
△ *Juliana Top*   **Guiana**   Inini
1230
Pontoetoe

Serra Tumucumaque

Lourenço   Calçoene
Amapá   *Ilha de*
Maracá

Macapá   *Mouths of the*
Porto Santana   *Amazon*
Arere   Mazagão   Chaves   *Ilha*
Caviana   *Cabo*
Oriximiná   Almeirim   *Ilha de*   Salinópolis
Óbidos   *Marajó*   Bragança
Juruti   Breves   **Belém**   Viseu
Parintins   Monte   Portel   Mirinú   Castanhal   Gurupu
cuntuba   Alegre   Cametá   Acará   Pinheiro   Camocim
Santarém   *Xingu*   Tucuruí   **São Luís**
Altamira   *Capim*   Vizeu   **Parnaíba**
Itaituba   *Represa*   Santa   Bacabal   Itapicuru   Luziânia   Sobral   **Fortaleza**
Tucuruí   Luzia   Mirim   Tianguá   Caucaia   Cascavel
acareacanga   Jacunda   Pedreiras   Codó   Piripiri   Campo Maior   Canindé   Aracati
Marabá   Pres. Dutra   Caxias   Timon   **Teresina**   Crateús   Boa   Quixadá   Macau   Mossoró
Araras   Imperatriz   Grajaú   Buriti Bravo   Taua   Viagem   Iguatu   **Natal**
Manuelzinho   *São*   Tocantinópolis   Barra do   Palmeirais   Açude Boa   Icó   Campina
Félix   Xinguara   Porto Franco   Corda   Floriano   *Esperança*   Sousa   Grande   Mamanguape
Araguaína   Jerumenha   Picos   Crato   **João**
Balsas   Oeiras   Juazeiro   **Pessoa**
Conceição   Carolina   Canto do Buriti   do Norte   Jaboatão   Olinda
do Araguaia   Uruçuí   Paulistana   **Recife**
Santa Maria   Pedro   São Raimundo   Floresta   Salgueiro   Caruaru   *Cabo*
das Barreiras   Afonso   Caracol   Nonato   Petrolina   Garanhuns   Rio Largo
Peixoto de   Gilbués   Nova   Juazeiro   Paulo   **Maceió**
Azevedo   Palmas   Remanso   Afonso   Monte Santo   Arapiraca
Porto Artur   Porto Nacional   Corrente   Xique   Lagarto   Aracaju
Diamantino   *Ilha do*   Dianópolis   *Barragem de*   Xique   Jacobina   Estância
Rosário Oeste   *Bananal*   *Sobradinho*   Irecê   Serrinha
Barra do Bugres   *São*   Gurupi   Natividade   Barreiras   Ibotirama   Feira   Alagoinhas
Cuiabá   *Félix*   Ibotirama   de Santana   Camaçari
Porangatu   Cavalcante   Santana   Bom Jesus   Itaberaba   **Salvador**
Rondonópolis   Correntina   da Lapa   Santo Antônio de Jesus
Planalto   Uruaçu   Posse   Brumado   Jequié   Iaçu
Coxim   *do*   Niquelândia   Guanambi   Itabuna   Ubaitaba
Itiquira   *Mato Grosso*   Barra do   Formosa   Januária   Espinosa   Vitória da   Ilhéus
Serra do   Garças   Goiás   **BRASÍLIA**   Arinos   Conquista   Itapetinga   Una
Alto   Iporá   Luziânia   Janaúba   Almenara   Porto Seguro
Itumbiara   Garças   Trindade   Unaí   Montes   Salinas
Rio Verde de Mato Grosso   Jataí   Itumbiara   **Goiânia**   Claros   Teófilo   Alcobaça
Coxim   Rio Verde   Paraúna   Caracatu   Jequitaí   Otôni
Araguari   Patos   *Serra do Espinhaço*
Uberlândia   de Minas

D   50°   E   40°   F

2

3

10°

4

Serra
do Cachimbo
Cáceres

Serra
do Caiapó

© Collins Bartholomew Ltd

0   200   400   600 KILOMETRES

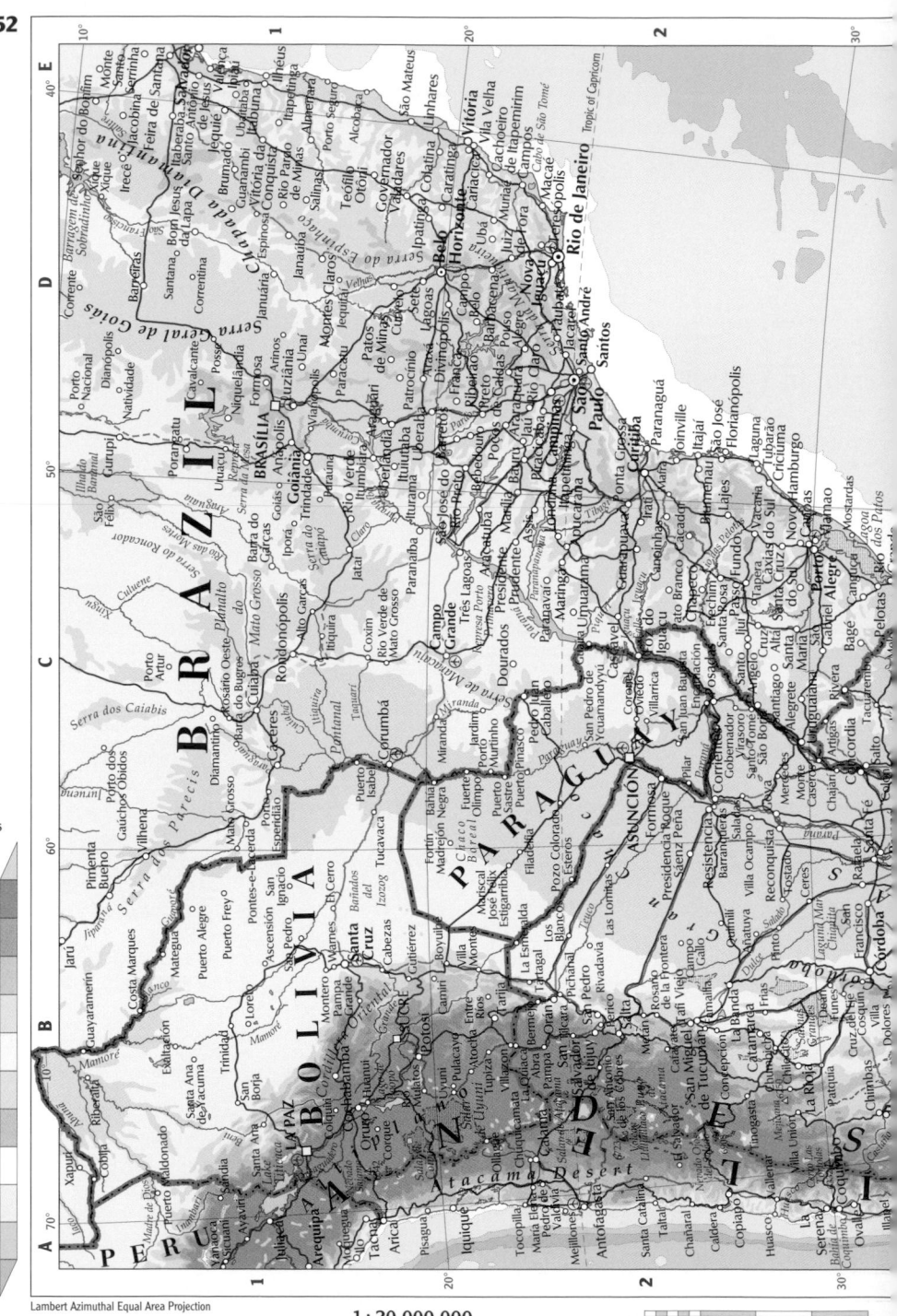

METRES / FEET

5000	16404
3000	9843
2000	6562
1000	3281
500	1640
200	656
0	0
Land below sea level	
200	656
4000	13124
6000	19686

Lambert Azimuthal Equal Area Projection

1 : 20 000 000

MILES 0   100   200   300   400

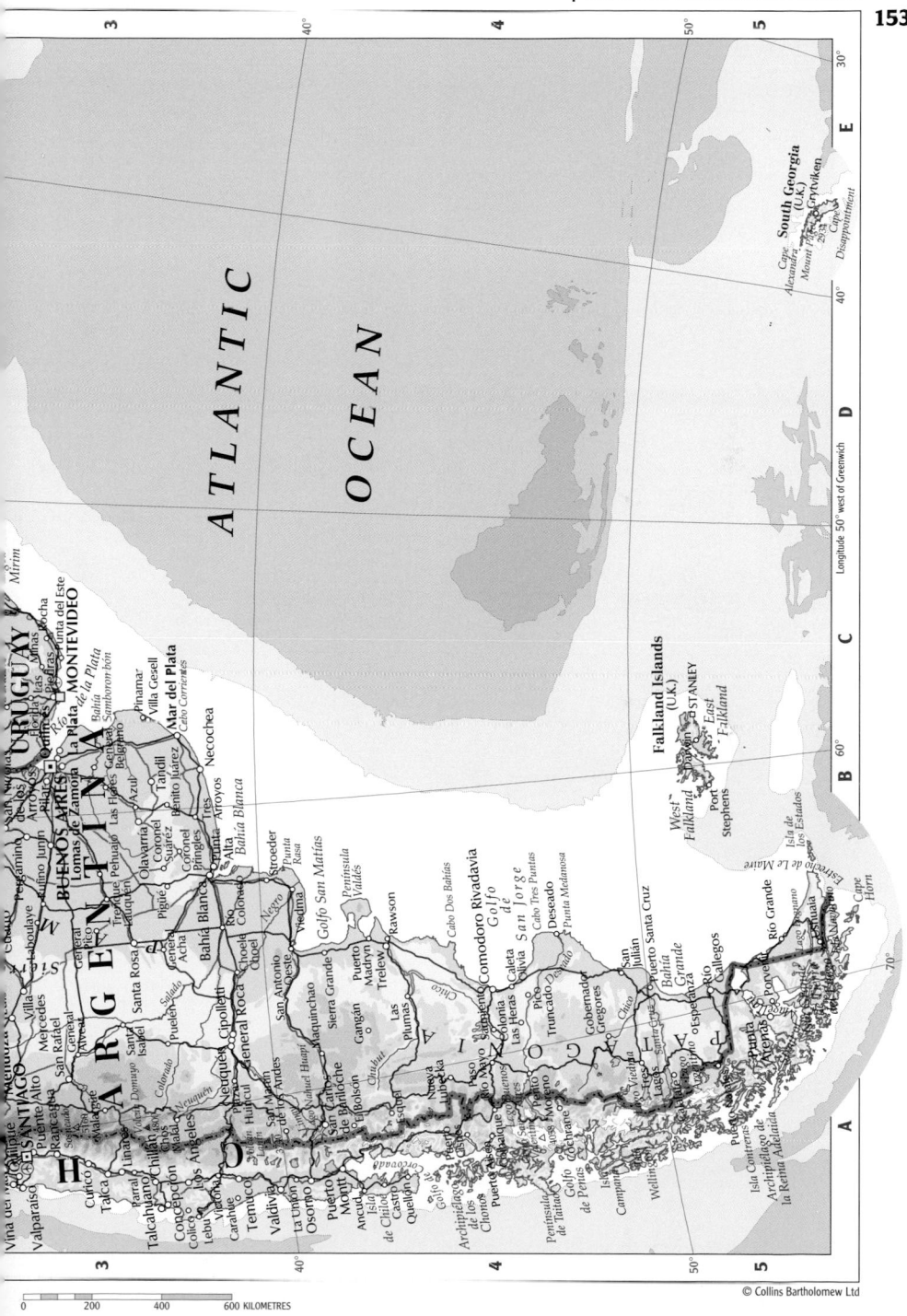

ATLANTIC

OCEAN

URUGUAY

MONTEVIDEO

ARGENTINA

BUENOS AIRES

PATAGONIA

CHILE

South Georgia
(U.K.)

Falkland Islands
(U.K.)

West
Falkland

East
Falkland

STANLEY

Port
Stephens

Isla de
los Estados

Estrecho de Le Maire

Cape
Horn

Longitude 50° west of Greenwich

© Collins Bartholomew Ltd

0   200   400   600 KILOMETRES

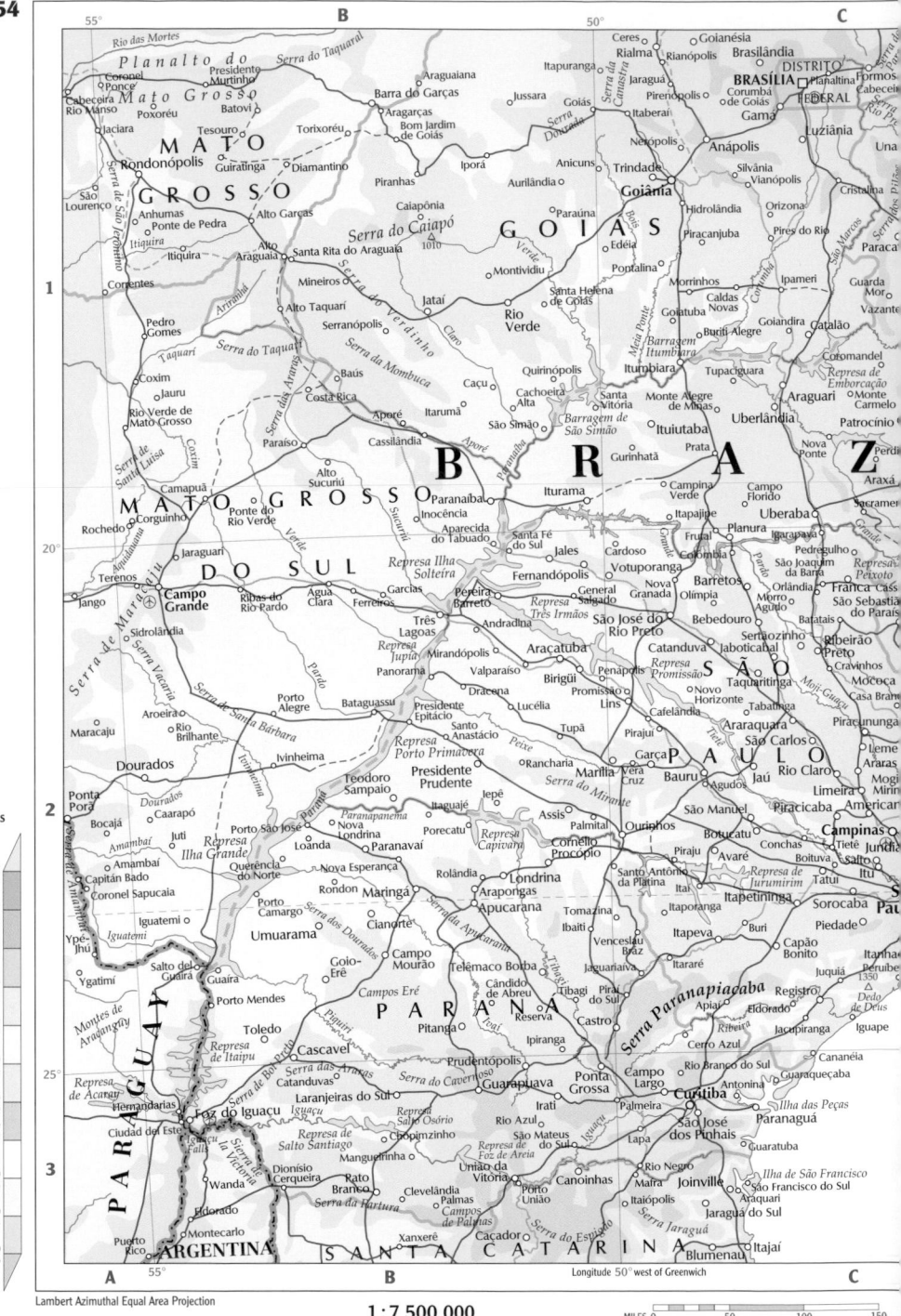

METRES
FEET

5000	16404
3000	9843
2000	6562
1000	3281
500	1640
200	656
0	0
Land below sea level	
200	656
4000	13124
6000	19686

Lambert Azimuthal Equal Area Projection

1 : 7 500 000

MILES 0   50   100   150

Longitude 50° west of Greenwich

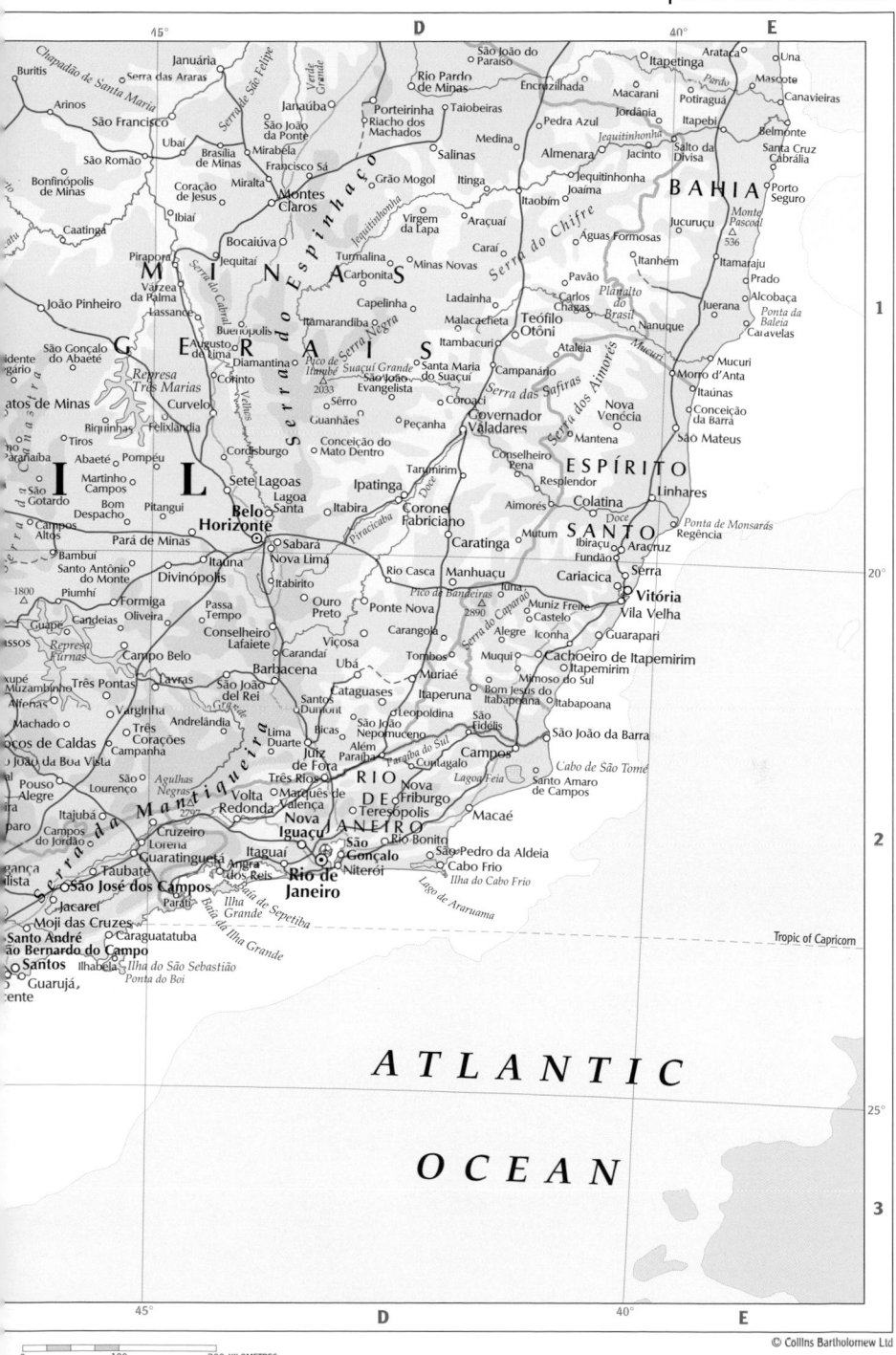

0   100   200 KILOMETRES

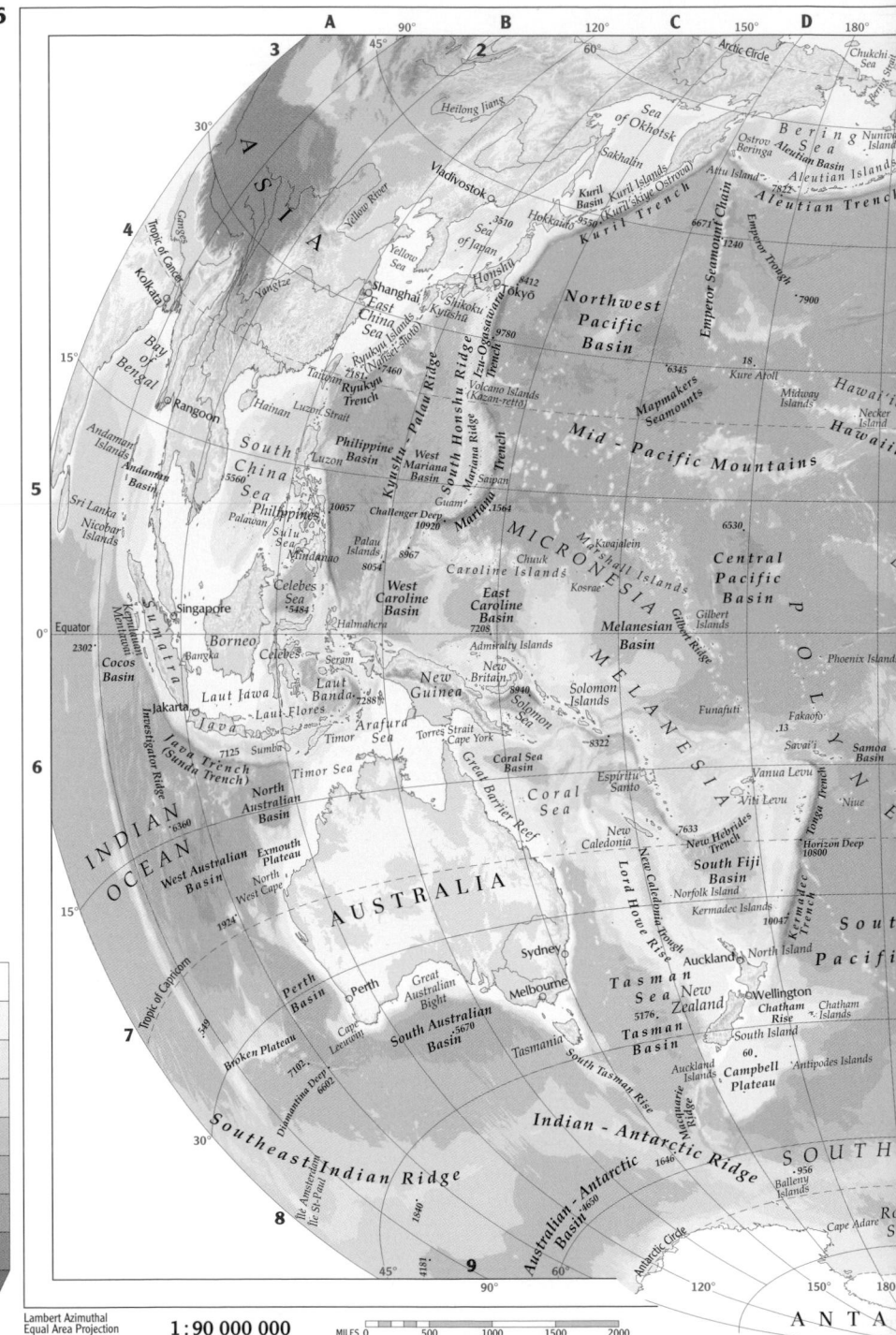

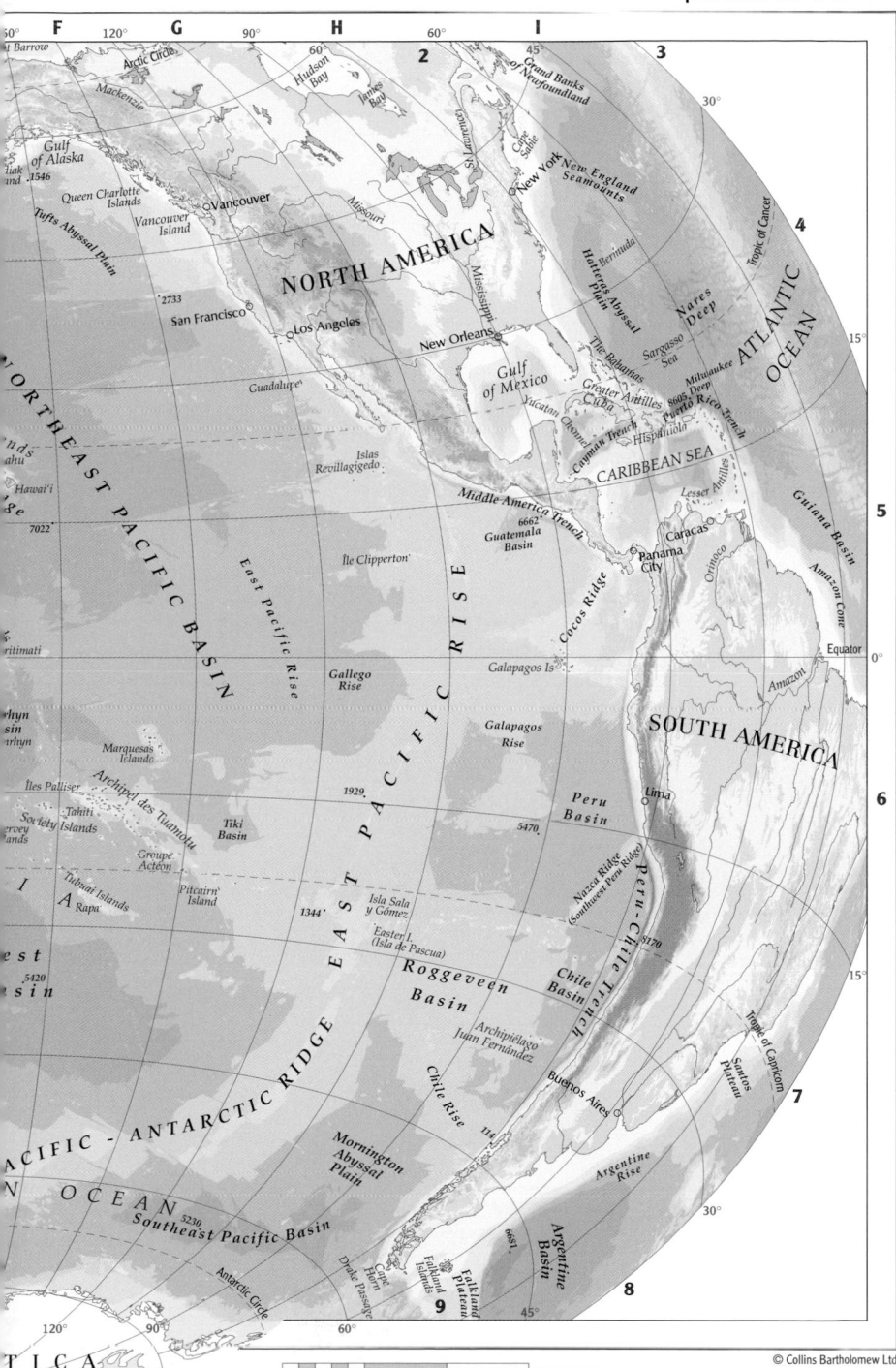

F 120° G 90° H 60° I

Barrow

Arctic Circle

Mackenzie

Hudson Bay

James Bay

Grand Banks of Newfoundland

30°

2

3

Gulf of Alaska

.1546

Kodiak Island

Queen Charlotte Islands

Vancouver Island

Vancouver

Missouri

Louisiana Is.

Sable

New York

New England Seamounts

Bermuda

Tropic of Cancer

ATLANTIC OCEAN

4

Tufts Abyssal Plain

2733

San Francisco

Los Angeles

NORTH AMERICA

Mississippi

Hatteras Abyssal Plain

Nares Deep

15°

NORTHEAST PACIFIC BASIN

nds

ahu

Hawai'i

7022

Guadalupe

Islas Revillagigedo

New Orleans

Gulf of Mexico

Yucatan

Greater Antilles

Cuba

Cayman Trench

The Bahamas

Sargasso Sea

8605 Milwaukee Deep

Puerto Rico Trench

Lesser Antilles

Sea

Hispaniola

CARIBBEAN SEA

Guiana Basin

5

ritimati

EAST PACIFIC BASIN

East Pacific Rise

Middle America Trench

6662

Guatemala Basin

Cocos Ridge

Caracas

Panama City

Orinoco

Amazon Cone

Guiana Basin

Île Clipperton

EAST PACIFIC RISE

Galapagos Is.

Equator 0°

Amazon

rhyn sin

rhyn

Marquesas Islands

Îles Palliser

Archipel des Tuamotu

Gallego Rise

Galapagos Rise

SOUTH AMERICA

6

Society Islands

Tahiti

1929,

Tiki Basin

Peru Basin

Lima

Groupe Actéon

Tubuai Islands

5420

Rapa

Pitcairn Island

1344

Isla Sala y Gómez

Easter I. (Isla de Pascua)

5470

Nazca Ridge

Southeast Peru Ridge

Peru-Chile Trench

8170

15°

sin

A

I

est

Roggeveen Basin

Chile Basin

PACIFIC - ANTARCTIC RIDGE

Archipiélago Juan Fernández

Chile Rise

114

Santos Plateau

Tropic of Capricorn

7

Buenos Aires

OCEAN

5230

Southeast Pacific Basin

Mornington Abyssal Plain

Argentine Rise

Argentine Basin

30°

Antarctic Circle

Cape Horn

Drake Passage

Falkland Islands

Falkland Plateau

6697

8

120° 90° 60° 45°

9

TICA

© Collins Bartholomew Ltd

0 1000 2000 3000 KILOMETRES

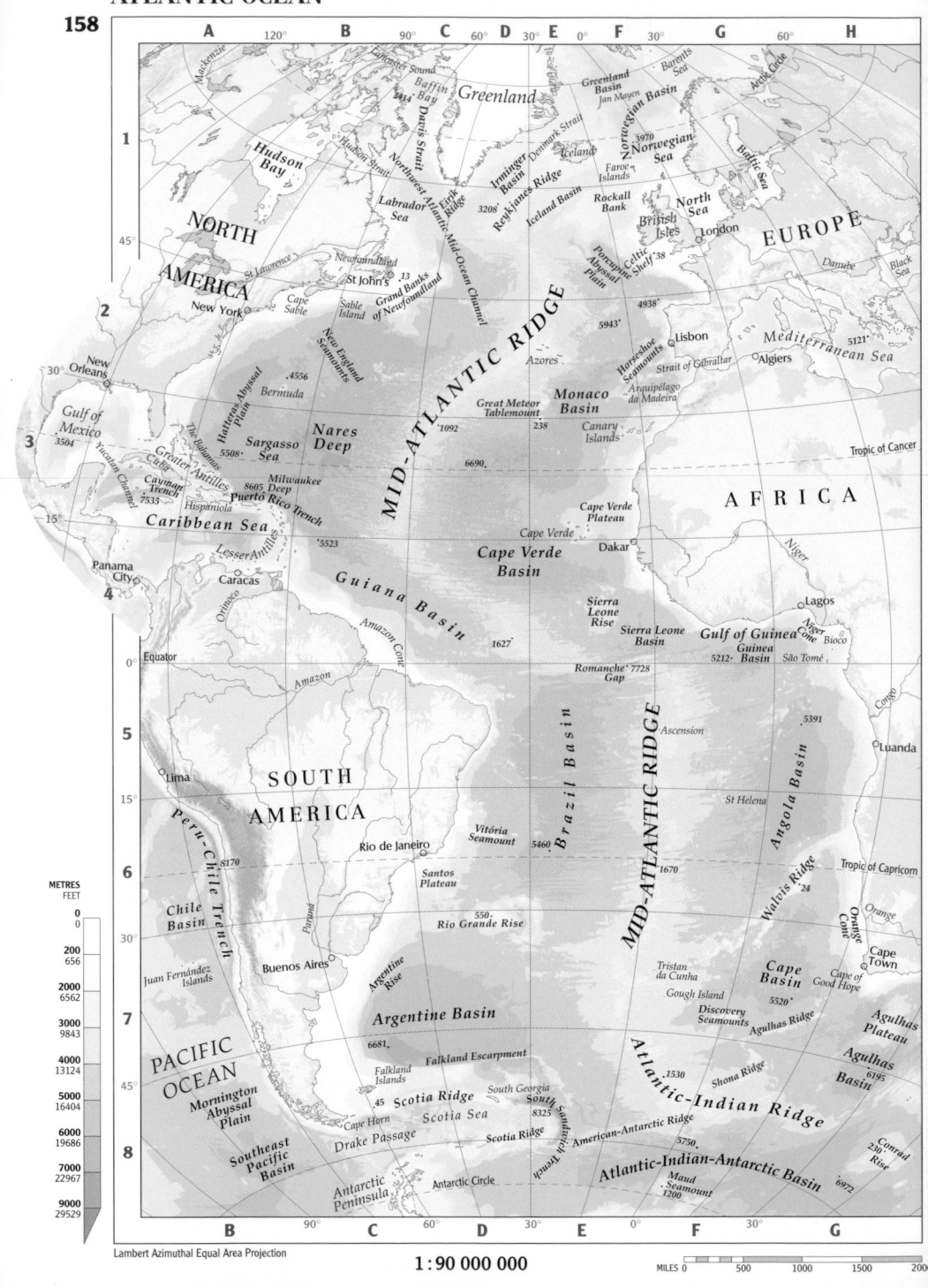

ATLANTIC OCEAN

A 120° B 90° C 60° D 30° E 0° F 30° G 60° H

Mackenzie

Lancaster Sound

Baffin Bay

Greenland

Greenland Basin Jan Mayen Barents Sea Arctic Circle

Davis Strait

Hudson Bay

Hudson Strait

Northwest Atlantic Mid-Ocean Channel

Baffin Bay 3414

Eirik Ridge

Irminger Basin 3208'

Denmark Strait

Iceland

Norwegian Basin 3970

Barents Sea

Norwegian Sea

Baltic Sea

NORTH 45°

Labrador Sea

Reykjanes Ridge

Faroe Islands

Rockall Bank

North Sea

British Isles 38

London

EUROPE

Black Sea

AMERICA

St Lawrence

Newfoundland

St John's J3

Grand Banks of Newfoundland

Iceland Basin

Celtic Shelf

Porcupine Abyssal Plain 4938'

Danube

New York

Cape Sable

Sable Island

MID-ATLANTIC RIDGE

5943'

Horseshoe Seamounts

Lisbon

Mediterranean Sea 5121'

New Orleans 30°

New England Seamounts

.4556

Azores

Monaco Basin

Strait of Gibraltar Algiers

Gulf of Mexico 3504

Hatteras Abyssal Plain

Bermuda

Great Meteor Tablemount

238

Arquipélago da Madeira

The Bahamas

Sargasso Sea

Nares Deep

'1092

Canary Islands'

Tropic of Cancer

Greater Antilles Cuba

5508'

6690.

AFRICA

Cayman Trench 7535'

Milwaukee Deep 8605

Puerto Rico Trench

Cape Verde Plateau

Hispaniola

Caribbean Sea Lesser Antilles

'5523

Cape Verde

Dakar

Panama City

Caracas

Guiana Basin

Cape Verde Basin

Niger

Orinoco

1627'

Sierra Leone Rise

Lagos

Amazon Cone

Sierra Leone Basin

Gulf of Guinea Niger Cone Bioco

Equator 0°

Amazon

Romanche' 7728 Gap

5212· Guinea Basin São Tomé

Congo

SOUTH 15°

Lima

Brazil Basin

Ascension

.5391

Luanda

AMERICA

Peru-Chile Trench 8170

St Helena

Angola Basin

MID-ATLANTIC RIDGE

Rio de Janeiro

Vitória Seamount 5460

'1670

Walvis Ridge

Tropic of Capricorn

Santos Plateau

Orange Cone

Chile Basin 30°

550· Rio Grande Rise

Cape Town

Buenos Aires

Argentine Rise

Tristan da Cunha

Cape Basin

Cape of Good Hope

Juan Fernández Islands

6681.

Gough Island

Discovery Seamounts 5520'

Agulhas Plateau

Argentine Basin

Falkland Escarpment

Agulhas Ridge

Agulhas Basin 6195

PACIFIC 45°

Falkland Islands

45

Scotia Ridge

South Georgia 8325

.1530 Shona Ridge

Atlantic-Indian Ridge

OCEAN

Mornington Abyssal Plain

Scotia Sea

Cape Horn

Scotia Ridge

American-Antarctic Ridge

5750.

Conrad Rise 230·

Southeast Pacific Basin

Drake Passage

Atlantic-Indian-Antarctic Basin '697'

Antarctic Peninsula

Antarctic Circle

Maud Seamount 1200

MILES 0 500 1000 1500 2000

B 90° C 60° D 30° E 0° F 30° G

METRES / FEET

0 / 0
200 / 656
2000 / 6562
3000 / 9843
4000 / 13124
5000 / 16404
6000 / 19686
7000 / 22967
9000 / 29529

Lambert Azimuthal Equal Area Projection

1 : 90 000 000

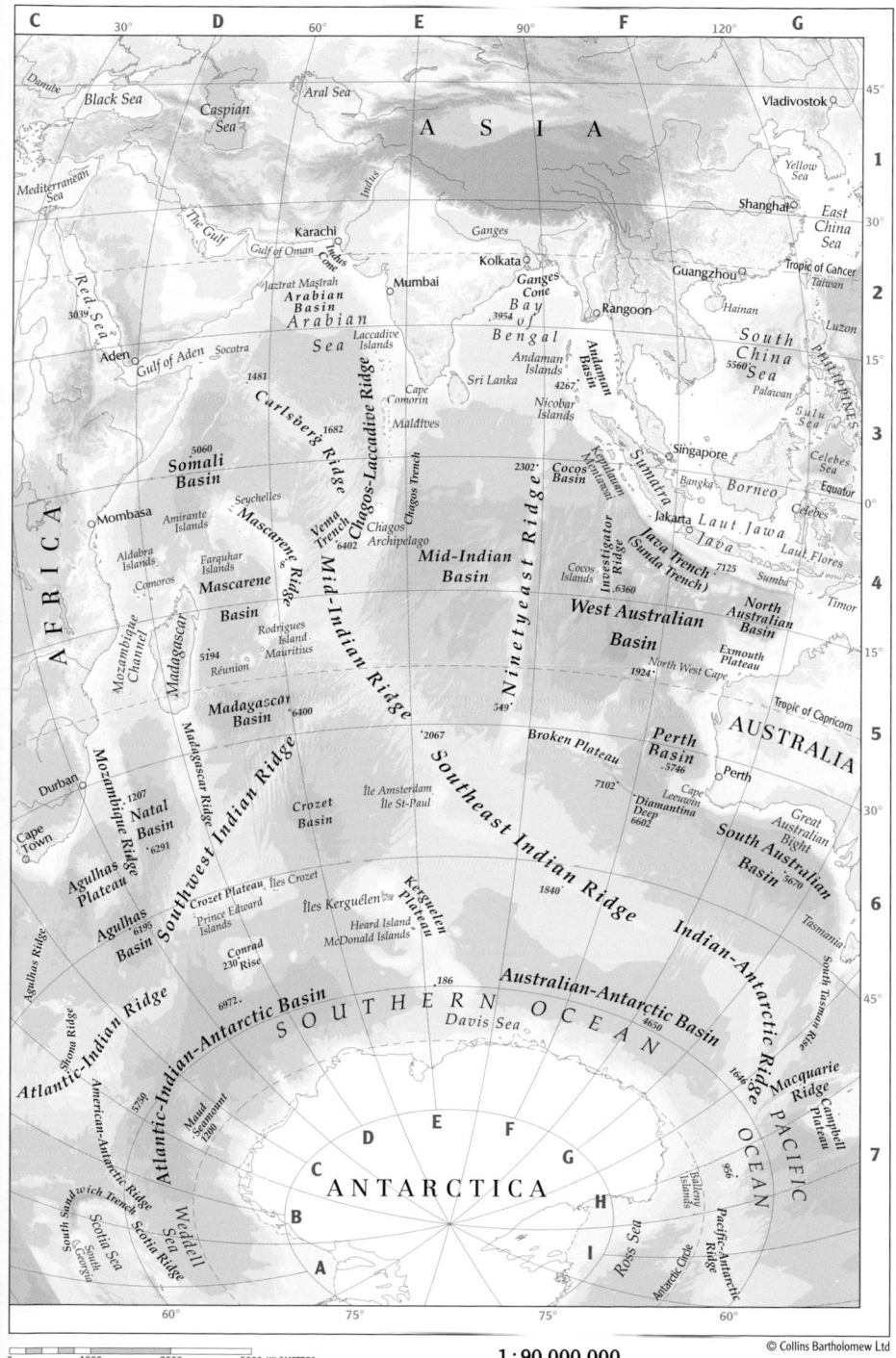

0   1000   2000   3000 KILOMETRES

1 : 90 000 000

A 160° B 180° C 160° D

PACIFIC OCEAN

Pribilof Islands
Nunivak Island
St Matthew Island
St Lawrence Island
Bering Sea
Kamchatka Basin
3703
140°
Kodiak Island
1546
60°
Sea of Okhotsk

Gulf of Alaska
Anchorage
Yukon
Nome
Bering Strait
40
Point Hope
R
Arctic Circle
Chukchi Sea

Mackenzie
70°
Barrow
Point Barrow
Wrangel Island
East Siberian Sea
1
A S I A
E
120°
3990
Beaufort Sea
Mendeleyev Ridge
New Siberia Islands
Amundsen Gulf
Canada Basin
80°
60
Lena
Ostrov Bol'shoy
Q
Laptev Sea
F
Victoria Island
Banks Island
3700
North Magnetic Pole (2006)
Alpha Ridge
4097
Makarov Basin
Lomonosov Ridge
Severnaya Zemlya
Ostrov Komsomolets
100°
Melville Island
Prince Patrick Island
Queen Elizabeth Islands
1
North Pole
4100
P
3
Parry Islands
Ellesmere Island
North Geomagnetic Pole (2006)
Amundsen Basin
4449
1
Arctic Mid-Ocean Ridge
3018
Nansen Basin
Zemlya Frantsa-Josifa
2
G
Yenisey
80°
Baffin Island
Lancaster Sound
Nares Strait
Novaya Zemlya
Kara Sea
H
Baffin Bay
2414
Station Nord
Barents Sea
O
Davis Strait
Greenland
Greenland Sea
5608
Spitsbergen
60°
Nuuk
3884
26
Bjørnøya
Greenland Basin
Nordkapp
Murmansk
Arctic Circle
Archangel
I

METRES / FEET
0 / 0
200 / 656
2000 / 6562
3000 / 9843
4000 / 13124
5000 / 16404
6000 / 19686
7000 / 22967
9000 / 29529

N
Jan Mayen
3322
Tromsø
Eirik Ridge
Nansen Island
Denmark Strait
Icelandic Plateau
Voring Plateau 1275
Bergen
Norwegian Sea
Baltic Sea
E U R O P E
Irminger Basin
Reykjavik
3208
Iceland
3970
Norwegian Basin

40°
ATLANTIC OCEAN
Reykjanes Ridge
Iceland Basin
Faroe Islands
Bergen
Rockall Bank
British Isles
North Sea

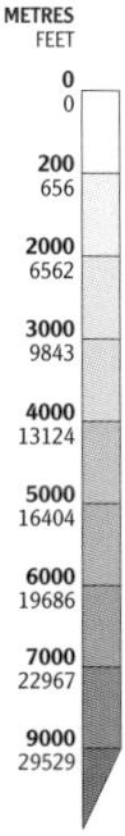

M 20° L Greenwich 0° meridian K 20° J

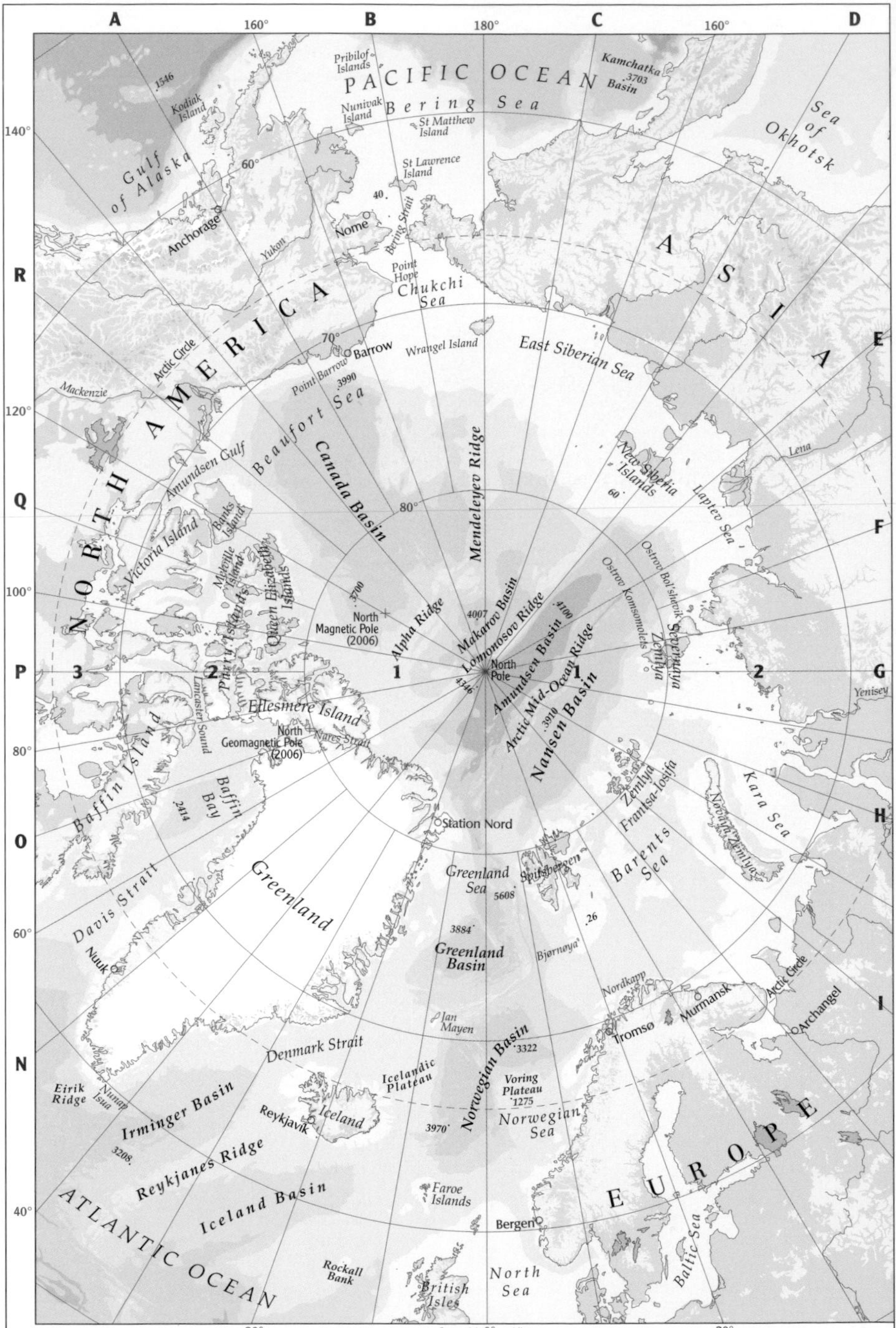

Polar Stereographic Projection

1 : 45 000 000

MILES 0   250   500   750
0   500   1000 KILOMETRES

INTRODUCTION TO THE INDEX

The index includes all names shown on the maps in the Atlas of the World. Names are referenced by page number and by a grid reference. The grid reference correlates to the alphanumeric values which appear within each map frame. Each entry also includes the country or geographical area in which the feature is located. Entries relating to names appearing on insets are indicated by a small box symbol: □, followed by a grid reference if the inset has its own alphanumeric values.

Name forms are as they appear on the maps, with additional alternative names or name forms included as cross-references which refer the user to the entry for the map form of the name. Names beginning with Mc or Mac are alphabetized exactly as they appear. The terms Saint, Sainte, Sankt, etc, are abbreviated to St, Ste, St, etc, but alphabetized as if in the full form.

Names of physical features beginning with generic geographical terms are permuted – the descriptive term is placed after the main part of the name. For example, Lake Superior is indexed as Superior, Lake; Mount Everest as Everest, Mount. This policy is applied to all languages.

Entries, other than those for towns and cities, include a descriptor indicating the type of geographical feature. Descriptors are not included where the type of feature is implicit in the name itself.

Administrative divisions are included to differentiate entries of the same name and feature type within the one country. In such cases, duplicate names are alphabetized in order of administrative division. Additional qualifiers are also included for names within selected geographical areas.

INDEX ABBREVIATIONS

admin. div.	administrative division	g.	gulf	Port.	Portugal
Afgh.	Afghanistan	Ger.	Germany	prov.	province
Alg.	Algeria	Guat.	Guatemala	pt	point
Arg.	Argentina	hd	headland	r.	river
Austr.	Australia	Hond.	Honduras	r. mouth	river mouth
aut. comm.	autonomous community	i.	island	reg.	region
aut. reg.	autonomous region	imp. l.	impermanent lake	resr	reservoir
aut. rep.	autonomous republic	Indon.	Indonesia	rf	reef
Azer.	Azerbaijan	is.	islands	Rus. Fed.	Russian Federation
b.	bay	isth.	isthmus	S.	South
B.I.O.T.	British Indian Ocean	Kazakh.	Kazakhstan	salt l.	salt lake
	Territory	Kyrg.	Kyrgyzstan	sea chan.	sea channel
Bangl.	Bangladesh	l.	lake	special admin. reg.	special administrative region
Bol.	Bolivia	lag.	lagoon		
Bos.-Herz.	Bosnia Herzegovina	Lith.	Lithuania	str.	strait
Bulg.	Bulgaria	Lux.	Luxembourg	Switz.	Switzerland
c.	cape	Madag.	Madagascar	Tajik.	Tajikistan
Can.	Canada	Maur.	Mauritania	Tanz.	Tanzania
C.A.R.	Central African Republic	Mex.	Mexico	terr.	territory
Col.	Colombia	Moz.	Mozambique	Thai.	Thailand
Czech Rep.	Czech Republic	mt.	mountain	Trin. and Tob.	Trinidad and Tobago
Dem. Rep.	Democratic	mts	mountains	Turkm.	Turkmenistan
Congo	Republic of the Congo	mun.	municipality	U.A.E.	United Arab Emirates
depr.	depression	N.	North	U.K.	United Kingdom
des.	desert	Neth.	Netherlands	Ukr.	Ukraine
Dom. Rep.	Dominican Republic	Neth. Antilles	Netherland Antilles	union terr.	union territory
Equat.	Equatorial Guinea	Nic.	Nicaragua	Uru.	Uruguay
Guinea		N.Z.	New Zealand	U.S.A.	United States of America
esc.	escarpment	Pak.	Pakistan	Uzbek.	Uzbekistan
est.	estuary	Para.	Paraguay	val.	valley
Eth.	Ethiopia	pen.	peninsula	Venez.	Venezuela
Fin.	Finland	Phil.	Philippines	vol.	volcano
for.	forest	plat.	plateau	vol. crater	volcanic crater
Fr. Guiana	French Guiana	P.N.G.	Papua New Guinea		
Fr. Polynesia	French Polynesia	Pol.	Poland		

A

93 E4 Aabenraa Denmark
100 C2 Aachen Ger.
93 E4 Aalborg Denmark
102 C2 Aalen Ger.
100 B2 Aalst Belgium
93 I3 Äänekoski Fin.
105 D2 Aarau Switz.
100 B2 Aarschot Belgium
70 A2 Aba China
119 D2 Aba Dem. Rep. Congo
115 C4 Aba Nigeria
81 C2 Ābādān Iran
81 D2 Ābādeh Iran
81 D3 Ābādeh Ţashk Iran
114 B1 Abadla Alg.
155 C1 Abaeté Brazil
　　 Abagnar Qi China see
　　 Xilinhot
135 E3 Abajo Peak U.S.A.
115 C4 Abakaliki Nigeria
83 H3 Abakan Rus. Fed.
150 B4 Abancay Peru
81 D2 Abarqū Iran
66 D2 Abashiri Japan
66 D2 Abashiri-wan b. Japan
59 D3 Abau P.N.G.
　　 Abaya, Lake Eth. see
　　 Lake Abaya
　　 Ābay Wenz r. Eth. see
　　 Blue Nile
83 H3 Abaza Rus. Fed.
108 A2 Abbasanta Sardinia Italy
104 C1 Abbeville France
141 C2 Abbeville AL U.S.A.
140 B3 Abbeville LA U.S.A.
97 B2 Abbeyfeale Ireland
55 R2 Abbot Ice Shelf Antarctica
74 B1 Abbottabad Pak.
115 E3 Abéché Chad
114 B4 Abengourou Côte d'Ivoire
114 C4 Abeokuta Nigeria
99 A3 Aberaeron U.K.
96 C2 Aberchirder U.K.
　　 Abercorn Zambia see
　　 Mbala
99 B4 Aberdare U.K.
99 A3 Aberdaron U.K.
53 D2 Aberdeen Austr.
122 B3 Aberdeen S. Africa
96 C2 Aberdeen U.K.
139 D3 Aberdeen MD U.S.A.
137 D1 Aberdeen SD U.S.A.
134 B1 Aberdeen WA U.S.A.
129 E1 Aberdeen Lake Can.
96 C2 Aberfeldy U.K.
96 B2 Aberfoyle U.K.
99 B4 Abergavenny U.K.
　　 Abergwaun U.K. see
　　 Fishguard
　　 Aberhonddu U.K. see
　　 Brecon
143 C2 Abernathy U.S.A.
134 B2 Abert, Lake U.S.A.
　　 Abertawe U.K. see
　　 Swansea
　　 Aberteifi U.K. see
　　 Cardigan
99 B3 Abertillery U.K.
99 A3 Aberystwyth U.K.
86 F2 Abez' Rus. Fed.
78 B3 Abhā Saudi Arabia
81 C2 Abhar Iran
　　 Abiad, Bahr el r.
　　 Sudan/Uganda see
　　 White Nile
114 B4 Abidjan Côte d'Ivoire
137 D3 Abilene KS U.S.A.
143 D2 Abilene TX U.S.A.
99 C4 Abingdon U.K.
138 C3 Abingdon U.S.A.
91 D3 Abinsk Rus. Fed.
130 B3 Abitibi, Lake Can.
　　 Åbo Fin. see Turku
74 B1 Abohar India
114 B4 Aboisso Côte d'Ivoire
114 C4 Abomey Benin
60 A1 Abongabong, Gunung mt.
　　 Indon.
118 B2 Abong Mbang Cameroon
64 A3 Aborlan Phil.
115 D3 Abou Déia Chad
106 B2 Abrantes Port.
152 B2 Abra Pampa Arg.
142 A3 Abreojos, Punta pt Mex.
116 B2 'Abri Sudan
136 A2 Absaroka Range mts
　　 U.S.A.

81 C1 Abşeron Yarımadası pen.
　　 Azer.
78 B3 Abū 'Arīsh Saudi Arabia
116 A2 Abū Ballāş hill Egypt
79 C2 Abu Dhabi U.A.E.
116 B3 Abu Hamed Sudan
116 B3 Abu Haraz Sudan
115 C4 Abuja Nigeria
81 C2 Abū Kamāl Syria
118 C2 Abumombazi
　　 Dem. Rep. Congo
152 B1 Abunã r. Bol.
150 C3 Abunã Brazil
74 B2 Abu Road India
78 B2 Abū Şādi, Jabal hill
　　 Saudi Arabia
116 B2 Abū Sunbul Egypt
116 A3 Abu Zabad Sudan
　　 Abū Ẓabī U.A.E. see
　　 Abu Dhabi
117 A4 Abyei Sudan
145 B2 Acambaro Mex.
120 B2 Acampamento de Caça
　　 do Mucusso Angola
106 B1 A Cañiza Spain
144 B2 Acaponeta Mex.
145 C3 Acapulco Mex.
151 E3 Acará Brazil
154 A3 Acaray, Represa de resr
　　 Para.
150 C2 Acarigua Venez.
110 B1 Acâş Romania
145 C3 Acatlan Mex.
145 C3 Acayucán Mex.
114 B4 Accra Ghana
98 B3 Accrington U.K.
74 B2 Achalpur India
97 A2 Achill Island Ireland
101 D1 Achim Ger.
96 B2 Achnasheen U.K.
91 D2 Achuyevo Rus. Fed.
111 C3 Acıpayam Turkey
109 C3 Acireale Sicily Italy
147 C2 Acklins Island Bahamas
153 A3 Aconcagua, Cerro mt.
　　 Arg.
106 B1 A Coruña Spain
108 A2 Acqui Terme Italy
103 D2 Ács Hungary
49 N6 Actéon, Groupe is
　　 Fr. Polynesia
145 C2 Actopán Mex.
143 D2 Ada U.S.A.
　　 Adabazar Turkey see
　　 Adapazarı
79 C2 Adam Oman
111 B3 Adamas Greece
135 B3 Adams Peak U.S.A.
　　 'Adan Yemen see Aden
80 B2 Adana Turkey
111 D2 Adapazarı Turkey
97 B2 Adare Ireland
55 M2 Adare, Cape Antarctica
108 A1 Adda r. Italy
78 B2 Ad Dafinah Saudi Arabia
78 B2 Ad Dahnā' des.
　　 Saudi Arabia
79 B2 Ad Dahnā' des.
　　 Saudi Arabia
114 A2 Ad Dakhla Western Sahara
　　 Ad Dammām Saudi Arabia
　　 see Dammam
78 A2 Ad Dār al Ḥamrā'
　　 Saudi Arabia
78 B3 Ad Darb Saudi Arabia
78 B2 Ad Dawādimī Saudi Arabia
　　 Ad Dawḥah Qatar see
　　 Doha
　　 Ad Ḍiffah Egypt see
　　 Libyan Plateau
78 B2 Ad Dilam Saudi Arabia
78 B2 Ad Dir'īyah Saudi Arabia
117 B4 Addis Ababa Eth.
81 C2 Ad Dīwānīyah Iraq
141 D2 Adel U.S.A.
52 A2 Adelaide Austr.
55 A3 Adelaide Island Antarctica
50 C1 Adelaide River Austr.
101 D2 Adelebsen Ger.
55 K2 Adélie Land Antarctica
78 B3 Aden Yemen
116 C3 Aden, Gulf of
　　 Somalia/Yemen
100 C2 Adenau Ger.
115 C3 Aderbissinat Niger
79 C2 Adh Dhayd U.A.E.
59 C3 Adi i. Indon.
116 B3 Ādī Ārk'ay Eth.
108 B1 Adige r. Italy
116 B3 Ādīgrat Eth.
78 A3 Adi Keyih Eritrea

74 B3 Adilabad India
115 D2 Adiri Libya
139 E2 Adirondack Mountains
　　 U.S.A.
　　 Ādīs Ābeba Eth. see
　　 Addis Ababa
81 C2 Ādīs Alem Eth.
80 B2 Adıyaman Turkey
110 C1 Adjud Romania
50 B1 Admiralty Gulf Austr.
128 A2 Admiralty Island U.S.A.
59 D3 Admiralty Islands P.N.G.
73 B3 Adoni India
104 B3 Adour r. France
106 C2 Adra Spain
114 B2 Adrar Alg.
138 C2 Adrian MI U.S.A.
143 C1 Adrian TX U.S.A.
108 B2 Adriatic Sea Europe
　　 Adua Eth. see Ādwa
116 B3 Ādwa Eth.
83 K2 Adycha r. Rus. Fed.
91 D3 Adygeysk Rus. Fed.
114 B4 Adzopé Côte d'Ivoire
111 B3 Aegean Sea
　　 Greece/Turkey
101 D1 Aerzen Ger.
106 B1 A Estrada Spain
116 B3 Afabet Eritrea
　　 Affreville Alg. see
　　 Khemis Miliana
76 C3 Afghanistan country Asia
78 B2 'Afif Saudi Arabia
136 A2 Afton U.S.A.
80 B2 Afyon Turkey
115 C3 Agadez Niger
114 B1 Agadir Morocco
77 D2 Agadyr' Kazakh.
113 I7 Agalega Islands Mauritius
　　 Agana Guam see Hagåtña
106 B1 A Gándara de Altea Spain
74 B2 Agar India
116 B3 Āgaro Eth.
75 D2 Agartala India
81 C2 Ağdam Azer.
105 C3 Agde France
　　 Agedabia Libya see
　　 Ajdābiyā
104 C3 Agen France
122 A2 Aggeneys S. Africa
111 C3 Agia Varvara Greece
111 B3 Agios Dimitrios Greece
111 C3 Agios Efstratios i. Greece
111 C3 Agios Kirykos Greece
111 C3 Agios Nikolaos Greece
78 A3 Agirwat Hills Sudan
123 C2 Agisanang S. Africa
110 B1 Agnita Romania
74 B2 Agra India
81 C2 Ağrı Turkey
　　 Ağrı Dağı mt. Turkey see
　　 Ararat, Mount
108 B3 Agrigento Sicily Italy
111 B3 Agrinio Greece
109 B2 Agropoli Italy
87 E3 Agryz Rus. Fed.
144 B2 Agua Brava, Laguna lag.
　　 Mex.
154 B2 Água Clara Brazil
145 C3 Aguada Mex.
146 B4 Aguadulce Panama
144 B2 Aguanaval r. Mex.
144 B1 Agua Prieta Mex.
144 B2 Aguascalientes Mex.
155 D1 Águas Formosas Brazil
154 C2 Águdos Brazil
106 B1 Águeda Port.
106 B1 Aguelhok Mali
106 C1 Aguilar de Campóo Spain
107 C2 Águilas Spain
144 B3 Aguililla Mex.
122 B3 Agulhas, Cape S. Africa
158 F7 Agulhas Basin sea feature
　　 Southern Ocean
155 D2 Agulhas Negras mt. Brazil
158 F7 Agulhas Plateau
　　 sea feature Southern Ocean
158 F7 Agulhas Ridge sea feature
　　 S. Atlantic Ocean
111 C2 Ağva Turkey
81 C2 Ahar Iran
100 C1 Ahaus Ger.
81 C2 Ahlat Turkey
100 C2 Ahlen Ger.
74 B2 Ahmadabad India
74 B3 Ahmadnagar India
74 B2 Ahmadpur East Pak.
74 B1 Ahmadpur Sial Pak.
117 C4 Ahmar Eth.
　　 Ahmedabad India see
　　 Ahmadabad

　　 Ahmednagar India see
　　 Ahmadnagar
144 B2 Ahome Mex.
81 D3 Ahram Iran
101 E1 Ahrensburg Ger.
104 C2 Ahun France
93 F4 Åhus Sweden
81 C2 Ahvāz Iran
　　 Ahvenanmaa is Fin. see
　　 Åland Islands
122 A2 Ai-Ais Namibia
80 B2 Aigialousa Cyprus
111 B3 Aigio Greece
　　 Aihui China see Heihe
　　 Aijal India see Aizawl
141 D2 Aiken U.S.A.
155 D1 Aimorés Brazil
155 D1 Aimorés, Serra dos hills
　　 Brazil
105 D2 Ain r. France
107 E2 Aïn Azel Alg.
115 C1 Aïn Beïda Alg.
114 B2 'Aïn Ben Tili Maur.
107 D2 Aïn Defla Alg.
114 B1 Aïn Sefra Alg.
136 D2 Ainsworth U.S.A.
　　 Aintab Turkey see
　　 Gaziantep
107 D2 Aïn Taya Alg.
107 D2 Aïn Tédélès Alg.
107 C2 Aïn Temouchent Alg.
115 C3 Aïr, Massif de l' mts Niger
60 A1 Airbangis Indon.
128 C2 Airdrie Can.
96 C3 Airdrie U.K.
104 B3 Aire-sur-l'Adour France
101 E3 Aisch r. Ger.
128 A1 Aishihik Lake Can.
100 A3 Aisne r. France
59 D3 Aitape P.N.G.
137 E1 Aitkin U.S.A.
110 B1 Aiud Romania
105 D3 Aix-en-Provence France
　　 Aix-la-Chapelle Ger. see
　　 Aachen
105 D2 Aix-les-Bains France
75 D2 Aizawl India
88 C2 Aizkraukle Latvia
88 B2 Aizpute Latvia
67 C3 Aizu-Wakamatsu Japan
105 D3 Ajaccio Corsica France
　　 Ajayameru India see Ajmer
115 E1 Ajdābiyā Libya
79 C2 'Ajman U.A.E.
74 B2 Ajmer India
　　 Ajmer-Merwara India see
142 A2 Ajmer
119 D2 Ajo U.S.A.
　　 Ak'ak'i Beseka Eth.
　　 Akamagaseki Japan see
　　 Shimonoseki
54 B2 Akaroa N.Z.
87 E3 Akbulak Rus. Fed.
80 B2 Akçakale Turkey
114 A3 Akchār reg. Maur.
111 C3 Akdağ mt. Turkey
80 B2 Akdağmadeni Turkey
88 A2 Åkersberga Sweden
118 C2 Aketi Dem. Rep. Congo
81 C1 Akhalk'alak'i Georgia
81 C1 Akhalts'ikhe Georgia
79 C2 Akhdar, Jabal mts Oman
111 C3 Akhisar Turkey
87 D4 Akhtubinsk Rus. Fed.
118 B3 Akiéni Gabon
130 B2 Akimiski Island Can.
66 D3 Akita Japan
114 A3 Akjoujt Maur.
　　 Akkerman Ukr. see
　　 Bilhorod-Dnistrovs'kyy
77 D1 Akkol' Kazakh.
　　 Ak-Mechet Kazakh. see
　　 Kyzylorda
88 B2 Akmenrags pt Latvia
　　 Akmola Kazakh. see
　　 Astana
　　 Akmolinsk Kazakh. see
　　 Astana
67 B4 Akō Japan
117 B4 Akobo Sudan
74 B2 Akola India
118 B2 Akonolinga Cameroon
78 A3 Akordat Eritrea
131 D1 Akpatok Island Can.
77 D2 Akqi China
92 □A3 Akranes Iceland
136 C2 Akron CO U.S.A.
138 C2 Akron OH U.S.A.
75 B1 Aksai Chin terr. Asia
80 B2 Aksaray Turkey
86 F2 Aksarka Rus. Fed.

76 B1 **Aksay** Kazakh.
91 D2 **Aksay** Rus. Fed.
80 B2 **Akşehir** Turkey
78 C2 **Akshiganak** Kazakh.
77 E2 **Aksu** China
116 B3 **Aksum** Eth.
76 B2 **Aktau** Kazakh.
76 B1 **Aktobe** Kazakh.
77 D2 **Aktogay** Kazakh.
88 C3 **Aktsyabrski** Belarus
Aktyubinsk Kazakh. *see*
Aktobe
67 B4 **Akune** Japan
115 C4 **Akure** Nigeria
92 □B2 **Akureyri** Iceland
Akyab Myanmar *see* Sittwe
111 D2 **Akyazı** Turkey
77 C2 **Akzhaykyn, Ozero** *salt l.*
Kazakh.
140 C2 **Alabama** *r.* U.S.A.
140 C2 **Alabama** *state* U.S.A.
140 B2 **Alabaster** U.S.A.
111 C3 **Alaçatı** Turkey
145 D2 **Alacrán, Arrecife** *rf* Mex.
81 C1 **Alagir** Rus. Fed.
151 F4 **Alagoinhas** Brazil
107 C1 **Alagón** Spain
77 E2 **Al Aḥmadī** Kuwait
77 E2 **Alakol', Ozero** *salt l.*
Kazakh.
92 J2 **Alakurtti** Rus. Fed.
78 B3 **Al 'Alayyah** Saudi Arabia
81 C2 **Al 'Amādīyah** Iraq
81 C2 **Al 'Amārah** Iraq
80 A2 **Al 'Āmiriyah** Egypt
143 C3 **Alamitos, Sierra de los**
mt. Mex.
135 C3 **Alamo** U.S.A.
142 D2 **Alamogordo** U.S.A.
144 B2 **Alamos** Mex.
144 B2 **Alamos** Mex.
144 B2 **Alamos** *r.* Mex.
136 B3 **Alamosa** U.S.A.
Åland Fin. *see*
80 B2 **Åland Islands** *is* Fin.
93 G3 **Åland Islands** *is* Fin.
80 B2 **Alanya** Turkey
Alappuzha India *see*
Alleppey
80 B3 **Al 'Aqabah** Jordan
78 B2 **Al 'Aqiq** Saudi Arabia
107 C2 **Alarcón, Embalse de** *resr*
Spain
80 B2 **Al 'Arish** Egypt
78 B2 **Al Arṭāwīyah** Saudi Arabia
61 C2 **Alas** Indon.
111 C3 **Alaşehir** Turkey
128 A2 **Alaska** *state* U.S.A.
124 D4 **Alaska, Gulf of** U.S.A.
126 B3 **Alaska Peninsula** U.S.A.
126 C2 **Alaska Range** *mts* U.S.A.
81 C2 **Älät** Azer.
87 D3 **Alatyr'** Rus. Fed.
150 B2 **Alausí** Ecuador
93 H3 **Alavus** Fin.
52 B2 **Alawoona** Austr.
79 C2 **Al 'Ayn** U.A.E.
108 A2 **Alba** Italy
107 C2 **Albacete** Spain
78 A2 **Al Badā'i'** Saudi Arabia
78 B2 **Al Badī'** Saudi Arabia
110 B1 **Alba Iulia** Romania
106 B2 **Albania** *country* Europe
50 A3 **Albany** Austr.
130 B2 **Albany** *r.* Can.
141 D2 **Albany** *GA* U.S.A.
139 E2 **Albany** *NY* U.S.A.
134 B2 **Albany** *OR* U.S.A.
115 E1 **Al Bardī** Libya
Al Başrah Iraq *see* Basra
51 D1 **Albatross Bay** Austr.
116 A2 **Al Bawīṭī** Egypt
115 E1 **Al Bayḍā'** Libya
78 B3 **Al Bayḍā'** Yemen
141 D1 **Albemarle** U.S.A.
141 E1 **Albemarle Sound**
sea chan. U.S.A.
108 A2 **Albenga** Italy
52 C2 **Alberga** *watercourse* Austr.
119 D2 **Albert, Lake**
Dem. Rep. Congo/Uganda
128 C2 **Alberta** *prov.* Can.
100 B2 **Albert Kanaal** *canal*
Belgium
137 E2 **Albert Lea** U.S.A.
117 B4 **Albert Nile** *r.*
Sudan/Uganda
123 C2 **Alberton** S. Africa
Albertville
Dem. Rep. Congo *see*
Kalemie

105 D2 **Albertville** France
104 C3 **Albi** France
151 D2 **Albina** Suriname
78 A2 **Al Bi'r** Saudi Arabia
78 B3 **Al Birk** Saudi Arabia
78 B2 **Al Biyāḍh** *reg.*
Saudi Arabia
Alborz, Reshteh-ye Iran
see Elburz Mountains
107 C2 **Albox** Spain
106 B2 **Albufeira** Port.
142 B1 **Albuquerque** U.S.A.
79 C2 **Al Buraymī** Oman
53 C3 **Albury** Austr.
106 B2 **Alcácer do Sal** Port.
106 C1 **Alcalá de Henares** Spain
107 C2 **Alcalá la Real** Spain
78 A3 **Alcamo** *Sicily* Italy
107 C1 **Alcañiz** Spain
106 B2 **Alcántara** Spain
107 C2 **Alcantarilla** Spain
106 C2 **Alcaraz** Spain
106 C2 **Alcaraz, Sierra de** *mts*
Spain
115 C1 **Alcaudete** Spain
106 C2 **Alcázar de San Juan**
Spain
137 E2 **Alcazarquivir** Morocco *see*
Ksar el Kebir
91 D2 **Alchevs'k** Ukr.
155 E1 **Alcobaça** Brazil
107 C2 **Alcoy-Alcoi** Spain
107 D2 **Alcúdia** Spain
113 H6 **Aldabra Islands**
Seychelles
142 B3 **Aldama** Mex.
145 C2 **Aldama** Mex.
83 J3 **Aldan** Rus. Fed.
83 J2 **Aldan** *r.* Rus. Fed.
99 D3 **Aldeburgh** U.K.
95 C4 **Alderney** *i.* Channel Is
99 C4 **Aldershot** U.K.
114 A3 **Aleg** Maur.
155 D2 **Alegre** Brazil
152 C2 **Alegrete** Brazil
89 D1 **Alekhovshchina** Rus. Fed.
89 E2 **Aleksandrov** Rus. Fed.
Aleksandrovsk-
Sakhalinskiy Rus. Fed.
82 E1 **Aleksandry, Zemlya** *i.*
Rus. Fed.
91 D1 **Alekseyevka** Kazakh. *see*
Akkol'
91 D1 **Alekseyevka** Rus. Fed.
89 E3 **Aleksin** Rus. Fed.
109 D2 **Aleksinac** Serbia
118 B3 **Alèmbé** Gabon
155 D2 **Além Paraíba** Brazil
93 F3 **Ålen** Norway
104 C2 **Alençon** France
80 B2 **Aleppo** Syria
150 B4 **Alerta** Peru
128 B2 **Alert Bay** Can.
105 C3 **Alès** France
110 B1 **Aleşd** Romania
108 A2 **Alessandria** Italy
93 E3 **Ålesund** Norway
156 D2 **Aleutian Basin** *sea feature*
Bering Sea
124 A4 **Aleutian Islands** U.S.A.
83 L3 **Alevina, Mys** *c.* Rus. Fed.
128 A2 **Alexander Archipelago** *is*
U.S.A.
122 A2 **Alexander Bay** S. Africa
140 C2 **Alexander City** U.S.A.
55 A2 **Alexander Island**
Antarctica
53 C3 **Alexandra** Austr.
54 A3 **Alexandra** N.Z.
153 E5 **Alexandra, Cape**
S. Georgia
Alexandra Land *i.*
Rus. Fed. *see*
Aleksandry, Zemlya
111 B2 **Alexandreia** Greece
116 A1 **Alexandria** Egypt
110 C2 **Alexandria** Romania
123 C3 **Alexandria** S. Africa
96 B3 **Alexandria** U.K.
140 B2 **Alexandria** *LA* U.S.A.
137 D1 **Alexandria** *MN* U.S.A.
139 D3 **Alexandria** *VA* U.S.A.
52 A3 **Alexandrina, Lake** Austr.
111 C2 **Alexandroupoli** Greece
131 E2 **Alexis** *r.* Can.

128 B2 **Alexis Creek** Can.
77 E1 **Aleysk** Rus. Fed.
107 C1 **Alfaro** Spain
81 C3 **Al Fāw** Iraq
80 B3 **Al Fayyum** Egypt
101 D2 **Alfeld (Leine)** Ger.
155 D2 **Alfenas** Brazil
96 C2 **Al Fujayrah** U.A.E. *see*
Fujairah
Al Furāt *r.* Iraq/Syria *see*
Euphrates
93 E4 **Ålgård** Norway
106 B2 **Algarve** *reg.* Port.
106 B2 **Algeciras** Spain
107 C2 **Algemesí** Spain
78 A3 **Algena** Eritrea
Alger Alg. *see* Algiers
114 C2 **Algeria** *country* Africa
79 C3 **Al Ghaydah** Yemen
108 A2 **Alghero** *Sardinia* Italy
116 B2 **Al Ghurdaqah** Egypt
79 B2 **Al Ghwaybiyah**
Saudi Arabia
115 C1 **Algiers** Alg.
123 C3 **Algoa Bay** S. Africa
137 E2 **Algona** U.S.A.
106 C1 **Algorta** Spain
Algueirao Moz. *see*
Hacufera
81 C2 **Al Hadīthah** Iraq
79 C2 **Al Ḥajar al Gharbī** *mts*
Oman
115 D2 **Al Hamādah al Ḥamrā'**
plat. Libya
107 C2 **Alhama de Murcia** Spain
80 A2 **Al Ḥammām** Egypt
78 B2 **Al Ḥanākīyah** Saudi Arabia
81 C2 **Al Ḥasakah** Syria
78 B2 **Al Ḥawīyah** Saudi Arabia
81 C2 **Al Ḥayy** Iraq
78 B3 **Al Ḥazm al Jawf** Yemen
79 C3 **Al Ḥibāk** *des.* Saudi Arabia
Al Ḥillah Iraq *see* Hillah
78 B2 **Al Ḥillah** Saudi Arabia
79 B2 **Al Ḥinnāh** Saudi Arabia
Al Ḥudaydah Yemen *see*
Hodeidah
79 B2 **Al Ḥufūf** Saudi Arabia
115 D2 **Al Hulayq al Kabīr** *hills*
Libya
79 C2 **'Alīābād** Iran
111 C3 **Aliağa** Turkey
111 B2 **Aliakmonas** *r.* Greece
81 C2 **'Alī Bayramlı** Azer.
107 C2 **Alicante** Spain
143 D3 **Alice** U.S.A.
109 C3 **Alice, Punta** *pt* Italy
51 C2 **Alice Springs** Austr.
77 D3 **Alichur** Tajik.
74 B2 **Aligarh** India
81 C2 **Aligūdarz** Iran
69 E1 **Alihe** China
118 B3 **Alima** *r.* Congo
118 C2 **Alindao** C.A.R.
111 C3 **Aliova** *r.* Turkey
74 B2 **Alirajpur** India
117 C3 **Ali Sabieh** Djibouti
78 A1 **'Isāwiyah** Saudi Arabia
Al Iskandarīyah Egypt *see*
Alexandria
116 B1 **Al Ismā'īlīyah** Egypt
123 C3 **Aliwal North** S. Africa
115 E2 **Al Jaghbūb** Libya
78 B2 **Al Jahrah** Kuwait
79 C2 **Al Jamalīyah** Qatar
79 C2 **Al Jawf** Libya
115 E2 **Al Jawsh** Libya
Al Jīzah Egypt *see* Giza
79 B2 **Al Jubayl** Saudi Arabia
78 B2 **Al Jubaylah** Saudi Arabia
115 D2 **Al Jufrah** Libya
78 B2 **Al Junaynah** Saudi Arabia
106 B2 **Aljustrel** Port.
78 B2 **Al Kahfah** Saudi Arabia
79 C2 **Al Kāmil** Oman
80 B2 **Al Karak** Jordan
81 C2 **Al Kāzimīyah** Iraq
79 C2 **Al Khābūrah** Oman
78 B2 **Al Khamāsīn** Saudi Arabia
116 B2 **Al Khārijah** Egypt
79 B2 **Al Khasab** Oman
78 B3 **Al Khawkhah** Yemen
79 C2 **Al Khawr** Qatar
115 D1 **Al Khums** Libya
79 B2 **Al Kidan** *well* Saudi Arabia
79 C2 **Al Kir'ānah** Qatar
100 B1 **Alkmaar** Neth.
115 E2 **Al Kufrah** Libya

81 C2 **Al Kūt** Iraq
Al Kuwayt Kuwait *see*
Kuwait
Al Lādhiqīyah Syria *see*
Latakia
75 C2 **Allahabad** India
83 K2 **Allakh-Yun'** Rus. Fed.
78 A2 **'Allāqi, Wādī al**
watercourse Egypt
79 C2 **Allegheny** *r.* U.S.A.
139 C3 **Allegheny Mountains**
U.S.A.
97 B1 **Allen, Lough** *l.* Ireland
145 B2 **Allende** Mex.
145 B2 **Allende** Mex.
139 D2 **Allentown** U.S.A.
73 B4 **Alleppey** India
101 D1 **Aller** *r.* Ger.
136 C2 **Alliance** *NE* U.S.A.
138 C2 **Alliance** *OH* U.S.A.
78 B2 **Al Lith** Saudi Arabia
96 C2 **Alloa** U.K.
131 C3 **Alma** Can.
Alma-Ata Kazakh. *see*
Almaty
106 C2 **Almada** Port.
106 C2 **Almadén** Spain
Al Madīnah Saudi Arabia
see Medina
80 B2 **Al Mafraq** Jordan
114 B2 **Al Mahbas**
Western Sahara
78 B3 **Al Maḥwīt** Yemen
78 B2 **Al Majma'ah** Saudi Arabia
116 B2 **Al Maks al Baḥri** Egypt
Al Manāmah Bahrain *see*
Manama
135 B2 **Almanor, Lake** U.S.A.
107 C2 **Almansa** Spain
80 B2 **Al Manşūrah** Egypt
79 C2 **Al Mariyyah** U.A.E.
115 E1 **Al Marj** Libya
77 D2 **Almaty** Kazakh.
Al Mawşil Iraq *see* Mosul
81 C2 **Al Mayādīn** Syria
106 C1 **Almazán** Spain
151 D3 **Almeirim** Brazil
100 C1 **Almelo** Neth.
155 D1 **Almenara** Brazil
106 B1 **Almendra, Embalse de**
resr Spain
106 B2 **Almendralejo** Spain
106 C2 **Almería** Spain
106 C2 **Almería, Golfo de** *b.*
Spain
87 E3 **Al'met'yevsk** Rus. Fed.
78 D2 **Al Mindak** Saudi Arabia
116 B2 **Al Minyā** Egypt
79 B2 **Al Mish'āb** Saudi Arabia
106 B2 **Almodôvar** Port.
106 B2 **Almonte** Spain
75 B2 **Almora** India
79 B2 **Al Mubarrez** Saudi Arabia
79 C2 **Al Muḍaibī** Oman
80 B3 **Al Mudawwarah** Jordan
79 C3 **Al Mukallā** Yemen
Mukalla
78 B3 **Al Mukhā** Yemen *see*
Mocha
106 C2 **Almuñécar** Spain
81 C2 **Al Muqdādīyah** Iraq
78 A2 **Al Musayjid** Saudi Arabia
78 A2 **Al Muwaylih** Saudi Arabia
111 B3 **Almyros** Greece
96 B2 **Alness** U.K.
98 C2 **Alnwick** U.K.
62 A1 **Along** India
111 B3 **Alonnisos** *i.* Greece
59 C3 **Alor** *i.* Indon.
59 C3 **Alor, Kepulauan** *is* Indon.
60 B1 **Alor Setar** Malaysia
Alor Star Malaysia *see*
Alor Setar
Alost Belgium *see* Aalst
59 E3 **Alotau** P.N.G.
86 C2 **Alozero** Rus. Fed.
138 C1 **Alpena** U.S.A.
160 Q1 **Alpha Ridge** *sea feature*
Arctic Ocean
100 B1 **Alphen aan den Rijn**
Neth.
142 B2 **Alpine** *AZ* U.S.A.
143 C2 **Alpine** *TX* U.S.A.
105 D2 **Alps** *mts* Europe
84 E4 **Al Qa'āmiyāt** *reg.*
79 B3 **Al Qa'āmīyat** *reg.*
Saudi Arabia
115 D1 **Al Qaddāḥiyah** Libya
78 B2 **Al Qāhirah** Egypt *see*
Cairo
78 B2 **Al Qā'iyah** Saudi Arabia
81 C2 **Al Qāmishlī** Syria

Al Qaryatayn

164

80 B2 **Al Qaryatayn** Syria
79 B2 **Al Qaşab** Saudi Arabia
116 A2 **Al Qaşr** Egypt
79 B3 **Al Qaţn** Yemen
115 D2 **Al Qaţrūn** Libya
106 B2 **Alqueva, Barragem de** *resr* Port.
80 B2 **Al Qunayţirah** Syria
78 B3 **Al Qunfidhah** Saudi Arabia
116 B2 **Al Quşayr** Egypt
78 B2 **Al Quwārah** Saudi Arabia
78 B2 **Al Quwayīyah** Saudi Arabia
101 D2 **Alsfeld** Ger.
98 B2 **Alston** U.K.
92 H2 **Alta** Norway
92 H2 **Altaelva** *r.* Norway
68 B1 **Altai Mountains** Asia
141 D2 **Altamaha** *r.* U.S.A.
151 D3 **Altamira** Brazil
109 C2 **Altamura** Italy
144 A1 **Altar, Desierto de** *des.* Mex.
77 E2 **Altay** China
68 C1 **Altay** Mongolia
105 D2 **Altdorf** Switz.
107 C2 **Altea** Spain
92 H1 **Alteidet** Norway
101 F2 **Altenburg** Ger.
100 C2 **Altenkirchen (Westerwald)** Ger.
101 F1 **Altentreptow** Ger.
111 C3 **Altınoluk** Turkey
111 D3 **Altıntaş** Turkey
152 B1 **Altiplano** *plain* Bol.
96 B1 **Altnaharra** U.K.
154 B1 **Alto Araguaia** Brazil
107 C1 **Alto del Moncayo** *mt.* Spain
154 B1 **Alto Garças** Brazil
121 C2 **Alto Ligonha** Moz.
121 C2 **Alto Molócuè** Moz.
99 C4 **Alton** U.K.
137 E3 **Alton** U.S.A.
129 E3 **Altona** Can.
139 D2 **Altoona** U.S.A.
154 B1 **Alto Sucuriú** Brazil
154 B1 **Alto Taquarí** Brazil
102 C2 **Altötting** Ger.
68 C2 **Altun Shan** *mt.* China
68 B2 **Altun Shan** *mts* China
134 B2 **Alturas** U.S.A.
143 D2 **Altus** U.S.A.
88 C2 **Alūksne** Latvia
78 A2 **Al 'Ulā** Saudi Arabia
115 D1 **Al 'Uqaylah** Libya
Al Uqşur Egypt *see* **Luxor**
91 C3 **Alushta** Ukr.
115 E2 **Al 'Uwaynāt** Libya
143 D1 **Alva** U.S.A.
145 C3 **Alvarado** Mex.
93 F3 **Älvdalen** Sweden
93 F3 **Älvdalen** *val.* Sweden
92 H2 **Älvsbyn** Sweden
78 A2 **Al Wajh** Saudi Arabia
79 C2 **Al Wakrah** Qatar
74 B2 **Alwar** India
81 C2 **Al Widyān** *plat.* Iraq/Saudi Arabia
Alxa Youqi China *see* **Ehen Hudag**
Alxa Zuoqi China *see* **Bayan Hot**
51 C1 **Alyangula** Austr.
88 B3 **Alytus** Lith.
136 C1 **Alzada** U.S.A.
101 D3 **Alzey** Ger.
50 C2 **Amadeus, Lake** *salt flat* Austr.
127 H2 **Amadjuak Lake** Can.
106 B2 **Amadora** Port.
78 B2 **Amā'ir** Saudi Arabia
67 B4 **Amakusa-Shimo-shima** *i.* Japan
93 F4 **Åmål** Sweden
111 B3 **Amaliada** Greece
59 D3 **Amamapare** Indon.
154 A2 **Amambaí** Brazil
154 B2 **Amambaí** *r.* Brazil
154 A2 **Amambaí, Serra de** *hills* Brazil/Para.
69 E3 **Amami-Ō-shima** *i.* Japan
69 E3 **Amami-shotō** *is* Japan
77 C1 **Amangel'dy** Kazakh.
109 C3 **Amantea** Italy
123 D3 **Amanzimtoti** S. Africa
151 D2 **Amapá** Brazil
106 B2 **Amareleja** Port.
88 B2 **Āmari** Estonia
143 C1 **Amarillo** U.S.A.
108 B2 **Amaro, Monte** *mt.* Italy
80 B1 **Amasya** Turkey
150 D2 **Amazon** *r.* S. America
151 E2 **Amazon, Mouths of the** Brazil
Amazonas *r.* S. America *see* **Amazon**
157 I5 **Amazon Cone** *sea feature* S. Atlantic Ocean
74 B1 **Ambala** India
121 □D3 **Ambalavao** Madag.
121 □D2 **Ambanja** Madag.
104 B3 **Ambarès-et-Lagrave** France
150 B3 **Ambato** Ecuador
121 □D2 **Ambato Boeny** Madag.
121 □D3 **Ambato Finandrahana** Madag.
121 □D2 **Ambatolampy** Madag.
121 □D2 **Ambatondrazaka** Madag.
101 E3 **Amberg** Ger.
146 B3 **Ambergris Cay** *i.* Belize
75 C2 **Ambikapur** India
121 □D2 **Ambilobe** Madag.
98 C2 **Amble** U.K.
98 B2 **Ambleside** U.K.
121 □D3 **Amboasary** Madag.
121 □D2 **Ambodifotatra** Madag.
121 □D2 **Ambohidratrimo** Madag.
121 □D3 **Ambohimahasoa** Madag.
Amboina Indon. *see* **Ambon**
59 C3 **Ambon** Indon.
59 C3 **Ambon** *i.* Indon.
121 □D3 **Ambositra** Madag.
121 □D3 **Ambovombe** Madag.
135 C4 **Amboy** U.S.A.
Ambre, Cap d' *c.* Madag. *see* **Bobaomby, Tanjona**
120 A1 **Ambriz** Angola
Ambrizete Angola *see* **N'zeto**
86 F2 **Amderma** Rus. Fed.
Amdo China *see* **Lharigarbo**
145 B2 **Amealco** Mex.
144 B2 **Ameca** Mex.
100 B1 **Ameland** *i.* Neth.
154 C2 **Americana** Brazil
55 D4 **American-Antarctic Ridge** *sea feature* S. Atlantic Ocean
134 D2 **American Falls** U.S.A.
134 D2 **American Falls Reservoir** U.S.A.
135 D2 **American Fork** U.S.A.
49 J5 **American Samoa** *terr.* S. Pacific Ocean
141 D2 **Americus** U.S.A.
100 B1 **Amersfoort** Neth.
55 H2 **Amery Ice Shelf** Antarctica
137 E2 **Ames** U.S.A.
111 B3 **Amfissa** Greece
83 J2 **Amga** Rus. Fed.
66 C1 **Amgu** Rus. Fed.
115 C2 **Amguid** Alg.
83 K3 **Amgun'** *r.* Rus. Fed.
131 D3 **Amherst** Can.
104 C2 **Amiens** France
79 C3 **Amilhayt, Wādī al** *r.* Oman
73 B3 **Amindivi Islands** India
122 A1 **Aminuis** Namibia
74 A2 **Amir Chah** Pak.
129 D2 **Amisk Lake** Can.
143 C3 **Amistad Reservoir** Mex./U.S.A.
98 A3 **Amlwch** U.K.
80 B2 **'Ammān** Jordan
127 J2 **Ammassalik** Greenland
78 B3 **Am Nābiyah** Yemen
81 D2 **Amol** Iran
111 C3 **Amorgos** *i.* Greece
140 C2 **Amory** U.S.A.
130 C3 **Amos** Can.
Amoy China *see* **Xiamen**
121 □D3 **Ampanihy** Madag.
155 C2 **Amparo** Brazil
121 □D2 **Ampasimanolotra** Madag.
107 D1 **Amposta** Spain
78 B3 **'Amrān** Yemen
Amraoti India *see* **Amravati**
74 B2 **Amravati** India
74 B2 **Amreli** India
74 B1 **Amritsar** India
100 B1 **Amstelveen** Neth.
100 B1 **Amsterdam** Neth.
123 D2 **Amsterdam** S. Africa
156 A8 **Amsterdam, Île** *i.* Indian Ocean
103 C2 **Amstetten** Austria
115 E3 **Am Timan** Chad
76 B2 **Amudar'ya** *r.* Asia
126 F1 **Amund Ringnes Island** Can.
55 J3 **Amundsen, Mount** Antarctica
160 H1 **Amundsen Basin** *sea feature* Arctic Ocean
126 D2 **Amundsen Gulf** Can.
55 P2 **Amundsen Ridges** *sea feature* Southern Ocean
55 P2 **Amundsen Sea** Antarctica
61 C2 **Amuntai** Indon.
Amur *r.* China/Rus. Fed. *see* **Heilong Jiang**
78 A3 **'Amur, Wadi** *watercourse* Sudan
61 D2 **Anabanua** Indon.
83 I2 **Anabar** *r.* Rus. Fed.
83 I2 **Anabarskiy Zaliv** *b.* Rus. Fed.
150 C2 **Anaco** Venez.
134 D1 **Anaconda** U.S.A.
134 B1 **Anacortes** U.S.A.
143 D1 **Anadarko** U.S.A.
80 B1 **Anadolu Dağları** *mts* Turkey
83 M2 **Anadyr'** Rus. Fed.
83 M2 **Anadyr'** *r.* Rus. Fed.
81 C2 **'Ānah** Iraq
145 B2 **Anáhuac** Mex.
73 B3 **Anai Mudi Peak** India
121 □D2 **Analalava** Madag.
121 □D3 **Analavelona** *mts* Madag.
60 B1 **Anambas, Kepulauan** *is* Indon.
137 E2 **Anamosa** U.S.A.
80 B2 **Anamur** Turkey
67 B4 **Anan** Japan
73 B3 **Anantapur** India
74 B1 **Anantnag** Jammu and Kashmir
90 B2 **Anan'yiv** Ukr.
91 D3 **Anapa** Rus. Fed.
154 C1 **Anápolis** Brazil
81 D2 **Anār** Iran
152 B2 **Añatuya** Arg.
65 B2 **Anbyon** N. Korea
104 B2 **Ancenis** France
126 C2 **Anchorage** U.S.A.
108 B2 **Ancona** Italy
153 A4 **Ancud** Chile
Anda China *see* **Daqing**
93 E3 **Åndalsnes** Norway
106 C2 **Andalucía** *reg.* Spain
Andalusia *reg.* Spain *see* **Andalucía**
140 C2 **Andalusia** U.S.A.
159 F3 **Andaman Basin** *sea feature* Indian Ocean
73 D3 **Andaman Islands** India
63 A2 **Andaman Sea** Indian Ocean
121 □D2 **Andapa** Madag.
100 B2 **Andelst** Neth.
92 G2 **Andenes** Norway
100 B2 **Andenne** Belgium
100 B2 **Anderlecht** Belgium
105 D2 **Andermatt** Switz.
126 D2 **Anderson** *r.* Can.
126 C2 **Anderson** *AK* U.S.A.
138 B2 **Anderson** *IN* U.S.A.
141 D2 **Anderson** *SC* U.S.A.
148 C3 **Andes** *mts* S. America
77 D2 **Andijon** Uzbek.
121 □D2 **Andilamena** Madag.
121 □D2 **Andilanatoby** Madag.
Andizhan Uzbek. *see* **Andijon**
74 A1 **Andkhvoy** Afgh.
121 □D2 **Andoany** Madag.
Andong China *see* **Dandong**
65 B2 **Andong** S. Korea
104 C3 **Andorra** *country* Europe
104 C3 **Andorra la Vella** Andorra
99 C4 **Andover** U.K.
154 B2 **Andradina** Brazil
89 D2 **Andreapol'** Rus. Fed.
155 D2 **Andrelândia** Brazil
143 C2 **Andrews** U.S.A.
109 C2 **Andria** Italy
121 □D3 **Androka** Madag.
Andropov Rus. Fed. *see* **Rybinsk**
146 C2 **Andros** *i.* Bahamas
111 B3 **Andros** Greece
111 B3 **Andros** *i.* Greece
141 E4 **Andros Town** Bahamas
73 B3 **Andrott** *i.* India
90 B1 **Andrushivka** Ukr.
92 G2 **Andselv** Norway
106 C2 **Andújar** Spain
120 A2 **Andulo** Angola
114 C3 **Anéfis** Mali
147 D3 **Anegada Passage** Virgin Is (U.K.)
114 C4 **Aného** Togo
107 D1 **Aneto** *mt.* Spain
115 D3 **Aney** Niger
83 H3 **Angara** *r.* Rus. Fed.
68 C1 **Angarsk** Rus. Fed.
93 G3 **Ånge** Sweden
Angel, Salto del *waterfall* Venez. *see* **Angel Falls**
144 A2 **Ángel de la Guarda, Isla** *i.* Mex.
64 B2 **Angeles** Phil.
150 C2 **Angel Falls** Venez.
93 F4 **Ängelholm** Sweden
92 G3 **Ångermanälven** *r.* Sweden
104 B2 **Angers** France
129 E1 **Angikuni Lake** Can.
52 B3 **Anglesea** Austr.
98 A3 **Anglesey** *i.* U.K.
121 C2 **Angoche** Moz.
79 C2 **Angohrān** Iran
120 A2 **Angola** *country* Africa
138 C2 **Angola** U.S.A.
158 F6 **Angola Basin** *sea feature* S. Atlantic Ocean
128 A2 **Angoon** U.S.A.
104 C2 **Angoulême** France
155 D2 **Angra dos Reis** Brazil
77 D2 **Angren** Uzbek.
147 D3 **Anguilla** *terr.* West Indies
75 C2 **Angul** India
93 F4 **Anholt** *i.* Denmark
71 B3 **Anhua** China
70 B2 **Anhui** *prov.* China
154 B1 **Anhumas** Brazil
Anhwei *prov.* China *see* **Anhui**
154 C1 **Anicuns** Brazil
66 D1 **Aniva, Mys** *c.* Rus. Fed.
66 D1 **Aniva, Zaliv** *b.* Rus. Fed.
88 C1 **Anjalankoski** Fin.
104 B2 **Anjou** *reg.* France
65 B2 **Anjŭ** N. Korea
70 A2 **Ankang** China
80 B2 **Ankara** Turkey
121 □D3 **Ankazoabo** Madag.
121 □D2 **Ankazobe** Madag.
137 E2 **Ankeny** U.S.A.
102 C1 **Anklam** Ger.
121 □D2 **Ankofa** *mt.* Madag.
70 B2 **Anlu** China
55 G3 **Ann, Cape** Antarctica
139 E2 **Ann, Cape** U.S.A.
89 F3 **Anna** Rus. Fed.
115 C1 **Annaba** Alg.
101 F2 **Annaberg-Buchholtz** Ger.
80 B2 **An Nabk** Syria
78 B2 **An Nafūd** *des.* Saudi Arabia
150 D2 **Annai** Guyana
81 C2 **An Najaf** Iraq
63 B2 **Annam Highlands** *mts* Laos/Vietnam
96 C3 **Annan** U.K.
139 D3 **Annapolis** U.S.A.
75 C2 **Annapurna I** *mt.* Jammu and Kashmir/Nepal
138 C2 **Ann Arbor** U.S.A.
150 D2 **Anna Regina** Guyana
An Nás Ireland *see* **Naas**
81 C2 **An Nāşirīyah** Iraq
115 D1 **An Nawfalīyah** Libya
105 D2 **Annecy** France
78 B3 **An Nimāş** Saudi Arabia
71 A3 **Anning** China
140 C2 **Anniston** U.S.A.
105 C2 **Annonay** France
79 B2 **An Nu'ayrīyah** Saudi Arabia
121 □D2 **Anorontany, Tanjona** *hd* Madag.
71 B3 **Anpu** China
70 B2 **Anqing** China
65 B2 **Ansan** S. Korea
101 E3 **Ansbach** Ger.
70 C1 **Anshan** China
71 A3 **Anshun** China
78 A1 **An Sirhān, Wādī** *watercourse* Saudi Arabia
143 D2 **Anson** U.S.A.
114 C3 **Ansongo** Mali
96 C2 **Anstruther** U.K.
150 B4 **Antabamba** Peru
80 B2 **Antakya** Turkey
121 □E2 **Antalaha** Madag.

101 E2 Bad Berka Ger.
101 D2 Bad Berleburg Ger.
101 E1 Bad Bevensen Ger.
101 D3 Bad Dürkheim Ger.
100 C2 Bad Ems Ger.
103 D2 Baden Austria
102 B2 Baden-Baden Ger.
101 E2 Bad Harzburg Ger.
101 D2 Bad Hersfeld Ger.
102 C2 Bad Hofgastein Austria
101 D2 Bad Homburg vor der Höhe Ger.
101 D1 Bad Iburg Ger.
74 A2 Badin Pak.
Bādiyat ash Shām des. Asia see Syrian Desert
101 E2 Bad Kissingen Ger.
100 C2 Bad Kreuznach Ger.
136 C1 Badlands reg. ND U.S.A.
136 C2 Badlands reg. SD U.S.A.
101 E2 Bad Lauterberg im Harz Ger.
101 D2 Bad Lippspringe Ger.
101 D3 Bad Mergentheim Ger.
101 D2 Bad Nauheim Ger.
100 C2 Bad Neuenahr-Ahrweiler Ger.
101 E2 Bad Neustadt an der Saale Ger.
101 D2 Bad Oldesloe Ger.
101 D1 Bad Pyrmont Ger.
78 A2 Badr Ḩunayn Saudi Arabia
101 D1 Bad Salzuflen Ger.
101 E2 Bad Salzungen Ger.
102 C1 Bad Schwartau Ger.
101 E2 Bad Segeberg Ger.
100 C3 Bad Sobernheim Ger.
73 C4 Badulla Sri Lanka
101 D1 Bad Zwischenahn Ger.
106 C2 Baeza Spain
114 A3 Bafatá Guinea-Bissau
127 H2 Baffin Bay sea Can./Greenland
127 H2 Baffin Island Can.
118 B2 Bafia Cameroon
114 A3 Bafing r. Guinea/Mali
114 A3 Bafoulabé Mali
118 B2 Bafoussam Cameroon
81 D2 Bāfq Iran
80 B1 Bafra Turkey
79 C2 Bāft Iran
119 C2 Bafwasende Dem. Rep. Congo
119 D3 Bagamoyo Tanz.
Bagan Datoh Malaysia see Bagan Datuk
60 B1 Bagan Datuk Malaysia
64 B3 Baganga Phil.
120 B2 Bagani Namibia
60 B1 Bagansiapiapi Indon.
118 B3 Bagata Dem. Rep. Congo
91 E2 Bagayevskiy Rus. Fed.
142 A2 Bagdad U.S.A.
152 C3 Bagé Brazil
81 C2 Baghdād Iraq
79 C1 Bāghīn Iran
77 C3 Baghlān Afgh.
104 C3 Bagnères-de-Luchon France
105 C3 Bagnols-sur-Cèze France
Bago Myanmar see Pegu
88 B3 Bagrationovsk Rus. Fed.
Bagrax China see Bohu
64 B2 Baguio Phil.
115 C3 Bagzane, Monts mts Niger
146 C2 Bahamas, The country West Indies
75 C2 Baharampur India
Bahariya Oasis Egypt see Waḥāt al Baḥrīyah
76 B3 Baharly Turkm.
60 B1 Bahau Malaysia
74 B2 Bahawalnagar Pak.
74 B2 Bahawalpur Pak.
Bahia Brazil see Salvador
155 E1 Bahia state Brazil
146 B3 Bahía, Islas de la is Hond.
153 B3 Bahía Blanca Arg.
144 A2 Bahía Kino Mex.
152 C2 Bahía Negra Para.
144 A2 Bahía Tortugas Mex.
117 B3 Bahir Dar Eth.
79 C2 Bahlā Oman
75 C2 Bahraich India
79 C2 Bahrain country Asia
81 D2 Bāhū Kālāt Iran
89 D3 Bahushewsk Belarus
120 A2 Baía dos Tigres Angola
110 C2 Baia Romania
110 B1 Baia Mare Romania

118 B2 Baïbokoum Chad
69 E1 Baicheng China
Baidoa Somalia see Baydhabo
Baie-aux-Feuilles Can. see Tasiujaq
131 D3 Baie-Comeau Can.
Baie-du-Poste Can. see Mistissini
131 C3 Baie-St-Paul Can.
131 E2 Baie Verte Can.
62 A1 Baihanchang China
65 B1 Baihe China
69 D1 Baikal, Lake Rus. Fed.
Baile Átha Cliath Ireland see Dublin
110 B2 Băilești Romania
68 C2 Baima China
141 D2 Bainbridge U.S.A.
Baingoin China see Porong
48 I3 Bairiki Kiribati
Bairin Youqi China see Daban
53 C3 Bairnsdale Austr.
65 B1 Baishan Jilin China
65 B1 Baishanzhen Jilin China
120 A2 Baixo-Longa Angola
70 A2 Baiyin China
116 B3 Baiyuda Desert Sudan
103 D2 Baja Hungary
144 A1 Baja California pen. Mex.
61 D2 Bajawa Indon.
78 B3 Bājil Yemen
115 D3 Bajoga Nigeria
109 D2 Bajram Curri Albania
114 A3 Bakel Senegal
135 C3 Baker CA U.S.A.
140 B2 Baker LA U.S.A.
136 C1 Baker MT U.S.A.
134 C2 Baker OR U.S.A.
134 B1 Baker, Mount vol. U.S.A.
129 E1 Baker Foreland hd Can.
49 J3 Baker Island terr. N. Pacific Ocean
129 E1 Baker Lake Can.
129 E1 Baker Lake l. Can.
135 C3 Bakersfield U.S.A.
Bakharden Turkm. see Baharly
91 C3 Bakhchysaray Ukr.
91 C1 Bakhmach Ukr.
Bakhmut Ukr. see Artemivs'k
Bākhtarān Iran see Kermānshāh
Baku Azer. see Bakı
111 C2 Bakırköy Turkey
92 □C2 Bakkaflói b. Iceland
118 C2 Bakouma C.A.R.
81 C1 Bakı Azer.
99 B3 Bala U.K.
64 A3 Balabac Phil.
64 A3 Balabac i. Phil.
61 C1 Balabac Strait Malaysia/Phil.
75 C2 Balaghat India
60 C2 Balaiberkuak Indon.
52 A2 Balaklava Austr.
91 C3 Balaklava Ukr.
91 D2 Balakliya Ukr.
87 D3 Balakovo Rus. Fed.
76 C3 Bālā Morghāb Afgh.
145 C3 Balancán Mex.
111 C3 Balan Dağı hill Turkey
64 B2 Balanga Phil.
87 D3 Balashov Rus. Fed.
Balaton, Lake Hungary see Lake Balaton
103 D2 Balatonboglár Hungary
150 D3 Balbina, Represa de resr Brazil
97 C2 Balbriggan Ireland
52 A2 Balcanoona Austr.
110 C2 Balchik Bulg.
54 A3 Balclutha N.Z.
143 C3 Balcones Escarpment U.S.A.
129 E2 Baldock Lake Can.
138 D2 Baldwin U.S.A.
129 D2 Baldy Mountain hill Can.
142 B2 Baldy Peak U.S.A.
Baleares, Islas is Spain see Balearic Islands
107 D2 Balearic Islands is Spain
155 E1 Baleia, Ponta da pt Brazil
130 C2 Baleine, Grande Rivière de la r. Can.
131 D2 Baleine, Rivière à la r. Can.
75 C2 Baleshwar India

50 B2 Balgo Austr.
79 B3 Bālḩaf Yemen
61 C2 Bali i. Indon.
115 D4 Bali Nigeria
60 A1 Balige Indon.
75 C2 Baliguda India
111 C3 Balıkesir Turkey
61 C2 Balikpapan Indon.
64 A3 Balimbing Phil.
59 D3 Balimo P.N.G.
102 B2 Balingen Ger.
64 B2 Balintang Channel Phil.
Bali Sea Indon. see Laut Bali
78 B3 Baljurshi Saudi Arabia
76 B3 Balkanabat Turkm.
110 B2 Balkan Mountains Bulg./Serbia
77 C1 Balkashino Kazakh.
77 D2 Balkhash Kazakh.
77 D2 Balkhash, Lake Kazakh.
Balkhash, Ozero l. Kazakh. see Balkhash, Lake
Balla Balla Zimbabwe see Mbalabala
96 B2 Ballachulish U.K.
50 B3 Balladonia Austr.
97 B2 Ballaghaderreen Ireland
92 G2 Ballangen Norway
96 B3 Ballantrae U.K.
52 B3 Ballarat Austr.
50 B2 Ballard, Lake salt flat Austr.
96 C2 Ballater U.K.
114 B3 Ballé Mali
55 M3 Balleny Islands Antarctica
53 D1 Ballina Austr.
97 B1 Ballina Ireland
97 B2 Ballinasloe Ireland
97 B3 Ballineen Ireland
143 D2 Ballinger U.S.A.
97 B2 Ballinrobe Ireland
97 B1 Ballycastle Ireland
97 C1 Ballycastle U.K.
97 D1 Ballyclare U.K.
97 B1 Ballyhaunis Ireland
97 C1 Ballymena U.K.
97 C1 Ballymoney U.K.
97 D1 Ballynahinch U.K.
97 B1 Ballyshannon Ireland
95 B2 Ballyvoy U.K.
52 D3 Balmoral Austr.
143 C2 Balmorhea U.S.A.
120 A2 Balombo Angola
51 D2 Balonne r. Austr.
74 B2 Balotra India
77 D2 Balpyk Bi Kazakh.
75 C2 Balrampur India
52 B2 Balranald Austr.
110 B2 Balș Romania
151 E3 Balsas Brazil
145 C3 Balsas Mex.
145 B3 Balsas r. Mex.
90 B2 Bălți Moldova
93 G4 Baltic Sea g. Europe
80 B2 Baltim Egypt
97 B3 Baltimore Ireland
123 C1 Baltimore S. Africa
139 D3 Baltimore U.S.A.
97 C2 Baltinglass Ireland
88 A3 Baltiysk Rus. Fed.
75 C2 Balu India
52 A2 Balumbah Austr.
88 C2 Balvi Latvia
77 D2 Balykchy Kyrg.
87 E4 Balykshi Kazakh.
79 C2 Bam Iran
68 C2 Bama China
51 D1 Bamaga Austr.
130 A2 Bamaji Lake Can.
114 B3 Bamako Mali
118 C2 Bambari C.A.R.
118 B2 Bambio C.A.R.
119 C2 Bambouti C.A.R.
155 C2 Bambuí Brazil
98 C2 Bamburgh U.K.
118 B2 Bamenda Cameroon
77 C3 Bāmīān Afgh.
79 D2 Bampūr Iran
79 D2 Bampūr watercourse Iran
152 B1 Bañados del Izozog swamp Bol.
119 C2 Banalia Dem. Rep. Congo
71 A3 Banan China
151 D4 Bananal, Ilha do i. Brazil
74 B2 Banas r. India

111 C3 Banaz Turkey
62 B2 Ban Ban Laos
97 C1 Banbridge U.K.
99 C3 Banbury U.K.
96 C2 Banchory U.K.
130 C3 Bancroft Can.
Bancroft Zambia see Chililabombwe
119 C2 Banda Dem. Rep. Congo
75 C2 Banda India
59 C3 Banda, Kepulauan is Indon.
59 C3 Banda, Laut Indon.
60 A1 Banda Aceh Indon.
Bandar India see Machilipatnam
Bandar Abbas Iran see Bandar-e 'Abbās
75 D2 Bandarban Bangl.
79 C2 Bandar-e 'Abbās Iran
81 C2 Bandar-e Anzalī Iran
79 C2 Bandar-e Chārak Iran
81 C2 Bandar-e Emām Khomeynī Iran
79 C2 Bandar-e Lengeh Iran
79 C2 Bandar-e Maqām Iran
Bandar-e Pahlavī Iran see Bandar-e Anzalī
Bandar-e Shāhpūr Iran see Bandar-e Emām Khomeynī
60 B2 Bandar Lampung Indon.
61 C1 Bandar Seri Begawan Brunei
Banda Sea Indon. see Banda, Laut
155 D2 Bandeiras, Pico de mt. Brazil
123 C1 Bandelierkop S. Africa
144 B2 Banderas, Bahía de b. Mex.
114 B3 Bandiagara Mali
111 C2 Bandırma Turkey
Bandjarmasin Indon. see Banjarmasin
97 B3 Bandon Ireland
97 B3 Bandon r. Ireland
118 B3 Bandundu Dem. Rep. Congo
60 B2 Bandung Indon.
128 C2 Banff Can.
96 C2 Banff U.K.
114 B3 Banfora Burkina
64 B3 Banga Phil.
73 B3 Bangalore India
118 C2 Bangassou C.A.R.
61 D2 Banggai Indon.
59 C3 Banggai, Kepulauan is Indon.
61 D2 Banggi, Kepulauan is Indon.
61 C1 Banggi i. Sabah Malaysia
Banghāzī Libya see Benghazi
60 B2 Bangka i. Indon.
60 B2 Bangka, Selat sea chan. Indon.
61 C2 Bangkalan Indon.
60 B1 Bangkinang Indon.
60 B1 Bangko Indon.
63 B2 Bangkok Thai.
75 C2 Bangladesh country Asia
63 B2 Ba Ngoi Vietnam
97 D1 Bangor Northern Ireland U.K.
98 A3 Bangor Wales U.K.
139 F2 Bangor U.S.A.
63 A2 Bang Saphan Yai Thai.
64 B2 Bangued Phil.
118 B2 Bangui C.A.R.
64 B2 Bangui Phil.
121 B2 Bangweulu, Lake Zambia
80 B2 Banhā Egypt
62 B2 Ban Huai Khon Thai.
118 C2 Bani C.A.R.
80 B3 Banī Mazār Egypt
116 B2 Banī Suwayf Egypt
115 D1 Banī Walīd Libya
80 B2 Bāniyās Syria
109 C2 Banja Luka Bos.-Herz.
61 C2 Banjarmasin Indon.
114 A3 Banjul Gambia
63 A3 Ban Khok Kloi Thai.
128 A2 Banks Island B.C. Can.
126 D2 Banks Island N.W.T. Can.
48 H5 Banks Islands Vanuatu
129 E1 Banks Lake Can.
54 B2 Banks Peninsula N.Z.
75 D4 Banks Strait Austr.
75 C2 Bankura India
62 A1 Banmauk Myanmar

138 C3 Beckley U.S.A.
17 B4 Bedelë Eth.
99 C3 Bedford U.K.
138 B3 Bedford U.S.A.
98 C2 Bedlington U.K.
100 C1 Bedum Neth.
53 C3 Beechworth Austr.
53 D2 Beecroft Peninsula Austr.
101 F1 Beelitz Ger.
53 D1 Beenleigh Austr.
80 B2 Beersheba Israel
Be'ér Sheva' Israel see Beersheba
143 D3 Beeville U.S.A.
121 D2 Befandriana Avaratra Madag.
53 C3 Bega Austr.
107 D1 Begur, Cap de c. Spain
81 D2 Behbehän Iran
81 D2 Behshahr Iran
69 E1 Bei'an China
71 A3 Beihai China
70 B2 Beijing China
100 C1 Beilen Neth.
18 B2 Béinamar Chad
96 B3 Beinn an Oir hill U.K.
96 A2 Beinn Mhòr hill U.K.
Beinn na Faoghlia i. U.K. see Benbecula
121 C2 Beira Moz.
80 B2 Beirut Lebanon
123 C1 Beitbridge Zimbabwe
106 B2 Beja Port.
115 C1 Bejaïa Alg.
106 B1 Béjar Spain
74 A2 Beji r. Pak.
103 E2 Békés Hungary
103 E2 Békéscsaba Hungary
121 D3 Bekily Madag.
66 D2 Bekkai Japan
114 B4 Bekwai Ghana
75 C2 Bela India
74 A2 Bela Pak.
123 C1 Bela-Bela S. Africa
118 B2 Bélabo Cameroon
109 D2 Bela Crkva Serbia
61 C1 Belaga Sarawak Malaysia
88 C3 Belarus country Europe
123 C1 Bela Vista Moz.
60 A1 Belawan Indon.
83 M2 Belaya r. Rus. Fed.
103 D1 Bełchatów Pol.
Bełchatow Pol. see Bełchatów
130 C2 Belcher Islands Can.
87 F3 Belebey Rus. Fed.
117 C4 Beledweyne Somalia
118 B2 Bélèl Cameroon
151 E3 Belém Brazil
142 B2 Belen U.S.A.
110 C2 Belene Bulg.
89 E3 Belev Rus. Fed.
97 D1 Belfast U.K.
139 F2 Belfast U.S.A.
136 C1 Belfield U.S.A.
105 D2 Belfort France
73 B3 Belgaum India
Belgian Congo country Africa see Congo, Democratic Republic of the
100 B2 Belgium country Europe
91 D1 Belgorod Rus. Fed.
109 D2 Belgrade Serbia
134 D1 Belgrade U.S.A.
109 C1 Beli Manastir Croatia
60 B2 Belinyu Indon.
60 B2 Belitung i. Indon.
118 B3 Belize Angola
146 B3 Belize Belize
146 B3 Belize country Central America
83 K1 Bel'kovskiy, Ostrov i. Rus. Fed.
128 B2 Bella Bella Can.
104 C2 Bellac France
128 B2 Bella Coola Can.
73 B3 Bellary India
53 C1 Bellata Austr.
138 C3 Bellefontaine U.S.A.
136 C2 Belle Fourche U.S.A.
136 C2 Belle Fourche r. U.S.A.
141 D3 Belle Glade U.S.A.
104 B2 Belle-Île i. France
131 E2 Belle Isle i. Can.
131 E2 Belle Isle, Strait of Can.
130 C3 Belleville Can.
138 B3 Belleville U.S.A.
137 D3 Belleville KS U.S.A.
134 D2 Bellevue ID U.S.A.
134 B1 Bellevue WA U.S.A.

53 D2 Bellin Can. see Kangirsuk
134 B1 Bellingen Austr.
55 B2 Bellingham U.S.A.
Bellingshausen Sea Antarctica
105 D2 Bellinzona Switz.
96 C2 Bell Rock i. U.K.
Belluno Italy
122 A3 Bellville S. Africa
53 D2 Belmont Austr.
155 E1 Belmonte Brazil
146 B3 Belmopan Belize
97 B1 Belmullet Ireland
69 E1 Belogorsk Rus. Fed.
121 D3 Beloha Madag.
155 D1 Belo Horizonte Brazil
138 B2 Beloit U.S.A.
86 C2 Belomorsk Rus. Fed.
89 E3 Beloomut Rus. Fed.
91 D3 Belorechensk Rus. Fed.
Belorechenskaya Rus. Fed. see Belorechensk
87 E3 Beloretsk Rus. Fed.
Belorussia country Europe see Belarus
Belorusskaya S.S.R. country Europe see Belarus
Belostok Pol. see Białystok
121 D3 Belo Tsiribihina Madag.
86 F2 Beloyarskiy Rus. Fed.
89 E1 Beloye, Ozero l. Rus. Fed.
Beloye More sea Rus. Fed. see White Sea
89 E1 Belozersk Rus. Fed.
52 A2 Belton Austr.
143 D2 Belton U.S.A.
Bel'ts' Moldova see Bălţi
Bel'tsy Moldova see Bălţi
97 C1 Belturbet Ireland
77 E2 Belukha, Gora mt. Kazakh./Rus. Fed.
86 D2 Belush'ye Rus. Fed.
138 B2 Belvidere U.S.A.
51 D2 Belyando r. Austr.
89 D2 Belyy Rus. Fed.
82 F2 Belyy, Ostrov i. Rus. Fed.
101 F1 Belzig Ger.
137 E1 Bemidji U.S.A.
118 C3 Bena Dibele Dem. Rep. Congo
53 C3 Benalla Austr.
Benares India see Varanasi
115 D1 Ben Arous Tunisia
118 C3 Bena-Sungu Dem. Rep. Congo
106 B1 Benavente Spain
96 A2 Benbecula i. U.K.
134 B2 Bend U.S.A.
123 C3 Bendearg mt. S. Africa
Bender Moldova see Tighina
Bendery Moldova see Tighina
52 B3 Bendigo Austr.
121 C2 Bene Moz.
102 C2 Benešov Czech Rep.
109 B2 Benevento Italy
73 C3 Bengal, Bay of sea Indian Ocean
Bengaluru India see Bangalore
70 B2 Bengbu China
115 E1 Benghazi Libya
60 B1 Bengkalis Indon.
60 B1 Bengkayang Indon.
60 B2 Bengkulu Indon.
120 A2 Benguela Angola
Benha Egypt see Banhā
96 B1 Ben Hope hill U.K.
152 B1 Beni r. Bol.
119 C2 Beni Dem. Rep. Congo
114 B1 Beni Abbès Alg.
107 C2 Benidorm Spain
114 B1 Beni Mellal Morocco
114 C1 Benin country Africa
114 C4 Benin, Bight of g. Africa
115 C4 Benin City Nigeria
107 C2 Beni Saf Alg.
Beni Suef Egypt see Banī Suwayf
153 C3 Benito Juárez Arg.
Benjamin Constant Brazil
144 A1 Benjamín Hill Mex.
59 C3 Benjina Indon.
136 C2 Benkelman U.S.A.
96 B1 Ben Lawers mt. U.K.
96 B2 Ben Lomond hill U.K.

96 C2 Ben Macdui mt. U.K.
98 A2 Ben More hill U.K.
96 C2 Ben More mt. U.K.
54 B2 Benmore, Lake N.Z.
96 B1 Ben More Assynt hill U.K.
128 A2 Bennett Can.
83 K1 Bennetta, Ostrov i. Rus. Fed.
Bennett Island Rus. Fed. see Bennetta, Ostrov
96 B2 Ben Nevis mt. U.K.
139 E2 Bennington U.S.A.
123 C2 Benoni S. Africa
115 D4 Bénoye Chad
101 D3 Bensheim Ger.
114 B1 Ben Slimane Morocco
142 A2 Benson U.S.A.
61 D2 Benteng Indon.
117 A4 Bentiu Sudan
138 B2 Benton Harbor U.S.A.
140 B1 Bentonville U.S.A.
63 B2 Bên Tre Vietnam
115 C4 Benue r. Nigeria
97 B1 Benwee Head hd Ireland
96 B2 Ben Wyvis mt. U.K.
70 C1 Benxi China
Beograd Serbia see Belgrade
75 C2 Beohari India
114 B4 Béoumi Côte d'Ivoire
67 B4 Beppu Japan
100 C2 Berane Montenegro
109 C2 Berat Albania
59 C3 Berau, Teluk b. Indon.
116 B3 Berber Sudan
117 C3 Berbera Somalia
118 B2 Berbérati C.A.R.
104 C1 Berck France
91 D2 Berdyans'k Ukr.
91 D2 Berdychiv Ukr.
90 A2 Berehove Ukr.
59 D3 Bereina P.N.G.
76 B3 Bereket Turkm.
129 E2 Berens River Can.
137 D2 Beresford U.S.A.
91 D2 Berezanskaya Rus. Fed.
90 A2 Berezhany Ukr.
90 C2 Berezivka Ukr.
90 B1 Berezne Ukr.
86 D2 Bereznik Rus. Fed.
86 E3 Berezniki Rus. Fed.
Berezov Rus. Fed. see Berezovo
86 F2 Berezovo Rus. Fed.
107 D1 Berga Spain
111 C3 Bergama Turkey
108 A1 Bergamo Italy
102 C1 Bergen Ger.
101 D1 Bergen Ger.
100 B1 Bergen Neth.
93 E3 Bergen Norway
100 B2 Bergen op Zoom Neth.
104 C3 Bergerac France
100 C2 Bergheim (Erft) Ger.
100 C2 Bergisch Gladbach Ger.
122 A1 Bergland Namibia
93 G3 Bergsjö Sweden
92 H2 Bergsviken Sweden
Berhampur India see Baharampur
83 M3 Beringa, Ostrov i. Rus. Fed.
100 B2 Beringen Belgium
124 A4 Bering Sea N. Pacific Ocean
124 B3 Bering Strait Rus. Fed./U.S.A.
100 C1 Berkel r. Neth.
135 B3 Berkeley U.S.A.
100 B1 Berkhout Neth.
55 B2 Berkner Island Antarctica
110 B2 Berkovitsa Bulg.
92 I1 Berlevåg Norway
101 F1 Berlin Ger.
139 E2 Berlin U.S.A.
101 E2 Berlingerode Ger.
53 D1 Bermagui Austr.
144 B2 Bermejillo Mex.
152 B2 Bermejo Bol.
131 D2 Bermen, Lac l. Can.
125 L6 Bermuda terr. N. Atlantic Ocean
105 D2 Bern Switz.
101 E2 Bernburg (Saale) Ger.
127 G2 Bernier Bay Can.
100 C3 Bernkastel-Kues Ger.
121 D3 Beroroha Madag.
52 B2 Berri Austr.
115 C1 Berriane Alg.
53 C3 Berrigan Austr.

107 D2 Berrouaghia Alg.
53 D2 Berry Austr.
146 C2 Berry Islands Bahamas
122 A2 Berseba Namibia
101 C1 Bersenbrück Ger.
90 B2 Bershad' Ukr.
131 D2 Berté, Lac l. Can.
118 B2 Bertoua Cameroon
150 C3 Beruri Brazil
98 B2 Berwick-upon-Tweed U.K.
91 C2 Beryslav Ukr.
121 D2 Besalampy Madag.
105 D2 Besançon France
81 D3 Beshneh Iran
129 D2 Besnard Lake Can.
140 C2 Bessemer U.S.A.
76 B2 Besshoky, Gora hill Kazakh.
100 B2 Best Neth.
121 D2 Betafo Madag.
106 B1 Betanzos Spain
118 B2 Bétaré Oya Cameroon
122 A2 Bethanie Namibia
100 B3 Bétheny France
139 D3 Bethesda U.S.A.
123 C2 Bethlehem S. Africa
139 D2 Bethlehem U.S.A.
123 C3 Bethulie S. Africa
105 C1 Béthune France
121 D3 Betioky Madag.
51 D2 Betoota Austr.
77 D2 Betpak-Dala plain Kazakh.
121 D3 Betroka Madag.
131 D3 Betsiamites Can.
137 E2 Bettendorf U.S.A.
75 C2 Bettiah India
74 B2 Betul India
74 B2 Betwa r. India
99 B3 Betws-y-coed U.K.
100 C2 Betzdorf Ger.
136 C1 Beulah U.S.A.
98 C3 Beverley U.K.
101 D2 Beverungen Ger.
100 B1 Beverwijk Neth.
99 D4 Bexhill U.K.
111 C3 Beykoz Turkey
114 B4 Beyla Guinea
76 B2 Beyneu Kazakh.
80 B1 Beypazarı Turkey
Beyrouth Lebanon see Beirut
80 B2 Beyşehir Turkey
80 B2 Beyşehir Gölü l. Turkey
91 D2 Beysug r. Rus. Fed.
Beysugskiy Liman lag. Rus. Fed.
88 C2 Bezhanitsy Rus. Fed.
89 E2 Bezhetsk Rus. Fed.
105 C3 Béziers France
Bhadgaon Nepal see Bhaktapur
75 C2 Bhadrak India
73 B3 Bhadravati India
75 C2 Bhagalpur India
74 A2 Bhairi Hol mt. Pak.
74 B1 Bhakkar Pak.
75 C2 Bhaktapur Nepal
62 A1 Bhamo Myanmar
75 C3 Bhanjanagar India
74 B2 Bharatpur India
74 B2 Bharuch India
74 B2 Bhavnagar India
75 C3 Bhawanipatna India
123 D2 Bhekuzulu S. Africa
74 B1 Bhera India
74 B2 Bhilwara India
73 B3 Bhima r. India
74 B2 Bhind India
75 C2 Bhiwani India
123 C3 Bhongweni S. Africa
74 B2 Bhopal India
75 C2 Bhubaneshwar India
Bhubaneswar India see Bhubaneshwar
74 A2 Bhuj India
74 B2 Bhusawal India
75 D2 Bhutan country Asia
62 B2 Bia, Phou mt. Laos
Biafra, Bight of g. Africa see Benin, Bight of
59 C3 Biak Indon.
59 D3 Biak i. Indon.
103 E1 Biała Podlaska Pol.
103 D1 Białogard Pol.
103 E1 Białystok Pol.
109 C2 Bianco Italy
74 B2 Biaora India
104 B3 Biarritz France

105 D2	Biasca Switz.
66 D2	Bibai Japan
120 A2	Bibala Angola
53 C3	Bibbenluke Austr.
102 B2	Biberach an der Riß Ger.
155 D2	Bicas Brazil
73 B3	Bid India
115 C4	Bida Nigeria
73 B3	Bidar India
139 E2	Biddeford U.S.A.
96 B2	Bidean nam Bian mt. U.K.
99 A4	Bideford U.K.
	Bideford Bay U.K. see Barnstaple Bay
	Bié Angola see Kuito
120 A2	Bié, Planalto do Angola
101 D2	Biedenkopf Ger.
105 D2	Biel Switz.
101 D1	Bielefeld Ger.
108 A1	Biella Italy
103 D2	Bielsko-Biała Pol.
63 B2	Biên Hoa Vietnam
130 C2	Bienville, Lac l. Can.
100 B3	Bièvre Belgium
118 B3	Bifoun Gabon
111 C2	Biga Turkey
134 D1	Big Belt Mountains U.S.A.
123 D2	Big Bend Swaziland
129 D2	Biggar Can.
96 C3	Biggar U.K.
99 C3	Biggleswade U.K.
134 D1	Big Hole r. U.S.A.
134 E1	Bighorn r. U.S.A.
136 B1	Bighorn r. U.S.A.
136 B2	Bighorn Mountains U.S.A.
143 C2	Big Lake U.S.A.
138 B2	Big Rapids U.S.A.
129 D2	Big River Can.
129 E2	Big Sand Lake Can.
137 D2	Big Sioux r. U.S.A.
143 C2	Big Spring U.S.A.
134 E1	Big Timber U.S.A.
130 B2	Big Trout Lake Can.
130 A2	Big Trout Lake l. Can.
109 C2	Bihać Bos.-Herz.
75 C2	Bihar state India
75 C2	Bihar Sharif India
110 B1	Bihor, Vârful mt. Romania
114 A3	Bijagós, Arquipélago dos is Guinea-Bissau
73 B3	Bijapur India
81 C2	Bijār Iran
109 C2	Bijeljina Bos.-Herz.
109 C2	Bijelo Polje Montenegro
71 A3	Bijie China
74 B2	Bikaner India
66 B1	Bikin Rus. Fed.
66 B1	Bikin r. Rus. Fed.
118 B3	Bikoro Dem. Rep. Congo
79 C2	Bilād Banī Bū 'Alī Oman
75 C2	Bilaspur India
81 C2	Biläsuvar Azer.
90 C2	Bila Tserkva Ukr.
63 A2	Bilauktaung Range mts Myanmar/Thai.
106 C1	Bilbao Spain
109 C2	Bileća Bos.-Herz.
111 C2	Bilecik Turkey
103 E1	Biłgoraj Pol.
119 D3	Bilharamulo Tanz.
90 C2	Bilhorod-Dnistrovs'kyy Ukr.
119 C2	Bili Dem. Rep. Congo
83 M2	Bilibino Rus. Fed.
109 D2	Bilisht Albania
104 B3	Billère France
134 E1	Billings U.S.A.
99 B4	Bill of Portland hd U.K.
142 A1	Bill Williams Mountain U.S.A.
115 D3	Bilma Niger
51 E2	Biloela Austr.
91 C2	Bilohirs'k Ukr.
90 B1	Bilohir"ya Ukr.
91 C1	Bilopillya Ukr.
91 D2	Bilovods'k Ukr.
140 C2	Biloxi U.S.A.
51 C2	Bilpa Morea Claypan salt flat Austr.
101 E2	Bilshausen Ger.
115 E3	Biltine Chad
90 C2	Bilyayivka Ukr.
114 C4	Bimbila Ghana
118 B2	Bimbo C.A.R.
141 E3	Bimini Islands Bahamas
74 B2	Bina-Etawa India
59 C3	Binaija, Gunung mt. Indon.
53 C1	Bindle Austr.
118 B3	Bindu Dem. Rep. Congo
121 C2	Bindura Zimbabwe
107 D1	Binéfar Spain
120 B2	Binga Zimbabwe
53 D1	Bingara Austr.
100 C3	Bingen am Rhein Ger.
114 B4	Bingerville Côte d'Ivoire
139 F1	Bingham U.S.A.
139 D2	Binghamton U.S.A.
115 D2	Bin Ghanīmah, Jabal hills Libya
81 C2	Bingöl Turkey
62 A1	Bingzhongluo China
60 A1	Binjai Indon.
53 C2	Binnaway Austr.
60 B1	Bintan i. Indon.
60 B2	Bintuhan Indon.
61 C1	Bintulu Sarawak Malaysia
115 C3	Bin-Yauri Nigeria
70 B2	Binzhou China
118 A2	Bioco i. Equat. Guinea
109 C2	Biograd na Moru Croatia
155 C1	Biquinhas Brazil
115 D2	Birāk Libya
118 C1	Birao C.A.R.
75 C2	Biratnagar Nepal
52 B3	Birchip Austr.
128 C2	Birch Mountains Can.
51 C2	Birdsville Austr.
80 B2	Birecik Turkey
	Birendranagar Nepal see Surkhet
60 A1	Bireun Indon.
75 C2	Birganj Nepal
117 B3	Birhan mt. Eth.
154 B2	Birigüi Brazil
118 C2	Birini C.A.R.
76 B3	Birjand Iran
98 B3	Birkenhead U.K.
99 C3	Birmingham U.K.
140 C2	Birmingham U.S.A.
114 A2	Bir Mogreïn Maur.
115 C3	Birnin-Kebbi Nigeria
115 C3	Birnin Konni Niger
69 E1	Birobidzhan Rus. Fed.
97 C2	Birr Ireland
96 C1	Birsay U.K.
78 A2	Bi'r Shalatayn Egypt
88 B2	Biržai Lith.
75 B2	Bisalpur India
142 B2	Bisbee U.S.A.
104 A2	Biscay, Bay of sea France/Spain
141 D3	Biscayne Bay U.S.A.
102 C2	Bischofshofen Austria
77 D2	Bishkek Kyrg.
135 C3	Bishop U.S.A.
98 C1	Bishop Auckland U.K.
69 E1	Bishui China
150 C2	Bisinaca Col.
115 C1	Biskra Alg.
64 B3	Bislig Phil.
136 C1	Bismarck U.S.A.
59 D3	Bismarck Archipelago is P.N.G.
59 D3	Bismarck Sea P.N.G.
107 D2	Bissa, Djebel mt. Alg.
114 A3	Bissau Guinea-Bissau
129 E2	Bissett Can.
128 C2	Bistcho Lake Can.
110 B1	Bistriţa Romania
110 C1	Bistriţa r. Romania
100 C3	Bitburg Ger.
105 D2	Bitche France
115 D3	Bitkine Chad
81 C2	Bitlis Turkey
111 B2	Bitola Macedonia
	Bitolj Macedonia see Bitola
109 C2	Bitonto Italy
101 F2	Bitterfeld Ger.
122 A3	Bitterfontein S. Africa
134 D1	Bitterroot r. U.S.A.
134 C1	Bitterroot Range mts U.S.A.
89 E3	Bityug r. Rus. Fed.
115 D3	Biu Nigeria
67 C3	Biwa-ko l. Japan
77 E1	Biysk Rus. Fed.
115 C1	Bizerte Tunisia
	Bizerta Tunisia see Bizerte
92 □A2	Bjargtangar hd Iceland
92 G3	Bjästa Sweden
109 C1	Bjelovar Croatia
92 G2	Bjerkvik Norway
	Björneborg Fin. see Pori
82 C2	Bjørnøya Arctic Ocean
114 B3	Bla Mali
137 E3	Black r. U.S.A.
51 D2	Blackall Austr.
98 B2	Blackburn U.K.
134 D2	Blackfoot U.S.A.
102 B2	Black Forest mts Ger.
136 C2	Black Hills U.S.A.
96 B2	Black Isle pen. U.K.
129 D2	Black Lake Can.
129 D2	Black Lake l. Can.
99 B4	Black Mountains hills U.K.
142 A1	Black Mountains U.S.A.
98 B3	Blackpool U.K.
142 B2	Black Range mts U.S.A.
62 B1	Black River r. Vietnam
138 A2	Black River Falls U.S.A.
134 C2	Black Rock Desert U.S.A.
138 C3	Blacksburg U.S.A.
80 B1	Black Sea Asia/Europe
131 D3	Blacks Harbour Can.
97 A1	Blacksod Bay Ireland
97 C2	Blackstairs Mountains hills Ireland
114 B4	Black Volta r. Africa
51 D2	Blackwater Austr.
97 C2	Blackwater r. Ireland
128 B1	Blackwater Lake Can.
50 A3	Blackwood r. Austr.
87 D4	Blagodarnyy Rus. Fed.
111 B2	Blagoevgrad Bulg.
69 E1	Blagoveshchensk Rus. Fed.
129 D2	Blaine Lake Can.
137 D2	Blair U.S.A.
96 C2	Blair Atholl U.K.
96 C2	Blairgowrie U.K.
141 D2	Blakely U.S.A.
105 D2	Blanc, Mont mt. France/Italy
153 B3	Blanca, Bahía b. Arg.
52 A1	Blanche, Lake salt flat Austr.
152 B1	Blanco r. Bol.
134 B2	Blanco, Cape U.S.A.
131 E2	Blanc-Sablon Can.
92 □A2	Blanda r. Iceland
99 B4	Blandford Forum U.K.
135 E3	Blanding U.S.A.
107 D1	Blanes Spain
60 A1	Blangkejeren Indon.
100 A2	Blankenberge Belgium
100 C2	Blankenheim Ger.
100 C2	Blankenrath Ger.
147 D3	Blanquilla, Isla i. Venez.
103 D2	Blansko Czech Rep.
121 C2	Blantyre Malawi
97 B3	Blarney Ireland
98 C2	Blaydon U.K.
53 C2	Blayney Austr.
54 B2	Blenheim N.Z.
115 C1	Blida Alg.
130 B3	Blind River Can.
123 C2	Bloemfontein S. Africa
123 C2	Bloemhof S. Africa
123 C2	Bloemhof Dam S. Africa
104 C2	Blois France
92 □A2	Blönduós Iceland
97 B1	Bloody Foreland pt Ireland
142 B1	Bloomfield U.S.A.
138 B2	Bloomington IL U.S.A.
138 B3	Bloomington IN U.S.A.
102 B2	Bludenz Austria
137 E2	Blue Earth U.S.A.
138 C3	Bluefield U.S.A.
146 B3	Bluefields Nic.
53 C2	Blue Mountains Austr.
134 C1	Blue Mountains U.S.A.
116 B3	Blue Nile r. Eth./Sudan
126 E2	Bluenose Lake Can.
138 C3	Blue Ridge mts U.S.A.
128 C2	Blue River Can.
97 B1	Blue Stack Mountains hills Ireland
54 A3	Bluff N.Z.
135 E3	Bluff U.S.A.
154 C3	Blumenau Brazil
52 A2	Blyth Austr.
98 C2	Blyth U.K.
135 D4	Blythe U.S.A.
140 C1	Blytheville U.S.A.
114 A4	Bo Sierra Leone
64 B2	Boac Phil.
146 B3	Boaco Nic.
151 E3	Boa Esperança, Açude resr Brazil
134 C1	Boardman U.S.A.
123 C1	Boatlaname Botswana
151 F3	Boa Viagem Brazil
150 C2	Boa Vista Brazil
53 C2	Bobadah Austr.
71 B3	Bobai China
121 □D2	Bobaomby, Tanjona c. Madag.
114 B3	Bobo-Dioulasso Burkina
121 B3	Bobonong Botswana
	Bobriki Rus. Fed. see Novomoskovsk
89 F3	Bobrov Rus. Fed.
91 C1	Bobrovytsya Ukr.
91 C2	Bobrynets' Ukr.
121 □D3	Boby mt. Madag.
150 C3	Boca do Acre Brazil
155 D1	Bocaiúva Brazil
154 A2	Bocajá Brazil
118 B2	Bocaranga C.A.R.
141 D3	Boca Raton U.S.A.
146 B4	Bocas del Toro Panama
103 E2	Bochnia Pol.
100 C2	Bocholt Belgium
100 C2	Bocholt Ger.
100 C2	Bochum Ger.
123 C1	Bochum S. Africa
101 E1	Bockenem Ger.
110 B1	Bocşa Romania
118 B2	Boda C.A.R.
83 I3	Bodaybo Rus. Fed.
96 D2	Boddam U.K.
115 D3	Bodélé reg. Chad
92 H2	Boden Sweden
	Bodensee l. Ger./Switz. see Constance, Lake
99 A4	Bodmin U.K.
99 A4	Bodmin Moor moorland U.K.
92 F2	Bodø Norway
111 C3	Bodrum Turkey
118 C3	Boende Dem. Rep. Congo
63 A2	Bogale Myanmar
140 C2	Bogalusa U.S.A.
114 B3	Bogandé Burkina
118 B2	Bogangolo C.A.R.
80 B2	Boğazlıyan Turkey
68 B2	Bogda Shan mts China
53 D1	Boggabilla Austr.
53 D2	Boggabri Austr.
97 B2	Boggeragh Mountains hills Ireland
	Boghari Alg. see Ksar el Boukhari
59 D3	Bogia P.N.G.
100 B3	Bogny-sur-Meuse France
97 C2	Bog of Allen reg. Ireland
53 C3	Bogong, Mount Austr.
60 B2	Bogor Indon.
89 E3	Bogoroditsk Rus. Fed.
150 B2	Bogotá Col.
83 G3	Bogotol Rus. Fed.
	Bogoyavlenskoye Rus. Fed. see Pervomayskoye
83 H3	Boguchany Rus. Fed.
91 E2	Boguchar Rus. Fed.
114 A3	Bogué Maur.
70 B2	Bo Hai g. China
100 A3	Bohain-en-Vermandois France
70 B2	Bohai Wan b. China
	Bohemian Forest mts Ger. see Böhmer Wald
123 C2	Bohlokong S. Africa
101 F3	Böhmer Wald mts Ger.
91 D1	Bohodukhiv Ukr.
64 B3	Bohol i. Phil.
64 B3	Bohol Sea Phil.
77 E2	Bohu China
155 C2	Boi, Ponta do pt Brazil
123 C2	Boikhutso S. Africa
154 B3	Boi Preto, Serra de hills Brazil
154 B1	Bois r. Brazil
126 E2	Bois, Lac des l. Can.
134 C2	Boise U.S.A.
143 C1	Boise City U.S.A.
129 D3	Boissevain Can.
123 C2	Boitumelong S. Africa
154 C2	Boituva Brazil
101 E1	Boizenburg Ger.
76 B3	Bojnūrd Iran
75 C2	Bokaro India
118 B3	Bokatola Dem. Rep. Congo
114 A3	Boké Guinea
118 C3	Bokele Dem. Rep. Congo
93 E4	Boknafjorden sea chan. Norway
115 D3	Bokoro Chad
63 A2	Bokpyin Myanmar
89 D2	Boksitogorsk Rus. Fed.
122 B2	Bokspits S. Africa
118 C3	Bokungu Dem. Rep. Congo
115 D3	Bol Chad
114 A3	Bolama Guinea-Bissau
75 C2	Bolangir India
104 C2	Bolbec France
77 E2	Bole China
118 C3	Boleko Dem. Rep. Congo
114 B3	Bolgatanga Ghana

Brigham City
171

90 B2 **Bolhrad** Ukr.
66 B1 **Boli** China
118 B3 **Bolia** Dem. Rep. Congo
92 H3 **Boliden** Sweden
110 C2 **Bolintin-Vale** Romania
137 E3 **Bolivar** *MO* U.S.A.
140 C1 **Bolivar** *TN* U.S.A.
150 B2 **Bolívar, Pico** *mt.* Venez.
152 B1 **Bolivia** *country* S. America
89 E3 **Bolkhov** Rus. Fed.
105 C3 **Bollène** France
93 G3 **Bollnäs** Sweden
53 C1 **Bollon** Austr.
101 E2 **Bollstedt** Ger.
93 F4 **Bolmen** *l.* Sweden
118 B3 **Bolobo** Dem. Rep. Congo
108 B2 **Bologna** Italy
89 D2 **Bologovo** Rus. Fed.
89 D2 **Bologoye** Rus. Fed.
123 C2 **Bolokanang** S. Africa
118 B2 **Bolomba** Dem. Rep. Congo
63 B2 **Bolovens, Phouphieng** *plat.* Laos
108 B2 **Bolsena, Lago di** *l.* Italy
83 H1 **Bol'shevik, Ostrov** *i.* Rus. Fed.
86 E2 **Bol'shezemel'skaya Tundra** *lowland* Rus. Fed.
83 L2 **Bol'shoy Aluy** *r.* Rus. Fed.
66 B2 **Bol'shoy Kamen'** Rus. Fed.
Bol'shoy Kavkaz *mts* Asia/Europe *see* **Caucasus**
83 K2 **Bol'shoy Lyakhovskiy, Ostrov** *i.* Rus. Fed.
Bol'shoy Tokmak Kyrg. *see* **Tokmok**
Bol'shoy Tokmak Ukr. *see* **Tokmak**
100 B1 **Bolsward** Neth.
98 B3 **Bolton** U.K.
80 B1 **Bolu** Turkey
59 E3 **Bolubolu** P.N.G.
92 □A2 **Bolungarvík** Iceland
108 B1 **Bolzano** Italy
118 B3 **Boma** Dem. Rep. Congo
53 D2 **Bomaderry** Austr.
53 C3 **Bombala** Austr.
Bombay India *see* **Mumbai**
155 C1 **Bom Despacho** Brazil
75 D2 **Bomdila** India
154 B1 **Bom Jardim de Goiás** Brazil
151 E4 **Bom Jesus da Lapa** Brazil
155 D2 **Bom Jesus do Itabapoana** Brazil
115 D1 **Bon, Cap** *c.* Tunisia
147 D3 **Bonaire** *i.* Neth. Antilles
134 C1 **Bonaparte, Mount** U.S.A.
50 D1 **Bonaparte Archipelago** *is* Austr.
131 E3 **Bonavista** Can.
131 E3 **Bonavista Bay** Can.
118 C2 **Bondo** Dem. Rep. Congo
114 B4 **Bondoukou** Côte d'Ivoire
Bône Alg. *see* **Annaba**
61 D2 **Bonerate, Kepulauan** *is* Indon.
155 C1 **Bonfinópolis de Minas** Brazil
117 B4 **Bonga** Eth.
75 D2 **Bongaigaon** India
118 C2 **Bongandanga** Dem. Rep. Congo
122 B2 **Bongani** S. Africa
118 C2 **Bongo, Massif des** *mts* C.A.R.
121 □D2 **Bongolava** *mts* Madag.
115 D3 **Bongor** Chad
114 B4 **Bongouanou** Côte d'Ivoire
63 B2 **Bông Sơn** Vietnam
143 D2 **Bonham** U.S.A.
105 D3 **Bonifacio** *Corsica* France
108 A2 **Bonifacio, Strait of** France/Italy
69 F3 **Bonin Islands** *is* Japan
100 C2 **Bonn** Ger.
134 C1 **Bonners Ferry** U.S.A.
105 D2 **Bonneville** France
50 A3 **Bonnie Rock** Austr.
129 C2 **Bonnyville** Can.
108 A2 **Bonorva** *Sardinia* Italy
53 D1 **Bonshaw** Austr.
61 C1 **Bontang** Indon.
114 A4 **Bonthe** Sierra Leone
64 B2 **Bontoc** Phil.
61 C2 **Bontosunggu** Indon.
123 C3 **Bontrug** S. Africa
53 C1 **Boolba** Austr.
52 B2 **Booligal** Austr.
53 C1 **Boomi** Austr.
53 D1 **Boonah** Austr.
137 E2 **Boone** U.S.A.
140 C2 **Booneville** U.S.A.
137 E3 **Boonville** U.S.A.
52 B3 **Booroorban** Austr.
53 C2 **Boorowa** Austr.
117 C3 **Boosaaso** Somalia
126 G2 **Boothia, Gulf of** Can.
126 F2 **Boothia Peninsula** Can.
118 B3 **Booué** Gabon
100 C2 **Boppard** Ger.
144 B2 **Boquilla, Presa de la** *resr* Mex.
109 D2 **Bor** Serbia
117 B4 **Bor** Sudan
80 B2 **Bor** Turkey
93 F4 **Borås** Sweden
81 D3 **Borāzjān** Iran
150 D3 **Borba** Brazil
104 B3 **Bordeaux** France
126 E1 **Borden Island** Can.
127 G2 **Borden Peninsula** Can.
52 B3 **Bordertown** Austr.
107 D2 **Bordj Bou Arréridj** Alg.
107 D2 **Bordj Bounaama** Alg.
114 B2 **Bordj Flye Ste-Marie** Alg.
115 C1 **Bordj Messaouda** Alg.
114 C2 **Bordj Mokhtar** Alg.
Bordj Omar Driss Alg. *see* **Bordj Omer Driss**
115 C2 **Bordj Omer Driss** Alg.
94 B1 **Borðoy** *i.* Faroe Is
Borgå Fin. *see* **Porvoo**
92 □A3 **Borgarnes** Iceland
143 C1 **Borger** U.S.A.
93 G4 **Borgholm** Sweden
100 B2 **Borgloon** Belgium
108 A1 **Borgosesia** Italy
87 D3 **Borisoglebsk** Rus. Fed.
89 E2 **Borisoglebskiy** Rus. Fed.
91 D1 **Borisovka** Rus. Fed.
119 C2 **Bo River Post** Sudan
100 C2 **Borken** Ger.
92 G2 **Borkenes** Norway
100 C1 **Borkum** Ger.
100 C1 **Borkum** *i.* Ger.
93 G3 **Borlänge** Sweden
101 F2 **Borna** Ger.
100 C1 **Borne** Neth.
61 C1 **Borneo** *i.* Asia
93 F4 **Bornholm** *i.* Denmark
111 C3 **Bornova** Turkey
90 B1 **Borodyanka** Ukr.
77 E2 **Borohoro Shan** *mts* China
114 B3 **Boron** Mali
89 D2 **Borovichi** Rus. Fed.
89 E2 **Borovsk** Rus. Fed.
76 C1 **Borovskoy** Kazakh.
51 C1 **Borroloola** Austr.
110 B1 **Borşa** Romania
76 B2 **Borsakelmas sho'rxogi** *salt marsh* Uzbek.
90 B2 **Borshchiv** Ukr.
69 D1 **Borshchovochnyy Khrebet** *mts* Rus. Fed.
101 E1 **Börßum** Ger.
Bortala China *see* **Bole**
81 C2 **Borūjerd** Iran
90 A2 **Boryslav** Ukr.
90 C1 **Boryspil'** Ukr.
91 C1 **Borzna** Ukr.
69 D1 **Borzya** Rus. Fed.
109 C1 **Bosanska Dubica** Bos.-Herz.
109 C1 **Bosanska Gradiška** Bos.-Herz.
109 C2 **Bosanska Krupa** Bos.-Herz.
109 C1 **Bosanski Novi** Bos.-Herz.
109 C2 **Bosansko Grahovo** Bos.-Herz.
71 A3 **Bose** China
123 C2 **Boshof** S. Africa
109 C2 **Bosnia-Herzegovina** *country* Europe
118 B2 **Bosobolo** Dem. Rep. Congo
111 C2 **Bosporus** *str.* Turkey
142 B2 **Bosque** U.S.A.
118 B2 **Bossangoa** C.A.R.
118 B2 **Bossembélé** C.A.R.
140 B2 **Bossier City** U.S.A.
122 A2 **Bossiesvlei** Namibia
68 B2 **Bosten Hu** *l.* China
99 C3 **Boston** U.K.
139 E2 **Boston** U.S.A.
140 B1 **Boston Mountains** U.S.A.
53 D2 **Botany Bay** Austr.
120 B3 **Boteti** *r.* Botswana
110 B2 **Botev** *mt.* Bulg.
80 A1 **Botevgrad** Bulg.
92 C3 **Bothnia, Gulf of** Fin./Sweden
110 C1 **Botoşani** Romania
70 B2 **Botou** China
123 C2 **Botshabelo** S. Africa
120 B3 **Botswana** *country* Africa
109 C3 **Botte Donato, Monte** *mt.* Italy
136 C1 **Bottineau** U.S.A.
100 C2 **Bottrop** Ger.
154 C2 **Botucatu** Brazil
114 B4 **Bouaké** Côte d'Ivoire
118 B2 **Bouar** C.A.R.
114 B1 **Bouârfa** Morocco
131 D3 **Bouctouche** Can.
107 E2 **Bougaa** Alg.
48 G4 **Bougainville Island** P.N.G.
Bougie Alg. *see* **Bejaïa**
114 B3 **Bougouni** Mali
100 B3 **Bouillon** Belgium
107 D2 **Bouira** Alg.
114 A2 **Boujdour** Western Sahara
50 B3 **Boulder** Austr.
136 B2 **Boulder** *CO* U.S.A.
134 D1 **Boulder** *MT* U.S.A.
135 D3 **Boulder City** U.S.A.
Boulhaut Morocco *see* **Ben Slimane**
51 C2 **Boulia** Austr.
104 C2 **Boulogne-Billancourt** France
104 C1 **Boulogne-sur-Mer** France
118 C2 **Boulouba** C.A.R.
118 B3 **Boumango** Gabon
118 B2 **Boumba** *r.* Cameroon
107 D2 **Boumerdes** Alg.
114 B4 **Bouna** Côte d'Ivoire
114 B4 **Boundiali** Côte d'Ivoire
134 D2 **Bountiful** U.S.A.
49 I8 **Bounty Islands** N.Z.
114 B3 **Bourem** Mali
104 C2 **Bourganeuf** France
105 D2 **Bourg-en-Bresse** France
104 C2 **Bourges** France
Bourgogne *reg.* France *see* **Burgundy**
105 D2 **Bourgoin-Jallieu** France
53 C2 **Bourke** Austr.
99 C3 **Bourne** U.K.
99 C4 **Bournemouth** U.K.
118 C1 **Bourtoutou** Chad
115 C1 **Bou Saâda** Alg.
115 D3 **Bousso** Chad
100 A2 **Boussu** Belgium
114 A3 **Boutilimit** Maur.
128 C3 **Bow** *r.* Can.
Bowa China *see* **Muli**
51 D2 **Bowen** Austr.
53 C3 **Bowen, Mount** Austr.
129 C3 **Bow Island** Can.
138 B3 **Bowling Green** *KY* U.S.A.
137 E3 **Bowling Green** *MO* U.S.A.
138 C2 **Bowling Green** *OH* U.S.A.
136 C1 **Bowman** U.S.A.
53 D2 **Bowral** Austr.
101 D3 **Boxberg** Ger.
100 B2 **Boxtel** Neth.
80 B1 **Boyabat** Turkey
71 B3 **Boyang** China
97 B2 **Boyle** Ireland
97 C2 **Boyne** *r.* Ireland
136 B2 **Boysen Reservoir** U.S.A.
152 B2 **Boyuibe** Bol.
111 C3 **Bozburun** Turkey
111 C3 **Bozcaada** *i.* Turkey
111 C3 **Bozdağ** *mt.* Turkey
111 C3 **Boz Dağları** *mts* Turkey
111 C3 **Bozdoğan** Turkey
134 D1 **Bozeman** U.S.A.
118 B2 **Bozoum** C.A.R.
111 D3 **Bozüyük** Turkey
109 C2 **Brač** *i.* Croatia
130 C3 **Bracebridge** Can.
93 G3 **Bräcke** Sweden
99 C4 **Bracknell** U.K.
109 C2 **Bradano** *r.* Italy
141 D3 **Bradenton** U.S.A.
98 C3 **Bradford** U.K.
139 D2 **Bradford** U.S.A.
147 D3 **Brades** Montserrat
143 D2 **Brady** U.S.A.
96 C2 **Braemar** U.K.
106 B1 **Braga** Port.
151 E3 **Bragança** Brazil
106 B1 **Bragança** Port.
155 C2 **Bragança Paulista** Brazil
89 D3 **Brahin** Belarus
75 D2 **Brahmanbaria** Bangl.
75 C3 **Brahmapur** India
62 A1 **Brahmaputra** *r.* China/India
53 C3 **Braidwood** Austr.
110 C1 **Brăila** Romania
137 E1 **Brainerd** U.S.A.
99 D4 **Braintree** U.K.
100 B2 **Braives** Belgium
101 D1 **Brake (Unterweser)** Ger.
122 A1 **Brakwater** Namibia
98 B2 **Brampton** U.K.
101 D1 **Bramsche** Ger.
150 C3 **Branco** *r.* Brazil
101 F1 **Brandenburg** Ger.
129 E3 **Brandon** Can.
140 C2 **Brandon** U.S.A.
97 A2 **Brandon Mountain** *hill* Ireland
122 B3 **Brandvlei** S. Africa
103 D1 **Braniewo** Pol.
130 B3 **Brantford** Can.
53 D2 **Branxton** Austr.
131 D3 **Bras d'Or Lake** Can.
155 D1 **Brasil, Planalto do** *plat.* Brazil
154 C1 **Brasilândia** Brazil
154 C1 **Brasília** Brazil
155 D1 **Brasília de Minas** Brazil
88 C2 **Braslaw** Belarus
110 C1 **Braşov** Romania
103 D2 **Bratislava** Slovakia
83 H3 **Bratsk** Rus. Fed.
102 C2 **Braunau am Inn** Austria
101 E1 **Braunschweig** Ger.
92 □A2 **Brautarholt** Iceland
Bravo del Norte, Río *r.* Mex./U.S.A. *see* **Rio Grande**
135 C4 **Brawley** U.S.A.
97 C2 **Bray** Ireland
150 D2 **Brazil** *country* S. America
158 E6 **Brazil Basin** *sea feature* S. Atlantic Ocean
143 D3 **Brazos** *r.* U.S.A.
118 B3 **Brazzaville** Congo
109 C2 **Brčko** Bos.-Herz.
96 C2 **Brechin** U.K.
100 B2 **Brecht** Belgium
143 D2 **Breckenridge** U.S.A.
103 D2 **Břeclav** Czech Rep.
99 B4 **Brecon** U.K.
99 B4 **Brecon Beacons** *reg.* U.K.
100 B2 **Breda** Neth.
122 B3 **Bredasdorp** S. Africa
102 B2 **Bregenz** Austria
92 H1 **Breivikbotn** Norway
92 E3 **Brekstad** Norway
101 D1 **Bremen** Ger.
101 D1 **Bremerhaven** Ger.
Bremersdorp Swaziland *see* **Manzini**
134 B1 **Bremerton** U.S.A.
101 D1 **Bremervörde** Ger.
143 D2 **Brenham** U.S.A.
108 B1 **Brennero** Italy
102 C2 **Brenner Pass** Austria/Italy
99 D4 **Brentwood** U.K.
108 B1 **Brescia** Italy
100 A2 **Breskens** Neth.
108 B1 **Bressanone** Italy
96 □ **Bressay** *i.* U.K.
104 B2 **Bressuire** France
88 B3 **Brest** Belarus
104 B2 **Brest** France
Brest-Litovsk Belarus *see* **Brest**
Bretagne *reg.* France *see* **Brittany**
140 C3 **Breton Sound** *b.* U.S.A.
151 D3 **Breves** Brazil
53 C1 **Brewarrina** Austr.
134 C1 **Brewster** U.S.A.
89 E2 **Breytovo** Rus. Fed.
Brezhnev Rus. Fed. *see* **Naberezhnyye Chelny**
109 C1 **Brezovo Polje** *hill* Croatia
118 C2 **Bria** C.A.R.
105 D3 **Briançon** France
90 B2 **Briceni** Moldova
Brichany Moldova *see* **Briceni**
99 B4 **Bridgend** U.K.
139 E2 **Bridgeport** *CT* U.S.A.
136 C2 **Bridgeport** *NE* U.S.A.
147 E3 **Bridgetown** Barbados
131 D3 **Bridgewater** Can.
99 B3 **Bridgnorth** U.K.
99 B4 **Bridgwater** U.K.
99 B4 **Bridgwater Bay** U.K.
98 C2 **Bridlington** U.K.
98 C2 **Bridlington Bay** U.K.
99 B4 **Bridport** U.K.
105 D2 **Brig** Switz.
134 D2 **Brigham City** U.S.A.

154 C1 **Cabeceiras** Brazil
106 B2 **Cabeza del Buey** Spain
152 B1 **Cabezas** Bol.
150 B1 **Cabimas** Venez.
120 A1 **Cabinda** Angola
118 B3 **Cabinda** prov. Angola
151 F3 **Cabo** Brazil
155 D2 **Cabo Frio** Brazil
155 D2 **Cabo Frio, Ilha do** i. Brazil
130 C3 **Cabonga, Réservoir** resr Can.
53 D1 **Caboolture** Austr.
150 B3 **Cabo Pantoja** Peru
121 C2 **Cabora Bassa, Lake** resr Moz.
144 A1 **Caborca** Mex.
131 D3 **Cabot Strait** Can.
106 C2 **Cabra** Spain
155 D1 **Cabral, Serra do** mts Brazil
107 D2 **Cabrera, Illa de** i. Spain
106 B1 **Cabrera, Sierra de la** mts Spain
107 C2 **Cabri** Can.
107 C2 **Cabriel** r. Spain
155 D2 **Caçador** Brazil
109 D2 **Čačak** Serbia
108 A2 **Caccia, Capo** c. Sardinia Italy
106 B2 **Cacém** Port.
151 D4 **Cáceres** Brazil
106 B2 **Cáceres** Spain
120 D2 **Cache Creek** Can.
114 A3 **Cacheu** Guinea-Bissau
151 D3 **Cachimbo, Serra do** hills Brazil
154 B1 **Cachoeira Alta** Brazil
155 D2 **Cachoeiro de Itapemirim** Brazil
114 A3 **Cacine** Guinea-Bissau
120 A2 **Cacolo** Angola
120 A2 **Caconda** Angola
154 B1 **Caçu** Brazil
103 D2 **Čadca** Slovakia
101 D1 **Cadenberge** Ger.
145 B2 **Cadereyta** Mex.
138 B2 **Cadillac** U.S.A.
64 B2 **Cadiz** Phil.
106 B2 **Cádiz** Spain
106 B2 **Cádiz, Golfo de** g. Spain
128 C2 **Cadotte Lake** Can.
104 B2 **Caen** France
Caerdydd U.K. see **Cardiff**
Caerfyrddin U.K. see **Carmarthen**
Caergybi U.K. see **Holyhead**
98 A3 **Caernarfon** U.K.
99 A3 **Caernarfon Bay** U.K.
Caernarvon U.K. see **Caernarfon**
152 B2 **Cafayate** Arg.
154 B2 **Cafelândia** Brazil
64 B3 **Cagayan de Oro** Phil.
64 A3 **Cagayan de Tawi-Tawi** i. Phil.
108 B2 **Cagli** Italy
108 A3 **Cagliari** Sardinia Italy
108 A3 **Cagliari, Golfo di** b. Sardinia Italy
76 B2 **Çağyl** Turkm.
120 A2 **Cahama** Angola
97 B3 **Caha Mountains** Ireland
97 A3 **Cahermore** Ireland
97 C2 **Cahir** Ireland
97 A3 **Cahirciveen** Ireland
Cahora Bassa, Lago de resr Moz. see **Cabora Bassa, Lake**
97 C2 **Cahore Point** Ireland
104 C3 **Cahors** France
90 B2 **Cahul** Moldova
121 C2 **Caia** Moz.
151 D4 **Caiabis, Serra dos** hills Brazil
120 B2 **Caianda** Angola
154 B1 **Caiapó, Serra do** mts Brazil
147 C2 **Caiapônia** Brazil
147 C2 **Caicos Islands** Turks and Caicos Is
96 C2 **Cairngorm Mountains** U.K.
96 B3 **Cairnryan** U.K.
51 C1 **Cairns** Austr.
116 B1 **Cairo** Egypt
Caisleán an Bharraigh Ireland see **Castlebar**
98 C3 **Caistor** U.K.
120 A2 **Caiundo** Angola
150 B3 **Cajamarca** Peru

109 C1 **Čakovec** Croatia
123 C3 **Cala** S. Africa
115 C4 **Calabar** Nigeria
150 C2 **Calabozo** Venez.
110 B2 **Calafat** Romania
153 A5 **Calafate** Arg.
107 C1 **Calahorra** Spain
120 A2 **Calai** Angola
104 C1 **Calais** France
139 F1 **Calais** U.S.A.
152 B2 **Calama** Chile
64 A2 **Calamian Group** is Phil.
107 C1 **Calamocha** Spain
120 A1 **Calandula** Angola
60 A1 **Calang** Indon.
64 B2 **Calapan** Phil.
110 C2 **Călăraşi** Romania
107 C1 **Calatayud** Spain
64 B2 **Calayan** i. Phil.
64 B2 **Calbayog** Phil.
151 F3 **Calcanhar, Ponta do** pt Brazil
151 D2 **Calçoene** Brazil
Calcutta India see **Kolkata**
106 B2 **Caldas da Rainha** Port.
154 C1 **Caldas Novas** Brazil
152 B3 **Caldera** Chile
51 D2 **Caldervale** Austr.
134 C2 **Caldwell** U.S.A.
123 C3 **Caledon** r. Lesotho/S. Africa
122 A3 **Caledon** S. Africa
153 B4 **Caleta Olivia** Arg.
98 A2 **Calf of Man** i. Isle of Man
128 C2 **Calgary** Can.
150 B2 **Cali** Col.
73 B3 **Calicut** India
135 D3 **Caliente** U.S.A.
135 B2 **California** state U.S.A.
144 A1 **California, Gulf of** g. Mex.
135 B3 **California Aqueduct** canal U.S.A.
81 C2 **Călilabad** Azer.
122 B3 **Calitzdorp** S. Africa
145 C2 **Calkiní** Mex.
52 B1 **Callabonna, Lake** salt flat Austr.
135 C3 **Callaghan, Mount** U.S.A.
97 C2 **Callan** Ireland
96 B2 **Callander** U.K.
150 B4 **Callao** Peru
99 A4 **Callington** U.K.
108 B3 **Caltagirone** Sicily Italy
108 B3 **Caltanissetta** Sicily Italy
120 A1 **Calulo** Angola
120 B2 **Calunda** Angola
120 A2 **Caluquembe** Angola
117 D3 **Caluula** Somalia
105 D3 **Calvi** Corsica France
107 D2 **Calvià** Spain
144 B2 **Calvillo** Mex.
122 A3 **Calvinia** S. Africa
100 C2 **Calvo, Monte** mt. Italy
151 F4 **Camaçari** Brazil
144 B2 **Camacho** Mex.
120 A2 **Camacupa** Angola
146 C2 **Camagüey** Cuba
146 C2 **Camagüey, Archipiélago de** is Cuba
150 B4 **Camana** Peru
120 B2 **Camanongue** Angola
154 B1 **Camapuã** Brazil
145 C2 **Camargo** Mex.
63 B3 **Ca Mau** Vietnam
Cambay India see **Khambhat**
63 B2 **Cambodia** country Asia
99 A4 **Camborne** U.K.
105 C1 **Cambrai** France
99 B3 **Cambrian Mountains** hills U.K.
138 C2 **Cambridge** Can.
54 C1 **Cambridge** N.Z.
99 D3 **Cambridge** U.K.
139 E2 **Cambridge** MA U.S.A.
139 D3 **Cambridge** MD U.S.A.
137 E1 **Cambridge** MN U.S.A.
138 C2 **Cambridge** OH U.S.A.
126 E2 **Cambridge Bay** Can.
120 B1 **Cambulo** Angola
53 D2 **Camden** Austr.
140 B2 **Camden** AR U.S.A.
139 F2 **Camden** ME U.S.A.
139 D3 **Camden** NJ U.S.A.
137 E3 **Camdenton** U.S.A.
137 E3 **Cameron** U.S.A.
118 B2 **Cameroon** country Africa
118 B2 **Cameroon Highlands** slope Cameroon/Nigeria

118 A2 **Cameroun, Mont** vol. Cameroon
151 E3 **Cametá** Brazil
64 B2 **Camiguin** i. Phil.
64 B3 **Camiguin** i. Phil.
152 B2 **Camiri** Bol.
151 E3 **Camocim** Brazil
51 C1 **Camooweal** Austr.
73 B3 **Camorta** i. India
153 A4 **Campana, Isla** i. Chile
155 D1 **Campanário** Brazil
155 C2 **Campanha** Brazil
122 B2 **Campbell** S. Africa
54 B2 **Campbell, Cape** N.Z.
48 H9 **Campbell Island** N.Z.
156 D9 **Campbell Plateau** sea feature S. Pacific Ocean
128 B2 **Campbell River** Can.
138 B3 **Campbellsville** U.S.A.
131 D3 **Campbellton** Can.
53 D2 **Campbelltown** Austr.
96 B3 **Campbeltown** U.K.
145 C3 **Campeche** Mex.
145 C3 **Campeche, Bahía de** g. Mex.
52 B3 **Camperdown** Austr.
110 C1 **Câmpina** Romania
151 F3 **Campina Grande** Brazil
154 C2 **Campinas** Brazil
154 C1 **Campina Verde** Brazil
108 B2 **Campobasso** Italy
155 C2 **Campo Belo** Brazil
154 C1 **Campo Florido** Brazil
152 B2 **Campo Gallo** Arg.
154 B2 **Campo Grande** Brazil
154 C3 **Campo Largo** Brazil
151 E3 **Campo Maior** Brazil
106 B2 **Campo Maior** Port.
150 B1 **Campo Mara** Venez.
155 D2 **Campos** Brazil
155 C1 **Campos Altos** Brazil
155 C2 **Campos do Jordão** Brazil
110 C1 **Câmpulung** Romania
142 A2 **Camp Verde** U.S.A.
63 B2 **Cam Ranh, Vinh** b. Ba Ngoi
63 B2 **Cam Ranh, Vinh** Vietnam
Cam Ranh Bay Vietnam see **Cam Ranh, Vinh**
128 C2 **Camrose** Can.
129 D2 **Camsell Portage** Can.
111 C2 **Can** Turkey
126 F2 **Canada** country N. America
160 A2 **Canada Basin** sea feature Arctic Ocean
143 C1 **Canadian** U.S.A.
143 D1 **Canadian** r. U.S.A.
111 C2 **Çanakkale** Turkey
144 A1 **Cananea** Mex.
154 C2 **Cananéia** Brazil
114 A2 **Canary Islands** terr. N. Atlantic Ocean
154 C2 **Canastra, Serra da** mts Goiás Brazil
155 C1 **Canastra, Serra da** mts Minas Gerais Brazil
144 B2 **Canatlán** Mex.
141 D3 **Canaveral, Cape** U.S.A.
155 E1 **Canavieiras** Brazil
53 C2 **Canberra** Austr.
145 D2 **Cancún** Mex.
111 C3 **Çandarlı** Turkey
155 C2 **Candeias** Brazil
145 C3 **Candelaria** Mex.
154 C3 **Cândido de Abreu** Brazil
129 D2 **Candle Lake** Can.
137 D1 **Cando** U.S.A.
120 A1 **Cangamba** Angola
106 B1 **Cangas** Spain
106 B1 **Cangas del Narcea** Spain
120 B2 **Cangombe** Angola
152 C3 **Canguçu** Brazil
70 B2 **Cangzhou** China
131 D2 **Caniapiscau** Can.
131 D2 **Caniapiscau** r. Can.
131 C1 **Caniapiscau, Réservoir de** l. Can.
Caniçado Moz. see **Guija**
108 B3 **Canicattì** Sicily Italy
151 F3 **Canindé** Brazil
144 B2 **Cañitas de Felipe Pescador** Mex.
80 B1 **Çankırı** Turkey
128 C2 **Canmore** Can.
96 A2 **Canna** i. U.K.

73 B3 **Cannanore** India
105 D3 **Cannes** France
99 B3 **Cannock** U.K.
53 C3 **Cann River** Austr.
152 C2 **Canoas** Brazil
129 D2 **Canoe Lake** Can.
154 B3 **Canoinhas** Brazil
136 B3 **Canon City** U.S.A.
52 B2 **Canopus** Austr.
129 D2 **Canora** Can.
53 C2 **Canowindra** Austr.
131 D3 **Canso** Can.
Cantabrian Mountains Spain see **Cantábrica, Cordillera**
Cantabrian Sea Spain see **Cantábrico, Mar**
106 C1 **Cantábrica, Cordillera** mts Spain
106 B1 **Cantábrico, Mar** sea Spain
99 D4 **Canterbury** U.K.
54 B2 **Canterbury Bight** b. N.Z.
54 B2 **Canterbury Plains** N.Z.
63 B2 **Cần Thơ** Vietnam
151 E3 **Canto do Buriti** Brazil
Canton China see **Guangzhou**
137 E2 **Canton** MO U.S.A.
140 C2 **Canton** MS U.S.A.
139 D2 **Canton** NY U.S.A.
138 C2 **Canton** OH U.S.A.
143 C1 **Canyon** U.S.A.
134 D1 **Canyon Ferry Lake** U.S.A.
134 B2 **Canyonville** U.S.A.
62 B1 **Cao Bằng** Vietnam
109 C2 **Capaccio** Italy
154 C2 **Capão Bonito** Brazil
155 D2 **Caparaó, Serra do** mts Brazil
139 E1 **Cap-de-la-Madeleine** Can.
51 D4 **Cape Barren Island** Austr.
158 F7 **Cape Basin** sea feature S. Atlantic Ocean
52 A3 **Cape Borda** Austr.
131 D3 **Cape Breton Island** Can.
141 D3 **Cape Canaveral** U.S.A.
139 D3 **Cape Charles** U.S.A.
114 B4 **Cape Coast** Ghana
139 E2 **Cape Cod Bay** U.S.A.
141 D3 **Cape Coral** U.S.A.
127 G2 **Cape Dorset** Can.
141 E2 **Cape Fear** r. U.S.A.
137 F3 **Cape Girardeau** U.S.A.
155 D1 **Capelinha** Brazil
100 B2 **Capelle aan de IJssel** Neth.
Capelongo Angola see **Kuvango**
139 F3 **Cape May Point** U.S.A.
120 A1 **Capenda-Camulemba** Angola
122 A3 **Cape Town** S. Africa
158 E3 **Cape Verde** country N. Atlantic Ocean
158 D4 **Cape Verde Basin** sea feature N. Atlantic Ocean
51 D1 **Cape York Peninsula** Austr.
147 C3 **Cap-Haïtien** Haiti
151 E3 **Capim** r. Brazil
58 D1 **Capitol Hill** N. Mariana Is
154 B2 **Capivara, Represa** resr Brazil
109 C2 **Čapljina** Bos.-Herz.
108 B3 **Capo d'Orlando** Sicily Italy
108 A2 **Capraia, Isola di** i. Italy
108 A2 **Caprara, Punta** pt Sardinia Italy
108 B2 **Capri, Isola di** i. Italy
51 E2 **Capricorn Channel** Austr.
120 A2 **Caprivi Strip** reg. Namibia
143 C2 **Cap Rock Escarpment** U.S.A.
143 C1 **Capulin** U.S.A.
150 C3 **Caquetá** r. Col.
110 B2 **Caracal** Romania
150 D2 **Caracarai** Brazil
150 B1 **Caracas** Venez.
151 E3 **Caracol** Brazil
155 C2 **Caraguatatuba** Brazil
153 A3 **Carahue** Chile
155 D1 **Caraí** Brazil
155 D2 **Carajás, Serra dos** hills Brazil
155 D2 **Carandaí** Brazil
155 D2 **Carangola** Brazil
110 B1 **Caransebeş** Romania

105 D2 Chambéry France
121 C2 Chambeshi Zambia
121 D2 Chambeshi r. Zambia
Chamdo China see Qamdo
119 D2 Ch'amo Häyk' l. Eth.
105 D2 Chamonix-Mont-Blanc France
105 C2 Champagne reg. France
138 B2 Champaign U.S.A.
139 E2 Champlain, Lake Can./U.S.A.
145 C3 Champotón Mex.
Chanak Turkey see Çanakkale
152 A2 Chañaral Chile
Chanda India see Chandrapur
126 C2 Chandalar r. U.S.A.
140 C3 Chandeleur Islands U.S.A.
74 B1 Chandigarh India
131 D3 Chandler Can.
142 A2 Chandler U.S.A.
75 D2 Chandpur Bangl.
75 B3 Chandrapur India
63 B2 Chang, Ko i. Thai.
Chang'an China see Rong'an
121 C3 Changane r. Moz.
121 C2 Changara Moz.
65 B1 Changbai China
65 B1 Changbai Shan mts China/N. Korea
Changchow China see Zhangzhou
Changchow China see Changzhou
69 E2 Changchun China
71 B3 Changde China
65 B2 Ch'angdo N. Korea
70 B2 Changge China
71 C3 Changhua Taiwan
65 B3 Changhŭng S. Korea
Chang Jiang r. China see Yangtze
Changjiang Kou r. mouth China see Yangtze, Mouth of the
65 B1 Changjin N. Korea
65 B1 Changjin-gang r. N. Korea
Changkiang China see Zhanjiang
Changning China see Xunwu
Ch'ang-pai Shan mts China/N. Korea see Changbai Shan
71 B3 Changsha China
70 C2 Changshu China
65 B2 Changsŏng S. Korea
Changteh China see Changde
71 B3 Changting Fujian China
66 A2 Changting Heilong. China
65 A1 Changtu China
146 B4 Changuinola Panama
65 B2 Ch'angwŏn S. Korea
65 B2 Changyŏn N. Korea
70 B2 Changyuan China
70 B2 Changzhi China
70 B2 Changzhou China
111 B3 Chania Greece
95 C4 Channel Islands English Chan.
135 C4 Channel Islands U.S.A.
131 E3 Channel-Port-aux-Basques Can.
106 B1 Chantada Spain
63 B2 Chanthaburi Thai.
104 C2 Chantilly France
137 D3 Chanute U.S.A.
82 G3 Chany, Ozero salt l. Rus. Fed.
70 B2 Chaohu China
71 B3 Chaoyang Guangdong China
Chaoyang China see Huinan
70 C1 Chaoyang Liaoning China
71 B3 Chaozhou China
144 B2 Chapala, Laguna de l. Mex.
76 B1 Chapayev Kazakh.
87 D3 Chapayevsk Rus. Fed.
152 C2 Chapecó Brazil
141 E1 Chapel Hill U.S.A.
130 B3 Chapleau Can.
89 E3 Chaplygin Rus. Fed.
91 C2 Chaplynka Ukr.
Chapra India see Chhapra
145 B2 Charcas Mex.
99 B4 Chard U.K.
Chardzhev Turkm. see Türkmenabat
Chardzhou Turkm. see Türkmenabat
104 B2 Charente r. France
118 B1 Chari r. Cameroon/Chad
77 C3 Chārīkār Afgh.
86 E2 Charkayuvom Rus. Fed.
Charkhlik China see Ruoqiang
100 B2 Charleroi Belgium
139 D3 Charles, Cape U.S.A.
139 E1 Charlesbourg Can.
137 E2 Charles City U.S.A.
138 B3 Charleston IL U.S.A.
137 F3 Charleston MO U.S.A.
141 E2 Charleston SC U.S.A.
138 C3 Charleston WV U.S.A.
135 C3 Charleston Peak U.S.A.
51 D2 Charleville Austr.
105 C2 Charleville-Mézières France
138 B1 Charlevoix U.S.A.
141 D1 Charlotte U.S.A.
141 D3 Charlotte Harbor b. U.S.A.
139 D3 Charlottesville U.S.A.
131 D3 Charlottetown Can.
52 B3 Charlton Austr.
130 C2 Charlton Island Can.
51 D2 Charters Towers Austr.
104 C2 Chartres France
128 C2 Chase Can.
88 C3 Chashniki Belarus
54 A3 Chaslands Mistake c. N.Z.
65 B1 Chasŏng N. Korea
104 B2 Chassiron, Pointe de pt France
104 B2 Châteaubriant France
104 C2 Château-du-Loir France
104 C2 Châteaudun France
104 B2 Château-Gontier France
104 B2 Châteaulin France
105 D3 Châteauneuf-les-Martigues France
104 C2 Châteauneuf-sur-Loire France
104 C2 Châteauroux France
105 C2 Château-Thierry France
128 C2 Chateh Can.
100 B2 Châtelet Belgium
104 C2 Châtellerault France
138 C2 Chatham Ont. Can.
99 D4 Chatham U.K.
49 J8 Chatham Islands N.Z.
105 C2 Châtillon-sur-Seine France
141 D2 Chattahoochee r. U.S.A.
141 C1 Chattanooga U.S.A.
63 B2 Châu Đôc Vietnam
62 A1 Chauk Myanmar
105 D2 Chaumont France
105 C2 Chauny France
Chau Phu Vietnam see Châu Đôc
151 E3 Chaves Brazil
106 B1 Chaves Port.
130 C2 Chavigny, Lac l. Can.
89 D3 Chavusy Belarus
89 E2 Chayevo Rus. Fed.
86 E3 Chaykovskiy Rus. Fed.
140 C2 Cheaha Mountain hill U.S.A.
102 C1 Cheb Czech Rep.
87 D3 Cheboksary Rus. Fed.
138 C1 Cheboygan U.S.A.
65 B2 Chech'ŏn S. Korea
140 A1 Checotah U.S.A.
Chefoo China see Yantai
126 B2 Chefornak U.S.A.
114 B2 Chegga Maur.
121 C2 Chegutu Zimbabwe
134 B1 Chehalis U.S.A.
65 B3 Cheju S. Korea
65 B3 Cheju-do i. S. Korea
65 B3 Cheju-haehyŏp sea chan. S. Korea
89 E2 Chekhov Rus. Fed.
Chekiang prov. China see Zhejiang
134 B1 Chelan, Lake U.S.A.
103 E1 Chełm Pol.
99 D4 Chelmer r. U.K.
103 D1 Chełmno Pol.
99 D4 Chelmsford U.K.
99 B4 Cheltenham U.K.
87 F3 Chelyabinsk Rus. Fed.
83 H1 Chelyuskin Rus. Fed.
101 F2 Chemnitz Ger.
Chemulpo S. Korea see Inch'ŏn
134 B2 Chemult U.S.A.
74 B2 Chenab r. India/Pak.
114 B2 Chenachane Alg.
134 C1 Cheney U.S.A.
Chengchow China see Zhengzhou
70 B1 Chengde China
70 A2 Chengdu China
Chengjiang China see Taihe
71 B4 Chengmai China
Chengshou China see Yingshan
Chengtu China see Chengdu
70 A2 Chengxian China
Chengxiang China see Wuxi
Chengxiang China see Mianning
Chengyang China see Juxian
73 C3 Chennai India
Chenstokhov Pol. see Częstochowa
71 B3 Chenzhou China
99 B4 Chepstow U.K.
141 E2 Cheraw U.S.A.
104 B2 Cherbourg France
Cherchen China see Qiemo
89 E3 Cheremisinovo Rus. Fed.
68 C1 Cheremkhovo Rus. Fed.
89 E2 Cherepovets Rus. Fed.
91 C2 Cherkasy Ukr.
87 D4 Cherkessk Rus. Fed.
89 E3 Chern' Rus. Fed.
91 C1 Chernihiv Ukr.
91 D2 Cherninivka Ukr.
90 B2 Chernivtsi Ukr.
68 C1 Chernogorsk Rus. Fed.
90 B1 Chernyakhiv Ukr.
88 B3 Chernyakhovsk Rus. Fed.
89 E3 Chernyanka Rus. Fed.
69 D1 Chernyshevsk Rus. Fed.
83 I2 Chernyshevskiy Rus. Fed.
Chernyy Rynok Rus. Fed. see Kochubey
137 D2 Cherokee U.S.A.
83 L2 Cherskiy Rus. Fed.
83 K2 Cherskogo, Khrebet mts Rus. Fed.
91 E2 Chertkovo Rus. Fed.
Chervonoarmeyskoye Ukr. see Vil'nyans'k
Chervonoarmiys'k Ukr. see Krasnoarmiys'k
Chervonoarmiys'k Ukr. see Radyvyliv
90 A1 Chervonohrad Ukr.
88 C3 Chervyen' Belarus
89 D3 Cherykaw Belarus
139 D3 Chesapeake Bay U.S.A.
86 D2 Cheshskaya Guba b. Rus. Fed.
98 B3 Chester U.K.
138 B3 Chester IL U.S.A.
141 D2 Chester SC U.S.A.
139 D3 Chester VA U.S.A.
98 C3 Chesterfield U.K.
137 E3 Chesterfield U.S.A.
129 E1 Chesterfield Inlet Can.
129 E1 Chesterfield Inlet inlet Can.
139 F1 Chesuncook Lake U.S.A.
108 A3 Chetaïbi Alg.
131 D3 Chéticamp Can.
145 D3 Chetumal Mex.
128 B2 Chetwynd Can.
98 B2 Cheviot Hills U.K.
119 D2 Che'w Bahir salt l. Eth.
136 C2 Cheyenne U.S.A.
136 C2 Cheyenne r. U.S.A.
136 C3 Cheyenne Wells U.S.A.
75 C2 Chhapra India
75 B2 Chhatarpur India
75 C2 Chhattisgarh state India
74 B2 Chhindwara India
75 C2 Chhukha Bhutan
71 C3 Chiai Taiwan
62 A2 Chiang Dao Thai.
120 A2 Chiange Angola
62 A2 Chiang Mai Thai.
62 A2 Chiang Rai Thai.
145 C3 Chiapa Mex.
108 A1 Chiavenno Italy
69 F2 Chiba Japan
70 B3 Chibi China
Chibizovka Rus. Fed. see Zherdevka
121 C3 Chiboma Moz.
130 C3 Chibougamau Can.
123 D1 Chibuto Moz.
138 B2 Chicago U.S.A.
128 A2 Chichagof Island U.S.A.
99 C4 Chichester U.K.
50 A2 Chichester Range mts Austr.
143 D1 Chickasha U.S.A.
106 B2 Chiclana de la Frontera Spain
150 B3 Chiclayo Peru
153 B4 Chico r. Arg.
153 B4 Chico r. Arg.
135 B3 Chico U.S.A.
139 E2 Chicopee U.S.A.
64 B2 Chico Sapocoy, Mount Phil.
131 C3 Chicoutimi Can.
131 D1 Chidley, Cape Can.
63 A3 Chieo Lan, Ang Kep Nam Thai.
108 B2 Chieti Italy
145 C3 Chietla Mex.
70 B1 Chifeng China
155 D1 Chifre, Serra do mts Brazil
121 C2 Chifunde Moz.
77 D2 Chiganak Kazakh.
145 C3 Chignahuapán Mex.
121 C3 Chigubo Moz.
62 A1 Chigu Co l. China
144 B2 Chihuahua Mex.
77 C2 Chiili Kazakh.
88 C2 Chikhachevo Rus. Fed.
67 C3 Chikuma-gawa r. Japan
128 B2 Chilanko r. Can.
74 B1 Chilas Jammu and Kashmir
143 C2 Childress U.S.A.
153 A3 Chile country S. America
158 C6 Chile Basin sea feature S. Pacific Ocean
152 B2 Chilecito Arg.
157 G8 Chile Rise sea feature S. Pacific Ocean
77 D2 Chilik Kazakh.
75 C3 Chilika Lake India
121 B2 Chililabombwe Zambia
128 B2 Chilko r. Can.
128 B2 Chilko Lake Can.
153 A3 Chillán Chile
138 B2 Chillicothe IL U.S.A.
137 E3 Chillicothe MO U.S.A.
138 C3 Chillicothe OH U.S.A.
128 B3 Chilliwack Can.
153 A4 Chiloé, Isla de i. Chile
145 C3 Chilpancingo Mex.
53 C3 Chiltern Austr.
99 C4 Chiltern Hills U.K.
120 B1 Chiluage Angola
71 C3 Chilung Taiwan
119 D3 Chimala Tanz.
121 C2 Chimanimani Zimbabwe
152 B3 Chimbas Arg.
150 B3 Chimborazo mt. Ecuador
150 B3 Chimbote Peru
76 B2 Chimboy Uzbek.
Chimishliya Moldova see Cimişlia
Chimkent Kazakh. see Shymkent
121 C2 Chimoio Moz.
77 C3 Chimtargha, Qullai mt. Tajik.
68 C2 China country Asia
145 C2 China Mex.
150 B4 Chincha Alta Peru
128 C2 Chinchaga r. Can.
145 D3 Chinchorro, Banco sea feature Mex.
121 C2 Chinde Moz.
65 B3 Chindo S. Korea
65 B3 Chin-do i. S. Korea
68 C2 Chindu China
62 A1 Chindwin r. Myanmar
65 B2 Chinghwa N. Korea
121 B2 Chingola Zambia
120 A2 Chinguar Angola
65 B2 Chinhae S. Korea
121 C2 Chinhoyi Zimbabwe
Chini India see Kalpa
Chining China see Jining
74 B1 Chiniot Pak.
144 B2 Chinipas Mex.
65 B2 Chinju S. Korea
118 C2 Chinko r. C.A.R.
142 B1 Chinle U.S.A.
71 B3 Chinmen Taiwan
Chinnamp'o N. Korea see Namp'o

134 B2 Cottage Grove U.S.A.
102 C1 Cottbus Ger.
105 D3 Cottian Alps *mts* France/Italy
104 B2 Coubre, Pointe de la *pt* France
52 A3 Couedic, Cape du Austr.
105 C2 Coulommiers France
137 D2 Council Bluffs U.S.A.
88 B2 Courland Lagoon *b.* Lith./Rus. Fed.
100 A3 Courmelles France
128 B3 Courtenay Can.
104 B2 Coutances France
104 B2 Coutras France
100 B2 Couvin Belgium
99 C3 Coventry U.K.
106 B1 Covilhã Port.
141 D2 Covington *GA* U.S.A.
138 C3 Covington *KY* U.S.A.
138 C3 Covington *VA* U.S.A.
50 B3 Cowan, Lake *salt flat* Austr.
96 C2 Cowdenbeath U.K.
52 A2 Cowell Austr.
53 C3 Cowes Austr.
134 B1 Cowlitz *r.* U.S.A.
53 C2 Cowra Austr.
154 B1 Coxim Brazil
154 B1 Coxim *r.* Brazil
75 D2 Cox's Bazar Bangl.
145 B3 Coyuca de Benítez Mex.
145 D2 Cozumel Mex.
145 D2 Cozumel, Isla de *i.* Mex.
52 A2 Cradock Austr.
123 C3 Cradock S. Africa
136 B2 Craig U.S.A.
102 C2 Crailsheim Ger.
110 B2 Craiova Romania
129 D2 Cranberry Portage Can.
53 C3 Cranbourne Austr.
128 C3 Cranbrook Can.
151 E3 Crateús Brazil
151 F3 Crato Brazil
154 C2 Cravinhos Brazil
136 C2 Crawford U.S.A.
138 B2 Crawfordsville U.S.A.
99 C4 Crawley U.K.
134 D1 Crazy Mountains U.S.A.
129 D2 Cree *r.* Can.
144 B2 Creel Mex.
129 D2 Cree Lake Can.
129 D2 Creighton Can.
104 C2 Creil France
100 B1 Creil Neth.
108 A1 Crema Italy
108 B1 Cremona Italy
108 B2 Cres *i.* Croatia
134 B2 Crescent City U.S.A.
53 D2 Crescent Head Austr.
135 E3 Crescent Junction U.S.A.
128 C3 Creston Can.
137 E2 Creston U.S.A.
140 C2 Crestview U.S.A.
111 B3 Crete *i.* Greece
107 D1 Creus, Cap de *c.* Spain
107 C2 Crevillente Spain
98 B3 Crewe U.K.
96 B2 Crianlarich U.K.
152 D2 Criciúma Brazil
96 C2 Crieff U.K.
108 B1 Crikvenica Croatia
91 C2 Crimea *pen.* Ukr.
101 F2 Crimmitschau Ger.
96 B2 Crinan U.K.
118 B2 Cristal, Monts de *mts* Equat. Guinea/Gabon
154 C1 Cristalina Brazil
110 B1 Crişul Alb *r.* Romania
101 E1 Crivitz Ger.
Crna Gora *country* Europe *see* Montenegro
109 C1 Črnomelj Slovenia
97 B2 Croagh Patrick *hill* Ireland
109 C1 Croatia *country* Europe
61 C1 Crocker, Banjaran *mts* Malaysia
143 D2 Crockett U.S.A.
59 C3 Croker Island Austr.
96 B2 Cromarty U.K.
99 D3 Cromer U.K.
54 A3 Cromwell N.Z.
147 C2 Crooked Island Bahamas
137 D1 Crookston U.S.A.
53 C2 Crookwell Austr.
53 D1 Croppa Creek Austr.
136 C1 Crosby U.S.A.
141 D3 Cross City U.S.A.
140 B2 Crossett U.S.A.
98 B2 Cross Fell *hill* U.K.
129 E2 Cross Lake Can.

141 C1 Crossville U.S.A.
109 C3 Crotone Italy
134 E1 Crow Agency U.S.A.
99 D4 Crowborough U.K.
140 B2 Crowley U.S.A.
53 D1 Crows Nest Austr.
128 C3 Crowsnest Pass Can.
159 D7 Crozet, Îles *is* Indian Ocean
146 C3 Cruz, Cabo *c.* Cuba
152 C2 Cruz Alta Brazil
152 B3 Cruz del Eje Arg.
155 D2 Cruzeiro Brazil
150 B3 Cruzeiro do Sul Brazil
52 A2 Crystal Brook Austr.
143 D3 Crystal City U.S.A.
138 B1 Crystal Falls U.S.A.
140 B2 Crystal Springs U.S.A.
103 E2 Csongrád Hungary
103 D2 Csorna Hungary
121 C2 Cuamba Moz.
120 B2 Cuando *r.* Angola/Zambia
120 A2 Cuangar Angola
118 B3 Cuango *r.* Angola/Dem. Rep. Congo
120 A1 Cuanza *r.* Angola
144 B2 Cuatro Ciénegas Mex.
144 B2 Cuauhtémoc Mex.
145 C3 Cuautla Mex.
146 B2 Cuba *country* West Indies
120 A2 Cubal Angola
120 B2 Cubango *r.* Angola/Namibia
150 B2 Cúcuta Col.
73 B3 Cuddalore India
73 B3 Cuddapah India
50 A2 Cue Austr.
106 C1 Cuéllar Spain
120 A2 Cuemba Angola
150 B3 Cuenca Ecuador
107 C1 Cuenca Spain
107 C1 Cuenca, Serranía de *mts* Spain
145 C3 Cuernavaca Mex.
143 D3 Cuero U.S.A.
104 C3 Cugnaux France
151 D4 Cuiabá Brazil
151 D4 Cuiabá *r.* Brazil
96 A2 Cuillin Sound *sea chan.* U.K.
120 A1 Cuilo Angola
120 B2 Cuito *r.* Angola
120 A2 Cuito Cuanavale Angola
60 B1 Cukai Malaysia
64 B2 Culasi Phil.
53 C3 Culcairn Austr.
100 B2 Culemborg Neth.
53 C1 Culgoa *r.* Austr.
144 B2 Culiacán Mex.
64 A2 Culion *i.* Phil.
107 C2 Cullera Spain
140 C2 Cullman U.S.A.
97 C1 Cullybackey U.K.
139 D3 Culpeper U.S.A.
151 D4 Culuene *r.* Brazil
54 B2 Culverden N.Z.
150 C1 Cumaná Venez.
139 D3 Cumberland U.S.A.
138 B3 Cumberland *r.* U.S.A.
141 D2 Cumberland Island U.S.A.
129 D2 Cumberland Lake Can.
127 H2 Cumberland Peninsula Can.
140 C1 Cumberland Plateau U.S.A.
127 H2 Cumberland Sound *sea chan.* Can.
96 C3 Cumbernauld U.K.
135 B3 Cummings U.S.A.
96 B3 Cumnock U.K.
144 B1 Cumpas Mex.
145 C3 Cunduacán Mex.
108 A2 Cuneo Italy
53 C1 Cunnamulla Austr.
108 A1 Cuorgnè Italy
96 C2 Cupar U.K.
110 B2 Ćuprija Serbia
147 D3 Curaçao *i.* Neth. Antilles
150 B3 Curaray *r.* Ecuador
153 A3 Curicó Chile
154 C3 Curitiba Brazil
52 A2 Curnamona Austr.
135 C3 Currant U.S.A.
51 D3 Currie Austr.
135 D2 Currie U.S.A.
51 E2 Curtis Island Austr.
151 D3 Curuá *r.* Brazil
60 B2 Curup Indon.
151 E3 Cururupu Brazil
155 D1 Curvelo Brazil
150 B4 Cusco Peru

97 C1 Cushendun U.K.
143 D1 Cushing U.S.A.
136 C2 Custer U.S.A.
134 D1 Cut Bank U.S.A.
75 C2 Cuttack India
120 A2 Cuvelai Angola
101 D1 Cuxhaven Ger.
64 B2 Cuyo Islands Phil.
Cuzco Peru *see* Cusco
99 B4 Cwmbrân U.K.
119 C3 Cyangugu Rwanda
111 B3 Cyclades *is* Greece
129 C3 Cypress Hills Can.
80 B2 Cyprus *country* Asia
80 B2 Cyprus *i.* Asia
102 C2 Czech Republic *country* Europe
103 D1 Czersk Pol.
103 D1 Częstochowa Pol.

D

Đa, Sông *r.* Vietnam *see* Black River
69 D2 Daban China
103 D2 Dabas Hungary
118 B3 Dabola Guinea
103 D1 Dąbrowa Górnicza Pol.
110 B2 Dăbuleni Romania
Dacca Bangl. *see* Dhaka
102 C2 Dachau Ger.
Dachuan China *see* Dazhou
141 D3 Dade City U.S.A.
Dadong China *see* Donggang
Dadra India *see* Achalpur
74 B2 Dadra and Nagar Haveli *union terr.* India
74 A2 Dadu Pak.
Daegu S. Korea *see* Taegu
64 B2 Daet Phil.
114 A3 Dagana Senegal
119 D2 Daga Post Sudan
88 C2 Dagda Latvia
64 B2 Dagupan Phil.
74 B3 Dahanu India
69 D2 Da Hinggan Ling *mts* China
116 C3 Dahlak Archipelago *is* Eritrea
100 C2 Dahlem Ger.
78 B3 Dahm, Ramlat *des.* Saudi Arabia/Yemen
74 B2 Dahod India
Dahomey *country* Africa *see* Benin
Dahra Senegal *see* Dara
81 C2 Dahūk Iraq
60 B2 Daik Indon.
106 C2 Daimiel Spain
Dairen China *see* Dalian
51 C2 Dajarra Austr.
70 A2 Dajing China
114 A3 Dakar Senegal
117 C4 Daketa Shet' *watercourse* Eth.
Dakhla Oasis Egypt *see* Wāḥat ad Dākhilah
63 A3 Dakoank India
88 C3 Dakol'ka *r.* Belarus
109 D2 Đakovica Serbia
109 C1 Đakovo Croatia
120 B2 Dala Angola
70 A1 Dalain Hob China
93 G3 Dalälven *r.* Sweden
111 C3 Dalaman Turkey
111 C3 Dalaman *r.* Turkey
68 C2 Dalandzadgad Mongolia
64 B2 Dalanganem Islands Phil.
63 B2 Đa Lat Vietnam
74 A2 Dalbandin Pak.
96 C3 Dalbeattie U.K.
53 D1 Dalby Austr.
93 E3 Dale Norway
141 C1 Dale Hollow Lake U.S.A.
53 C3 Dalgety Austr.
143 C1 Dalhart U.S.A.
131 D3 Dalhousie Can.
62 B1 Dali China
70 C2 Dalian China
96 C3 Dalkeith U.K.
143 D2 Dallas U.S.A.
128 A2 Dall Island U.S.A.

Dalmacija *reg.* Croatia *see* Dalmatia
96 B2 Dalmally U.K.
109 C2 Dalmatia *reg.* Croatia
96 B3 Dalmellington U.K.
66 C2 Dal'negorsk Rus. Fed.
66 B1 Dal'nerechensk Rus. Fed.
Dalny China *see* Dalian
114 B4 Daloa Côte d'Ivoire
71 A3 Dalou Shan *mts* China
51 D2 Dalrymple, Mount Austr.
92 □A3 Dalsmynni Iceland
75 C2 Daltenganj India
141 D2 Dalton U.S.A.
Daltonganj India *see* Daltenganj
60 B1 Daludalu Indon.
71 B3 Daluo Shan *mt.* China
92 □B2 Dalvík Iceland
96 B2 Dalwhinnie U.K.
50 C1 Daly *r.* Austr.
51 C1 Daly Waters Austr.
74 B2 Daman India
74 B2 Daman and Diu *union terr.* India
116 B1 Damanhūr Egypt
59 C3 Damar *i.* Indon.
118 B2 Damara C.A.R.
80 B2 Damascus Syria
115 D3 Damaturu Nigeria
76 B3 Damāvand, Qolleh-ye *mt.* Iran
120 A1 Damba Angola
118 B1 Damboa Nigeria
81 D2 Damghan Iran
Damietta Egypt *see* Dumyāţ
79 C2 Dammam Saudi Arabia
101 D1 Damme Ger.
75 B2 Damoh India
114 B4 Damongo Ghana
50 A2 Dampier Austr.
59 C3 Dampir, Selat *sea chan.* Indon.
75 D1 Damxung China
114 B4 Danané Côte d'Ivoire
63 B2 Đa Nẵng Vietnam
139 E2 Danbury U.S.A.
70 C1 Dandong China
117 B3 Dangila Eth.
146 B3 Dangriga Belize
70 B2 Dangshan China
89 F2 Danilov Rus. Fed.
89 E2 Danilovskaya Vozvyshennost' *hills* Rus. Fed.
70 B2 Danjiangkou China
79 C2 Dank Oman
89 E3 Dankov Rus. Fed.
146 B3 Danlí Hond.
101 E1 Dannenberg (Elbe) Ger.
54 C2 Dannevirke N.Z.
62 B2 Dan Sai Thai.
110 A1 Danube *r.* Europe
110 C1 Danube Delta Romania
138 B2 Danville *IL* U.S.A.
138 C3 Danville *KY* U.S.A.
139 D3 Danville *VA* U.S.A.
Danxian China *see* Danzhou
71 A4 Danzhou China
Danzig, Gulf of Pol./Rus. Fed. *see* Gdańsk, Gulf of
70 B2 Daojiang China
Daoxian
115 D2 Dao Timmi Niger
Daoud Alg. *see* Aïn Beïda
114 B4 Daoukro Côte d'Ivoire
71 B3 Daoxian China
64 B3 Dapa Phil.
114 C3 Dapaong Togo
64 B3 Dapitan Phil.
62 A1 Da Qaidam Zhen China
69 E1 Daqing China
114 A3 Dara Senegal
80 B2 Dar'ā Syria
81 D3 Dārāb Iran
115 D1 Daraj Libya
81 D2 Dārān Iran
109 D2 Đaravica *mt.* Serbia
75 C2 Darbhanga India
Dardo China *see* Kangding
119 D3 Dar es Salaam Tanz.
117 A3 Darfur *reg.* Sudan
74 B1 Dargai Pak.
54 B1 Dargaville N.Z.
53 C3 Dargo Austr.
68 D1 Darhan Mongolia
150 B2 Darién, Golfo del *g.* Col.
Darjeeling India *see* Darjiling
Darjiling

75 C2 Darjiling India
68 C2 Darlag China
52 B2 Darling r. Austr.
53 C1 Darling Downs hills Austr.
50 A3 Darling Range hills Austr.
98 C2 Darlington U.K.
53 C2 Darlington Point Austr.
103 D1 Darłowo Pol.
101 D3 Darmstadt Ger.
115 E1 Darnah Libya
52 B2 Darnick Austr.
55 H3 Darnley, Cape Antarctica
107 C1 Daroca Spain
99 D4 Dartford U.K.
99 A4 Dartmoor hills U.K.
131 D3 Dartmouth Can.
99 B4 Dartmouth U.K.
59 D3 Daru P.N.G.
59 C2 Daruba Indon.
50 C1 Darwin Austr.
153 C5 Darwin Falkland Is
79 C2 Dārzin Iran
65 A1 Dashiqiao China
Dashkhovuz Turkm. see Daşoguz
74 A2 Dasht r. Pak.
76 B2 Daşoguz Turkm.
61 C1 Datadian Indon.
111 C3 Datça Turkey
66 D2 Date Japan
71 B3 Datian China
70 D1 Datong China
64 R3 Datu Piang Phil.
74 B1 Daud Khel Pak.
88 B2 Daugava r. Latvia
88 C2 Daugavpils Latvia
100 C2 Daun Ger.
129 E2 Dauphin Can.
129 E2 Dauphin Lake Can.
73 B3 Davangere India
64 B3 Davao Phil.
64 B3 Davao Gulf Phil.
137 E2 Davenport U.S.A.
99 C3 Daventry U.K.
123 C2 Daveyton S. Africa
146 B4 David Panama
129 D2 Davidson Can.
126 F3 Davidson Lake Can.
135 B3 Davis Austr.
131 D2 Davis Inlet Can.
55 I3 Davis Sea sea Antarctica
160 P3 Davis Strait str. Can./Greenland
105 D2 Davos Switz.
88 C3 Davyd-Haradok Belarus
78 A2 Dawmat al Jandal Saudi Arabia
79 C3 Dawqah Oman
78 B3 Dawqah Saudi Arabia
126 C2 Dawson Can.
141 D2 Dawson U.S.A.
128 B2 Dawson Creek Can.
128 B2 Dawsons Landing Can.
68 C2 Dawu China
Dawukou China see Shizuishan
79 C2 Dawwah Oman
104 B3 Dax France
Daxian China see Dazhou
68 C2 Da Xueshan mts China
52 B3 Daylesford Austr.
Dayong China see Zhangjiajie
81 C2 Dayr az Zawr Syria
138 C3 Dayton U.S.A.
141 D3 Daytona Beach U.S.A.
71 B3 Dayu China
70 B2 Da Yunhe canal China
71 B3 Dayyer Iran
70 A2 Dazhou China
70 B2 Dazhou China
122 B3 De Aar S. Africa
141 D3 Deadman Bay U.S.A.
80 B2 Dead Sea salt l. Asia
99 D4 Deal U.K.
152 B3 De'an China
152 B3 Deán Funes Arg.
128 B2 Dease Lake Can.
128 B2 Dease Strait Can.
135 C3 Death Valley depr. U.S.A.
104 C2 Deauville France
61 C1 Debak Sarawak Malaysia
109 D2 Debar Macedonia
111 B3 Dębica Pol.
103 E1 Dęblin Pol.
114 B3 Débo, Lac l. Mali
103 E2 Debrecen Hungary
117 B3 Debre Markos Eth.
117 B3 Debre Sina Eth.
117 B3 Debre Tabor Eth.
117 B4 Debre Zeyit Eth.
140 C2 Decatur AL U.S.A.

138 B3 Decatur IL U.S.A.
73 B3 Deccan plat. India
53 D1 Deception Bay Austr.
71 A3 Dechang China
102 C1 Děčín Czech Rep.
137 E2 Decorah U.S.A.
154 C2 Dedo de Deus mt. Brazil
88 C2 Dedovichi Rus. Fed.
121 C2 Dedza Malawi
99 B3 Dee r. England/Wales U.K.
96 C2 Dee r. Scotland U.K.
130 C3 Deep River Can.
53 D1 Deepwater Austr.
131 E3 Deer Lake Can.
134 D1 Deer Lodge U.S.A.
138 C2 Defiance U.S.A.
140 C2 De Funiak Springs U.S.A.
68 C2 Dêgê China
117 C4 Degeh Bur Eth.
139 F1 Dégelis Can.
102 C2 Deggendorf Ger.
91 E2 Degtevo Rus. Fed.
81 C2 Dehlorān Iran
74 B1 Dehra Dun India
75 C2 Dehri India
69 E2 Dehui China
100 A2 Deinze Belgium
110 B1 Dej Romania
138 B2 De Kalb U.S.A.
116 B3 Dekemhare Eritrea
118 C3 Dekese Dem. Rep. Congo
118 B2 Dékoa C.A.R.
141 D3 De Land U.S.A.
135 C3 Delano U.S.A.
135 D3 Delano Peak U.S.A.
48 I3 Delap-Uliga-Djarrit Marshall Is
74 A1 Delārām Afgh.
123 C2 Delareyville S. Africa
129 D2 Delaronde Lake Can.
138 C2 Delaware U.S.A.
139 D3 Delaware r. U.S.A.
139 D3 Delaware state U.S.A.
139 D3 Delaware Bay U.S.A.
53 C3 Delegate Austr.
118 C2 Délembé C.A.R.
105 D2 Delémont Switz.
100 B1 Delft Neth.
100 C1 Delfzijl Neth.
121 D2 Delgado, Cabo c. Moz.
68 C2 Delhi China
74 B2 Delhi India
60 B2 Deli i. Indon.
128 B1 Déline Can.
Delingha China see Delhi
101 F2 Delitzsch Ger.
107 D2 Dellys Alg.
135 C4 Del Mar U.S.A.
101 D1 Delmenhorst Ger.
109 B1 Delnice Croatia
136 B3 Del Norte U.S.A.
83 L1 De-Longa, Ostrova is Rus. Fed.
De Long Islands Rus. Fed. see De-Longa, Ostrova
49 M5 De Long Strait Rus. Fed. see Longa, Proliv
129 D3 Deloraine Can.
111 B3 Delphi tourist site Greece
141 B4 Delray Beach U.S.A.
143 C3 Del Rio U.S.A.
136 B3 Delta CO U.S.A.
135 D3 Delta UT U.S.A.
126 C2 Delta Junction U.S.A.
109 D3 Delvinë Albania
106 C1 Demanda, Sierra de la mts Spain
118 C3 Demba Dem. Rep. Congo
119 D1 Dembech'a Eth.
117 B4 Dembi Dolo Eth.
Demerara Guyana see Georgetown
91 C3 Demerdzhi mt. Ukr.
89 D2 Demidov Rus. Fed.
142 B2 Deming U.S.A.
111 C3 Demirci Turkey
111 C2 Demirköy Turkey
102 C1 Demmin Ger.
140 C2 Demopolis U.S.A.
60 B2 Dempo, Gunung vol. Indon.
89 D2 Demyansk Rus. Fed.
122 B3 De Naawte S. Africa
117 B4 Denakil reg. Eritrea/Eth.
98 B3 Denbigh U.K.
100 B1 Den Burg Neth.
62 B1 Den Chai Thai.
60 B2 Dendang Indon.
100 B2 Dendermonde Belgium

100 B2 Dendre r. Belgium
Dengjiabu China see Yujiang
70 A1 Dengkou China
Dengxian China see Dengzhou
70 B2 Dengzhou China
Dengzhou China see Penglai
Den Haag Neth. see The Hague
50 A2 Denham Austr.
100 B1 Den Helder Neth.
107 D2 Denia Spain
52 B3 Deniliquin Austr.
134 C2 Denio U.S.A.
137 D2 Denison IA U.S.A.
143 D2 Denison TX U.S.A.
111 C3 Denizli Turkey
53 D2 Denman Austr.
50 A3 Denmark Austr.
93 E4 Denmark country Europe
84 B2 Denmark Strait Greenland/Iceland
77 C3 Denov Uzbek.
61 C2 Denpasar Indon.
143 D2 Denton U.S.A.
50 A3 D'Entrecasteaux, Point Austr.
59 E3 D'Entrecasteaux Islands P.N.G.
141 D2 Dentsville U.S.A.
136 B3 Denver U.S.A.
75 C2 Deogarh Orissa India
74 B2 Deogarh Rajasthan India
75 C2 Deoghar India
138 B2 De Pere U.S.A.
83 K2 Deputatskiy Rus. Fed.
62 A1 Dêqên China
140 B2 De Queen U.S.A.
74 A2 Dera Bugti Pak.
74 B1 Dera Ghazi Khan Pak.
74 B1 Dera Ismail Khan Pak.
87 D4 Derbent Rus. Fed.
50 B1 Derby Austr.
99 C3 Derby U.K.
137 D3 Derby U.S.A.
99 D3 Dereham U.K.
97 B2 Derg, Lough l. Ireland
91 D1 Derhachi Ukr.
140 B2 De Ridder U.S.A.
91 D2 Derkul' r. Rus. Fed./Ukr.
75 B1 Dêrub China
116 B3 Derudeb Sudan
122 B3 De Rust S. Africa
109 C2 Derventa Bos.-Herz.
98 C2 Derwent r. England U.K.
98 C3 Derwent r. England U.K.
98 B2 Derwent Water l. U.K.
77 C1 Derzhavinsk Kazakh.
Derzhavinskiy Kazakh. see Derzhavinsk
152 B1 Desaguadero r. Bol.
49 M5 Désappointement, Îles du is Fr. Polynesia
134 B1 Deschutes r. U.S.A.
117 B3 Desê Eth.
153 B4 Deseado Arg.
153 B4 Deseado r. Arg.
142 A2 Desemboque Mex.
137 E2 Des Moines U.S.A.
137 E2 Des Moines r. U.S.A.
91 C1 Desna r. Rus. Fed./Ukr.
89 D3 Desnogorsk Rus. Fed.
101 F2 Dessau Ger.
Dessye Eth. see Desê
128 A1 Destruction Bay Can.
149 C5 Desventurados, Islas de los is S. Pacific Ocean
128 C1 Dete Zimbabwe
101 D2 Detmold Ger.
138 C2 Detroit U.S.A.
137 D1 Detroit Lakes U.S.A.
Dett Zimbabwe see Dete
100 B2 Deurne Neth.
110 B1 Deva Romania
96 C2 Deveron r. U.K.
103 D2 Devét Skal hill Czech Rep.
137 D1 Devil's Lake U.S.A.
128 A2 Devil's Paw mt. U.S.A.
99 C4 Devizes U.K.
74 B2 Devli India
110 C2 Devnya Bulg.
128 C2 Devon Can.
126 F1 Devon Island Can.
51 D4 Devonport Austr.
74 B2 Dewas India
137 F3 Dexter U.S.A.

70 A2 Deyang China
59 D3 Deyong, Tanjung pt Indon.
81 D2 Dezfūl Iran
70 B2 Dezhou China
79 C2 Dhahran Saudi Arabia
75 D2 Dhaka Bangl.
78 B3 Dhamār Yemen
75 C2 Dhamtari India
75 C2 Dhanbad India
74 B2 Dhandhuka India
75 C2 Dhankuta Nepal
74 B2 Dhar India
75 D2 Dharmanagar India
73 B3 Dharmapuri India
75 C2 Dharmjaygarh India
114 B3 Dhar Oualâta hills Maur.
114 B3 Dhar Tichît hills Maur.
73 B3 Dharwad India
Dharwar India see Dharwad
74 B2 Dhasa India
75 C2 Dhaulagiri mt. Nepal
78 B3 Dhubāb Yemen
74 B2 Dhule India
Dhulia India see Dhule
117 C4 Dhuusa Marreeb Somalia
144 A1 Diablo, Picacho del mt. Mex.
142 B2 Diablo Plateau U.S.A.
121 C2 Diaca Moz.
51 C2 Diamantina watercourse Austr.
155 D1 Diamantina Brazil
151 E4 Diamantina, Chapada plat. Brazil
159 F6 Diamantina Deep sea feature Indian Ocean
154 B1 Diamantino Brazil
151 D4 Diamantino Brazil
71 B3 Dianbai China
151 E4 Dianópolis Brazil
114 B4 Dianra Côte d'Ivoire
114 C3 Diapaga Burkina
79 C2 Dibā al Ḩiṣn U.A.E.
79 C2 Dibab Oman
118 C3 Dibaya Dem. Rep. Congo
122 B2 Dibeng S. Africa
72 D2 Dibrugarh India
136 C1 Dickinson U.S.A.
140 C1 Dickson U.S.A.
Dicle r. Turkey see Tigris
105 D3 Die France
Diedenhofen France see Thionville
129 D2 Diefenbaker, Lake Can.
Diégo Suarez Madag. see Antsirañana
114 B3 Diéma Mali
101 D2 Diemel r. Ger.
62 B1 Điện Biên Phu Vietnam
62 B1 Điện Châu Vietnam
101 D1 Diepholz Ger.
104 C2 Dieppe France
100 B2 Diest Belgium
115 D3 Diffa Niger
131 D2 Digby Can.
105 D3 Digne-les-Bains France
105 C2 Digoin France
64 B3 Digos Phil.
59 D3 Digul r. Indon.
105 D2 Dijon France
115 D4 Dik Chad
117 C3 Dikhil Djibouti
111 C3 Dikili Turkey
100 A2 Diksmuide Belgium
82 G2 Dikson Rus. Fed.
115 D3 Dikwa Nigeria
59 C3 Dili East Timor
101 D2 Dillenburg Ger.
117 A3 Dilling Sudan
126 A3 Dillingham U.S.A.
134 D1 Dillon MT U.S.A.
141 E2 Dillon SC U.S.A.
118 C4 Dilolo Dem. Rep. Congo
72 D2 Dimapur India
Dimashq Syria see Damascus
52 B3 Dimboola Austr.
110 C2 Dimitrovgrad Bulg.
87 D3 Dimitrovgrad Rus. Fed.
Dimitrovo Bulg. see Pernik
64 B2 Dinagat i. Phil.
75 C2 Dinajpur Bangl.
104 B2 Dinan France
100 B2 Dinant Belgium
111 D3 Dinar Turkey
81 D2 Dīnār, Kūh-e mt. Iran
104 B2 Dinard France
Dinbych U.K. see Denbigh
73 B3 Dindigul India

Dindima
180

118 B1 Dindima Nigeria
123 D1 Dindiza Moz.
101 E2 Dingelstädt Ger.
97 A2 Dingle Ireland
97 A2 Dingle Bay Ireland
71 B3 Dingnan China
102 C2 Dingolfing Ger.
114 A3 Dinguiraye Guinea
96 B2 Dingwall U.K.
70 A2 Dingxi China
75 C2 Dinngyê China
123 C1 Dinokwe Botswana
91 D2 Dinskaya Rus. Fed.
100 C2 Dinslaken Ger.
135 C3 Dinuba U.S.A.
114 B3 Dioïla Mali
154 B3 Dionísio Cerqueira Brazil
114 A3 Diourbel Senegal
75 D2 Diphu India
74 B1 Dir Pak.
51 D1 Direction, Cape Austr.
117 C4 Dirē Dawa Eth.
120 B2 Dirico Angola
50 A2 Dirk Hartog Island Austr.
53 C1 Dirranbandi Austr.
78 B3 Ḑirs Saudi Arabia
153 E5 Disappointment, Cape S. Georgia
134 B1 Disappointment, Cape U.S.A.
50 B2 Disappointment, Lake salt flat Austr.
52 B3 Discovery Bay Austr.
Disko i. Greenland see Qeqertarsuaq
141 E1 Dismal Swamp U.S.A.
99 D3 Diss U.K.
154 C1 Distrito Federal admin. dist. Brazil
108 B3 Dittaino r. Sicily Italy
74 B2 Diu India
155 D2 Divinópolis Brazil
87 D4 Divnoye Rus. Fed.
114 B4 Divo Côte d'Ivoire
80 B2 Divriği Turkey
74 A2 Diwana Pak.
138 B2 Dixon U.S.A.
128 A2 Dixon Entrance sea chan. Can./U.S.A.
81 C2 Diyarbakır Turkey
74 A2 Diz Pak.
115 D2 Djado Niger
115 D2 Djado, Plateau du Niger
Djakarta Indon. see Jakarta
118 B3 Djambala Congo
115 C2 Djanet Alg.
115 D3 Djédaa Chad
115 C1 Djelfa Alg.
119 C2 Djéma C.A.R.
114 B3 Djenné Mali
114 B3 Djibo Burkina
117 C3 Djibouti country Africa
117 C3 Djibouti Djibouti
Djidjelli Alg. see Jijel
118 C2 Djolu Dem. Rep. Congo
114 C4 Djougou Benin
118 B2 Djoum Cameroon
115 D3 Djourab, Erg du des. Chad
92 □C3 Djúpivogur Iceland
89 F3 Dmitriyevka Rus. Fed.
89 E3 Dmitriyev-L'govskiy Rus. Fed.
Dmitriyevsk Ukr. see Makiyivka
89 E2 Dmitrov Rus. Fed.
Dmytriyevs'k Ukr. see Makiyivka
Dnepr r. Rus. Fed. see Dnieper
89 D3 Dnieper r. Rus. Fed.
91 C2 Dnieper r. Ukr.
90 B2 Dniester r. Ukr.
Dnipro r. Ukr. see Dnieper
91 C2 Dniprodzerzhyns'k Ukr.
91 D2 Dnipropetrovs'k Ukr.
91 C2 Dniprorudne Ukr.
Dnister r. Ukr. see Dniester
90 C2 Dnistrov'ky Lyman l. Ukr.
88 C2 Dno Rus. Fed.
121 C2 Doa Moz.
115 D4 Doba Chad
88 B2 Dobele Latvia
101 F2 Döbeln Ger.
59 C3 Doberai, Jazirah pen. Indon.
Doberai Peninsula Indon. see Doberai, Jazirah
59 C3 Dobo Indon.
109 C2 Doboj Bos.-Herz.
103 E1 Dobre Miasto Pol.
110 C2 Dobrich Bulg.
89 F3 Dobrinka Rus. Fed.
89 E3 Dobroye Rus. Fed.
89 D3 Dobrush Belarus
86 E3 Dobryanka Rus. Fed.
155 E1 Doce r. Brazil
145 B2 Doctor Arroyo Mex.
144 B2 Doctor Belisario Domínguez Mex.
Doctor Petru Groza Romania see Ştei
111 C3 Dodecanese is Greece
Dodekanisos is Greece see Dodecanese
136 C3 Dodge City U.S.A.
119 D3 Dodoma Tanz.
100 C1 Doesburg Neth.
100 C2 Doetinchem Neth.
59 C3 Dofa Indon.
75 C1 Dogai Coring salt l. China
128 B2 Dog Creek Can.
67 B3 Dōgo i. Japan
115 C3 Dogondoutchi Niger
81 C2 Doğubeyazıt Turkey
79 C2 Doha Qatar
62 A2 Doi Saket Thai.
81 D2 Dokali Iran
100 B1 Dokkum Neth.
88 C3 Dokshytsy Belarus
91 D2 Dokuchayevs'k Ukr.
142 A1 Dolan Springs U.S.A.
130 C3 Dolbeau-Mistassini Can.
104 B2 Dol-de-Bretagne France
105 D2 Dole France
91 D2 Dolgaya, Kosa spit Rus. Fed.
99 B3 Dolgellau U.K.
89 E3 Dolgorukovo Rus. Fed.
89 E3 Dolgoye Rus. Fed.
69 F1 Dolinsk Rus. Fed.
103 D2 Dolný Kubín Slovakia
59 D3 Dolok, Pulau i. Indon.
108 B1 Dolomites mts Italy
Dolomiti mts Italy see Dolomites
70 B1 Dolonnur China
117 C4 Dolo Odo Eth.
144 A2 Dolores Mex.
126 E2 Dolphin and Union Strait Can.
90 A2 Dolyna Ukr.
102 C2 Domažlice Czech Rep.
93 E3 Dombås Norway
103 D2 Dombóvár Hungary
Dombrovitsa Ukr. see Dubrovytsya
Dombrowa Pol. see Dąbrowa Górnicza
128 B2 Dome Creek Can.
147 D3 Dominica country West Indies
147 C3 Dominican Republic country West Indies
118 C3 Domiongo Dem. Rep. Congo
117 C4 Domo Eth.
89 E2 Domodedovo Rus. Fed.
111 B3 Domokos Greece
61 C2 Dompu Indon.
153 A3 Domuyo, Volcán vol. Arg.
142 B3 Don Mex.
89 E3 Don r. Rus. Fed.
96 C2 Don r. U.K.
97 D1 Donaghadee U.K.
52 B3 Donald Austr.
Donau r. Austria/Ger. see Danube
102 C2 Donauwörth Ger.
106 B2 Don Benito Spain
98 C3 Doncaster U.K.
120 A1 Dondo Angola
121 C2 Dondo Moz.
73 C4 Dondra Head hd Sri Lanka
97 B1 Donegal Ireland
97 B1 Donegal Bay Ireland
91 D2 Donets'k Ukr.
91 D2 Donets'kyy Kryazh hills Rus. Fed./Ukr.
118 B2 Donga Nigeria
50 A2 Dongara Austr.
71 A4 Dongfang China
66 B1 Dongfanghong China
61 C2 Donggala Indon.
65 A2 Donggang China
Donggou China see Donggang
71 B3 Dongguan China
71 B3 Dongguan China
62 B2 Đông Ha Vietnam
Dong Hai sea N. Pacific Ocean see East China Sea
62 B2 Đông Hơi Vietnam
116 B3 Dongola Sudan
118 B2 Dongou Congo
Dong Phaya Yen Range mts Thai. see San Khao Phang Hoei
63 B2 Dong Phraya Yen esc. Thai.
Dongping China see Anhua
71 B3 Dongshan China
Dongsheng China see Ordos
70 C2 Dongtai China
71 B3 Dongting Hu l. China
Dong Ujimqin Qi China see Uliastai
71 C3 Dongyang China
70 B2 Dongying China
143 D3 Donna U.S.A.
54 B1 Donnellys Crossing N.Z.
100 C3 Donnersberg hill Ger.
107 C1 Donostia-San Sebastián Spain
81 D1 Donyztau, Sor dry lake Kazakh.
51 C1 Doomadgee Austr.
138 B2 Door Peninsula U.S.A.
117 C4 Dooxo Nugaaleed val. Somalia
50 B2 Dora, Lake salt flat Austr.
99 B4 Dorchester U.K.
122 A1 Dordabis Namibia
104 B2 Dordogne r. France
100 B2 Dordrecht Neth.
123 C3 Dordrecht S. Africa
122 A1 Doreenville Namibia
129 D2 Doré Lake Can.
101 D1 Dorfmark Ger.
114 B3 Dori Burkina
122 A3 Doring r. S. Africa
100 C2 Dormagen Ger.
96 B2 Dornoch U.K.
96 B2 Dornoch Firth est. U.K.
114 B3 Doro Mali
89 D3 Dorogobuzh Rus. Fed.
110 C1 Dorohoi Romania
68 C1 Döröö Nuur salt l. Mongolia
92 G3 Dorotea Sweden
50 A2 Dorre Island Austr.
53 D2 Dorrigo Austr.
100 C2 Dorsten Ger.
100 C2 Dortmund Ger.
100 C2 Dortmund-Ems-Kanal canal Ger.
153 B4 Dos Bahías, Cabo c. Arg.
101 F1 Dosse r. Ger.
114 C3 Dosso Niger
141 C2 Dothan U.S.A.
101 D1 Dötlingen Ger.
105 C1 Douai France
118 A2 Douala Cameroon
104 B2 Douarnenez France
105 D2 Doubs r. France/Switz.
54 A3 Doubtful Sound N.Z.
114 B3 Douentza Mali
98 A2 Douglas Isle of Man
122 B2 Douglas S. Africa
128 A2 Douglas AK U.S.A.
142 B2 Douglas AZ U.S.A.
141 D2 Douglas GA U.S.A.
136 B2 Douglas WY U.S.A.
104 C1 Doullens France
154 B1 Dourada, Serra hills Brazil
154 B2 Dourados Brazil
154 B2 Dourados r. Brazil
154 B2 Dourados, Serra dos hills Brazil
106 B1 Douro r. Port.
99 D4 Dover U.K.
139 D3 Dover U.S.A.
95 D3 Dover, Strait of France/U.K.
139 F1 Dover-Foxcroft U.S.A.
99 B3 Dovey r. U.K.
121 C2 Dowa Malawi
81 D3 Dowlatābād Iran
79 C2 Dowlatābād Iran
97 D1 Downpatrick U.K.
81 C2 Dow Rūd Iran
77 C3 Dowshī Afgh.
67 B3 Dōzen is Japan
130 C3 Dozois, Réservoir resr Can.
114 B2 Drâa, Hamada du plat. Alg.
154 B2 Dracena Brazil
100 C1 Drachten Neth.
110 B2 Drăgănești-Olt Romania
110 B2 Drăgășani Romania
105 D3 Draguignan France
88 C3 Drahichyn Belarus
53 D1 Drake Austr.
123 C2 Drakensberg mts Lesotho/S. Africa
123 C2 Drakensberg mts S. Africa
149 C8 Drake Passage S. Atlantic Ocean
111 B2 Drama Greece
93 F4 Drammen Norway
109 C1 Drava r. Europe
128 C2 Drayton Valley Can.
101 D2 Dreieich Ger.
102 C1 Dresden Ger.
104 C2 Dreux France
100 B1 Driemond Neth.
98 C2 Driffield U.K.
137 D1 Drift Prairie reg. U.S.A.
109 C2 Drina r. Bos.-Herz./Serbia
140 B2 Driskill Mountain hill U.S.A.
Drissa Belarus see Vyerkhnyadzvinsk
109 C2 Drniš Croatia
110 B2 Drobeta-Turnu Severin Romania
90 B2 Drochia Moldova
101 D1 Drochtersen Ger.
97 C2 Drogheda Ireland
90 A2 Drohobych Ukr.
99 B3 Droitwich Spa U.K.
Drokiya Moldova see Drochia
97 B1 Dromahair Ireland
97 C1 Dromore U.K.
100 B1 Dronten Neth.
74 B1 Drosh Pak.
53 C3 Drouin Austr.
128 C2 Drumheller Can.
138 C1 Drummond Island U.S.A.
131 C3 Drummondville Can.
96 B3 Drummore U.K.
96 B2 Drumnadrochit U.K.
Druskieniki Lith. see Druskininkai
88 B3 Druskininkai Lith.
88 C2 Druya Belarus
91 D2 Druzhkivka Ukr.
88 D2 Druzhnaya Gorka Rus. Fed.
89 D3 Drybin Belarus
130 A3 Dryden Can.
50 B1 Drysdale r. Austr.
147 C3 Duarte, Pico mt. Dom. Rep.
78 A2 Ḑubā Saudi Arabia
79 C2 Dubai U.A.E.
90 B2 Dubăsari Moldova
129 D1 Dubawnt Lake Can.
Dubayy U.A.E. see Dubai
78 A2 Dubbagh, Jabal ad mt. Saudi Arabia
53 C2 Dubbo Austr.
Dubesar' Moldova see Dubăsari
97 C2 Dublin Ireland
141 D2 Dublin U.S.A.
89 E2 Dubna Rus. Fed.
90 B1 Dubno Ukr.
139 D2 Du Bois U.S.A.
Dubossary Moldova see Dubăsari
114 A4 Dubréka Guinea
109 C2 Dubrovnik Croatia
90 B1 Dubrovytsya Ukr.
89 D3 Dubrowna Belarus
137 E2 Dubuque U.S.A.
63 B2 Đức Bôn Vietnam
135 D2 Duchesne U.S.A.
129 D2 Duck Bay Can.
101 E2 Duderstadt Ger.
82 G2 Dudinka Rus. Fed.
99 B3 Dudley U.K.
106 B1 Duero r. Spain
48 H4 Duff Islands Solomon Is
131 C2 Duffreboy, Lac l. Can.
96 C2 Dufftown U.K.
109 C2 Dugi Otok i. Croatia
109 C2 Dugi Rat Croatia
100 C2 Duisburg Ger.
123 D1 Duiwelskloof S. Africa
123 C3 Dukathole S. Africa
117 B4 Duk Fadiat Sudan
79 C2 Dukhān Qatar
89 D2 Dukhovshchina Rus. Fed.
Dukou China see Panzhihua
88 C2 Dūkštas Lith.

71 B3 **Fuzhou** China
71 B3 **Fuzhou** China
93 F4 **Fyn** i. Denmark
96 B3 **Fyne, Loch** inlet U.K.
F.Y.R.O.M. country Europe see **Macedonia**

G

117 C4 **Gaalkacyo** Somalia
120 A2 **Gabela** Angola
Gaberones Botswana see **Gaborone**
115 D1 **Gabès** Tunisia
115 D1 **Gabès, Golfe de** g. Tunisia
118 B3 **Gabon** country Africa
123 C1 **Gaborone** Botswana
79 C2 **Gäbrik** Iran
110 C2 **Gabrovo** Bulg.
114 A3 **Gabú** Guinea-Bissau
73 B3 **Gadag** India
75 C2 **Gadchiroli** India
101 E1 **Gadebusch** Ger.
140 C2 **Gadsden** U.S.A.
118 B2 **Gadzi** C.A.R.
110 C2 **Gãeşti** Romania
108 B2 **Gaeta** Italy
108 B2 **Gaeta, Golfo di** g. Italy
141 D1 **Gaffney** U.S.A.
115 C1 **Gafsa** Tunisia
89 E2 **Gagarin** Rus. Fed.
109 C3 **Gagliano del Capo** Italy
114 B4 **Gagnoa** Côte d'Ivoire
131 D2 **Gagnon** Can.
Gago Coutinho Angola see **Lumbala N'guimbo**
81 C1 **Gagra** Georgia
122 A2 **Gaiab** watercourse Namibia
111 C3 **Gaïdouronisi** i. Greece
104 C3 **Gaillac** France
Gaillimh Ireland see **Galway**
141 D3 **Gainesville** FL U.S.A.
141 D2 **Gainesville** GA U.S.A.
143 D2 **Gainesville** TX U.S.A.
98 C3 **Gainsborough** U.K.
52 A2 **Gairdner, Lake** salt flat Austr.
96 B2 **Gairloch** U.K.
122 B2 **Gakarosa** mt. S. Africa
119 E3 **Galana** r. Kenya
103 D2 **Galanta** Slovakia
Galápagos, Islas is Pacific Ocean see **Galapagos Islands**
125 I10 **Galapagos Islands** is Pacific Ocean
157 G6 **Galapagos Rise** sea feature Pacific Ocean
96 C3 **Galashiels** U.K.
110 C1 **Galaţi** Romania
93 E3 **Galdhøpiggen** mt. Norway
145 B2 **Galeana** Mex.
128 C2 **Galena Bay** Can.
138 A2 **Galesburg** U.S.A.
122 A3 **Galeshewe** S. Africa
89 F2 **Galich** Rus. Fed.
106 B1 **Galicia** reg. Spain
78 A3 **Gallabat** Sudan
140 C1 **Gallatin** U.S.A.
157 G6 **Galle** Sri Lanka
Gallego Rise sea feature Pacific Ocean
150 B1 **Gallinas, Punta** pt Col.
109 C2 **Gallipoli** Italy
111 C2 **Gallipoli** Turkey
92 H2 **Gällivare** Sweden
142 B1 **Gallup** U.S.A.
114 A2 **Galtat Zemmour** Western Sahara
97 B2 **Galtymore** hill Ireland
143 E3 **Galveston** U.S.A.
143 E3 **Galveston Bay** U.S.A.
143 E3 **Galveston Island** U.S.A.
97 B2 **Galway** Ireland
97 B2 **Galway Bay** Ireland
154 C1 **Gamá** Brazil
123 D3 **Gamalakhe** S. Africa
117 B4 **Gambēla** Eth.
114 A3 **Gambia** r. Gambia
114 A3 **Gambia, The** country Africa
49 N6 **Gambier, Îles** is Fr. Polynesia
52 A3 **Gambier Islands** Austr.
131 E3 **Gambo** Can.
118 D3 **Gamboma** Congo

92 H2 **Gammelstaden** Sweden
142 B1 **Ganado** U.S.A.
81 C1 **Gäncä** Azer.
61 C2 **Gandadiwata, Bukit** mt. Indon.
118 C3 **Gandajika** Dem. Rep. Congo
131 E3 **Gander** Can.
131 E3 **Gander** r. Can.
101 D1 **Ganderkesee** Ger.
107 D1 **Gandesa** Spain
74 B2 **Gandhidham** India
74 B2 **Gandhinagar** India
74 B2 **Gandhi Sagar** resr India
107 C2 **Gandía** Spain
Ganga r. Bangl./India see **Ganges**
153 B4 **Gangán** Arg.
74 B2 **Ganganagar** India
62 A1 **Gangaw** Myanmar
68 C2 **Gangca** China
75 C1 **Gangdisê Shan** mts China
75 D2 **Ganges** r. Bangl./India
105 C3 **Ganges** France
75 C2 **Ganges, Mouths of the** Bangl./India
159 E2 **Ganges Cone** sea feature Indian Ocean
75 C2 **Gangtok** India
75 C2 **Ganjam** India
71 B3 **Gan Jiang** r. China
71 A3 **Gânliú** China
105 C2 **Gannat** France
136 B2 **Gannett Peak** U.S.A.
122 A3 **Gansbaai** S. Africa
70 A1 **Gansu** prov. China
115 D4 **Ganye** Nigeria
71 B3 **Ganzhou** China
73 B3 **Gao** Mali
Gaoleshan China see **Xianfeng**
114 B3 **Gaoua** Burkina
114 A3 **Gaoual** Guinea
70 B2 **Gaoyou** China
70 B2 **Gaoyou Hu** l. China
105 D3 **Gap** France
64 B2 **Gapan** Phil.
75 C1 **Gar** China
72 C1 **Gar** China
97 B2 **Gara, Lough** l. Ireland
76 C3 **Garabil Belentligi** hills Turkm.
76 B2 **Garabogaz** Turkm.
76 B2 **Garabogazköl** Turkm.
76 B2 **Garabogazköl Aýlagy** b. Turkm.
117 C4 **Garacad** Somalia
53 C1 **Garah** Austr.
151 F3 **Garanhuns** Brazil
123 C2 **Ga-Rankuwa** S. Africa
118 C1 **Garar, Plaine de** plain Chad
117 C4 **Garbahaarrey** Somalia
135 B2 **Garberville** U.S.A.
81 D2 **Garbosh, Küh-e** mt. Iran
101 D1 **Garbsen** Ger.
154 C2 **Garça** Brazil
154 B2 **Garcias** Brazil
108 B1 **Garda, Lake** l. Italy
108 A3 **Garde, Cap de** c. Alg.
101 E1 **Gardelegen** Ger.
136 C3 **Garden City** U.S.A.
129 E2 **Garden Hill** Can.
77 C3 **Gardēz** Afgh.
139 F2 **Gardiner** U.S.A.
Gardner atoll Micronesia see **Faraulep**
135 C3 **Gardnerville** U.S.A.
136 B3 **Garfield** U.S.A.
88 B2 **Gargždai** Lith.
123 C3 **Gariep Dam** resr S. Africa
122 A3 **Garies** S. Africa
119 D3 **Garissa** Kenya
88 B2 **Garkalne** Latvia
143 D2 **Garland** U.S.A.
102 C2 **Garmisch-Partenkirchen** Ger.
52 B2 **Garnpung Lake** imp. l. Austr.
104 B3 **Garonne** r. France
117 C4 **Garoowe** Somalia
74 B2 **Garoth** India
118 B2 **Garoua** Cameroon
118 B2 **Garoua Boulai** Cameroon
Garqêntang China see **Sog**
96 B2 **Garry** r. U.K.
126 F2 **Garry Lake** Can.
119 E3 **Garsen** Kenya
76 B2 **Garşy** Turkm.
122 A2 **Garub** Namibia

60 B2 **Garut** Indon.
138 B2 **Gary** U.S.A.
145 B2 **Garza García** Mex.
68 C2 **Garzê** China
Gascogne reg. France see **Gascony**
Gascogne, Golfe de g. France/Spain see **Gascony, Gulf of**
104 B3 **Gascony** reg. France
104 B3 **Gascony, Gulf of** France/Spain
50 A2 **Gascoyne** r. Austr.
118 B2 **Gashaka** Nigeria
115 D3 **Gashua** Nigeria
59 E3 **Gasmata** P.N.G.
131 D3 **Gaspé** Can.
131 D3 **Gaspésie, Péninsule de la** pen. Can.
141 E1 **Gaston, Lake** U.S.A.
141 D1 **Gastonia** U.S.A.
107 C2 **Gata, Cabo de** c. Spain
88 D2 **Gatchina** Rus. Fed.
98 C2 **Gateshead** U.K.
143 D2 **Gatesville** U.S.A.
139 D1 **Gatineau** Can.
130 C3 **Gatineau** r. Can.
Gatooma Zimbabwe see **Kadoma**
53 D1 **Gatton** Austr.
129 E2 **Gauer Lake** Can.
93 E4 **Gausta** mt. Norway
123 C2 **Gauteng** prov. S. Africa
79 C2 **Gävbandi** Iran
111 B3 **Gavdos** i. Greece
93 G3 **Gävle** Sweden
93 G3 **Gävlebukten** b. Sweden
89 F2 **Gavrilov Posad** Rus. Fed.
89 E2 **Gavrilov-Yam** Rus. Fed.
122 A2 **Gawachab** Namibia
62 A1 **Gawai** Myanmar
52 A2 **Gawler** Austr.
52 A2 **Gawler Ranges** hills Austr.
75 C2 **Gaya** India
114 C3 **Gaya** Niger
114 C3 **Gayéri** Burkina
138 C1 **Gaylord** U.S.A.
86 E2 **Gayny** Rus. Fed.
116 B1 **Gaza** terr. Asia
80 B2 **Gaza** Gaza
80 B2 **Gaziantep** Turkey
76 C2 **Gazojak** Turkm.
114 B4 **Gbarnga** Liberia
118 A2 **Gboko** Nigeria
103 D1 **Gdańsk** Pol.
88 A3 **Gdańsk, Gulf of** Pol./Rus. Fed.
88 C2 **Gdov** Rus. Fed.
103 D1 **Gdynia** Pol.
116 B3 **Gedaref** Sudan
101 D2 **Gedern** Ger.
111 C3 **Gediz** Turkey
111 C3 **Gediz** r. Turkey
93 F4 **Gedser** Denmark
100 B2 **Geel** Belgium
52 B3 **Geelong** Austr.
101 E1 **Geesthacht** Ger.
75 C1 **Gê'gyai** China
129 D2 **Geikie** r. Can.
93 E3 **Geilo** Norway
119 D3 **Geita** Tanz.
71 A3 **Gejiu** China
108 B3 **Gela** Sicily Italy
108 B3 **Gela, Golfo di** g. Sicily Italy
91 D3 **Gelendzhik** Rus. Fed.
Gelibolu Turkey see **Gallipoli**
100 C2 **Gelsenkirchen** Ger.
118 B2 **Gemena** Dem. Rep. Congo
111 C2 **Gemlik** Turkey
108 B1 **Gemona del Friuli** Italy
117 C4 **Genalē Wenz** r. Eth.
81 D3 **Genāveh** Iran
153 B4 **General Acha** Arg.
153 B4 **General Alvear** Arg.
153 C4 **General Belgrano** Arg.
144 B2 **General Cepeda** Mex.
General Freire Angola see **Muxaluando**
General Machado Angola see **Camacupa**
153 B3 **General Pico** Arg.
153 B4 **General Roca** Arg.
154 B2 **General Salgado** Brazil
64 B3 **General Santos** Phil.
139 E2 **Genesee** r. U.S.A.
138 B2 **Geneseo** IL U.S.A.
139 D2 **Geneseo** NY U.S.A.
105 D2 **Geneva** Switz.
139 D2 **Geneva** U.S.A.

105 D2 **Geneva, Lake** l. France/Switz.
Genève Switz. see **Geneva**
106 B2 **Genil** r. Spain
100 B2 **Genk** Belgium
53 C3 **Genoa** Austr.
108 A2 **Genoa** Italy
108 A2 **Genoa, Gulf of** g. Italy
Genova Italy see **Genoa**
Gent Belgium see **Ghent**
61 C2 **Genteng** i. Indon.
101 F1 **Genthin** Ger.
50 A3 **Geographe Bay** Austr.
131 D2 **George** r. Can.
122 B3 **George** S. Africa
52 A3 **George, Lake** Austr.
141 D3 **George, Lake** FL U.S.A.
139 E2 **George, Lake** NY U.S.A.
146 C2 **George Town** Bahamas
114 A3 **Georgetown** Gambia
151 D2 **Georgetown** Guyana
60 B1 **George Town** Malaysia
138 C3 **Georgetown** KY U.S.A.
141 F2 **Georgetown** SC U.S.A.
143 D2 **Georgetown** TX U.S.A.
55 L2 **George V Land** reg. Antarctica
81 C1 **Georgia** country Asia
141 D2 **Georgia** state U.S.A.
130 B3 **Georgian Bay** Can.
51 C2 **Georgina** watercourse Austr.
Georgiu-Dezh Rus. Fed. see **Liski**
77 E2 **Georgiyevka** Kazakh.
87 D4 **Georgiyevsk** Rus. Fed.
101 F2 **Gera** Ger.
151 E4 **Geral de Goiás, Serra** hills Brazil
54 B2 **Geraldine** N.Z.
50 A2 **Geraldton** Austr.
80 B1 **Gerede** Turkey
76 C3 **Gereshk** Afgh.
102 C2 **Geretsried** Ger.
135 C2 **Gerlach** U.S.A.
103 E2 **Gerlachovský štít** mt. Slovakia
139 D3 **Germantown** U.S.A.
102 C1 **Germany** country Europe
100 C2 **Gerolstein** Ger.
101 E3 **Gerolzhofen** Ger.
53 D2 **Gerringong** Austr.
101 D2 **Gersfeld (Rhön)** Ger.
Géryville Alg. see **El Bayadh**
75 C1 **Gêrzê** China
106 C1 **Getafe** Spain
139 D3 **Gettysburg** PA U.S.A.
136 D1 **Gettysburg** SD U.S.A.
55 P2 **Getz Ice Shelf** Antarctica
111 B3 **Gevgelija** Macedonia
111 C3 **Geyikli** Turkey
122 B2 **Ghaap Plateau** S. Africa
Ghadames Libya see **Ghadāmis**
115 C1 **Ghadāmis** Libya
75 C2 **Ghaghara** r. India
76 C2 **Ghalkarteniz, Solonchak** salt marsh Kazakh.
114 B4 **Ghana** country Africa
120 B3 **Ghanzi** Botswana
115 C1 **Ghardaïa** Alg.
78 A2 **Ghārib, Jabal** mt. Egypt
115 D1 **Gharyān** Libya
115 D2 **Ghāt** Libya
75 C2 **Ghatal** India
75 B2 **Ghaziabad** Uttar Prad. India
75 C2 **Ghazipur** India
77 C3 **Ghazni** Afgh.
78 B2 **Ghazzālah** Saudi Arabia
100 A2 **Ghent** Belgium
Gheorghe Gheorghiu-Dej Romania see **Oneşti**
110 B1 **Gheorgheni** Romania
110 B1 **Gherla** Romania
105 D3 **Ghisonaccia** Corsica France
74 A2 **Ghotaru** India
74 A2 **Ghotki** Pak.
75 C2 **Ghugri** r. India
76 C3 **Ghurian** Afgh.
91 E1 **Giaginskaya** Rus. Fed.
97 C1 **Giant's Causeway** lava field U.K.
61 C2 **Gianyar** Indon.
108 A1 **Giaveno** Italy
122 A2 **Gibeon** Namibia
106 B2 **Gibraltar** terr. Europe
106 B2 **Gibraltar, Strait of** Morocco/Spain

131 D3 Grande-Rivière Can.
152 B3 Grandes, Salinas salt marsh Arg.
131 D3 Grand Falls N.B. Can.
131 E3 Grand Falls-Windsor Nfld. Can.
128 C3 Grand Forks Can.
137 D1 Grand Forks U.S.A.
138 B2 Grand Haven U.S.A.
128 C1 Grandin, Lac l. Can.
137 D2 Grand Island U.S.A.
140 B3 Grand Isle U.S.A.
136 B3 Grand Junction U.S.A.
114 B4 Grand-Lahou Côte d'Ivoire
131 D3 Grand Lake N.B. Can.
131 E3 Grand Lake Nfld. Can.
137 E1 Grand Marais U.S.A.
130 C3 Grand-Mère Can.
106 B2 Grândola Port.
129 E2 Grand Rapids Can.
138 B2 Grand Rapids MI U.S.A.
137 E1 Grand Rapids MN U.S.A.
136 A2 Grand Teton mt. U.S.A.
147 C2 Grand Turk Turks and Caicos Is
129 D2 Grandview Can.
134 C1 Grandview U.S.A.
134 C1 Grangeville U.S.A.
128 B2 Granisle Can.
137 D2 Granite Falls U.S.A.
134 E1 Granite Peak MT U.S.A.
134 C2 Granite Peak NV U.S.A.
108 B3 Granitola, Capo c. Sicily Italy
93 F4 Gränna Sweden
101 F1 Gransee Ger.
99 C2 Grantham U.K.
96 C2 Grantown-on-Spey U.K.
142 B1 Grants U.S.A.
134 B2 Grants Pass U.S.A.
129 D2 Granville France
129 D2 Granville Lake Can.
155 D1 Grão Mogol Brazil
123 D1 Graskop S. Africa
105 D3 Grasse France
50 B3 Grass Patch Austr.
107 D1 Graus Spain
92 F2 Gravdal Norway
104 B2 Grave, Pointe de pt France
129 D3 Gravelbourg Can.
130 C3 Gravenhurst Can.
53 D1 Gravesend Austr.
99 D4 Gravesend U.K.
105 D2 Gray France
141 D1 Gray U.S.A.
138 C2 Grayling U.S.A.
99 D4 Grays U.K.
103 D2 Graz Austria
146 C2 Great Abaco i. Bahamas
50 B3 Great Australian Bight g. Austr.
146 C2 Great Bahama Bank sea feature Bahamas
54 C1 Great Barrier Island N.Z.
51 D1 Great Barrier Reef Austr.
134 C3 Great Basin U.S.A.
128 C1 Great Bear Lake Can.
93 F4 Great Belt sea chan. Denmark
137 D3 Great Bend U.S.A.
63 A2 Great Coco Island Cocos Is
53 B3 Great Dividing Range mts Austr.
Great Eastern Erg des. Alg. see Grand Erg Oriental
146 B2 Greater Antilles is Caribbean Sea
Greater Khingan Mountains China see Da Hinggan Ling
58 A3 Greater Sunda Islands Indon.
134 D1 Great Falls U.S.A.
123 C3 Great Fish r. S. Africa
123 C3 Great Fish Point S. Africa
147 C2 Great Inagua i. Bahamas
123 C3 Great Karoo plat. S. Africa
123 C3 Great Kei r. S. Africa
99 B4 Great Malvern U.K.
122 A2 Great Namaqualand reg. Namibia
73 D4 Great Nicobar i. India
98 B3 Great Ormes Head hd U.K.
99 D4 Great Ouse r. U.K.
136 C2 Great Plains U.S.A.
119 D3 Great Rift Valley Africa
119 D3 Great Ruaha r. Tanz.

134 D2 Great Salt Lake U.S.A.
134 D2 Great Salt Lake Desert U.S.A.
116 A2 Great Sand Sea des. Egypt/Libya
50 B2 Great Sandy Desert Austr.
128 C1 Great Slave Lake Can.
141 D1 Great Smoky Mountains U.S.A.
99 A4 Great Torrington U.K.
50 B2 Great Victoria Desert Austr.
70 B1 Great Wall tourist site China
Great Western Erg des. Alg. see Grand Erg Occidental
99 D3 Great Yarmouth U.K.
106 B1 Gredos, Sierra de mts Spain
111 B3 Greece country Europe
136 C2 Greeley U.S.A.
82 F1 Greem-Bell, Ostrov i. Rus. Fed.
138 F1 Green r. Can.
138 B3 Green r. KY U.S.A.
136 B3 Green r. WY U.S.A.
138 B2 Green Bay U.S.A.
138 B1 Green Bay b. U.S.A.
138 C3 Greenbrier r. U.S.A.
138 B3 Greencastle U.S.A.
141 D1 Greeneville U.S.A.
139 E2 Greenfield U.S.A.
129 D2 Green Lake Can.
127 J2 Greenland terr. N. America
160 L2 Greenland Basin sea feature Arctic Ocean
160 R2 Greenland Sea sea Greenland/Svalbard
96 B3 Greenock U.K.
97 C1 Greenore Ireland
135 D3 Green River UT U.S.A.
136 B2 Green River WY U.S.A.
138 B3 Greensburg IN U.S.A.
139 D2 Greensburg PA U.S.A.
141 E2 Green Swamp U.S.A.
142 A2 Green Valley U.S.A.
114 B4 Greenville Liberia
140 C2 Greenville AL U.S.A.
139 F1 Greenville ME U.S.A.
140 B2 Greenville MS U.S.A.
141 E1 Greenville NC U.S.A.
141 D2 Greenville SC U.S.A.
143 D2 Greenville TX U.S.A.
53 D2 Greenwell Point Austr.
131 D3 Greenwood Can.
140 B2 Greenwood MS U.S.A.
141 D2 Greenwood SC U.S.A.
50 B2 Gregory, Lake salt flat Austr.
51 D1 Gregory Range hills Austr.
102 C1 Greifswald Ger.
101 F2 Greiz Ger.
86 C2 Gremikha Rus. Fed.
93 F4 Grenå Denmark
140 C2 Grenada U.S.A.
147 D3 Grenada country West Indies
104 C3 Grenade France
93 F4 Grenen spit Denmark
53 C2 Grenfell Austr.
129 D2 Grenfell Can.
105 D2 Grenoble France
51 D1 Grenville, Cape Austr.
134 B1 Gresham U.S.A.
140 B3 Gretna LA U.S.A.
139 D3 Gretna VA U.S.A.
100 C1 Greven Ger.
111 B3 Grevena Greece
100 C2 Grevenbroich Ger.
101 E1 Grevesmühlen Ger.
136 B2 Greybull U.S.A.
128 A1 Grey Hunter Peak Can.
131 E2 Grey Islands Can.
54 B2 Greymouth N.Z.
52 B1 Grey Range hills Austr.
97 C2 Greystones Ireland
54 C2 Greytown N.Z.
91 E1 Gribanovskiy Rus. Fed.
118 B2 Gribingui r. C.A.R.
101 D3 Griesheim Ger.
141 D2 Griffin U.S.A.
53 C2 Griffith Austr.
88 C3 Grigiškės Lith.
118 C2 Grimari C.A.R.
101 F2 Grimma Ger.
102 C1 Grimmen Ger.
98 C3 Grimsby U.K.
128 C2 Grimshaw Can.

92 □B2 Grimsstaðir Iceland
93 E4 Grimstad Norway
92 □A3 Grindavík Iceland
93 E4 Grindsted Denmark
137 E2 Grinnell U.S.A.
123 C3 Griqualand East reg. S. Africa
122 B2 Griqualand West reg. S. Africa
122 B2 Griquatown S. Africa
127 G1 Grise Fiord Can.
Grishino Ukr. see Krasnoarmiys'k
99 D4 Gris Nez, Cap c. France
96 C1 Gritley U.K.
123 C2 Groblersdal S. Africa
122 B2 Groblershoop S. Africa
Grodno Belarus see Hrodna
103 D1 Grodzisk Wielkopolski Pol.
92 □A3 Gröf Iceland
104 B2 Groix, Île de i. France
100 C1 Gronau (Westfalen) Ger.
92 F3 Grong Norway
100 C1 Groningen Neth.
122 B3 Groot Brakrivier S. Africa
122 B2 Grootdrink S. Africa
51 C1 Groote Eylandt i. Austr.
120 A2 Grootfontein Namibia
122 A2 Groot Karas Berg plat. Namibia
122 B3 Groot Swartberge mts S. Africa
122 B2 Grootvloer salt pan S. Africa
122 B3 Groot Winterberg mt. S. Africa
101 D2 Großenlüder Ger.
101 E2 Großer Beerberg hill Ger.
102 C2 Großer Rachel mt. Ger.
103 C2 Grosser Speikkogel mt. Austria
108 B2 Grosseto Italy
101 D3 Groß-Gerau Ger.
102 C2 Großglockner mt. Austria
100 C1 Groß-Hesepe Ger.
101 E2 Großlohra Ger.
122 A1 Gross Ums Namibia
136 A2 Gros Ventre Range mts U.S.A.
131 E2 Groswater Bay Can.
130 B3 Groundhog r. Can.
135 B3 Grover Beach U.S.A.
140 B3 Groves U.S.A.
139 E2 Groveton U.S.A.
87 D4 Groznyy Rus. Fed.
109 D1 Grubišno Polje Croatia
Grudovo Bulg. see Sredets
103 D1 Grudziądz Pol.
122 A2 Grünau Namibia
92 □A3 Grundarfjörður Iceland
Gruzinskaya S.S.R. country Asia see Georgia
89 E3 Gryazi Rus. Fed.
89 F2 Gryazovets Rus. Fed.
103 D1 Gryfice Pol.
102 C1 Gryfino Pol.
153 E5 Grytviken S. Georgia
146 C2 Guacanayabo, Golfo de b. Cuba
144 B2 Guadalajara Mex.
106 C1 Guadalajara Spain
48 H4 Guadalcanal i. Solomon Is
107 C1 Guadalope r. Spain
106 B2 Guadalquivir r. Spain
132 B4 Guadalupe i. Mex.
106 B2 Guadalupe, Sierra de mts Spain
142 C2 Guadalupe Peak U.S.A.
144 B2 Guadalupe Victoria Mex.
144 B2 Guadalupe y Calvo Mex.
106 C1 Guadarrama, Sierra de mts Spain
147 D3 Guadeloupe terr. West Indies
147 D3 Guadeloupe Passage Caribbean Sea
106 B2 Guadiana r. Port./Spain
106 C2 Guadix Spain
154 B2 Guaíra Brazil
147 C3 Guajira, Península de la pen. Col.
150 B3 Gualaceo Ecuador
59 D2 Guam terr. N. Pacific Ocean
144 B3 Guamúchil Mex.
144 B2 Guanacevi Mex.
151 E4 Guanambi Brazil
150 C2 Guanare Venez.
146 B2 Guane Cuba

70 A2 Guang'an China
71 B3 Guangchang China
71 B3 Guangdong prov. China
Guanghua China see Laohekou
71 A3 Guangxi Zhuangzu Zizhiqu aut. reg. China
70 A2 Guangyuan China
71 B3 Guangzhou China
155 D1 Guanhães Brazil
147 D4 Guanipa r. Venez.
71 A3 Guanling China
65 A1 Guanshui China
Guansuo China see Guanling
147 C2 Guantánamo Cuba
155 C2 Guapé Brazil
150 C4 Guaporé r. Bol./Brazil
155 D2 Guarapari Brazil
154 B3 Guarapuava Brazil
155 C2 Guaratinguetá Brazil
154 C3 Guaratuba Brazil
106 B1 Guarda Port.
Guardafui, Cape Somalia see Gwardafuy, Gees
154 C1 Guarda Mor Brazil
106 C1 Guardo Spain
155 C2 Guarujá Brazil
144 B2 Guasave Mex.
146 A3 Guatemala country Central America
Guatemala Guat. see Guatemala City
157 G5 Guatemala Basin sea feature N. Pacific Ocean
146 A3 Guatemala City Guat.
150 C2 Guaviare r. Col.
155 C2 Guaxupé Brazil
150 B3 Guayaquil Ecuador
150 A3 Guayaquil, Golfo de g. Ecuador
152 B1 Guayaramerín Bol.
144 A2 Guaymas Mex.
117 B3 Guba Eth.
86 E1 Guba Dolgaya Rus. Fed.
108 B2 Gubbio Italy
89 E3 Gubkin Rus. Fed.
73 C3 Gudivada India
Gudur India
Guecho Spain see Algorta
114 A2 Guelb er Richât hill Maur.
115 C1 Guelma Alg.
114 A2 Guelmine Morocco
130 B3 Guelph Can.
145 C2 Guémez Mex.
104 B2 Guérande France
115 E2 Guerende Libya
104 C2 Guéret France
95 C4 Guernsey i. Channel Is
95 C4 Guernsey terr. Channel Is
144 A2 Guerrero Negro Mex.
131 D2 Guers, Lac l. Can.
158 D4 Guiana Basin sea feature N. Atlantic Ocean
150 C2 Guiana Highlands mts Guyana/Venez.
Guichi China see Chizhou
118 B2 Guider Cameroon
108 B2 Guidonia-Montecelio Italy
71 A3 Guigang China
100 A3 Guignicourt France
123 D1 Guija Moz.
71 B3 Guildford U.K.
71 B3 Guilin China
130 C2 Guillaume-Delisle, Lac l. Can.
106 B1 Guimarães Port.
114 A3 Guinea country Africa
113 D5 Guinea, Gulf of Africa
114 A3 Guinea-Bissau country Africa
104 B2 Guingamp France
104 B2 Guipavas France
154 B1 Guiratinga Brazil
150 C1 Güiria Venez.
150 C2 Guisanbourg Fr. Guiana
98 C2 Guisborough U.K.
100 A3 Guise France
64 B2 Guiuan Phil.
71 A3 Guiyang China
71 A3 Guizhou prov. China
104 B3 Gujan-Mestras France
74 B2 Gujarat state India
Gujerat state India see Gujarat
74 B1 Gujranwala Pak.
74 B1 Gujrat Pak.
91 D2 Gukovo Rus. Fed.
70 A2 Gulang China

93 G3	Härnösand Sweden
69 E1	Har Nur China
68 C1	Har Nuur l. Mongolia
96 ▫	Haroldswick U.K.
114 B4	Harper Liberia
101 D1	Harpstedt Ger.
130 C2	Harricana, Rivière d' r. Can.
53 D2	Harrington Austr.
131 E2	Harrington Harbour Can.
96 A2	Harris pen. U.K.
96 A2	Harris, Sound of sea chan. U.K.
138 B3	Harrisburg IL U.S.A.
134 B2	Harrisburg OR U.S.A.
139 D2	Harrisburg PA U.S.A.
123 C2	Harrismith S. Africa
140 B1	Harrison U.S.A.
131 E2	Harrison, Cape Can.
126 B2	Harrison Bay U.S.A.
139 D3	Harrisonburg U.S.A.
128 B3	Harrison Lake Can.
137 E3	Harrisonville U.S.A.
98 C3	Harrogate U.K.
110 C2	Hârșova Romania
92 G2	Harstad Norway
122 B2	Hartbees watercourse S. Africa
103 D2	Hartberg Austria
139 E2	Hartford CT U.S.A.
137 D2	Hartford SD U.S.A.
99 A4	Hartland Point U.K.
98 C2	Hartlepool U.K.
	Hartley Zimbabwe see Chegutu
128 B2	Hartley Bay Can.
123 B2	Harts r. S. Africa
141 D2	Hartwell Reservoir U.S.A.
68 C1	Har Us Nuur l. Mongolia
136 C1	Harvey U.S.A.
99 D4	Harwich U.K.
74 B2	Haryana state India
101 E2	Harz hills Ger.
101 E2	Harzgerode Ger.
78 B2	Hasan, Jabal hill Saudi Arabia
80 B2	Hasan Daği mts Turkey
99 C4	Haslemere U.K.
73 B3	Hassan India
100 B2	Hasselt Belgium
101 E2	Haßfurt Ger.
115 C2	Hassi Bel Guebbour Alg.
115 C1	Hassi Messaoud Alg.
93 F4	Hässleholm Sweden
100 B2	Hastière-Lavaux Belgium
53 C3	Hastings Vic. Austr.
54 C1	Hastings N.Z.
99 D4	Hastings U.K.
137 E2	Hastings MN U.S.A.
137 D2	Hastings NE U.S.A.
	Hatay Turkey see Antakya
142 B2	Hatch U.S.A.
129 D2	Hatchet Lake Can.
110 R1	Haţeg Romania
52 B2	Hatfield Austr.
68 C1	Hatgal Mongolia
62 B2	Ha Tinh Vietnam
52 B2	Hattah Austr.
141 E1	Hatteras, Cape U.S.A.
157 H3	Hatteras Abyssal Plain sea feature S. Atlantic Ocean
140 C2	Hattiesburg U.S.A.
100 C2	Hattingen Ger.
63 B3	Hat Yai Thai.
117 C4	Haud reg. Eth.
93 E4	Haugesund Norway
93 E4	Haukeligrend Norway
92 I2	Haukipudas Fin.
54 C1	Hauraki Gulf N.Z.
114 B1	Hauroko, Lake N.Z.
131 D3	Hauterive Can.
	Haute-Volta country Africa see Burkina
114 B1	Hauts Plateaux Alg.
146 B2	Havana Cuba
99 C4	Havant U.K.
101 E1	Havel r. Ger.
101 F1	Havelberg Ger.
54 B2	Havelock N.Z.
	Havelock Swaziland see Bulembu
54 C1	Havelock North N.Z.
99 A4	Haverfordwest U.K.
100 C2	Havixbeck Ger.
	Havlíčkův Brod Czech Rep.
92 H1	Havøysund Norway
111 C3	Havran Turkey
134 E1	Havre U.S.A.
131 D3	Havre-Aubert Can.
131 D2	Havre-St-Pierre Can.
49 L2	Hawai'i i. U.S.A.
156 E4	Hawai'ian Islands is N. Pacific Ocean
78 B2	Hawallī Kuwait
98 B2	Hawarden U.K.
54 A2	Hawea, Lake N.Z.
54 B1	Hawera N.Z.
98 B2	Hawes U.K.
96 C3	Hawick U.K.
54 C1	Hawke Bay N.Z.
52 A2	Hawker Austr.
52 B1	Hawkers Gate Austr.
123 A3	Hawston S. Africa
135 C3	Hawthorne U.S.A.
52 B2	Hay Austr.
128 C1	Hay r. Can.
100 C3	Hayange France
134 C1	Hayden U.S.A.
129 E2	Hayes r. Man. Can.
126 F2	Hayes r. Nunavut Can.
79 C3	Hoymā' Oman
77 C2	Hayotboshi tog'i mt. Uzbek.
111 C2	Hayrabolu Turkey
128 C1	Hay River Can.
137 D3	Hays U.S.A.
78 B3	Hays Yemen
90 B2	Haysyn Ukr.
135 B3	Hayward U.S.A.
99 C4	Haywards Heath U.K.
81 D2	Hazar Turkm.
74 A1	Hazarajat reg. Afgh.
138 C3	Hazard U.S.A.
75 C2	Hazaribagh India
75 C2	Hazaribagh Range mts India
104 C1	Hazebrouck France
128 B2	Hazelton Can.
139 D2	Hazleton U.S.A.
135 B3	Healdsburg U.S.A.
53 C3	Healesville Austr.
159 E7	Heard Island Indian Ocean
143 D2	Hearne U.S.A.
130 B3	Hearst Can.
55 A3	Hearst Island Antarctica
70 B2	Hebei prov. China
53 C1	Hebel Austr.
140 B1	Heber Springs U.S.A.
70 B2	Hebi China
101 D2	Hebron Can.
128 A2	Hecate Strait Can.
71 A3	Hechi China
100 B2	Hechtel Belgium
54 C2	Hector, Mount N.Z.
93 F3	Hede Sweden
100 C1	Heerde Neth.
100 B1	Heerenveen Neth.
100 B1	Heerhugowaard Neth.
100 B2	Heerlen Neth.
	Hefa Israel see Haifa
70 B2	Hefei China
70 B3	Hefeng China
69 E1	Hegang China
119 D1	Heiban Sudan
102 B1	Heide Ger.
122 A1	Heide Namibia
101 D3	Heidelberg Ger.
122 B3	Heidelberg S. Africa
69 E1	Heihe China
102 B2	Heilbronn Ger.
69 E1	Heilong Jiang r. China/Rus. Fed.
93 I3	Heinola Fin.
	Hejaz reg. Saudi Arabia see Hijaz
92 A3	Hekla vol. Iceland
92 F3	Helagsfjället mt. Sweden
70 A2	Helan Shan mts China
140 B2	Helena AR U.S.A.
134 D1	Helena MT U.S.A.
96 B2	Helensburgh U.K.
102 B1	Helgoland i. Ger.
102 B1	Helgoländer Bucht b. Ger. see Helgoland
	Helgoland i. Ger. see Helgoländer Bucht
	Heligoland Bight b. Ger. see Helgoländer Bucht
92 □A3	Hella Iceland
100 B2	Hellevoetsluis Neth.
107 C2	Hellín Spain
	Hell-Ville Madag. see Andoany
76 C3	Helmand r. Afgh.
101 E2	Helmbrechts Ger.
122 A2	Helmeringhausen Namibia
100 B2	Helmond Neth.
96 C1	Helmsdale U.K.
96 C1	Helmsdale r. U.K.
98 C2	Helmsley U.K.
101 E1	Helmstedt Ger.
65 B1	Helong China
143 D3	Helotes U.S.A.
93 F4	Helsingborg Sweden
	Helsingfors Fin. see Helsinki
93 F4	Helsingør Denmark
93 H3	Helsinki Fin.
99 A4	Helston U.K.
97 C2	Helvick Head hd Ireland
99 C4	Hemel Hempstead U.K.
101 D1	Hemmoor Ger.
92 F2	Hemnesberget Norway
70 B2	Henan prov. China
111 D2	Hendek Turkey
138 B3	Henderson KY U.S.A.
141 E1	Henderson NC U.S.A.
135 D3	Henderson NV U.S.A.
143 E2	Henderson TX U.S.A.
49 O6	Henderson Island Pitcairn Is
141 D1	Hendersonville U.S.A.
99 C4	Hendon U.K.
62 A1	Hengduan Shan mts China
100 C1	Hengelo Neth.
	Hengnan China see Hengyang
71 B3	Hongehan China
70 B2	Hengshui China
71 A3	Hengxian China
71 B3	Hengyang China
	Hengzhou China see Hengxian
91 C2	Heniches'k Ukr.
139 D3	Henlopen, Cape U.S.A.
100 C2	Hennef (Sieg) Ger.
130 B2	Henrietta Maria, Cape Can.
	Henrique de Carvalho Angola see Saurimo
139 D3	Henry, Cape U.S.A.
143 D1	Henryetta U.S.A.
127 H2	Henry Kater, Cape Can.
101 D1	Henstedt-Ulzburg Ger.
120 A3	Hentiesbaai Namibia
101 D3	Heppenheim (Bergstraße) Ger.
71 B3	Hepu China
76 C3	Herāt Afgh.
129 D2	Herbert Can.
54 C2	Herbertville N.Z.
101 D2	Herbstein Ger.
109 C2	Herceg-Novi Montenegro
99 B3	Hereford U.K.
143 C2	Hereford U.S.A.
101 D2	Herford Ger.
100 C2	Herkenbosch Neth.
96 □	Herma Ness hd U.K.
122 A3	Hermanus S. Africa
53 C2	Hermidale Austr.
134 C1	Hermiston U.S.A.
59 U3	Herit Islands P.N.G.
144 B2	Hermosillo Mex.
154 B3	Hernandarias Para.
100 C2	Herne Ger.
93 E4	Herning Denmark
104 B2	Hérouville-St-Clair France
106 B2	Herrera del Duque Spain
139 D2	Hershey U.S.A.
99 C4	Hertford U.K.
123 C2	Hertzogville S. Africa
51 E2	Hervey Bay Austr.
101 F2	Herzberg Ger.
101 E3	Herzogenaurach Ger.
71 A3	Heshan China
135 C4	Hesperia U.S.A.
128 A1	Hess r. Can.
101 E1	Hessen land Ger.
101 D2	Hessisch Lichtenau Ger.
136 C1	Hettinger U.S.A.
101 E2	Hettstedt Ger.
98 B1	Hexham U.K.
81 C2	Heydarābad Iran
98 B2	Heysham U.K.
71 B3	Heyuan China
52 B3	Heywood Austr.
70 B2	Heze China
71 B3	Hezhou China
141 D3	Hialeah U.S.A.
137 D3	Hiawatha U.S.A.
137 E1	Hibbing U.S.A.
141 D1	Hickory U.S.A.
54 C1	Hicks Bay N.Z.
66 D2	Hidaka-sanmyaku mts Japan
145 C2	Hidalgo Mex.
145 C2	Hidalgo Mex.
144 B2	Hidalgo del Parral Mex.
154 C1	Hidrolândia Brazil
67 A4	Higashi-suidō sea chan. Japan
	High Atlas mts Morocco see Haut Atlas
134 B2	High Desert U.S.A.
128 C2	High Level Can.
141 E1	High Point U.S.A.
128 C2	High Prairie Can.
128 C2	High River Can.
129 D2	Highrock Lake Can.
	High Tatras mts Pol./Slovakia see Tatry
99 C4	High Wycombe U.K.
88 B2	Hiiumaa i. Estonia
78 A2	Hijaz reg. Saudi Arabia
54 C1	Hikurangi mt. N.Z.
101 E2	Hildburghausen Ger.
100 C2	Hilden Ger.
101 E2	Hilders Ger.
101 D1	Hildesheim Ger.
81 C2	Hillah Iraq
100 B1	Hillegom Neth.
100 C2	Hillesheim Ger.
138 C3	Hillsboro OH U.S.A.
143 D2	Hillsboro TX U.S.A.
53 C2	Hillston Austr.
96 □	Hillswick U.K.
49 L2	Hilo U.S.A.
141 D2	Hilton Head Island U.S.A.
100 B1	Hilversum Neth.
74 B1	Himachal Pradesh state India
68 B2	Himalaya mts Asia
74 B2	Himatnagar India
67 B4	Himeji Japan
123 C2	Himeville S. Africa
67 C3	Himi Japan
	Ḥimş Syria see Homs
147 C3	Hinche Haiti
51 D1	Hinchinbrook Island Austr.
52 B3	Hindmarsh, Lake dry lake Austr.
74 A1	Hindu Kush mts Afgh./Pak.
73 B3	Hindupur India
134 C2	Hines U.S.A.
141 D2	Hinesville U.S.A.
74 B2	Hinganghat India
81 C2	Hınıs Turkey
92 G2	Hinnøya i. Norway
106 B2	Hinojosa del Duque Spain
100 C1	Hinte Ger.
62 A2	Hinthada Myanmar
128 C2	Hinton Can.
75 C2	Hirakud Reservoir India
	Hîrlău Romania see Hârlău
66 D2	Hiroo Japan
66 D2	Hirosaki Japan
67 B4	Hiroshima Japan
101 E3	Hirschaid Ger.
101 E2	Hirschberg Ger.
105 C2	Hirson France
	Hîrşova Romania see Hârşova
93 E4	Hirtshals Denmark
74 B2	Hisar India
147 C2	Hispaniola i. Caribbean Sea
81 C2	Hīt Iraq
67 D3	Hitachi Japan
67 D3	Hitachinaka Japan
92 E3	Hitra i. Norway
49 N4	Hiva Oa i. Fr. Polynesia
93 G3	Hjälmaren l. Sweden
129 D1	Hjalmar Lake Can.
93 F4	Hjørring Denmark
123 D2	Hlabisa S. Africa
92 □B2	Hlíð Iceland
91 C2	Hlobyne Ukr.
123 C2	Hlohlowane S. Africa
123 C2	Hlotse Lesotho
91 C1	Hlukhiv Ukr.
88 C3	Hlusk Belarus
88 C3	Hlybokaye Belarus
114 C4	Ho Ghana
62 B2	Hoa Binh Vietnam
122 A1	Hoachanas Namibia
120 A2	Hoanib watercourse Namibia
120 A2	Hoarusib watercourse Namibia
51 D4	Hobart Austr.
143 D1	Hobart U.S.A.
143 C2	Hobbs U.S.A.
93 E4	Hobro Denmark
117 C4	Hobyo Somalia
	Hô Chi Minh Vietnam see Ho Chi Minh City
63 B2	Ho Chi Minh City Vietnam

114 B3 Hôḍ reg. Maur.
117 D3 Hodda mt. Somalia
78 B3 Hodeidah Yemen
103 E2 Hódmezóvásárhely Hungary
Hoek van Holland Neth. see Hook of Holland
65 B2 Hoeyang N. Korea
101 E2 Hof Ger.
101 E2 Hofheim in Unterfranken Ger.
92 □B3 Höfn Iceland
92 □A2 Höfn Iceland
92 □B3 Hofsjökull ice cap Iceland
67 B4 Hōfu Japan
115 C2 Hoggar plat. Alg.
93 G4 Högsby Sweden
93 E3 Høgste Breakulen mt. Norway
101 D2 Hohe Rhön mts Ger.
100 C2 Hohe Venn moorland Belgium
70 B1 Hohhot China
75 C1 Hoh Xil Shan mts China
63 B2 Hôi An Vietnam
119 D2 Hoima Uganda
75 D2 Hojai India
54 B2 Hokitika N.Z.
66 D2 Hokkaidō i. Japan
91 C2 Hola Prystan' Ukr.
128 B2 Holberg Can.
53 C3 Holbrook Austr.
142 A2 Holbrook U.S.A.
137 D2 Holdrege U.S.A.
146 C2 Holguín Cuba
92 □B2 Hóll Iceland
103 D2 Hollabrunn Austria
138 B2 Holland U.S.A.
Hollandia Indon. see Jayapura
135 B3 Hollister U.S.A.
103 E2 Hollóháza Hungary
93 I3 Hollola Fin.
100 B1 Hollum Neth.
140 C2 Holly Springs U.S.A.
134 C4 Hollywood U.S.A.
141 D3 Hollywood U.S.A.
92 F2 Holm Norway
126 E2 Holman Can.
92 H3 Holmsund Sweden
122 A2 Holoog Namibia
93 E4 Holstebro Denmark
141 D1 Holston r. U.S.A.
98 A3 Holyhead U.K.
98 C2 Holy Island England U.K.
98 A3 Holy Island Wales U.K.
136 C2 Holyoke U.S.A.
Holy See Europe see Vatican City
101 D2 Holzminden Ger.
62 A1 Homalin Myanmar
101 D2 Homberg (Efze) Ger.
114 B3 Hombori Mali
100 C3 Homburg Ger.
127 H2 Home Bay Can.
140 B2 Homer U.S.A.
141 D3 Homestead U.S.A.
92 F3 Hommelvik Norway
141 D3 Homosassa Springs U.S.A.
80 B2 Homs Syria
89 D3 Homyel' Belarus
Honan prov. China see Henan
122 A3 Hondeklipbaai S. Africa
145 D3 Hondo r. Belize/Mex.
142 B2 Hondo NM U.S.A.
143 D3 Hondo TX U.S.A.
146 B3 Honduras country Central America
146 B3 Honduras, Gulf of Belize/Hond.
93 F3 Hønefoss Norway
135 B2 Honey Lake U.S.A.
104 C2 Honfleur France
70 B3 Honghu China
71 A3 Hongjiang China
71 B3 Hong Kong China
71 B3 Hong Kong special admin. reg. China
Hongqizhen China see Wuzhishan
131 D3 Honguedo, Détroit d' sea chan. Can.
65 B1 Hongwŏn N. Korea
70 B2 Hongze Hu l. China
48 H4 Honiara Solomon Is
99 B4 Honiton U.K.
66 D3 Honjō Japan
92 I1 Honningsvåg Norway
49 L1 Honolulu U.S.A.

67 B3 Honshū i. Japan
134 B1 Hood, Mount vol. U.S.A.
50 A3 Hood Point Austr.
134 B1 Hood River U.S.A.
100 B2 Hoogerheide Neth.
100 C1 Hoogeveen Neth.
100 C1 Hoogezand-Sappemeer Neth.
100 C2 Hoog-Keppel Neth.
100 B2 Hook of Holland Neth.
128 A2 Hoonah U.S.A.
123 C2 Hoopstad S. Africa
100 B1 Hoorn Neth.
49 J5 Hoorn, Îles de is Wallis and Futuna Is
128 B3 Hope Can.
140 B2 Hope U.S.A.
83 N2 Hope, Point U.S.A.
131 D2 Hopedale Can.
Hopei prov. China see Hebei
145 D2 Hopelchén Mex.
131 D2 Hope Mountains Can.
Hopes Advance Bay Can. see Aupaluk
52 B3 Hopetoun Austr.
122 B3 Hopetown S. Africa
139 D3 Hopewell U.S.A.
130 C2 Hopewell Islands Can.
50 B2 Hopkins, Lake salt flat Austr.
138 B3 Hopkinsville U.S.A.
134 B1 Hoquiam U.S.A.
81 C1 Horasan Turkey
93 F4 Hörby Sweden
89 D3 Horki Belarus
91 D2 Horlivka Ukr.
79 D2 Hormak Iran
79 C2 Hormuz, Strait of Iran/Oman
103 D2 Horn Austria
92 □A2 Horn c. Iceland
153 B5 Horn, Cape Chile
139 D2 Hornell U.S.A.
130 B3 Hornepayne Can.
Hornos, Cabo de c. Chile see Horn, Cape
53 D2 Hornsby Austr.
98 C3 Hornsea U.K.
90 B2 Horodenka Ukr.
91 C1 Horodnya Ukr.
90 B2 Horodok Ukr.
90 A2 Horodok Ukr.
90 A1 Horokhiv Ukr.
Horqin Youyi Qianqi China see Ulanhot
131 E2 Horse Islands Can.
52 B3 Horsham Austr.
99 C4 Horsham U.K.
93 F4 Horten Norway
126 E2 Horton r. Can.
117 B4 Hosa'ina Eth.
74 A2 Hoshab Pak.
74 B1 Hoshiarpur India
142 B1 Hosta Butte mt. U.S.A.
75 C1 Hotan China
122 B2 Hotazel S. Africa
92 G3 Hoting Sweden
140 C2 Hot Springs AR U.S.A.
136 C2 Hot Springs SD U.S.A.
Hot Springs see Truth or Consequences
128 C1 Hottah Lake Can.
100 B2 Houffalize Belgium
138 B1 Houghton U.S.A.
139 F1 Houlton U.S.A.
70 B2 Houma China
140 B3 Houma U.S.A.
128 B2 Houston Can.
143 D3 Houston U.S.A.
50 A2 Houtman Abrolhos is Austr.
122 B3 Houwater S. Africa
68 C1 Hovd Mongolia
99 C4 Hove U.K.
90 A2 Hoverla, Hora mt. Ukr.
68 C1 Hövsgöl Nuur l. Mongolia
68 C2 Hövüün Mongolia
116 A3 Howar, Wadi watercourse Sudan
98 C3 Howden U.K.
53 C3 Howe, Cape Austr.
123 D2 Howick S. Africa
49 J3 Howland Island terr. N. Pacific Ocean
53 C3 Howlong Austr.
Howrah India see Haora
140 B1 Hoxie U.S.A.
101 D2 Höxter Ger.
96 C1 Hoy i. U.K.
93 E3 Høyanger Norway

102 C1 Hoyerswerda Ger.
62 A2 Hpapun Myanmar
103 D1 Hradec Králové Czech Rep.
109 C2 Hrasnica Bos.-Herz.
92 □B2 Hraun Iceland
91 C1 Hrebinka Ukr.
88 B3 Hrodna Belarus
62 A1 Hsi-hseng Myanmar
71 C3 Hsinchu Taiwan
71 C3 Hsinying Taiwan
62 A1 Hsipaw Myanmar
70 A2 Huachi China
150 B4 Huacho Peru
70 B1 Huade China
65 B1 Huadian China
70 B2 Huai'an China
70 B2 Huaibei China
70 B2 Huai He r. China
71 A3 Huaihua China
70 B2 Huainan China
70 B2 Huaiyang China
145 C3 Huajuápan de León Mex.
59 C3 Huaki Indon.
71 C3 Hualien Taiwan
150 B3 Huallaga r. Peru
120 A2 Huambo Angola
150 B4 Huancavelica Peru
150 B4 Huancayo Peru
Huangcaoba China see Xingyi
70 B2 Huangchuan China
Huang Hai sea N. Pacific Ocean see Yellow Sea
Huang He r. China see Yellow River
71 A4 Huangliu China
70 B2 Huangshan China
70 B2 Huangshi China
70 A2 Huangtu Gaoyuan plat. China
71 C3 Huangyan China
70 A2 Huangyuan China
65 B1 Huanren China
150 B3 Huánuco Peru
152 B1 Huanuni Bol.
150 B4 Huaral Peru
150 B3 Huaráz Peru
150 B4 Huarmey Peru
152 A1 Huasco Chile
152 A2 Huasco r. Chile
144 B2 Huatabampo Mex.
145 C3 Huatusco Mex.
71 A3 Huayuan China
62 B1 Huayxay Laos
70 B2 Hubei prov. China
73 B3 Hubli India
100 C2 Hückelhoven Ger.
99 C3 Hucknall U.K.
98 C3 Huddersfield U.K.
93 G3 Hudiksvall Sweden
139 E2 Hudson r. U.S.A.
129 D2 Hudson Bay Can.
127 G3 Hudson Bay sea Can.
128 B2 Hudson's Hope Can.
127 H2 Hudson Strait Can.
63 B2 Huê Vietnam
146 A3 Huehuetenango Guat.
144 B2 Huehueto, Cerro mt. Mex.
145 C2 Huejutla Mex.
106 B2 Huelva Spain
107 C2 Huércal-Overa Spain
107 C1 Huesca Spain
106 C2 Huéscar Spain
51 D2 Hughenden Austr.
50 B3 Hughes Austr.
75 C2 Hughli r. mouth India
143 D2 Hugo U.S.A.
Huhehot China see Hohhot
122 B2 Huhudi S. Africa
122 A2 Huib-Hoch Plateau Namibia
71 B3 Huichang China
Huicheng China see Huilai
65 B1 Huich'ŏn N. Korea
120 A2 Huíla, Planalto da Angola
71 B3 Huilai China
71 A3 Huili China
70 B2 Huimin China
69 E2 Huinan China
Huinan China see Nanhui
93 H3 Huittinen Fin.
145 C3 Huixtla Mex.
71 A3 Huize China
68 C1 Hujirt Mongolia
78 B2 Hujr Saudi Arabia
122 B1 Hukuntsi Botswana
78 B2 Hulayfah Saudi Arabia
66 B1 Hulin China
130 C3 Hull Can.

70 C1 Huludao China
69 D1 Hulun Buir China
69 D1 Hulun Nur l. China
91 D2 Hulyaypole Ukr.
69 E1 Huma China
150 C3 Humaitá Brazil
122 B3 Humansdorp S. Africa
98 C2 Humber est. U.K.
143 D3 Humble U.S.A.
129 D2 Humboldt Can.
135 C2 Humboldt NV U.S.A.
140 C1 Humboldt TN U.S.A.
135 C2 Humboldt r. U.S.A.
103 E2 Humenné Slovakia
53 C3 Hume Reservoir Austr.
142 A1 Humphreys Peak U.S.A.
115 D1 Hūn Libya
92 □A2 Húnaflói b. Iceland
71 B3 Hunan prov. China
65 C1 Hunchun China
110 B1 Hunedoara Romania
101 D2 Hünfeld Ger.
103 D2 Hungary country Europe
52 B1 Hungerford Austr.
65 B2 Hŭngnam N. Korea
65 A1 Hun He r. China
Hunjiang China see Baishan
99 D3 Hunstanton U.K.
101 D1 Hunte r. Ger.
48 I6 Hunter Island S. Pacific Ocean
51 D4 Hunter Islands Austr.
99 C3 Huntingdon U.K.
138 B2 Huntingdon IN U.S.A.
138 C3 Huntington WV U.S.A.
135 C4 Huntington Beach U.S.A.
54 C1 Huntly N.Z.
96 C1 Huntly U.K.
130 C3 Huntsville Can.
140 C2 Huntsville AL U.S.A.
143 D2 Huntsville TX U.S.A.
Hunyani r. Moz./Zimbabwe see Manyame
59 D3 Huon Peninsula P.N.G.
Huoxian China see Huozhou
70 B2 Huozhou China
Hupeh prov. China see Hubei
Hurghada Egypt see Al Ghurdaqah
137 D2 Huron U.S.A.
138 C2 Huron, Lake Can./U.S.A.
135 D3 Hurricane U.S.A.
100 C2 Hürth Ger.
92 □B2 Húsavík Iceland
110 C1 Huşi Romania
126 B2 Huslia U.S.A.
78 B3 Husn Āl 'Abr Yemen
102 B1 Husum Ger.
68 C1 Hutag Mongolia
60 A1 Hutanopan Indon.
137 D3 Hutchinson U.S.A.
141 D3 Hutchinson Island U.S.A.
70 B2 Hutuo He r. China
100 B2 Huy Belgium
70 C2 Huzhou China
92 □C3 Hvalnes Iceland
92 □B3 Hvannadalshnúkur vol. Iceland
109 C2 Hvar Croatia
109 C2 Hvar i. Croatia
91 C2 Hvardys'ke Ukr.
120 B2 Hwange Zimbabwe
Hwang Ho r. China see Yellow River
136 C2 Hyannis U.S.A.
68 C1 Hyargas Nuur salt l. Mongolia
50 A3 Hyden Austr.
73 B3 Hyderabad India
74 A2 Hyderabad Pak.
Hydra i. Greece see Ydra
105 D3 Hyères France
105 D3 Hyères, Îles d' is France
65 B1 Hyesan N. Korea
128 B2 Hyland Post Can.
67 B3 Hyōno-sen mt. Japan
99 D4 Hythe U.K.
67 B4 Hyūga Japan
93 H3 Hyvinkää Fin.

I

114 B2 Iabès, Erg des. Alg.
150 C3 Iaco r. Brazil
110 C2 Ialomiţa r. Romania
110 C1 Ianca Romania

77 C1 **Kokshetau** Kazakh.
131 D2 **Koksoak** r. Can.
103 D1 **Kokstad** S. Africa
123 C3 **Koktokay** China see Fuyun
61 D2 **Kolaka** Indon.
86 C2 **Kola Peninsula** Rus. Fed.
92 H2 **Kolari** Fin.
Kolarovgrad Bulg. see Shumen
114 A3 **Kolda** Senegal
93 E4 **Kolding** Denmark
119 C2 **Kole** Dem. Rep. Congo
107 D2 **Koléa** Alg.
86 D2 **Kolguyev, Ostrov** i. Rus. Fed.
73 B3 **Kolhapur** India
88 B2 **Kolkasrags** pt Latvia
75 C2 **Kolkata** India
Kollam India see Quilon
100 C1 **Kollum** Neth.
Köln Ger. see Cologne
103 D1 **Koło** Pol.
103 D1 **Kołobrzeg** Pol.
114 B3 **Kolokani** Mali
89 E2 **Kolomna** Rus. Fed.
90 B2 **Kolomyya** Ukr.
114 B3 **Kolondiéba** Mali
61 D2 **Kolonedale** Indon.
122 B2 **Kolonkwaneng** Botswana
82 G3 **Kolpashevo** Rus. Fed.
89 E3 **Kolpny** Rus. Fed.
Kol'skiy Poluostrov pen. Rus. Fed. see Kola Peninsula
78 B3 **Koluli** Eritrea
92 F3 **Kolvereid** Norway
119 C4 **Kolwezi** Dem. Rep. Congo
83 L2 **Kolyma** r. Rus. Fed.
Kolyma Lowland Rus. Fed. see Kolymskaya Nizmennost'
Kolyma Range mts Rus. Fed. see Kolymskiy, Khrebet
83 L2 **Kolymskaya Nizmennost'** lowland Rus. Fed.
83 M2 **Kolymskiy, Khrebet** mts Rus. Fed.
122 A2 **Komaggas** S. Africa
67 C3 **Komaki** Japan
83 M3 **Komandorskiye Ostrova** is Rus. Fed.
103 D2 **Komárno** Slovakia
123 D2 **Komati** r. Swaziland
123 D2 **Komatipoort** S. Africa
67 C3 **Komatsu** Japan
120 A2 **Kombat** Namibia
119 C3 **Kombe** Dem. Rep. Congo
Komintern Ukr. see Marhanets'
90 C2 **Kominternivs'ke** Ukr.
109 C2 **Komiža** Croatia
103 D2 **Komló** Hungary
Kommunarsk Ukr. see Alchevs'k
118 B3 **Komono** Congo
111 C2 **Komotini** Greece
Kompong Som Cambodia see Sihanoukville
Komrat Moldova see Comrat
122 B3 **Komsberg** mts S. Africa
83 H1 **Komsomolets, Ostrov** i. Rus. Fed.
89 F2 **Komsomol'sk** Rus. Fed.
91 C2 **Komsomol's'k** Ukr.
83 M2 **Komsomol'skiy** Rus. Fed.
Komsomol'skiy Rus. Fed. see Yugorsk
87 D4 **Komsomol'skiy** Rus. Fed.
83 K3 **Komsomol'sk-na-Amure** Rus. Fed.
89 E2 **Konakovo** Rus. Fed.
75 C3 **Kondagaon** India
86 F2 **Kondinskoye** Rus. Fed.
Kondinskoye Rus. Fed. see Oktyabr'skoye
119 D3 **Kondoa** Tanz.
89 F2 **Kondopoga** Rus. Fed.
89 E3 **Kondrovo** Rus. Fed.
127 J2 **Kong Christian IX Land** reg. Greenland
127 K2 **Kong Christian X Land** reg. Greenland
127 J2 **Kong Frederik VI Kyst** coastal area Greenland
65 B2 **Kongju** S. Korea
119 C3 **Kongolo** Dem. Rep. Congo
93 E4 **Kongsberg** Norway
93 F3 **Kongsvinger** Norway
77 U3 **Kongur Shan** mt. China

100 C2 **Königswinter** Ger.
103 D1 **Konin** Pol.
109 C2 **Konjic** Bos.-Herz.
122 A2 **Konkiep** watercourse Namibia
86 D2 **Konosha** Rus. Fed.
91 C1 **Konotop** Ukr.
103 E1 **Końskie** Pol.
Konstantinograd Ukr. see Krasnohrad
102 B2 **Konstanz** Ger.
115 C3 **Kontagora** Nigeria
63 B2 **Kon Tum** Vietnam
63 B2 **Kon Tum, Cao Nguyên** Vietnam
80 B2 **Konya** Turkey
77 D2 **Konyrat** Kazakh.
100 C3 **Konz** Ger.
86 E3 **Konzhakovskiy Kamen', Gora** mt. Rus. Fed.
134 C1 **Kooskia** U.S.A.
128 C3 **Kootenay Lake** Can.
53 D2 **Kootingal** Austr.
122 B3 **Kootjieskolk** S. Africa
92 B2 **Kópasker** Iceland
108 B1 **Koper** Slovenia
93 G4 **Köping** Sweden
123 C1 **Kopong** Botswana
93 G4 **Kopparberg** Sweden
109 C1 **Koprivnica** Croatia
89 F3 **Korablino** Rus. Fed.
73 C3 **Koraput** India
101 D2 **Korbach** Ger.
109 D2 **Korçë** Albania
109 C2 **Korčula** Croatia
109 C2 **Korčula** i. Croatia
65 B1 **Korea, North** country Asia
65 B2 **Korea, South** country Asia
70 C2 **Korea Bay** g. China/N. Korea
65 B3 **Korea Strait** Japan/S. Korea
89 D3 **Korenëvo** Rus. Fed.
91 D2 **Korenovsk** Rus. Fed.
Korenovskaya Rus. Fed. see Korenovsk
90 B1 **Korets'** Ukr.
111 C2 **Körfez** Turkey
114 B4 **Korhogo** Côte d'Ivoire
Korinthos Greece see Corinth
103 D2 **Koris-hegy** hill Hungary
109 D2 **Koritnik** mt. Albania
Koritsa Albania see Korçë
67 D3 **Kōriyama** Japan
87 F3 **Korkino** Rus. Fed.
111 D3 **Korkuteli** Turkey
77 E2 **Korla** China
103 D2 **Körmend** Hungary
49 I5 **Koro** i. Fiji
114 B3 **Koro** Mali
131 D2 **Koroc** r. Can.
91 D1 **Korocha** Rus. Fed.
119 D3 **Korogwe** Tanz.
103 E2 **Körös** r. Romania
90 B1 **Korosten'** Ukr.
90 B1 **Korostyshiv** Ukr.
115 D3 **Koro Toro** Chad
93 H3 **Korpo** Fin.
66 D1 **Korsakov** Rus. Fed.
91 C2 **Korsun'-Shevchenkivs'kyy** Ukr.
103 E1 **Korsze** Pol.
116 B3 **Korti** Sudan
100 A2 **Kortrijk** Belgium
83 L3 **Koryakskaya, Sopka** vol. Rus. Fed.
83 M2 **Koryakskiy Khrebet** mts Rus. Fed.
86 D2 **Koryazhma** Rus. Fed.
65 B2 **Koryŏng** S. Korea
91 C1 **Koryukivka** Ukr.
111 C3 **Kos** Greece
111 C3 **Kos** i. Greece
91 D2 **Kosa Biryuchyy Ostriv** i. Ukr.
65 B2 **Kosan** N. Korea
103 D1 **Kościan** Pol.
Kosciusko, Mount Austr. see Kosciuszko, Mount
53 C3 **Kosciuszko, Mount** Austr.
77 E2 **Kosh-Agach** Rus. Fed.
67 A4 **Koshikijima-rettō** is Japan
103 E2 **Košice** Slovakia
92 H2 **Koskullskulle** Sweden
65 B2 **Kosŏng** N. Korea
109 D2 **Kosovo** prov. Serbia
109 D2 **Kosovska Mitrovica** Serbia

48 H3 **Kosrae** atoll Micronesia
114 B4 **Kossou, Lac de** l. Côte d'Ivoire
76 C1 **Kostanay** Kazakh.
110 B2 **Kostenets** Bulg.
123 C2 **Koster** S. Africa
116 B3 **Kosti** Sudan
92 J3 **Kostomuksha** Rus. Fed.
90 B1 **Kostopil'** Ukr.
89 F2 **Kostroma** Rus. Fed.
89 F2 **Kostroma** r. Rus. Fed.
102 C1 **Kostrzyn** Pol.
91 D2 **Kostyantynivka** Ukr.
103 D1 **Koszalin** Pol.
103 D2 **Kőszeg** Hungary
74 B2 **Kota** India
60 B2 **Kotaagung** Indon.
61 C2 **Kotabaru** Indon.
61 C1 **Kota Belud** Sabah Malaysia
60 B1 **Kota Bharu** Malaysia
60 B2 **Kotabumi** Indon.
61 C1 **Kota Kinabalu** Sabah Malaysia
75 C3 **Kotaparh** India
61 C1 **Kota Samarahan** Sarawak Malaysia
86 D3 **Kotel'nich** Rus. Fed.
87 D4 **Kotel'nikovo** Rus. Fed.
83 K1 **Kotel'nyy, Ostrov** i. Rus. Fed.
91 C1 **Kotel'va** Ukr.
101 E2 **Köthen (Anhalt)** Ger.
119 D2 **Kotido** Uganda
93 I3 **Kotka** Fin.
86 D2 **Kotlas** Rus. Fed.
126 B2 **Kotlik** U.S.A.
115 C3 **Kotorkoshi** Nigeria
109 C2 **Kotor Varoš** Bos.-Herz.
87 D3 **Kotovo** Rus. Fed.
91 E1 **Kotovsk** Rus. Fed.
90 B2 **Kotovs'k** Ukr.
73 C3 **Kottagudem** India
118 C2 **Kotto** r. C.A.R.
83 H2 **Kotuy** r. Rus. Fed.
126 B2 **Kotzebue** U.S.A.
126 B2 **Kotzebue Sound** sea chan. U.S.A.
114 A3 **Koubia** Guinea
100 A2 **Koudekerke** Neth.
114 B3 **Koudougou** Burkina
122 B3 **Kougaberge** mts S. Africa
118 B3 **Koulamoutou** Gabon
114 B3 **Koulikoro** Mali
118 B2 **Koum** Cameroon
118 B2 **Koumra** Chad
114 A3 **Koundâra** Guinea
Kounradskiy Kazakh. see Konyrat
151 D2 **Kourou** Fr. Guiana
114 B3 **Kouroussa** Guinea
115 D3 **Kousséri** Cameroon
114 B3 **Koutiala** Mali
93 I3 **Kouvola** Fin.
109 D1 **Kovačica** Serbia
92 J2 **Kovdor** Rus. Fed.
90 A1 **Kovel'** Ukr.
Kovno Lith. see Kaunas
89 F2 **Kovrov** Rus. Fed.
51 D1 **Kowanyama** Austr.
54 B2 **Kowhitirangi** N.Z.
111 C3 **Köyceğiz** Turkey
86 D2 **Koyda** Rus. Fed.
126 B2 **Koyukuk** r. U.S.A.
111 B2 **Kozani** Greece
90 C1 **Kozelets'** Ukr.
89 E3 **Kozel'sk** Rus. Fed.
Kozhikode India see Calicut
90 B2 **Kozyatyn** Ukr.
114 C4 **Kpalimé** Togo
63 A2 **Kra, Isthmus of** Thai.
63 A3 **Krabi** Thai.
63 A2 **Kra Buri** Thai.
63 B2 **Krâchéh** Cambodia
93 E4 **Kragerø** Norway
100 B1 **Kraggenburg** Neth.
109 D2 **Kragujevac** Serbia
60 B2 **Krakatau** i. Indon.
103 D1 **Kraków** Pol.
109 D2 **Kraljevo** Serbia
91 D2 **Kramators'k** Ukr.
93 G3 **Kramfors** Sweden
111 B3 **Kranidi** Greece
108 B1 **Kranj** Slovenia
123 G3 **Kranskop** S. Africa
91 E2 **Krasino** Rus. Fed.
88 C2 **Krāslava** Latvia
101 F2 **Kraslice** Czech Rep.
89 D3 **Krasnapollye** Belarus
89 D3 **Krasnaya Gora** Rus. Fed.

89 F2 **Krasnaya Gorbatka** Rus. Fed.
Krasnoarmeysk Kazakh. see Tayynsha
87 D3 **Krasnoarmeysk** Rus. Fed.
Krasnoarmeyskaya Rus. Fed. see Poltavskaya
91 D2 **Krasnoarmiys'k** Ukr.
86 D2 **Krasnoborsk** Rus. Fed.
91 D2 **Krasnodar** Rus. Fed.
91 D2 **Krasnodon** Ukr.
88 C2 **Krasnogorodskoye** Rus. Fed.
91 D1 **Krasnogvardeyskoye** Rus. Fed.
91 D2 **Krasnohrad** Ukr.
91 C2 **Krasnohvardiys'ke** Ukr.
86 E3 **Krasnokamsk** Rus. Fed.
89 D2 **Krasnomayskiy** Rus. Fed.
91 C2 **Krasnoperekops'k** Ukr.
87 D3 **Krasnoslobodsk** Rus. Fed.
86 F3 **Krasnotur'insk** Rus. Fed.
86 E3 **Krasnoufimsk** Rus. Fed.
86 E2 **Krasnovishersk** Rus. Fed.
Krasnovodsk Turkm. see Türkmenbaşy
83 H3 **Krasnoyarsk** Rus. Fed.
89 E3 **Krasnoye** Rus. Fed.
83 M2 **Krasnoye, Ozero** l. Rus. Fed.
89 F2 **Krasnoye-na-Volge** Rus. Fed.
103 E1 **Krasnystaw** Pol.
89 D3 **Krasnyy** Rus. Fed.
Krasnyy Kamyshanik Rus. Fed. see Komsomol'skiy
89 E2 **Krasnyy Kholm** Rus. Fed.
91 D2 **Krasnyy Luch** Ukr.
91 C2 **Krasnyy Sulin** Rus. Fed.
90 B2 **Krasyliv** Ukr.
Kraulshavn Greenland see Nuussuaq
100 C2 **Krefeld** Ger.
91 C2 **Kremenchuk** Ukr.
91 C2 **Kremenchuts'ka Vodoskhovyshche** resr Ukr.
90 B1 **Kremenets'** Ukr.
103 D2 **Kremešník** hill Czech Rep.
Kremges Ukr. see Svitlovods'k
91 D2 **Kreminna** Ukr.
136 B2 **Kremmling** U.S.A.
103 D2 **Krems an der Donau** Austria
89 D2 **Kresttsy** Rus. Fed.
88 B2 **Kretinga** Lith.
100 C2 **Kreuzau** Ger.
101 C2 **Kreuztal** Ger.
118 A2 **Kribi** Cameroon
123 C2 **Kriel** S. Africa
111 B3 **Krikellos** Greece
66 D1 **Kril'on, Mys** c. Rus. Fed.
111 B3 **Krios, Akrotirio** pt Greece
73 C3 **Krishna** r. India
73 C3 **Krishna, Mouths of the** India
75 C2 **Krishnanagar** India
93 E4 **Kristiansand** Norway
93 F4 **Kristianstad** Sweden
92 E3 **Kristiansund** Norway
93 F4 **Kristinehamn** Sweden
Kristinopol' Ukr. see Chervonohrad
127 J2 **Kronprins Frederik Bjerge** nunataks Greenland
123 C2 **Kroonstad** S. Africa
91 E2 **Kropotkin** Rus. Fed.
103 E2 **Krosno** Pol.
103 D1 **Krotoszyn** Pol.
61 C2 **Krui** Indon.
122 B3 **Kruisfontein** S. Africa
109 C2 **Krujë** Albania
111 C2 **Krumovgrad** Bulg.
Krung Thep Thai. see Bangkok

97 C1 Lisburn U.K.
97 B2 Liscannor Bay Ireland
97 B2 Lisdoonvarna Ireland
Lishi China see Dingnan
71 B3 Lishui China
104 C2 Lisieux France
99 A4 Liskeard U.K.
89 E3 Liski Rus. Fed.
53 D1 Lismore Austr.
97 C1 Lismore Ireland
97 C1 Lisnaskea U.K.
97 B2 Listowel Ireland
71 A3 Litang Guangxi China
68 C2 Litang Sichuan China
138 B3 Litchfield IL U.S.A.
137 E1 Litchfield MN U.S.A.
53 D2 Litghow Austr.
111 B3 Lithino, Akrotirio pt Greece
88 B2 Lithuania country Europe
111 B2 Litochoro Greece
102 C1 Litoměřice Czech Rep.
Litovskaya S.S.R. country Europe see Lithuania
146 C2 Little Abaco i. Bahamas
73 D3 Little Andaman i. India
141 E3 Little Bahama Bank sea feature Bahamas
93 E4 Little Belt sea chan. Denmark
146 B3 Little Cayman i. Cayman Is
142 A1 Little Colorado r. U.S.A.
138 C I Little Current Can.
137 E1 Little Falls U.S.A.
143 C2 Littlefield U.S.A.
99 C4 Littlehampton U.K.
122 A2 Little Karas Berg plat. Namibia
122 B3 Little Karoo plat. S. Africa
96 A2 Little Minch sea chan. U.K.
136 C1 Little Missouri r. U.S.A.
73 D4 Little Nicobar i. India
140 B2 Little Rock U.S.A.
139 E2 Littleton U.S.A.
121 C2 Litunde Moz.
90 B2 Lityn Ukr.
Liuchow China see Liuzhou
70 B2 Liujiachang China
Liupanshui China see Lupanshui
121 C2 Liupo Moz.
71 A3 Liuzhou China
113 B3 Livadeia Greece
88 C2 Livâni Latvia
142 C1 Live Oak U.S.A.
50 B1 Liveringa Austr.
53 D2 Livermore, Mount U.S.A.
131 D3 Liverpool Austr.
98 B3 Liverpool Can.
98 B3 Liverpool U.K.
127 G2 Liverpool, Cape Can.
53 C2 Liverpool Range mts Austr.
96 C3 Livingston U.K.
134 D1 Livingston MT U.S.A.
143 E2 Livingston TX U.S.A.
143 D2 Livingston, Lake U.S.A.
120 B2 Livingstone Zambia
55 A3 Livingston Island Antarctica
109 C2 Livno Bos.-Herz.
89 E3 Livny Rus. Fed.
138 C2 Livonia U.S.A.
108 B2 Livorno Italy
119 D3 Liwale Tanz.
99 A5 Lizard Point U.K.
108 B1 Ljubljana Slovenia
93 G3 Ljungan r. Sweden
93 F4 Ljungby Sweden
93 G3 Ljusdal Sweden
93 G3 Ljusnan r. Sweden
99 B4 Llandeilo U.K.
99 B4 Llandovery U.K.
99 B3 Llandrindod Wells U.K.
98 B3 Llandudno U.K.
99 A4 Llanelli U.K.
106 C1 Llanes Spain
98 A3 Llangefni U.K.
99 B3 Llangollen U.K.
99 B3 Llangurig U.K.
143 C2 Llano Estacado plain U.S.A.
150 C2 Llanos reg. Col./Venez.
107 D1 Lleida Spain
99 A3 Lleyn Peninsula U.K.
107 C2 Lliria Spain
106 C1 Llodio Spain
128 B2 Lloyd George, Mount Can.

129 D2 Lloyd Lake Can.
129 C2 Lloydminster Can.
152 B2 Llullaillaco, Volcán vol. Chile
154 B2 Loanda Brazil
123 C2 Lobatse Botswana
103 D1 Łobez Pol.
120 A2 Lobito Angola
101 F1 Loburg Ger.
96 B2 Lochaber mts U.K.
96 B2 Lochaline U.K.
96 A1 Loch a' Tuath U.K.
Loch Baghasdail U.K. see Lochboisdale
96 A2 Lochboisdale U.K.
104 C2 Loches France
96 B2 Lochgilphead U.K.
96 B1 Lochinver U.K.
96 A2 Lochmaddy U.K.
96 C2 Lochnagar mt. U.K.
Loch nam Madadh U.K. see Lochmaddy
96 B3 Lochranza U.K.
52 A2 Lock Austr.
96 C3 Lockerbie U.K.
53 C3 Lockhart Austr.
143 D3 Lockhart U.S.A.
51 D1 Lockhart River Austr.
139 D2 Lock Haven U.S.A.
139 D2 Lockport U.S.A.
63 B2 Lôc Ninh Vietnam
105 C3 Lodève France
86 C2 Lodeynoye Pole Rus. Fed.
74 B2 Lodhran Pak.
108 A1 Lodi Italy
135 B3 Lodi U.S.A.
92 F2 Loding Norway
92 G2 Lødingen Norway
118 C3 Lodja Dem. Rep. Congo
119 D2 Lodwar Kenya
103 D1 Łódź Pol.
62 B2 Loei Thai.
122 A3 Loeriesfontein S. Africa
92 F2 Lofoten is Norway
134 D2 Logan U.S.A.
128 A1 Logan, Mount Can.
138 B2 Logansport U.S.A.
108 B1 Logatec Slovenia
115 D3 Logone r. Africa
106 C1 Logroño Spain
93 H3 Lohja Fin.
101 D1 Löhne Ger.
101 D1 Lohne (Oldenburg) Ger.
62 A2 Loikaw Myanmar
62 A2 Loi Lan mt. Myanmar/Thai.
93 H3 Loimaa Fin.
104 B2 Loire r. France
150 B3 Loja Ecuador
106 C2 Loja Spain
92 I2 Lokan tekojärvi i. Fin.
100 B2 Lokeren Belgium
122 B1 Lokgwabe Botswana
91 C1 Lokhvytsya Ukr.
119 D2 Lokichar Kenya
119 D2 Lokichokio Kenya
93 F4 Løkken Denmark
89 D2 Loknya Rus. Fed.
115 C4 Lokoja Nigeria
89 D3 Lokot' Rus. Fed.
88 C2 Loksa Estonia
127 H2 Loks Land i. Can.
114 B4 Lola Guinea
93 F5 Lolland i. Denmark
119 D3 Lollondo Tanz.
118 C2 Lolo Dem. Rep. Congo
122 B2 Lolwane S. Africa
110 B2 Lom Bulg.
93 E3 Lom Norway
119 C2 Lomami r. Dem. Rep. Congo
153 C3 Lomas de Zamora Arg.
50 B1 Lombardina Austr.
61 C2 Lombok i. Indon.
61 C2 Lombok, Selat sea chan. Indon.
114 C4 Lomé Togo
118 C3 Loméla r. Dem. Rep. Congo
100 B2 Lommel Belgium
96 B2 Lomond, Loch l. U.K.
88 C2 Lomonosov Rus. Fed.
160 A1 Lomonosov Ridge sea feature Arctic Ocean
61 C2 Lompobattang, Gunung mt. Indon.
135 B4 Lompoc U.S.A.
63 B2 Lom Sak Thai.
103 E1 Łomża Pol.
130 B3 London Can.
99 C4 London U.K.
138 C3 London U.S.A.

97 C1 Londonderry U.K.
50 B1 Londonderry, Cape Austr.
154 B2 Londrina Brazil
135 C3 Lone Pine U.S.A.
83 M2 Longa, Proliv sea chan. Rus. Fed.
61 C1 Long Akah Sarawak Malaysia
141 E2 Long Bay U.S.A.
135 C4 Long Beach U.S.A.
71 A3 Longchang China
99 C3 Long Eaton U.K.
97 C2 Longford Ireland
96 C1 Longhope U.K.
119 D3 Longido Tanz.
61 C2 Longiram Indon.
147 C2 Long Island Bahamas
130 C2 Long Island Can.
59 D3 Long Island P.N.G.
139 E2 Long Island U.S.A.
130 B3 Longlac Can.
130 B3 Long Lake Can.
71 A3 Longli China
71 A3 Longming China
136 B2 Longmont U.S.A.
70 A2 Longnan China
Longping China see Longli
138 C2 Long Point Can.
71 B3 Longquan China
131 E3 Long Range Mountains Can.
51 D2 Longreach Austr.
Longshan China see Longli
99 D3 Long Stratton U.K.
98 B2 Longtown U.K.
105 D2 Longuyon France
143 E2 Longview TX U.S.A.
134 B1 Longview WA U.S.A.
61 C1 Longwai Malaysia
70 A2 Longxi China
Longxian China see Wengyuan
71 B3 Longxi Shan mt. China
63 B2 Long Xuyên Vietnam
71 B3 Longyan China
82 C1 Longyearbyen Svalbard
108 B1 Lonigo Italy
100 C1 Löningen Ger.
105 D2 Lons-le-Saunier France
141 E2 Lookout, Cape U.S.A.
119 D3 Loolmalasin vol. crater Tanz.
50 B3 Loongana Austr.
97 B2 Loop Head hd Ireland
Lopasnya Rus. Fed. see Chekhov
63 B2 Lop Buri Thai.
64 B2 Lopez Phil.
118 A3 Lopez, Cap c. Gabon
68 C2 Lop Nur salt l. China
110 D2 Lopori r. Dem. Rep. Congo
92 H1 Lopphavet b. Norway
106 B2 Lora del Río Spain
138 C2 Lorain U.S.A.
74 A1 Loralai Pak.
107 C2 Lorca Spain
51 E3 Lord Howe Island Austr.
142 B2 Lordsburg U.S.A.
155 C2 Lorena Brazil
59 D3 Lorengau P.N.G.
59 D3 Lorentz r. Indon.
152 B1 Loreto Bol.
144 A2 Loreto Mex.
104 B2 Lorient France
96 B2 Lorn, Firth of est. U.K.
52 B3 Lorne Austr.
105 D2 Lorraine reg. France
142 B1 Los Alamos U.S.A.
143 D3 Los Aldamas Mex.
153 A3 Los Ángeles Chile
135 C4 Los Angeles U.S.A.
135 B3 Los Banos U.S.A.
152 B3 Los Blancos Arg.
89 F3 Losevo Rus. Fed.
108 B2 Lošinj i. Croatia
144 B2 Los Mochis Mex.
118 B2 Losombo Dem. Rep. Congo
106 B2 Los Pedroches plat. Spain
147 D3 Los Roques, Islas is Venez.
96 C1 Lossiemouth U.K.
150 C1 Los Teques Venez.
59 E3 Losuia P.N.G.
152 A3 Los Vilos Chile
104 C2 Lot r. France
96 C1 Loth U.K.
134 D1 Lothair U.S.A.

Lothringen reg. France see Lorraine
119 D2 Lotikipi Plain Kenya
118 C3 Loto Dem. Rep. Congo
89 E2 Lotoshino Rus. Fed.
62 B1 Louangnamtha Laos
62 B2 Louangphabang Laos
118 B3 Loubomo Congo
104 B2 Loudéac France
71 B3 Loudi China
118 B3 Loudima Congo
114 A3 Louga Senegal
99 C3 Loughborough U.K.
97 B2 Loughrea Ireland
105 D2 Louhans France
97 B2 Louisburgh Ireland
51 E1 Louisiade Archipelago is P.N.G.
140 B2 Louisiana state U.S.A.
138 B3 Louisville KY U.S.A.
140 C2 Louisville MS U.S.A.
86 C2 Loukhi Rus. Fed.
118 B3 Loukoléla Congo
106 B2 Loulé Port.
118 A2 Loum Cameroon
130 C2 Loups Marins, Lacs des lakes Can.
104 B3 Lourdes France
151 D2 Lourenço Brazil
Lourenço Marques Moz. see Maputo
119 B2 Lousã Port.
53 C2 Louth Austr.
98 C3 Louth U.K.
Louvain Belgium see Leuven
122 A1 Louwater-Suid Namibia
89 D2 Lovat' r. Rus. Fed.
110 B2 Lovech Bulg.
136 B2 Loveland U.S.A.
136 B2 Lovell U.S.A.
135 C2 Lovelock U.S.A.
88 C1 Loviisa Fin.
143 C2 Lovington U.S.A.
86 C2 Lovozero Rus. Fed.
119 C3 Lowa Dem. Rep. Congo
139 E2 Lowell U.S.A.
119 D2 Lowelli Sudan
128 C3 Lower Arrow Lake Can.
Lower California pen. Mex. see Baja California
54 B2 Lower Hutt N.Z.
97 C1 Lower Lough Erne l. U.K.
128 B2 Lower Post Can.
137 E1 Lower Red Lake U.S.A.
Lower Tunguska r. Rus. Fed. see Nizhnyaya Tunguska
99 D3 Lowestoft U.K.
103 D1 Łowicz Pol.
139 D2 Lowville U.S.A.
52 B2 Luxton Austr.
Loyang China see Luoyang
48 H6 Loyauté, Îles New Caledonia
89 D3 Loyew Belarus
92 F2 Løypskardtinden mt. Norway
109 C2 Loznica Serbia
91 D2 Lozova Ukr.
120 B2 Luacano Angola
70 B2 Lu'an China
120 A1 Luanda Angola
63 B3 Luang, Thale lag. Thai.
121 C2 Luangwa r. Zambia
121 B2 Luanshya Zambia
Luau Angola see Luau
106 B1 Luarca Spain
120 B2 Luau Angola
103 E1 Lubaczów Pol.
103 D1 Lubań Pol.
64 A2 Lubang Islands Phil.
120 A2 Lubango Angola
119 C3 Lubao Dem. Rep. Congo
103 E1 Lubartów Pol.
101 D1 Lübbecke Ger.
102 C1 Lübben Ger.
143 C2 Lubbock U.S.A.
101 E1 Lübeck Ger.
69 E1 Lubei China
77 C1 Lubenka Kazakh.
119 C3 Lubero Dem. Rep. Congo
103 D1 Lubin Pol.
103 E1 Lublin Pol.
91 C1 Lubny Ukr.
61 C1 Lubok Antu Sarawak Malaysia
101 E1 Lübow Ger.
101 E1 Lübtheen Ger.
119 C3 Lubudi Dem. Rep. Congo
60 B2 Lubuklinggau Indon.

119 C4 **Lubumbashi** Dem. Rep. Congo
120 B2 **Lubungu** Zambia
119 C3 **Lubutu** Dem. Rep. Congo
120 A1 **Lucala** Angola
97 C2 **Lucan** Ireland
120 B1 **Lucapa** Angola
108 B2 **Lucca** Italy
96 B3 **Luce Bay** U.K.
154 B2 **Lucélia** Brazil
64 B2 **Lucena** Phil.
106 C2 **Lucena** Spain
103 D2 **Lučenec** Slovakia
109 C2 **Lucera** Italy
105 D2 **Lucerne** Switz.
66 B1 **Luchegorsk** Rus. Fed.
101 E1 **Lüchow** Ger.
120 A2 **Lucira** Angola
Łuck Ukr. *see* Luts'k
101 F1 **Luckenwalde** Ger.
122 B2 **Luckhoff** S. Africa
75 C2 **Lucknow** India
120 A1 **Lucunga** Angola
120 B2 **Lucusse** Angola
Lüda China *see* Dalian
100 C2 **Lüdenscheid** Ger.
101 E1 **Lüder** Ger.
120 A3 **Lüderitz** Namibia
119 D4 **Ludewa** Tanz.
74 B1 **Ludhiana** India
138 B2 **Ludington** U.S.A.
99 B3 **Ludlow** U.K.
135 C4 **Ludlow** U.S.A.
110 C2 **Ludogorie** *reg.* Bulg.
93 G3 **Ludvika** Sweden
102 B2 **Ludwigsburg** Ger.
101 F1 **Ludwigsfelde** Ger.
101 D3 **Ludwigshafen am Rhein** Ger.
101 E1 **Ludwigslust** Ger.
88 C2 **Ludza** Latvia
118 C3 **Luebo** Dem. Rep. Congo
120 A2 **Luena** Angola
70 A2 **Lüeyang** China
71 B3 **Lufeng** China
119 C3 **Lufira** *r.* Dem. Rep. Congo
143 E2 **Lufkin** U.S.A.
88 C2 **Luga** Rus. Fed.
88 C2 **Luga** *r.* Rus. Fed.
105 D2 **Lugano** Switz.
121 C2 **Lugenda** *r.* Moz.
97 C2 **Lugnaquilla** *hill* Ireland
106 B1 **Lugo** Spain
110 B1 **Lugoj** Romania
91 D2 **Luhans'k** Ukr.
119 D3 **Luhombero** Tanz.
90 B1 **Luhyny** Ukr.
120 B2 **Luiana** Angola
Luichow Peninsula China *see* Leizhou Bandao
118 C3 **Luilaka** *r.* Dem. Rep. Congo
Luimneach Ireland *see* Limerick
105 D2 **Luino** Italy
92 I2 **Luiro** *r.* Fin.
118 C3 **Luiza** Dem. Rep. Congo
70 B2 **Lujiang** China
Lukapa Angola *see* Lucapa
109 C2 **Lukavac** Bos.-Herz.
118 B3 **Lukenie** *r.* Dem. Rep. Congo
142 A2 **Lukeville** U.S.A.
89 E3 **Lukhovitsy** Rus. Fed.
Lukou China *see* Zhuzhou
103 E1 **Łuków** Pol.
120 B2 **Lukulu** Zambia
92 H2 **Luleå** Sweden
92 H2 **Luleälven** *r.* Sweden
111 C2 **Lüleburgaz** Turkey
70 B2 **Lüliang Shan** *mts* China
143 D3 **Luling** U.S.A.
Luluabourg Dem. Rep. Congo *see* Kananga
61 C2 **Lumajang** Indon.
75 C1 **Lumajangdong Co** *salt l.* China
Lumbala Angola *see* Lumbala N'guimbo
Lumbala Kaquengue Angola *see* Lumbala Kaquengue
120 B2 **Lumbala Kaquengue** Angola
120 B2 **Lumbala N'guimbo** Angola
140 C2 **Lumberton** MS U.S.A.
141 E2 **Lumberton** NC U.S.A.
61 C1 **Lumbis** Indon.
106 B1 **Lumbrales** Spain
63 B2 **Lumphăt** Cambodia

129 D2 **Lumsden** Can.
54 A3 **Lumsden** N.Z.
93 F4 **Lund** Sweden
121 C2 **Lundazi** Zambia
99 A4 **Lundy** U.K.
101 E1 **Lüneburg** Ger.
101 E1 **Lüneburger Heide** *reg.* Ger.
100 C2 **Lünen** Ger.
105 D2 **Lunéville** France
120 B2 **Lunga** *r.* Zambia
114 A4 **Lungi** Sierra Leone
Lungleh India *see* Lunglei
75 D2 **Lunglei** India
120 B2 **Lungwebungu** *r.* Zambia
74 B2 **Luni** *r.* India
88 C3 **Luninyets** Belarus
104 C3 **L'Union** France
114 A4 **Lunsar** Sierra Leone
77 E2 **Luntai** China
71 A3 **Luodian** China
71 B3 **Luoding** China
70 B2 **Luohe** China
70 B2 **Luoyang** China
118 B3 **Luozi** Dem. Rep. Congo
121 B2 **Lupane** Zimbabwe
71 A3 **Lupanshui** China
110 B1 **Lupeni** Romania
121 C2 **Lupilichi** Moz.
101 F2 **Luppa** Ger.
95 B3 **Lurgan** U.K.
Luring China *see* Gêrzê
121 D2 **Lúrio** Moz.
121 D2 **Lurio** *r.* Moz.
92 F2 **Lurøy** Norway
121 B2 **Lusaka** Zambia
118 C3 **Lusambo** Dem. Rep. Congo
109 C2 **Lushnjë** Albania
70 C2 **Lüshun** China
123 C3 **Lusikisiki** S. Africa
136 C2 **Lusk** U.S.A.
Luso Angola *see* Luena
101 F2 **Lutherstadt Wittenberg** Ger.
99 C4 **Luton** U.K.
61 C1 **Lutong** Sarawak Malaysia
129 C1 **Łutselk'e** Can.
90 B1 **Luts'k** Ukr.
55 F3 **Lützow-Holm Bay** Antarctica
122 B2 **Lutzputs** S. Africa
122 A3 **Lutzville** S. Africa
117 C4 **Luuq** Somalia
137 D2 **Luverne** U.S.A.
119 C3 **Luvua** *r.* Dem. Rep. Congo
120 B2 **Luvuei** Angola
123 D1 **Luvuvhu** *r.* S. Africa
119 D3 **Luwego** *r.* Tanz.
119 D2 **Luwero** Uganda
61 D2 **Luwuk** Indon.
100 C3 **Luxembourg** *country* Europe
100 C3 **Luxembourg** Lux.
105 D2 **Luxeuil-les-Bains** France
62 A1 **Luxi** China
123 C3 **Luxolweni** S. Africa
116 B2 **Luxor** Egypt
100 B2 **Luyksgestel** Neth.
86 D2 **Luza** Rus. Fed.
Luzern Switz. *see* Lucerne
62 B1 **Luzhai** China
71 A3 **Luzhi** China
71 A3 **Luzhou** China
154 C1 **Luziânia** Brazil
151 E3 **Luzilândia** Brazil
64 B2 **Luzon** *i.* Phil.
64 B1 **Luzon Strait** Phil.
109 C3 **Luzzi** Italy
90 A2 **L'viv** Ukr.
L'vov Ukr. *see* L'viv
Lwów Ukr. *see* L'viv
88 C3 **Lyakhavichy** Belarus
Lyallpur Pak. *see* Faisalabad
89 D2 **Lychkovo** Rus. Fed.
92 G3 **Lycksele** Sweden
55 C2 **Lyddan Island** Antarctica
123 D2 **Lydenburg** S. Africa
88 C3 **Lyel'chytsy** Belarus
88 C3 **Lyepyel'** Belarus
136 A2 **Lyman** U.S.A.
99 B4 **Lyme Bay** U.K.
99 B4 **Lyme Regis** U.K.
139 D3 **Lynchburg** U.S.A.
53 D2 **Lyndhurst** Austr.
129 D2 **Lynn Lake** Can.
134 B1 **Lynnwood** U.S.A.
129 D1 **Lynx Lake** Can.
105 C2 **Lyon** France
Lyons France *see* Lyon

89 D2 **Lyozna** Belarus
103 E1 **Łysica** *hill* Pol.
86 E3 **Lys'va** Rus. Fed.
91 D2 **Lysychans'k** Ukr.
87 D3 **Lysyye Gory** Rus. Fed.
98 B3 **Lytham St Anne's** U.K.
88 C3 **Lyuban'** Belarus
90 C2 **Lyubashivka** Ukr.
89 E2 **Lyubertsy** Rus. Fed.
90 B1 **Lyubeshiv** Ukr.
89 F2 **Lyubim** Rus. Fed.
91 D2 **Lyubotyn** Ukr.
89 D2 **Lyubytino** Rus. Fed.
89 D3 **Lyudinovo** Rus. Fed.

M

80 B2 **Ma'ān** Jordan
70 B2 **Ma'anshan** China
88 C2 **Maardu** Estonia
78 B3 **Ma'āriḍ, Bani** *des.* Saudi Arabia
80 B2 **Ma'arrat an Nu'mān** Syria
100 B1 **Maarssen** Neth.
100 B2 **Maas** *r.* Neth.
100 B2 **Maaseik** Belgium
64 B2 **Maasin** Phil.
100 B2 **Maastricht** Neth.
121 C3 **Mabalane** Moz.
78 B3 **Ma'bar** Yemen
150 D2 **Mabaruma** Guyana
98 D3 **Mablethorpe** U.K.
123 C2 **Mabopane** S. Africa
121 C3 **Mabote** Moz.
122 B2 **Mabule** Botswana
122 B1 **Mabutsane** Botswana
155 D2 **Macaé** Brazil
121 C2 **Macaloge** Moz.
126 F2 **McAlpine Lake** Can.
71 B3 **Macao** *special admin. reg.* China
151 D2 **Macapá** Brazil
150 B3 **Macará** Ecuador
155 D1 **Macarani** Brazil
Macassar Indon. *see* Makassar
Macassar Strait Indon. *see* Makassar, Selat
121 C2 **Macatanja** Moz.
151 F3 **Macau** Brazil
121 C3 **Maccaretane** Moz.
98 B3 **Macclesfield** U.K.
50 B2 **Macdonald, Lake** *salt flat* Austr.
50 C2 **Macdonnell Ranges** *mts* Austr.
130 A2 **MacDowell Lake** Can.
96 C2 **Macduff** U.K.
106 B1 **Macedo de Cavaleiros** Port.
52 B3 **Macedon** *mt.* Austr.
111 B2 **Macedonia** *country* Europe
151 F3 **Maceió** Brazil
108 B2 **Macerata** Italy
52 A2 **Macfarlane, Lake** *salt flat* Austr.
97 B3 **Macgillycuddy's Reeks** *mts* Ireland
74 A2 **Mach** Pak.
155 C2 **Machado** Brazil
121 C3 **Machaila** Moz.
119 D3 **Machakos** Kenya
150 B3 **Machala** Ecuador
121 C3 **Machanga** Moz.
Machaze Moz. *see* Chitobe
70 B2 **Macheng** China
138 B2 **Machesney Park** U.S.A.
139 F2 **Machias** U.S.A.
73 C3 **Machilipatnam** India
121 C2 **Machinga** Malawi
150 B1 **Machiques** Venez.
150 A3 **Machu Picchu** Peru
99 B3 **Machynlleth** U.K.
123 D2 **Macia** Moz.
Macias Nguema *i.* Equat. Guinea *see* Bioco
110 C1 **Măcin** Romania
114 B3 **Macina** Mali
53 D1 **Macintyre** *r.* Austr.
51 D2 **Mackay** Austr.
50 B2 **Mackay, Lake** *salt flat* Austr.
128 C1 **MacKay Lake** Can.
128 B2 **Mackenzie** Can.
128 B2 **Mackenzie** *r.* Can.
128 A1 **Mackenzie** Guyana *see* Linden

Mackenzie *atoll* Micronesia *see* Ulithi
55 H3 **Mackenzie Bay** Antarctica
126 C2 **Mackenzie Bay** Can.
126 E1 **Mackenzie King Island** Can.
128 A1 **Mackenzie Mountains** Can.
Mackillop, Lake *salt flat* Austr. *see* Yamma Yamma, Lake
129 D2 **Macklin** Can.
53 D2 **Macksville** Austr.
53 D1 **Maclean** Austr.
123 C3 **Maclear** S. Africa
50 A2 **MacLeod, Lake** *imp. l.* Austr.
138 A2 **Macomb** U.S.A.
108 A2 **Macomer** Sardinia Italy
121 D2 **Macomia** Moz.
105 C2 **Mâcon** France
141 D2 **Macon** GA U.S.A.
137 E3 **Macon** MO U.S.A.
140 C2 **Macon** MS U.S.A.
53 C2 **Macquarie** *r.* Austr.
48 G9 **Macquarie Island** S. Pacific Ocean
53 C2 **Macquarie Marshes** Austr.
53 C2 **Macquarie Mountain** Austr.
156 D9 **Macquarie Ridge** *sea feature* S. Pacific Ocean
55 H2 **Mac. Robertson Land** *reg.* Antarctica
97 B3 **Macroom** Ireland
52 A1 **Macumba** *watercourse* Austr.
145 C3 **Macuspana** Mex.
144 B2 **Macuzari, Presa** *resr* Mex.
123 D2 **Madadeni** S. Africa
121 □D3 **Madagascar** *country* Africa
159 D5 **Madagascar Ridge** *sea feature* Indian Ocean
115 D2 **Madama** Niger
111 B2 **Madan** Bulg.
59 D3 **Madang** P.N.G.
139 D1 **Madawaska** *r.* Can.
62 A1 **Madaya** Myanmar
150 D3 **Madeira** *r.* Brazil
114 A1 **Madeira** *terr.* N. Atlantic Ocean
131 D3 **Madeleine, Îles de la** *is* Can.
99 B3 **Madeley** U.K.
144 B2 **Madera** Mex.
135 B3 **Madera** U.S.A.
73 B3 **Madgaon** India
74 B2 **Madhya Pradesh** *state* India
123 C2 **Madibogo** S. Africa
118 B3 **Madingou** Congo
121 □D2 **Madirovalo** Madag.
138 B3 **Madison** IN U.S.A.
137 D2 **Madison** SD U.S.A.
138 B2 **Madison** WI U.S.A.
138 C3 **Madison** WV U.S.A.
134 D1 **Madison** *r.* U.S.A.
138 B3 **Madisonville** U.S.A.
61 C2 **Madiun** Indon.
119 D2 **Mado Gashi** Kenya
68 C2 **Madoi** China
88 C2 **Madona** Latvia
78 A2 **Madrakah** Saudi Arabia
79 C3 **Madrakah, Ra's** *c.* Oman
Madras India *see* Chennai
134 B2 **Madras** U.S.A.
145 C2 **Madre, Laguna** *lag.* Mex.
143 D3 **Madre, Laguna** *lag.* U.S.A.
150 C4 **Madre de Dios** *r.* Peru
145 B3 **Madre del Sur, Sierra** *mts* Mex.
144 B2 **Madre Occidental, Sierra** *mts* Mex.
145 B2 **Madre Oriental, Sierra** *mts* Mex.
106 C1 **Madrid** Spain
106 C2 **Madridejos** Spain
61 C2 **Madura** *i.* Indon.
61 C2 **Madura, Selat** *sea chan.* Indon.
73 B4 **Madurai** India
121 B2 **Madziwadzido** Zimbabwe
67 C3 **Maebashi** Japan
62 A2 **Mae Hong Son** Thai.
62 A1 **Mae Sai** Thai.
62 A2 **Mae Sariang** Thai.
99 B4 **Maesteg** U.K.
62 A2 **Mae Suai** Thai.

Ref	Name	Ref	Name	Ref	Name	Ref	Name
121 ☐D2	Maevatanana Madag.	07 C3	Maizuru Japan	119 C3	Malela Dem. Rep. Congo	117 A4	Manda, Jebel mt. Sudan
	Mafeking S. Africa see	109 C2	Maja Jezercë mt. Albania	116 A3	Malha Sudan	121 ☐D3	Mandabe Madag.
	Mafikeng	61 C2	Majene Indon.	134 C2	Malheur Lake U.S.A.	93 E4	Mandal Norway
123 C2	Mafeteng Lesotho	119 D2	Maji Eth.	114 B3	Mali country Africa	59 D3	Mandala, Puncak mt.
53 C3	Maffra Austr.	107 D2	Majorca i. Spain	114 A3	Mali Guinea		Indon.
119 D3	Mafia Island Tanz.		Majunga Madag. see	59 C3	Maliana East Timor	62 A1	Mandalay Myanmar
123 C2	Mafikeng S. Africa		Mahajanga	58 C3	Malili Indon.	68 D1	Mandalgovi Mongolia
119 D3	Mafinga Tanz.	123 C2	Majwemasweu S. Africa	97 C1	Malin Ireland	136 C1	Mandan U.S.A.
154 C3	Mafra Brazil	118 B3	Makabana Congo	119 E3	Malindi Kenya	118 B1	Mandara Mountains
83 L3	Magadan Rus. Fed.	61 C2	Makale Indon.	97 C1	Malin Head hd Ireland		Cameroon/Nigeria
	Magallanes Chile see	119 C3	Makamba Burundi	97 B1	Malin More Ireland	108 A3	Mandas Sardinia Italy
	Punta Arenas	77 E2	Makanchi Kazakh.	111 C2	Malkara Turkey	119 E2	Mandera Kenya
	Magallanes, Estrecho de	118 B2	Makanza	88 C3	Mal'kavichy Belarus	100 C2	Manderscheid Ger.
	Chile see Magellan,		Dem. Rep. Congo	110 C2	Malko Tŭrnovo Bulg.	74 B1	Mandi India
	Strait of	90 B1	Makariv Ukr.	53 C3	Mallacoota Austr.	114 B3	Mandiana Guinea
150 B2	Magangue Col.	69 F1	Makarov Rus. Fed.	53 C3	Mallacoota Inlet b. Austr.	74 B1	Mandi Burewala Pak.
140 B1	Magazine Mountain U.S.A.	160 B1	Makarov Basin	96 B2	Mallaig U.K.		Mandidzuzure Zimbabwe
114 A4	Magburaka Sierra Leone		sea feature Arctic Ocean	116 B2	Mallawī Egypt		see Chimanimani
69 E1	Magdagachi Rus. Fed.	109 C2	Makarska Croatia	129 E1	Mallery Lake Can.	75 C2	Mandla India
144 A1	Magdalena Mex.	61 C2	Makassar Indon.		Mallorca i. Spain see	121 ☐D2	Mandritsara Madag.
142 B2	Magdalena U.S.A.	61 C2	Makassar, Selat Indon.		Majorca	74 B2	Mandsaur India
144 A2	Magdalena, Bahía b. Mex.	76 B2	Makat Kazakh.	97 B2	Mallow Ireland	50 A3	Mandurah Austr.
101 E1	Magdeburg Ger.	119 D3	Makatapora Tanz.	92 F3	Malm Norway	73 B3	Mandya India
153 A5	Magellan, Strait of	123 D2	Makatini Flats lowland	92 H2	Malmberget Sweden	108 B1	Manerbio Italy
	sea chan. Chile		S. Africa	100 C2	Malmédy Belgium	90 B1	Manevychi Ukr.
	Maggiore, Lago Italy see	114 A4	Makeni Sierra Leone	122 A3	Malmesbury S. Africa	109 C2	Manfredonia Italy
	Maggiore, Lake	120 B3	Makgadikgadi salt pan	93 F4	Malmö Sweden	109 C2	Manfredonia, Golfo di g.
108 A1	Maggiore, Lake l. Italy		Botswana	71 A3	Malong China		Italy
116 B2	Maghāghah Egypt	87 D4	Makhachkala Rus. Fed.	118 C4	Malonga Dem. Rep. Congo	114 B3	Manga Burkina
97 C1	Magherafelt U.K.	123 C1	Makhado S. Africa	86 C2	Maloshuyka Rus. Fed.	118 B3	Mangai Dem. Rep. Congo
87 E3	Magnitogorsk Rus. Fed.	76 B2	Makhambet Kazakh.	93 E3	Måløy Norway	49 L6	Mangaia i. Cook Is
140 B2	Magnolia U.S.A.	119 D3	Makindu Kenya	89 F2	Maloyaroslavets Rus. Fed.	54 C1	Mangakino N.Z.
121 C2	Màgoé Moz.	77 D1	Makinsk Kazakh.	89 E2	Maloye Borisovo	110 C2	Mangalia Romania
130 C3	Magog Can.	91 D2	Makiyivka Ukr.		Rus. Fed.	73 B3	Mangalore India
131 D2	Magpie, Lac l. Can.		Makkah Saudi Arabia see	86 D2	Malozemel'skaya Tundra	123 C2	Mangaung S. Africa
114 A3	Magta' Lahjar Maur.		Mecca		lowland Rus. Fed.	60 B2	Manggar Indon.
81 D2	Magtymguly Turkm.	131 E2	Makkovik Can.	125 J9	Malpelo, Isla de i.		Mangghyshlaq Kazakh.
119 D3	Magu Tanz.	103 E2	Makó Hungary		N. Pacific Ocean		see Mangystau
151 E3	Maguarinho, Cabo c.	118 B2	Makokou Gabon	84 F5	Malta country Europe	61 C1	Mangkalihat, Tanjung pt
	Brazil	119 D3	Makongolosi Tanz.	88 C2	Malta Latvia		Indon.
123 D2	Magude Moz.	122 B2	Makopong Botswana	134 E1	Malta U.S.A.	68 C2	Mangnai China
90 B2	Măgura, Dealul hill	119 C2	Makoro Dem. Rep. Congo	122 A1	Maltahöhe Namibia	121 C2	Mangochi Malawi
	Moldova	118 B3	Makoua Congo	98 C2	Malton U.K.	121 ☐D3	Mangoky r. Madag.
62 A1	Magwe Myanmar	111 B3	Makrakomi Greece		Maluku is Indon. see	59 C3	Mangole i. Indon.
81 C2	Mahābād Iran	79 D2	Makran reg. Iran/Pak.		Moluccas	54 B1	Mangonui N.Z.
74 B2	Mahajan India	74 A2	Makran Coast Range mts	93 F3	Malung Sweden		Mangshi China see Luxi
121 ☐D2	Mahajanga Madag.		Pak.	123 C2	Maluti Mountains Lesotho	106 B1	Manguéide Port.
61 C2	Mahakam r. Indon.	89 E2	Maksatikha Rus. Fed.	73 B3	Malvan India	154 B3	Mangueirinha Brazil
123 C1	Mahalapye Botswana	81 C2	Mākū Iran	140 B2	Malvern U.S.A.	69 E1	Mangui China
121 ☐D2	Mahalevona Madag.	62 A1	Makum India	117 B4	Malwal Sudan		Mangyshlak Kazakh. see
121 ☐D2	Mahanadi r. India	67 B4	Makurazaki Japan	90 B1	Malyn Ukr.		Mangystau
121 ☐D2	Mahanoro Madag.	115 C4	Makurdi Nigeria	83 L2	Malyy Anyuy r. Rus. Fed.	76 B2	Mangystau Kazakh.
74 B3	Maharashtra state India	92 G2	Malå Sweden		Malyy Kavkaz mts Asia	137 D3	Manhattan U.S.A.
63 B2	Maha Sarakham Thai.	146 B4	Mala, Punta pt Panama		see Lesser Caucasus	121 C3	Manhica Moz.
121 ☐D2	Mahavavy r. Madag.	73 B3	Malabar Coast India	83 K2	Malyy Lyakhovskiy,	155 D2	Manhuaçu Brazil
68 B3	Mahbubnagar India	118 A2	Malabo Equat. Guinea		Ostrov i. Rus. Fed.	121 ☐D2	Mania r. Madag.
78 B2	Mahd adh Dhahab	155 D1	Malacacheta Brazil	123 C2	Mamafubedu S. Africa	108 B1	Maniago Italy
	Saudi Arabia		Malacca Malaysia see	151 F3	Mamanguape Brazil	121 C2	Maniamba Moz.
107 D2	Mahdia Alg.		Melaka	64 B3	Mambajao Phil.	150 B3	Manicoré Brazil
150 D2	Mahdia Guyana	60 A1	Malacca, Strait of	119 C2	Mambasa Dem. Rep.	131 D2	Manicouagan r. Can.
113 I6	Mahé i. Seychelles		Indon./Malaysia		Congo	131 D2	Manicouagan, Réservoir
75 C3	Mahendragiri mt. India	134 D2	Malad City U.S.A.	118 B2	Mambéré r. C.A.R.		resr Can.
119 D3	Mahenge Tanz.	88 C3	Maladzyechna Belarus	64 B2	Mamburao Phil.	79 B2	Manifah Saudi Arabia
54 B3	Maheno N.Z.	106 C2	Málaga Spain	123 C2	Mame!odi S. Africa	49 K5	Manihiki atoll Cook Is
74 B2	Mahesana India		Malagasy Republic	118 A2	Mamfe Cameroon	64 B2	Manila Phil.
74 B2	Mahi r. India		country Africa see	135 A2	Mammoth Lakes U.S.A.	53 D2	Manilla Austr.
54 C1	Mahia Peninsula N.Z.		Madagascar	88 A3	Mamonovo Rus. Fed.		Manipur India see Imphal
89 D3	Mahilyow Belarus	121 ☐D3	Malaimbandy Madag.	150 C4	Mamoré r. Bol./Brazil	111 C3	Manisa Turkey
129 D2	Mahón Spain	48 H4	Malaita i. Solomon Is	114 A3	Mamou Guinea	107 C2	Manises Spain
114 B3	Mahou Mali	117 B4	Malakal Sudan	121 C2	Mampong Ghana	138 B2	Manistee U.S.A.
	Mahsana India see	48 H5	Malakula i. Vanuatu	61 C2	Mamuju Indon.	138 B2	Manistique U.S.A.
	Mahesana	61 C2	Malamala Indon.	114 B4	Man Côte d'Ivoire	129 E2	Manitoba prov. Can.
74 B2	Mahuva India	61 C2	Malang Indon.	98 A2	Man, Isle of i. Irish Sea	129 E2	Manitoba, Lake Can.
111 C2	Mahya Dağı mt. Turkey	120 A1	Malange Angola see	150 C3	Manacapuru Brazil	138 B1	Manitou Islands U.S.A.
106 B1	Maia Port.		Malanje	107 D2	Manacor Spain	130 B3	Manitoulin Island Can.
	Maiaia Moz. see Nacala	120 A1	Malanje Angola	59 C2	Manado Indon.	136 C3	Manitou Springs U.S.A.
147 C3	Maicao Col.	93 G4	Mälaren l. Sweden	146 B3	Managua Nic.	130 B3	Manitouwadge Can.
129 D2	Maidstone Can.	153 B3	Malargüe Arg.	121 ☐D3	Manakara Madag.	138 B2	Manitowoc U.S.A.
99 D4	Maidstone U.K.	130 C3	Malartic Can.	78 B3	Manākhah Yemen	130 C3	Maniwaki Can.
115 D3	Maiduguri Nigeria	88 B3	Malaryta Belarus	79 C2	Manama Bahrain	150 B2	Manizales Col.
74 B2	Maijdi Bangl.	80 B2	Malatya Turkey	59 D3	Manam Island P.N.G.	121 ☐D3	Manja Madag.
75 C2	Mailani India	121 C2	Malawi country Africa	121 ☐D3	Mananara r. Madag.	121 C3	Manjacaze Moz.
101 D2	Main r. Ger.		Malawi, Lake Africa see	121 ☐D2	Mananara Avaratra	137 E2	Mankato U.S.A.
118 B3	Mai-Ndombe, Lac l.		Nyasa, Lake		Madag.	114 B4	Mankono Côte d'Ivoire
	Dem. Rep. Congo	89 D2	Malaya Vishera Rus. Fed.	121 ☐D3	Mananjary Madag.	129 D3	Mankota Can.
101 E3	Main-Donau-Kanal canal	64 B3	Malaybalay Phil.	114 A3	Manantali, Lac de l. Mali	73 C4	Mankulam Sri Lanka
	Ger.	81 C2	Malāyer Iran	54 A3	Manapouri, Lake N.Z.	74 B2	Manmad India
139 F1	Maine state U.S.A.	60 B1	Malaysia country Asia	77 E2	Manas Hu l. China	52 A2	Mannahill Austr.
131 D3	Maine, Gulf of Can./U.S.A.	81 C2	Malazgirt Turkey	75 C2	Manaslu mt. Nepal	73 B4	Mannar Sri Lanka
62 A1	Maingkwan Myanmar	103 D1	Malbork Pol.		Manastir Macedonia see	73 B4	Mannar, Gulf of
96 C1	Mainland i.	101 F1	Malchin Ger.		Bitola		India/Sri Lanka
	Orkney Is, Scotland U.K.	100 A3	Maldegem Belgium	59 C3	Manatuto East Timor	101 D3	Mannheim Ger.
96 ☐	Mainland i.	48 L4	Malden Island Kiribati	62 A2	Man-aung Kyun Myanmar	128 C2	Manning Can.
	Shetland Is, Scotland U.K.	56 C5	Maldives country	150 C3	Manaus Brazil	52 A2	Mannum Austr.
121 ☐D2	Maintirano Madag.		Indian Ocean	80 B2	Manavgat Turkey	129 C2	Mannville Can.
101 D2	Mainz Ger.	99 D4	Maldon U.K.	116 A3	Manawashei Sudan	118 C3	Manono Dem. Rep. Congo
150 C1	Maiquetía Venez.	56 I9	Male Maldives	98 B3	Manchester U.K.	119 C3	Manosque France
120 B3	Maitengwe Botswana	111 B3	Maleas, Akrotirio pt	139 E2	Manchester CT U.S.A.	63 A2	Manoron Myanmar
53 D2	Maitland N.S.W. Austr.		Greece	139 E2	Manchester NH U.S.A.	105 D3	Manosque France
52 A2	Maitland S.A. Austr.	103 D2	Malé Karpaty hills	140 C1	Manchester TN U.S.A.	131 C2	Manouane, Lac l. Can.
146 B3	Maíz, Islas del is Nic.		Slovakia	81 D3	Mand, Rūd-e r. Iran	65 B1	Manp'o N. Korea

137 E1	Mesabi Range *hills* U.S.A.
109 C2	Mesagne Italy
142 B2	Mescalero U.S.A.
143 C2	Mescalero Ridge U.S.A.
101 D2	Meschede Ger.
89 E3	Meshchovsk Rus. Fed.
	Meshed Iran *see* Mashhad
91 E2	Meshkovskaya Rus. Fed.
142 B2	Mesilla U.S.A.
111 B2	Mesimeri Greece
111 B3	Mesolongi Greece
115 C1	Messaad Alg.
121 D2	Messalo *r.* Moz.
109 C3	Messina *Sicily* Italy
109 C3	Messina, Strait of *str.* Italy
	Messina, Stretta di Italy *see* Messina, Strait of
111 B3	Messini Greece
111 B3	Messiniakos Kolpos *b.* Greece
111 B2	Mesta *r.* Bulg.
	Mesta *r.* Greece *see* Nestos
150 C2	Meta *r.* Col./Venez.
130 C3	Métabetchouan Can.
127 H2	Meta Incognita Peninsula Can.
140 B3	Metairie U.S.A.
152 B2	Metán Arg.
111 B3	Methoni Greece
109 C2	Metković Croatia
121 C2	Metoro Moz.
60 B2	Metro Indon.
100 C3	Mettlach Ger.
135 C3	Mettler U.S.A.
117 B4	Metu Eth.
105 D2	Metz France
100 B2	Meuse *r.* Belgium/France
143 D2	Mexia U.S.A.
144 A1	Mexicali Mex.
144 B2	Mexico *country* Central America
	México Mex. *see* Mexico City
137 E3	Mexico U.S.A.
125 I7	Mexico, Gulf of Mex./U.S.A.
145 C3	Mexico City Mex.
81 D2	Meybod Iran
101 F1	Meyenburg Ger.
76 C3	Meymaneh Afgh.
83 M2	Meynypil'gyno Rus. Fed.
86 D2	Mezen' Rus. Fed.
86 D2	Mezen' *r.* Rus. Fed.
86 E1	Mezhdusharskiy, Ostrov *i.* Rus. Fed.
103 E2	Mezőtúr Hungary
132 C4	Mezquital *r.* Mex.
144 B2	Mezquitic Mex.
88 C2	Mežvidi Latvia
121 C2	Mfuwe Zambia
89 D3	Mglin Rus. Fed.
123 D2	Mhlume Swaziland
74 B2	Mhow India
145 C3	Miahuatlán Mex.
106 B2	Miajadas Spain
141 D3	Miami *FL* U.S.A.
143 E1	Miami *OK* U.S.A.
141 D3	Miami Beach U.S.A.
81 C2	Miāndowāb Iran
121 □D2	Miandrivazo Madag.
81 C2	Miāneh Iran
71 A3	Mianning China
74 B1	Mianwali Pak.
	Mianyang China *see* Xiantao
70 A2	Mianyang China
121 □D2	Miarinarivo Madag.
87 F3	Miass Rus. Fed.
103 D1	Miastko Pol.
128 C2	Mica Creek Can.
103 E2	Michalovce Slovakia
138 B1	Michigan *state* U.S.A.
138 B2	Michigan, Lake U.S.A.
138 B2	Michigan City U.S.A.
138 B1	Michipicoten Bay Can.
130 B3	Michipicoten Island Can.
130 B3	Michipicoten River Can.
	Michurin Bulg. *see* Tsarevo
89 F3	Michurinsk Rus. Fed.
156 D5	Micronesia *is* Pacific Ocean
48 G3	Micronesia, Federated States of *country* N. Pacific Ocean
158 E6	Mid-Atlantic Ridge *sea feature* Atlantic Ocean
100 A2	Middelburg Neth.
123 C3	Middelburg *E. Cape* S. Africa

123 C2	Middelburg *Mpumalanga* S. Africa
100 B2	Middelharnis Neth.
134 B2	Middle Alkali Lake U.S.A.
73 D3	Middle Andaman *i.* India
	Middle Congo *country* Africa *see* Congo
136 D2	Middle Loup *r.* U.S.A.
138 C3	Middlesboro U.S.A.
98 C2	Middlesbrough U.K.
139 E2	Middletown *NY* U.S.A.
138 C3	Middletown *OH* U.S.A.
78 B3	Midi Yemen
130 C3	Midland Can.
138 C2	Midland *MI* U.S.A.
143 C2	Midland *TX* U.S.A.
97 B3	Midleton Ireland
	Midnapore India *see* Medinipur
94 B1	Miðvágur Faroe Is
	Midway Oman *see* Thamarīt
57 T7	Midway Islands *terr.* N. Pacific Ocean
109 D2	Midzhur *mt.* Bulg./Serbia
103 E1	Mielec Pol.
110 C1	Miercurea-Ciuc Romania
106 B1	Mieres Spain
101 E1	Mieste Ger.
75 D1	Migriggyangzham Co *l.* China
145 C3	Miguel Alemán, Presa *resr* Mex.
144 B2	Miguel Auza Mex.
144 B2	Miguel Hidalgo, Presa *resr* Mex.
63 A2	Migyaunglaung Myanmar
67 B4	Mihara Japan
89 E3	Mikhaylov Rus. Fed.
	Mikhaylovgrad Bulg. *see* Montana
66 B2	Mikhaylovka Rus. Fed.
	Mikhaylovka Rus. Fed. *see* Kimovsk
87 D3	Mikhaylovka Rus. Fed.
77 D1	Mikhaylovskiy Rus. Fed.
93 I3	Mikkeli Fin.
86 E2	Mikun' Rus. Fed.
67 C3	Mikuni-sanmyaku *mts* Japan
67 C4	Mikura-jima *i.* Japan
73 B4	Miladhunmadulu Atoll Maldives
108 A1	Milan Italy
121 C2	Milange Moz.
	Milano Italy *see* Milan
111 C3	Milas Turkey
137 D1	Milbank U.S.A.
99 D3	Mildenhall U.K.
52 B2	Mildura Austr.
71 A3	Mile China
128 B2	100 Mile House Can.
136 B1	Miles City U.S.A.
139 D3	Milford *DE* U.S.A.
135 D3	Milford *UT* U.S.A.
99 A4	Milford Haven U.K.
54 A2	Milford Sound N.Z.
	Milḩ, Baḩr al *l.* Iraq *see* Razzāzah, Buḩayrat ar
107 D2	Miliana Alg.
50 C1	Milikapiti Austr.
51 C1	Milingimbi Austr.
134 E1	Milk *r.* U.S.A.
116 B3	Milk, Wadi el *watercourse* Sudan
83 L3	Mil'kovo Rus. Fed.
128 C3	Milk River Can.
105 C3	Millau France
141 D2	Milledgeville U.S.A.
137 E1	Mille Lacs *lakes* U.S.A.
130 A3	Mille Lacs, Lac des *l.* Can.
	Millennium Island Kiribati *see* Caroline Island
137 D2	Miller U.S.A.
91 E2	Millerovo Rus. Fed.
52 A2	Millers Creek Austr.
96 B3	Milleur Point U.K.
52 B3	Millicent Austr.
140 C1	Millington U.S.A.
139 F1	Millinocket U.S.A.
55 J3	Mill Island Antarctica
53 D1	Millmerran Austr.
98 B2	Millom U.K.
136 B2	Mills U.S.A.
128 C1	Mills Lake Can.
111 B3	Milos *i.* Greece
89 E3	Miloslavskoye Rus. Fed.
91 E2	Milove Ukr.
52 B1	Milparinka Austr.
54 A3	Milton N.Z.

99 C3	Milton Keynes U.K.
138 B2	Milwaukee U.S.A.
158 C3	Milwaukee Deep *sea feature* Caribbean Sea
104 B3	Mimizan France
118 B3	Mimongo Gabon
155 D2	Mimoso do Sul Brazil
79 C2	Mīnāb Iran
61 D1	Minahasa, Semenanjung *pen.* Indon.
	Minahassa Peninsula Indon. *see* Minahasa, Semenanjung
79 C2	Mina Jebel Ali U.A.E.
	Minaker Can. *see* Prophet River
60 B1	Minas Indon.
153 C3	Minas Uru.
79 B2	Minā' Sa'ūd Kuwait
155 D1	Minas Gerais *state* Brazil
155 D1	Minas Novas Brazil
145 C3	Minatitlán Mex.
62 A1	Minbu Myanmar
64 B3	Mindanao *i.* Phil.
52 B2	Mindarie Austr.
101 D1	Minden Ger.
140 B2	Minden *LA* U.S.A.
137 D2	Minden *NE* U.S.A.
64 B3	Mindoro *i.* Phil.
64 A2	Mindoro Strait Phil.
118 B3	Mindouli Congo
99 B4	Minehead U.K.
154 B1	Mineiros Brazil
143 D2	Mineral Wells U.S.A.
75 C1	Minfeng China
119 C4	Minga Dem. Rep. Congo
81 C1	Mingäçevir Azer.
131 D2	Mingan Can.
52 B2	Mingary Austr.
70 B2	Mingguang China
62 A1	Mingin Myanmar
107 C2	Minglanilla Spain
119 D4	Mingoyo Tanz.
69 E1	Mingshui China
96 A2	Mingulay *i.* U.K.
71 B3	Mingxi China
	Mingzhou China *see* Suide
70 A2	Minhe China
73 B4	Minicoy *i.* India
50 A2	Minilya Austr.
114 B3	Mininian Côte d'Ivoire
131 D2	Minipi Lake Can.
130 A2	Miniss Lake Can.
52 A2	Minlaton Austr.
115 C4	Minna Nigeria
137 E2	Minneapolis U.S.A.
129 E2	Minnedosa Can.
137 E2	Minnesota *state* U.S.A.
137 E1	Minnesota *state* U.S.A.
106 B1	Miño *r.* Port./Spain
107 D1	Minorca *i.* Spain
136 C1	Minot U.S.A.
88 C3	Minsk Belarus
103 E1	Mińsk Mazowiecki Pol.
96 D2	Mintlaw U.K.
131 D3	Minto Can.
130 C2	Minto, Lac *l.* Can.
68 C1	Minusinsk Rus. Fed.
62 A1	Minutang India
70 A2	Minxian China
155 D1	Mirabela Brazil
155 D1	Miralta Brazil
131 D2	Miramichi Can.
111 C3	Mirampellou, Kolpos *b.* Greece
152 C2	Miranda Brazil
152 C1	Miranda *r.* Brazil
	Miranda Moz. *see* Macaloge
106 C1	Miranda de Ebro Spain
106 B1	Mirandela Port.
154 B2	Mirandópolis Brazil
154 B2	Mirante, Serra do *hills* Brazil
79 C3	Mirbāţ Oman
61 C1	Miri Sarawak Malaysia
153 C3	Mirim, Lagoa *l.* Brazil
79 D2	Mīrjāveh Iran
89 D3	Mirnyy Rus. Fed.
83 I2	Mirnyy Rus. Fed.
101 F1	Mirow Ger.
74 A2	Mirpur Khas Pak.
	Mirtoan Sea Greece *see* Mirtoö Pelagos
111 B3	Mirtoö Pelagos *sea* Greece
65 B2	Miryang S. Korea

75 C2	Mirzapur India
77 E3	Misalay China
66 B1	Mishan China
51 E1	Misima Island P.N.G.
146 B3	Miskitos, Cayos *is* Nic.
103 E2	Miskolc Hungary
59 C3	Misoöl *i.* Indon.
115 D1	Mişrātah Libya
130 B2	Missinaibi *r.* Can.
130 B3	Missinaibi Lake Can.
128 B3	Mission Can.
130 B2	Missisa Lake Can.
140 C3	Mississippi *r.* U.S.A.
140 C3	Mississippi *state* U.S.A.
140 C3	Mississippi Delta U.S.A.
140 C2	Mississippi Sound *sea chan.* U.S.A.
	Missolonghi Greece *see* Mesolongi
134 D1	Missoula U.S.A.
137 E3	Missouri *r.* U.S.A.
137 E3	Missouri *state* U.S.A.
130 C3	Mistassibi *r.* Can.
130 C2	Mistassini, Lac *l.* Can.
131 D2	Mistastin Lake Can.
103 D2	Mistelbach Austria
131 D2	Mistinibi, Lac *l.* Can.
130 C2	Mistissini Can.
51 D2	Mitchell Austr.
51 D1	Mitchell *r.* Austr.
136 C2	Mitchell *NE* U.S.A.
137 D2	Mitchell *SD* U.S.A.
97 B2	Mitchelstown Ireland
74 A2	Mithi Pak.
67 D3	Mito Japan
119 D3	Mitole Tanz.
53 D2	Mittagong Austr.
101 E2	Mittelhausen Ger.
101 D1	Mittellandkanal *canal* Ger.
101 F3	Mitterteich Ger.
	Mittimatalik Can. *see* Pond Inlet
150 B2	Mitú Col.
119 C4	Mitumba, Chaîne des *mts* Dem. Rep. Congo
119 C3	Mitumba, Monts *mts* Dem. Rep. Congo
119 C3	Mitwaba Dem. Rep. Congo
118 B3	Mitzic Gabon
78 B2	Miyah, Wādī al *watercourse* Saudi Arabia
67 C4	Miyake-jima *i.* Japan
66 D3	Miyako Japan
67 B4	Miyakonojō Japan
76 B2	Miyaly Kazakh.
	Miyang China *see* Mile
67 B4	Miyazaki Japan
67 C3	Miyazu Japan
115 D1	Mizdah Libya
97 B3	Mizen Head *hd* Ireland
90 A2	Mizhhir"ya Ukr.
	Mizo Hills *state* India *see* Mizoram
	Mizoram *state* India
93 G4	Mjölby Sweden
93 F3	Mjøsa *l.* Norway
119 D3	Mkomazi Tanz.
103 C1	Mladá Boleslav Czech Rep.
109 D2	Mladenovac Serbia
103 E1	Mława Pol.
109 C2	Mljet *i.* Croatia
123 C3	Mlungisi S. Africa
90 B1	Mlyniv Ukr.
123 C2	Mmabatho S. Africa
123 C2	Mmathethe Botswana
93 E3	Mo Norway
135 E3	Moab U.S.A.
123 D2	Moamba Moz.
54 B2	Moana N.Z.
118 B3	Moanda Gabon
97 C2	Moate Ireland
119 C3	Moba Dem. Rep. Congo
118 C2	Mobayi-Mbongo Dem. Rep. Congo
137 E3	Moberly U.S.A.
140 C2	Mobile U.S.A.
140 C2	Mobile Bay U.S.A.
140 C2	Mobile Point U.S.A.
136 C1	Mobridge U.S.A.
	Mobutu, Lake Dem. Rep. Congo/Uganda *see* Albert, Lake
	Mobutu Sese Seko, Lake Dem. Rep. Congo/Uganda *see* Albert, Lake
121 C2	Moçambicano, Planalto *plat.* Moz.
121 D2	Moçambique Moz.
	Moçâmedes Angola *see* Namibe

62 B1 Môc Châu Vietnam
78 B3 Mocha Yemen
123 C1 Mochudi Botswana
121 D2 Mocimboa da Praia Moz.
101 D3 Möckmühl Ger.
150 B2 Mocoa Col.
154 C2 Mococa Brazil
144 B2 Mocorito Mex.
144 B1 Moctezuma Mex.
144 B2 Moctezuma Mex.
144 B2 Moctezuma Mex.
121 C2 Mocuba Moz.
105 D2 Modane France
122 B2 Modder r. S. Africa
108 B2 Modena Italy
135 B3 Modesto U.S.A.
109 B3 Modica Sicily Italy
105 C3 Modimolle S. Africa
53 C3 Moe Austr.
Moero, Lake Dem. Rep. Congo/Zambia see Mweru, Lake
100 C2 Moers Ger.
96 C3 Moffat U.K.
117 C4 Mogadishu Somalia
Mogador Morocco see Essaouira
106 B1 Mogadouro, Serra de mts Port.
123 C1 Mogalakwena r. S. Africa
62 A1 Mogaung Myanmar
Mogilev Belarus see Mahilyow
154 C2 Mogi-Mirim Brazil
83 I3 Mogocha Rus. Fed.
123 C1 Mogoditshane Botswana
62 A1 Mogok Myanmar
142 A2 Mogollon Plateau U.S.A.
103 D2 Mohács Hungary
123 C3 Mohale's Hoek Lesotho
107 D2 Mohammadia Alg.
142 A2 Mohave Mountains U.S.A.
139 E2 Mohawk r. U.S.A.
62 A1 Mohnyin Myanmar
119 D3 Mohoro Tanz.
90 B2 Mohyliv Podil's'kyy Ukr.
123 C1 Moijabana Botswana
110 C1 Moineşti Romania
Mointy Kazakh. see Moyynty
92 F2 Mo i Rana Norway
88 C2 Mõisaküla Estonia
104 C3 Moissac France
135 C3 Mojave U.S.A.
135 C3 Mojave Desert U.S.A.
62 B1 Mojiang China
155 C2 Moji das Cruzes Brazil
154 C2 Moji-Guaçu r. Brazil
109 C2 Mojkovac Montenegro
54 B1 Mokau N.Z.
123 C2 Mokhotlong Lesotho
83 J2 Mokhsogollokh Rus. Fed.
118 B1 Mokolo Cameroon
123 C2 Mokopane S. Africa
65 B3 Mokp'o S. Korea
145 C2 Mola di Bari Italy
Molango Mex.
Moldavia country Europe see Moldova
Moldavskaya S.S.R. country Europe see Moldova
93 E3 Molde Norway
90 B2 Moldova country Europe
110 B2 Moldova Nouă Romania
110 B1 Moldoveanu, Vârful mt. Romania
Moldovei, Podişul plat. Romania
90 B2 Molepolole Botswana
123 C1 Molepolole Botswana
88 C2 Molėtai Lith.
109 C2 Molfetta Italy
Molière Alg. see Bordj Bounaama
107 C1 Molina de Aragón Spain
107 C2 Molina de Segura Spain
119 D3 Moliro Dem. Rep. Congo
150 B4 Mollendo Peru
93 F4 Mölnlycke Sweden
91 D2 Molochna r. Ukr.
89 E2 Molokovo Rus. Fed.
53 C2 Molong Austr.
122 B2 Molopo watercourse Botswana/S. Africa
Molotov Rus. Fed. see Perm'
Molotovsk Rus. Fed. see Severodvinsk

Molotovsk Rus. Fed. see Nolinsk
118 B2 Moloundou Cameroon
59 C3 Moluccas is Indon.
Molucca Sea Indon. see Laut Maluku
52 B2 Momba Austr.
119 D3 Mombasa Kenya
154 B1 Mombuca, Serra da hills Brazil
111 C2 Momchilgrad Bulg.
93 F4 Møn i. Denmark
105 D2 Monaco country Europe
96 B2 Monadhliath Mountains U.K.
97 C1 Monaghan Ireland
143 C2 Monahans U.S.A.
147 D3 Mona Passage Dom. Rep./Puerto Rico
120 A1 Mona Quimbundo Angola
Monastir Macedonia see Bitola
89 D3 Monastyrshchina Rus. Fed.
90 B2 Monastyryshche Ukr.
118 B2 Monatélé Cameroon
66 D2 Monbetsu Japan
108 A1 Moncalieri Italy
86 C2 Monchegorsk Rus. Fed.
100 C2 Mönchengladbach Ger.
144 B2 Monclova Mex.
131 D3 Moncton Can.
106 B1 Mondego r. Port
118 C2 Mondjamboli Dem. Rep. Congo
123 D2 Mondlo S. Africa
108 A2 Mondovì Italy
111 B3 Monemvasia Greece
66 D1 Moneron, Ostrov i. Rus. Fed.
139 D1 Monet Can.
137 E3 Monett U.S.A.
108 B1 Monfalcone Italy
106 B1 Monforte de Lemos Spain
119 D2 Mongbwalu Dem. Rep. Congo
62 B1 Mông Cai Vietnam
62 A1 Mong Hang Myanmar
129 D2 Monghyr India see Munger
75 C2 Mongla Bangl.
62 B1 Mong Lin Myanmar
62 A1 Mong Nawng Myanmar
115 D3 Mongo Chad
68 C1 Mongolia country Asia
74 B1 Mongora Pak.
62 A1 Mong Pawk Myanmar
62 A1 Mong Ping Myanmar
107 D1 Mongu Zambia
123 C3 Monitor Range mts U.S.A.
52 A1 Mońki Pol.
99 B4 Monmouth U.K.
114 C4 Mono r. Togo
135 C3 Mono Lake U.S.A.
109 C2 Monopoli Italy
107 C1 Monreal del Campo Spain
140 B2 Monroe LA U.S.A.
138 C2 Monroe MI U.S.A.
138 B2 Monroe WI U.S.A.
140 C2 Monroeville U.S.A.
114 A4 Monrovia Liberia
100 A2 Mons Belgium
155 E1 Monsarás, Ponta de pt Brazil
100 C2 Montabaur Ger.
122 B3 Montagu S. Africa
109 C3 Montalto mt. Italy
110 B2 Montana Bulg.
134 E1 Montana state U.S.A.
105 C2 Montargis France
104 C3 Montauban France
139 E2 Montauk Point U.S.A.
123 C2 Mont-aux-Sources mt. Lesotho
105 C2 Montbard France
105 D2 Montbéliard France
105 C2 Montbrison France
100 B3 Montcornet France
104 B3 Mont-de-Marsan France
104 C2 Montdidier France
151 D3 Monte Alegre Brazil
154 C1 Monte Alegre de Minas Brazil
139 E1 Montebello Can.
154 B3 Montecarlo Arg.
105 D3 Monte-Carlo Monaco
154 C1 Monte Carmelo Brazil
152 C3 Monte Caseros Arg.
123 C1 Monte Cristo S. Africa
108 B2 Montecristo, Isola di i. Italy
146 C3 Montego Bay Jamaica

105 C3 Montélimar France
109 C2 Montella Italy
145 C2 Montemorelos Mex.
104 B2 Montendre France
109 C2 Montenegro country Europe
121 C2 Montepuez Moz.
108 B2 Montepulciano Italy
135 B3 Monterey U.S.A.
135 B3 Monterey Bay U.S.A.
150 B2 Montería Col.
152 B1 Montero Bol.
145 B2 Monterrey Mex.
109 C2 Montesano sulla Marcellana Italy
109 C2 Monte Sant'Angelo Italy
151 F4 Monte Santo Brazil
108 A2 Monte Santu, Capo di c. Sardinia Italy
155 D1 Montes Claros Brazil
153 C3 Montevideo Uru.
137 D2 Montevideo U.S.A.
136 B3 Monte Vista U.S.A.
140 C2 Montgomery U.S.A.
100 B3 Monthermé France
105 D2 Monthey Switz.
140 B2 Monticello AR U.S.A.
141 D2 Monticello FL U.S.A.
135 E3 Monticello UT U.S.A.
104 C2 Montignac France
100 B2 Montignies-le-Tilleul Belgium
105 D2 Montigny-le-Roi France
106 B2 Montijo Port.
106 B2 Montijo Spain
106 C2 Montilla Spain
154 B1 Montividiu Brazil
131 D3 Mont-Joli Can.
130 C3 Mont-Laurier Can.
104 C2 Montluçon France
131 C3 Montmagny Can.
104 C2 Montmorillon France
51 E2 Monto Austr.
134 D2 Montpelier ID U.S.A.
139 E2 Montpelier VT U.S.A.
105 C3 Montpellier France
130 C3 Montréal Can.
129 D2 Montreal Lake Can.
129 D2 Montreal Lake l. Can.
99 D4 Montreuil France
105 D2 Montreux Switz.
96 C2 Montrose U.K.
136 B3 Montrose U.S.A.
147 D3 Montserrat terr. West Indies
62 A1 Monywa Myanmar
108 A1 Monza Italy
107 D1 Monzón Spain
123 C1 Mookane Botswana
52 A1 Moolawatana Austr.
52 B1 Moomba Austr.
53 D1 Moonie Austr.
53 C1 Moonie r. Austr.
52 A2 Moonta Austr.
50 A3 Moora Austr.
50 A2 Moore, Lake salt flat Austr.
137 D1 Moorhead U.S.A.
53 C3 Mooroopna Austr.
122 A3 Moorreesburg S. Africa
130 B2 Moose r. Can.
130 B2 Moose Factory Can.
139 F1 Moosehead Lake U.S.A.
129 D2 Moose Jaw Can.
137 E1 Moose Lake U.S.A.
129 D2 Moosomin Can.
130 B2 Moosonee Can.
52 B2 Mootwingee Austr.
123 C1 Mopane S. Africa
114 B3 Mopti Mali
150 B4 Moquegua Peru
103 D2 Mór Hungary
118 B1 Mora Cameroon
93 F3 Mora Sweden
137 E1 Mora U.S.A.
74 B2 Moradabad India
121 □D2 Morafenobe Madag.
136 A2 Moran U.S.A.
51 D2 Moranbah Austr.
103 D2 Morava r. Europe
96 B2 Moray Firth b. U.K.
100 C3 Morbach Ger.
74 B2 Morbi India
93 G4 Mörbylånga Sweden
104 B3 Morcenx France
69 E1 Mordaga China
129 D3 Morden Can.
89 F3 Mordovo Rus. Fed.
98 B2 Morecambe U.K.
98 B2 Morecambe Bay U.K.

53 C1 Moree Austr.
59 D3 Morehead P.N.G.
138 C3 Morehead U.S.A.
141 E2 Morehead City U.S.A.
145 B3 Morelia Mex.
107 C1 Morella Spain
74 B2 Morena India
106 B2 Morena, Sierra mts Spain
110 C2 Moreni Romania
142 A3 Moreno Mex.
128 A2 Moresby, Mount Can.
128 A2 Moresby Island Can.
53 D1 Moreton Island Austr.
52 A2 Morgan Austr.
140 B3 Morgan City U.S.A.
141 D1 Morganton U.S.A.
139 D3 Morgantown U.S.A.
105 D2 Morges Switz.
68 C2 Mori China
66 D2 Mori Japan
53 C1 Moriarty's Range hills Austr.
128 B2 Morice Lake Can.
66 D3 Morioka Japan
53 D2 Morisset Austr.
104 B2 Morlaix France
98 C3 Morley U.K.
157 G9 Mornington Abyssal Plain sea feature S. Atlantic Ocean
51 C1 Mornington Island Austr.
59 U3 Morobe P.N.G.
114 C1 Morocco country Africa
119 D3 Morogoro Tanz.
64 B3 Moro Gulf Phil.
122 B2 Morokweng S. Africa
121 □D3 Morombe Madag.
68 C1 Mörön Mongolia
121 □D3 Morondava Madag.
106 B2 Morón de la Frontera Spain
121 C2 Moroni Comoros
59 C2 Morotai i. Indon.
119 D2 Moroto Uganda
98 C2 Morpeth U.K.
140 B1 Morrilton U.S.A.
154 C1 Morrinhos Brazil
54 C1 Morrinsville N.Z.
129 E3 Morris Can.
137 D1 Morris U.S.A.
141 D1 Morristown U.S.A.
154 C2 Morro Agudo Brazil
155 E1 Morro d'Anta Brazil
55 K3 Morse, Cape Antarctica
87 D3 Morshanka Rus. Fed.
Morshansk Rus. Fed. see Morshanka
151 C3 Mortes, Rio das r. Brazil
52 B3 Mortlake Austr.
48 G3 Mortlock Islands Micronesia
138 B2 Morton U.S.A.
53 C2 Morundah Austr.
53 D3 Moruya Austr.
96 B2 Morvern reg. U.K.
Morvi India see Morbi
53 C3 Morwell Austr.
101 D3 Mosbach Ger.
89 E2 Moscow Rus. Fed.
134 C1 Moscow U.S.A.
100 C2 Mosel r. Ger.
122 B2 Moselebe watercourse Botswana
105 D2 Moselle r. France
134 C1 Moses Lake U.S.A.
92 □A3 Mosfellsbær Iceland
54 B3 Mosgiel N.Z.
88 C2 Moshchnyy, Ostrov i. Rus. Fed.
89 D2 Moshenskoye Rus. Fed.
119 D3 Moshi Tanz.
92 F2 Mosjøen Norway
Moskva Rus. Fed. see Moscow
103 D2 Mosonmagyaróvár Hungary
146 B4 Mosquitos, Golfo de los b. Panama
93 F4 Moss Norway
Mossâmedes Angola see Namibe
122 B3 Mossel Bay S. Africa
122 B3 Mossel Bay b. S. Africa
118 B3 Mossendjo Congo
51 D1 Mossman Austr.
151 F3 Mossoró Brazil
53 D2 Moss Vale Austr.
102 C1 Most Czech Rep.
114 C1 Mostaganem Alg.

143 E2	Nacogdoches U.S.A.
144 B1	Nacozari de García Mex.
74 D2	Nada China see Danzhou
90 A2	Nadiad India
86 C2	Nadvirna Ukr.
86 G2	Nadvoitsy Rus. Fed.
93 F4	Nadym Rus. Fed.
111 B3	Næstved Denmark
111 B3	Nafpaktos Greece
115 D1	Nafplio Greece
78 B2	Nafūsah, Jabal hills Libya
64 B2	Nafy Saudi Arabia
130 B2	Naga Phil.
67 C3	Nagagami r. Can.
67 C3	Nagano Japan
75 D2	Nagaoka Japan
74 B1	Nagaon India
74 B2	Nagar India
67 A4	Nagar Parkar Pak.
67 B4	Nagasaki Japan
74 B2	Nagato Japan
73 B4	Nagaur India
74 A2	Nagercoil India
74 B2	Nagha Kalat Pak.
67 C3	Nagina India
75 B2	Nagoya Japan
75 D1	Nagpur India
141 E1	Naggu China
82 E1	Nags Head U.S.A.
103 D2	Nagurskiy Rus. Fed.
103 D2	Nagyatád Hungary
128 B1	Nagykanizsa Hungary
81 C2	Nahanni Butte Can.
101 E1	Nahāvand Iran
153 A4	Nahrendorf Ger.
	Nahuel Huapí, Lago l. Arg.
141 D2	Nahunta U.S.A.
131 D2	Nain Can.
81 D2	Nā'īn Iran
121 C2	Naiopué Moz.
96 C2	Nairn U.K.
119 D3	Nairobi Kenya
	Naissus Serbia see Niš
119 D3	Naivasha Kenya
81 D2	Najafābād Iran
78 B2	Najd reg. Saudi Arabia
106 C1	Nájera Spain
65 C1	Najin N. Korea
78 B3	Najrān Saudi Arabia
119 D2	Nakasongola Uganda
67 C3	Nakatsugawa Japan
78 A3	Nakfa Eritrea
66 B2	Nakhodka Rus. Fed.
63 B2	Nakhon Nayok Thai.
63 B2	Nakhon Pathom Thai.
62 B2	Nakhon Phanom Thai.
63 B2	Nakhon Ratchasima Thai.
63 B2	Nakhon Sawan Thai.
63 A3	Nakhon Si Thammarat Thai.
	Nakhrachi Rus. Fed. see Kondinskoye
130 B2	Nakina Can.
126 B3	Naknek U.S.A.
121 C1	Nakonde Zambia
93 F5	Nakskov Denmark
119 D3	Nakuru Kenya
128 C2	Nakusp Can.
75 D2	Nalbari India
87 D4	Nal'chik Rus. Fed.
115 D1	Nālūt Libya
123 C2	Namaacha Moz.
123 C2	Namahadi S. Africa
81 D2	Namak, Daryācheh-ye salt flat Iran
76 B3	Namak, Kavīr-e salt flat Iran
79 C1	Namakzar-e Shadad salt flat Iran
77 D2	Namangan Uzbek.
119 D3	Namanyere Tanz.
122 A2	Namaqualand reg. S. Africa
51 E2	Nambour Austr.
53 D2	Nambucca Heads Austr.
63 B3	Năm Căn Vietnam
75 D1	Nam Co salt l. China
62 B1	Nam Đinh Vietnam
121 C2	Namialo Moz.
120 A3	Namib Desert Namibia
120 A2	Namibe Angola
120 A3	Namibia country Africa
72 D2	Namjagbarwa Feng mt. China
59 C3	Namlea Indon.
62 B2	Nam Ngum Reservoir Laos
53 C2	Namoi r. Austr.
134 C2	Nampa U.S.A.
114 B3	Nampala Mali
65 B2	Namp'o N. Korea
121 C2	Nampula Moz.
72 D2	Namrup India
62 A1	Namsang Myanmar
92 F3	Namsos Norway
92 F3	Namsskogan Norway
62 A1	Nam Tok Thai.
63 A2	Namtsy Rus. Fed.
83 J2	Namtu Myanmar
62 A1	Namtu Myanmar
121 C2	Namuno Moz.
100 B2	Namur Belgium
120 B2	Namwala Zambia
65 B2	Namwŏn S. Korea
62 A1	Namya Ra Myanmar
62 B2	Nan Thai.
128 B3	Nanaimo Can.
71 B3	Nan'an China
122 A1	Nananib Plateau Namibia
	Nan'ao China see Dayu
67 C3	Nanao Japan
71 B3	Nanchang .Jiangxi China
71 B3	Nanchang Jiangxi China
71 B3	Nancheng China
70 A2	Nanchong China
63 A3	Nancowry i. India
105 D2	Nancy France
75 C1	Nanda Devi mt. India
71 A3	Nandan China
74 B3	Nanded India
	Nander India see Nanded
53 D2	Nandewar Range mts Austr.
74 D2	Nandurbar India
73 R3	Nandyal India
71 B3	Nanfeng China
62 A1	Nang China
118 B2	Nanga Eboko Cameroon
61 C2	Nangahpinoh Indon.
77 D3	Nanga Parbat mt. Jammu and Kashmir
61 C2	Nangatayap Indon.
63 A2	Nangin Myanmar
65 B1	Nangnim-sanmaek mts N. Korea
70 B2	Nangong China
119 D3	Nangulangwa Tanz.
70 C2	Nanhui China
70 B2	Nanjing China
	Nanking China see Nanjing
67 B4	Nankoku Japan
120 A2	Nankova Angola
70 B2	Nanle China
71 B3	Nan Ling mts China
71 A3	Nanning China
127 I2	Nanortalik Greenland
71 A3	Nanpan Jiang r. China
75 C2	Nanpara India
71 B3	Nanping China
	Nanpu China see Pucheng
	Nansei-shotō Japan see Ryukyu Islands
160 I1	Nansen Sound sea chan. Can.
104 B2	Nantes France
70 C2	Nantong China
130 C2	Nantucket U.S.A.
139 F2	Nantucket Island U.S.A.
99 B3	Nantwich U.K.
49 I4	Nanumea i. Tuvalu
155 D1	Nanuque Brazil
64 B3	Nanusa, Kepulauan is Indon.
71 B3	Nanxiong China
70 B2	Nanyang China
119 D3	Nanyuki Kenya
70 B2	Nanzhang China
	Nanzhao China see Zhao'an
107 D2	Nao, Cabo de la c. Spain
131 C2	Naococane, Lac l. Can.
74 A2	Naokot Pak.
71 B3	Naozhou Dao i. China
135 B3	Napa U.S.A.
126 E2	Napaktulik Lake Can.
139 D2	Napanee Can.
127 I2	Napasoq Greenland
137 F2	Naperville U.S.A.
54 C1	Napier N.Z.
108 B2	Naples Italy
141 D3	Naples U.S.A.
150 B3	Napo r. Ecuador
	Napoli Italy see Naples
114 B3	Nara Mali
88 C3	Narach Belarus
52 B3	Naracoorte Austr.
53 C2	Naradhan Austr.
145 C2	Naranjos Mex.
63 B3	Narathiwat Thai.
74 B3	Narayanganj India
105 C3	Narbonne France
63 A2	Narcondam Island India
127 H1	Nares Strait Can./Greenland
103 E1	Narew r. Pol.
122 A1	Narib Namibia
87 D4	Narimanov Rus. Fed.
67 D3	Narita Japan
74 B2	Narmada r. India
74 B2	Narnaul India
108 B2	Narni Italy
86 F2	Narodnaya, Gora mt. Rus. Fed.
90 B1	Narodychi Ukr.
89 E2	Naro-Fominsk Rus. Fed.
53 D3	Narooma Austr.
88 C3	Narowlya Belarus
93 H3	Närpes Fin.
53 C2	Narrabri Austr.
53 C2	Narrandera Austr.
53 C2	Narromine Austr.
67 B4	Naruto Japan
88 C2	Narva Estonia
	Narva Bay Estonia/Rus. Fed.
92 G2	Narvik Norway
88 C2	Narvskoye Vodokhranilishche resr Estonia/Rus. Fed.
86 E2	Nar'yan-Mar Rus. Fed.
77 D2	Naryn Kyrg.
139 E2	Nashua U.S.A.
140 C1	Nashville U.S.A.
137 E1	Nashwauk U.S.A.
109 C1	Našice Croatia
117 B4	Nasir Sudan
	Nasirabad Bangl. see Mymensingh
119 C4	Nasondoye Dem. Rep. Congo
76 B3	Naşrābād Iran
128 B2	Nass r. Can.
146 C2	Nassau Bahamas
116 B2	Nasser, Lake resr Egypt
93 F4	Nässjö Sweden
130 C1	Nastapoca r. Can.
130 C1	Nastapoka Islands Can.
89 D2	Nasva Rus. Fed.
120 B3	Nata Botswana
151 F3	Natal Brazil
60 A1	Natal Indon.
	Natal prov. S. Africa see KwaZulu-Natal
159 D6	Natal Basin sea feature Indian Ocean
143 D3	Natalia U.S.A.
131 D2	Natashquan Can.
131 D2	Natashquan r. Can.
140 B2	Natchez U.S.A.
140 B2	Natchitoches U.S.A.
53 C3	Nathalia Austr.
114 C3	Natitingou Benin
151 E4	Natividade Brazil
67 D3	Natori Japan
119 D3	Natron, Lake salt l. Tanz.
60 B1	Natuna, Kepulauan is Indon.
60 B1	Natuna Besar i. Indon.
122 A1	Nauchas Namibia
101 F1	Nauen Ger.
64 B2	Naujan Phil.
88 B2	Naujoji Akmenė Lith.
101 E2	Naumburg (Saale) Ger.
48 H34	Nauru country S. Pacific Ocean
145 C2	Nauta Mex.
145 C2	Nautla Mex.
106 B2	Navahrudak Belarus
106 B2	Navalmoral de la Mata Spain
106 B2	Navalvillar de Pela Spain
97 C2	Navan Ireland
88 C2	Navapolatsk Belarus
83 M2	Navarin, Mys c. Rus. Fed.
153 B5	Navarino, Isla i. Chile
107 C1	Navarre aut. comm. Spain see Navarra
96 B1	Naver r. U.K.
73 B3	Navi Mumbai India
89 D3	Navlya Rus. Fed.
110 C2	Năvodari Romania
77 C2	Navoiy Uzbek.
144 B2	Navojoa Mex.
144 B2	Navolato Mex.
74 A2	Nawabshah Pak.
75 C2	Nawada India
62 A1	Nawnghkio Myanmar
62 A1	Nawngleng Myanmar
81 C2	Naxçıvan Azer.
111 C3	Naxos Greece
111 C3	Naxos i. Greece
144 B2	Nayar Mex.
66 D2	Nayoro Japan
62 A2	Naypyidaw Myanmar
80 B2	Nazareth Israel
144 B2	Nazas Mex.
144 B2	Nazas r. Mex.
150 B4	Nazca Peru
157 H7	Nazca Ridge sea feature S. Pacific Ocean
	Nazerat Israel see Nazareth
111 C3	Nazilli Turkey
117 B4	Nazrēt Eth.
79 C2	Nazwá Oman
121 B1	Nchelenge Zambia
122 B1	Ncojane Botswana
120 A1	N'dalatando Angola
118 C2	Ndélé C.A.R.
118 B3	Ndendé Gabon
115 D3	Ndjamena Chad
118 A3	Ndogo, Lagune lag. Gabon
121 B2	Ndola Zambia
97 C1	Neagh, Lough l. U.K
50 C2	Neale, Lake salt flat Austr.
111 B3	Neapoli Greece
111 B3	Nea Roda Greece
99 B4	Neath U.K.
119 D2	Nebbi Uganda
53 C1	Nebine Creek r. Austr.
150 C2	Neblina, Pico da mt. Brazil
135 D3	Nebo, Mount U.S.A.
89 D2	Nebolchi Rus. Fed.
136 C2	Nebraska state U.S.A.
137 D2	Nebraska City U.S.A.
108 B3	Nebrodi, Monti mts Sicily Italy
143 E3	Neches r. U.S.A.
156 E4	Necker Island U.S.A.
153 C3	Necochea Arg.
143 E3	Nederland U.S.A.
100 B2	Neder Rijn r. Neth.
130 C2	Nedlouc, Lac l. Can.
139 E2	Needham U.S.A.
135 D4	Needles U.S.A.
74 B2	Neemuch India
129 E2	Neepawa Can.
87 E3	Neftekamsk Rus. Fed.
82 F2	Nefteyugansk Rus. Fed.
108 A3	Nefza Tunisia
120 A1	Negage Angola
117 B4	Negēlē Eth.
109 D2	Negotin Serbia
111 B2	Negotino Macedonia
150 A3	Negra, Punta pt Peru
155 D1	Negra, Serra mts Brazil
153 B4	Negrais, Cape Myanmar
150 D3	Negro r. Arg.
152 C3	Negro r. S. America
152 C3	Negro r. Uru.
106 B2	Negro, Cabo c. Morocco
64 B3	Negros i. Phil.
79 D1	Nehbandān Iran
69 E1	Nehe China
70 B2	Neijiang China
129 D2	Neilburg Can.
150 D2	Neiva Col.
129 E2	Nejanilini Lake Can.
	Nejd reg. Saudi Arabia see Najd
117 B4	Nek'emtē Eth.
89 F2	Nekrasovskoye Rus. Fed.
89 D2	Nelidovo Rus. Fed.
73 B3	Nellore India
128 C3	Nelson Can.
129 E2	Nelson r. Can.
54 B2	Nelson N.Z.
52 B3	Nelson, Cape Austr.
53 D2	Nelson Bay Austr.
130 C2	Nelson House Can.
134 E1	Nelson Reservoir U.S.A.
123 C3	Nelspruit S. Africa
114 B3	Néma Maur.
88 B2	Neman Rus. Fed.
105 C2	Nemours France
66 D2	Nemuro Japan
90 B2	Nemyriv Ukr.
97 B2	Nenagh Ireland
99 D3	Nene r. U.K.
69 E1	Nenjiang China
137 E3	Neosho U.S.A.
75 C2	Nepal country Asia
75 C2	Nepalganj Nepal
139 D1	Nepean Can.

89 E2 Noginsk Rus. Fed.
83 K3 Nogliki Rus. Fed.
74 B2 Nohar India
100 C3 Nohfelden Ger.
104 B2 Noires, Montagnes *hills* France
104 B2 Noirmoutier, Île de *i.* France
104 B2 Noirmoutier-en-l'Île France
67 C4 Nojima-zaki *c.* Japan
74 B2 Nokha India
93 H3 Nokia Fin.
74 A2 Nok Kundi Pak.
118 B2 Nola C.A.R.
86 D3 Nolinsk Rus. Fed.
126 A2 Nome U.S.A.
123 C3 Nomonde S. Africa
123 D2 Nondweni S. Africa
Nonghui China *see* Guang'an
62 B2 Nong Khai Thai.
75 D2 Nongstoin India
52 A2 Nonning Austr.
144 B2 Nonoava Mex.
65 R2 Nonsan S. Korea
63 B2 Nonthaburi Thai.
122 B3 Nonzwakazi S. Africa
100 B1 Noordwijk-Binnen Neth.
77 C3 Norak Tajik.
130 C3 Noranda Can.
82 C1 Nordaustlandet *i.* Svalbard
128 C2 Nordegg Can.
100 C1 Norden Ger.
83 H1 Nordenshel'da, Arkhipelag *is* Rus. Fed.
Nordenskjold Archipelago *is* Rus. Fed. *see* Nordenshel'da, Arkhipelag
100 C1 Norderney Ger.
100 C1 Norderney *i.* Ger.
101 E1 Norderstedt Ger.
93 E3 Nordfjordeid Norway
Nordfriesische Inseln Ger. *see* North Frisian Islands
101 E2 Nordhausen Ger.
101 D1 Nordholz Ger.
100 C1 Nordhorn Ger.
Nordkapp Norway *see* North Cape
92 F3 Nordli Norway
102 C2 Nördlingen Ger.
92 G3 Nordmaling Sweden
94 B1 Norðoyar *i.* Faroe Is
97 C2 Nore *r.* Ireland
88 B3 Noreikiškės Lith.
137 D2 Norfolk *NC* U.S.A.
139 D3 Norfolk *VA* U.S.A.
48 H6 Norfolk Island *terr.* S. Pacific Ocean
93 E3 Norheimsund Norway
82 G2 Noril'sk Rus. Fed.
75 C2 Norkyung China
143 D1 Norman U.S.A.
Normandes, Îles *is* English Chan. *see* Channel Islands
150 D2 Normandia Brazil
Normandie *reg.* France *see* Normandy
104 B2 Normandy *reg.* France
51 D1 Normanton Austr.
128 B1 Norman Wells Can.
93 G4 Norrköping Sweden
93 G4 Norrtälje Sweden
50 B3 Norseman Austr.
92 G3 Norsjö Sweden
55 M2 Norsk Rus. Fed.
North, Cape Antarctica
98 C2 Northallerton U.K.
50 A3 Northam Austr.
50 A2 Northampton Austr.
99 C3 Northampton U.K.
73 D3 North Andaman *i.* India
159 F4 North Australian Basin *sea feature* Indian Ocean
129 D2 North Battleford Can.
130 C3 North Bay Can.
130 C2 North Belcher Islands Can.
96 C2 North Berwick U.K.
North Borneo *state* Malaysia *see* Sabah
92 I1 North Cape *c.* Norway
54 B1 North Cape N.Z.
130 A2 North Caribou Lake Can.
141 E1 North Carolina *state* U.S.A.
130 B3 North Channel *lake channel* Can.

96 A3 North Channel U.K.
141 E2 North Charleston U.S.A.
128 B3 North Cowichan Can.
136 C1 North Dakota *state* U.S.A.
99 C4 North Downs *hills* U.K.
157 E3 Northeast Pacific Basin *sea feature* N. Pacific Ocean
141 E3 Northeast Providence Channel Bahamas
101 D2 Northeim Ger.
122 A2 Northern Cape *prov.* S. Africa
Northern Dvina *r.* Rus. Fed. *see* Severnaya Dvina
129 E2 Northern Indian Lake Can.
97 C1 Northern Ireland *prov.* U.K.
59 D1 Northern Mariana Islands *terr.* N. Pacific Ocean
Northern Rhodesia *country* Africa *see* Zambia
50 C1 Northern Territory *admin. div.* Austr.
Northern Transvaal *prov.* S. Africa *see* Limpopo
96 C2 North Esk *r.* U.K.
137 E2 Northfield U.S.A.
99 D4 North Foreland *c.* U.K.
102 B1 North Frisian Islands *is* Ger.
54 B1 North Island N.Z.
129 E2 North Knife Lake Can.
65 B1 North Korea *country* Asia
72 D2 North Lakhimpur India
North Land *is* Rus. Fed. *see* Severnaya Zemlya
128 B1 North Nahanni *r.* Can.
136 C2 North Platte U.S.A.
136 C2 North Platte *r.* U.S.A.
96 C1 North Ronaldsay *i.* U.K.
129 D2 North Saskatchewan *r.* Can.
94 D2 North Sea Europe
63 A2 North Sentinel Island India
130 A2 North Spirit Lake Can.
53 D1 North Stradbroke Island Austr.
131 D3 North Sydney Can.
54 B1 North Taranaki Bight *b.* N.Z.
130 U2 North Twin Island Can.
98 B2 North Tyne *r.* U.K.
96 A2 North Uist *i.* U.K.
131 D3 Northumberland Strait Can.
99 D3 North Walsham U.K.
123 C2 North West *prov.* S. Africa
158 D1 Northwest Atlantic Mid-Ocean Channel *sea chan.* N. Atlantic Ocean
50 A2 North West Cape Austr.
156 D3 Northwest Pacific Basin *sea feature* N. Pacific Ocean
141 E3 Northwest Providence Channel Bahamas
131 E2 North West River Can.
128 B1 Northwest Territories *admin. div.* Can.
98 C2 North York Moors *moorland* U.K.
138 C3 Norton U.S.A.
121 C2 Norton Zimbabwe
Norton de Matos Angola *see* Balombo
126 B2 Norton Sound *sea chan.* U.S.A.
55 L2 Norvegia, Cape Antarctica
138 C2 Norwalk U.S.A.
93 F3 Norway *country* Europe
129 E2 Norway House Can.
160 L3 Norwegian Basin *sea feature* N. Atlantic Ocean
92 E2 Norwegian Sea N. Atlantic Ocean
99 D3 Norwich U.K.
139 E2 Norwich *CT* U.S.A.
139 D2 Norwich *NY* U.S.A.
66 D2 Noshiro Japan
91 C1 Nosivka Ukr.
122 B2 Nosop *watercourse* Africa
86 E2 Nosovaya Rus. Fed.
79 C2 Noṣratābād Iran
121 □D2 Nosy Bé *i.* Madag.
121 □E2 Nosy Boraha *i.* Madag.
103 D1 Noteć *r.* Pol.

93 E4 Notodden Norway
67 C3 Noto-hantō *pen.* Japan
131 D3 Notre-Dame, Monts *mts* Can.
131 E3 Notre Dame Bay Can.
130 C2 Nottaway *r.* Can.
99 C3 Nottingham U.K.
114 A2 Nouâdhibou Maur.
114 A3 Nouakchott Maur.
114 A3 Nouâmghâr Maur.
63 B2 Nouei Vietnam
48 H6 Nouméa New Caledonia
114 B3 Nouna Burkina
122 B3 Noupoort S. Africa
Nouveau-Comptoir Can. *see* Wemindji
114 B3 Nouvelle Anvers Dem. Rep. Congo *see* Makanza
Nouvelles Hébrides *country* S. Pacific Ocean *see* Vanuatu
Nova Chaves Angola *see* Muconda
164 B2 Nova Esperança Brazil
81 D2 Nova Freixa Moz. *see* Cuamba
155 D2 Nova Friburgo Brazil
109 C1 Nova Gradiška Croatia
154 C2 Nova Granada Brazil
155 D2 Nova Iguaçu Brazil
91 C2 Nova Kakhovka Ukr.
155 D1 Nova Lima Brazil
Nova Lisboa Angola *see* Huambo
154 B2 Nova Londrina Brazil
91 C2 Nova Odesa Ukr.
154 C1 Nova Paraíso Brazil
154 C1 Nova Ponte Brazil
108 A1 Novara Italy
151 E3 Nova Remanso Brazil
131 D3 Nova Scotia *prov.* Can.
155 D1 Nova Venécia Brazil
83 K1 Novaya Sibir', Ostrov *i.* Rus. Fed.
86 E1 Novaya Zemlya *is* Rus. Fed.
107 C2 Novelda Spain
103 D2 Nové Zámky Slovakia
Novgorod Rus. Fed. *see* Veliky Novgorod
91 C1 Novhorod-Sivers'kyy Ukr.
110 B2 Novi Iskŭr Bulg.
66 D1 Novikovo Rus. Fed.
108 A2 Novi Ligure Italy
109 D2 Novi Pazar Serbia
109 C1 Novi Sad Serbia
Novoalekseyevka Kazakh. *see* Khobda
87 D3 Novoanninskiy Rus. Fed.
150 C3 Novo Aripuanã Brazil
91 D2 Novoazovs'k Ukr.
91 E2 Novocherkassk Rus. Fed.
89 D2 Novodugino Rus. Fed.
86 D2 Novodvinsk Rus. Fed.
Novoekonomicheskoye Ukr. *see* Dymytrov
152 C2 Novo Hamburgo Brazil
154 C2 Novo Horizonte Brazil
90 B1 Novohrad-Volyns'kyy Ukr.
Novokazalinsk Kazakh. *see* Ayteke Bi
91 E1 Novokhopersk Rus. Fed.
68 B1 Novokuznetsk Rus. Fed.
109 C1 Novo Mesto Slovenia
91 D3 Novomikhaylovskiy Rus. Fed.
89 E3 Novomoskovsk Rus. Fed.
91 D2 Novomoskovs'k Ukr.
91 C2 Novomyrhorod Ukr.
Novonikolayevsk Rus. Fed. *see* Novosibirsk
91 C2 Novooleksiyivka Ukr.
91 C2 Novopokrovskaya Rus. Fed.
91 D2 Novopskov Ukr.
Novo Redondo Angola *see* Sumbe
91 D2 Novorossiysk Rus. Fed.
88 C2 Novorzhev Rus. Fed.
87 D3 Novosergiyevka Rus. Fed.
91 D2 Novoshakhtinsk Rus. Fed.
82 G3 Novosibirsk Rus. Fed.
Novosibirskiye Ostrova *is* Rus. Fed. *see* New Siberia Islands
89 E3 Novosil' Rus. Fed.
89 E3 Novosokol'niki Rus. Fed.
91 C2 Novotroyits'ke Ukr.
91 C2 Novoukrayinka Ukr.
90 A1 Novovolyns'k Ukr.

89 E3 Novovoronezh Rus. Fed.
Novovoronezhskiy Rus. Fed. *see* Novovoronezh
89 D3 Novozybkov Rus. Fed.
103 D2 Nový Jičín Czech Rep.
86 E2 Novyy Bor Rus. Fed.
91 C2 Novyy Buh Ukr.
Novyy Donbass Ukr. *see* Dymytrov
Novyye Petushki Rus. Fed. *see* Petushki
86 G2 Novyy Margelan Uzbek. *see* Farg'ona
89 E2 Novyy Nekouz Rus. Fed.
91 D1 Novyy Oskol Rus. Fed.
86 G2 Novyy Port Rus. Fed.
86 G2 Novyy Urengoy Rus. Fed.
69 E1 Novyy Urgal Rus. Fed.
Novyy Uzen' Kazakh. *see* Zhanaozen
103 D1 Nowogard Pol.
Noworadomsk Pol. *see* Radomsko
53 D2 Nowra Austr.
81 D2 Nowshahr Iran
74 B1 Nowshera Pak.
103 E2 Nowy Sącz Pol.
103 E2 Nowy Targ Pol.
82 G2 Noyabr'sk Rus. Fed.
105 C2 Noyon France
121 C2 Nsanje Malawi
121 B2 Nsombo Zambia
118 B3 Ntandembele Dem. Rep. Congo
111 B3 Ntha S. Africa
111 B3 Ntoro, Kavo *pt* Greece
118 A2 Ntoum Gabon
119 D3 Ntungamo Uganda
Nuanetsi *r.* Zimbabwe *see* Mwenezi
79 C2 Nu'aym *reg.* Oman
116 B2 Nubian Desert Sudan
150 B4 Nudo Coropuna *mt.* Peru
143 D3 Nueces *r.* U.S.A.
129 E1 Nueltin Lake Can.
153 A4 Nueva Lubecka Arg.
145 B2 Nueva Rosita Mex.
144 B1 Nuevo Casas Grandes Mex.
144 B2 Nuevo Ideal Mex.
145 C2 Nuevo Laredo Mex.
117 C4 Nugaal *watercourse* Somalia
105 C2 Nuits-St-Georges France
Nu Jiang *r.* China/Myanmar *see* Salween
Nukha Azer. *see* Şäki
49 J6 Nuku'alofa Tonga
49 M4 Nuku Hiva *i.* Fr. Polynesia
48 G4 Nukumanu Islands P.N.G.
76 B2 Nukus Uzbek.
50 B2 Nullagine Austr.
50 C3 Nullarbor Austr.
50 B3 Nullarbor Plain Austr.
115 D4 Numan Nigeria
67 C3 Numazu Japan
51 C1 Numbulwar Austr.
93 E3 Numedal *val.* Norway
59 C3 Numfoor *i.* Indon.
53 C3 Numurkah Austr.
Nunap Isua *c.* Greenland *see* Farewell, Cape
127 G2 Nunavik *reg.* Can.
129 E1 Nunavut *admin. div.* Can.
99 C3 Nuneaton U.K.
126 A3 Nunivak Island U.S.A.
106 B1 Nuñomoral Spain
108 A2 Nuoro Sardinia Italy
78 B2 Nuqrah Saudi Arabia
77 C1 Nura *r.* Kazakh.
101 E3 Nuremberg Ger.
52 A2 Nuriootpa Austr.
92 I3 Nurmes Fin.
Nürnberg Ger. *see* Nuremberg
53 C2 Nurri, Mount *hill* Austr.
62 A1 Nu Shan *mts* China
74 A2 Nushki Pak.
127 I2 Nuuk Greenland
127 I2 Nuussuaq Greenland
127 I2 Nuussuaq *pen.* Greenland
80 B3 Nuwaybi' al Muzayyinah Egypt
122 A3 Nuwerus S. Africa
122 B3 Nuweveldberge *mts* S. Africa
86 F2 Nyagan' Rus. Fed.
75 D1 Nyainqêntanglha Feng *mt.* China

146 B2 **Pinar del Río** Cuba
64 B2 **Pinatubo, Mount** vol. Phil.
103 E1 **Pińczów** Pol.
151 E3 **Pindaré** r. Brazil
Pindos Greece see
Pindus Mountains
111 B3 **Pindus Mountains** mts
Greece
140 B2 **Pine Bluff** U.S.A.
136 C2 **Pine Bluffs** U.S.A.
50 C1 **Pine Creek** Austr.
136 B2 **Pinedale** U.S.A.
86 D2 **Pinega** Rus. Fed.
129 C2 **Pinehouse Lake** Can.
111 B3 **Pineios** r. Greece
141 D3 **Pine Islands** FL U.S.A.
141 D4 **Pine Islands** FL U.S.A.
128 C1 **Pine Point** Can.
136 C2 **Pine Ridge** U.S.A.
108 A2 **Pinerolo** Italy
Pines, Isle of i. Cuba see
Juventud, Isla de la
123 C2 **Pinetown** S. Africa
140 B2 **Pineville** U.S.A.
70 B2 **Pingdingshan** China
70 B2 **Pingdu** China
62 B1 **Pingguo** China
71 B3 **Pingjiang** China
70 A2 **Pingliang** China
70 B1 **Pingquan** China
71 C3 **P'ingtung** Taiwan
Pingxi China see Yuping
71 A3 **Pingxiang** Guangxi China
71 B3 **Pingxiang** Jiangxi China
70 B2 **Pingyin** China
155 C2 **Pinhal** Brazil
151 E3 **Pinheiro** Brazil
52 B3 **Pinnaroo** Austr.
101 D1 **Pinneberg** Ger.
Pinos, Isla de i. Cuba see
Juventud, Isla de la
145 C3 **Pinotepa Nacional** Mex.
48 H6 **Pins, Île des** i.
New Caledonia
88 C3 **Pinsk** Belarus
152 B2 **Pinto** Arg.
135 D3 **Pioche** U.S.A.
119 C3 **Piodi** Dem. Rep. Congo
108 B2 **Piombino** Italy
86 F2 **Pionerskiy** Rus. Fed.
103 E1 **Pionki** Pol.
103 D1 **Piotrków Trybunalski** Pol.
137 D2 **Pipestone** U.S.A.
131 C3 **Pipmuacan, Réservoir**
resr Can.
154 B2 **Piquiri** r. Brazil
154 C1 **Piracanjuba** Brazil
154 C2 **Piracicaba** Brazil
155 D1 **Piracicaba** r. Brazil
154 C2 **Piraçununga** Brazil
111 B3 **Piraeus** Greece
154 C2 **Piraí do Sul** Brazil
154 C2 **Piraju** Brazil
154 C2 **Pirajuí** Brazil
154 B1 **Piranhas** Brazil
151 F3 **Piranhas** r. Brazil
155 D1 **Pirapora** Brazil
154 C1 **Pirenópolis** Brazil
154 C1 **Pires do Rio** Brazil
Pirineos mts Europe see
Pyrenees
151 E3 **Piripiri** Brazil
109 C2 **Pirot** Serbia
59 C3 **Piru** Indon.
108 B2 **Pisa** Italy
152 A1 **Pisagua** Chile
150 B4 **Pisco** Peru
102 C2 **Písek** Czech Rep.
79 D2 **Pishin** Iran
74 A1 **Pishin** Pak.
145 C3 **Pisté** Mex.
109 C2 **Pisticci** Italy
108 B2 **Pistoia** Italy
106 C1 **Pisuerga** r. Spain
134 B2 **Pit** r. U.S.A.
114 A3 **Pita** Guinea
154 B2 **Pitanga** Brazil
155 D1 **Pitangui** Brazil
49 O6 **Pitcairn Island**
S. Pacific Ocean
49 O6 **Pitcairn Islands** terr.
S. Pacific Ocean
92 H2 **Piteå** Sweden
92 H2 **Piteälven** r. Sweden
110 B2 **Piteşti** Romania
75 C2 **Pithoragarh** India
142 A2 **Pitiquito** Mex.
86 C2 **Pitkyaranta** Rus. Fed.
96 C2 **Pitlochry** U.K.
128 B2 **Pitt Island** Can.
137 E3 **Pittsburg** U.S.A.

138 D2 **Pittsburgh** U.S.A.
139 E2 **Pittsfield** U.S.A.
155 C2 **Piumhi** Brazil
150 A3 **Piura** Peru
90 C2 **Pivdennyy Buh** r. Ukr.
131 E3 **Placentia** Can.
135 B3 **Placerville** U.S.A.
146 C2 **Placetas** Cuba
143 C2 **Plains** U.S.A.
143 C2 **Plainview** U.S.A.
60 B2 **Plaju** Indon.
61 C2 **Plampang** Indon.
154 C1 **Planaltina** Brazil
137 D2 **Plankinton** U.S.A.
143 D2 **Plano** U.S.A.
154 C2 **Planura** Brazil
140 B2 **Plaquemine** U.S.A.
106 B1 **Plasencia** Spain
109 C1 **Plaški** Croatia
68 B2 **Plateau of Tibet** plat.
China
147 C4 **Plato** Col.
137 D2 **Platte** r. U.S.A.
138 A2 **Platteville** U.S.A.
139 E2 **Plattsburgh** U.S.A.
101 F1 **Plau** Ger.
101 F2 **Plauen** Ger.
101 F1 **Plauer See** l. Ger.
89 E3 **Plavsk** Rus. Fed.
106 B2 **Playa de Castilla**
coastal area Spain
129 E2 **Playgreen Lake** Can.
63 B2 **Plây Ku** Vietnam
153 B3 **Plaza Huincul** Arg.
143 D3 **Pleasanton** U.S.A.
54 B2 **Pleasant Point** N.Z.
138 C2 **Pleasure Ridge Park**
U.S.A.
104 C2 **Pleaux** France
130 B2 **Pledger Lake** Can.
54 C1 **Plenty, Bay of** g. N.Z.
136 C1 **Plentywood** U.S.A.
86 D2 **Plesetsk** Rus. Fed.
131 C2 **Plétipi, Lac** l. Can.
100 C2 **Plettenberg** Ger.
122 B3 **Plettenberg Bay** S. Africa
110 B2 **Pleven** Bulg.
Plevlja Montenegro see **Pljevlja**
109 C2 **Pljevlja** Montenegro
108 A2 **Ploaghe** Sardinia Italy
109 C2 **Ploče** Croatia
103 D1 **Płock** Pol.
109 C2 **Pločno** mt. Bos.-Herz.
104 B2 **Ploemeur** France
Ploeşti Romania see
Ploieşti
110 C2 **Ploieşti** Romania
89 F2 **Ploskoye** Rus. Fed.
104 B2 **Plouzané** France
110 B2 **Plovdiv** Bulg.
Plozk Pol. see Płock
121 B3 **Plumtree** Zimbabwe
88 B2 **Plungė** Lith.
144 B2 **Plutarco Elías Calles,**
Presa resr Mex.
88 C3 **Plyeshchanitsy** Belarus
147 D3 **Plymouth** Montserrat
99 A4 **Plymouth** U.K.
138 B2 **Plymouth** U.S.A.
99 B3 **Plynlimon** hill U.K.
88 C2 **Plyussa** Rus. Fed.
102 C2 **Plzeň** Czech Rep.
114 B3 **Pô** Burkina
108 B1 **Po** r. Italy
61 C1 **Po, Tanjung** pt Malaysia
77 M2 **Pobeda Peak** China/Kyrg.
Pobedy, Pik mt. China/
Kyrg. see Pobeda Peak
140 B1 **Pocahontas** U.S.A.
134 D2 **Pocatello** U.S.A.
90 B1 **Pochayiv** Ukr.
89 D3 **Pochep** Rus. Fed.
89 D3 **Pochinok** Rus. Fed.
145 C3 **Pochutla** Mex.
139 D3 **Pocomoke City** U.S.A.
155 C2 **Poços de Caldas** Brazil
89 D2 **Poddor'ye** Rus. Fed.
91 D1 **Podgorenskiy** Rus. Fed.
109 C2 **Podgorica** Montenegro
82 G3 **Podgornoye** Rus. Fed.
83 H2 **Podkamennaya Tunguska**
r. Rus. Fed.
89 E2 **Podol'sk** Rus. Fed.
109 D2 **Podujevo** Serbia
122 A2 **Pofadder** S. Africa
89 D3 **Pogar** Rus. Fed.
105 E3 **Poggibonsi** Italy
109 D2 **Pogradec** Albania
66 B2 **Pogranichnyy** Rus. Fed.
Po Hai g. China see Bo Hai

65 B2 **P'ohang** S. Korea
48 G3 **Pohnpei** atoll Micronesia
90 B2 **Pohrebyshche** Ukr.
110 B2 **Poiana Mare** Romania
118 C3 **Poie** Dem. Rep. Congo
118 B3 **Pointe-Noire** Congo
126 A2 **Point Hope** U.S.A.
128 C1 **Point Lake** Can.
138 C3 **Point Pleasant** U.S.A.
104 C2 **Poitiers** France
104 C2 **Poitou, Plaines et Seuil**
du plain France
74 B2 **Pokaran** India
53 C1 **Pokataroo** Austr.
75 C2 **Pokhara** Nepal
119 C2 **Poko** Dem. Rep. Congo
83 J2 **Pokrovsk** Rus. Fed.
91 D2 **Pokrovskoye** Rus. Fed.
Pola Croatia see Pula
142 A1 **Polacca** U.S.A.
106 B1 **Pola de Lena** Spain
106 B1 **Pola de Siero** Spain
103 D1 **Poland** country Europe
55 C1 **Polar Plateau** Antarctica
80 B2 **Polatlı** Turkey
88 C2 **Polatsk** Belarus
77 C3 **Pol-e Khomrī** Afgh.
61 C2 **Polewali** Indon.
118 B2 **Poli** Cameroon
102 C1 **Police** Pol.
109 C2 **Policoro** Italy
105 D2 **Poligny** France
64 B2 **Polillo Islands** Phil.
80 B2 **Polis** Cyprus
90 B1 **Polis'ke** Ukr.
109 C3 **Polistena** Italy
103 D1 **Polkowice** Pol.
107 D2 **Pollença** Spain
109 C3 **Pollino, Monte** mt. Italy
86 F2 **Polnovat** Rus. Fed.
91 D2 **Polohy** Ukr.
123 C1 **Polokwane** S. Africa
90 B1 **Polonne** Ukr.
134 D1 **Polson** U.S.A.
91 C2 **Poltava** Ukr.
66 B2 **Poltavka** Rus. Fed.
91 D2 **Poltavskaya** Rus. Fed.
88 C2 **Põltsamaa** Estonia
88 C2 **Põlva** Estonia
Polyanovgrad Bulg. see
Karnobat
91 D2 **Polyarnyy** Rus. Fed.
86 C2 **Polyarnyye Zori** Rus. Fed.
111 B2 **Polygyros** Greece
111 B2 **Polykastro** Greece
156 E6 **Polynesia** is Pacific
Ocean
106 B2 **Pombal** Port.
102 C1 **Pomeranian Bay** b.
Ger./Pol.
108 B2 **Pomezia** Italy
Pommersche Bucht b.
Ger. see Pomeranian Bay
92 I2 **Pomokaira** reg. Fin.
110 C2 **Pomorie** Bulg.
Pomorska, Zatoka b. Pol.
see Pomeranian Bay
155 D1 **Pompéu** Brazil
143 D1 **Ponca City** U.S.A.
147 D3 **Ponce** Puerto Rico
Pondicherry India see
Puducherry
127 G2 **Pond Inlet** Can.
Ponds Bay Can. see
Pond Inlet
106 B1 **Ponferrada** Spain
117 A4 **Pongo** watercourse Sudan
123 D2 **Pongola** r. S. Africa
123 D2 **Pongolapoort Dam** l.
S. Africa
128 C2 **Ponoka** Can.
154 B3 **Ponta Grossa** Brazil
154 C1 **Pontalina** Brazil
105 D2 **Pont-à-Mousson** France
154 A2 **Ponta Porã** Brazil
105 D2 **Pontarlier** France
102 B2 **Pontcharra** France
140 B2 **Pontchartrain, Lake**
U.S.A.
154 B1 **Ponte de Pedra** Brazil
106 B2 **Ponte de Sor** Port.
154 B1 **Ponte do Rio Verde**
Brazil
98 C3 **Pontefract** U.K.
129 D3 **Ponteix** Can.
155 D2 **Ponte Nova** Brazil
150 D4 **Pontes-e-Lacerda** Brazil
106 B1 **Pontevedra** Spain
Ponthierville Dem. Rep.
Congo see Ubundu
138 B2 **Pontiac** IL U.S.A.

138 C2 **Pontiac** MI U.S.A.
60 B2 **Pontianak** Indon.
Pontine Islands is Italy
see Ponziane, Isole
104 B2 **Pontivy** France
151 D2 **Pontoetoe** Suriname
104 C2 **Pontoise** France
129 E2 **Ponton** Can.
99 B4 **Pontypool** U.K.
99 B4 **Pontypridd** U.K.
108 B2 **Ponziane, Isole** is Italy
99 C4 **Poole** U.K.
Poona India see Pune
52 B2 **Pooncarie** Austr.
152 B1 **Poopó, Lago de** l. Bol.
150 B2 **Popayán** Col.
83 I2 **Popigay** r. Rus. Fed.
52 B2 **Popiltah** N.S.W. Austr.
129 E2 **Poplar** r. U.S.A.
137 E3 **Poplar Bluff** U.S.A.
118 B3 **Popokabaka** Dem. Rep.
Congo
Popovichskaya Rus. Fed.
see Kalininskaya
110 C2 **Popovo** Bulg.
103 E2 **Poprad** Slovakia
151 E4 **Porangatu** Brazil
74 A2 **Porbandar** India
126 C2 **Porcupine** r. Can./U.S.A.
108 B1 **Pordenone** Italy
108 B1 **Poreč** Croatia
154 B2 **Porecatu** Brazil
114 C3 **Porga** Benin
93 H3 **Pori** Fin.
54 B2 **Porirua** N.Z.
88 C2 **Porkhov** Rus. Fed.
104 B2 **Pornic** France
83 K3 **Poronaysk** Rus. Fed.
75 D1 **Porong** China
111 B3 **Poros** Greece
92 I1 **Porsangerfjorden**
sea chan. Norway
93 E4 **Porsgrunn** Norway
111 D3 **Porsuk** r. Turkey
97 C1 **Portadown** U.K.
97 C1 **Portaferry** U.K.
138 B2 **Portage** U.S.A.
129 E3 **Portage la Prairie** Can.
128 B3 **Port Alberni** Can.
106 B2 **Portalegre** Port.
143 C2 **Portales** U.S.A.
128 A2 **Port Alexander** U.S.A.
128 B2 **Port Alice** Can.
140 B2 **Port Allen** U.S.A.
134 B1 **Port Angeles** U.S.A.
97 C2 **Portarlington** Ireland
51 D4 **Port Arthur** Austr.
Port Arthur China see
Lüshun
143 E3 **Port Arthur** U.S.A.
96 A3 **Port Askaig** U.K.
52 A2 **Port Augusta** Austr.
147 C3 **Port-au-Prince** Haiti
131 E2 **Port aux Choix** Can.
122 B3 **Port Beaufort** S. Africa
73 D3 **Port Blair** India
52 B3 **Port Campbell** Austr.
131 D2 **Port-Cartier** Can.
54 B3 **Port Chalmers** N.Z.
141 D3 **Port Charlotte** U.S.A.
147 C3 **Port-de-Paix** Haiti
128 A2 **Port Edward** Can.
155 D1 **Porteirinha** Brazil
151 D3 **Portel** Brazil
130 B3 **Port Elgin** Can.
123 C3 **Port Elizabeth** S. Africa
96 A3 **Port Ellen** U.K.
98 A2 **Port Erin** Isle of Man
122 A3 **Porterville** S. Africa
135 C3 **Porterville** U.S.A.
Port Étienne Maur. see
Nouâdhibou
52 B3 **Port Fairy** Austr.
54 C1 **Port Fitzroy** N.Z.
Port Francqui
Dem. Rep. Congo see Ilebo
118 A3 **Port-Gentil** Gabon
115 C4 **Port Harcourt** Nigeria
128 B2 **Port Hardy** Can.
Port Harrison Can. see
Inukjuak
131 D3 **Port Hawkesbury** Can.
99 B4 **Porthcawl** U.K.
50 A2 **Port Hedland** Austr.
Port Herald Malawi see
Nsanje
99 A3 **Porthmadog** U.K.
131 E2 **Port Hope Simpson**
Can.
138 C2 **Port Huron** U.S.A.
106 B2 **Portimão** Port.

Puerto Presidente Stroessner Para. *see* Ciudad del Este
64 A3 Puerto Princesa Phil.
154 A3 Puerto Rico Arg.
147 D3 Puerto Rico *terr.* West Indies
158 C3 Puerto Rico Trench *sea feature* Caribbean Sea
146 A3 Puerto San José Guat.
153 B5 Puerto Santa Cruz Arg.
152 C2 Puerto Sastre Para.
144 B2 Puerto Vallarta Mex.
87 D3 Pugachev Rus. Fed.
74 B2 Pugal India
54 B2 Pukaki, Lake N.Z.
49 K5 Pukapuka *atoll* Cook Is
129 D2 Pukatawagan Can.
65 B1 Pukchin N. Korea
65 B1 Pukch'ŏng N. Korea
109 C2 Pukë Albania
54 B1 Pukekohe N.Z.
65 B1 Puksubaek-san *mt.* N. Korea
Pula China *see* Nyingchi
108 B2 Pula Croatia
108 A3 Pula *Sardinia* Italy
152 B2 Pulacayo Bol.
103 E1 Puławy Pol.
92 I3 Pulkkila Fin.
134 C1 Pullman U.S.A.
64 B2 Pulog, Mount Phil.
64 B3 Pulutan Indon.
150 A3 Puná, Isla *i.* Ecuador
54 B2 Punakaiki N.Z.
123 D1 Punda Maria S. Africa
73 B3 Pune India
65 B1 P'ungsan N. Korea
121 C2 Púnguè *r.* Moz.
119 C3 Punia Dem. Rep. Congo
74 B1 Punjab *state* India
153 B3 Punta Alta Arg.
153 A5 Punta Arenas Chile
108 A2 Punta Balestrieri *mt. Sardinia* Italy
153 C3 Punta del Este Uru.
146 B3 Punta Gorda Belize
146 B3 Puntarenas Costa Rica
150 B1 Punto Fijo Venez.
92 I3 Puolanka Fin.
Puqi China *see* Chibi
82 G2 Pur *r.* Rus. Fed.
75 C3 Puri India
100 B1 Purmerend Neth.
Purnea India *see* Purnia
75 C2 Purnia India
75 C2 Puruliya India
150 B3 Purus *r.* Peru
61 B2 Purwakarta Indon.
61 C2 Purwodadi Indon.
65 B1 Puryŏng N. Korea
74 B3 Pusad India
65 B2 Pusan S. Korea
89 E3 Pushchino Rus. Fed.
Pushkino Azer. *see* Biläsuvar
89 E2 Pushkino Rus. Fed.
88 C2 Pushkinskiye Gory Rus. Fed.
88 C2 Pustoshka Rus. Fed.
62 A1 Putao Myanmar
71 B3 Putian China
Puting China *see* De'an
61 C2 Puting, Tanjung *pt* Indon.
101 F1 Putlitz Ger.
60 B1 Putrajaya Malaysia
122 B2 Putsonderwater S. Africa
102 C1 Puttgarden Ger.
150 B3 Putumayo *r.* Col.
61 C1 Putusibau Indon.
90 B2 Putyla Ukr.
91 C1 Putyvl' Ukr.
93 I3 Puula I. Fin.
130 C1 Puvirnituq Can.
70 B2 Puyang China
104 C3 Puylaurens France
119 C3 Pweto Dem. Rep. Congo
99 A3 Pwllheli U.K.
92 J2 Pyaozerskiy Rus. Fed.
63 A2 Pyapon Myanmar
83 G2 Pyasina *r.* Rus. Fed.
87 D4 Pyatigorsk Rus. Fed.
91 C2 P"yatykhatky Ukr.
62 A2 Pyè Myanmar
88 C3 Pyetrykaw Belarus
93 H3 Pyhäjärvi *l.* Fin.
92 H3 Pyhäjoki *r.* Fin.
92 I3 Pyhäsalmi Fin.
62 A1 Pyingaing Myanmar
62 A2 Pyinmana Myanmar
62 A1 Pyin-U-Lwin Myanmar

65 B2 Pyŏksŏng N. Korea
65 B2 P'yŏnggang N. Korea
65 B2 P'yŏngsan N. Korea
65 B2 P'yŏngsong N. Korea
65 B2 P'yŏngt'aek S. Korea
65 B2 P'yŏngyang N. Korea
135 C2 Pyramid Lake U.S.A.
80 B3 Pyramids of Giza *tourist site* Egypt
107 D1 Pyrenees *mts* Europe
111 B3 Pyrgetos Greece
111 C3 Pyrgi Greece
111 B3 Pyrgos Greece
91 C1 Pyryatyn Ukr.
103 C1 Pyrzyce Pol.
88 C2 Pytalovo Rus. Fed.
111 B3 Pyxaria *mt.* Greece

Q

Qaanaaq Greenland *see* Thule
Qabqa China *see* Gonghe
123 C3 Qacha's Nek Lesotho
69 D2 Qagan Nur China
Qahremānshahr Iran *see* Kermānshāh
68 C2 Qaidam Pendi *basin* China
79 C2 Qalamat Abū Shafrah Saudi Arabia
78 A2 Qal'at al Azlam Saudi Arabia
78 A2 Qal'at al Mu'azzam Saudi Arabia
78 B2 Qal'at Bishah Saudi Arabia
76 C3 Qal'eh-ye Now Afgh.
129 E1 Qamanirjuaq Lake Can.
Qamanittuaq Can. *see* Baker Lake
79 C3 Qamar, Ghubbat al *b.* Yemen
78 C3 Qamar, Ghubbat al *b.* Yemen
68 C2 Qamdo China
78 B3 Qam Hadil Saudi Arabia
127 I2 Qaqortoq Greenland
80 A3 Qārah Egypt
Qarkilik China *see* Ruoqiang
77 C3 Qarshi Uzbek.
78 B2 Qaryat al Ulyā Saudi Arabia
127 I2 Qasigiannguit Greenland
116 A2 Qaşr al Farāfirah Egypt
79 D2 Qasr-e Qand Iran
81 C2 Qaşr-e Shīrīn Iran
127 I2 Qassimiut Greenland
78 B3 Qa'tabah Yemen
79 C2 Qatar *country* Asia
116 A2 Qattara Depression Egypt
Qausuittuq Can. *see* Resolute
76 B3 Qāyen Iran
81 C1 Qazax Azer.
81 C1 Qazımämmäd Azer.
81 C2 Qazvīn Iran
127 I2 Qeqertarsuaq Greenland
127 I2 Qeqertarsuaq *i.* Greenland
127 I2 Qeqertarsuatsiaat Greenland
127 I2 Qeqertarsuup Tunua *b.* Greenland
79 C2 Qeshm Iran
74 A1 Qeyşār, Kūh-e *mt.* Afgh.
70 A3 Qianjiang *Chongqing* China
70 B2 Qianjiang *Hubei* China
69 E1 Qianjin China
65 A1 Qian Shan *mts* China
71 A3 Qianxi China
70 C2 Qidong China
77 E3 Qiemo China
71 A3 Qijiang China
68 C2 Qijiaojing China
127 H2 Qikiqtarjuaq Can.
68 C2 Qila Ladgasht Pak.
68 C2 Qilian Shan *mts* China
127 J2 Qillak *i.* Greenland
70 B3 Qimen China
127 H1 Qimusseriarsuaq *b.* Greenland
116 B2 Qinā Egypt
Qincheng China *see* Nanfeng
70 C2 Qingdao China

68 C2 Qinghai Hu *salt l.* China
68 C2 Qinghai Nanshan *mts* China
Qingjiang China *see* Huai'an
Qingjiang China *see* Zhangshu
70 B2 Qingshuihe China
70 A2 Qingtongxia China
70 A2 Qingyang China
71 B3 Qingyuan *Guangdong* China
Qingyuan China *see* Yizhou
65 A1 Qingyuan *Liaoning* China
Qingzang Gaoyuan China *see* Tibet, Plateau of
70 B2 Qingzhou China
70 B2 Qinhuangdao China
Qinjiang China *see* Shicheng
70 A2 Qin Ling *mts* China
70 B2 Qinting China *see* Lianhua
71 A3 Qinzhou China
71 B4 Qionghai China
70 A2 Qionglai Shan *mts* China
71 B4 Qiongshan China
71 A4 Qiongzhong China
69 E1 Qiqihar China
81 D3 Qīr Iran
Qishan China *see* Qimen
79 C3 Qishn Yemen
66 B1 Qītaihe China
70 B2 Qixian *Henan* China
70 B2 Qixian *Shanxi* China
Qogir Feng *mt.* China/ Jammu and Kashmir *see* K2
81 D2 Qom Iran
Qomishēh Iran *see* Shahrezā
Qomolangma Feng *mt.* China/Nepal *see* Everest, Mount
76 B2 Qo'ng'irot Uzbek.
Qoqek China *see* Tacheng
77 D2 Qo'qon Uzbek.
76 B2 Qoraqalpog'iston Kazakh.
80 B2 Qornet es Saouda *mt.* Lebanon
81 C2 Qorveh Iran
79 C2 Qotbābād Iran
101 C1 Quakenbrück Ger.
53 C2 Quambone Austr.
63 B2 Quang Ngai Vietnam
63 B2 Quang Tri Vietnam
62 B1 Quan Hoa Vietnam
Quan Long Vietnam *see* Ca Mau
Quan Phu Quoc *i.* Vietnam *see* Phu Quôc, Đao
71 B3 Quanzhou *Fujian* China
71 B3 Quanzhou *Guangxi* China
108 A3 Quartu Sant'Elena *Sardinia* Italy
142 A2 Quartzsite U.S.A.
81 C1 Quba Azer.
76 B3 Quchan Iran
53 C3 Queanbeyan Austr.
131 C3 Québec Can.
131 C3 Québec *prov.* Can.
101 E2 Quedlinburg Ger.
Queen Adelaide Islands Chile *see* Reina Adelaida, Archipiélago de la
128 A2 Queen Charlotte Can.
128 A2 Queen Charlotte Islands Can.
128 B2 Queen Charlotte Sound *sea chan.* Can.
128 B2 Queen Charlotte Strait Can.
126 E1 Queen Elizabeth Islands Can.
55 I2 Queen Mary Land *reg.* Antarctica
126 F2 Queen Maud Gulf Can.
55 E2 Queen Maud Land *reg.* Antarctica
55 P1 Queen Maud Mountains Antarctica
52 B3 Queenscliff Austr.
52 B1 Queensland *state* Austr.
51 D4 Queenstown Austr.
Queenstown Ireland *see* Cobh
54 A3 Queenstown N.Z.
123 C3 Queenstown S. Africa
121 C2 Quelimane Moz.
153 A4 Quellón Chile

Quelpart Island S. Korea *see* Cheju-do
142 B2 Quemado U.S.A.
Que Que Zimbabwe *see* Kwekwe
154 B2 Queréncia do Norte Brazil
145 B2 Querétaro Mex.
101 E2 Querfurt Ger.
128 B2 Quesnel Can.
128 B2 Quesnel Lake Can.
74 A1 Quetta Pak.
146 A3 Quetzaltenango Guat.
64 A3 Quezon Phil.
64 B2 Quezon City Phil.
120 A2 Quibala Angola
150 B2 Quibdó Col.
104 B2 Quiberon France
120 A2 Quilengues Angola
104 C3 Quillan France
153 C3 Quilmes Arg.
73 B4 Quilon India
51 D2 Quilpie Austr.
153 A3 Quilpué Chile
120 A1 Quimbele Angola
152 B2 Quimili Arg.
104 B2 Quimper France
104 B2 Quimperlé France
135 B3 Quincy *CA* U.S.A.
141 D2 Quincy *FL* U.S.A.
137 E3 Quincy *IL* U.S.A.
139 E2 Quincy *MA* U.S.A.
107 C1 Quinto Spain
121 D2 Quionga Moz.
120 A2 Quirima Angola
53 D2 Quirindi Austr.
154 B1 Quirinópolis Brazil
131 D3 Quispamsis Can.
121 C3 Quissico Moz.
120 A2 Quitapa Angola
150 B3 Quito Ecuador
151 F3 Quixadá Brazil
71 A3 Qujing China
75 D1 Qumar He *r.* China
123 C3 Qumrha S. Africa
115 E1 Qunayyin, Sabkhat al *salt marsh* Libya
129 E1 Quoich *r.* Can.
52 A2 Quorn Austr.
79 C2 Qurayat Oman
77 C3 Qürghonteppa Tajik.
Quxar China *see* Lhazê
Quyang China *see* Jingzhou
63 B2 Quy Nhon Vietnam
71 B3 Quzhou China
Qyteti Stalin Albania *see* Kuçovë
Qyzyltū Kazakh. *see* Kishkenekol'

R

103 D2 Raab *r.* Austria
92 H3 Raahe Fin.
100 C1 Raalte Neth.
61 C2 Raas *i.* Indon.
61 C2 Raba Indon.
114 B1 Rabat Morocco
59 E3 Rabaul P.N.G.
50 C2 Rabbit Flat Austr.
78 A2 Rābigh Saudi Arabia
103 D2 Rabka Pol.
103 B2 Rabka Moldova *see* Rîbniţa
Rîbniţa
Rabyānah, Ramlat *des.* Libya *see* Rebiana Sand Sea
131 E3 Race, Cape Can.
140 B3 Raceland U.S.A.
139 E2 Race Point U.S.A.
63 B3 Rach Gia Vietnam
103 D1 Racibórz Pol.
138 B2 Racine U.S.A.
78 B3 Radā' Yemen
110 C1 Rădăuţi Romania
138 B3 Radcliff U.S.A.
74 B2 Radhanpur India
130 C2 Radisson Can.
103 E1 Radom Pol.
103 D1 Radomsko Pol.
90 B1 Radomyshl' Ukr.
111 B2 Radoviš Macedonia
88 B2 Radviliškis Lith.
78 A2 Raḍwá, Jabal *mt.* Saudi Arabia
90 B1 Radyvyliv Ukr.
75 C2 Rae Bareli India
128 C1 Rae-Edzo Can.
128 C1 Rae Lakes Can.

139 E2 Rumford U.S.A.
103 D1 Rumia Pol.
105 D2 Rumilly France
50 C1 Rum Jungle Austr.
66 D2 Rumoi Japan
121 C2 Rumphi Malawi
54 B2 Runanga N.Z.
98 B3 Runcorn U.K.
120 A2 Rundu Namibia
119 C2 Rungu Dem. Rep. Congo
119 D3 Rungwa Tanz.
68 B2 Ruoqiang China
130 C2 Rupert r. Can.
134 D2 Rupert U.S.A.
130 C2 Rupert Bay Can.
       Rusaddir N. Africa see
       Melilla
121 C2 Rusape Zimbabwe
110 C2 Ruse Bulg.
137 E1 Rush City U.S.A.
121 C2 Rushinga Zimbabwe
77 D3 Rushon Tajik.
136 C2 Rushville U.S.A.
53 C3 Rushworth Austr.
129 D2 Russell Can.
54 B1 Russell N.Z.
137 D3 Russell U.S.A.
140 C2 Russellville AL U.S.A.
140 B1 Russellville AR U.S.A.
138 B3 Russellville KY U.S.A.
101 D2 Rüsselsheim Ger.
82 F2 Russian Federation
       country Asia/Europe
81 C1 Rust'avi Georgia
123 C2 Rustenburg S. Africa
140 B2 Ruston U.S.A.
61 D2 Ruteng Indon.
98 B3 Ruthin U.K.
139 E2 Rutland U.S.A.
       Rutog China see Dêrub
119 C3 Rutshuru
       Dem. Rep. Congo
119 E4 Ruvuma r. Moz./Tanz.
79 C2 Ruweis U.A.E.
89 E2 Ruza Rus. Fed.
77 C1 Ruzayevka Kazakh.
87 D3 Ruzayevka Rus. Fed.
119 C3 Rwanda country Africa
89 E3 Ryazan' Rus. Fed.
89 F3 Ryazhsk Rus. Fed.
86 C2 Rybachiy, Poluostrov pen.
       Rus. Fed.
       Rybach'ye Kyrg. see
       Balykchy
89 E2 Rybinsk Rus. Fed.
89 E2 Rybinskoye
       Vodokhranilishche resr
       Rus. Fed.
103 D1 Rybnik Pol.
       Rybnitsa Moldova see
       Ribnița
89 E3 Rybnoye Rus. Fed.
99 D4 Rye U.K.
       Rykovo Ukr. see
       Yenakiyeve
89 D3 Ryl'sk Rus. Fed.
67 C3 Ryojun China see Lüshun
69 E3 Ryōtsu Japan
89 D3 Ryukyu Islands is Japan
103 E1 Ryzhikovo Rus. Fed.
103 E1 Rzeszów Pol.
91 E1 Rzhaksa Rus. Fed.
89 D2 Rzhev Rus. Fed.

S

79 C2 Sa'ādatābād Iran
101 E2 Saale r. Ger.
101 E2 Saalfeld Ger.
134 B1 Saanich Can.
100 C3 Saar r. Ger.
102 B2 Saarbrücken Ger.
88 B2 Sääre Estonia
88 B2 Saaremaa i. Estonia
92 I2 Saarenkylä Fin.
93 I3 Saarijärvi Fin.
100 C3 Saarlouis Ger.
80 B2 Sab' Abar Syria
107 D1 Sabadell Spain
67 C3 Sabae Japan
61 C1 Sabah state Malaysia
61 C2 Sabalana i. Indon.
146 B2 Sabana, Archipiélago de
       is Cuba
150 B1 Sabanalarga Col.
60 A1 Sabang Indon.
155 D1 Sabará Brazil
108 B2 Sabaudia Italy
83 B3 Sabelo S. Africa

119 D2 Sabena Desert Kenya
115 D2 Sabhā Libya
123 D2 Sabie r. Moz./S. Africa
123 D2 Sabie S. Africa
145 B2 Sabinas Mex.
145 B2 Sabinas Hidalgo Mex.
143 E3 Sabine r. U.S.A.
131 D3 Sable, Cape Can.
141 D3 Sable, Cape U.S.A.
131 E3 Sable Island Can.
106 B1 Sabugal Port.
78 B3 Şabyā Saudi Arabia
76 B3 Sabzevār Iran
137 D2 Sac City U.S.A.
120 A2 Sachanga Angola
130 A2 Sachigo Lake Can.
65 B3 Sach'on S. Korea
126 D2 Sachs Harbour Can.
154 C1 Sacramento Brazil
135 B3 Sacramento U.S.A.
135 B3 Sacramento r. U.S.A.
142 B2 Sacramento Mountains
       U.S.A.
135 B2 Sacramento Valley U.S.A.
110 B1 Săcueni Romania
123 C3 Sada S. Africa
107 C1 Sádaba Spain
       Sá da Bandeira Angola
       see Lubango
78 B3 Şa'dah Yemen
63 B3 Sadao Thai.
79 B3 Şadārah Yemen
63 B2 Sa Đec Vietnam
74 D2 Sadiqabad Pak.
72 D2 Sadiya India
67 C3 Sadoga-shima i. Japan
107 D2 Sa Dragonera i. Spain
81 D2 Safāshahr Iran
93 F4 Säffle Sweden
142 B2 Safford U.S.A.
99 D3 Saffron Walden U.K.
114 B1 Safi Morocco
76 C3 Safīd Kūh mts Afgh.
155 D1 Safiras, Serra das mts
       Brazil
86 D2 Safonovo Rus. Fed.
89 D2 Safonovo Rus. Fed.
78 B2 Safrā' as Sark esc.
       Saudi Arabia
75 C2 Saga China
67 B4 Saga Japan
62 A1 Sagaing Myanmar
67 C3 Sagamihara Japan
74 B2 Sagar India
       Sagarmatha mt.
       China/Nepal see
       Everest, Mount
138 C2 Saginaw U.S.A.
138 C2 Saginaw Bay U.S.A.
       Saglouc Can. see Salluit
106 B2 Sagres Port.
146 B2 Sagua la Grande Cuba
139 F1 Saguenay r. Can.
107 C2 Sagunto Spain
76 B2 Sagyndyk, Mys pt Kazakh.
106 B1 Sahagún Spain
114 C3 Sahara des. Africa
       Sahara el Gharbīya des.
       Egypt see Western Desert
       Sahara el Sharqīya des.
       Egypt see Eastern Desert
       Saharan Atlas mts Alg.
       see Atlas Saharien
74 B2 Saharanpur India
75 C2 Saharsa India
114 B3 Sahel reg. Africa
74 B1 Sahiwal Pak.
144 B2 Sahuayo Mex.
78 B2 Şāḥūq reg. Saudi Arabia
114 C1 Saïda Alg.
       Saïda Lebanon see Sidon
75 C2 Saidpur Bangl.
67 B3 Saigō Japan
       Saigon Vietnam see
       Ho Chi Minh City
75 D2 Saiha India
70 B1 Saihan Tal China
67 B4 Saiki Japan
93 I3 Saimaa l. Fin.
144 B2 Sain Alto Mex.
96 C3 St Abb's Head hd U.K.
131 E3 St Alban's Can.
99 C4 St Albans U.K.
138 C3 St Albans U.S.A.
       St Alban's Head hd U.K.
       see St Aldhelm's Head
99 B4 St Aldhelm's Head
       U.K.
       St-André, Cap c Madag.
       see Vilanandro, Tanjona
96 C2 St Andrews U.K.

131 E2 St Anthony Can.
134 D2 St Anthony U.S.A.
52 B3 St Arnaud Austr.
131 E2 St-Augustin Can.
131 E2 St Augustin r. Can.
141 D3 St Augustine U.S.A.
99 A4 St Austell U.K.
104 C2 St-Avertin France
147 D3 St-Barthélemy i.
       West Indies
98 B2 St Bees Head hd U.K.
105 D3 St-Bonnet-en-
       Champsaur France
99 A4 St Bride's Bay U.K.
104 B2 St-Brieuc France
130 C3 St Catharines Can.
141 D2 St Catherines Island
       U.S.A.
99 C4 St Catherine's Point U.K.
137 E3 St Charles U.S.A.
138 C2 St Clair, Lake Can./U.S.A.
105 D2 St-Claude France
99 A4 St Clears U.K.
137 E1 St Cloud U.S.A.
99 A4 St Croix r. U.S.A.
147 D3 St Croix Virgin Is (U.S.A.)
99 A4 St David's U.K.
99 A4 St David's Head hd U.K.
113 I8 St-Denis
104 C2 St-Denis France
       St-Denis-du-Sig Alg. see
       Sig
104 D2 St-Dié France
105 C2 St-Dizier France
130 C3 Ste-Adèle Can.
131 D3 Ste-Anne-des-Monts Can.
139 E1 Ste-Foy France
105 D2 St-Égrève France
128 A1 St Elias Mountains Can.
131 D2 Ste-Marguerite r. Can.
139 E1 Ste-Marie Can.
       Ste-Marie, Cap c. Madag.
       see Vohimena, Tanjona
       Sainte-Marie, Île i.
       Madag. see Nosy Boraha
       Ste-Rose-du-Dégelé Can.
       see Dégelis
129 E2 Sainte Rose du Lac Can.
104 B2 Saintes France
105 C2 St-Étienne France
104 B2 St-Étienne-du-Rouvray
       France
130 C3 St-Félicien Can.
97 D1 Saintfield U.K.
105 D3 St-Florent Corsica France
105 C2 St-Flour France
136 C3 St Francis U.S.A.
104 C3 St-Gaudens France
53 C1 St George Austr.
135 D3 St George U.S.A.
141 D3 St George Island U.S.A.
131 C3 St-Georges Can.
147 D3 St George's Grenada
131 E3 St George's Bay Can.
97 C3 St George's Channel
       Ireland/U.K.
105 D2 St Gotthard Pass pass
       Switz.
113 C7 St Helena terr.
       S. Atlantic Ocean
122 A3 St Helena Bay S. Africa
122 A3 St Helena Bay b. S. Africa
98 B3 St Helens U.K.
134 B1 St Helens, Mount vol.
       U.S.A.
95 C4 St Helier Channel Is
100 B2 St-Hubert Belgium
139 E1 St-Hyacinthe Can.
138 C1 St Ignace U.S.A.
130 B3 St Ignace Island Can.
99 A4 St Ives U.K.
       St Jacques, Cap Vietnam
       see Vung Tau
128 A2 St James, Cape Can.
130 C3 St-Jean, Lac l. Can.
104 B3 St-Jean-d'Angély France
104 C3 St-Jean-de-Luz France
104 C2 St-Jean-de-Monts France
130 C3 St-Jean-sur-Richelieu
       Can.
131 C3 St-Jérôme Can.
134 C1 St Joe r. U.S.A.
131 D3 Saint John Can.
131 D3 St John r. U.S.A.
147 D3 St John's Antigua
131 E3 St John's Can.
138 C3 St Johns U.S.A.
141 D3 St Johns r. U.S.A.
139 E2 St Johnsbury U.S.A.
137 E3 St Joseph U.S.A.

130 A2 St Joseph, Lake Can.
       St-Joseph-d'Alma Can.
       see Alma
130 B3 St Joseph Island Can.
139 E1 St-Jovité Can.
104 C2 St-Junien France
94 B2 St Kilda i. U.K.
147 D3 St Kitts and Nevis
       country West Indies
151 D2 St-Laurent-du-Maroni
       Fr. Guiana
131 E3 St Lawrence Can.
131 D3 St Lawrence inlet Can.
131 D3 St Lawrence, Gulf of Can.
126 A2 St Lawrence Island U.S.A.
104 B2 St-Lô France
114 A3 St-Louis Senegal
137 E3 St Louis U.S.A.
137 E1 St Louis r. U.S.A.
147 D3 St Lucia country
       West Indies
147 D3 St Lucia Channel
       Martinique/St Lucia
123 D2 St Lucia Estuary S. Africa
147 D3 St Maarten i. West Indies
96 ☐ St Magnus Bay U.K.
104 B2 St-Malo France
104 B2 St-Malo, Golfe de g.
       France
147 C3 St-Marc Haiti
       St Mark's S. Africa see
       Cofimvaba
147 D3 St-Martin i. West Indies
122 A3 St Martin, Cape S. Africa
129 E2 St Martin, Lake Can.
139 D2 St Marys U.S.A.
124 A3 St Matthew Island U.S.A.
59 D3 St Matthias Group is
       P.N.G.
130 C3 St-Maurice r. Can.
130 C3 St-Michel-des-Saints
       Can.
104 B2 St-Nazaire France
104 C1 St-Omer France
129 C2 St Paul Can.
137 E2 St Paul U.S.A.
156 A8 St-Paul, Île i. Indian Ocean
137 E2 St Peter U.S.A.
95 C4 St Peter Port Channel Is
141 D3 St Petersburg U.S.A.
131 E3 St-Pierre
       St Pierre and Miquelon
131 E3 St-Pierre, Lac l. Can.
131 C0 St Pierre and Miquelon
       terr. N. America
104 B2 St-Pierre-d'Oléron France
105 C2 St-Pourçain-sur-Sioule
       France
131 C3 St Quentin Can.
104 C2 St-Quentin France
105 D3 St-Raphaël France
122 B3 St Sebastian Bay S. Africa
104 B2 St-Sébastien-sur-Loire
       France
131 D3 St-Siméon Can.
129 E2 St Theresa Point Can.
130 B3 St Thomas Can.
105 D3 St-Tropez France
105 D3 St-Tropez, Cap de c.
       France
       St Vincent, Cape Port. see
       São Vicente, Cabo de
52 A3 St Vincent, Gulf Austr.
147 D3 St Vincent and the
       Grenadines country
       West Indies
147 D3 St Vincent Passage
       St Lucia/St Vincent
129 D2 St Walburg Can.
104 C2 St-Yrieix-la-Perche
       France
59 D1 Saipan i. N. Mariana Is
152 B1 Sajama, Nevado mt. Bol.
122 B2 Sak watercourse S. Africa
67 C4 Sakai Japan
67 C4 Sakaide Japan
78 B2 Sakākah Saudi Arabia
136 C1 Sakakawea, Lake U.S.A.
       Sakarya Turkey see
       Adapazarı
111 D2 Sakarya r. Turkey
66 C3 Sakata Japan
65 B1 Sakchu N. Korea
76 C1 Sakhalin i. Rus. Fed.
123 C2 Sakhile S. Africa
81 C1 Şäki Azer.
88 B3 Sakiai Lith.
69 E3 Sakishima-shotō is Japan
62 B2 Sakon Nakhon Thai.
74 A2 Sakrand Pak.
122 B3 Sakrivier S. Africa

Savu Sea Indon. see Laut Sawu
74 B2 Sawai Madhopur India
62 A1 Sawan Myanmar
62 A2 Sawankhalok Thai.
136 B3 Sawatch Range mts U.S.A.
116 B2 Sawhāj Egypt
121 B2 Sawmills Zimbabwe
79 C3 Şawqirah, Dawḥat b. Oman
Şawqirah Bay Oman see Şawqirah, Dawḥat
53 D2 Sawtell Austr.
134 C2 Sawtooth Range mts U.S.A.
68 C1 Sayano-Shushenskoye Vodokhranilishche resr Rus. Fed.
76 C3 Saýat Turkm.
79 C3 Sayhūt Yemen
93 I3 Säynätsalo Fin.
69 D2 Saynshand Mongolia
139 D2 Sayre U.S.A.
144 B3 Sayula Mex.
145 C3 Sayula Mex.
128 B2 Sayward Can.
Sayyod Turkm. see Saýat
89 E2 Sazonovo Rus. Fed.
114 B2 Sbaa Alg.
98 B2 Scafell Pike hill U.K.
109 C3 Scalea Italy
96 □ Scalloway U.K.
108 B2 Scandicci Italy
96 C1 Scapa Flow inlet U.K.
96 B2 Scarba i. U.K.
130 C3 Scarborough Can.
147 D3 Scarborough Trin. and Tob.
98 C2 Scarborough U.K.
64 A2 Scarborough Shoal sea feature Phil.
96 A2 Scarinish U.K.
Scarpanto i. Greece see Karpathos
100 C3 Schaerbeek Belgium
105 D2 Schaffhausen Switz.
100 B1 Schagen Neth.
102 C2 Schärding Austria
100 A2 Scharendijke Neth.
101 D1 Scharhörn sea feature Ger.
101 D1 Scheeßel Ger.
131 D2 Schefferville Can.
135 D3 Schell Creek Range mts U.S.A.
139 E2 Schenectady U.S.A.
143 D3 Schertz U.S.A.
101 E3 Scheßlitz Ger.
100 C1 Schiermonnikoog i. Neth.
100 B2 Schilde Belgium
108 B1 Schio Italy
101 F2 Schkeuditz Ger.
101 E1 Schladen Ger.
102 C2 Schladming Austria
101 E2 Schleiz Ger.
102 B1 Schleswig Ger.
101 D2 Schloss Holte-Stukenbrock Ger.
101 D2 Schlüchtern Ger.
101 E3 Schlüsselfeld Ger.
101 D2 Schmallenberg Ger.
Schmidt Island Rus. Fed. see Shmidta, Ostrov
101 F2 Schmölln Ger.
101 D1 Schneverdingen Ger.
101 E1 Schönebeck (Elbe) Ger.
101 E1 Schöningen Ger.
100 B2 Schoonhoven Neth.
59 D3 Schouten Islands P.N.G.
97 B3 Schull Ireland
101 E3 Schwabach Ger.
102 B2 Schwäbische Alb mts Ger.
101 F3 Schwandorf Ger.
61 C2 Schwaner, Pegunungan mts Indon.
101 E1 Schwarzenbek Ger.
101 F2 Schwarzenberg Ger.
122 A2 Schwarzrand mts Namibia
Schwarzwald mts Ger. see Black Forest
102 C2 Schwaz Austria
102 C1 Schwedt an der Oder Ger.
101 E2 Schweinfurt Ger.
101 E1 Schwerin Ger.
101 E1 Schweriner See l. Ger.
105 D2 Schwyz Switz.
108 B3 Sciacca Sicily Italy
95 B4 Scilly, Isles of U.K.
138 C3 Scioto r. U.S.A.

136 B1 Scobey U.S.A.
53 D2 Scone Austr.
110 B2 Scornicești Romania
55 C3 Scotia Ridge sea feature S. Atlantic Ocean
149 F8 Scotia Sea S. Atlantic Ocean
96 C2 Scotland admin. div. U.K.
128 B2 Scott, Cape Can.
123 D3 Scottburgh S. Africa
136 C3 Scott City U.S.A.
136 C2 Scottsbluff U.S.A.
140 C2 Scottsboro U.S.A.
96 B1 Scourie U.K.
139 D2 Scranton U.S.A.
98 C3 Scunthorpe U.K.
105 E2 Scuol Switz.
Scutari Albania see Shkodër
99 D4 Seaford U.K.
98 C2 Seaham U.K.
129 E2 Seal r. Can.
122 B3 Seal, Cape S. Africa
52 B3 Sea Lake Austr.
143 D3 Sealy U.S.A.
140 B1 Searcy U.S.A.
98 B1 Seascale U.K.
134 B1 Seattle U.S.A.
139 E2 Sebago Lake U.S.A.
144 A2 Sebastián Vizcaíno, Bahía b. Mex.
Sebastopol' Ukr. see Sevastopol'
Šebenico Croatia see Šibenik
110 B1 Sebeș Romania
60 B2 Sebeși i. Indon.
88 C2 Sebezh Rus. Fed.
80 B1 Şebinkarahisar Turkey
141 D3 Sebring U.S.A.
61 C2 Sebuku i. Indon.
128 B3 Sechelt Can.
150 A3 Sechura Peru
73 B3 Secunderabad India
137 E3 Sedalia U.S.A.
105 C2 Sedan France
54 B2 Seddon N.Z.
114 A3 Sédhiou Senegal
142 A2 Sedona U.S.A.
101 E2 Seeburg Ger.
101 E1 Seehausen (Altmark) Ger.
122 A2 Seeheim Namibia
104 C2 Sées France
101 E2 Seesen Ger.
101 E1 Seevetal Ger.
114 A4 Sefadu Sierra Leone
123 C1 Sefare Botswana
93 F3 Segalstad Norway
60 B1 Segamat Malaysia
86 C2 Segezha Rus. Fed.
114 B3 Ségou Mali
106 C1 Segovia Spain
86 C2 Segozerskoye, Ozero resr Rus. Fed.
115 D2 Séguédine Niger
114 B4 Séguéla Côte d'Ivoire
143 D3 Seguin U.S.A.
107 C2 Segura r. Spain
106 C2 Segura, Sierra de mts Spain
120 B3 Sehithwa Botswana
93 H3 Seinäjoki Fin.
104 C2 Seine r. France
104 B2 Seine, Baie de b. France
105 C2 Seine, Val de val. France
103 E1 Sejny Pol.
60 B2 Sekayu Indon.
114 B4 Sekondi Ghana
134 B1 Selah U.S.A.
59 C3 Selaru i. Indon.
61 C2 Selatan, Tanjung pt Indon.
126 B2 Selawik U.S.A.
98 C3 Selby U.K.
136 C1 Selby U.S.A.
111 C3 Selçuk Turkey
114 B3 Sélingué, Lac de l. Mali
89 D2 Selizharovo Rus. Fed.
93 E4 Seljord Norway
129 E2 Selkirk Can.

96 C3 Selkirk U.K.
128 C2 Selkirk Mountains Can.
142 A2 Sells U.S.A.
140 C2 Selma AL U.S.A.
135 C3 Selma CA U.S.A.
105 D2 Selongey France
99 C4 Selsey Bill hd U.K.
89 D3 Sel'tso Rus. Fed.
Selukwe Zimbabwe see Shurugwi
150 B3 Selvas reg. Brazil
134 C1 Selway r. U.S.A.
129 D1 Selwyn Lake Can.
128 A1 Selwyn Mountains Can.
51 C2 Selwyn Range hills Austr.
60 B2 Semangka, Teluk b. Indon.
61 C2 Semarang Indon.
60 B1 Sematan Sarawak Malaysia
118 B2 Sembé Congo
81 C2 Şemdinli Turkey
91 C1 Semenivka Ukr.
87 D3 Semenov Rus. Fed.
61 C2 Semeru, Gunung vol. Indon.
91 E2 Semikarakorsk Rus. Fed.
89 E3 Semiluki Rus. Fed.
136 B2 Seminoe Reservoir U.S.A.
143 C2 Seminole U.S.A.
141 D2 Seminole, Lake U.S.A.
77 E1 Semipalatinsk Kazakh.
61 C1 Semitau Indon.
Sem Kolodezey Ukr. see Lenine
81 D2 Semnān Iran
61 C1 Semporna Sabah Malaysia
105 C2 Semur-en-Auxois France
Semyonovskoye Rus. Fed. see Bereznik
Semyonovskoye Rus. Fed. see Ostrovskoye
150 C3 Sena Madureira Brazil
120 B2 Senanga Zambia
67 B4 Sendai Japan
67 D3 Sendai Japan
141 D2 Seneca U.S.A.
114 A3 Senegal country Africa
114 A3 Sénégal r. Maur./Senegal
102 C1 Senftenberg Ger.
119 D3 Sengerema Tanz.
151 E4 Senhor do Bonfim Brazil
103 D2 Senica Slovakia
108 B2 Senigallia Italy
109 B2 Senj Croatia
92 G2 Senja i. Norway
122 B2 Senlac S. Africa
105 C2 Senlis France
63 B2 Senmonorom Cambodia
116 B3 Sennar Sudan
130 C3 Senneterre Can.
123 C3 Senqu r. Lesotho
105 C2 Sens France
109 D1 Senta Serbia
128 B2 Sentinel Peak Can.
75 B2 Seoni India
65 B2 Seoul S. Korea
155 D2 Sepetiba, Baía de b. Brazil
59 D3 Sepik r. P.N.G.
61 C1 Sepinang Indon.
131 D2 Sept-Îles Can.
87 D4 Serafimovich Rus. Fed.
100 B2 Seraing Belgium
59 C3 Seram i. Indon.
60 B2 Serang Indon.
60 B1 Serasan, Selat sea chan. Indon.
109 D2 Serbia country Europe
76 B3 Serdar Turkm.
117 C3 Serdo Eth.
89 E3 Serebryanyye Prudy Rus. Fed.
60 B1 Seremban Malaysia
119 D3 Serengeti Plain Tanz.
121 C2 Serenje Zambia
90 B2 Seret r. Ukr.
87 D3 Sergach Rus. Fed.
86 F2 Sergino Rus. Fed.
89 E2 Sergiyev Posad Rus. Fed.
Sergo Ukr. see Stakhanov
74 A1 Serhetabat Turkm.
61 C1 Seria Brunei
61 C1 Serian Sarawak Malaysia
111 B3 Serifos i. Greece
80 B2 Serik Turkey
59 C3 Serinata, Kepulauan is Indon.
Sernyy Zavod Turkm. see Kükürtli
86 F3 Serov Rus. Fed.

120 B3 Serowe Botswana
106 B2 Serpa Port.
Serpa Pinto Angola see Menongue
89 E3 Serpukhov Rus. Fed.
155 D2 Serra Brazil
155 C1 Serra das Araras Brazil
108 A3 Serramanna Sardinia Italy
154 B1 Serranópolis Brazil
100 A3 Serre r. France
111 B2 Serres Greece
151 F4 Serrinha Brazil
155 C1 Sêrro Brazil
154 C2 Sertãozinho Brazil
59 D3 Serui Indon.
120 B3 Serule Botswana
61 C2 Seruyan r. Indon.
68 C2 Sêrxü China
120 A2 Sesfontein Namibia
108 B2 Sessa Aurunca Italy
108 A2 Sestri Levante Italy
105 C3 Sète France
155 D1 Sete Lagoas Brazil
92 G2 Setermoen Norway
93 E4 Setesdal val. Norway
115 C1 Sétif Alg.
67 B4 Seto-naikai sea Japan
114 B1 Settat Morocco
98 B2 Settle U.K.
106 B2 Setúbal Port.
106 B2 Setúbal, Baía de b. Port.
130 A2 Seul, Lac l. Can.
81 C1 Sevan Armenia
76 A2 Sevana, Lake Armenia
Sevana Lich l. Armenia see Sevan, Lake
91 C3 Sevastopol' Ukr.
Seven Islands Can. see Sept-Îles
131 D2 Seven Islands Bay Can.
99 D4 Sevenoaks U.K.
105 C3 Sévérac-le-Château France
130 B2 Severn r. Can.
122 B2 Severn S. Africa
99 B4 Severn r. U.K.
86 D2 Severnaya Dvina r. Rus. Fed.
83 H1 Severnaya Zemlya is Rus. Fed.
86 D2 Severnyy Rus. Fed.
86 F2 Severnyy Rus. Fed.
83 I3 Severobaykal'sk Rus. Fed.
86 C2 Severodvinsk Rus. Fed.
83 L3 Severo-Kuril'sk Rus. Fed.
92 J2 Severomorsk Rus. Fed.
86 C2 Severoonezhsk Rus. Fed.
83 H2 Severo-Yeniseyskiy Rus. Fed.
91 D3 Severskaya Rus. Fed.
135 D3 Sevier r. U.S.A.
135 D3 Sevier Lake U.S.A.
Sevilla Spain see Seville
106 B2 Seville Spain
Sevlyush Ukr. see Vynohradiv
89 D3 Sevsk Rus. Fed.
126 C2 Seward U.S.A.
126 B2 Seward Peninsula U.S.A.
128 A2 Sewell Inlet Can.
128 C2 Sexsmith Can.
144 B2 Sextín r. Mex.
86 G1 Seyakha Rus. Fed.
113 I6 Seychelles country Indian Ocean
92 □C2 Seyðisfjörður Iceland
Seyhan Turkey see Adana
80 B2 Seyhan r. Turkey
91 C1 Seym r. Rus. Fed./Ukr.
83 L2 Seymchan Rus. Fed.
53 C3 Seymour Austr.
123 C3 Seymour S. Africa
138 B3 Seymour IN U.S.A.
143 D2 Seymour TX U.S.A.
105 C2 Sézanne France
108 B2 Sezze Italy
110 C1 Sfântu Gheorghe Romania
115 D1 Sfax Tunisia
Sfîntu Gheorghe Romania see Sfântu Gheorghe
's-Gravenhage Neth. see The Hague
96 A2 Sgurr Alasdair hill U.K.
70 A2 Shaanxi prov. China
Shaba Zimbabwe see Zvishavane
91 D2 Shabel'sk Rus. Fed.
77 D2 Shache China
55 C1 Shackleton Range mts Antarctica

Silgarhi

75 C2 Silgarhi Nepal
80 B2 Silifke Turkey
75 C1 Siling Co salt l. China
110 C2 Silistra Bulg.
111 C2 Silivri Turkey
93 F3 Siljan l. Sweden
93 E4 Silkeborg Denmark
88 C2 Sillamäe Estonia
98 B2 Silloth U.K.
140 B1 Siloam Springs U.S.A.
123 D2 Silobela S. Africa
60 B1 Siluas Indon.
88 B2 Šilutė Lith.
81 C2 Silvan Turkey
154 C1 Silvânia Brazil
74 B2 Silvassa India
137 E1 Silver Bay U.S.A.
142 B2 Silver City U.S.A.
136 B3 Silverton U.S.A.
62 B1 Simao China
130 C3 Simard, Lac l. Can.
111 C3 Simav Turkey
111 C3 Simav Dağları mts Turkey
118 C2 Simba Dem. Rep. Congo
138 C2 Simcoe Can.
139 D2 Simcoe, Lake Can.
78 A3 Simën Eth.
60 A1 Simeulue i. Indon.
91 C3 Simferopol' Ukr.
75 C2 Simikot Nepal
135 C4 Simi Valley U.S.A.
Simla India see Shimla
110 B1 Şimleu Silvaniei Romania
100 C3 Şimmern (Hunsrück) Ger.
92 I2 Simo Fin.
129 D2 Simonhouse Can.
60 B2 Simpang Indon.
51 C2 Simpson Desert Austr.
93 F4 Simrishamn Sweden
60 A1 Sinabang Indon.
116 B2 Sinai pen. Egypt
105 E3 Sinalunga Italy
71 A3 Sinan China
65 B2 Sinanju N. Korea
62 A1 Sinbo Myanmar
62 A1 Sinbyugyun Myanmar
150 B2 Sincelejo Col.
60 B2 Sindangbarang Indon.
111 C3 Sındırgı Turkey
86 E2 Sindor Rus. Fed.
111 C2 Sinekçi Turkey
106 B2 Sines Port.
106 B2 Sines, Cabo de c. Port.
116 B3 Singa Sudan
75 C2 Singahi India
60 B1 Singapore country Asia
61 C2 Singaraja Indon.
63 B2 Sing Buri Thai.
119 D3 Singida Tanz.
62 A1 Singkaling Hkamti Myanmar
61 D2 Singkang Indon.
60 B1 Singkawang Indon.
60 B2 Singkep i. Indon.
60 A1 Singkil Indon.
53 D2 Singleton Austr.
Sin'gosan N. Korea see Kosan
62 A1 Singu Myanmar
Sining China see Xining
108 A2 Siniscola Sardinia Italy
109 C2 Sinj Croatia
61 D2 Sinjai Indon.
116 B3 Sinkat Sudan
151 D2 Sinnamary Fr. Guiana
Sînnicolau Mare Romania see Sânnicolau Mare
Sinoia Zimbabwe see Chinhoyi
80 B1 Sinop Turkey
65 B1 Sinp'o N. Korea
61 C1 Sintang Indon.
100 B2 St Anthonis Neth.
100 A2 St-Laureins Belgium
100 B2 St-Niklaas Belgium
143 D3 Sinton U.S.A.
100 C2 St-Vith Belgium
65 A1 Sinŭiju N. Korea
64 B3 Siocon Phil.
103 D2 Siófok Hungary
105 D2 Sion Switz.
137 D2 Sioux Center U.S.A.
137 D2 Sioux City U.S.A.
137 D2 Sioux Falls U.S.A.
130 A2 Sioux Lookout Can.
65 A1 Siping China
129 E2 Sipiwesk Lake Can.
55 P2 Siple, Mount Antarctica
55 P2 Siple Island Antarctica
Sipolilo Zimbabwe see Guruve

60 A2 Sipura i. Indon.
64 B3 Siquijor Phil.
93 E4 Sira r. Norway
Siracusa Italy see Syracuse
51 C1 Sir Edward Pellew Group is Austr.
110 C1 Siret Romania
110 C1 Siret r. Romania
79 C2 Sirik Iran
61 C1 Sirik, Tanjung pt Malaysia
62 B2 Siri Kit, Khuan Thai.
128 B1 Sir James MacBrien, Mount Can.
79 C2 Sirjän Iran
81 C2 Şırnak Turkey
74 B2 Sirohi India
60 A1 Sirombu Indon.
74 B2 Sirsa India
115 D1 Sirte Libya
115 D1 Sirte, Gulf of Libya
88 B2 Širvintos Lith.
109 C1 Sisak Croatia
63 B2 Sisaket Thai.
145 C2 Sisal Mex.
122 B2 Sishen S. Africa
81 C2 Sisian Armenia
127 I2 Sisimiut Greenland
129 D2 Sisipuk Lake Can.
63 B2 Sisŏphŏn Cambodia
105 D3 Sisteron France
Sitang China see Sinan
75 C2 Sitapur India
111 C3 Siteia Greece
123 D2 Siteki Swaziland
128 A2 Sitka U.S.A.
100 B2 Sittard Neth.
62 A1 Sittaung Myanmar
62 A2 Sittaung r. Myanmar
62 A1 Sittwe Myanmar
61 C2 Situbondo Indon.
80 B2 Sivas Turkey
111 C3 Sivaslı Turkey
80 B2 Siverek Turkey
88 D2 Siverskiy Rus. Fed.
91 D2 Sivers'kyy Donets' r. Ukr.
80 B2 Sivrihisar Turkey
116 A2 Siwah Egypt
75 B1 Siwalik Range mts India/Nepal
Siwa Oasis Egypt see Wāḩāt Sīwah
105 D3 Six-Fours-les-Plages France
70 B2 Sixian China
123 C2 Siyabuswa S. Africa
Sjælland i. Denmark see Zealand
109 D2 Sjenica Serbia
92 G2 Sjøvegan Norway
91 C2 Skadovs'k Ukr.
93 F4 Skagen Denmark
93 E4 Skagerrak str. Denmark/Norway
134 B1 Skagit r. U.S.A.
128 A2 Skagway U.S.A.
92 G2 Skaland Norway
93 F4 Skara Sweden
74 B1 Skardu Jammu and Kashmir
103 E1 Skarżysko-Kamienna Pol.
103 D2 Skawina Pol.
114 A2 Skaymat Western Sahara
128 B1 Skeena r. Can.
128 B2 Skeena Mountains Can.
98 D3 Skegness U.K.
92 H3 Skellefteå Sweden
92 H3 Skellefteälven r. Sweden
97 C2 Skerries Ireland
93 F4 Ski Norway
111 B3 Skiathos i. Greece
97 B3 Skibbereen Ireland
92 □B2 Skiðadals-jökull glacier Iceland
98 B2 Skiddaw hill U.K.
93 E4 Skien Norway
103 E1 Skierniewice Pol.
115 C1 Skikda Alg.
52 B3 Skipton Austr.
98 B3 Skipton U.K.
93 F4 Skive Denmark
93 E4 Skjervøy Norway
Skobelev Uzbek. see Farg'ona
111 B3 Skopelos i. Greece
89 E3 Skopin Rus. Fed.
111 B2 Skopje Macedonia
111 C3 Skoutaros Greece
93 F4 Skövde Sweden
83 J3 Skovorodino Rus. Fed.
139 F2 Skowhegan U.S.A.

92 H2 Skröven Sweden
88 B2 Skrunda Latvia
128 A1 Skukum, Mount Can.
123 D1 Skukuza S. Africa
88 B2 Skuodas Lith.
90 B2 Skvyra Ukr.
96 A2 Skye i. U.K.
111 B3 Skyros Greece
111 B3 Skyros i. Greece
93 F4 Slagelse Denmark
60 B2 Slamet, Gunung vol. Indon.
97 C2 Slaney r. Ireland
88 C2 Slantsy Rus. Fed.
109 C1 Slatina Croatia
110 B2 Slatina Romania
143 C2 Slaton U.S.A.
129 C1 Slave r. Can.
114 C4 Slave Coast Africa
128 C2 Slave Lake Can.
77 D1 Slavgorod Rus. Fed.
88 C2 Slavkovichi Rus. Fed.
Slavonska Požega Croatia see Požega
109 C1 Slavonski Brod Croatia
90 B1 Slavuta Ukr.
90 C1 Slavutych Ukr.
66 B2 Slavyanka Rus. Fed.
Slavyanskaya Rus. Fed. see Slavyansk-na-Kubani
91 D2 Slavyansk-na-Kubani Rus. Fed.
89 D3 Slawharad Belarus
103 D1 Sławno Pol.
99 C3 Sleaford U.K.
97 A2 Slea Head hd Ireland
130 C2 Sleeper Islands Can.
97 D1 Slieve Donard hill U.K.
97 B1 Slieve Gamph hills Ireland
96 A2 Sligachan U.K.
Sligeach Ireland see Sligo
97 B1 Sligo Ireland
97 B1 Sligo Bay Ireland
93 G4 Slite Sweden
110 C2 Sliven Bulg.
Sloboda Rus. Fed. see Ezhva
110 C2 Slobozia Romania
128 C3 Slocan Can.
88 C3 Slonim Belarus
100 B1 Sloten Neth.
99 C4 Slough U.K.
103 D2 Slovakia country Europe
108 B1 Slovenia country Europe
91 D2 Slov"yans'k Ukr.
102 C1 Słubice Pol.
90 B1 Sluch r. Ukr.
100 A2 Sluis Neth.
103 D1 Słupsk Pol.
88 C3 Slutsk Belarus
97 A2 Slyne Head hd Ireland
68 C1 Slyudyanka Rus. Fed.
131 D2 Smallwood Reservoir Can.
88 C3 Smalyavichy Belarus
88 C3 Smarhon' Belarus
129 D2 Smeaton Can.
109 D2 Smederevo Serbia
109 D2 Smederevska Palanka Serbia
91 C2 Smila Ukr.
88 C3 Smilavichy Belarus
88 C2 Smiltene Latvia
137 D3 Smith Center U.S.A.
128 B2 Smithers Can.
141 E1 Smithfield NC U.S.A.
134 D2 Smithfield UT U.S.A.
139 D3 Smith Mountain Lake U.S.A.
130 C3 Smiths Falls Can.
53 D2 Smithton Austr.
53 D2 Smoky Cape Austr.
137 D3 Smoky Hills U.S.A.
92 E3 Smøla i. Norway
89 D3 Smolensk Rus. Fed.
89 D3 Smolensko-Moskovskaya Vozvyshennost' hills Rus. Fed.
111 B2 Smolyan Bulg.
66 B2 Smolyoninovo Rus. Fed.
130 B3 Smooth Rock Falls Can.
Smyrna Turkey see İzmir
91 D2 Smyrnove Ukr.
92 □B3 Snæfell mt. Iceland
98 A2 Snaefell hill Isle of Man
128 A1 Snag Can.
134 C1 Snake r. U.S.A.
134 D2 Snake River Plain U.S.A.
Snare Lakes Can. see Wekweti
92 F3 Snåsvatn l. Norway

100 B1 Sneek Neth.
97 B3 Sneem Ireland
122 B3 Sneeuberge mts S. Africa
Snegurovka Ukr. see Tetiyiv
103 D1 Snežka mt. Czech Rep.
108 B1 Snežnik mt. Slovenia
103 E1 Śniardwy, Jezioro l. Pol.
Sniečkus Lith. see Visaginas
91 C2 Snihurivka Ukr.
93 E3 Snøhetta mt. Norway
Snovsk Ukr. see Shchors
129 D1 Snowbird Lake Can.
99 A3 Snowdon mt. U.K.
Snowdrift Can. see Łutselk'e
129 C1 Snowdrift r. Can.
142 A2 Snowflake U.S.A.
129 D2 Snow Lake Can.
134 C1 Snowshoe Peak U.S.A.
52 A2 Snowtown Austr.
53 C3 Snowy r. Austr.
53 C3 Snowy Mountains Austr.
143 C2 Snyder U.S.A.
121 □D2 Soalala Madag.
121 □D2 Soanierana-Ivongo Madag.
90 B2 Sob r. Ukr.
65 B2 Sobaek-sanmaek mts S. Korea
117 B4 Sobat r. Sudan
89 F2 Sobinka Rus. Fed.
151 E4 Sobradinho, Barragem de resr Brazil
151 E3 Sobral Brazil
91 D3 Sochi Rus. Fed.
65 B2 Sŏch'ŏn S. Korea
49 L5 Society Islands Fr. Polynesia
150 B2 Socorro Col.
142 B2 Socorro NM U.S.A.
142 B2 Socorro TX U.S.A.
144 A3 Socorro, Isla i. Mex.
56 B4 Socotra i. Yemen
63 B3 Soc Trăng Vietnam
106 C2 Socuéllamos Spain
92 I2 Sodankylä Fin.
134 D2 Soda Springs U.S.A.
93 G3 Söderhamn Sweden
93 G4 Södertälje Sweden
116 A3 Sodiri Sudan
117 B4 Sodo Eth.
93 G3 Södra Kvarken str. Fin./Sweden
123 C1 Soekmekaar S. Africa
Soerabaia Indon. see Surabaya
101 D2 Soest Ger.
53 C2 Sofala Austr.
110 B2 Sofia Bulg.
121 □D2 Sofia r. Madag.
Sofiya Bulg. see Sofia
Sofiyivka Ukr. see Vil'nyans'k
75 D1 Sog China
93 E3 Sognefjorden inlet Norway
111 D2 Söğüt Turkey
Sohâg Egypt see Sawhāj
Sohar Oman see Şuḩār
100 B2 Soignies Belgium
105 C2 Soissons France
90 A1 Sokal' Ukr.
65 B2 Sokch'o S. Korea
111 C3 Söke Turkey
81 C1 Sokhumi Georgia
114 C4 Sokodé Togo
89 F2 Sokol Rus. Fed.
101 F2 Sokolov Czech Rep.
115 C3 Sokoto Nigeria
115 C3 Sokoto r. Nigeria
90 B2 Sokyryany Ukr.
73 B3 Solapur India
135 B3 Soledad U.S.A.
89 F2 Soligalich Rus. Fed.
99 C3 Solihull U.K.
86 E3 Solikamsk Rus. Fed.
87 E3 Sol'-Iletsk Rus. Fed.
100 C2 Solingen Ger.
122 A1 Solitaire Namibia
92 G3 Sollefteå Sweden
93 G4 Sollentuna Sweden
107 D2 Sóller Spain
101 D2 Solling hills Ger.
89 E2 Solnechnogorsk Rus. Fed.
60 B2 Solok Indon.
Solomon Islands country S. Pacific Ocean
48 G4 Solomon Sea P.N.G./Solomon Is
61 D2 Solor, Kepulauan is Indon.

118 B3 **Tshela** Dem. Rep. Congo
118 C3 **Tshikapa**
Dem. Rep. Congo
118 C3 **Tshikapa** r.
Dem. Rep. Congo
123 C2 **Tshing** S. Africa
123 D1 **Tshipise** S. Africa
118 C3 **Tshitanzu**
Dem. Rep. Congo
120 B3 **Tshootsha** Botswana
118 C3 **Tshuapa** r.
Dem. Rep. Congo
Tshwane S. Africa see
Pretoria
87 D4 **Tsimlyanskoye**
Vodokhranilishche resr
Rus. Fed.
Tsinan China see Jinan
Tsingtao China see
Qingdao
Tsining China see Jining
121 □D2 **Tsiroanomandidy** Madag.
76 A2 **Ts'khinvali** Georgia
123 C3 **Tsomo** S. Africa
67 C4 **Tsu** Japan
67 D3 **Tsuchiura** Japan
66 D2 **Tsugarū-kaikyō** str. Japan
Tsugaru Strait Japan see
Tsugarū-kaikyō
120 A2 **Tsumeb** Namibia
122 A1 **Tsumis Park** Namibia
120 B2 **Tsumkwe** Namibia
67 C3 **Tsuruga** Japan
66 C3 **Tsuruoka** Japan
67 A4 **Tsushima** is Japan
67 B3 **Tsuyama** Japan
123 C2 **Tswelelang** S. Africa
88 C3 **Tsyelyakhany** Belarus
91 C2 **Tsyurupyns'k** Ukr.
Tthenaagoo Can. see
Nahanni Butte
59 C3 **Tual** Indon.
97 B2 **Tuam** Ireland
49 M5 **Tuamotu Islands** is
Fr. Polynesia
54 A3 **Tuapeka Mouth** N.Z.
91 D3 **Tuapse** Rus. Fed.
54 A3 **Tuatapere** N.Z.
142 A1 **Tuba City** U.S.A.
61 C2 **Tuban** Indon.
152 D2 **Tubarão** Brazil
102 B2 **Tübingen** Ger.
115 F1 **Tubruq** Libya
49 L6 **Tubuai Islands** is
Fr. Polynesia
144 A1 **Tubutama** Mex.
72 C1 **Tucavaca** Bol.
128 B1 **Tuchitua** Can.
142 A2 **Tucson** U.S.A.
143 C1 **Tucumcari** U.S.A.
150 C2 **Tucupita** Venez.
151 E3 **Tucuruí** Brazil
151 E3 **Tucuruí, Represa** resr
Brazil
107 C1 **Tudela** Spain
106 B1 **Tuela** r. Port.
157 F2 **Tufts Abyssal Plain**
sea feature
N. Pacific Ocean
123 D2 **Tugela** r. S. Africa
64 B2 **Tuguegarao** Phil.
106 B1 **Tui** Spain
59 C3 **Tukangbesi, Kepulauan** is
Indon.
126 D2 **Tuktoyaktuk** Can.
88 B2 **Tukums** Latvia
119 D3 **Tukuyu** Tanz.
145 C2 **Tula** Mex.
89 E3 **Tula** Rus. Fed.
Tulach Mhór Ireland see
Tullamore
145 C2 **Tulancingo** Mex.
135 C3 **Tulare** U.S.A.
142 B2 **Tularosa** U.S.A.
110 C1 **Tulcea** Romania
90 B2 **Tul'chyn** Ukr.
Tuléar Madag. see Toliara
129 F1 **Tulemalu Lake** Can.
143 C2 **Tulia** U.S.A.
128 B1 **Tulita** Can.
140 C1 **Tullahoma** U.S.A.
53 C2 **Tullamore** Austr.
97 C2 **Tullamore** Ireland
104 C2 **Tulle** France
97 C2 **Tullow** Ireland
51 D1 **Tully** Austr.
143 D1 **Tulsa** U.S.A.
126 B2 **Tuluksak** U.S.A.
83 H3 **Tulun** Rus. Fed.
150 B2 **Tumaco** Col.

123 C2 **Tumahole** S. Africa
93 G4 **Tumba** Sweden
118 B3 **Tumba, Lac** l.
Dem. Rep. Congo
61 C2 **Tumbangtiti** Indon.
53 C3 **Tumbarumba** Austr.
150 A3 **Tumbes** Peru
128 B2 **Tumbler Ridge** Can.
52 A2 **Tumby Bay** Austr.
65 B1 **Tumen** China
150 C2 **Tumereng** Guyana
64 A3 **Tumindao** i. Phil.
74 A2 **Tump** Pak.
151 D2 **Tumucumaque, Serra** hills
Brazil
53 C3 **Tumut** Austr.
99 D4 **Tunbridge Wells, Royal**
U.K.
80 B2 **Tunceli** Turkey
53 D2 **Tuncurry** Austr.
118 A1 **Tundun-Wada** Nigeria
119 D3 **Tunduru** Tanz.
110 C2 **Tundzha** r. Bulg.
115 D1 **Tunis** Tunisia
108 B3 **Tunis, Golfe de** g. Tunisia
115 C1 **Tunisia** country Africa
150 B2 **Tunja** Col.
92 F3 **Tunnsjøen** l. Norway
Tunxi China see Huangshan
154 B2 **Tupã** Brazil
154 C1 **Tupaciguara** Brazil
140 C2 **Tupelo** U.S.A.
152 B2 **Tupiza** Bol.
83 H2 **Tura** Rus. Fed.
86 F3 **Tura** r. Rus. Fed.
78 B2 **Turabah** Saudi Arabia
83 J3 **Turana, Khrebet** mts
Rus. Fed.
54 C1 **Turangi** N.Z.
76 B2 **Turan Lowland** Asia
77 D2 **Turar Ryskulov** Kazakh.
78 A1 **Turayf** Saudi Arabia
88 B2 **Turba** Estonia
74 A2 **Turbat** Pak.
150 B2 **Turbo** Col.
110 B1 **Turda** Romania
Turfan China see Turpan
76 C2 **Turgay** Kazakh.
76 C1 **Turgayskaya Stolovaya**
Strana reg. Kazakh.
110 C2 **Türgovishte** Bulg.
111 C3 **Turgutlu** Turkey
80 B1 **Turhal** Turkey
107 C2 **Turia** r. Spain
108 A1 **Turin** Italy
86 F3 **Turinsk** Rus. Fed.
90 A1 **Turiya** r. Ukr.
90 A1 **Turiys'k** Ukr.
90 A2 **Turka** Ukr.
119 D2 **Turkana, Lake** salt l.
Eth./Kenya
77 C2 **Turkestan** Kazakh.
103 E2 **Túrkeve** Hungary
80 B2 **Turkey** country
Asia/Europe
50 B1 **Turkey Creek** Austr.
76 C3 **Türkmenabat** Turkm.
76 B2 **Türkmenbaşy** Turkm.
76 B2 **Turkmenistan** country
Asia
Turkmeniya country Asia
see Turkmenistan
Turkmenskaya S.S.R.
country Asia see
Turkmenistan
147 C2 **Turks and Caicos Islands**
terr. West Indies
147 C2 **Turks Islands**
Turks and Caicos Is
93 H3 **Turku** Fin.
119 D2 **Turkwel** watercourse
Kenya
135 B3 **Turlock** U.S.A.
155 D1 **Turmalina** Brazil
54 C2 **Turnagain, Cape** N.Z.
146 B3 **Turneffe Islands** Belize
100 B2 **Turnhout** Belgium
129 D2 **Turnor Lake** Can.
Túrnovo Bulg. see
Veliko Túrnovo
110 B2 **Turnu Măgurele** Romania
68 B2 **Turpan** China
96 C2 **Turriff** U.K.
64 A3 **Turtle Islands** Phil.
77 D2 **Turugart Pass** China/Kyrg.
82 G2 **Turukhansk** Rus. Fed.
154 C1 **Tuscaloosa** U.S.A.
140 C2 **Tuskegee** U.S.A.
81 C2 **Tutak** Turkey
89 E2 **Tutayev** Rus. Fed.

73 B4 **Tuticorin** India
121 C1 **Tutubu** Tanz.
49 J5 **Tutuila** i. American Samoa
120 B3 **Tutume** Botswana
93 H3 **Tuusula** Fin.
49 I4 **Tuvalu** country
S. Pacific Ocean
78 B2 **Tuwayq, Jabal** hills
Saudi Arabia
78 B2 **Tuwayq, Jabal** mts
Saudi Arabia
78 A2 **Tuwwal** Saudi Arabia
144 B2 **Tuxpan** Mex.
145 C2 **Tuxpan** Mex.
145 C3 **Tuxtla Gutiérrez** Mex.
62 B1 **Tuyên Quang** Vietnam
63 B2 **Tuy Hoa** Vietnam
80 B2 **Tuz, Lake** salt l. Turkey
Tuz, Lake
80 B2 **Tuz Gölü** salt l. Turkey see
Tuz, Lake
81 C2 **Tuz Khurmātū** Iraq
109 C2 **Tuzla** Bos.-Herz.
91 E2 **Tuzlov** r. Rus. Fed.
89 E2 **Tver'** Rus. Fed.
98 B2 **Tweed** r. U.K.
53 D1 **Tweed Heads** Austr.
122 A2 **Twee Rivier** Namibia
135 C4 **Twentynine Palms** U.S.A.
131 E3 **Twillingate** Can.
134 D2 **Twin Falls** U.S.A.
54 B2 **Twizel** South I. N.Z.
137 E1 **Two Harbors** U.S.A.
120 C2 **Two Hills** Can.
Tyddewi U.K. see
St David's
143 D2 **Tyler** U.S.A.
83 J3 **Tynda** Rus. Fed.
96 B2 **Tyndrum** U.K.
98 C2 **Tyne** r. England U.K.
95 C2 **Tyne** r. Scotland U.K.
93 F3 **Tynset** Norway
80 B2 **Tyre** Lebanon
69 E1 **Tyrma** Rus. Fed.
111 B3 **Tyrnavos** Greece
52 B3 **Tyrrell, Lake** dry lake
Austr.
108 B2 **Tyrrhenian Sea**
France/Italy
76 B2 **Tyub-Karagan, Mys** pt
Kazakh.
87 E3 **Tyul'gan** Rus. Fed.
86 F3 **Tyumen'** Rus. Fed.
83 J2 **Tyung** r. Rus. Fed.
Tyuratam Kazakh. see
Baykonyr
99 A4 **Tywi** r. U.K.
123 D1 **Tzaneen** S. Africa

U

Uaco Congo Angola see
Waku-Kungo
120 B2 **Uamanda** Angola
150 C3 **Uarini** Brazil
150 C3 **Uaupés** Brazil
155 D2 **Ubá** Brazil
155 D1 **Ubaí** Brazil
151 F4 **Ubaitaba** Brazil
118 B3 **Ubangi** r.
C.A.R./Dem. Rep. Congo
Ubangi-Shari country
Africa see Central
African Republic
67 B4 **Ube** Japan
106 C2 **Úbeda** Spain
154 C1 **Uberaba** Brazil
154 C1 **Uberlândia** Brazil
123 D2 **Ubombo** S. Africa
63 B2 **Ubon Ratchathani** Thai.
119 C3 **Ubundu** Dem. Rep. Congo
150 B3 **Ucayali** r. Peru
100 B2 **Uccle** Belgium
74 B2 **Uch** Pak.
77 E2 **Ucharal** Kazakh.
66 D2 **Uchiura-wan** b. Japan
76 C2 **Uchquduq** Uzbek.
83 J3 **Uchur** r. Rus. Fed.
100 C1 **Uckfield** U.K.
128 B3 **Ucluelet** Can.
89 E2 **Udachnyy** Rus. Fed.
73 B3 **Udaipur** India
91 C1 **Uday** r. Ukr.
93 F4 **Uddevalla** Sweden
92 G2 **Uddjaure** l. Sweden
100 B2 **Uden** Neth.
74 B1 **Udhampur**
Jammu and Kashmir

108 B1 **Udine** Italy
89 E2 **Udomlya** Rus. Fed.
62 B2 **Udon Thani** Thai.
73 B3 **Udupi** India
83 K3 **Udyl', Ozero** l. Rus. Fed.
67 C3 **Ueda** Japan
61 D2 **Uekuli** Indon.
118 C2 **Uele** r. Dem. Rep. Congo
83 N2 **Uelen** Rus. Fed.
101 E1 **Uelzen** Ger.
119 C2 **Uere** r. Dem. Rep. Congo
87 E3 **Ufa** Rus. Fed.
119 D3 **Ugalla** r. Tanz.
119 D2 **Uganda** country Africa
69 F1 **Uglegorsk** Rus. Fed.
89 E2 **Uglich** Rus. Fed.
89 D2 **Uglovka** Rus. Fed.
66 B2 **Uglovoye** Rus. Fed.
89 D3 **Ugra** Rus. Fed.
103 D2 **Uherské Hradiště**
Czech Rep.
Uibhist a' Deas i. U.K. see
South Uist
Uibhist a' Tuath i. U.K. see
North Uist
101 E2 **Uichteritz** Ger.
96 A2 **Uig** U.K.
120 A1 **Uige** Angola
65 B2 **Ŭijŏngbu** S. Korea
65 A1 **Ŭiju** N. Korea
135 D2 **Uinta Mountains** U.S.A.
120 A3 **Uis Mine** Namibia
65 B2 **Ŭisŏng** S. Korea
123 C3 **Uitenhage** S. Africa
100 C1 **Uithuizen** Neth.
131 D2 **Uivak, Cape** Can.
Ujiyamada Japan see Ise
74 B2 **Ujjain** India
Ujung Pandang Indon. see
Makassar
89 F3 **Ukholovo** Rus. Fed.
Ukhta Rus. Fed. see
Kalevala
86 E2 **Ukhta** Rus. Fed.
135 B3 **Ukiah** U.S.A.
127 I2 **Ukkusissat** Greenland
88 B2 **Ukmergė** Lith.
90 C2 **Ukraine** country Europe
Ukrainskaya S.S.R.
country Europe see
Ukraine
Ulaanbaatar Mongolia see
Ulan Bator
68 C1 **Ulaangom** Mongolia
59 E3 **Ulamona** P.N.G.
70 A2 **Ulan** China
69 D1 **Ulan Bator** Mongolia
Ulanhad China see
Chifeng
69 E1 **Ulanhot** China
87 D4 **Ulan-Khol** Rus. Fed.
69 D1 **Ulan-Ude** Rus. Fed.
75 D1 **Ulan Ul Hu** l. China
65 B2 **Ulchin** S. Korea
Uleåborg Fin. see Oulu
88 C2 **Ülenurme** Estonia
74 B3 **Ulhasnagar** India
69 D1 **Uliastai** China
68 C1 **Uliastay** Mongolia
59 D2 **Ulithi** atoll Micronesia
53 D3 **Ulladulla** Austr.
96 B2 **Ullapool** U.K.
98 B2 **Ullswater** l. U.K.
65 C2 **Ullŭng-do** i. S. Korea
102 B2 **Ulm** Ger.
65 B2 **Ulsan** S. Korea
95 □ **Ulsta** U.K.
97 C1 **Ulster** reg. Ireland/U.K.
52 B3 **Ultima** Austr.
145 C3 **Ulúa** r. Hond.
111 C3 **Ulubey** Turkey
111 D3 **Uluborlu** Turkey
111 C3 **Uludağ** mt. Turkey
123 D2 **Ulundi** S. Africa
77 E2 **Ulungur Hu** l. China
Uluqsaqtuuq Can. see
Holman
50 C2 **Uluru** hill Austr.
98 B2 **Ulverston** U.K.
90 C2 **Ul'yanovka** Ukr.
87 D3 **Ul'yanovsk** Rus. Fed.
136 C3 **Ulysses** U.S.A.
90 C2 **Uman'** Ukr.
86 E2 **Umba** Rus. Fed.
59 D3 **Umboi** i. P.N.G.
92 H3 **Umeå** Sweden
92 H3 **Umeälven** r. Sweden
123 D2 **Umhlanga Rocks** S. Africa
127 J2 **Umiiviip Kangertiva** inlet
Greenland